Philosophical Perspectives on Music

WAYNE D. BOWMAN

New York   Oxford
OXFORD UNIVERSITY PRESS
1998

To
the memory of
my mother,
Frances C. Gibson Bowman

Oxford University Press

Oxford   New York
Athens   Auckland   Bangkok   Bogota   Bombay   Buenos Aires
Calcutta   Cape Town   Dar es Salaam   Delhi   Florence   Hong Kong
Istanbul   Karachi   Kuala Lumpur   Madras   Madrid   Melbourne
Mexico City   Nairobi   Paris   Singapore   Taipei   Tokyo   Toronto   Warsaw

and associated companies in
Berlin   Ibadan

Published by Oxford University Press, Inc.
198 Madison Avenue, New York, New York 10016

Oxford is a registered trademark of Oxford University Press

Library of Congress Cataloging-in-Publication Data
Bowman, Wayne D., 1947–
Philosophical perspectives on music / Wayne D. Bowman.
p.   cm.
Includes bibliographical references and indexes.
ISBN 0-19-511296-2
1. Music—Philosophy and aesthetics.   I. Title.
ML3800.B79   1998
781'.1—dc21   97-25601
                                               CIP
                                               MN

1 3 5 7 9 8 6 4 2

Printed in the United States of America
on acid-free paper

Convictions are more dangerous enemies of truth than lies.
                                    —*Friedrich Nietzsche*

Contents

Acknowledgments

I am grateful to these publishers for having generously granted me permission to reprint portions of materials to which they hold copyright: Continuum Publishing Company, for Adorno's *Introduction to the Sociology of Music*; Dover Publications, Inc., for Schopenhauer's *The World as Will and Representation* (Payne translation); Encyclopaedia Britannica, Inc., for *Great Books of the Western World*, my source for *The Works of Aristotle* (Ross translation) and *The Dialogues of Plato* (Jowett translation); Hackett Publishing Company, Inc., for Goodman's *Languages of Art* and Hanslick's *On the Musically Beautiful* (Payzant translation); Harvard University Press, for Langer's *Philosophy in a New Key*; Johns Hopkins University Press, for Langer's *Mind: An Essay on Human Feeling*; Northwestern University Press, for Dufrenne's *The Phenomenology of Aesthetic Experience* (Casey translation); Oxford University Press, for Kant's *Critique of Judgement* (Meredith translation), *The Works of Aristotle* (Ross translation), *The Dialogues of Plato* (Jowett translation), and David Burrows' "On Hearing Things" (from *Musical Quarterly*, where parts of *Sound, Speech, and Music* first appeared); Princeton University Press, for Nattiez's *Music and Discourse: Toward a Semiology of Music* (Abbate translation); Telos Press, Ltd., for Adorno's "On the Social Significance of Music"; University of Chicago Press, for Meyer's *Music, the Arts, and Ideas*; University of Massachusetts Press, for parts of Burrow's *Sound, Speech, and Music*; University of Minnesota Press, for Attali's *Noise: The Political Economy of Music* (Massumi translation); and Yale University Press, for Clifton's *Music as Heard: A Study in Applied Phenomenology*.

My preparation of this book was aided significantly by a year's sabbatical leave from Brandon University; by access to Columbia University's library facilities during that leave, graciously arranged by Harold Abeles; and by the remarkable resources to which I had access during two stimulating years as Visiting Professor at the University of Toronto.

Interaction and exchanges with colleagues and students played a significant role in the development of this project. To Earl Davey, in particular, I wish to express my sincere gratitude for stimulating and insightful dialogue, criticism, and support at a time when they were sorely needed. I am grateful to Roberta Lamb (ever a source of provocative ideas and readings) for much-needed criticism of an early draft of the final chapter. I am also appreciative of David Elliott's helpful comments as the manuscript neared completion. I want to convey my gratitude to the many students who have, over the years, shared with me the excitement of exploring new and challenging ideas. Their questions, curiosity, and enthusiasm about music philosophy has kept me convinced unwaveringly of its relevance to today's music students. Special thanks are due Deborah Bradley, Nancy Flood, and Teresa Lee for their comments on the manuscript, and to Melissa Bowman for her diligent technical assistance.

I am grateful to a number of anonymous readers recruited by Oxford University Press for their insightful comments and criticisms, and to Maribeth Payne and OUP for taking this project on. Finally, I am profoundly indebted to all those whose ideas I explore here—for the challenge and stimulation of their insights, and for the way they have enriched my understanding of these rich and diverse undertakings we call music.

Above all, to my family—Emily, Melissa, and Benjamin, to whom this project must have often seemed something of an unwanted sibling, and my wife and dear friend, Ann—thank you for your patience, and support.

Toronto, Ontario   W. D. B.
January, 1997

Music and Philosophy

Aims and Assumptions

Musicians interested in becoming acquainted with philosophical reflections on their field encounter a vast, complex, and contradictory body of literature whose language is challenging, frequently arcane, and sometimes seemingly impenetrable. To the practice-oriented musician in particular, the issues music philosophers choose to explore can often seem remote and abstract, of little immediate relevance or consequence. Add to this the fact that philosophers' claims on music's behalf can seem bewildering and bizarre, and it is not entirely surprising that to many musicians philosophical inquiry remains a remote and mysterious undertaking. But that is quite unfortunate. For as mysterious as philosophy may be to the musician, so has music long been to the philosopher. We stand to learn a lot from each other. For thousands of years philosophers have puzzled over this uniquely human preoccupation called music, and what they have had to say is in many ways crucial to an informed appreciation of music's significance and value. Philosophy's importance to the musician is not limited, however, to abstract, theoretical issues: indeed, as we shall see, the practical implications of what may at first seem largely theoretical can be surprisingly direct and far-reaching.

This book offers to help demystify this puzzling world of music philosophy, to provide the serious student of music a basic understanding of what the fuss is about, where the important issues lie, and where, to employ a very strained metaphor, some of the mines are buried. It seeks to provide an orientation to the field, a fuller understanding of its scope and potential relevance to the concerns of contemporary musicians. The basic strategy is a simple one. We will explore from a number of different perspectives two fundamental, yet remarkably challenging, questions about music—questions that have fascinated and perplexed philosophers since earliest recorded history.

Just what is music?
And what is its significance or importance?

Or more concisely yet,

What is the nature and value of music?

These seemingly simple questions have generated, and indeed continue to generate, an astonishing array of responses. But amidst the striking diversity there do exist discernible patterns, convergences of perspective, recurrent disputes and problems. Exploring some of these in detail will help us develop the kind of familiarity with landmarks necessary for further navigation of the field, an inclination to which it is hoped this book may also contribute.

The book is written for the musician or the curious nonmusician without an extensive background in philosophy or musical aesthetics. It endeavors to examine a broad range of music philosophical terrain, showing the philosopher's reasons for holding beliefs that can strike nonphilosophers as little short of preposterous. As we begin to understand the bases for these seemingly strange ideas, the reader would do well to anticipate some conceptual discomfort, as comforting commonsense truths are subjected to scrutiny and stress they seldom encounter in casual conversation. Philosophy has a way of undermining the obvious, defamiliarizing the familiar, complicating the apparently simple.

Likewise, the reader is forewarned that the study we are about to undertake will not culminate in definitive answers or neatly resolve all the issues it raises. It is my belief that questions like the ones explored here have no single, definitive answer. Yet it is my further firm conviction that this by no means renders pointless the philosophical quest for answers. While none of the perspectives we will explore here—none of these attempts to describe music's nature and worth— is wholly adequate, neither is any of them devoid of insight. There are, in other words, a number of ways music may reasonably be construed to be, each with its valuable insights and its inevitable biases or blind spots. There is not one 'essential' way all music 'is' or may be found to be. On this more will be said shortly.

This book seeks to situate itself between brief and accessible introductions to music philosophy and erudite scholarly monographs written by and for professional philosophers. Useful though the former are, their brevity and accessibility inevitably deprive them of the richness and flavor that makes philosophy compelling. And crucial though the latter are, the newcomer to music philosophy often finds them abstruse, obscure, and pedantic. Students of philosophy and aesthetic theory are well served by detailed, rigorous resources and by curricula designed to pursue primary resources in detail; but the substantial majority of North American music students engage in predominantly 'practical' pursuits, in curricula which offer little if any opportunity for reflection upon what they do, why they do it, or what its broader significance may be. I believe we are professionally the worse for that.[1] Music philosophy is not the study of dead voices from the past, but rather of intriguing ideas and issues with continuing relevance and practical significance for musicians. As we explore various and divergent views of what counts as music, how it works, and what its value(s) may be, we will attempt to get sufficiently 'inside' those views to enable an appreciation of their persuasiveness and, in a surprising number of instances, their enduring influence.

Among the many preliminary points to be made here, one is absolutely crucial: this book is conceived as an introduction to, not a substitute for, the primary sources from which it is drawn. When finished with it (or better still, alongside it) I earnestly hope readers will use my analyses, comments, and references to orient firsthand examination of at least some of the original texts upon which I have drawn here. I urge readers not just to "take my word for it" but to examine the original texts and reach their own conclusions. Those who do so will be rewarded richly with depth of detail and delightful quirkiness of style at which my accounts can only hint. It has been necessary here to gloss over and sometimes omit important points. Ideas have been filtered through my own interpretive frameworks, and rearticulated in words I hope readers may more readily grasp. The dangers of oversimplifying and distorting rich, complex ideas in a project like this are ones to which I am quite sensitive. I am also acutely aware that I have not been entirely able to avoid those dangers. Yet I have persisted, believing that the potential for distortion is outweighed by an even more undesirable alternative: the continued neglect of music philosophy within postsecondary music study, a failure to capitalize on an extraordinarily valuable intellectual resource.

Where I have fallen short of my goal of making complex ideas accessible, it is not for lack of effort. Philosophy often yields to paraphrase as gracefully as poetry—which is to say, of course, that it does not—and quite often, complex ideas simply cannot be coaxed or coerced into simpler language. Philosophers often choose their words with the utmost precision, and tinkering with carefully chosen words always alters meanings. Where my words mislead, or where they gloss over important issues, I trust my colleagues to clarify, elaborate, supplement, or challenge them. The benefits to be accrued from this endeavor hardly require that we be in full accord on all issues.

This is not a book about aesthetic theory or philosophy of art, but specifically and explicitly philosophy of music. That is, it seeks to bring together in one place a wide range of ideas that shed light on the nature and value of music in particular. There is no shortage of books that undertake consideration of music as one among 'the arts', emphasizing the continuities and similarities that have preoccupied 'aesthetic' inquiry since its inception in the eighteenth century. But attention to supposed commonality exacts an unacceptable cost to consideration of what is unique and distinctive about music and musical experience, conveying the assumption, however implicitly, that the distinctively musical is only incidental—of less importance than what music shares with putatively related endeavors. I believe that appreciation of the uniquely and distinctly musical is of crucial significance to music students, and that addressing such concerns is among music philosophy's most fundamental obligations.

Even so delimited, though, music philosophy remains a vast terrain that can be charted many ways. The way I have chosen is in certain respects arbitrary. I have deliberately excluded the ideas of philosophers, composers, and musicians some will regard as essential to an introduction to the field. But this is not an exhaustive survey, it is an introduction intended to give students a sufficiently detailed acquaintance with the great and lasting issues in music philosophy that they may begin to see its relevance to their own musical beliefs, values, and undertakings. Cogency has thus been a higher priority than comprehensiveness; and where my omissions are deemed unacceptable, I am fully confident that colleagues will see to their rectification.[2]

Readers who look to this book for conclusive answers will probably experience frustration at my disinclination to provide them. But my determination to proceed as I have is deliberate and strategic: for while philosophy is rightly conceived as a quest for truth, its very nature is such that no one achieves it completely. Many people get a piece of it; nobody has it all. And that, as it turns out, is at least partly because musical practices are not the kind of affairs for which there is an 'all'. The whole of music is as ephemeral an idea as is the whole of truth, and we must learn to be content with insights that are provisional and temporary instead of absolute and timeless. Though partial and contingent, such insights are of inestimable help in providing direction along the path of continuing inquiry. Put differently, none of the thinkers whose ideas we will examine here gets things wholly right; but that is an unrealistic expectation of philosophy. More important is a willingness to entertain the possibility that none gets things wholly wrong. It is my hope, then, that as readers explore each of the perspectives examined here they may find themselves sympathetically inclined toward certain features at the same time they are skeptical of others. In my view, that attitude is more characteristic of the spirit of philosophical inquiry than identifying winners and losers.

Given musicians' notorious penchant for the 'practical', I anticipate that many readers will wish I had devoted more time to exploration of the many concrete, practical issues of relevance to music's various professional disciplines. Since philosophical inquiry's pragmatic utility is indeed among the most important reasons for engaging in it, such concerns are entirely valid. One's philosophical convictions can manifest startling 'practical' implications, and it would be gratifying to explore all these at length. But the cost of fuller attention to practical and professional issues would be a drastic reduction in the range and depth of philosophical coverage. And since in all likelihood different musicians will find the issues explored here significant in different ways, I have resisted the temptation to direct the book to the specific concerns of any single musical discipline. I must therefore ask my readers and their teachers to keep foremost in their minds these critically important pragmatic questions:

> If this idea, this claim, this way of looking at music were valid, what might it imply for the kind of music-related practices in which I engage? What difference might it make for me, for how I conceive of and execute my various musical undertakings?

Although the matters they encompass are far too diverse to be adequately addressed here, answers to questions like these represent the single most important outcome of this project.

Further, an appeal to patience. Since philosophical ideas sometimes reveal their sense slowly and in response to considerable effort, it will be prudent in the pages ahead to attempt to suspend the impatience toward abstraction for which musicians are often notorious. Instant gratification and quick fixes are not conspicuous characteristics of philosophy. But without the kind of theoretical deliberation and heightened awareness philosophy seeks to engender, practice can be aimless and blind. And unless we become more fully informed and articulate, decisions affecting music will be made by the less informed, guided more by economic and political agendas than by musical and rational ones.

Characteristic Concerns of Philosophical Discourse

Although most of us have a general notion of what philosophy is about, such notions often diverge significantly from what those seriously engaged in philosophy understand it to be: a situation known all too well by musicians in relation to their own field. Among these mistaken assumptions, perhaps the most pervasive is the idea that philosophy amounts to the expression of arbitrarily held opinion, personal views rooted in nothing more substantial than sentiment. On this view, philosophy reduces to rhetoric, a practice devoted to argumentation and persuasion. The stereotype of philosophy as personal opinion buttressed by rhetorical skills may contain a grain of truth, but little more. For as a practice— as opposed to a body of doctrine or ideology—philosophy is more properly regarded as the systematic and critical examination of the grounds for belief. It characteristically aspires to something quite a bit more ambitious than the rhetorical and political, and presumes to be based on something considerably more substantial than mere assertion.[3] Derived from the Greek *philosophia*, or 'love of wisdom', philosophical inquiry is driven by a passion for things like insight, understanding, and truth.

Philosophy is thus founded in the human need to make sense of the world and our place in it. What distinguishes it from mere personal opinion and credulity is its rejection of passionate convictions as sufficient grounds for belief and action, and its commitment to careful analysis and systematic reasoning. In the words of H. B. Redfern, philosophy involves a "passion for clarity" and a disdain for "devices which blur and confuse and seek to influence without inviting critical reflection."[4] As I have written elsewhere, "Philosophy works to render the implicit explicit, with the ultimate intent of enriching both understanding and perception. Among its greatest allies is a persistent curiosity. Its enemies are the habitual, the stereotypical, the unexamined, the acritical, the 'common sense' assumption or assertion. The philosophical mind critically challenges and explores received doctrine, renounces the security and comfort of dogma, exposes inconsistencies, weighs and evaluates alternatives. It explores, probes, and questions, taking very little for granted."[5] Although just how much philosophy takes for granted is a contentious issue in some quarters,[6] these ideals and attitudes are certainly descriptive of the philosophical disposition as it has been conventionally understood. At the same time they help explain why, to the exasperation of those new to philosophy, it never quite succeeds in finding the ultimate, irrefutable, universally acknowledged truths traditionally presumed to be the measure of its worth. Simply put, subscription to a common set of doctrines ranks relatively low among the priorities of those engaged in philosophical inquiry. Rather than a uniform body of doctrine, philosophy manifests itself in an ongoing process of critically examining and refining the grounds for our beliefs and actions, the ideas we recognize as true, as deserving our loyalty and commitment. As well, the philosophical attitude is marked by a determination to stand out from what Northrop Frye once called "the uniform bleating of the herd."[7] Such independence of mind seldom manifests itself in uncontested agreement.

To those unaccustomed to thinking this way, philosophy can sometimes seem a nuisance. Philosophers are inveterate askers of questions, people who find intractable problems and issues in what to others seems obvious and utterly uncontroversial. It is not for no reason that the philosopher has been considered (to put it politely) a gadfly. So to approach the study of music philosophy with the expectation of finding a coolly dispassionate endeavor governed by strict laws of logic and marked by widespread agreement on fundamental issues is to seriously misunderstand its nature and underestimate its difficulty. Philosophy is no mere marshaling of views, no purveyor of irrefutable, absolute truths. It is, rather, a messy and disquieting process in which cherished beliefs and comfortable assumptions are subjected to critical scrutiny.

Although music philosophy is sometimes equated with musical aesthetics, the two are not the same: philosophy of music is broader than musical aesthetics, and subsumes it. The study of musical aesthetics takes its lead from general aesthetic theory, the field of discourse that arose in the eighteenth century in an effort to describe presumed commonalties among the arts and, more broadly, instances of beauty. Accordingly, while musical aesthetics is sometimes regarded as the effort to describe what is distinctive about music and musical experience, it has frequently based its claims on a rather restricted range of evidence—those musical practices recently regarded in the Western world as 'art'. Unfortunately, situating music within a class of endeavors called 'the arts' begs the questions of what music is, what purposes it serves, and what its values are: for to call it an 'art' almost invariably removes from consideration an extensive range of musical practices not regarded as 'artistic'—practices and pieces that do not evince 'aesthetic value' in high degree. That is to say, musical aesthetics often tends to confer global validity upon characteristics that are in fact local, specific to a relatively narrow range of musics. As Francis Sparshott puts it, aesthetic accounts of music attribute universality to what is in fact a normative theory of taste, one which emphasizes orderliness and trained perception over other modes of musical engagement. They assume that music's inherent value lies in its capacity to sustain appreciative, contemplative experience in "a privileged group of consumers, not themselves musicians . . ."[8] Moreover, the evolution of musical aesthetics has been intimately entangled with the idea of musical value's 'intrinsicality', a concept that erects rather rigid and impermeable boundaries between the range of the properly musical and an (often vast) 'extramusical' residue. Each of these tendencies restricts the range of musical experiences and practices deemed relevant to questions of music's nature and value—with results that seriously compromise our understanding of the phenomena at hand.

As I see it, then, music philosophy addresses considerably broader ranges of concern, and philosophical contexts considerably more inclusive, than those historically envisioned by musical aesthetics. Since aesthetic orientations, like the musics that arose and evolved in tandem with them, are historically factual, music philosophy is obliged to recognize them. It need not, however, accept their claims to ultimacy, or their assumptions of music's 'autonomy' and 'intrinsicality', or of listening's status as the quintessentially musical mode of engagement. Indeed, it often does not. Music philosophy explores areas musical aesthetics often regards as musically incidental: matters epistemological, ethical, social, cultural, and political.

Music philosophy should not be regarded as a hermetic discipline, restricted in its rightful purview to theoretical exploration of abstract propositions about 'music proper'. Its interests overlap with and extend deeply into quite a number of related intellectual disciplines. The most immediately apparent of these is music criticism. The relationship between music philosophy and music criticism is sometimes described as one between theory and practice, philosophy addressing music more comprehensively and abstractly while criticism concerns itself with the merits of specific musical works and endeavors. Criticism, in this view, is a kind of applied philosophy—general beliefs brought to bear on particular and concrete musical undertakings. While the distinction between philosophy and criticism is helpful, it is not a good idea to draw too sharp a distinction between the two: for they work dialectically with each other, they inform one another in important ways, and their basic orientations are in many respects quite similar. As I have suggested elsewhere, "philosophy is to belief as criticism is to music."[9] Both seek to explore beliefs, undo habitual stereotypes and prejudices, enhance imagination, and reveal previously hidden aspects of the given. The good critic, wrote T. S. Eliot, is one "who can make me look at something I have never looked at before, or looked at only with eyes clouded with prejudice."[10] The same is true of philosophers, although their focus is more often conceptual than perceptual. Both philosophy and criticism seek to educate sensibilities and enhance critical awareness, endeavors that, it should be noted, ultimately reduce esteem for the pedestrian and the commonplace.

Criticism usually draws liberally on philosophical convictions, while philosophy can and frequently does seek to examine specific musical practices. For those to whom 'philosophy' connotes unbridled abstraction and speculation, the 'groundedness' of criticism in perception is understandably attractive. Yet it is hardly possible to engage in criticism without employing, at least implicitly, beliefs as to what constitutes good or proper musical practice: beliefs whose formulation and examination are explicitly philosophical undertakings. Although the scope of music criticism is generally more concretely and specifically musical than philosophy, it is not invariably so, and never purely so. Nor—and here I admittedly part company with many—need philosophy operate necessarily and invariably on the level of generalities. The relation between philosophy and criticism is not one of diametrical opposition, nor is there a fixed, stable boundary between the two. In fact, where the idea of a mutually exclusive relationship between music 'itself' and its sociocultural 'context' is denied, the differences between criticism and philosophy become rather ephemeral.

It may be well to acknowledge a few other disciplinary convergences and affinities in passing. Music psychology, for instance, departs rather decisively from music philosophy in its markedly empirical proclivities, and is thus typically preoccupied with the mechanisms behind musical perception, preference, response, and the like. Yet it shares philosophy's keen interest in judgments of musical value, the distinctively affective character of musical experience, and the like. Thus, psychology's investigations often build implicitly or explicitly on ideas rightly regarded as philosophical. Social psychology casts its net more widely, seeking to examine how social influences shape musical judgments, meanings, and responses. Again, music philosophy shares those concerns. The convergence between psychological interests and philosophy will be most evident here in phenomenology's exploration of music's lived, experiential basis, and in Meyer's and Langer's struggles to illuminate the relation of feeling to musical experience.

Music philosophy also has significant affinities with sociology and social theory, as will become apparent in the later chapters of this book. Music's inextricable cultural situatedness, its deep involvement in shaping and maintaining human social orders, and the profound extent to which its meanings are socially mediated and constructed are each pivotal concerns for contemporary music philosophers, many of whom increasingly regard the distinction between the musical and the social as a serious mistake.

Still other disciplines—music theory and the nascent field of music cognition for instance—have roots that extend deeply into the realm of music philosophy, even if those roots are not always explicitly acknowledged or fully appreciated. And others still—music education, for instance—are profoundly reliant upon music philosophy for fundamental direction: without an adequate prior grasp of music philosophy, the fabrication of an applied professional philosophy is bound to be a highly precarious undertaking.

The point is not that all these various disciplines are merely derivative, or that their distinctive character is illusory; far from it. The broader point is simply that music philosophy must not be regarded as an insular, esoteric realm whose interests and endeavors have little significance or relevance beyond the confines of philosophy in and of itself. As an endeavor which commits itself to uncovering and scrutinizing beliefs about music's nature and value, its potential sphere of influence and relevance extends wherever human beliefs manifest themselves in musical practices. It offers to help us reexamine, clarify, and reconstruct musical beliefs, and in turn the many practices with which they are intimately entwined. As such, it is a grievous mistake to conceive of it as an obscurely marginal practice, with little immediate importance for the making, experience, or teaching of music.

This points to another important reason for music philosophy's divergence and diversity: since its roots interlace so extensively with those of other domains, it is hardly surprising that the ways of conducting philosophical inquiry and the kind of 'products' they generate vary considerably. Both the way questions are posed and the kind of answers deemed relevant often differ substantially. And yet, at least on a general level, the questions that concern music philosophy tend to align themselves in relatively clear patterns and configurations. Just what sort of thing is music? What purpose(s) does music serve? How may judgments of musical worth be grounded or substantiated? How is it that such a universal and distinctive presence in human culture and experience seems so resistant to explanation, so perpetually in need of justification? How does music relate to and differ from things like noise, speech, language—that is, nonmusical sonorous experience? How do musical experiences differ from merely sensuous experience? What human needs and interests can music be shown to serve? How do musical practices relate to and differ from other areas of human endeavor, including those characteristic of the other 'arts' and nonmusical experiences? In what senses can music be said to 'mean' something? In what sense might music be considered a kind of knowing, a manifestation of human intelligence? What has music to do with feeling or emotion? Does music have the power to shape people's character, to make them better or worse? Or is it, rather, a mere amusement, a diversion?

These are but a few of the many provocative and daunting questions to which music philosophy directs our attention. Yet, among them are two that subsume most of the others and that will serve to orient us in the explorations undertaken in the ensuing chapters of this book. They are of course the questions introduced above: What is music? What is its value?

The Value of Music Philosophy to the Musician

To repeat, comforting though it would be if music philosophy were able to provide us with ultimate answers to questions like these, that is an unrealistic expectation. Music assumes too many forms, serves too many diverse functions, and is too deeply embedded in the dynamic flux and mutation of sociocultural life to be exhaustively explained by theoretical undertakings that are not similarly dynamic, diverse, and fluid. Simply and directly put, philosophy is simply not that kind of creature.[11] But that hardly means music philosophy is wholly useless; fortunately, its value to the musician does not rest on its capacity to arm us with the kind of definitive answers that obtain for all musics, everywhere, for all time.

It is sometimes claimed that among philosophy's benefits is its capacity to inspire, to instill in people a sense of purpose and direction. People who have a clear understanding of what they do and its value, it is maintained, function more effectively; and people whose understanding of music is based on systematic exploration and analysis—as opposed to platitudes, aphorisms, and slogans, for instance—are better equipped to demonstrate and explain the true significance of their undertakings to others. These are not insignificant considerations in a time when music seems so widely regarded as an insubstantial indulgence, an entertaining diversion. Yet, while music philosophy is indeed capable of shaping, expanding, and strengthening minds, it can "blow" them as well.[12] It may indeed affirm and inspire, but its capacity to reveal the inadequacy of reassuring convictions and beliefs can also confuse and disturb. There are those, in fact, who would maintain that philosophical inquiry which fails to disturb and disrupt has not truly done its job. In other words, it probably misrepresents philosophical inquiry to suggest that its primary value lies in some unconditional capacity to strengthen and inspire. For among the things it reveals are sometimes matters we might prefer not to have confronted.

If music philosophy does not deliver final answers, if it does not automatically and invariably deliver inspiration, if it can bolster confidence and security but undermine them as well, then what good is it? That ultimate, inspiring truths are not what music philosophy is about, that it is as interested in questions as it is in answers, that it is more characterized by persistent curiosity than by once-and-for-all explanations: all these mean that philosophy's value to the musician must be conceived more broadly. Its practical value lies not in its revelation of the hidden truth about music's innermost essence but rather in its power to expose unexamined assumptions, to enrich one's understanding of music's many roles in human experience, thereby making one's various musical doings better informed and more fully subject to conscious direction. Subjecting habits and assumptions to critical, systematic examination leads to practice that is better 'theorized', more fully guided by explicit consideration of beliefs about what music is and what it should be. The decisions and actions that shape musical practices often are undertaken without such scrutiny. But such practices are likely to be haphazard and considerably less effective than we might hope. Even more to the point, they may inadvertently serve ends quite different from those we envisage. One's choice, in other words, is not so much between doing and reflecting as it is between practice that unthinkingly replicates an unexamined status quo and practice guided by critical awareness of carefully considered ends. The choice, to put it another way, is between skillful technical execution and wholly mindful agency.

Whether one is more immediately concerned with the making and doing of music, with the study of its inner workings, with teaching others about it, or with helping people develop the requisite skills for particular musical practices, music philosophy seeks to refine critically the system of beliefs and values that guide professional choices and decisions. To invent a philosophy 'from scratch' or build it piecemeal without the benefit of previous inquiry into foundational questions about music's nature and value would be inefficient and irresponsible. In the first place, familiarity with a range of philosophical or theoretical alternatives—their strengths and shortcomings, and the ways they may have influenced current beliefs and practices—is a crucial part of the distinction between being educated and merely being trained. And in the second place, a shared understanding of foundational beliefs and values is vital to any claim to truly professional status. To neglect music philosophy—to leave philosophical dispositions and understandings to unguided, casual development—is a mistake with implications that are far-reaching and serious.

It might seem that this need for philosophical grounding could be adequately met by simply subscribing to an explanation crafted for us by authorities in the field, without going through the messy business of exploring and weighing alternatives ourselves. Unfortunately, such shortcuts short-circuit the philosophical process and fail to nurture the habits of mind that are among philosophical inquiry's greatest potential benefits. And the idea of building a professional philosophy on a single point of view without critically examining other alternatives imputes both to music and to philosophy a static, unchanging character quite at odds with the character of either. Worse yet, it risks replacing philosophy with ideology and dogma: a significant concern, one would think, in a field where the dominant mode of training is imitative apprenticeship.

In short, basic acquaintance with the ways music shapes and is shaped by culture—what it is, and what its values may be—is fundamentally important to becoming musically educated. Extensive training in specialized skills is necessary, but not sufficient: to be educated is to be more broadly prepared. Music philosophy's role in that preparation lies in its assurance that we do what we do in light of foreseen consequences, in light of ends we envision as fully and accurately as possible.

Yet, as my disinclination to equate philosophy with advocacy and inspiration, or true education with training, may suggest, even this claim sounds more clear-cut than it probably is. For the nature of philosophical inquiry is such that we can never know precisely where it may lead: it *is* that kind of creature. Perhaps another analogy will help clarify the point: advocacy is to philosophy as training is to education. Advocacy and inspiration, like training, assume clearly defined ends, ends by which the adequacy of the means can be clearly gauged. On the other hand, where endeavors like philosophy and education will lead can never be fully determinate. One commits to a process in which one has faith. Beyond that one takes one's chances.

Music from Divergent Perspectives

One of the perennial dangers in exploring ideas is their tendency to harden into dogma, a tendency which converts intriguing possibilities into seemingly definitive absolutes. In this process, dynamic conceptual confluences and divergences somehow ossify into bewildering arrays of mutually exclusive 'isms' that seem to vie with one another for people's total allegiance. As suggested earlier, though, philosophers—despite undeniable affinities—are usually resolute individualists. Grouping their ideas into philosophical 'schools' of thought, while a useful orienting strategy, often distorts as much as it illuminates. Stressing differences and contrasts can lead to the neglect of subtle but important connections and relations; stressing similarities can obscure the uniqueness and particularity of individual voices. Since divergent perspectives serve as an organizational strategy in the pages ahead, it is important we candidly acknowledge and recognize the distortive potential of that strategy. The perspectives explored here are heuristic devices, idealizations. Few of those whose ideas we will explore are perfect matches to the perspectives with which I associate them, and some might be characterized quite differently simply by stressing other affinities and tendencies. Still, identifiable landmarks are essential when finding one's way in new territory, and highlighting certain patterns and trends is a useful organizational modus operandi so long as we remember why we are doing it and resist taking them too literally. Despite the profound differences that exist among philosophies of music, remarkable strains of continuity also exist. It is fascinating, in fact, to see how many of the roots of contemporary ideas extend back hundreds — sometimes thousands — of years. Indeed, ancient Greek writings on music raised in their basic form many of the issues that have occupied music philosophy ever since. Music's capacity to influence character, its special relation to human feeling, the nature of its contribution to human knowledge, the philosophical problems posed by its peculiar transience, its seemingly unique situation between the physical and spiritual worlds: these are but a few of the issues with which contemporary philosophy continues to wrestle that can be traced back to the time of Plato, and even earlier.

Another cluster of recurrent themes in music philosophy concerns music's distinctive abstractness (especially that of instrumental music), a quality that has led many philosophers to characterize it as insubstantial and illusory. Others, however, find in that same quality a unique capacity to reveal reality's innermost secrets, especially because of its special relationship with the realms of feeling or spirituality. Then, against the excesses of these expressivist theories, there arise equally ardent formalist theories, determined to link music's significance strictly to its sonorous patterns, patterns whose perception has by some been attributed to a wholly unique musical faculty of mind. Against the insularity of formalism's emphasis upon music's autonomy, still other philosophers — particularly in the twentieth century — mount cogent, sophisticated accounts of music as a potent social, psychological, and political force.

Changing fashions in music philosophy do not mean it is aimless, pointless, or outdated, however. In fact, given the radical changes in musical practices over thousands of years, it is remarkable philosophy has remained as stable and consistent as it has. It would also be quite misguided to assume that music philosophy is narrowly concerned with musical endeavor, for debates over music's meaning and value implicate many of philosophy's most durable, intractable problems: mind and body, reason and sensation, unity and plurality, uniformity and diversity, form and feeling, subjectivity and objectivity, freedom and constraint, tradition and innovation, and truth and illusion, to mention but a few. In short, the existence of philosophical differences hardly means music philosophy is arbitrary or irrelevant. To be sure, it is not a linear, progressive process, inexorably advancing toward some ultimate, irrefutable truth. The temptation to dismiss past philosophy as outdated is one that should be strenuously resisted: indeed, as will become apparent in the pages ahead, what past philosophers have had to say about music can often be remarkably cogent and illuminating. Perhaps the best way to make sense of all this is simply to acknowledge that however much things like music and philosophy change, they remain human endeavors. And since on some level, human needs, interests, and tendencies remain relatively constant even across the millennia, to dismiss categorically the relevance of the musical or philosophical past would be quite precipitous.

The second chapter of this book introduces the music philosophies of Plato and Aristotle, tracing their influence with sufficient detail to establish that their ideas are not simply quaint artifacts of a bygone era. For the ancient Greeks, music was not the entertaining diversion it often seems today, but a profoundly important part of their sociocultural, intellectual, and spiritual life. The discovery of mathematical explanations for pitch by the Pythagoreans led to a widespread conviction that music was deeply implicated in the mysteries of cosmic order. This, in conjunction with a belief that music could exert a profound influence on character, earned for it a place of paramount importance in education. But interestingly, at the same time, music's power and potency were apparently presumed to be such that they could not be entrusted to its own practitioners. The wrong music in the hands of the naive musician could undermine personal character, moral rectitude, social order, even state security. Furthermore, since music was considered an imitative phenomenon, the Greeks went to great ends to explain what kind of imitation it was, and to speculate about its veracity or trustworthiness. Music thus figured centrally in an important philosophical debate over the relation between the material and the ideal, between sense and reason, a debate that influenced musical thought and practice for centuries and whose residual influence is still evident today.

Among the many important philosophical issues prefigured in ancient Greek thought is the dispute over where to draw the line between music's inherent nature and its supposed effects, between what music is and what it does, between the musical and the extramusical. To those inclined to regard it as a fundamentally mental or cognitive affair, what is most noteworthy about music is its capacity to deliver something outside itself: a distinctive kind of knowledge for instance, or some insight into the true nature of reality. In the third chapter, we will explore influential efforts to portray music as a distinctive realm of 'idea'. Motivated by deep belief in the inherent mindfulness of the human condition, philosophers of an 'idealistic' bent struggled to articulate and clarify the differences among rational, moral, and aesthetic judgments, to define the relation between music's formal qualities and sensual effects, and to show exactly what kind of awareness a thing like music might be said to afford.

The view that music's significance is strictly (or primarily) autonomous, internal, or formal is taken up in the fourth chapter. For those who espouse this point of view, music's significance lies in its own unique qualities rather than in its connections to anything outside itself. Since its 'content' is wholly and exclusively musical, the musical relevance of anything but distinctive tones and structural configurations is often strenuously denied. As philosophers of a formalistic bent struggle to illuminate music's innermost core, the realm of musical meaning becomes an insular affair to which everything outside music's sonorous patterns relates—at best—as 'context.'

From these debates over whether musical meaning is formal or expressive, autonomous or heteronomous, there emerges in the twentieth century yet another strategy for substantiating music's cognitive status. On these views, music is among the signs and symbols by which humans order their worlds and construct their conceptions of reality. The fifth chapter explores symbolic and semiotic accounts of music as an instrument by which people conceive reality or construct their representations of it: the ways in which musical experience mediates interpretation of the world. Since symbolism requires a relation between two different kinds of thing, one that symbolizes or signifies and another that is symbolized or signified, the dualistic tensions between the musically intrinsic and extrinsic figure prominently in symbolic theories, as do questions about interpretive latitude.

A sixth chapter explores the nature and value of music from the perspective of the distinctive experience it affords, in a way that tries to neutralize the dualistic tensions to which we have just alluded. Suspending 'logical' belief in the opposition of subject and object, inside and outside, mind and body, phenomenologists explore music from the perspective of the lived, bodily experience—from the interpreter's point of view, one might say. By attempting to set aside the binary oppositions that fuel debates between autonomists and heteronomists, phenomenology offers a perspective that is strikingly fresh and richly resonant with music as a lived, human process.

The seventh chapter examines several theories that situate music not so much within the psychological domain of personal experience as in the broader realm of social experience, a realm intimately connected to issues of power and political influence. Music, it is argued, is no 'natural' phenomenon but rather a human construction. As such, what music is and means can never escape the fundamental facts of historical and cultural relativity. Its value must be gauged by the social ends it serves—by how its practitioners and participants come to relate to each other through and as a result of their musical engagements. On these views, music is an undertaking with significant moral and ethical ramifications, as well as a fundamentally 'historied' affair that defies the universal explanations commonly believed to be the ultimate aim of philosophy. From the social perspective, music can have many functions, and its value can only be assessed in light of the desirability of those functions. Music is thus a force whose power and influence are radically underestimated by views that reduce it to orderly successions of pleasing sound, or that attempt to account for its significance in strictly psychological terms.

The eighth and final chapter examines late-twentieth-century perspectives that are still nascent, yet highly provocative and controversial, presenting challenges that promise to transform radically both the philosophical process and the character of its philosophical 'product'. Feminist theory takes up phenomenological and sociocultural themes and presses them into a divergent array of theories undergirded by a common commitment to heightened awareness of women's experience in patriarchal social orders. Postmodernists, on the other hand, take seeming delight in shattering comfortable distinctions and blurring disciplinary boundaries, delivering music philosophy to unpredictable frontiers where the very possibility of philosophy is called into question.

Perspectivism Versus the God's-eye View[13]

Of the many developments in music philosophy, few seem to generate more conceptual strain (at least for traditional sensibilities and institutions) than the apparent erosion of belief in music's unity, purity, insularity, and autonomy.

Recognition of the radical diversity and sociocultural situatedness of musical practices, awareness of the historicity and contingency of musical values, and a growing awareness that the boundaries of 'the musical' are negotiable and fluid: each of these disturbs comforting beliefs—in music's uniformity, and in the existence of a range of value that is strictly and purely musical. Separating the realm of music from the rest of human experience is both arbitrary and reductive. Their roots in a slow-changing human physiology notwithstanding, the social and political worlds within which music is constructed and from which it derives its significance are extraordinarily dynamic, radically multiple. As a sociocultural phenomenon, music's meanings and values are culturally specific, culturally relative, culturally negotiated. The cultural centrism that once presumed to project onto all musics the qualities and values of a particular range of practice is no longer fashionable.[14]

Therefore, the notion of philosophy as an endeavor devoted to constructing grand metaphysical narratives and edifices from irrefutable absolutes and foundational truths has begun to show signs of considerable strain. Belief in historically and culturally invariant truths is slowly giving way to more modest and pragmatic assumptions.[15] On these latter views, the elusiveness of impersonal absolutes and ultimate, definitive explanations is no mere temporary state of affairs, something to be overcome by more rigorous philosophizing. The idea of philosophy as a purveyor of all-encompassing answers is one we need to learn to get along without—for a host of reasons, not the least of which is its tendency to curtail rather than invite extensive participation.

Among the convictions that has guided the writing of this book is a belief that musicians are ill served by the idea of philosophy as a spectator or consumer activity devoted to transmitting and acquiring others' views, and that philosophy is more fruitfully conceived as a personal quest rooted in continuously expanding intellectual experience. As Scheffler reminds, philosophy's "starting points are not fixed and its paths and destinations are plural."[16] The examinations and analyses found in the following chapters are not undertaken with the purpose of winning converts to a particular position. The goal is rather to contribute in some way to the development of philosophical dispositions, philosophical habits of mind. To approach this book expecting only to commit to memory neat summaries is, then, to misconstrue its purpose fundamentally. The philosophical mind, says Scheffler, eschews "untrammeled coherence" and "blind certainty." "Doctrine," he continues, is "the death of theory," and "the quest for certainty is the quest for an end to inquiry."[17]

Contrary to popular assumptions, philosophy does not consist of formulas, platitudes, or slogans. Slogans may inspire and motivate, but their appeal is often more emotional than thoughtful. They reduce complex, dynamic ideas to succinct, simple phrases; and far too often, they become political weapons in factious struggles that are philosophically counterproductive. To approach philosophy with the assumption that it gets things either wholly right or wholly wrong is to subscribe to a one-eyed view lacking perspectival depth. Incomplete and partial though all perspectives are, in the end they are all we have. It is unrealistic to expect philosophy to achieve the view from everywhere—the point-of-view-without-point-of-view sought by those who turn to it for exhaustive explanations that transcend place and time. All philosophies are perspectival, and to that extent limited in what they can tell us about music. No perspective can be all-inclusive, and no philosophy serves all ends equally well.

These points are important enough to warrant repetition. The promise of ultimate explanations and absolute truths has fallen, for good reason, into disrepute. Music philosophy is not so much a quest for the universal or the definitive as it is a dynamic, ongoing process with no single point of arrival. Instead of explaining, interpreting, comparing, and evaluating, contemporary philosophy increasingly seeks to describe,[18] to engage in a grounded endeavor whose validity is consensual, local, and perhaps only temporary. Potential fallibility or partiality of purview are not philosophical flaws. Nor are philosophies necessarily the kind of things that supersede and overcome each other. Nor is the continuing evolution of philosophical thought invariably a matter of right replacing wrong, of old wearing out and being replaced by new. It is more a matter of orienting and reorienting, of refining, of assessing and reassessing descriptive adequacy in light of musical practices that are radically plural, diverse, divergent, and constantly changing.

Anyone interested in music who commits to systematic reflection on that interest engages in activity that is to some degree philosophical. Accordingly, the question is not whether to engage in it, but how to do it well. And we would do well to remember that there is more than one way to do it well.

The word 'music' is not the name of any single entity or 'thing' to which we can point in the world; nor is there a single way it all is, or a single end it all serves. Because 'music' is an abstraction, there are many ways it may reasonably be construed—each partially valid, none absolutely or unconditionally so. Accounts that focus on sensation, for instance, often neglect music's mindful nature, while accounts that emphasize mind often neglect music's corporeal roots. Accounts that stress music's bodily or psychological dimensions frequently overlook its social nature. Accounts that portray music as works or pieces often slight musical action and the crucial fact of human agency. Accounts that stress emotion, feeling, or music's commonalties with 'other arts' frequently undervalue the uniqueness of music's sonorous character. And accounts that regard music as a unified, uniform practice often disregard the field's diversity and difference.

Neither music philosophy nor music are static things. Philosophy's historical perspectives are no more lodged in some remote and distant past than venerated musical practices we continue to enjoy centuries after they were created. Philosophy's voices continue to speak to us, and they have a great deal to say if only we try to understand their assumptions. They promise to inform our understanding not only of what music has been, but of what it is today and perhaps what it is now in the process of becoming. So the reader is urged to approach the accounts that follow not as quaint historical artifacts, but as living ideas; to think of philosophy not as a set of answers or propositions, but as a set of tools designed to clarify the grounds for one's beliefs and actions. Like tools, particular philosophical orientations serve some ends better than others. If, when

I am working at a task, the tool I need is not close at hand, I frequently use whatever is within reach: I have been known, for instance, to hammer with a wrench or to chisel with a screwdriver. Sometimes it works; other times, it makes quite a mess. But a wrench's limited utility as a hammer does not mean it is a bad wrench. It just means one would be well advised to bring along a toolbox when the task at hand looks complex and intricate. Attempting to come to grips with the nature and value of music meets both those criteria—complexity and intricacy—and then some.

If we envision the diverse philosophical perspectives explored here as tools for clarifying and enriching our understanding of music and its significance, we should not be tempted to dismiss them for failing to account for all aspects of all musical practices everywhere. What we are seeking to identify are not so much criteria for, as symptoms of, the musical. Our progress in this important pursuit will be enhanced immeasurably by committing to attitudes and goals I believe to be representative of philosophical inquiry at its best:

- Willingness to take conceptual risks, trying new ways of conceiving of music and its value;
- Commitment to clarity, balanced by acceptance of complexity and relativity;
- Openness to and respect for divergent ideas, provided they are subjected to critical reflection and supported by reasons that are themselves the products of careful deliberation;
- Conviction that is not dogmatic or doctrinaire;
- A desire to see things as they are, tempered by awareness that most things 'are' many ways.[19]

With this as background, it is time to see how well these attitudes serve us as we explore various ways of conceiving of music and its significance. As the next chapter looks back thousands of years to the musical philosophies of the ancient Greeks, the reader is invited to look for ideas that resonate richly with our current situation despite their antiquity.

DISCUSSION QUESTIONS

1. Traditionally, it is maintained that what distinguishes philosophical questions from others is their generality and their foundational nature. Critics of this view, however, sometimes accuse its adherents of 'plethorophobia,'[20] of fear of multiplicity and difference. Does the conventional understanding of philosophy exclude from 'properly philosophical' discourse musical issues you think belong there? Explain.

2. Discuss the similarities and differences among interpretation, explanation, and description. Is description more securely grounded than explanation? Is it possible to describe something without also interpreting it in some way?

3. State in your own words the 'pragmatic question' posed in this chapter. What does this question appear to imply about the relationship between theory and practice?

4. How does music philosophy differ from musical aesthetics?

5. Discuss the difference between conceiving of philosophy as a process and as an entity—an action and a body of knowledge. In what ways is the development of philosophical habits and dispositions more important than defining or subscribing to 'a philosophy'?

6. How does criticism resemble and differ from philosophy? Do you think one is better suited than the other to dealing with music's plurality? Why?

7. Why is the author wary about linking philosophy to advocacy and inspiration? to universals and absolutes? Do you agree? Why or why not?

8. It is often maintained that 'relativism' is self-negating, because to insist meanings and values are 'relative' is to make an absolute (nonrelative) assertion. Do you agree? Why or why not?

9. This chapter implies that divergent perspectives work together to create conceptual depth, just as having two eyes or two ears yields perceptual depth. On the other hand, contradiction can and often does end in confusion. How would you explain the difference between conceptual tension that is constructive and that which results in confusion?

10. It is often maintained that an important benefit of philosophical inquiry is heightened conviction and confidence in the validity of one's beliefs. How can we know whether a belief is justified or not?

11. Classical Greeks distinguished between three kinds of knowledge: *theoria* (the theoretical), *techne* (the productive), and *praxis* (the practical).[21] *Theoria* was contemplative: knowledge of things unchanging and eternal. *Techne* was workmanlike skill or craft, manifest in technical capacity to make things whose nature and value were stable and clear. Unlike the self-containedness of rational theory and theoryless execution, *praxis* was concerned with 'right action': knowledge of what to do in relation to the highly variable norms and standards of human conduct. With which of these is the philosophical orientation of this book most closely allied? What might be the consequences of conceiving of music in each of these three ways?

Music as Imitation

To the ancient Greeks, or at least to the philosophers through which we know of them, music was an essentially imitative art. Belief that music's significance lay in its resemblances to other things—to harmonious balance and unity, to attributes of human character or the soul, and so forth—led them to speculate lavishly about and attribute extraordinary power and significance to music. Music was paramount among the characteristics of 'civilized' community, and to call people unmusical was tantamount to calling them uneducated. As one prominent scholar observes, "Music in one form or other impinged on everyone in Greek society. There was no one who was not exposed to it, and no one who did not think that it was in principle a good thing . . ."[1] In striking contrast to its status in our 'advanced' society, music was an utterly essential part of education, for both moral and rational reasons.

Yet, music's undisputed power and importance precipitated more than a little concern about its potentially adverse effects: its sensuality, its capacity to deceive, its capacity to influence human character subtly but powerfully, and indeed, even its capacity to undermine state security. The music of the ancient Greeks is irretrievably lost. But most of their concerns about music remain vitally relevant today, and so deep and indelible has been the impact of their ideas over the centuries that an adequate grasp of contemporary musical issues is scarcely conceivable without consideration of what they had to say.

For all our musical and philosophical sophistication, it seems that the Greeks 'lived' their musics far more deeply than we do ours. Difficult though it may be for us to think of music as the kind of thing capable of revealing important fundamental truths about the world, for the ancient Greeks there seems to have been little doubt. And for good reason: their world was, after all, a fundamentally musical one.

Appearance and Reality, Deception and Truth: Plato's Music Philosophy

Introductory Remarks: Understanding Plato

In the history of philosophical reflection on music there are a handful of pivotal figures whose ideas have left such an indelible mark that virtually all subsequent discussions of music's nature and value are forced to contend with them. Among such figures, **Plato** (427–347 B.C.) may well be the most prominent. In fact, it would be difficult to identify anyone in the history of philosophical reflection on music whose influence has been more enduring. Music was but one among a vast array of concerns to which he devoted attention, but it was such a ubiquitous presence in ancient Greece that his writings return to it time and again. Accordingly, Plato leaves us a number of subtly differing perspectives on music's nature and value, perspectives that do not exactly cohere into the tight philosophical system one might expect of someone writing on the subject today. In fact, because music is associated with such a wide range of issues for Plato, his claims can seem confused and contradictory. It helps, then, to recognize two things at the outset: first, that music was not a specialized, insular enterprise for the Greeks, but something that pervaded virtually every aspect of their lives; and second, that music was therefore something Plato took very, very seriously — more seriously, perhaps, than even modern musicians can fully grasp. Because of its potency, and because it was an inextricable part of society, education, and practically all facets of life, music was something toward which Plato was deeply ambivalent. His attitude toward it was one of both profound respect and deep suspicion. Extreme though his views sometimes sound, however, many of our current concerns and attitudes toward music are scarcely less ambivalent, as we shall see in due course.

What Plato has to say about music is not always pleasing or endearing. Some of his claims sound quaint, naive, or antiquated; others are simply offensive. But we would do well to resist the temptation to dismiss what he says as outmoded, outgrown, and utterly irrelevant to current concerns. It is remarkable how many of the fundamental questions with which modern music philosophy continues to wrestle find their first formulation in the writings of Plato. His belief in music's power to shape character for good and ill, or to enhance or undermine the security of society and state, his advocacy of musical censorship, and his disdain for musical innovation — all these seem extreme to modern sensibilities. And perhaps they are. But again, it is important to remember that these beliefs were linked to an unwavering belief in music's centrality to a good life and a just society. A fuller understanding of his reasons for taking the positions he did may help us examine some of the things we take for granted, and perhaps judge his views a bit less impatiently.

Because they are part of a far reaching philosophical system, Plato's views on music can only be fully understood in light of the attitudes, assumptions, and values that underlie that system. Among these, one conviction is crucially important: the unexamined life, Plato believes, is simply not worth living; the key to a good life and a just society is reason. Living well requires that all practical and moral matters be guided by rationality. Even at its most theoretical and abstract, then, Plato's thought never strays far from the pressing matters of what is true, right, and trustworthy, and the implications of these concerns for individual and social action. From these two basic strands, reason and moral rectitude, Plato weaves a delicate philosophical tapestry that probes many of the most fundamental concerns of philosophy: What is the relationship between perception and conception, the material and the mental world, the world given the senses and the world given the mind? What role do the senses play in the acquisition or verification of knowledge? What are the grounds for knowledge? What is the difference between mere appearance and reality, between knowledge and opinion? How do we get beyond the particularity of individual experience and personal perspective to the kind of truths that are timeless and universal? Whose version of the truth ought we be obliged to acknowledge? By whose rules should society and human social relations be governed? And why?

Provocative musical counterparts to many of these questions spring readily to mind: How does music relate to reason and morality? Is it more closely allied with reality or illusion, truth or opinion? Can it be considered knowing in any legitimate sense or is it only illusory, a distraction? What is music good for? Does its sensual and expressive character contribute anything of lasting significance to human knowledge? Or is its value exhausted in whatever transient pleasure it gives? Has it anything to offer education, or is it an entertaining frill, a release, a diversion? Worse yet, can it cause us harm?

Again, the answers Plato offers are not always entirely clear. But ambiguity is to be expected where new terrain is being explored, and it would hardly be fair to expect him to speak to us in terms we find immediately meaningful. Our world and our musics are separated from his by an immense semantic gulf, and if his claims are to be understood, we must at least meet him halfway. Even our most fundamental and familiar of concepts—'art' and 'music', for instance—lack precise parallels in Greek language and experience. Ancient Greeks did not draw strong distinctions among what we know as the arts. Nor did they distinguish between the kind of activity we call artistic and other kinds of making, between arts and crafts. The term *techne* described them all. Nor does there appear to have been a strong demarcation between music per se and other areas of human endeavor. The Greek *mousike* was freely employed in contexts most moderns would have great difficulty conceiving of as musical. Add to these important realizations the fact that the idea of a distinctly 'aesthetic' realm of experience would not emerge for nearly two thousand years, and we can begin to appreciate how wrong it would be to approach Plato demanding the kind of precision and clarity we do of contemporary philosophers. The enormous chasm that separates our cultures, our languages, and our musical practices should alert us to a serious potential for distortion when applying his words to our situations and practices.

Even ascribing to Plato a philosophy of 'music' introduces a degree of distortion, since to the ancient Greek mind music, poetry, drama, and often dance were practically inseparable from one another. The boundary we like to draw between matters musical and extramusical is likewise probably not one with which Plato would be comfortable, since musical, social, political, and moral concerns were for him intimately connected. Music for Plato was such an indissoluble part of human activity and interaction that his accounts of it are invariably linked to concerns about reason, morality, the good society, and the good life. In short, musical experience as Plato conceived of it was never an autonomous affair, isolable from other (as we know them) arts or the important business of daily living.

One of the great impediments to understanding Plato adequately, then, is what might be called cultural chauvinism: the assumption that our historical vantage point somehow gives us privileged insight into the nature of music that eluded the classical Greeks because of the primitivity of their music and language. Athenian culture was hardly primitive. Indeed, one might well argue that in many respects theirs is the richer conception of music, and ours the poorer: that our sophisticated ideas and practices are profoundly lacking in the concreteness, immediacy, expressive vitality, and deeply social significance so central to the Greek musical experience. To the Greek mind, life and culture were inconceivable without music. Music was not so much the name of a thing as a quality, one which could be found in a tremendously broad range of human activity. For precisely this reason, numerous scholars and musicians persuasively maintain that ancient Greek culture achieved the ideal union of art and experience.

Thus, appreciating Plato's ideas about music requires an attitude of respect, perhaps even humility, toward the civilization within and about which he wrote. Rather than criticizing his inclination to blur what for us are comfortable distinctions, we would do well to accept it as a reflection of a culture and a world in many respects richer than ours: one in which the segregation of art from life was unthinkable, in which music was not an idle diversion or pastime but essential to living, the mark of an educated individual, an expectation of virtually every member of society, a presence that vivified all endeavors from the mundane to the most supremely intellectual.

Other Influences

While Plato's is the first comprehensive philosophy of which we have extensive documentation, it hardly emerged from a vacuum. Understanding his various claims on matters pertaining to music requires a general orientation to his motives, influences, and predilections. It is important to understand, for instance, that Plato was decidedly not what we might call a 'democrat': committed to egalitarian principles and the supremacy of individual rights. He was, rather, an aristocrat who was not particularly enamored with democratic governance, and whose faith in the common person was not particularly keen. Most people's capacity to judge what is best, he believed, is clouded by self-interests that lead them to neglect the greater needs of society at large. Not without reason did he hold these views. He lived during a period when the glory of the Athenian empire had begun to fade, and in his view the blame for the moral, economic, social, and cultural decay lay with the democratic institutions of his day. In fact, the death of his long-time friend and mentor, **Socrates** (469–399 B.C.), was for Plato vivid evidence that ordinary people were ill prepared for just, rational decisions. Accused by a democratic government of sedition, Socrates had been forced to choose between recanting his philosophical convictions or fleeing to avoid persecution. Rather than betray the truth, Socrates ended his life by drinking poison hemlock. As far as Plato was concerned, then, the shallow, popular, easily influenced views of the masses were no basis for a government dedicated to important principles like justice, wisdom, and truth, and to the preservation of Greece's illustrious heritage. Situated at the threshold of the great Athenian empire's demise, as one writer puts it, Plato peered "prophetically into the gloom and [threw] all the energies of his heroic mind into the task of averting it."[2] Since neither tradition nor democracy could be relied upon to achieve the important business at hand, Plato placed his trust in reason and rationality. The ideal state, he firmly believed, should be ruled by philosophers—individuals with the intellectual acumen to distinguish needs from mere wants, and to govern with the best interests of a just society at heart. The good life, in other words, was fundamentally reliant upon superior reason; and reason, of course, was without question the domain of philosophy.

A short digression will show the potential relevance of these convictions and dispositions to music philosophy. As Plato sees it, the same kind of authority that governs affairs of state should determine matters of musical value: what music—whose music—is good, and why? On such matters, musicians are generally less democratic, less pluralistic, and less egalitarian than on questions of governance. Loath though we might be to condone authoritative imposition, we are hardly inclined to entrust estimates of musical value to egalitarian principles—to popularity polls. Does a commitment to pluralistic and egalitarian principles in social affairs implicate a similar orientation to musical ones? Under what conditions and on what grounds might the imposition of musical values or standards be justified? Surely, not all assessments of musical value are equally valid: some, for instance, are grounded in informed perception, while others seem to be rooted in nothing more substantial than familiarity, than unreflective 'likes' and 'dislikes'. But does it follow that judgments of musical worth should be deferred to 'authority'? Who might such authorities be? How is that authority established and maintained? What kind of principles should guide musical judgments—or are all such judgments mere expressions of personal taste? Although not all these questions were directly posed by Plato, it is important to keep them in mind as we examine what he has to say: for such questions are hardly less controversial today than they were two thousand years ago, as the final chapter of this book will demonstrate.

Another significant influence on Plato's philosophical orientation was an animated debate among his predecessors over whether reality consists of the multiplicity of particular things we encounter in the world, or whether underlying this manifold was one basic substance of which 'the many' were transformations or variations. Queer though this controversy over 'the one and the many' may sound to our ears, it is not really so archaic as it first seems: the underlying issue is, after all, not far removed from more modern scientific theories that suggest the apparently uniform is actually radically manifold—comprised, for instance, of molecules, atoms, and even electrically charged subatomic particles. Opposing sides in the ancient (fifth century B.C.) debate were championed by Heraclitus and Parmenides. The former argued that the essence of reality was change itself, a perpetual state of flux, and that stability or uniformity was only apparent: rather like a flame in a constant process of regeneration. It was Heraclitus who pointed out the impossibility of setting foot in the same river twice, urging that plurality and change were more fundamental than unity and permanence. Parmenides, on the other hand, argued that reality was a durable, changeless affair, and that change was illusory and apparent. Parmenides' 'truth' was an absolute which somehow lay behind the fleeting world of appearances: it was inaccessible to the senses, and could be attained only through reason. As we shall see, each of these positions figures prominently in Plato's accounts of music.

Plato's thought was also significantly influenced by the teachings of the Sophists, who were influential advocates of rhetorical persuasion. Widely traveled and conversant in the ways of the world (in a word, 'sophisticated'), the Sophists were what some might today call relativists. Pointing to reason's capacity for reaching diametrically opposite conclusions from the seemingly identical 'givens', as the debate between Heraclitus and Parmenides illustrates, they tended to downplay reason's power to deliver genuine or ultimate 'truth'. Truth is relative, they maintained; and the authority claimed by moral laws is just a way of consolidating sociopolitical control. Although ambivalence toward absolutes is a salient feature of modern thought, most people continue to believe in certain unconditional, universal truths—that things like genocide and terrorism are morally reprehensible, for instance. With issues like these in mind, then, it is easier to comprehend the utter disdain in which Plato held the Sophists: for their polished rhetorical skills, like those of modern lawyers and politicians, stressed style over substance, delivery over idea. Such relativism was clearly linked in his mind to the disintegration of values he was so profoundly committed to averting.

The ancient doctrines of **Pythagoras** (sixth century B.C.) were also strong influences on Plato's musical ideas. Thanks to the musical authority Damon, close personal advisor to Pericles, the founder of the Athenian empire, Pythagorean ideas were solidly institutionalized at the time Plato wrote. Students of music will recognize Pythagoras as discoverer of the relationship between pitch and the length of vibrating bodies, and of the fact that intervals could be expressed as the ratios between those lengths (the octave 2:1, the fifth 3:2, the fourth 4:3, and so forth). In addition to these important acoustical discoveries, Pythagoras proffered a decidedly less empirical body of ideas buttressed by the seemingly magical relationship between sound and number. Notable among these was a doctrine to the effect that planets and stars of different sizes emit different pitches, all merging in a vast, but unheard, cosmic music. Thus, sound and music attained important status as clues to the nature of the universe, each in turn being inextricably and mysteriously associated with number and ratio,

which, as if by magic, could exist apart from material things. Numbers and ratios were the presumed essence of concrete, sense-perceived reality.

Pythagorean theory also had it that changes or modulations in numbers and
their attendant harmonies could affect changes in personal character, so that
moral and spiritual life were intimately wed to musical phenomena. Belief that
number and ratio were sources of important insight into ultimate reality, divine
gifts with the power to mediate truths inaccessible to sense perception, led the
Pythagoreans further and further from the practice and sound of music itself.
The numbers behind the sound, capable of being grasped by the mind alone,
were of greater musical significance than musical experience per se. Accordingly, music's educational value had little to do with sounds heard, or music
made. As one modern commentator explains, "The ear hears sounds, but only
mind can interpret them and grasp their harmony."[3] Thus, curiously, while on
the one hand Pythagorean beliefs secured music a position of unsurpassed prominence in Greek education because of its capacity to shape character, music's
primary significance had little to do with the 'doing' or enjoyment of music. Its
real significance was in its mathematical nature: an idea that was to dominate
musical thought throughout antiquity and the middle ages and whose vestiges
can be easily observed even today.

In short, the foundation on which Plato's accounts of music are built consists of an unwavering belief in the centrality of reason to the good life and the
just society. And that foundation is comprised of a host of underlying, dualistic
tensions between authority and popularity, tradition and innovation, stability and
change, uniformity and diversity, universality and particularity, discipline and
pleasure, and idea and sense. In each instance, it is the former with which Plato
casts his lot.

Reality, Reason, and the Good Life

We are now ready to examine the remarkable synthesis which Plato forged from
these various influences. Plato's conception of reality is fundamentally dualistic, a precarious integration of the opposing views of Heraclitus and Parmenides.
Both were mistaken, he believed, to assume that all reality was of a single, unitary fabric, whether changing or permanent. Yet each had been partially correct. Reality is essentially twofold. There exists a reality which consists of particularity and transience, of the individual physical things given to sense
experience; and there exists as well a reality which is unchanging and permanent, one which confers unity upon diversity and multiplicity. The former is the
world of concrete, tangible, perceptible things—the world of particularity in
which no two things or events are exactly alike. It is a transitory world of fleeting appearances, known through sense impressions. In it, nothing endures.

But there exists as well a higher reality, the immutable world of Forms—of
archetypes, or universals, a reality given only to the intellect or mind or idea.
'Ideal' reality is the world of abstractions, which bring together particular things
into classes based upon common features. We might say, for instance, that among

the things that populate the ideal realm is a universal, all-inclusive concept of (say) music; and the numerous specific instances of 'music' that we actually hear and experience each partake of that ideal 'musicality' to one degree or another (are, we might say, more or less musical), depending upon their adequacy in relation to that universal form. Ideals are the eternal models by which all particular instances or concrete occurrences are recognized or evaluated. Since in this account of things particulars always fall short of their archetype, the universal of which they are particular examples, all particular things in the world are in some way or other imitations of their ideals. This is the Platonic doctrine of mimesis. Plato's world, then, consists of varying degrees or levels of reality, the ideal that are most real, faithful imitations that are 'somewhat' real, and faulty imitations or outright deceptions that only distort and falsify.

Unfortunately, this ideal realm is never wholly accessible, never directly knowable. It is approached most closely through reason, but one cannot know with certainty whether a given conception is true or merely apparent. Thus, although one's grasp of the ideal may be more or less complete, more or less adequate, it is not at all a product of people's beliefs. Ideals are not constructions of human imagination, but the very essences of things, their innermost reality. They exist whether we know them or not. They are no mere conventions, relative to communities of like-minded individuals, as many moderns might be tempted to describe them. Indeed, such relativistic inclinations were precisely why Plato felt it necessary to establish that the ideal realm was immutable: there had to be, he believed, something enduring, trustworthy, and absolute, beyond the world of flux.

Note carefully, then, that for Plato all reality is not created equal. That which is given to the senses is transitory and of a distinctly lower order than the ideal or universal. It can and often does deceive. In short, and in many respects science has borne Plato out on this point, things are not necessarily what they appear to be. Although this does not in itself rule out all possibility of the sensible revealing something of the ideal, Plato appears to have been too anxious to establish an absolute foundation for knowledge and moral action to make such a concession. More often than not, he claims the images and objects given to the senses cannot be reliable indications of reality as it ultimately is—a disposition, as we shall see, with ominous implications for a sense-based thing like music.

Plato's allegory of the cave[4] illustrates vividly the implications of this dualistic metaphysical stance for his epistemology, or theory of knowledge. In it, Socrates (Plato) describes prisoners held captive deep within a cave, bound from birth, and unable to look or move about. Behind them burns a fire, the light from which casts on the cave wall before the prisoners shadow-images of people and objects that pass behind them. Since their perceptions of their world are mediated entirely by these shadowy images, they come to constitute reality as the prisoners know it. However cleverly or consistently they may learn to discern or distinguish among these shadow images, they remain, as shadows, illusory.

Now suppose one of the prisoners were somehow freed to turn toward the fire, and ultimately to make the ascent from the cave to the light of day. Growing accustomed to the light would require radical reorientation, learning to see all over again. Like all educational experience, the new at first appears illusory, becoming comprehensible only with considerable pain and effort. And should this prisoner return to the cave to share her enlightenment with the others, they would in all likelihood reject her as a heretic rather than accept the illusory nature of their existence (a clear allusion to the circumstances that led to Socrates' demise).

Our purposes do not demand we follow the allegory further. But we should take careful note of the radically different kinds of knowledge here described: one of shadows mistaken for reality; the other of the things or substances themselves. Shadow-reality, that which we know empirically from sense experience, is of a lower order than knowledge of the world as it is in itself. True knowledge is only to be had by the painful and difficult ascent from the cave into the full light of the sun, by turning one's back on what is apparent, obvious, or commonsense.

This theory is presented elsewhere in more technical fashion. Represent reality, Plato suggests, by a vertical line[5] divided into two unequal segments, one representing the realm of the visible or sensible, the other the intelligible. These correspond to the world of images, impressions, or opinion (the greater, lower segment), and the world of genuine knowledge (the shorter, higher segment). Then further divide each segment into two more segments, also of unequal proportions. The first or lowest segment consists of perceptions of the shadows, reflections, and images of things; the second consists of perceptions of actual things, "the animals which we see, and everything that grows or is made."[6] Both these divisions, being sense mediated, fall below our initial division of the line, although direct perception is of a higher order than imagining or perceiving imitations of objects.

The third segment of the line transcends sensibility, entering the intelligible realm of reason. Unlike imagination and sense perception, it consists in the conceptual grasp of things and relations. It grasps the unchanging characteristics of things: the 'triangularity' a triangle shares with all other triangles, for instance. Finally we ascend to the highest level, that of absolute and immutable truths untainted by particularity or concreteness. As Plato says in *Timaeus*, the realm of self-existent ideas is "always the same, uncreated and indestructible, never receiving anything into itself from without, nor itself going out to any other, but invisible and imperceptible by any sense, and of which the contemplation is granted to intelligence only."[7]

Each successive rung on this ladder of knowledge attains a greater degree of clarity and trustworthiness than the previous rung. Each step in its ascent thus represents a step closer to the ideal, which is, paradoxically to our minds, the most real by virtue of its unchanging character. At the lowest level one encounters a world of fancy and imagination; at the second, the world of belief, faith, or opinion. Neither quite qualifies as knowledge, and the most one can hope to attain in these realms is true or accurate opinion. At the third level one attains understanding, and at the fourth, purely abstract reason. There is a decisive qualitative difference between mere 'true opinion' and the higher realm of mind. They have different origins and are of different natures. "[T]he one is implanted in us by instruction, the other by persuasion; the one is always accompanied by true reason, the other is without reason; the one cannot be overcome by persuasion, but the other can; and lastly, every man may be said to share in true opinion, but mind is the attribute of the gods and of very few men."[8] Ideas and ultimate understanding are exclusively affairs of mind. The realm of opinion and sense consist, by contrast, of merely transitory things and events. And finally, there is a realm comprised of images modeled after a reality not their own: since the image "exists ever as the fleeting shadow of some other," and is apprehended only "by a kind of spurious reason," its dreamlike character is "hardly real."[9]

This Platonic account runs rather contrary to our commonsense manner of thinking. The empirical world of the senses is 'real'; yet, because the senses alone cannot provide true knowledge, their significance pales in comparison to the 'light' (note the visual metaphor) of the rational realm. The highest reality, the most real, is ideal.

Although Plato holds that ideas constitute the highest reality, it bears repeating that these ideas are not to be found in private, subjective states of mind. They are objective, the essence of any individual thing. Concrete, particular things are real only to the extent that they partake of or measure up to their universal forms. Since the nature of physical reality is such that no two objects or events are entirely identical, only ideas attain perfect, unchanging reality. To this ultimate state of perfection, everything else aspires, but necessarily falls short.

But if reason is the definitively human capacity, why do people behave irrationally? If people know what goodness is, why do they not behave in accordance with that knowledge? Because of unfortunate deformities in people's souls, Plato suggests. Human souls consist of three parts: the rational, the spirited, and bodily desires or appetites. Each part plays an essential role in maintaining an ordered and balanced soul. The properly balanced soul is virtuous and just, presumably because spirit and bodily appetites are kept in check by rationality. An imbalanced soul leads to vice, cowardice, or any number of other deformities, depending upon which part of the soul prevails. Although rationality plays a key regulative role (in convincing the spirited part of the soul to help it control the appetitive, for instance), true happiness requires a balance of the rational, the spirited, and bodily or corporeal. Thus, in conspicuous contrast to later Christian attitudes toward the ways of the flesh, Plato concedes rather important functions to the spirited and the appetitive. Rationality ever retains an upper hand, but the highest good lies in a harmonious balance among the soul's three faculties. In such concord lies the key to genuine happiness and the good life.

Plato's utopian city-state mirrors the soul's tripartite structure, consisting of three social classes, each with its distinctive attributes and responsibilities. The producer or worker class ideally consists of individuals in whom the appetitive part of the soul is dominant. The army, or guardian class, is comprised of those in whom the spirited (aggressive, animated) element is preeminent. The governing class is predominantly rational. The appetitive and spirited elements thus perform important roles, yet remain subservient to the rational so that society attains the same harmony as the ideally balanced soul. As we shall see shortly, these epistemological, ontological, and political convictions are profoundly influential in shaping Plato's conception of the nature and value of music, as well as of education.

Music Imitation: Mimesis

Recall that for Plato things are real to the extent they partake of their ideal essence, a 'partaking' which must, in the empirical world, always remain partial. The relationship between empirical things and their archetypal or ideal forms is, according to Plato, essentially imitative. This doctrine of mimesis raises a number of intriguing issues regarding the status of sense-based things like music. Do the imitations that comprise empirical experience help shape or clarify the ideals to which they relate? Or does the ideal realm rather consist strictly of a priori and immutable 'givens' that exist in hermetic isolation, organizing experience yet immune from its influence? Some evidence for both positions can be found in Plato's writings, but more often than not it seems the imitation has relatively little to say to the imitated, particularly those imitations that lie at furthest remove from the ideal. Although the issue may seem obscure at first, it has fairly significant implications for music. Since in Plato's view music is an imitative art, the relation between the imitation and the imitated has a significant bearing on our understanding of his philosophy of music. Precisely what kind of imitation is music? What does it imitate, and how? Given its imitative or representational capacity, does music have the potential to reveal anything of the Truth? Or is music merely entertaining and decorative? If it is a diversion, is it harmless? Or is it a dangerously attractive illusion?

There is not a short answer to these questions, at least not one which does justice to Plato. Music's mimetic character figures centrally both in his loftiest claims for music and in his most heated denunciations. At times he seems to imply that as an earthly manifestation of ideal or divine harmony music can give us vital, if fleeting, insights into its nature—that music tells us things about the harmony of the universe we could not otherwise know. He also seems to imply at times that music imitates the beauty of the harmoniously balanced soul. It is tempting, therefore, to conclude that music's beauty partakes of the ideal or perfect beauty it imitates, a beauty inaccessible in this world except through music's mimetic power. Without this positive interpretation of musical mimesis it is extremely difficult to account for the crucial roles Plato confers upon music in education, and in creating and sustaining the good life.

Unfortunately, his interpretation of the matter is not this simple or generous. While on the one hand he says, "poets are a divine race and often in their strains, by the aid of the Muses and the Graces, they attain truth,"[10] it is abundantly clear that 'often' is simply not good enough when it comes to the serious business of truth and morality. Music may indeed imitate ideal truth, harmony, and beauty, but it may just as easily misrepresent them. Since there is no foolproof way of distinguishing reliable imitations from deceitful ones, music's potential to mislead is a source of grave concern. The musician's inspiration is fundamentally irrational, a madness that cannot be given free reign in Plato's utopian city-state. In fact, music's irrationality poses such a threat that it has to be banished. So much for a divine race whose strains attain truth.

Perhaps Plato intends to point out the existence of a broad range of mimetic veracity, with the flawed and deceitful imitations of the shadow-realm on the one hand, and those that afford glimpses of true light on the other. But however much he valued music (and there is no doubt he did), his quest for certainty, for a reliable truth supported by reason, was his most pressing concern. Judged by that standard, musical imitations sink to the depths of the cave. They are third-rate copies, mere imitations of appearances. And regrettably, most musicians are not particularly concerned with the veracity of their imitations: "The imitative artist will be in a brilliant state of intelligence about his own creations? Nay, very much the reverse. And still he will go on imitating without knowing what makes a thing good or bad, and may be expected therefore to imitate only that which appears to be good to the ignorant multitude? Just so. Thus far then we are pretty well agreed that the imitator has no knowledge worth mentioning of what he imitates. Imitation is only a kind of play or sport. . . . And now tell me . . . has not imitation been shown by us to be concerned with that which is thrice removed from the truth? Certainly."[11] Musical imitations are clearly "a long way off the truth."[12]

Appetites, Pleasures, and Controls

Music's untrustworthiness and irrationality are not Plato's only worries. If they were, music might still earn its place in the utopian scheme of things as a source of harmless entertainment or diversion. But music has exceptional power to move and stir the emotions, a power that can be used for good or ill, to strengthen or weaken, to soothe or arouse. Music can nurture temperance and moderation, but it can also undermine self-control and disrupt the harmonious balance of the virtuous soul. Music can make people lethargic and indolent, or volatile and emotional. As much as Plato worried about the deceptiveness of musical imitations, he worried about their appetitive appeal, their seductive pleasure: "Then the imitative poet who aims at being popular is not by nature made, nor is his art intended, to please or affect the rational principle in the soul; but he will prefer the passionate and fitful temper which is easily imitated? Clearly."[13] Music, at least that which caters to popular demand, appeals less to the reasoned than to the appetitive part of the soul. It "feeds and waters the passions instead of drying them up; she lets them rule, although they ought to be controlled, if mankind are ever to increase in happiness and virtue."[14] If music's seductiveness is given free reign, "not law and the reason . . . but pleasure and pain will be the rulers in our State."[15]

Pleasure must be controlled, and used in service of proper moral ends so as to lead people "always to hate what you ought to hate, and love what you ought to love. . ."[16] Musical pleasure is not given us by the gods as a hedonistic end in itself, but rather as a means for developing our instincts and values along lines congruent with reason and moral uprightness. For these reasons, "those who seek for the best kind of song and music ought not to seek for that which is pleasant, but for that which is true . . ."[17] Music's emotional force needs to be grounded, linked in some concrete way to the True and the Good. Otherwise, people may wrongly conclude that musical value is merely a matter of personal preference or taste, a function of the degree of pleasure it affords. Although Plato does not reject musical pleasure altogether, he does go to great lengths to establish the insufficiency of pleasure to musical value; he denounces diversion, entertainment, and amusement in and of themselves. "[T]he equal is not equal or the symmetrical symmetrical because somebody thinks or likes something. . . . [W]hen anyone says that music is to be judged of by pleasure, his doctrine cannot be admitted; and if there be any music of which pleasure is the criterion, such music is not to be sought out or deemed to have any real excellence . . ."[18]

It is not so much that Plato disliked pleasure; but pleasure is a very subjective thing, and people with bad taste may take considerable pleasure in bad music. The situation is worsened by musicians' inclinations to pander to mass tastes, which reinforces the dangerous conviction that unreflective preferences are as valid as any, that the pleasure a music affords is a reasonable indication of its worth. Not just anyone's pleasure can count as a measure of musical worth: "[T]he fairest music is that which delights the best and best educated . . ."[19] Whatever the pleasure it affords, musical worth depends on three things: what is being imitated, the truth or fidelity of the imitation, and the expertise with which it is executed.[20] The best music must share the rational consistency and harmonious balance of ideal truth and goodness. Since sensuous pleasure is associated with both good and bad imitations, music requires special precautions: "Music is more celebrated than any other kind of imitation, and therefore requires the greatest care of them all. For if a man makes a mistake here, he may do himself the greatest of injury by welcoming evil dispositions, and the mistake may be very difficult to discern . . ."[21]

As we have noted, the propensities of performing musicians only seem to make matters worse. In their preoccupation with technical prowess, they too often neglect the imitated and the fidelity of the imitation. Such recklessness can deteriorate into vulgar and lawless innovation: "They were men of genius, but they had no perception of what is just and lawful in music; raging like Bacchanals and possessed with inordinate delights—mingling lamentations with hymns, and paeans with dythrambs . . . and making one general confusion; ignorantly affirming that music has no truth and, whether good or bad, can only be judged of rightly by the pleasure of the hearer. And by composing such licentious poems, and adding to them words as licentious, they have inspired the multitude with lawlessness and boldness, and made them fancy that they can judge for themselves about melody and song."[22]

Such blatant disregard for authority, such "insolent refusal to regard the opinion of the better, by reason of an overdaring sort of liberty,"[23] poses a dangerous threat to national security[24] and cannot be tolerated. There would be no pandering to mass taste in Plato's utopian city-state. So potent and far-reaching are music's powers that their influence cannot be left to chance. People cannot be trusted with music. And since even musicians are unreliable when it comes to monitoring music's use and abuse, the final court of appeal in musical matters must be authority. "[T]hose who are themselves good and also honourable in the state, creators of noble actions—let their poems be sung, even though they be not very musical."[25] "Art," as Beardsley puts it, "is too serious to be left to the artist."[26]

Plato's other strategic weapon in the battle to keep music's influence under control is tradition. The innovators of his day indulged in all manner of disturbing musical practices, among them the mixing of melodies and words of opposing character, and the mixing of "the voices and sounds of animals and of men and instruments, and every other sort of noise, as if they were all one." They engaged in panharmonic playing that obscured modal purity. They created "still further havoc by separating the rhythm and the figure of the dance from the melody, setting bare words to metre, and also separating the melody and the rhythm from the words, using the lyre or the [*aulos*] alone," a practice he considers "exceedingly coarse and tasteless" since it "leads to every sort of irregularity and trickery."[27] In contrast to such practices, traditional music is purer, its meanings clear and uncontaminated.

So profound is music's potential moral influence that Plato will stop at nothing to assure its proper use. Strict adherence to tradition helps, as does respect for the authority of the learned; but the persuasiveness of music must be controlled at any cost. The best melodies are those that are "expressive of virtue of soul or body, or of images of virtue . . ."[28] Upon people whose songs suggest bad people lead pleasant lives, or suggest there is gain to be had through immoral means, he would "inflict the heaviest penalties on any one in all the land . . ."[29] People who claim that ". . . wicked men are often happy, and the good miserable; and that injustice is profitable when undetected, but that justice is a man's own loss and another's gain—these things we shall forbid them to utter, and command them to sing and say the opposite."[30]

These rather depressing accounts of music as something ill understood by those who practice it, and as a static practice purged of innovation and creativity, are among the least endearing features of Plato's thought. Equally troubling is his belief in music's obligation to portray morally good acts. To be sure, music is accorded almost unlimited power, but at a tremendous cost.

Harmonia, Concord, and Unity

The idea of *harmonia*, of harmony, balance, and cohesiveness, is crucial to ancient Greek thought. Harmonia forges unity from diversity, pattern from randomness, relatedness from difference. Health, virtuous character, spiritual well-being, the well-ordered state, the interdependence and essential orderliness of the manifold parts of the universe: almost all things good, it seems, seem to have been attributable in some degree to the influence of this magical force.

The specifically musical *harmoniai*, the Greek modes, seem to have been perceptible embodiments of this mysterious force, affording glimpses of an ideal harmony otherwise unfathomable. Music's harmony was significant not only musically, but ethically, morally, politically, and socially as well. The more one experienced and understood properly harmonious music, the more one understood the harmony which lay at the center of virtually everything of value to the Greek mind. Music's remarkable unity, its capacity to bring together disparate parts into a beautiful, ordered whole, was thus one of the most vivid symbols of antiquity.

The precise structure and sound of the musical harmoniai is lost forever. We know, however, that each harmonia was believed to express and dispose a distinctive type of character. The ionian and lydian, Plato claims, dispose softness, indolence, and sentimentality; the tenor lydian, or mixolydian, expresses lamentation and sorrow; and the phrygian and dorian beget courage and temperance, respectively.[31] Precisely how this could be remains one of the great mysteries of musical history. Their expressive character was probably at least partly a result of differing tonal configurations, since some retuning of the lyre was apparently necessary to negotiate changes among them. Much of the historical speculation about the precise nature of these tonal patterns over the centuries has derived from the writings of Aristoxenus, whose Greater Perfect System has often been taken as the tonal basis for Greek musical practice. According to prominent scholars, however, Aristoxenus' system was probably a successor to the older Greek harmoniai, one that failed to retain many of their individuating qualities. In Anderson's view, in Aristoxenus' system, "instead of individual Harmoniai we now have segments of an extended Dorian scale pattern which begin on successive degrees of that scale. To call these segments modes and build a theory of modality on them, as has so often been done, is to make strange use of language."[32] Winnington-Ingram offers the same assessment: it is "impossible to take [the species of Aristoxenus] as they stand as representing the old modes adequately."[33] Thus, the standardized system of 'modes' differentiated only by the location of whole and half steps should not be equated with the individually distinct harmoniai that preceded it.

This being the case, musical harmoniai cannot be conceived of as tonal patterns whose identity and character remained stable throughout ancient Greek history. In pre-Platonic times, when the Pythagorean doctrines that eventually influenced Plato were most predominant, harmoniai may indeed have been sharply individuated, contrasted with each other in easily discernible ways. As they were absorbed into a body of common practice, though, they became increasingly standardized, losing much of their former distinctiveness. Thus, it is possible that the expressive character Plato imputes to the harmoniai had already eroded to a significant extent, and that the qualities and influences he attributes to them, though once apparent, were becoming less discernible. This gradual process of dissolution would make for ambiguity that would help explain Plato's seemingly prudish attitude toward musical innovation.

The original musical harmoniai were probably ethnic song styles or 'dialects',[34] distinguished from each other as much by rhythmic features, ornamentation, and other expressive devices as by scale pattern. Their character, suggests Anderson, was probably a function not only of intervals used, but also of tessitura, timbre, melodic cliché, and distinctive intervallic sequences.[35] Verbal associations and cultural/ethnic stereotypes could have had some bearing upon the character attributed to various harmoniai as well. As practices in a predominantly aural and improvised tradition, it would in fact be surprising had the harmoniai not been subject to the evolution and mutation characteristic of such traditions. Thus, the ancient harmoniai gradually became replaced by a system defined by a master scale pattern that enabled, among other things, the 'pan-harmonic playing' that so worried Plato. The absence of vertical sonorities also helps explain his concern about ambiguity, since without the ballast or sense of musical bearing reinforced by harmony in the modern, vertical sense, relatively minor rhythmic and melodic deviations may have been quite disorienting.

Some of Plato's boldest claims for music derive from his conception of music's generally harmonious nature. In *Timaeus* he says, "Moreover, so much of music as is adapted to the sound of the voice and to the sense of hearing is granted to us for the sake of harmony; and harmony, which has motions akin to the revolutions of our souls, is not . . . given . . . with a view to irrational pleasure . . . but . . . to correct any discord which may have arisen in the courses of the soul, and to be our ally in bringing her into harmony and agreement with herself . . ."[36] Music's harmony provides us with a profoundly important model of harmonious balance, unity, and integrity. Indeed, it goes beyond imitation to actually ". . . implant that harmony of which we speak."[37] Music can help balance the soul and thereby attune it to the ideal. As the universe blends and balances its opposing forces, music imparts harmony to thought and action, a capacity of tremendous significance, as ". . . the life of man in every part has need of harmony and rhythm."[38] In proper proportion, music and gymnastic bring concord to the human soul, each, like the strings of the lyre, being variously tightened and relaxed until the spirited and wisdom-loving parts of the soul are duly harmonized. Indeed, "he who mingles music with gymnastic in the fairest proportions, and best attempers them to the soul, may rightly be called the true musician and harmonist in a far higher sense than the tuner of strings."[39] On the other hand, the imbalance created by discordant music is for Plato as pernicious as harmony is good. As Portnoy puts it, ". . . bards who composed music incongruous with the natural order . . . were destroyers of souls and the fore-runners of social doom."[40]

Not all musical beauty consists of harmonia's balance of opposing tendencies. Plato does allow for simple music with simple beauty. In *Philebus* he writes, "When sounds are smooth and clear, and have a single pure tone, then I mean to say that they are not relatively but absolutely beautiful, and have natural pleasures associated with them."[41] If this sounds like a concession to intrinsically musical meaning and value, however, we should note that simple, nonimitative beauty appears to be of a lower order. In contrast to harmonious musical beauty that presents itself to both mind and sense, simple musical beauty is primarily sensual. And unfortunately, ". . . pleasure is not the first of possessions, nor yet the second . . ."[42]

Despite its sensible pleasures, musical harmony's primary value lies in what it does for mind and character. Music's heard harmony is less important than the study of harmonics it enables, of the (ideal) numbers and ratios that lie behind musical consonance. Musical harmony thus provides insight into the essentially harmonious nature of beauty, truth, and virtue. Here lies the crucial difference between the skilled performer and the true musician: performers' interests adhere to music's surfaces, placing ear before mind. Although they may "... investigate the numbers of the harmonies which are heard ... they never attain to problems—that is to say, they never reach the natural harmonies of number, or reflect why some numbers are harmonious and others not." Such musical endeavor is vital "... if sought with a view to the beautiful and good; but if pursued in any other spirit, useless."[43]

For Plato, music could exemplify concord with a vividness found few other places in the perceptible world. And yet, whether this is to music's ultimate advantage or disadvantage depends upon one's perspective. On the one hand, it confers rational status on something Plato otherwise considers primarily sensual and irrational. On the other hand, it radically separates musical practice from musical understanding. Since the highest reality lies beyond the particularity of empirical experience, harmony is better grasped through mathematical relation and proportion than through musical sounds and practices. Thus, musical science becomes severed from musical practice, and each is relegated to different levels of education. The higher education is rational, involving the intellectual study of musical harmonics and through them the natural order of beauty, virtue, and justice. The lower education, comprised of music making and gymnastic, is more psychological than logical. Through musical performance, music's harmony, balance, and temperance would become part of people's nature over time, to their personal benefit and to that of the state.

Since higher, ideal harmony is not so much heard as grasped by the mind, music's order and proportion earn it a place of prominence in the quadrivium alongside geometry, mathematics, and astronomy, with which it is closely allied. At the same time, music making habituates people's souls to harmony and measure, thereby discouraging unhealthy inclinations toward discord or immoderation. The two levels of musical study work in tandem, but the highest musical value lies in music's capacity to reflect natural order, rather than the pleasures of its practice.

Character Education: Musical Ethos and Paideia

As observed earlier, one of the more perplexing aspects of ancient Greek musical thought is the attribution of a specific character to each individual harmonia, and the belief that each could shape human character in its own distinctive way: the doctrine of ethos. Music's power to influence the development of human character makes it utterly indispensable in education, or *paideia*. Music's ethetic power figures centrally in the writings of every major Greek thinker who writes of music. Yet, although there is widespread agreement that music has ethetic influence, few accounts appear to agree on the particulars. Given the evolving character of the harmoniai to which ethetic influences were linked, disagreement over their precise nature is not surprising. As we have already commented, the theory itself may well have remained popular long after the music itself ceased to support it.

While Plato offers more specific accounts of ethos than many, his claims may not have reflected mainstream Greek musical thought on the matter. He appears to have taken the moral and educational implications of the theory a good deal more seriously than many of his contemporaries who, though they acknowledged music's ethetic influences, treated them rather more casually. For Plato, music's ethetic power made it an essential agent of moral training and education. Different musical effects could apparently be dispensed almost like drugs, calming the overly excited, animating the lethargic, and creating balanced moderation from excessiveness. These effects could penetrate to the very depths of the soul, taking permanent hold there, and shaping individual character: ". . . [M]usical training is a more potent instrument than any other, because rhythm and harmony find their way into the inward places of the soul, on which they mightily fasten, imparting grace, and making the soul of him who is rightly-educated graceful, or of him who is ill-educated ungraceful . . ."[44]

Neither music nor gymnastic, the mainstays of the lower education, were studied as ends in themselves but as endeavors that would balance the competing parts of the soul, thus fostering moral virtue. People so educated prefer and seek excellence in all human endeavors, rejecting the easy and the merely expedient. Making music was therefore 'lower' not in the sense of being less important, but in being less intellectually oriented than harmonics or philosophy, and in being particularly well suited to the young. Despite a subordinate and preparatory relation to higher education, music is utterly indispensable to paideia. It imparts something nothing else can, and its neglect cannot be compensated for by other means. Music making contributes to value and character formation in a way reason alone cannot. At the end of his life, according to Plato, Socrates recounted a recurrent dream: " 'Cultivate and make music,' said the dream. And hitherto I had imagined that this was only intended to exhort and encourage me in the study of philosophy, which has been the pursuit of my life, and is the noblest and best of music . . . But I was not certain of this; for the dream might have meant music in the popular sense of the word. . . ."[45]

The importance of value education to Plato is best understood in contrast to the opposing educational philosophy of the Sophists. Their 'new' educational model stressed intellectual development at the expense of virtue and moral rectitude. Rhetorical skill was the hallmark of the Sophist education: the development of skills devoted, says Hare, to "giving an ability to persuade courts and assemblies, and thus get one's political way. The new education played on the weaknesses of the old: the old produced ambitious but fundamentally upright people; the new fostered the ambitions, and held out greater hopes of realising them, but paid less attention to uprightness."[46]

For Plato, uprightness of character is paramount if the erosion of values to which he attributes the decay of Greek society is to be contained. Rationalist though he is in so many ways, such an important task cannot be entrusted to reason alone. It is necessary, rather, to confront the problem at its source by developing character and commitment to values. Thus paideia goes well beyond mere schooling. It is not abstract academic study, not technical or vocational training, not transmission of factual knowledge. Its most fundamental purpose is to teach people "how to choose the mean and avoid the extremes on either side . . . not only in this life but in all that which is to come. For this is the way of happiness."[47]

Under his paideutic program, the young are to ". . . dwell in a land of health, amid fair sights and sounds, and receive the good in everything; and beauty, the effluence of fair works, shall flow into the eye and ear, like a health-giving breeze from a purer region, and insensibly draw the soul from the earliest years into likeness and sympathy with the beauty of reason. There can be no nobler training than that . . ."[48] The recipient of this "true education of the inner being . . . will justly blame and hate the bad . . . even before he is able to know the reason why; and when reason comes he will recognise and salute the friend with whom his education has made him long familiar."[49] It is an education ". . . given by suitable habits to the first instincts of virtue," leading one always to hate and love what one ought.[50] Dedicated to the induction of the young into the deepest values of society, this educational program educates the inner being, not so much prescriptively as persuasively. It works on a preconceptual level, instilling values that, once intellectual understanding is developed, will be all the more valued for the beauty of their foundations. The conviction with which people hold many of their rational values derives in important ways from aesthetic support or reinforcement, and Plato is determined to use music's seductive and persuasive powers for precisely that kind of support.

Early paideia is thus designed to lay the foundation for 'right reason', and music is its most important vehicle because of its power to enchant us with its harmonies.[51] This use of music's ethetic power to shape the values of the young sounds propagandistic, but the process Plato envisions is one not so much of indoctrination as of persuasion, of using music to help fend off the nihilistic conception of values as strictly arbitrary things. Ideas developed through song are more warmly received ". . . than any others which we might address to them,"[52] he says. Song's combination of verbal and ethetic forces gives it far greater influence than prose alone could ever claim. Music has, in effect, the capacity to be truer than truth, persuading where reason alone might leave one unconvinced.

It is crucial that value education be undertaken as early as possible, since ". . . in infancy more than at any other time the character is engrained by habit."[53] Indeed, it is only for fear of appearing ridiculous, Plato says, that he does not insist pregnant women be carefully tended, keeping them from violent or excessive pleasures and deliberately cultivating gentleness, benevolence, and kindness.[54] "[T]he beginning is the most important part of any work, especially in the case of a young and tender thing," he says, "for that is the time when the character is being formed and the desired impression is more readily taken."[55] Moreover, "If a man be brought up from childhood to the age of discretion and maturity in the use of orderly and severe music, when he hears the opposite, he detests it, and calls it illiberal; but if trained in the sweet and vulgar music, he deems the severer kind cold and displeasing. So . . . while he who hears them gains no more pleasure from one than from the other, the one has the advantage of making those who are trained in it better men, whereas the other makes them worse."[56]

Since the idea of music as a powerful persuader seems somewhat dubious from a contemporary perspective, it is worthy of particular note that a great many modern-day persuaders continue to take it very seriously indeed. People from politicians to advertisers capitalize on music's power to enhance radically the persuasiveness of their messages, and to dispose an audience to endure even the most mindless of messages time and time again. For those whose livelihood depends upon the successful manipulation of mass opinion in their favor, the choice of music is seldom taken lightly. Music's capacity to make people believe, to tolerate the unpalatable, and to camouflage the distasteful are ideas taken up with considerable cogency by Theodor Adorno and Jacques Attali, whose ideas will be explored in a later chapter.

Contemporary attitudes also strongly favor unrestricted freedom of expression rather than blatant censorship of the kind Plato advocated, or the musically dreary fare generated when people attempt to create music for expressly sociopolitical ends. The evils that come of control, on the modern liberal view, are far more objectionable than any conceivable ill effects of free musical expression. Music is not really all that dangerous. Note, however, that such liberal tolerance often changes considerably when the music in question glorifies drug abuse, sexual license, or some other such threat to the greater good of society. The continued use of music to underscore the significance of social and political occasions both festive and solemn is further evidence that despite protestations to the contrary, Plato may not have been all that wide of the mark.

Although Plato sometimes overstates the specificity and directness of music's persuasive power, that power is no mere figment of ancient Greek fancy. Just how hyperbolic was Plato's contention that changes in music could ultimately affect even the security of the state? Among those who watched the breakup of the Soviet bloc are some who attribute that dissolution in no small part to the unchecked influence of rock music. The contemporary notion of music as a fundamentally artistic and aesthetic undertaking must not be permitted to obscure the significant role music always plays in reinforcing social and cultural values. To the extent that it fulfills such functions, music may be considered an essential component of the social cement that sustains cohesion and continuity, or indeed, that forges community in the first place.

There is yet another aspect of Plato's paideutic program that is important for understanding the extravagance of his claims on its behalf. Paideia, for Plato, was a highly personalized thing. Failure to properly personalize education can result in failure to acquire knowledge of "the most beautiful kind of song": ". . . you have your young men herding and feeding together like young colts. No one takes his own individual colt . . . and gives him a groom to attend to him alone, and trains and rubs him down privately, and gives him the qualities in education which will make him not only a good soldier, but also a governor. . . ."[57]

Whatever the efficacy of mass instruction for the crudely utilitarian ends of training, it is ill suited to educational aspirations as ambitious as Plato's. Character education requires close master-student interaction. The prescribed three years of lyre study must have been highly individualized in nature. Especially since musical practices of the time were predominantly aural and improvisatory, modeling and imitation between master and apprentice would have been essential. And since the nature of modeling is such that a good deal more than music proper gets transmitted in the process, it is not difficult to conceive of how paideia might have exerted the kind of influence upon character and values that Plato claims.

Thus, the success of character education derived in part from the age at which it was initiated, in part from its highly personal nature, and in part from music's capacity to render propositional truths more persuasive. But music's specific ethetic effects were central and had to be carefully controlled. The sad harmoniai needed to be excluded from paideia because "even to women who have a character to maintain they are of no use, and much less to men."[58] The relaxed character of the "drinking harmonies" had to be excluded because it would develop qualities "utterly unbecoming of our guardians." The "stern resolve" of the dorian and the temperate nature of the phrygian were apparently highly desirable, though. "These two harmonies I ask you to leave; the strain of necessity and the strain of freedom . . . the strain of courage, and the strain of temperance . . ."[59] Rhythms, too, must be carefully scrutinized, believes Plato. "[C]omplex systems of metre, or metres of every kind" are to be avoided in favor of those that express a "courageous and harmonious life."[60] It is important that paideia take into careful account "what rhythms are expressive of meanness, or insolence, or fury, or other unworthiness, and what are to be reserved for the expression of opposite feelings."[61]

Purity and simplicity are highly desirable attributes of music destined for paideia, lest its effects become diluted, mistaken, or confused. Instruments capable of panharmonic playing were therefore particularly troublesome. Of these, the *aulos*, a reed instrument with a shrill, sensuous timbre, was especially offensive. ". . . [W]e shall not want multiplicity of notes or a panharmonic scale? I suppose not. Then shall we not maintain the artificers of lyres with three corners and complex scales, or the makers of any other many-stringed curiously harmonised instruments? Certainly not. But what do you say to flute [aulos] makers, and flute players? Would you admit them into our State when you reflect that in this composite use of harmony the flute is worse than all the stringed instruments put together. . . ? Clearly not."[62]

Moreover, the auletes of the day were apparently fond of virtuosic display which, although it played quite well to the public, was extraordinarily untrustworthy. Sensuousness, panharmonic playing, and virtuosic display all conspired against that of which music at its best was capable. Musical pleasure is irrelevant when choosing music for paideia, since people like that with which they are familiar. Despite popular appeal, Plato cannot abide the purveyor of clever imitations: ". . . [W]e will fall down and worship him as a sweet and holy and wonderful being; but we must also inform him that in our State such as he are not permitted to exist . . . And . . . we shall send him away to another city. For we mean to employ for our soul's health the rougher and severer poet . . . who will imitate the style of the virtuous only. . . ."[63]

On balance, the pleasure of the 'honeyed muse'—the entertaining or agreeable as opposed to genuinely beautiful, to anticipate a distinction Kant will make — is more dangerous than beneficial. The indulgence of pleasure, as much as of pain, compromises people's use of their rational faculties.[64] Moreover, even soothing music may, in excess, cause the spirit to "melt and waste."[65] The commercial musician whose music caters to the passionate parts of the soul "feeds and waters the passions,"[66] and "impairs the reason."[67] Therefore, "we must remain firm in our conviction that hymns to the gods and praises of famous men are the only poetry which ought to be admitted into our State. For if you go beyond this and allow the honeyed muse to enter . . . pleasure and pain will be the rulers. . . ."[68]

Clearly, then, although Plato is quite willing to capitalize on music's seductive and persuasive power in paideia, these same powers necessitate the imposition of strict controls. He was fundamentally reliant upon the muses, yet vehement in his rejection of the honeyed muse who deals in the apparent rather than the actual, caters to sense rather than mind.

Plato's theory of paideutic ethos rests on two fundamental assumptions. First, music's expressive character resembles certain aspects of the inner life; its motions are akin to the "revolutions of our souls." Second, because of music's arousal and habituation of particular emotions, music shapes people's characters. Modern counterparts to the first assumption are easily found: in Dewey's assertion of the congruence between life's tension-release patterns and music's ebb and flow, in Langer's doctrine of music's isomorphism to the patterns of sentience, and in Pratt's assertion that music sounds like feelings feel. That music may, in virtue of such similarities, shape character and develop specific values is an idea whose endurance has been less remarkable.

However skeptically one views the details of Plato's argument for paideutic ethos, his educational commitment to the development of character and value remains one that is widely shared. If a significant role for music in that process seems like fanciful thinking, it is well worth asking whether that is due to a fundamental flaw in Plato's view or to a deficiency in our own. The words of John Dewey beg careful study within the context of Plato's seemingly lofty expectations: The arts "have the office . . . of all appreciation in fixing taste, in forming standards for the worth of later experiences. They arouse discontent with conditions which fall below their measure; they create a demand for surroundings to come up to their own level. They reveal a depth and range of meaning in experiences which otherwise might be mediocre and trivial. They supply, that is, organs of vision. . . . They are not luxuries of education, but emphatic expressions of that which makes any education worth while."[69]

The Case Against Music

Plato's ambivalence toward music is by now abundantly clear. Music's affective potency makes it both indispensable and extraordinarily dangerous. It cultivates character but can also seduce people into taking pleasure in bad things. It is potentially a purveyor of important insights, but it can trivialize the mind and the imagination as well. Having wrestled with the tension between pleasure and truth, people's wants and their needs, Plato says of music, "[W]e are very conscious of her charms; but we may not on that account betray the truth."[70] So troubling are his criticisms of music, so seemingly excessive his decision to ban 'our sweet friend' from the Republic, that they often overshadow his love for music and his lofty aspirations for it. Although Plato bans music, he does so reluctantly. He leaves the door slightly ajar, allowing for music's return if but one condition be met: "that she make a defence of herself in lyrical or some other metre."[71] "And we may further grant to those of her defenders who are lovers of poetry and yet not poets the permission to speak in prose on her behalf: let them show not only that she is pleasant but also useful to States and to human life, and we will listen in a kindly spirit; for if this can be proved we shall surely be the gainers—I mean if there is a use in poetry as well as a delight? Certainly. . . . If her defence fails, then, my dear friend, like other persons who are enamoured of something, but put a restraint upon themselves when they think their desires are opposed to their interests, so too must we after the manner of lovers give her up, though not without a struggle."[72]

That we take deep pleasure in music is clearly not in dispute; but pleasure is not enough. We must take pleasure in music for the right reasons. Pleasure, enthusiasm, and passion are not good in and of themselves, and such is music's power that a more substantial defense is required: one that shows a value beyond its capacity to arouse, delight, and entertain. The defense Plato wants is one that will buttress the two pillars of his philosophical system, reason and morality. He does not develop that defense himself, but that does not necessarily mean he thought the task impossible. In fact, his many discussions about music give important clues as to various ways one might proceed. Let us try to understand better the reasons he felt it necessary to turn music out, and use those to speculate about how a defense of music might take shape.

What does Plato find so worrisome about music, so dangerous that we would be better off deprived of its pleasure? How are we to understand such an extreme decision? One answer lies in music's status as an imitation, its relation to reason, and the kind of knowledge it affords. The "tribe of imitators,"[73] as Plato refers to them, includes both serious, faithful representers and those given to exaggeration and amusing effects. Musicians of this latter kind pander to popular tastes, giving people whatever they want, engaging them in experience that entertains by any means possible, without regard for what people may learn in that process. Such experience may be undeniably pleasant, but its superficiality wrongly encourages people to equate music's goodness with its ability to offer titillating diversion. It lacks experiential depth, deprives people of the kind of experience that extends beyond the surface, or that leaves behind anything more substantial than pleasure. Rather than cognitive nourishment, it offers pleasant experience. And its utter disregard for veracity or fidelity opens the door to deceit and illusion.

As an imitation, then, music fares poorly on several related counts. First, its imitations may be bad ones, introducing distortions that corrupt understanding. The mindless, servile copier—the thoughtless musical practitioner—generates imitations of imitations, heaps error upon error, at ever-increasing distance from the truth. And second, imitations may portray bad things in a good light, imparting an air of pleasantness to things that should not be experienced as such, and habituating people to accept as natural or inevitable things that are not. Good music is music that is associated with good things. But as Plato apparently sees it, people are oblivious to the powerful ways music influences habits of thought, action, and perception: music making is mostly an unreflective, untheorized kind of practice. It shapes thought, action, and perception in powerful ways to which most people, musicians included, are oblivious. Bad imitations and pleasing imitations of bad things are not the innocuous things people believe them to be. Because music that is discordant and ambiguous is as dangerous as harmonious unity is good, because imitation that portrays undesirable states of affairs in pleasant ways poses fundamental threats to the moral fiber of society, it requires strict controls.

Another major source of concern for Plato is music's affective or emotional character, which threatens to make people believe that sensation or hedonic pleasure are higher values than rational or moral ones. The emotional excitement it affords may act in tandem with its imitative function to develop the wrong kind of character, rendering people susceptible to beliefs and actions that are morally bad. Immoderation and hedonism are at odds with rationality, and indulging in musical pleasure for its own sake disposes people to value personal pleasure over the broader social good, sensual gratification over reason. People ruled by pleasure are disinclined to defer gratification for seemingly austere values like truth and justice, a state of affairs that poses a serious threat to social stability. "[F]or great is the issue at stake, greater than appears, whether a man is to be good or bad. And what will any one be profited if under the influence of money or power, aye, or under the excitement of poetry, he neglect justice and virtue?"[74] The possibility of sense taking the upper hand from reason, feeding and watering the passions instead of cultivating the higher values of mind and reason is obviously of great concern. Like mimesis, music's ethetic power can serve forces of both good and evil. It can strengthen the soul, individual character, and society at large, or it can weaken them.

So whether conceived mimetically or ethetically, music is simply too potent to be entrusted to the whims and caprices of mere musicians and common people. The best music is that which delights the tastes of the most educated, the most rational: those who look past music's capacity to excite and entertain, beyond sensual indulgence and superficial pleasure, to the greater interests of society as a whole. Not just any listener's preferences count; only those of the fully competent, responsible listener. Nor is inspiration enough; artistic inspiration must be critically informed, disciplined, rational. And though no one disputes music's capacity to stir the feelings, unbridled emotional indulgence and mindless pleasure are antithetical to music's deepest value. Since distinguishing good from bad music is so difficult for the average person, restraints on its use are thus essential. Its influence must be grounded, whether by lyrics, mathematics, authority, or tradition—and Plato relies to some degree on each of these. Mimetic and ethetic character must be clear, univocal, and dedicated to virtue. Convention and tradition must be honored, and innovation is deeply worrisome. The risks of unguarded, uncontrolled musical practice—moral decadence, superfluity, incomprehensibility, deceit, erosion of value, and ultimately, the demise of social order itself—are exceedingly dangerous. Thus, Plato banishes the honeyed muse and retains the severer poet to do his bidding. There is no place in his Republic for virtuosic pyrotechnics, for those who fail to exercise proper rational and moral restraint, or for those who treat music as a mere diversion or harmless pleasure. Music's power is much too valuable to squander, much to dangerous to ignore.

There are, of course, other, less generous ways of explaining Plato's attitudes toward music. It might be maintained, for instance, that the lack of clarity, precision, or purity that so troubles him simply provokes a conservative response to the creativity and change so fundamental to music. From this point of view, the worrisome virtuosic displays of the aulete and the panharmonic playing he finds so distressing were important musical innovations that challenged the perceptual habits of a nonmusician. Perhaps Plato's decision to ban the honeyed muse and his preoccupation with authenticity represent an unjustifiably extreme fear of stylistic change—an attitude of which we could probably identify many contemporary examples. His adverse reaction might also be attributed to his apparently overwhelming desire to unify and organize, an orientation that caused a near-phobic reaction to things like difference, diversity, and multiplicity. Order and stability were of paramount importance to Plato—elements threatened by such things as change and plurality. Perhaps, then, part of his ultraconservative disposition toward music was the result of his urgent quest to construct a coherent philosophical system with rationality and morality at its heart. Perhaps he simply 'painted himself into a corner' on matters of music and poetry. Taken one way, Plato was a prude; taken the other, he was a stern moral rationalist whose system got the better of him. Obviously, neither is particularly flattering. Equally obviously, he does not write from the perspective of the practicing musician. Music is much too important to be entrusted to such irrational, self-indulgent people, people who engage in it simply for the pleasure it affords, with complete indifference to what else is made in and through that process. The threats immorality and corruption pose to civic order are much too severe for music to be entrusted to the capricious and irresponsible likes of musicians. It must be regulated by people less musically vulnerable—or perhaps, less musically sensitive—people who understand music's broader cultural and sociopolitical influences. What that creates, however, is a static music in a static world, its evolution prevented by strict controls upon innovation and complexity. The fact that such a radical move was prompted by Plato's belief in music's profound expressive power seems small consolation.

There is probably an element of truth in these criticisms. Yet, there are several other concerns that must be acknowledged in order to achieve a balanced understanding of this seemingly extreme attitude toward music. First, as Elias reminds,[75] ancient poet-musicians were not the pathetically marginal influences they often are today. Instead, they were often prominent community figures, comparable in visibility and influence to modern-day lawyers, journalists, advertisers, or religious leaders. Plato's attack makes a little more sense if we think of this civic group, since even modern societies impose constraints upon the freedom of civic leaders. We have laws requiring financial disclosure of public figures, punishing false advertising, requiring drug testing, prohibiting language which incites violence or hatred or racism, and punishing libel or slander. Plato's ban on music must be taken at least in part as a criticism of people who abuse their public trust and use their influence to the detriment of the public interest.

It is crucial, too, to remember that despite his suspicions and unkind words, Plato had his own very significant uses for music. It remains a central feature of paideia and an important influence for developing character and maintaining civic order. It was given, after all, precisely for the harmonization of the soul. Its study and practice, at least in moderation, could make people better, more noble, more virtuous. It was essential to the cultivation of the good life, the educated life, the balanced life. In the right hands and under the right conditions, music can capture important aspects of truth. At its best, it transcends particularity, diversity, and randomness, offering glimpses of divine harmony. Its capacity to forge unity and its exemplary coherence make it a highly desirable imitation, offering insight into the harmonious foundations of virtue, reason, and beauty alike. He did not, we must recall, ban all music from his Republic, only bad music. The offender is not music, but music pursued for pleasure's sake alone, music that merely entertains, music that caters to self-indulgence and appetitive gratification. The culprit is "an art having the tendencies which we have described . . . ,"[76] the honeyed muse. The severer poet may, indeed must, remain. As Collingwood observes, to understand Plato we must distinguish between music's 'amusement' and 'magical' uses.[77] The former, hedonistic use is the one Plato cannot abide. The magical use of music as a reinforcer and clarifier of important social values is not only tolerated, it enjoys a position of honor in Plato's utopian state. His distrust of music and musicians is unmistakable, but so is his respect for their profound power. He concedes music's 'charms', and is seemingly anxious to readmit it to the Republic if only someone can help resolve the dangers and rational inconsistencies created by its presence. Glibly asserting that Plato did not take his indictments of music all that seriously hardly constitutes the kind of defense he invited or that we have the right to expect. Let us speculate, then, as to what a defense of music might have looked like had Plato undertaken it.

Defending Music

Plato's conception of music revolves around its power and utility for ends it has become fashionable to regard as musically extrinsic. It is a decidedly heteronomous account of musical value, whose center of gravity lies considerably outside what is often now considered the realm of 'music proper'. Since his philosophy was fundamentally rationalistic and moralistic, knowledge and right action are his paramount concerns. By these criteria, music cannot but earn mixed reviews. Plato's most extravagant claims and stinging criticisms of music attend its rational and its emotional force, concerns he explores in his accounts of mimesis and ethos, respectively.

For the sake of argument, let us grant Plato's point that music involves more than 'music alone' and attempt to respond to his invitation for a defense—one that shows what, besides pleasure, music is good for, and why this 'honeyed muse' should be permitted to stay. Probably the best point of departure is music's role in paideia, where its affective power helps balance the soul and guide people toward right dispositions, attitudes, and actions. But this argument has rather negative consequences since in it music becomes something of a sugar coating for indemonstrable or otherwise unpalatable truths. The idea that music's expressive power strengthens the conviction with which people hold beliefs and values that are desirable yet in themselves unconvincing portrays music as a tool of ideological or propagandistic persuasion, a way of assuring that the rationally less-endowed believe the right things, behave the right way. Not only does this subordinate questions of musical value to nonmusical ends, it carries with it the potential for abuse that led Plato to contemplate strict controls in the first place. This is rather a weak and pathetic defense, one which, were it successful, would allow music back into the Republic under what Elias rightly judges "pretty rotten conditions."[78] However, a softer, less offensive version of this defense is possible, one in which music is not so much a seducer of the inept to ends ordained by an all-knowing power elite as something society collectively employs in ways that enhance and celebrate the events and ideas it most values. Viewed that way, music is not a coercive agent in service of politically sanctioned doctrines, yet it does perform the important function of highlighting and rendering vivid values that society holds collectively and consensually. Music remains, then, a powerful persuader, and plays an important role in creating and maintaining people's commitment to the common values essential to social cohesion. Its power imparts a special sense of significance to ideas, morals, and events of particular social importance, making them more compelling and memorable than they could ever be in and of themselves. If it be objected that this reduces music to second-class status, it need only be pointed out that without such assistance, society could scarcely exist.

Another line of defense would probably involve establishing that music is not a hopelessly irrational undertaking, because the senses do not stand utterly opposed to mind. It might be argued, for instance, that knowledge depends upon sensation in profoundly important ways, and that indeed, were it not for the novelty generated by sense and imagination, knowing would be a pretty vacuous affair. We might argue that music provides reason with important raw materials, patterns of thinking, and has the additional benefit of rejuvenating rational faculties dulled by habitual activity. Furthermore, if feeling (the 'passions') and rationality are not the mutually exclusive things Plato apparently takes them to be, we might argue that music represents a unique blend of the two, one with significant potential to remind us of the felt nature of knowing and of the rational roots of at least a certain range of feeling. We will see these lines of argument taken up energetically by subsequent music philosophers.

The charge that music imitates appearances only, that it is a merely decorative affair whose creations are thrice removed from ideal reality and truth, is more difficult to answer—especially since music is so fleeting and seemingly intangible. It is important to recall, however, that Plato censures only the servile copier of appearances, the purveyor of mindless entertainment. Of genuine musicians he clearly expects more: the capacity "to discern the true nature of the beautiful and graceful . . ."[79] The true musician is an imitator in the highly positive sense of revealing important aspects of the truth and beauty of the non-sensible realm. That musical inspiration can achieve revelation as well as deceit is a common and important response to Plato's allegations,[80] but that defense is more persuasive for music with some propositional content than it is for wordless music. That, of course, was part of what lay behind Plato's dismay at improvised technical displays. It might be argued, though, that 'instrumental' or 'absolute' music, while perhaps not a purveyor of insights that are clear and distinct, does nonetheless afford a kind of fuzzy knowledge: its insights may not constitute high reason, but neither are they wholly irrational. Perhaps music exercises mind's essential coherence-seeking propensities in ways that prepare it for rational, abstract knowing. Since this kind of claim has been pursued vigorously throughout the years—by those who insist, for instance, that music may be pre-conceptual, but is not pre-rational, and that it offers a special kind of knowing unavailable through any other medium—it is important to note several interesting issues. First, knowing remains the undisputed criterion by which music's value is argued, as other possibilities go unexplored. This has the effect, secondly, of conferring greater value on musics judged orderly, harmonious, and controlled. And third, it remains to be shown how this special 'knowing' or 'intelligence' is crucial to human or social development.

Another possible defense attempts to speak to this last issue, showing that music performs the valuable function of 'humanizing' the intellectually abstract. On this view, music renders knowledge fuller and more complete by conferring upon it the vitality or felt sense so crucial to important knowledge. It enhances our recognition of our role in knowing, renders ideas more alive, and infuses truth and goodness with the personal sense of value upon which our commitment to them ultimately relies. Music, then, is not an attractive addendum to a knowledge complete in itself, but makes knowledge human. In its peculiar fusion of cognition and feeling, sense and mind, music helps establish standards of cognitive efficacy that are truly worthy of humanity. Versions of this defense are taken up by philosophers like Schiller and Hegel, and remain central assumptions in many current views of musical value.

Another line of defense blends the claims to music's persuasive and cognitive powers, arguing that music is essential for even the most rational women and men because of the fundamental limitations of propositional, logical, conceptual knowledge. As Elias has argued, music (or, more broadly, expression that is poetic rather than prosaic) has the capacity to convince precisely where reason alone would fail. Indeed, in certain extraordinary passages, Plato himself sets logical argument aside in favor of high poetry. All systems, Elias explains, rest upon foundational 'givens' that cannot be logically proven or scrutinized in terms of the system's own framework. All thought and reason rest on indemonstrable presuppositions, assumptions which cannot be established propositionally because they themselves constitute the ground on which one stands in accepting or rejecting assertions within the system of rationality. Plato's myths are not shortcuts to ends he might have achieved by logical, expository means. "[E]very system proposed," argues Elias, "must contain some terms which are primitive, indemonstrable, asserted on faith; and because no rules can be given for their invention a touch of the poet is necessarily found in every such system."[81] Although Plato sought a purely rational knowledge, universal, self-sufficient, independent of a knower, and untainted by belief, his reliance upon poetry shows he did not find it. And this, urges Elias, is the strongest possible Platonic defense of things like poetry. Since all knowledge is supported at critical points by belief and commitment secured by this 'poet's touch', music plays an indispensable role in creating and sustaining cultural cohesion and stability.

Those who regard music's emancipation from nonmusical ends as the single most important development in thousands of years of philosophical inquiry are bound to be troubled by the functional or utilitarian emphasis of these defenses. To Plato, however, the idea of an inherent, intrinsic, and autonomous range of musical value would likely have been incomprehensible and morally irresponsible. His criticisms of music invite a defense that shows how it advances culture and makes people and society better. He insists that music not be construed as an end in itself, that it be recognized as a means to all manner of sociocultural ends. He insists on the primacy of education through music over education merely in and about it. Those who find persuasive this particular strand of Plato's thought would remind us, further, that music's survival apart from the social practices from which it derives its meaning is at best precarious. For music is an inalterably and profoundly social endeavor. To neglect this essential truth is to miss what is arguably most durable and fundamental about music — to miss the ultimate source of its value.

Regardless of one's disposition toward the business of defending music, several Platonic convictions are inescapable: that music at its best gives us stirring examples of excellence, creating standards or expectations to which all value experience will subsequently be held; that music cannot, without fundamentally compromising its essential nature, be extirpated from its broadly significant role in virtually every facet of human experience; and that music's value can scarcely be confined to an insular, aesthetic realm.

None of the defenses sketched here is definitive. Indeed, the history of musical philosophy is the record of, among other things, efforts to respond satisfactorily to Plato's challenges. The fact that Plato's thought precipitates such a broad range of speculation and controversy is an important reason both for its enduring attraction and for having selected it as a starting point for this study. The difficult questions with which his ideas force us to wrestle have lost surprisingly little of their cogency in the thousands of years since he first articulated them. Indeed, not only did their influence dominate musical philosophy for centuries, but their indelible impression can be detected in contemporary thought in ways of which we are often scarcely aware.

The Continuing Greek Legacy: Aristotle

Contrasting Temperaments: Plato and Aristotle

The similarities and differences between Plato and his student **Aristotle** (384–322 B.C.) make for fascinating study and debate. To the devout Platonist, Aristotle's views are indebted to Plato's exploratory work in most important ways, and his many criticisms of his teacher are attributable to misunderstanding or misinterpretation. Aristotle's closely reasoned analyses are no match for the comprehensive philosophical vision achieved by Plato. Aristotelians, on the other hand, find Plato charming but philosophically primitive, his moral preoccupations unpalatably conservative, and his poetic propensities alluring but hardly the equal of Aristotle's analytical rigor. Both sides make valid points, but the root of their disagreement probably has less to do with who is the better philosopher than with what philosophy should be. Aristotle and Plato represent two strikingly different temperaments, so different that it is sometimes said that everyone is born either a Platonist or an Aristotelian. Plato's vision was utopian; Aristotle built no utopias. Plato sought to unify knowledge into a rationally coherent system; Aristotle was more interested in exploring and describing what was distinctive about things than subsuming them under broad explanatory principles. Plato's ideals for knowledge and reality were the abstractions of mathematics; Aristotle was more inclined to careful description and organization, more the biologist than the mathematician.

As we have seen, Plato's was a profoundly dualistic world, radically divided between potentially illusory perceptions (appearances) and the 'ideal' realities they imitate. Aristotle contested this separation, arguing that only in thought are forms separable from entities. To his way of thinking, ideal forms or essences overlaid the concreteness and particularity of the material world with an unnecessary level of abstraction. He was more the realist than Plato, at least in his willingness to allow that appearances of things are reliable indexes of their true nature. He was temperamentally disposed to exploring the world as given to experience, the potential consequences of existing conditions, and the causes and interrelationships among things and events.

Believing Plato's ideal forms to be useless abstractions, he developed a philosophical perspective from the very concrete, individual things Plato had believed so unreliable. He doubted the existence of substances apart from perceptible qualities, of forms apart from concrete instances, of universals apart from individuals. The material and the formal, he believed, were causally related, and the task of philosophy was to understand these causes. Aristotle was not just more accepting of the sensible world of change than Plato had been; it became in one sense the foundation of his philosophical enterprise. To understand a thing was to see how its particular nature relates to its ultimate purpose. The key to understanding that relationship lay, he thought, in the answers to four fundamental questions: what is it? of what is it made? how was it made? why was it made?

Thus, where Plato had been interested in generalization, Aristotle was intrigued by differences and particularity. Where Plato had sought a comprehensive, ideal synthesis of knowledge, Aristotle savored analytical distinctions, and was fascinated by the delineation of systems. Aristotle was more the cautious observer than Plato, and his language rather more sober, prosaic, and logically incisive. As well, Plato had been a reformer, ever preoccupied with what ought to be. Aristotle's consuming interest was to describe what is. We must, he thought, deal with things as we find them, judging them in terms of their own distinctive nature. Plato the stern moral rationalist equated knowledge and virtue, believing that to know good was to be good. His system placed power in the hands of those he thought best knew good: authorities with superior rational power. Individual pleasures were always subjugated to the higher good of the community. Aristotle shared Plato's faith in reason, but recognized that people are always more than mind, that there is more to the good life than rational activity. He was thus more open, more accepting, more tolerant of personal pursuits and pleasures. The best way to know human nature, he believed, is to observe what makes humans happy; and the state exists to serve the individual. In short, where Plato was moralistic, Aristotle was humanistic.

Distinguishing Moral from Musical Value

Important though these contrasts are, the views of Plato and Aristotle on music were in many ways quite convergent: Aristotle obviously drew extensively upon the ideas of his teacher. However, one of Aristotle's more notable departures from Plato is his willingness to differentiate between musical goodness and the goodness of what music 'imitates'. Since in Plato's mind, beauty, truth, and virtue are coextensive, music's value is closely linked to the moral desirability of the imitated, and to the clarity with which it is represented. The goodness of the imitated is a more pressing concern than the excellence of the imitation. While Aristotle shares Plato's conception of music as an imitative art, he departs from Plato by specifically attending to the skills and artistry involved in creating imitations: exploring the artistic genesis of poetic or musical effect. In his *Poetics*, Aristotle undertakes to explore what makes literature (specifically, tragedy) good in its kind, apparently believing that moral questions of 'what ought to be' should follow the prior question of 'what is'. He examines poetry as poetry rather than as an imitation of something else.

To be clear, Aristotle did not undertake a specifically musical investigation in *Poetics*. However, many of his points are highly relevant. His most fundamental observation is that not all imitations are the same, for people seem to bring different assumptions and expectations to images than to the things they imitate. An important part of the pleasure people find in imitations comes from an appreciation of the skill and imagination with which they are made.

A poem or literary plot, he observes, is not simply a narrative segment but a well-structured, cohesive whole, comprised of a clearly perceptible beginning, middle, and end. A beginning and ending cannot be imposed at whatever point one might like.[82] Moreover, the poet must be selective about what is included: the poetic effect entails considerably more than narrative accuracy, and a good story entails more than accurately recounting detail. The parts of a successful poem must be "so closely connected that the transposal or withdrawal of any one of them will disjoin and dislocate the whole. For that which makes no perceptible difference by its presence or absence is no real part of the whole."[83] The dramatic unity and structural coherence of a work are of paramount concern. "[I]ncidents have the very greatest effect on the mind when they occur unexpectedly and at the same time in consequence of one another; there is more of the marvellous in them then than if they happened of themselves or by mere chance. Even matters of chance seem most marvellous if there is an appearance of design as it were in them . . ."[84] Plays may engage people's attention with spectacle and special effect, but the same can be achieved by "the very structure and incidents of the play—which is the better way and shows the better poet."[85] Thus, unlike Plato, Aristotle's perspective provides for both moral and artistic criteria for poetic (and, by extension, musical) value.

Moreover, poetry differs from history or journalism in that it does not so much attempt to describe actual events as "a kind of thing that might happen,"[86] which appears to relieve poetry of its onerous obligation under Plato to convey the truth at all times. In fact, although Aristotle agrees that in general, poetic description should strive to remain free from error, misrepresentation, and what he refers to as 'impossibilities', such concerns may apparently be tolerated provided they "serve the end of poetry itself—if . . . they make the effect . . . more astounding."[87]

In short, Aristotle maintains that judgments of poetic value should be made in light of poetry's distinctive nature and function. Otherwise, one invokes expectations inappropriate to it. What poetry 'ought' to do can only be determined in light of what kind of thing it really is. And apparently, it is not the kind of thing that is obligated above all else to tell the literal truth. Under certain circumstances, 'poetic effect' may even take precedence over veracity. Whether such license is justified is a determination to be made in light of concerns 'proper' to poetry, not 'foreign' to it: concerns like unity, structure, economy, impact, and so on. From an Aristotelian point of view, judgments of worth must be informed by a proper assessment of kind, and that requires direct examination of the thing itself rather than rationalistic Platonic abstraction or speculation. Thus, while *Poetics* did not address what we now call music per se, it did grant poetry its own distinctive purpose and proper end, a stance that has important implications for music. For on this view, questions about music's nature and value cannot be exhaustively addressed by attending to moral concerns. Music's 'goodness' and what it is 'good for' are two different issues.

Imitation and Pleasure

While Aristotle subscribed to the basic notion of music as an imitative phenomenon, he had relatively little sympathy for many of the other popular Pythagorean doctrines which Plato had embraced. Consistent with his belief in the trustworthiness of empirical experience, Aristotle vigorously contested Plato's numerological belief that numbers are substances, that the planets emit unheard sounds, and the like.[88] For Aristotle, harmonia was more a concrete experiential fact than a metaphysical affair, more a matter of notes and rhythms than of intangible ideals or imperceptible universals. In fact, in Anderson's estimation,

Aristotle's use of the term harmonia seems for the most part to imply the "interchangeable ... tempered modal complex which replaced the original modes,"[89] a state of affairs that probably reflects the continued evolution of the ancient harmoniai toward a more standardized system.

Concerning music's imitative nature and capacity to influence human character, however, Aristotle has relatively little to add to Plato. Music is fundamentally representative, Aristotle believes, and our souls do indeed undergo changes when we hear it. "There seems to be in us a sort of affinity to musical modes and rhythms," he says,[90] which gives music the power to shape the soul. But even so, Aristotle's attitude toward images and imitation is more tolerant and trusting than Plato's: "Imitation is natural to man from childhood, one of his advantages over the lower animals being this, that he is the most imitative creature in the world, and learns first by imitation. And it is also natural for all to delight in works of imitation. . . . [T]hough the objects themselves may be painful to see, we delight to view the most realistic representations of them in art. . . . The explanation is to be found in a further fact: to be learning something is the greatest of pleasures not only to the philosopher but also to the rest of mankind, however small their capacity for it; the reason of the delight in seeing the picture is that one is at the same time learning—gathering the meaning of things. . . ."[91] Instead of dangerously irrational pleasures and copies thrice removed from reality, then, images may apparently afford acceptable pleasures and, indeed, constitute instances of learning. Part of the pleasure people derive from imitations comes from their capacity to show "something fresh,"[92] something new and beneficial. What is imitated is not so important as the manner of its representation. And the pleasure of the experience is the understandable result of our having learned something, of appreciating a particularly imaginative perspective or manner of portrayal. That musical images may have the capacity to yield insight is a strong contrast to Plato's condemnations of their irrationality. Likewise, the notion that manner of execution and its attendant pleasures are positive things is far removed from Plato's worries about music feeding and watering the passions. Thus, in Aristotle's view, musical imitations do not seem to have the stigma they did for Plato.

Aristotle's allowance that taking pleasure in images is a natural human tendency also stands in contrast to Plato. To Aristotle, pleasure need not be fundamentally irrational and suspect. The nature and the significance of pleasure is as various as its attendant activities. Thus, Aristotle is more trusting of music's seductiveness and sensuality: not only is musical pleasure relatively 'safe', under some circumstances—toward certain ends—it may even be beneficial.

In *Nicomachean Ethics*, Aristotle argues that not all pleasure is of the kind that impedes activity. Indeed, pleasure often intensifies activity, and "what intensifies a thing is proper to it . . ."[93] People do what they do, by and large, neither out of their sense of moral obligation nor as the result of rational deliberation about foreseen consequences, but because they enjoy it. "Every activity is completed by the attendant pleasure,"[94] he reasons, and just as activities differ in kind, so will their attendant pleasures. Thought has its own distinctive, natural and "proper" pleasure, music its own, and so forth. Just as predominantly mental activities are different in kind from predominantly sensual ones, so are the pleasures that "complete them."[95] It is wrong, then, to construe pleasure as something invariably irrational and obstructive, since proper pleasures enhance activity. The pleasures inherent in rational and musical activity play significant roles in sustaining and refining their respective practices. What is more, authorities in a given area, the connoisseurs, are precisely those people who have cultivated its proper pleasures to a high degree. In a statement notable for its contrast to Plato's unwillingness to entrust judgments of musical worth to music's practitioners, Aristotle remarks, "[E]ach class of things is better judged of and brought to precision by those who engage in the activity with pleasure . . ."[96]

While activities are enhanced and intensified by proper pleasures, they "are hindered by pleasures arising from other sources."[97] Musical pleasure, Aristotle offers by way of example, may distract or disrupt a rational train of thought. So while "activities are made precise and more enduring and better by their proper pleasure," foreign pleasures have precisely the opposite effect: indeed, they "do pretty much what proper pains do."[98] Pleasures foreign to desirable activities have the capacity to disrupt or impede them. So pleasures proper to "worthy activities" are good and desirable, whereas those proper to unworthy activities are bad. "[A]ppetites for noble objects are laudable, those for base objects culpable."[99] In short, whether pleasure is good or bad can only be determined in light of the activity to which it is proper.

Aristotle's pluralistic way of looking at pleasure means that he can take a far more tolerant and sympathetic view of musical pleasure than Plato. Any assessment of the value of pleasure must follow from an understanding of its attendant activity. If pleasure enhances a desirable activity or impedes an undesirable one, it must be beneficial and valuable. Pleasure is neither good nor bad in itself, then. Even the most rational activity is sustained and rendered more precise by its proper pleasures, and corrupted by foreign pleasures. "Neither practical wisdom nor any state of being is impeded by the pleasure arising from it; it is foreign pleasures that impede, for the pleasures arising from thinking and learning will make us think and learn all the more."[100] Proper or inherent pleasure is essential to high levels of attainment in any undertaking, music presumably among them.

Since on one level musical pleasure is sensual in nature, it is noteworthy that even the relatively direct and immediate pleasure associated with the senses has a purpose in Aristotle's account of things. "Since every sense is active in relation to its object, and a sense which is in good condition acts perfectly in relation to the most beautiful of its objects . . . it follows that in the case of each sense the best activity is that of the best-conditioned organ in relation to the finest of its objects. . . . [T]he most complete [activity] is pleasantest, and that of a well-conditioned organ in relation to the worthiest of its objects is the most complete; and the pleasure completes the activity."[101] On this view, considered as the kind of experience that completes this important relationship between a well-conditioned organ and the worthiest of its objects, musical pleasure is not the suspicious thing Plato thought it was, but rather a perfectly natural and constitutive aspect of the process of listening done well.

Thus, Aristotle allows that pleasures vary in kind and that they play important roles in human activity. However, not all proper pleasures are equally good. There are different grades of proper pleasure, the highest being contemplative in nature. "We may assume," he says, "the distinction between bodily pleasures and those of the soul, such as love of honour and love of learning; for the lover of each of these delights in that of which he is a lover, the body being in no way affected, but rather the mind."[102] The pleasure of intellectual contemplation is best because "reason more than anything else *is* man," and because "we can contemplate truth more continuously than we can *do* anything."[103] Contemplative activity is also best because it "seems both to be superior in serious worth and to aim at no end beyond itself, and to have its pleasure proper to itself . . ."[104] Unlike bodily pleasures which are often pursued for instrumental ends, contemplative activity carries its pleasure entirely within the activity. Bodily pleasures may be pursued in excess, becoming injurious. In contrast, contemplative pleasure is "good without qualification."[105] Thus, we must apparently draw distinctions between intrinsic and extrinsic pleasure, and between contemplative and bodily pleasure. Aristotle shares some of Plato's suspicion of immoderate sensual pleasure, believing the best pleasures to be those that 'complete' contemplative activity.

The specific implications of these remarks on pleasure for music are not matters Aristotle explores. How specifically musical pleasure might fare in light of these observations, then, is something of an open question. If one construes music as purely sensual indulgence, its pleasures are perhaps not unlike those associated with sex or drink: relaxing and amusing, yet detrimental if pursued in excess. Conceived of along contemplative lines, as the ear's and mind's involvement with harmonious, well-proportioned beauty, it would fare considerably better. To be consistent with his pluralism, it seems Aristotle would need to hold that, since there exists quite a broad range of musics, each with appropriate attendant pleasures of different kinds, properly musical pleasures range from the corporeal to the cerebral, from hedonic pleasure to contemplative pleasure.

Indeed, Aristotle does allow that the arousal of feelings by music leads to emotional release that is both pleasant and valuable.[106] Even wildly irrational music, which indulges baser, bodily pleasures and caused Plato no end of worry, has its 'proper' place in Aristotle's scheme. As a result he is able to find value in a dramatically broader range of musical experience than Plato, even in the pleasures associated with Plato's seductive 'honeyed muse'. Still, there remains for him a definite hierarchy of musical values. His recognition of 'proper' pleasures hardly means all musical pleasures are equal in value. Tolerant though he is of music that actively engages feelings, such music remains inferior to musics that engage and sustain contemplation.

The Values of Music

"It is not easy," declares Aristotle in what often seems a significant understatement, "to determine the nature of music, or why any one should have a knowledge of it."[107] He entertains a number of alternatives, though. Like Plato, he

maintains that music "conduces to virtue . . . it can form our minds and habit-
uate us to true pleasures." Quite unlike Plato, he suggests that music has value
"for the sake of amusement or relaxation, like sleep or drinking, which are not
good in themselves, but are pleasant," as well as for leisure enjoyment, and mental cultivation. Beyond the serious business of character formation and education, then, Aristotle sees value in music's capacity to amuse, divert, and relax.
"[M]usic should be studied," he concludes, "not for the sake of one, but of many
benefits . . ."[108] Where Plato's conception of musical value revolved almost exclusively around its rational and moral uses, Aristotle observes that music "makes
the hearts of men glad . . . on this ground alone we may assume that the young
ought to be trained in it. For innocent pleasures are not only in harmony with
the perfect end of life, but they also provide relaxation."[109] Thus music's value
lies not only in future benefits it may confer, but in its capacity to provide relaxation and refreshment here and now. It can be a harmless diversion that contributes to the "alleviation of past toils and pains."[110]

Music need not necessarily be soothing and relaxing to confer psychological benefits, though. Even the wildest, most irrational music has value, says Aristotle. After exposure to "melodies that excite the soul to mystic frenzy," he observes, people become "restored as though they had found healing and
purgation." People's souls may be "lightened and delighted" by the "modes of
action and passion."[111] Music can either relax directly or provide a cathartic out-
let for pent-up tension. For Aristotle, both are harmless, 'innocent' musical pleasures.

Although the various modes should be used in different ways, as Aristotle
sees it all of them are useful in some context or other.[112] Indeed, he even sees
an acceptable use for bad music. Since people take pleasure in what is natural
to them, and since the tastes of educated nobility differ from those of the uneducated, the same music is not necessarily appropriate to both. Music suited to
educated people is not appropriate to the "vulgar crowd composed of mechan-
ics, labourers, and the like," people whose minds are "perverted from the natural state . . ."[113] For the untutored and unsophisticated, music of a "lower" type
is perfectly acceptable: music consisting of "perverted modes and highly strung
and unnaturally coloured melodies."[114] We might want to weigh Aristotle's laudable pluralism and musical tolerance against his apparent belief that inferior
music is fine for inferior people. At least Plato insisted on the same standard,
however austere, for everyone.

Interestingly, despite his endorsements of musical entertainment and amusement, Aristotle's musical tolerance does not carry over into the realm of paideia.
In fact, his accounts of paideutic ethos are almost indistinguishable from Plato's.
Music's power to shape character, he believes, is particularly well suited to educating the young, who "will not, if they can help, endure anything which is
not sweetened by pleasure, and music has a natural sweetness."[115] Only the ethical modes may be employed in paideia, because people's feelings "move in
sympathy" with music and it is imperative the right feelings be engaged. "[T]here
is clearly nothing which we are so much concerned to acquire and to cultivate
as the power of forming right judgments, and of taking delight in good disposi-

tions and noble actions. Rhythm and melody supply imitations of anger and gentleness, and also of courage and temperance, and of all the qualities contrary to these . . . [I]n listening to such strains our souls undergo a change. The habit of feeling pleasure or pain at mere representations is not far removed from the same feeling about realities. . . . The objects of no other sense . . . have any resemblance to moral qualities . . ."[116]

For Aristotle, as for Plato, music is central to paideia because of its capacity to nurture and sustain moral rectitude. Like Plato, he believes logic alone is insufficient to incline the young to virtuous conduct. Right reason follows, rather, from habituation to right character, and music is unique in its similarity to moral qualities. Since its influence may serve either desirable or undesirable ends, and since exercising appropriate restraint and moderation can seem unpleasant to the young, paideia must be carefully monitored by "philosophers who have had a musical education."[117]

On the ethetic character of individual modes, Aristotle is of essentially the same mind as his teacher. The musical modes differ essentially from one another, he says, and "even in mere melodies there is an imitation of character . . ."[118] Some modes, like the mixolydian, make people sad and grave, while others can "enfeeble the mind." The phrygian "inspires enthusiasm." And the dorian, which "produces a moderate and settled temper,"[119] is also the "manliest."[120] Despite his tolerance for musical amusement and catharsis, not just any modes are acceptable for paideia. Each of the modes may have its individual use, but education is not necessarily among them. In fact, on music's educational uses, Aristotle is as conservative as Plato.

On the role of musical performance in education, Aristotle is equally conservative. "[W]hy should we learn ourselves instead of enjoying the performances of others?" he asks.[121] Since professional performers are "vulgar," and "no freeman would play or sing unless he were intoxicated or in jest,"[122] music making is not the kind of thing that should be extensively pursued, particularly as an end in itself. To be sure, "there is a considerable difference made in the character by the actual practice of the art,"[123] and musical performance gives children "something to do" while it helps refine appreciation. But performance-based musical education is degrading and vulgarizing if pursued in excess. It is imperative, then, that music instruction "stop short of the arts which are practiced in professional contests, and . . . those fantastic marvels of execution which are now the fashion. . . . Let the young practice even such music as we have prescribed, only until they are able to feel delight in noble melodies and rhythms, and not merely in that common part of music in which every slave or child and even some animals find pleasure."[124]

The aulos in particular is unsuitable in paideia, and for reasons that help illuminate the presumed role of actual music making within the context of liberal education. In the first place, proficiency with the aulos apparently requires a degree of technical skill that is unrealistic for the general student. Then of course practitioners of the instrument were well known for virtuosic displays unbecoming of nobility. So the aulos seems to be the kind of instrument that is inherently prone to immoderation. Most importantly, however, the aulos is "not an instrument which is expressive of moral character," and it "contributes nothing to the mind."[125] Ultimately, it seems, Aristotle finds the aulos unsuitable on the same rational and moral grounds which Plato advanced.

Thus, Aristotle rejects "the professional instruments and also the professional mode of education in music . . . for in this the performer practises the art, not for the sake of his own improvement, but in order to give pleasure, and that of a vulgar sort, to his hearers."[126] However entertaining or therapeutic that might be in certain contexts, it is clearly inappropriate for the education of nobility. "[F]or the purposes of education . . . those modes and melodies should be employed which are ethical, such as the Dorian . . ."[127]

In summary, although Aristotle adds little to Plato's accounts of paideutic ethos, he does articulate important distinctions that his teacher either could not or would not. In so doing, Aristotle helps to counter the two primary strains of Plato's attack on music. To the charge that music "feeds and waters the passions," he replies in essence that such experience can help restore equilibrium, perhaps leaving people better prepared to engage calmly in other activities. Except perhaps in the context of paideia, there is nothing terribly wrong with enjoying music's capacity to arouse. To the charge that music is irrational, he seems to respond that musical experience may indeed be an instance of learning and potential insight.

Again, though Aristotle finds proper uses for both music's emotional force and its supposedly imitative function, he attempts no musical theory equivalent to the literary one offered in his *Poetics*. He stops well short of addressing the provocative question of what makes a piece of music good in itself. Are the feelings music arouses a constitutive part of its meaning or value, or are they only its effects? Does our musical pleasure derive from the quality and intensity of what we feel in hearing it, or rather from what we learn or come to understand in contemplating it? Is the essence of music arousal or portrayal? Or neither? Although these and other questions remain unaddressed by Aristotle, he did set in place a framework within which they might eventually be explored, and brought to the discussion of music a more accepting, open-minded disposition. Still, it was the spirit of his teacher, Plato, that would be the predominant force behind philosophical reflection on music during the next thousand years.

Neoplatonic Elaborations

Plotinus

Platonic philosophy continued to be taught throughout the Roman era and into the early Christian period. One of the most notable of the neoplatonists was **Plotinus** (A.D. 205–270), whose writings are an important link between antiquity and the conceptions of music which dominated the Middle Ages. Since Plotinus's writing is mystical and enigmatic (in one scholar's estimation, "frequently obscure, and sometimes almost impenetrably so"[128]), and since his ideas parallel Plato's in many respects, we will not undertake a detailed examination of his writings. But a brief examination of his modifications of the doctrines of imitation and of beauty will serve to illustrate the subtle changes that occurred as the profoundly influential ideas of Plato were passed through the centuries.

One of Plotinus's more noteworthy achievements is to soften somewhat Plato's rigidly dualistic opposition between the true and the illusory, between knowledge and belief. In Plotinus' writings the relation of the apparent to the ideal seems to become more of a continuum between opposing polarities than the dichotic situation so often described in Plato. Plotinus likens the ideal realm to a source of light, which is most intense near its source. The greater the distance from that source, the dimmer and more diffuse the light becomes. Even so, even at great distance when the light becomes exceedingly faint, the light source remains constant.[129]

For Plotinus, then, the sensible world of particular things and experiences is not quite so radically separated from the ideal realm as Plato implied it was. And the differences between various imitations is more a matter of degree than of kind. The ideal world is still marked by brilliance, purity, and absolute unity; and the sensible world at furthest remove from the ideal is indeed dilute, diffuse, and shadowy. But weak and attenuated though it may be by contrast to the potency of the ideal, the sensible realm is not utterly cut off from the ideal, or inherently illusory as Plato frequently implied it was. Despite their remoteness, it seems the appearances given to sense perception may be informed in some way by the ideal. The light grows dim at a distance, but it remains the light.

The possibility that sense experience may be partly trustworthy allows Plotinus to claim for musical experience a value that Plato had not quite been willing to allow. Music, writes Plotinus, is "the earthly representation of the music there is in . . . the Ideal Realm."[130] As its earthly representation, music may reveal aspects of the ideal it imitates. Therefore, music is not necessarily less real or more illusory than other, more tangible 'imitations'. Music is not a 'bare reproduction', an imitation of a natural thing that is itself an imitation of the ideal: rather, music "go[es] back to the Ideas from which Nature itself derives . . ." Indeed, much of what the arts do they do on their own: "[T]hey are holders of beauty and add where nature is lacking."[131]

If this is the case, then perhaps music is not necessarily that far removed from truth and reality, a mere imitation of an imitation. Rather, music is, like the inhabitants of the natural and sensible world, once removed. Plotinus hardly suggests the ideal realm is an open book: it remains as impenetrable by direct means as it was for Plato. And yet, in Plotinus's description, while music is hardly a window opening onto an otherwise inaccessible realm, neither is its relationship to ideals inferior to that of other imitations. Perhaps, then, music may reveal certain aspects of the ideal realm; and perhaps it may even add where nature herself is lacking. Pheidias's rendition of Zeus, for instance, was not modeled after anything given to the senses, according to Plotinus, but rather from an apprehension of the form Zeus would have taken had he made himself visible.[132] These sentiments are a remarkable contrast to the Plato of the *Republic*, conceding as they do that Pheidias imitates a higher realm. Pheidias's Zeus is not an imitation of an imitation, but of a realm inaccessible to sense. Apparently, then, artistic imitations are not doomed to prevarication. They have at least a limited capacity to reveal.

Plotinus thus states more explicitly what Plato's commitment to his broader philosophical agenda would not quite permit him to concede. Inspiration is not invariably dangerous, and music is not necessarily deceptive. Plato recognized that the source of poetic madness might be divine inspiration, but that was apparently a difficult and risky determination. Plotinus seems less worried. Music may reveal without necessarily copying anything in the natural world. Music may draw its inspiration from ideal sources.

The musician, too, seems to fare somewhat better in the writing of Plotinus. The musician is one who is by nature "exceedingly quick to beauty, drawn in a very rapture to it: somewhat slow to stir of his own impulse, he answers at once to the outer stimulus . . . all that offends against unison or harmony in melodies and rhythm repels him; he longs for measure and shapely pattern."[133] Being drawn quickly and rapturously to beauty, being offended by discord, and longing for measure and shapely pattern sound as if Plotinus is willing to grant musicians a good deal more integrity and responsibility for their activities than Plato.

And yet Plato's voice is conspicuous in the conclusion Plotinus draws from this seemingly generous characterization. These natural tendencies of the musician are only a starting point. Building on this foundation, the musician must develop the capacity to see beyond this concrete and sensuous beauty, to perceive the higher beauty "that manifests itself through these forms; he must be shown that what ravished him was no other than the Harmony of the Intellectual world and the Beauty in that sphere . . ."[134] Music may reveal, it seems; but what it reveals still stands in rather stark contrast to the sensible, material realm of music itself. Heard music is decidedly subordinate to the abstract, ideal beauty that resides in the mind and has no equivalent in the sensible world. Beauty is chiefly possessed by things seen and heard, says Plotinus. But "minds that lift themselves above the realm of sense to a higher order are aware of beauty in the conduct of life, in actions, in character, in the pursuits of the intellect; and there is the beauty of the virtues."[135] The value of sensible beauty is its capacity to help people to grasp ideal beauty.

The nature of the relationships and distinctions between sensible and ideal beauty is of considerable interest to Plotinus. What "gives comeliness to material forms and draws the ear to the sweetness perceived in sounds?" he wonders.[136] Is there one universal beauty of which all beautiful things partake, or is there a beauty specific to material objects and another to the "bodiless" beauties of the ideal realm? His conclusions, though not surprising, are interesting in light of his observation that musicians are attracted to measure and shapely pattern. Most people believe that beauty consists in "the symmetry of parts towards each other and towards a whole, with, besides, a certain charm of colour," and that beauty is therefore "essentially symmetrical, patterned."[137] But, Plotinus objects, this seems to deny beauty to simple things. Moreover, 'bodiless' beauties like virtue and truth are not notably symmetrical, and there exist many symmetrical things that are not considered beautiful. Therefore, symmetry and pattern are not necessary attributes of beauty.

This conclusion leads to an intriguing characterization of higher, ideal beauty consonant with Platonic doctrine. Because of the soul's "affiliation" with the "noblest Existents in the hierarchy of Being," he writes, whenever it encounters anything that shares even the slightest trace of that affiliation, the soul "thrills with an immediate delight," and "stirs anew to the sense of its nature and of all its affinity."[138] This, then, is the principle that subsumes both sensual and intellectual beauty, both material beauties and those that have "[n]o shape, no colour, no grandeur of mass," like the "hueless splendour of the virtues."[139] Ugliness, Plotinus asserts, exists where things are not completely "mastered by pattern, that is by Reason . . ." Where, on the other hand, ideal form prevails, it forges unity from diverse and disparate parts, rallying "confusion into cooperation." Since the ideal consists in harmonious unity, so must its material manifestation consist in perceived beauty.[140]

Unity, pattern, and coherence are all evidence that a thing has been 'mastered by Reason'. The experience of Beauty consists neither in structural configuration nor in a simple recognition of correspondence between material and ideal. Beauty consists, rather, in the sense of immediate delight at something so formed by Reason that it reveals the unity of our nature with its divine source. Beauty "gathers into unity what still remains fragmentary, catches it up and carries it within, no longer a thing of parts, and presents it to the Ideal-Principle as something concordant and congenial, a natural friend . . ."[141]

Thus, while on the one hand Plotinus seems to stress the relatedness between the sensible and the ideal, on the other he clearly subscribes to the belief that the ideal is inherently superior to the sensible. The "harmonies unheard in sound create the harmonies we hear," he says.[142] Indeed, its pleasures notwithstanding, sensual beauty remains "fugitive" beauty. People should rather seek after "earlier and loftier beauties," leaving sense in "its own low place."[143] People must strive to become "lovers of the beauty outside of sense,"[144] a state achieved by withdrawing into oneself, "foregoing all that is known by the eyes, turning away forever from the material beauty that once made [our] joy."[145]

Plotinus concludes, "[Y]ou must close the eyes and call instead upon another vision which is to be waked within you, a vision, the birthright of all, which few turn to use."[146] To sense beauty, then, is not to know beauty. One must ultimately, according to Plotinus, turn one's back on the pleasures of heard music. The primary value of sonorous beauty is realized only by undertaking the ascent to the rational, contemplative world, the ideal world of bodiless, immaterial, intellectual beauty. To be 'quick to musical beauty' is to "run after the outer never understanding that it is the inner which stirs us," to mistake the reflection for the genuine article.[147] Perceived beauty is "borrowed" beauty.[148] On balance it is clear that music's primary redeeming value for Plotinus is essentially its promise to bring ideal principles "down into contact with the sense-order . . ."[149] This having been done, people should turn inward toward the ideal, becoming "lovers of the beauty outside of sense."[150]

Augustine

Among the most urgent concerns of the early Christian church was to forge a coherent and compelling theological system, one secure from encroachment by pa-

gan religion and philosophy. This being the case, there appears to have been little time or inclination for extensive original thought about the nature of music.
The predominant ideas about music during the period therefore show unmistakable signs of Platonic lineage. One of the most consuming issues of the early
church was whether something as sensuous and 'earthly' as music was acceptable in worship, a debate whose Platonic roots should by now be conspicuous.

The strong influence of Platonic doctrine upon those who labored to lay
the foundation of the church is nowhere more apparent than in the writings of
Augustine (A.D. 354–430). As Chadwick observes, the Augustinian tradition of
Christian Platonism "domesticated within the Church a substantial part of the
old Platonic language about numbers and harmony as roads to the truth . . ."[151]
On the whole, Augustine's musical thought (as well as that of Boethius, to whom
we turn shortly) is derivative. In a world becoming increasingly dominated by
Latin, however, preserving the achievements of Greek thought had become a
scholarly pursuit of considerable urgency. As Greek texts disappeared, Latin writings by scholars like Augustine who had dawn heavily upon Greek ideas became
the sole link to the great philosophical achievements of antiquity for hundreds
of years.

Augustine's account of music resembles Plotinus's. However, Augustine is
strongly drawn to the ancient Pythagorean doctrines of number that so capti-
vated Plato in *Timaeus*. Number and numerical relationships are immutable in
the face of change, as Plato had shown, and thus must be the very essence of
music.[152] In fact, given that number confers form and order upon the indeterminate, it is constitutive of reason and beauty alike. The universe is forged into
a beautiful whole by number, the "lowest" numbers being directly accessible by
the higher senses, and the "higher" numbers being divine. It is therefore easy
to understand the interest and attraction of music's "sensible traces," although
these remain inferior to the "real places where it is free of all body."[153]

Each of the liberal arts partakes of number to its own degree and in its own
manner, each affording glimpses into the beauty of higher numerical laws. And
since music's proportion and order are of the same general nature as those in
the ideal realm, beautiful music reveals higher beauties and truths. But Augustine retains the fundamental ambivalence toward music so characteristic of Plato,
Aristotle, and Plotinus, and accords very low status to the process of making music. Music's pivotal position within the liberal arts curriculum derives from the
mathematical essence it shares with other subjects. Thus, Augustine's musical
education revolves almost exclusively around numerical attributes and principles. Its method is theoretical, contemplative, reflective, analytical.

Despite a revelatory power that enables music to approach divinity, its sensual side is distinctly inferior. Vision and hearing are higher than the 'lower'
bodily senses like smell or taste because they partake of order, proportion, number. The lower senses are direct and immediate. Therefore, what is given directly and immediately to hearing is of a lower order than experience that embodies higher formal principles. Sensual experience is inferior to the perception
of harmony and unity. Such principles, rather than their sensuous manifestations, are what make music a worthy object of study.

Like Aristotle and Plotinus, Augustine suggests that composers draw inspiration from intuitive insights into the way things ultimately ought to be in this world. Unlike mere copies, artistic images improve upon their objects by emphasizing certain attributes and downplaying others. Thus they are capable of producing "in the exercise of the imagination that which, as a whole, was never within the observation of any of the senses."[154] However, the primary value of material beauty is still, as Plotinus maintained, its capacity to yield insight into higher, immaterial beauty. Augustine, like Aristotle, allows for the occasional use of music as a means of relaxation and restoration. But experience that becomes arrested at the lower level, entertained by music's sensual effects, is wholly improper. Warns Augustine: ". . . [I]t is very proper to take it in from time to time. But to be taken in by it, even at times, is improper and disgraceful."[155]

In his *Confessions*, Augustine describes how the "delights of the ear" had lured him prior to his conversion to Christianity, and reflects upon the role of such delights in a properly Christian life. On one hand, he notes, minds are "more holily and fervently raised unto the flame of devotion by the holy words" when they are sung than when they are spoken. This is because "the several affectations of our spirit . . . have their own proper measures in the voice and singing, by some hidden correspondence wherewith they are stirred up. But this contentment of the flesh, to which the soul must not be given over to be enervated, doth oft beguile me, the sense not so waiting upon reason as patiently to follow her."[156] So beguiling is music's seductive charm at times that Augustine even wishes "the whole melody of sweet music which is used to David's Psalter banished from my ears . . ."[157]

Augustine is painfully aware of his ambivalence: "Thus I fluctuate between peril of pleasure, and approved wholesomeness," he writes, "inclined the rather . . . to approve the usage of singing in the church, that so, by the delight of the ears, the weaker minds may rise to the feeling of devotion." Even this approval is conditional, though: "[W]hen it befalls me to be more moved with the voice than the words sung, I confess to have sinned penally, and then had rather not hear music."[158]

So continues, in ever more exaggerated form, the curiously paradoxical concurrent elevation and denigration of music. The highest form of musical experience involves turning away from sound, the surface or sensory aspects of the music, and turning inward toward its true formal or mathematical nature. Authentic musical experience necessarily involves the secure rational foundation of science.[159] Knowing is inherently superior to doing. People who make music beautifully yet cannot say what its numbers are or mean are like nightingales, Augustine says: mere imitators, not true musicians. Similarly, people who take pleasure in listening, but who do so without science or insight into number, are little better than beasts. Performers also learn their skills like animals, by aping their masters. They fail to grasp the incorporeal truths that lie behind "the veil." Birds sing but lack music because they imitate rather than reason. True music is rational, not imitative.[160] As for people who make their livings performing music, Augustine concludes, there can be "no more degraded and abject discipline than this one."[161]

For Augustine as for Plotinus, if everything in the material realm borrows from the ideal, then everything has ideal attributes to some degree. Indeed, "these numbers can be less and less beautiful, but they can't lack beauty entirely."[162] Augustine's aphorism "per corporalia ad incorporalia"[163] commits him to revelatory capacity for the senses in much the same way. But Augustine comes nearly as close as Plotinus to betraying these sentiments—to implying that he really believes the path to the incorporeal leads from rather than through the corporeal. Music's true value depends upon our ability to turn away from its concrete, sensual presence, and toward the bodiless beauty of number and form.

So music earns its place of prominence among the liberal arts as a predominantly mathematical discipline, an exercise of the mind. However much they partake of the ideal or divine beauty, physical sense and action are always, by definition, lower. It is hard to avoid the conclusion that what Augustine values is more science or acoustics than music. In the view of at least one Augustinian scholar, this rationalization of music amounts to no less than "a quiet but firm imperative for art to sign its own death warrant."[164] And indeed, as a subsequent chapter will show, Hegel will eventually argue precisely that.

Yet here, in this from-to relationship, in this investiture of corporeal phenomena with incorporeal meaning lies both the end of the strict imitative account of music and the beginning of a 'symbolic' account of music which would dominate medieval thinking, eventually blossoming profusely in the thought of Romantic philosophers. Music consists in revelation, and its primary value resides in its capacity to convey successfully not simply itself, but the beauty of divine truth. The sensible is a springboard to the disincarnate, the active to the contemplative, the pleasurable to the intellectual, the heard to the understood. For Augustine, heard music could only hint at the highest beauty. Ultimate beauty can be beheld only within, by the mind, by whose rigorous standards all earthly beauty must be judged deficient.

There is yet another intriguing and subtle irony in Augustine's treatment of music, one we have seen in Plato as well: the apparent inability of his theories of art to explain what he thought he himself was doing. As with Plato, we might do well to qualify Augustine's deprecatory attitude toward art in light of his extensive reliance upon the very poetic skills his rational assumptions denigrate. Subsequent Christian interpreters made extensive use of Augustine's words to support restrictive political and theological dogma. It seems unlikely that Augustine would have approved. However deserving of the soul's contempt embodied beauty may be, it remains beauty. Music is the beauty of the divine realm rendered 'incarnate'. Its pleasures and its attractions should be tolerated, Augustine believed, though only so long as we exercise caution that it is we who take them in, and not they us.

Boethius

Boethius's *De institutio musica* was the authoritative document on music theory for nearly a millennium. "More than anyone else," writes Schrade, "did [Boethius] form the musical mind of medieval men."[165] In addition, his treatises on the liberal arts became the very foundation of medieval education, and even as recently as the nineteenth century any educated person would have been expected to be conversant in his writings. **Boethius** (c. A.D. 430–525) was less an originator than a compiler and translator. Like others of his day, Boethius was far less concerned with originality than with bringing Greek philosophy to the Latin world. Indeed, since the preservation and integrity of ancient Greek ideas was his paramount concern, there is conspicuous continuity between the writings of this influential musical scholar—the first of the Scholastics—and his Platonic inspiration.

De institutione musica is one of a series of treatises written to expound on the virtues of the quadrivium, the mathematical disciplines within the liberal arts. Augustine had identified seven liberal arts: grammar, rhetoric, logic, geometry, arithmetic, astronomy, and music. The latter four Boethius designated the quadrivium. The remainder would eventually become known as the trivium. Since, in true Platonic tradition, Boethius held the aim of education to be the development of understanding and wisdom, rather than technical or practical skill, the disciplines of the quadrivium were conceived not as ends in themselves but as means of preparing people for higher good, the love of wisdom, and abstract reasoning.

Obviously this conviction disposes Boethius (like Augustine before him) to a theoretical conception of musical value, a conviction that the actual 'doing' of music was a kind of manual labour unbefitting the learned aristocrat. Accordingly, the musical study outlined by Boethius is only tangentially concerned with creating or performing music. Like the other mathematical disciplines in the quadrivium, musical study is intended to free the mind from sensuous and material tethers. Without such preparation, one could never ascend to the "summit of perfection." So in Boethius's accounts, music finds itself in erudite, trustworthy company. However, let us examine more closely the nature of music so conceived.

Music's source, for Boethius, lies in the divine realm of unchanging numbers.[166] Its essence lies in numerical proportions, by virtue of their capacity to confer harmony and unity on things otherwise diverse and discrete. There are three kinds of music, three levels, he explains. *Musica mundana,* or cosmic music, emanates from the forms and motions of the spheres, sonorous yet inaudible on earth. *Musica humana,* the music of the human soul and body, involves the inaudible but harmonious blending of the higher and lower parts of the soul, a balancing of the rational and the irrational, of the mind and the senses. *Musica instrumentalis* is actual sonorous music, that given to the ear. Of instrumental music much of what Boethius has to say we have now heard repeatedly. He makes it abundantly clear that whatever else it may be, heard music is indeed fundamentally *instrumental*: a first step toward comprehending proportion, harmony, and balance in their loftier manifestations, a step toward the unheard harmonies of the soul and the universe—but only a first step.

Performers of music are laborers of a lower kind, unaware of the harmonic laws that lie behind their actions. Composers fare only a little better, since their inspiration apparently derives more extensively from hunch and instinct than reason. The true *musicus* is one who reasons, who understands. "How much no-bler," he writes, "is the study of music as a rational discipline than as composition and performance. It is as much nobler as the mind is superior to the body; for devoid of reason, one remains in servitude. . . . [A] musician is one who has gained knowledge of making music by weighing with the reason, not through the servitude of work, but through the sovereignty of speculation."[167] The philosopher is the true *musicus*, and philosophy the one true consolation in the face of death. Like Augustine before him, Boethius conceived of music not as art, but as science, its practice to be tolerated rather than cultivated. Thus, Boethius gave the ancient Pythagorean doctrine of cosmic harmony, accessible through the intellect rather than the ear, the impetus it required to dominate musical thought for centuries more. Even today, certain aspects of formal musical curricula and the condescending attitude of the learned toward 'merely intuitive' musicians are powerful testimony to the enduring influence of this perspective.

Belief in music's moral influence is predominant in Boethius as well. Unlike the other mathematical sciences of the quadrivium, music is an important shaper and guardian of virtue. Instrumental music has a direct and significant influence upon the harmony of the souls of those who hear it. "[M]usic is associated not only with speculation but with morality as well. For nothing is more characteristic of human nature than to be soothed by pleasant modes and disturbed by their opposites."[168] Boethius exhorts us, therefore, to study music which is "temperate, simple, and masculine, rather than effeminate, violent, or fickle."[169] Moreover, music can cure ills of both the mind and the body. Boethius recounts numerous legends of music's therapeutic powers—among them one in which Pythagoras supposedly subdues a dangerous drunk with nothing but a Phrygian melody.

Music may lead people to virtue or to vice, of course, but properly employed, music helps wean them away from the deceptive material world, directing them to wisdom and certain knowledge. As Chadwick summarizes, "Arithmetic directs the mind towards immutable truths unaffected by the contingencies of time and space. But music advances even further towards that 'summit of perfection' for which the quadrivium is a prerequisite. The theory of music is a penetration of the very heart of providence's ordering of things. . . . a central clue to the interpretation of the hidden harmony of God and nature . . ."[170]

Even though Boethius's accounts of music are not notably original, their historical influence was profound. The Platonic and Pythagorean doctrines he transmitted to the Latin world lent themselves admirably to the concerns of an emerging Christian church. As Portnoy aptly observes, the idea that music involved the integration of the mathematical and the moral was nicely compatible with the church's need to control and direct it, since "[a]ny departure from traditional musical forms or ecclesiastical church music . . . was both unscientific and iconoclastic."[171] Given their disposition toward the pagan culture of ancient Greece, the church fathers could hardly have turned to Plato directly for authoritative support of their positions. The ideas of a Roman like Boethius, though, could be safely and advantageously employed. The utility of Boethius's ideas for such ends was remarkably durable. Nearly eight hundred years after his death, the Church would still quote Boethius to denounce suspect musical practices of their day: "A person who is intrinsically sensuous will delight hearing in these indecent melodies, and one who listens to them frequently will be weakened thereby and lose his virility of soul."[172]

Concluding Remarks

The survey undertaken in this chapter encompasses more than one thousand years of philosophical reflection on music. The immense influence of this complex body of thought upon subsequent philosophy can hardly be overestimated. Conspicuous among the strands that comprise this body are the Pythagorean conceptions of music as a phenomenon wed to number, to harmony, and to ethos. We have seen how these beliefs disposed Plato to a deeply ambivalent stance toward music: to a distrust, on the one hand, of music's sensuousness and capacity to deceive, and on the other hand to strikingly lofty aspirations for music's influence—in the right hands—for the good. Music's sensory and material nature was decidedly inferior in his view to the abstract universality of the ideal realm. And yet, that very sensuous attractiveness was utterly essential for the attainment of virtue and reason, the penultimate concerns of his philosophy.

The latter sections of this chapter have explored the evolution of these attitudes and ideas through a brief, selective examination of influential philosophical perspectives during the ensuing millennium. The most notable departures from Plato appear in the thought of the individual historically closest to him: his student, Aristotle. Aristotle's personal and philosophical dispositions stand in stark contrast to Plato: he was ever the realist, the describer of things given to experience, and conspicuously impatient with Plato's propensity for metaphysical speculation. His greater acceptance of things as they appear, as they occur in human experience, disposed him to a less rigid, more pluralistic accounting of music and its associated pleasures. Music was neither inherently deceptive, it seems, nor were its pleasures necessarily evil. Thus, the value of music extends beyond the tightly circumscribed role conceived for it by Plato. Catharsis, and even simple diversion or entertainment, offered potentially valuable psychological benefits for the individual and for society. Aristotle even found it possible to distinguish, as Plato either could or would not, between the excellence of an imitation and the goodness of what it 'imitated'. At the same time, though, Aristotle's trusting, pluralistic stance disposed him to espouse a rather condescending attitude toward the musical tastes and preferences of the masses, a fact which must be carefully weighed against Plato's insistence upon the same standard for all, austere though it undeniably was. His distinctive perspective notwithstanding, Aristotle remains extensively and conspicuously Platonic in his conceptions of musical practice, musical ethos, and the specific (moralistic) role music should play within the serious context of paideia.

In the thought of Plotinus, Augustine, and Boethius, it is Plato's voice which predominates rather than Aristotle's. In Plotinus's hands, Plato's strict demarcations between the material and the ideal, belief and knowledge, experiential deceit and rational truth, are somewhat softened. Plotinus articulated what had remained largely implicit in Plato: that imitation may—at least in some instances—take its inspiration directly from the higher, ideal real, rather than chasing after the illusory appearances of the material world. Musical inspiration might thereby bypass the deceptive distractions of the world of experience, and attain to some fleeting degree glimpses of divine truth and beauty. And yet, paradoxically, the beauties of sense can never quite penetrate the veil through which higher beauty is perceived. The thrill and delight of worldly beauty is, even at its best, only 'fugitive', only 'borrowed'. Unheard harmony is sweeter than any melody given the ear. Musical beauty is a ladder by which one ascends to the unheard, ideal harmonies. When one arrives, that ladder must be gently but firmly pushed away. Only by turning away from the sensual pleasure of earthly beauty, by turning inward, does one encounter ideal beauty.

In Augustine, we witnessed the early Christian church's effort to come to grips with the sensuality and materiality of music, and remarked at the extensive resurrection of Pythagorean doctrines of number in music's defense. Number's abstract constancy, its seeming capacity to confer unity upon change and diversity, offered music the security its beguiling sensible traces never could. Augustine's personal record of his love-hate relationship with the 'delights of the ear' wielded considerable impact. Music continued its inexorable ascent as a science serving reason, and its simultaneous descent as experience: take music in, Augustine cautioned, but do not be taken in by the perils of pleasure that threaten to usurp mind's rightful supremacy. Unthinking enjoyment and performance of music is characteristic of animals, but is beneath human dignity. Knowing music is thus more important and valuable than performing it or hearing it, however seductive its sensual charms. Per corporalia ad incorporalia.

Boethius, too, found music essential for that ascent to the 'summit of perfection'. But true perfection is abstract, disembodied, unfettered by earthly constraints. Sense is inferior to mind, and its unguarded indulgence weakens the soul. Heard music, performed music, is 'instrumental' only; and the true *musicus* is one who reasons, who understands—the philosopher.

Thus does music find itself inextricably ensnared in a philosophical battle between sense and reason, between materiality and ideality, between the merely apparent and the true. Seemingly without exception, the more closely music is held to approach the latter, the more suspect become its roots in the former. As we close this chapter and prepare to turn to another era, we should not expect to find this ancient struggle magically resolved.

DISCUSSION QUESTIONS

1. One way to make sense of musical mimesis might be to say musics can evince, through their aural images and sonorous qualities, characteristics of the cultures and people whose musics they are. Can you explore this tendency in a foreign musical practice? from a contemporary popular culture ('hip-hop', say, or 'country and western')? What might western Euro-

pean art music be said to reveal or portray (to 'imitate') about the cultural milieu from which it emerged?

2. 'Imitations' may be judged for (a) the quality with which they are crafted—the skill or artistry apparent in them, (b) their fidelity to what they represent or portray, or (c) the desirability of the imitated. In your view, is any of these more 'inherently musical' than the others? Why or why not?

3. Contemporary research on social learning seems to support the contention that people learn by observing and imitating modeled behaviors: that, for instance, observed violence can encourage violent behavior. Do you believe music capable of modifying human character? Consider music that is (a) texted, (b) nontexted, (c) performed, and (d) listened to.

4. Music education philosophy sometimes distinguishes between educating 'in' and educating 'through' music. What kind of 'educating through' might result from 'educating in' music? Does the study of music in itself shape human character in desirable ways? potentially undesirable ways? Why or why not?

5. Is the imposition of musical values (either by indoctrination or 'negatively,' by censorship) justified under any circumstances? What is the difference between musical indoctrination and musical education? Do you believe there is an important difference between people's musical 'likes' or preferences and their musical 'needs'?

6. Can you identify in contemporary educational practices vestiges of the belief that music's primary value lies in its unheard harmonies or its mathematical proportionality? Are there important educational and cultural benefits to studying music of which its practitioners may be largely unaware?

7. Plato demeans the sensuous and undisciplined in favor of the rational and the controlled. Compare this to the purely sensuous 'aesthetic' espoused by John Cage and others. Is sensual music inferior to rational music? Is the composer's job (in composed musics) the creation of perceptible order?

8. Does music function as a means of social regulation and control? How and under what circumstances? Is this invariably the case?

9. Discuss Plato's conservative attitude toward innovation in light of current debates over authentic performance practice and musical appropriations. Is creativity fundamentally at odds with authenticity? When is stylistic borrowing musical appropriation?

10. Do you share Plato's concern over people's 'false consciousness' when it comes to music? In other words, is there reason to worry about the naiveté of uneducated musical experience? Or would you rather, like

Aristotle, be inclined to condone cathartic and indulgent musical experience? Under what circumstances? For whom?

11. M. L. West tells us that in ancient Greek writings, expressions like 'lyre-less' were used to describe the grimness of war and death, and 'songs' to signify good fortune and happiness. Discuss the claim that contemporary notions of musical 'autonomy' represent a degeneration from the socio-cultural richness of music in Classical Greece. Is the idea of music's formal integrity invariably attained at the expense of its intimate connection to the quotidian and people's ability to 'live into' their musics?

12. Plato's suspicion of the corporeal aspects of music points toward a contemplative, rational ideal that found even fuller elaboration in Aristotle. What do you make of the fact that so many of the world's musics prioritize neither rationality nor contemplation, and that most people seem to value music precisely for its corporeal sense?

13. Plato is clearly worried about the inclination of music's practitioners (performers) to engage in unreflective 'doing', oblivious to the broader significance of their actions. Do you think modern circumstances justify his concern in any way? Is there a sense in which the master-apprentice model which remains the predominant mode of formal musical instruction in western societies today is at odds with educational ideals like critically informed practice, individual autonomy, and empowerment? Is learning to make music a matter of 'aping' or imitating rather than understanding? Is this tension inevitable? Why or why not?

14. The imitations that most worried Plato were those that imitated appearances. Since the apparent is sense mediated, the most trustworthy imitations are those that imitate unsensed ideals or forms rather than things given to sensation. How might you use these assumptions and the fact that, as a sonorous phenomenon, music does not deal in (visual) 'appearances' at all to mount a defense of music's mimetic powers?

15. The ancient Greeks conferred higher status to knowing and understanding music than to making or doing it. Can you discern in the 'pecking order' of various musical disciplines in academe any vestiges of these assumptions? If so, where?

Music as Idea

Whatever else it may be, music is a product of human minds. This conviction, in the hands of philosophers for whom the mind is central to understanding the world and our place in it, has spawned an enormous body of
speculative thought about music which can be generally characterized as 'idealistic'. To the philosophical idealist (or 'idea-ist'), the key to music's nature and
value is its relation to other human mental activity. It is presumed that, as a cognitive phenomenon, music entails some kind of knowing or understanding. But
what do we actually come to know or understand through music? How does
music resemble and differ from other kinds of human cognitive activity? What
is to be made of its distinctively temporal character, its sensory foundation, the
uniquely feelingful quality of its experience? And how does this compare to the
kind of cognitive activity occasioned by other 'artistic' pursuits? The German
idealists' answers to questions like these range from noble and inspiring to critical and skeptical.

Building on a dualistic foundation with roots extending at least as far back
as Plato—one that precariously separates body from mind, knowing from feeling, reason from sense, the mental from the material or physical—the philosophers examined in this chapter wrestle with music's ephemeral, felt nature, seeking to explain how such ephemerality relates to the realm of ideas, and to show
how music differs from the baser, sensory experience in which it obviously originates. We must not embark on this study anticipating widespread agreement;
on many crucial issues, the theories explored here will advance strikingly divergent claims. However, *that* there is an underlying dualistic tension between
the ideal and the material is an assumption held in common. And more importantly for our purposes here, so is the belief that music somehow occupies a
very distinctive place in this bifurcated universe.

Although they are speculative, metaphysical, and sometimes quite vexing,
these accounts have influenced musical discourse and practices in extraordi-

narily important ways, as will become increasingly apparent in the course of this chapter. Their explorations of music's distinctive 'inwardness' and expressivity, for instance, and the metaphors of 'heart' and 'soul' with which these are often described, have become prominent features of the musical-philosophical landscape. And though most contemporary music philosophy struggles to disavow the dualistic assumptions of the idealists, struggle it often must: such assumptions are tightly woven into the fabric of much musical thought and discourse. They orient contemporary beliefs and talk about music in ways of which we are scarcely aware. For this reason, they warrant careful study.

In the philosophical system of **Immanuel Kant** (1724–1804), what proves most remarkable about music is its sensuality, its fleetingness or transience, and its unfortunate intrusiveness—features that earn it a less than flattering ranking among the arts. Still, we will examine Kant's philosophy in some detail, because its accounts of aesthetic experience and judgments of beauty have had an enormous impact on what people have come to believe things like music are supposed to be about, and how they supposedly relate to other important domains of human activity. Kant wrote three extraordinarily influential treatises or 'critiques' analyzing and exploring the ways mind and nature relate to each other: one devoted to theoretical knowing, or 'reason'; one devoted to 'practical' or moral judgments as to what ought to be; and one devoted to judgments of beauty, or 'aesthetic' judgments. Significantly, since each of these were deemed to be fundamentally important, judgments of beauty occupy a position of real significance in his philosophical system. These judgments and the 'aesthetic' experience associated with them are mindful, Kant believes, yet differ in crucial ways from intellectual undertakings. At the same time, while aesthetic encounters with beautiful things are indeed pleasant and sensual in origin, that pleasure differs from the kind that attends purely sensual experience or the satisfaction of human appetites. So Kant undertakes to illuminate exactly how this 'aesthetic' judgment works: how judgments of beauty—or of 'taste', as they are also known—differ from rational judgments, moral judgments, and everyday sensual experience.

What emerges is an account of aesthetic experience as contemplative delight in the imaginative perception of form—or perhaps more accurately, in the perception of imaginative form—an experience whose value has nothing to do with connections to anything outside itself, to anything else in the world; an experience at once feelingful and mindful, yet reducible to neither feeling nor mind. Judgments of taste (the capacity for proper appreciation of beauty) represent a kind of knowing of which intellect is incapable, a distinctive kind of cognitive activity mediated by natural and artistic beauty. This possibility, as we shall see, inspires other philosophers to create lavish speculative claims for music's unique revelatory power. For Kant, however, music earns more mixed and modest reviews. As an art of tones, it seems, music is somewhat more sensual than mindful, rather too fleeting to sustain properly contemplative delight in form, and rather too brash and intrusive to contribute substantially to the urbane culture of mind. Music is, for Kant, an agreeable art rather than a fine one.

As Kant strove to demarcate a distinctive realm for judgments of taste within the realm of human cognitive activity, **Friedrich Schiller** (1759–1805) worked to show the humanizing potential of such activity and, by extension, the cultural value of what were increasingly known collectively as 'the arts'. Like Kant, Schiller situates 'the aesthetic' midway between sense and reason. Unlike Kant, however, he seems to regard sense and reason as polar opposites — as opposing psychological states or drives, either of which if pursued exclusively or excessively creates an unbalanced person. Sensually indulgent people are slaves to nature; intellectually indulgent people are coldly cerebral. Aesthetic experience and commerce with artistic beauty, Schiller believes, impart balance and harmony to the human spirit. Art creates thought that is feelingful, feeling that is mindful.

What is distinctive about beauty, according to Schiller, is not the absence of sense and reason, as Kant had implied, but their integration and union. In the philosophy of **G. W. F. Hegel** (1770–1831), this idea assumes paramount importance. Artistic beauty differs from natural beauty, Hegel believes, in that it is fundamentally human: artistic beauty is borne of and infused with mind. And its experience plays an extremely important role in advancing human awareness and understanding. To Hegel, the history of the human world is one in which human mentality grows increasingly more aware of its rational-spiritual nature and in which the ultimate rationality and spirituality of the universe is progressively revealed to humankind. His philosophy thus centers around the ascent of human awareness toward an ultimate realm of 'absolute idea'. In that ascent it is art's important office to reveal the fundamental nature of ideality. Because of its capacity to give us truth in sensuous form, art is an important repository of humankind's most profound intuitions and insights, an utterly essential stage in the evolution of human understanding.

However, not all art is equally suited to this revelatory mission at each advancing stage. As human awareness becomes increasingly spiritual and profound, the artistic medium best suited to it changes. Those that are more concrete and objective, for instance, outwear their effectiveness and must give way to media more congruent with mind's growing awareness of its spirituality. To this end, music's distinctive temporality, immateriality, and 'inwardness' — the very features Kant saw as defects — are ideally suited. Music is, more than any other art, the art of soul. Because music deals not so much with the world 'out there' as 'in here', because its moving patterns seem to be experienced as vital parts of who we are, music is uniquely endowed with the capacity to advance self-awareness, to show us the innermost nature of reality. Yet, once music fulfills this mission, its moment passes. Important though music and art once were, Hegel believes, they have outlived their value.

While Hegel sees the world as a fundamentally rational place, **Arthur Schopenhauer** (1788–1860) takes precisely the opposite stance. In itself — before it gets overlaid with veneers of human ideas and representations — the world is wholly irrational, pure blind energy, a ceaseless striving devoid of meaning: 'Will', Schopenhauer calls it. Ideas are not the ultimate stuff of reality then, but rather Will is. But Will cannot be grasped by the rational mind; indeed, mind and reason distort everything they touch, imputing order, meaning, and purpose to what is at base pointless and meaningless. What art does, in Schopenhauer's view, is give us insights into the nature of the phenomenal world. Music, however, is unlike the other arts. It is a copy of the Will itself, a face-to-face encounter with the innermost nature of existence. Music thus has the power to communicate the incommunicable, to penetrate the rational veil of representation and appearances — to give us insight into truths more profound than reason can ever grasp.

Notably, then, the idealistic orientation, with its images of music as an inward, sensual, expressive phenomenon — idea-like, yet operating in a feelingful realm that is highly distinctive — maintains that musical experience offers both relief from the press of quotidian life and vital insights into the ineffable, inner nature of reality. It is well worth noting, however, that such important achievements do not come without a cost: they subtly remove music from its sociocultural context, creating a view of its significance that is individual and inward, rather than collective and intersubjective.

Rationalism and Empiricism

Even the casual student of music history will recognize that a leap from Boethius's time to the seventeenth century bypasses profoundly important events in the evolution of western musical practice. Yet, remarkably, the strains of philosophical thought explored in the previous chapter did not change nearly so dramatically. The Greeks' mistrust of music's sensual nature and concurrent fascination with its apparent affective power, their wariness of music detached from its verbal 'ballast', their belief in music's essentially mathematical nature, and their conception of music as an imitative phenomenon: each of these survived with remarkably little modification in the thought of seventeenth-century philosophers.

Understanding idealistic accounts of music is greatly enhanced by some familiarity with the two contrasting strains of Enlightenment thought which immediately preceded it: rationalism and empiricism. Rationalists held, after **René Descartes** (1596–1650), that mind rather than sense was the arbiter of trustworthy knowledge. They placed their trust not in the fruits of empirical investigation or the products of sense-experience, but rather in the clarity and distinctness of ideas. The rationalist's knowledge was logically and systematically derived from what were presumed to be invincible, self-evident truths. The key to trustworthy and secure knowledge, then, was reason. Enlightenment rationalists demanded more subtle accounts of music than those formulated by their ancient Pythagorean predecessors, but they shared the conviction that beneath music's kaleidoscopic surfaces and seductive charms lay some kind of orderly and rational principle accessible to human logic and reason.

Leibniz (1646–1716), for instance, characterized sensation as "confusedly known intellectual pleasures," and attributed musical beauty to a kind of intuitive or unconscious awareness of "the harmony of numbers and . . . the reckoning of the beats or vibrations of sounding bodies."[1] Musical experience's sensual richness derived from an ineffable yet mathematically based understanding—not a strictly intellectual or logical affair, but a kind of 'knowing' just the same. To the rationalist, musical experience could not be a matter of blind, sensual pleasure and indulgence. Rather, music is orderly, patterned, systematic, the product of rules and principles.

The doctrine of 'affections', which maintained music's capacity to portray particular emotions, was one notable manifestation of this disposition, assuming as it did the existence of logically discernible congruence between tonal and emotional patterns that could be systematically exploited by composer and appreciated by listener. Rameau's harmonic theories also reflect a rationalistic disposition by systematizing the principles of chordal and intervallic inversion, maintaining the lawful derivation of chords from the harmonic series, and explicating rules for common-practice harmonic progression. Rameau also maintained that music's patterns of consonance and dissonance, stability and instability, derived from innate propensities shared by all human minds. From the rationalistic perspective, discoveries like these were compelling proof of music's underlying rational nature.

Similarly, Alexander Baumgarten coined (in 1750) the term 'aesthetics' to designate an orientation that would accomplish for artistic activity what logic did for reason. 'Aesthetic' experience was construed as a kind of parallel to intellectual knowledge, but one that was perceptual rather than conceptual in nature. Because of its sensory roots, Baumgarten construed his "science of sensory cognition" as a "lower" mode of cognition, lacking intellect's characteristic distinctness. Although sensory perception might not claim both the clarity and distinctness Descartes thought necessary for trustworthy knowledge, it could indeed achieve vividness, coherence, and clarity. Baumgarten's 'aesthetic' was thus a realm of sensory-imaginative activity possessing some (though not all) of the essential characteristics of knowledge.

Against this backdrop, the convictions of Enlightenment empiricists stand out in bold relief. Where the rationalist sought certainty in innate or self-evident ideas, the empiricist rejected the very possibility of their existence. The human mind, **John Locke** (1632–1704) insisted, begins as a blank slate. **Thomas Hobbes** (1588–1679) argued, further, that there could be no conceptions or ideas except as mediated by the senses, and that therefore the notion of innately known truths is a rationalistic delusion. Empirical experience is the only source of secure knowledge, and whatever defies direct corroboration by sense and nature is therefore suspect. Knowledge arises only from associations among experiences, and the key to its advancement is accepting only ideas whose validity sense experience can verify. Empiricists, then, placed their trust in knowledge that faithfully conformed to the external, material world, and strove to purge knowledge of the 'subjective' distortions inherent in rationalistic speculation. Truth was to be systematically constructed from 'objective' evidence, not the fancies of unbridled speculation. In short, empirical validity is gauged not by the clarity or internal coherence of ideas, but by their correspondence to objective, experiential 'facts'.

To the ardent empiricist, musical experience was a response to a stimulus, more psychological than logical. Musical responses, it was sometimes claimed, are mediated by faculties of 'imagination' or 'taste' that are not so much functions of rationality as of sensory pleasure. Thus, empiricist accounts of music emphasized its sensory side, its capacity to arouse emotion: musical pleasures were more bodily than mindful. Where rationalists regarded music as sensory intellectual experience, empiricists considered it mere sense. They differed strenuously on judgments of beauty as well. Empiricists like **David Hume** (1711–1776) urged a distinction between 'judgment' and mere 'sentiment', maintaining that "Beauty is no quality in things themselves. It exists merely in the mind which contemplates them, and each mind perceives a different beauty."[2] To the empiricist, beauty was not the domain of judgment, but rather of individual predilections and dispositions that "can never reasonably be the object of dispute, because there is no standard by which they can be decided."[3] To the empiricist, music was not rational, but emotional and sensory—a matter of sentiment, not judgment. With this ideological struggle as background, let us turn to Immanuel Kant, whose philosophical enterprise was devoted to bridging this chasm, to forging a synthesis of the best each side had to offer.

Kant: 'Aesthetic' Experience, Beauty, and Taste

Sense and Reason

Kant's writings are achievements whose incisiveness and complexity are arguably without parallel in the history of philosophy. It is largely due to his influence that the area of aesthetics came to be regarded as an essential branch of philosophy. He articulated the basic premises which were to shape aesthetic inquiry for generations to come, exerting an extraordinary influence on the way music has come to be conceived. Although the conclusions he reached about music are quite unflattering, the line of reasoning by which he reached them is both fascinating and highly relevant to contemporary thought. For many, it would be exceptionally difficult to argue the value of music without resort to some aspect of Kant's characterization of aesthetic judgments.

Although this section is primarily concerned with Kant's third critique, the *Critique of Judgement*, that critique must be grounded in an understanding of his broader philosophical undertaking, a task that involves an excursion beyond his writings on music. Central to Kant's philosophy is his account of the mind's role in shaping human 'reality', his contention that people perceive data from the so-called external world only through categories which are the spontaneous work of their minds. The objects of consciousness are not mere sense data, or things as they 'actually are', but things shaped and structured by human cognitive activity. Even the most scrupulously 'objective' facts and observations bear the mind's imprint. As noted above, Kant's thought takes as its point of departure the opposing perspectives of rationalism and empiricism. When Hume's extreme skepticism (his contention, for instance, that even such apparently rational concepts as causality were not 'real' but only imputed to the world) jarred

Kant from what he described as a "dogmatic slumber," he set out to forge a synthesis of rationalist and empiricist perspectives that would transcend their differences: a 'transcendental' idealism.

In the *Critique of Pure Reason* Kant declared the entire rationalism-empiricism controversy misguided, and set out to elucidate the limits of both sense and reason—to illuminate both the presuppositions of empirical or scientific knowledge and the limitations of 'pure rationality'. In so doing, he hoped to find a balance between pure reason's potentially undisciplined freedom and empiricism's sense-based determinism. By setting out to describe the limits of pure reason, Kant hoped to free human rationality from the constrained, mechanistic role envisioned for it by empiricism.

His primary concern in the first critique is the relation between mental images (or 'representations') and their objects. Reason comprehends, he argues, only what is given it in a manner compatible with its own categories and structures. It demands, in effect, that nature present itself in ways which conform to the structure of mind. Empiricists assume that knowledge is shaped primarily by its objects, in a largely mechanical response to an objective stimulus. But that does not explain how we know anything beyond fragmented sense data. In a turn whose significance Kant compares to the Copernican revolution, he urges we begin with precisely the opposite assumption, that objects are 'adjusted to' our knowledge. Mind is not led around on a leash by nature, as strict empiricism would have it. Knowing is fundamentally reliant upon acts of imagination that shape the known. Instead of approaching nature after the manner of a docile pupil who passively records everything his instructor says, Kant argues, the mind requires that nature present itself in ways it can understand, answering questions the mind has formulated. Since all knowing is mind mediated, reality as it exists 'in itself' is not knowable. To this extent, human consciousness is free and autonomous.

Yet, 'reality' is not merely a mental fabrication. The fact that we cannot know things as they are in and of themselves does not mean they do not exist. Nor does it negate the possibility of valid, reliable knowledge. A knowledge which bears the impression of the imaginative act is not a tainted or contaminated knowledge, it is simply the only knowledge we have. The empirical sciences owe their conspicuous success to having correctly sought "what reason must learn from nature" in accordance with what reason 'projects' there—but not just anything the mind can conjure up.

The details of Kant's tightly reasoned analysis can be foregone for current purposes, but his conclusions are essential. There exists, he maintains, an important rational order beyond the sense-derived ideas of empiricism, a rational order that is not experience-derived but a priori. The proof of its existence lies in concepts like space and time, which constitute the defining ground for all experience and all knowledge. Neither space nor time is in itself (empirically) anything at all. But without them no object or event would be conceivable. They do not follow from experience, but precede and frame it. So too, cause-effect relationships: although strictly speaking, they defy observation, causal connections are essential frames of experience. They are the contribution of a mind to which connection is utterly essential in finding coherence or making sense of otherwise random sense events.

In other words, space, time, and causation are the cognitive schemata or templates that make such a thing as 'experience' possible, wresting it from the 'raw data' of natural or material reality. Among what we perceive to be nature's qualities are attributes that are purely the work of mind. More strongly yet, the world out there is partly within us. We often mistakenly attribute to the world what is really within us, a fact which is a major embarrassment to the empiricist's idea of sense-derived and sense-verifiable truth.

Yet this hardly constitutes an unqualified endorsement of rationalism. If a priori knowledge serves to frame experience, any effort to free it completely from the tethers of experience is precarious. Unbridled 'reason', reason employed without proper recognition of and respect for its limitations, can only lead to irresolvable confusion and paradox—to quests for things like the origin of time, or the cause of the universe. Since many of the world's apparent characteristics are ultimately products of the mind's own action, rational activity is not an incontrovertible method for ascertaining truth.

Thus, Kant's critique delimits both sense and reason. To Kant, the sense stuff of experience is a given, but human cognition imparts the structure and order that make it meaningful. Without mind's categorizing activity, the world would be chaos. In this strictly limited sense, mind constitutes reality, but only in this limited sense. Kant's is not an extreme subjective idealism on which the world is nothing but one's representation of it. The mind shapes what is given it, and is to that extent free. But thoughts devoid of content are empty, as are intuitions that do not submit to conceptual constraints. Reason shapes what is given it, but does not create the world out of nothing.

As a consequence of this compromise between rationalism and empiricism, however, Kant was forced to maintain that there exists a 'noumenal', in-itself world, one forever inaccessible to 'phenomenal' human experience because it does not conform to the schemata that would enable its conception or perception. Thus, Kant's philosophy remains fundamentally dualistic. And in this idea of an unknowable, noumenal realm of things as they 'really' are lie the seeds of many a future claim for music's distinctive nature and value.

Whereas Kant's first critique deals with theoretical reason's grounds for judgments about nature, reality, scientific validity, and the like, his second and third critiques explore other forms of reason. The *Critique of Practical Reason* ('practical' not in the sense of expediency, but rather of action) explores normative moral judgments: the grounds for our conviction that free individuals are subject to binding moral obligations. In other words, where 'pure' reason concerns itself with 'what is', 'practical' reason explores 'what ought to be'. In his third critique, the *Critique of Judgement*, Kant explores aesthetic and teleological judgments, judgments of design and purpose, of beauty and of 'taste'. Here, Kant explores the grounds for maintaining that judgments of beauty are a form of reason, developing the idea that aesthetic judgments are not mere expressions of subjective preference. This claim to the substance of aesthetic judgments has inspired many a subsequent idealistic philosopher to argue that musical experience affords glimpses into the 'noumenal' realm, privileged knowledge of a realm unknowable in any other way. As we shall see shortly, however, this was hardly Kant's conclusion.

The Critique of Judgment

Kant's aesthetic judgments (judgments of 'taste', or of 'beauty') are not a mere postscript to an otherwise complete philosophical system, but an indispensable part of his analysis of human cognitive faculties. Against the ancient view that truth, virtue, and beauty are largely coextensive, Kant's critiques introduce crucial distinctions and contrasts. At the same time, he creates for judgments of beauty a cognitively valid domain of their own, secure from their common confusion with intellectual or logical judgments on the one hand and with moral judgments on the other. Such important achievements, however, are not without cost. For at Kant's hand, sensation and emotion are radically devalued, and formal qualities attain paramount priority. One might say he liberates the aesthetic, but at music's expense: for he ultimately concludes that music's transience lacks the formal integrity necessary to universally valid judgments of beauty. Kant acknowledges music's 'agreeable' nature, but attributes it to music's capacity to stimulate or arouse. Since it is more a matter of sensual pleasure than of the 'contemplative delight' he places at the heart of aesthetic experience, music warrants, in his view, the very lowest ranking among the beautiful objects to which judgments of taste apply.

Kant explores the distinctive characteristics and grounds for judgments of beauty from four perspectives, or four 'moments': their quality, their quantity, their relation, and their modality. The quality of aesthetic judgments is, he says, *disinterested*. Their quantity is, though *conceptless, universal*. Their relation is *purposive* (while, strictly speaking, *purposeless*). And their modality is *exemplary*. Let us examine each in turn.

First consider Kant's claim that judgments of beauty are disinterested in quality, that they are evaluations made "by means of a delight or aversion *apart from any interest*."[4] His concern here is to establish that while such judgments are not purely capricious things, they are nonetheless undertaken freely. 'Interests', in Kant's mind, always answer to some further end in a way that aesthetic judgments do not. So one reason for calling them disinterested is to counter the implicit determinism of the sensualist perspective, a determinism that would compromise their status as 'judgments'. To counter the empiricist belief that judgments of beauty are just functions of sensual pleasure, Kant needs to distinguish the aesthetic experience from the knee-jerk response. Therefore, aesthetic judgments must be freely undertaken. On the other hand, however, they cannot be totally free. To remain 'judgments' they must be anchored to something more durable and substantial than whim or personal preference.

Thus, Kant hopes to avoid the respective pitfalls of empiricism and rationalism by conceding that pleasure enters importantly into estimations of beauty, while insisting on an important distinction between sensual and aesthetic pleasures. Sensation is 'interested' in the gratification its stimulus affords, and is therefore a matter of agreeable experience rather than beauty. Sensation dissipates the moment its source is withdrawn. Sensual gratification is simply too direct and immediate, too active and indulgent to be entertained as beauty.

At the same time, 'disinterestedness' distinguishes aesthetic judgments from intellectual or logical ones, the domain of rational understanding. Since the actuality of the objects of rational knowledge is a matter of fundamental concern to intellectual judgments, they are always essentially 'interested'. To judgments of beauty, on the other hand, questions of actuality or reality are beside the point. Whether an object exists materially or physically is of little relevance to judgments of its beauty. Thus, while the aesthetic way of judging is concerned with discriminating and with estimating, it "contributes nothing to knowledge."[5] Moreover, it is wholly subjective: the final court of appeal is the individual's feeling, the degree of contemplative satisfaction its object affords.

Thus, to declare something beautiful is not to be at the mercy of a sensual impulse, nor does it rest on a binding relation like that between logic and truth. Because of their disinterestedness and subjectivity, aesthetic judgments of beauty are fundamentally free. They consist in "pure disinterested delight,"[6] being neither materially determined nor logically implicated. They are unencumbered by questions of utility or validity, free to appraise their object exclusive of extraneous concerns. Judgments of beauty, then, afford "absolutely no (not even a confused) knowledge."[7] They are supremely unconcerned with anything beyond the immediate, presentational significance of particular images.[8] The aesthetic judgment finds its objects whole, final, complete in and of themselves, and beauty is thus securely grounded in nothing other than the contemplative pleasure it affords and by which it is gauged. Because they are disinterested and derive exclusively from the way things *impress* us, aesthetic judgments are free of the potential distortions of logic, stereotype, classification, as well as the determinacy of sensation.

Kant's second major point is that beauty is "that which, apart from a concept, pleases universally."[9] This claim to universal validity is a clear denial of the utter subjectivity attributed to judgments of taste by Hume and others. Yet at the same time, Kant yields no ground to Baumgarten's 'lower conceptual' claims. Calling aesthetic judgments subjective cannot mean they are strictly personal or private. Like the theoretical judgments of reason, and like moral judgments, judgments of beauty lay claim to universal assent, *imputing* agreement to all who will approach the object in the proper way (which is to say, aesthetically: without 'interest', and without conceptual mediation). Beauty is not merely in the beholder's eye, but something 'out there' that any competent observer should perceive. In other words, like logical and moral judgments, aesthetic judgments claim universality; only in the case of beauty, universal agreement is imputed only, not governed by explicit rule. Unlike conceptually mediated rational judgments they are not determinate or logically constrained, but free. The botanist who judges a particular flower beautiful, says Kant, makes absolutely no use of his or her store of conceptual knowledge.[10] Unlike logical and moral judgments, aesthetic judgments are conceptless.

And yet, there is something at least law*like* in judgments of beauty, because we do in fact presume that others will necessarily find beauty where we do if they assume the proper perceptual stance. All who are present to beauty *in the way Kant describes* will concur, because beauty necessarily ensues from congruence between the form of the object and the fundamental structure of the human mind we all share. Disagreements and disputes arise, but presumably they are the result of deploying 'interested' or 'conceptual' schemata instead of properly 'aesthetic' ones. Should two individuals fail to agree upon the beauty of a Mozart sonata, one of them is not listening 'aesthetically' — that is, without interest and without concepts.

Thirdly, Kant argues that the ground for judgments of beauty is design, pattern, or coherence: in short, unity. Beautiful objects please solely by virtue of their "formal finality."[11] This formal finality or sense of completeness is, however, also characteristic of judgments that are not, in Kant's estimation, aesthetic. Hence the need for further distinctions. When we value something for its utility in serving certain ends, for being 'practical', we attend to matters beyond the individual thing before us, invoking attitudes that are interested and conceptual. When, on the other hand, we value something for its perfection, for being outstanding in its kind, even though the judgment remains internal to the object, it entails a comparison between the individual thing and our conception of what it is supposed to be. This comparison, to the extent that it is conceptual, cannot be considered aesthetic. The ground of aesthetic pleasure is neither the "pathological ground of agreeableness" then, nor is it "the intellectual ground of the represented good," but rather, "the active engagement of the cognitive powers without ulterior aim."[12] Beauty "pleases by its form,"[13] not objectively, but subjectively. "No concept can be its determining ground, and hence not one of a definite end. Beauty, therefore, as a formal subjective finality, involves no thought whatsoever of the perfection of the object."[14] In this way, the judgments of beauty find their objects purposive, yet without giving any consideration whatsoever to any actual or imagined purpose.

Kant describes three distinct kinds of pleasure (of feeling, or 'delight') which we are now in a position to differentiate more clearly: pleasure in beauty, pleasure in sensation, and pleasure in utility. Sensuous pleasure is purely subjective and conceptless, like the experience of beauty; but unlike beauty, it involves interest. *Agreeable* or *appetitive* (sensuous) experience simply gratifies, involving absolutely "no cognition of the object."[15] Animals and humans enjoy these baser, appetitive pleasures, but humans alone take pleasure in beauty. Unlike aesthetic experience, agreeable experience is a private, personal affair, making no claim to exist beyond the insularity of purely individual experience. It does not require the grasp of its object the way beauty does, just an automatic response to a sensual stimulus. Thus, where beauty *pleases*, agreeable experience *gratifies*.[16] The pleasure that attends the satisfaction of hunger or sexual urges is a pleasure of sensation. Aesthetic pleasure is a pleasure of reflection.

When we take pleasure in the practical utility of something, our judgment is grounded in appreciation of its contribution to some further end. We have in mind some concept of end, use, or *purpose*: of what something is good *for*. To find something useful, in other words, involves an awareness of practical ends to which it is suited and an estimation of its utility toward those ends. Moral decisions, for instance, are taken in view of ends an appropriate action will demonstrably serve: ends that can be rationally derived and debated. So the agreeable gratifies, and usefulness is enjoyed for its relation to ends or purposes; but beauty simply satisfies: it is "the one and only disinterested and free delight; for, with it, no interest, whether of sense or reason, extorts approval."[17]

Where Kant's first three 'moments' argue freedom from interest, from concepts, and from purpose, the fourth attributes to judgments of beauty an "exemplary necessity."[18] When face to face with genuine beauty, we recognize undeniable regularity, the presence of a lawlike coherence that is more than a mental projection, that appeals to more than idiosyncratic personal preference. There is a quality of *necessity* in the judgment of beauty that derives from the indisputable presence of order and rule. Still, the rule it exemplifies cannot be specified, formulated, or logically deduced. The 'ought' of judgments of beauty, their claim to universal validity, must therefore be conditional in a way other judgments are not. But saying beauty's rule cannot be formulated is not the same as saying that something rule-like is not operating, only that it is free from intellectual or sensual determination. There must be, Kant concludes, a "subjective principle" of beauty:[19] one we see exemplified in beauty's purposive and seemingly rational designs; one whose manifestations we rightly presume all others can similarly see, since all human minds work in the same way; one whose appeal is to the distinctive feeling which is aesthetic experience.

Imagination and Understanding

Aesthetic experience is disinterested yet pleasant, conceptless yet putatively universal, purposive yet purposeless, and lawlike yet without rule. The keystone which keeps this precarious edifice from tumbling to the ground may now be lowered into place. It consists in yet another seeming paradox: that even though judgments of beauty "do not of themselves contribute a whit to the knowledge of things, they still belong wholly to the faculty of knowledge . . ."[20] Understanding Kant on this point requires an examination of his highly individual theory of the relationship between the two cognitive faculties of understanding and imagination, a theory which, if it can be sustained, promises that the experience of beauty may provide 'knowledge' of a sort inaccessible to the rational or practical mind.

According to Kant, aesthetic pleasure is the result of harmony or congruence between the two cognitive faculties of imagination and understanding, the result of their free play, altogether independent of ulterior aim or purpose. To perceive anything at all—for anything to become an object of cognition—requires the work of an imagination whose job is "bringing together the manifold of intuition,"[21] or more simply, to make order of an otherwise patternless bombardment by sense data.[22] Although understanding functions similarly, it confers (through concepts) unity upon the images presented to it by imagination.

The imagination is no servile copier, mechanically recording and collating what the senses convey to it. Its activity is fundamentally free, spontaneous, and creative. In the presence of beauty, however, imagination relinquishes some of its freedom, recognizing, in effect, that what is before it is the kind of orderly whole that might well be a product of the understanding. As a result, the faculties of imagination and understanding are brought into a state of subjective harmony mediated by feeling. In Kant's words, there is a "quickening of both faculties . . . to an indefinite, but . . . harmonious activity,"[23] a "feeling of freedom in the play of our cognitive faculties . . ."[24] This experience is ordered yet playful, at once structured and free: a distinctive kind of pleasure.

Its significance does not consist only in such pleasure, though. For the imagination is "a powerful agent for creating, as it were, another nature out of the material supplied to it by actual nature. It affords us entertainment where experience proves too commonplace; and we even use it to remodel experience . . . following principles which have a higher seat in reason . . ."[25] Imagination takes what nature provides and refashions it, transforms it into something that surpasses what understanding itself can know of nature. Imagination emulates the lawfulness of reason, but being free of understanding's conceptual tethers, can create a sense of "completeness of which nature affords no parallel."[26]

When employed in the service of understanding, imagination must acquiesce to the conceptual rules that obtain there. Such imaginative activity is neither free nor playful. In aesthetic experience on the other hand, the imagination is conceptually unconstrained, free to indulge and enjoy its rational propensities to whatever extent the orderly image (or piece of music) will allow. In the words of one analyst, imagination is influenced by the understanding in that its images are "formful and bound, like those representations of the imagination which become objects of cognition."[27] At the same time, understanding is enlivened, "guided and coaxed,"[28] given animation and spirit by the imagination. In aesthetic experience, then, imagination is cognitively grounded, but not objectively or intellectually determined. For its part, understanding is vivified by the imagination, but can never fully grasp or account for the products of imagination's free activity.

In effect, understanding recognizes in beautiful images the pattern, order, coherence, and unity characteristic of *its* normal activity. But since understanding cannot subsume such images within its customary general concepts, the mind simply delights in the free play and harmony between imagination and understanding. This is the key to Kant's claims for the universal validity and exemplary necessity of judgments of beauty: this particular subjective pleasure or delight is not a purely private affair. The pleasure beauty affords, if it is freely experienced, is the result of universally-shared processes of consciousness. As one interpreter puts it, "That my imagination is in accord with my understanding does not mean that the accord is limited to me, since we all have minds that are equivalent."[29]

To the old adage that there is no disputing matters of taste, Kant responds in effect, "Of course there is." Only not all tastes are identical. Appetitive tastes and preferences are purely personal matters about which argument is pointless, but aesthetic judgments are not. Although not based upon rational rules, judgments of beauty extend well beyond idiosyncratic preferences. The connection between the form of a beautiful object and the harmonious, free play of imagination and understanding can be shared. When mind intuitively recognizes the mindlike unity and seeming lawfulness of beautiful objects, the ensuing pleasure is neither essentially sensuous nor rational in nature. It is an emotion all its own, a purely aesthetic one, autonomous and subjectively universal. Judgments of beauty are not grounded in mere sense responses or common emotion, but in a particular and distinctive feeling that arises from harmonious resonance between cognitive faculties.

Thus, aesthetic judgments are quite unlike naive, sentimental claims to 'charm' advanced by the crude and the untutored. Appeals to charm are "positively subversive of the judgment of taste";[30] indeed, "[t]aste that requires an added element of charm and emotion for its delight . . . has not yet emerged from barbarism."[31] Beauty is a matter of design, "not what gratifies in sensation, but merely what pleases by its form."[32] Pure, authentic aesthetic judgments rest upon neither charm, nor emotion, nor sensation. Such conditions are neither necessary nor sufficient to beauty. Accordingly, Kant believes, something like the tone of a violin can be called beautiful only in a specious sense: it is more properly called agreeable. Beauty as such derives from form, and sensation is too transient and personal an affair to count.

The strength of Kant's endorsement of form sometimes tempts people to neglect feeling's role in his 'aesthetic' theory. Kant's appeal to formal coherence and unity derives from the need to establish that judgments of beauty are not wholly objective: they cannot be grounded in rule and logic like intellectual judgments; yet to be considered cognitive, they do require grounding. For Kant, this grounding lies in a particular range of feeling. Aesthetic judgment is not merely a function of feeling, but the operation of feeling is among the important distinctions between reason and taste. Pure reason or understanding is abstract and formal, and stands diametrically opposed to the realm of sensation. However, sensations constitute only a part of the range of feeling. And while sensations that are strictly personal have little to do with cognition, that is apparently not the case for sensations perceptibly patterned. Thus, Kant's reputed formalism retains a place of considerable importance for a particular range of feeling: in fact, the feeling of free play between our cognitive faculties (imagination and reason) is utterly essential to the 'aesthetic' bridge that seeks to span the gap between fact and value.

The key points of Kant's position, then, are these. Aesthetic judgment or the judgment of beauty is an estimation based upon "delight or aversion apart from any interest."[33] Beauty is that which pleases universally, yet apart from any concept.[34] It is "reason's indeterminate idea of a maximum," but can be represented "only in an individual presentation."[35] Beauty is a "formal subjective finality," whose only determining ground is "the feeling (of the internal sense) of the concert in the play of the mental powers,"[36] totally independent of any perceived end or purpose.[37] Aesthetic judgment lays claim to "necessity of the assent of all to a judgment regarded as exemplifying a universal rule incapable of formulation."[38] Beauty is, in short, "that which, apart from a concept, is cognized as object of necessary delight",[39] by virtue of its capacity to give the imagination "scope for unstudied and final play"[40] in a way that keeps its perception ever fresh.

Artistic and Musical Beauty

Beauty in its pure state is a formal thing for Kant, untarnished by either sensation or concept, though grounded in its own distinct kind of feeling. We respond to beauty as we do because of discernible formal relationships and patterns which in effect strike us as being the kind of things a mind, in its freedom, might well create. The experience is concept-free, purely disinterested, utterly free to enjoy the cognitive harmony occasioned by the beautiful object. Although this account suits things like sunsets and roses reasonably well, signs of strain begin to show when it is applied to art.

According to Kant, nature is beautiful when it looks like art, and art is beautiful if despite having been fabricated, it appears natural. Art must show evidence of rationality, some degree of regularity or perceptible pattern, for instance. But such features must not draw attention to themselves. Instead, they should appear as part of an organic whole. Overly formulaic or calculated formal design suggests the imposition of a rule, which, as we have seen, is contrary to beauty's essential freedom and apparent spontaneity. To be beautiful, then, art must be capable of sustaining an attitude that is disinterested and conceptless. But how does an artifact, the creation of a rational mind, achieve this natural, unrestrained appearance while still exemplifying the regularity and harmony which are equally essential to beauty? Not by rational or logical calculation, since that would be conceptual rather than aesthetic. Unlike reason, which is completed in the theoretical or conceptual, the artistic is completed only in action: in some kind of doing. If knowing or understanding were sufficient to produce a work of art, one might become a musician simply by reading a book or following a list of rules.

Doings that are governed by more or less explicit principles are not art but craft. Art's motivation, art's mode of production, and art's primary reward alike derive from imagination's free play. Craft on the other hand is utilitarian, 'industrial', concerned more with pay than play. However purposive art may appear, its beauty must be autonomous, independent, purposeless. Art consists more in the doing itself than in the pursuit of preconceived ends. The fundamental character of art lies in the fact that its products are not constrained by concepts (like science) or ends (like craft): it requires only the free, harmonious play of imagination and understanding.

But again, how does art maintain its freedom from conceptual determination yet still attain the coherence of presentation it must have to be experienced as beautiful? How does it achieve its purposive quality in the absence of any purpose, or come to appear lawlike in the absence of rules? Kant's answer is that genius "gives the rule to art."[41] Since artists cannot stipulate rules for producing works of art or determining their completion, artistic production derives from an intuitive gift, a special sensitivity to harmonious relations among cognitive faculties. Genius is talent for producing what cannot be taught. Since its products are necessarily novel or original, they cannot be encompassed by general rules. Each creation of genius stands as an individual, an exemplar, that presents its own particular rules.[42]

Freedom from constraint by rules neither confers absolute license upon genius nor gives imagination utterly free reign. Art is an achievement of a disciplined imagination. Genius's inspiration must be stabilized by the critical skills of informed taste and skills of impression, skills that are products of learning and training. Genius furnishes the necessary imaginative material, but "its elaboration and its form require a talent academically trained."[43] Genius is a productive talent, and taste, the critical capacity for estimating its achievements. Unrestrained genius, then, produces inspired works that lack taste, pieces whose novelty is too radical for contemplative perception. On the other hand, no amount of taste can compensate for music that is devoid of genius, derivative and conventional.[44] In proper balance, though, genius and taste generate what Kant calls an "aesthetic idea," a "representation of the imagination which induces much thought, yet without the possibility of any definite thought whatever . . . being adequate to it, and which language, consequently, can never get quite on level terms with or render completely intelligible."[45] Imagination creates from natural materials aesthetic ideas or images that transcend their material composition. These "strain after something lying out beyond the confines of experience," attempting to approximate in their presentation alone the manner of "rational concepts." To the extent that they succeed—to the extent their patterns accord with the conceptual realm—they present a "semblance of an objective reality."[46] Here, then, is Kant's idealism, an idealism every bit as conditional or qualified as his formalism. Imagination takes what is given it, and fashions it into something new: an image, a semblance which communicates something at once ineffable and cognitively significant by virtue of its formal congruence to our conceptual faculty.

By declaring beauty's freedom from conceptual and sensual determination, Kant sought to establish the autonomy of aesthetic judgments—to show that judgments of beauty were free in ways that those in other experiential domains were not. Although this claim to autonomy is a matter of some moment for the arts, it is not without its costs, particularly in music's case. Although music (particularly wordless, instrumental music) might have been expected to fare extraordinarily well against the criterion of conceptlessness, for instance, that is not quite how Kant saw things. Music may be conceptless, but it is also transient and fleeting, which fact undermines the formal relationships on which the experience of pure beauty relies. As well, music is too active and changeable to be properly disinterested. Apparently, music appeals not quite enough to the mind, and rather too much to sense.

Fine and Agreeable Art

In comparison to the utterly free beauties of nature, artistic beauty carries varying degrees of impurity. There are, on the one hand, 'fine' arts, arts that derive their beauty from formal relationships without resort to charm or sentiment. Fine art caters to the pleasure which ensues from the contemplation of form alone. Its judgment is distinctively calm, reflective, and detached, virtues in light of which it "has the effect of advancing the culture of the mental powers . . ."[47] On the other hand, there are 'agreeable' arts, arts that cater more predominantly to appetitive enjoyment. Agreeable art charms, entertains, diverts or amuses, but appeals mainly to sensation. Like dinner music, agreeable art is little more than "a quaint idea intended to act on the mind merely as an agreeable noise fostering a genial spirit. . . . [and] making the time pass by unheeded."[48]

Fine arts, like natural beauty, have "no business beyond appealing to the eye, in order to entertain the imagination in free play with ideas, and to engage actively the aesthetic judgment independently of any definite end."[49] Their beauty consists exclusively in the pleasure that attends contemplation of their formal configurations. But the arts of sensation, music paramount among them, are 'fine' only to the extent that their beauty derives from the "proportion of the different degrees of tension in the sense to which the sensation belongs."[50] There is, for Kant, an important distinction to be drawn between pleasures caused by agreeable sensations and those that ensue from agreeable play among sensations. Only to the extent that music involves an "estimate of form in the play of sensations" can it be considered 'fine', then. Sensual pleasure is beautiful only where it gives rise to pattern or configuration, because only pattern can be beautiful. Sensual pleasure by itself is only agreeable.

Poetry ranks first among the arts for Kant, because it is unparalleled in its capacity to give freedom to the imagination and thereby cultivate mental power. Poetry "invigorates the mind by letting it feel its faculty—free, spontaneous, and independent of determination by nature."[51] Despite its use of illusory images, poetry is not deceptive, because "its avowed pursuit is merely one of play" and no more. Rhetoric, by contrast, deploys sensuous presentations to "ensnare the understanding," to win over minds pre-reflectively and thereby "rob their verdict of its freedom." Such political uses of art are completely unacceptable to Kant even under the most altruistic circumstances, since "it is not enough to do what is right, but we should practise it solely on the grounds of its being right."[52]

Kant's arguments and assumptions here are revealing. Poetry is important in its capacity to expand and invigorate the mind. Even the pleasure of its felt freedom is valuable not so much aesthetically as cognitively—in its further capacity to vivify the mind. Moreover, rhetoric is found wanting not because it is less beautiful but because it threatens to deceive and cheat understanding. Since mental cultivation seems to take priority over the capacity to afford aesthetic experience, and since Kant's estimation of the relative worth of poetry and rhetoric draws on an 'interested' distinction between their presumed intentions, perhaps there is reason to question the sufficiency of aesthetic considerations to questions of artistic beauty and worth.

His claims about poetry bring into sharp relief Kant's views on music. The art of tone, music "speaks by means of mere sensations without concepts, and so does not, like poetry, leave behind it any food for reflection."[53] Its patterns vanish as quickly as they arise, leaving us only with sense traces, stimulation, but no enduring or substantial mental nourishment. Music's conceptlessness, which should have been, aesthetically speaking, a virtue, is an artistic defect since its forms are so sensual and fleeting. It probably warrants some credit for its capacity to stimulate the mind 'diversely' and 'intensely', however, "It is certainly . . . more a matter of enjoyment than of culture . . . and it possesses less worth in the eyes of reason than any other of the fine arts. Hence, like all enjoyment, it calls for constant change, and does not stand frequent repetition without inducing weariness."[54] Charm and mental stimulation, music's direct evocative power, are what Kant finds most salient about music—aside, that is, from its unfortunate inability to stand still. Its broad appeal owes mainly to the universality of sensation, and its distinctive power is primarily a matter of its general emotive quality. Music "only serves the purpose of giving an expression to the aesthetic idea of an integral whole of an unutterable wealth of thought that fills the measure of a certain theme forming the dominant affection in the piece."[55] Although this might sound like no mean achievement, Kant believes it is a rather modest achievement in comparison with the other arts. Music does what it does merely in light of an "accord of the sensations," an accord which derives from (imperceptible) "numerical relations of the vibrations of the air."[56] Kant finds little in such relationships that promise to enhance mind's higher culture.

Judged in terms of its charm, its evocative power, its capacity to stimulate feeling (judged, that is, as an *agreeable* art), music reigns supreme. Unfortunately, these characteristics lie at the very periphery of what Kant considers to be art. Music most itself—sense stimulating rather than thoughtful or contemplative—is least art. In terms of its contribution to the cognitive faculties, music is the lowest of the arts. The arts of form, by contrast, put imagination to work in ways more congruent with the understanding. In their free play, they carry forward the serious business of "promoting . . . the urbanity of the higher powers of cognition."[57] They have the enviable advantage of leaving enduring impressions, where music's are largely fleeting and evanescent. When tunes do linger in the mind, Kant suggests, the experience is "more annoying to us than agreeable."[58]

In short, Kant believes "music has a certain lack of urbanity about it. . . . it scatters its influence abroad to an uncalled-for extent . . . and thus . . . becomes obtrusive and deprives others, outside the musical circle, of their freedom."[59] Its obtrusiveness is like a heavy perfume, which "gives a treat to all around whether they like it or not." Lest there be any doubt that Kant counts himself outside this musical circle, consider this brief footnote to his text: "Those who have recommended the singing of hymns at family prayers have forgotten the amount of annoyance which they give to the general public by such noisy (and, as a rule, for that very reason, pharisaical) worship, for they compel their neighbors either to join in the singing or else abandon their meditations."[60] Thus, music is noisy, intrusive, transient, unsophisticated, and more sensation than intellect. But are these conclusions inescapably implicated by Kant's critique, or are they rather the indiscretions of a musically naive intellectual? Perhaps both, to some degree. Let us reexamine Kant's theory in light of his ultimate conclusions about music.

An Art of Tone, or of Time?

Since conceptlessness is so central to Kant's aesthetic, how is it that the least 'conceptual' of all the arts ends up at the bottom of the heap? Kant based his ideal of utterly free, conceptless, disinterested aesthetic judgments upon *natural* beauty, a domain in which it may be appropriate. But unlike judgments of natural beauty, judgments of artistic beauty are always adherent: they are relative to the particular kind of thing being contemplated. It is interesting to note, then, that Kant seems to base his ultimate assessments of artistic value less upon their aesthetic purity than upon their potential contributions to culture. He seems to have identified a theoretically possible mode of experience, and one that has at least a degree of plausibility in the case of contemplating natural beauty. But he appears to have been singularly unsuccessful in applying it to music, and to have wrongly faulted music instead of his theory.

One scholar urges that, had Kant actually applied his aesthetic theory to music (rather than psychological and 'cultural' criteria), he might well have found music highest among the arts instead of lowest.[61] After all, musical pleasure seems to consist precisely in imagination's free play in the presence of harmonious relations. Music is free of both logic's conceptual and craft's utilitarian constraints. Musical pleasure is the product of our free enjoyment of patterned play among sounds. By these criteria, music should have fared exceptionally well. "Of all the arts," Schueller writes, "music is the most exemplary of this self-maintaining play which is not related to rational concepts at all. . . . The order of ideas in music resembles the order of rational, intellectual ideas, but of course no concept can be adequate to musical . . . ideas as internal intuitions."[62]

But Kant's aesthetic ideal is an experience afforded by the intuition of form or pattern alone, one uncontaminated by intrusions by deterministic sensation, and ultimately even devoid of content—characteristics that seriously compromise art's vitality and relevance to life. This kind of utterly free experience is something art (and especially music) seldom sustains. A music emancipated from history, from science, from morality, and from sensation is ultimately a music emancipated from meaning itself—what one scholar has described as "a beautiful and *ineffectual* angel, beating in the void his luminous wings in vain . . ."[63] From the idealized perspective of 'free' beauty, maintaining music's utter autonomy is crucial. Music is most itself when it is least other things. But this means music fares most poorly precisely when it is purest, and truest to itself. To be conceptless and disinterested, music must eschew the very characteristics in light of which it might counter Kant's allegations that it is more charm than substance, more sensation than culture.

In certain respects, Kant's may be the most extreme formalism ever articulated: for its ideal of 'free' beauty excludes use, purpose, emotion, sensation, and indeed, even judgments of goodness or perfection. It is exclusively a matter of our mental enjoyment of form or coherence. Such utterly 'free' beauty is at odds with something so dependent as music upon sensual pleasure, something whose form seems to vanish the instant it arises. However agreeable such experience may be, it holds little promise for advancing the culture of the mental powers.

But music's incapacity to advance culture and mind is not an 'aesthetic' failure, at least as Kant defined it. Indeed, such instrumental contributions were explicitly excluded from questions of aesthetic worth.

If Kant's characterization of music as an 'art of tone' is accepted, his disparaging conclusions can be difficult to refute. If it is no more than a fleeting, sensuous experience, perhaps music is more appetitive than cultural. Perhaps it does have little to contribute to the (for Kant) all-important world of ideas. But perhaps, as others have argued, it is wrong to construe music primarily as an art of tone. Indeed, it has been suggested, one only has to turn to Kant's own *Critique of Pure Reason* to find a much more substantial basis for a claim to musical value than Kant appears to have found in tone and sensation. In the first critique, Kant established time as an a priori framer of experience, a pre-condition and necessary foundation for all general knowledge. Had he taken this as his point of departure, characterizing music as an 'art of time' rather than of tone, his conclusions about its standing among the arts might have been significantly different. As Dalhaus observes, Kant's theory "suffers from too narrow an idea of the function of time in music."[64] His own theories about time would have given him a far more secure basis for estimating music's claims both to beauty and to the advancement of "the culture of mental power" (attuning the mind to a priori truths). For temporal events have forms or gestalten which are quite compatible with Kant's broader theory, forms that would be more than sufficient to substantiate musical experience. If poetry advances culture by virtue of the congruence of its forms to our rational faculty, music does so no less significantly. Indeed, as Schueller puts it, ". . . time as a mode of human thought seems to occur in its purest form in music, of all the arts."[65] On this view, music is both cultural and urbane, a potentially profound shaper of new orders of cognitive experience.

One of the more earnest attempts to take up the (overlooked) Kantian conception of music—music as an art of time, rather than of tone—appears in Susanne Langer's *Feeling and Form*. Kant's influence is strikingly evident in her thesis that "Music makes time audible, and its form and continuity sensible."[66] Music's distinctive contribution to the culture of mind lies in its very capacity to transcend mere pattern, Langer believes, in a way that renders time's essential nature conceivable. Indeed, music is "change made perceivable,"[67] "the sonorous image of passage, abstracted from actuality to become free and plastic and entirely perceptible."[68]

One might hazard, drawing at least some support from his disparaging remarks about music's indiscretion and lack of 'urbanity', that Kant's failure to find redeeming formal coherence in music may have been as much personal as philosophical. There is little reason to doubt that music was, for him, fleeting and sensuous. Certainly, music's tones—conceived as material sense data—are quite transient. But tones perceived musically are no longer sense data, bearing as they do the imprint of mind. Music does not reside in the realm of pure materiality and sensation. Indeed, for those fluent in particular musical universes of discourse, music consists of processive patterns and configurations that are stable and secure. It is comprised not of evanescent tones, but of dynamic, temporal gestalten that deeply engage the mind. With Kant's apparent capacity to retain intellectual ideas better than musical ones, one can only commiserate.

Natural and Musical Beauty

We must confront one final problem with Kant's aesthetic theory, one that again results from his precarious application of a nature-derived aesthetic theory to art. His argument that judgments of beauty are fundamentally conceptless[69] appears to meet contradiction head-on in section 48, where he asserts that art "always presupposes an end . . . a concept of what the thing is intended to be." Clearly, judgments of musical beauty cannot be conceptless and yet reliant upon concepts; disinterested and yet concerned with ends; purposeless and yet wed to an understanding of purpose. If beauty follows from the perception of purposiveness without purpose, how may a piece be judged as exemplary—of contrapuntal technique, say, or of sonata allegro form? How, in other words, can something be judged particularly beautiful in its kind, yet remain independent of any concept or purpose?

Obviously artistic phenomena cannot. Nor, perhaps, did Kant fully intend them to. Recall that Kant introduced the idea of genius in order to help distinguish between judgments of natural and artistic beauty. "It is imperative at the outset," he states, "accurately to determine the difference between beauty of nature, which it only requires taste to estimate, and beauty of art which requires genius for its possibility (a possibility to which regard must also be paid in estimating such an object)."[70] Estimates of natural beauty, then, require no special understanding, either of the nature of their objects or of anyone's intentions. Natural beauty's form pleases purely on its own account. Estimates of artistic beauty, on the other hand, always require a degree of awareness or understanding of what kind of phenomenon is involved. "[I]n estimating beauty of art the perfection of the thing must be also taken into account," Kant concedes, "a matter which in estimating a beauty of nature . . . is quite irrelevant."[71] Judgments of natural and musical beauty are not identical. To judge music employing no more than the estimates of taste appropriate to natural beauty results in a naive dilettantism to which Kant was too shrewd to subscribe.

Accordingly, a distinction must be drawn between judgments of natural and of musical beauty. Estimates of musical beauty involve not an utterly free imagination, but disciplined imagination; not a disinterested contemplative perception of form, but a further estimate of its adequacy to its kind. Achievements of musical genius are exemplary in their kind, and mere estimates of beauty, without full awareness or appreciation of the end to which they aspire, can scarcely be considered musical. Clearly, aesthetic impression as Kant describes it is inadequate to the full comprehension of musical beauty. In music's case, appreciation of its beauty must embrace additional considerations like the effectiveness, economy, or elegance with which its ends have been attained. This being the case, it is probably wrong to reduce Kant's philosophy of music to a mere philosophy of beauty. Unlike 'pure' aesthetic judgments, musical judgments must be conceptually grounded or risk superficiality and even vacuity. Indeed, in a statement strongly reminiscent of Aristotle's *Poetics*, Kant suggests that art's superiority to nature lies "in the beautiful descriptions it gives of things that in nature would be ugly or displeasing."[72] The recognition of musical beauty involves much more than the kind of appreciation appropriate to roses and sunsets.

The significance of these distinctions is hardly 'academic'. The argument that judgments of genuinely musical beauty must be grounded in awareness of purpose, of kind, of style, genre, and convention, stands strongly opposed to assertions that knowledge about a piece's history, structure, creation, and intended function is irrelevant to aesthetic perception and thereby to musical experience. Knowledge of purpose is, while not sufficient to musical judgment, essential. Consider, Dalhaus offers, the superfluity of judgments that fault a melody of early classical origins for excessive arpeggiation, or a fugal subject for lack of lyricism.[73] Such lists could be extended indefinitely, to include things like berating plainsong for its lack of rhythmic vitality, for instance, or judging oral musical traditions by standards of complexity that obtain only for notated musics. " 'Immediacy' may be an attribute of aesthetic intuition," Dalhaus concludes, "but it is not so devoid of presuppositions as is wished by the apologists for the kind of naiveté that transcends itself by proclaiming itself naive, reflecting on itself, and bristling at intellectual sneers. It is not so much a starting-point as a point of arrival. . . . A 'purely' esthetic experience, appreciating in some object nothing but its beauty, is a thin abstraction."[74] If judgments of purpose and intention are irrelevant to 'pure' aesthetic judgment, they are utterly fundamental to genuinely musical judgment. Musical perception, says Dalhaus, consists in a "to-and-fro between contemplating and reflecting. . . . Intellectual features are no superfluous addenda; rather they are always an intrinsic part of esthetic perception."[75]

This is not to conclude, however, that musical experience is constitutively conceptual. It is a matter of engaging perceptual habits appropriate to the music at hand, and judgments of its value may often consist in pre-conceptual appreciation of the propriety or ingenuity of musical choices in light of stylistic possibilities. Although such perception and appreciation is not nonconceptual, neither is it strictly conceptual. 'Conceptual' and 'nonconceptual' do not exhaust the range of possibilities. Concepts may function nonconceptually when they are absorbed into the rich experiential fabric that enables musical perception, and musical experience always rests upon tacit awareness of the kind of musical situation of which a particular 'passing sonorous event' is an instance. Judgments and responses devoid of such awareness can scarcely claim musical status. Acoustical sense data are not music, and music always bears the imprint of mind.

Thus, those who would portray Kant as a champion of music's autonomy from concepts will find as little to sustain their position as those who see him as a champion of unqualified musical formalism. Musical experience has its roots in what Kant calls a "supersensuous substrate"—a realm inaccessible to understanding, yet whose existence we must concede for the simple reason that without it the knowledge we do hold and know to be true could not exist. In musical experience, imagination and understanding resonate sympathetically: imagination wrests pattern, coherence, and unity from sonorous sense-data, and understanding recognizes, appreciates, and enjoys the ingenuity of these relations as they temporally unfold—their remarkable affinity to understanding's own conceptual structures and processes. In musical experience, we take pleasure in perceptual activity's congruence with our 'higher' mental powers.

Kant's accounts of aesthetic judgments, art, and music are highly individual and complex. So, what can be concluded as to what does and does not 'count' in musical value judgments? However disinterested and free from conceptual determination 'judgments of taste' may be, an utterly free, disinterested, and conceptless experience of music is scarcely musical. And despite Kant's determination to entrust aesthetic judgments to form rather than sensual pleasure, form devoid of sensuous attributes and divorced from the kind of mental habits that frame musical perception is profoundly empty. Accordingly it has been suggested here that Kant did not construe music as a purely aesthetic phenomenon, but as one with distinctive 'aesthetic' characteristics. Musical value extends beyond Kant's pure aesthetic judgments, and music's forms are vital forms, forms vivified by the human imagination. They are not empty abstractions, but rich, concrete, temporally unfolding realities. A 'pure' aesthetic response, as defined by Kant, names a musical impossibility.

Schiller: 'Aesthetic' Education

A history of idealistic aesthetic theory would devote extensive attention to the thought of Friedrich Schiller, but because he had relatively little to say about music as such, it will be considered only in passing here. His influence upon efforts to chart the 'aesthetic' grounds supposedly shared by 'the fine arts', however, was deeply important for music, since it shaped what people thought it meant for music to be considered one of the undertakings known collectively as 'the arts'. We might say that philosophers like Schiller were instrumental in conceptualizing the significance of endeavors like music in aesthetic rather than in artistic terms, an achievement whose influence extended well beyond the theoretical realm of philosophy to the way musicians themselves conceived of what they did and, by extension, how they did it.

Schiller's thought is unabashedly Kantian in its main features. Indeed, part of its import lies in the enhanced accessibility it brought to certain of Kant's abstract, complex ideas. But Schiller was not merely derivative, and his ideas represent noteworthy extensions and modifications of territory Kant staked out. In Schiller's hands, the aesthetic realm was the domain of 'art'. In his *Letters on the Aesthetic Education of Man* he explored with passionate and inspiring conviction his belief that art had deep cultural value: that it was of broad and fundamental significance to humanity, both individually and collectively. His persuasive sincerity appealed to philosopher and artist alike, establishing him as a major influence in the Romantic period.

Schiller's Letters build upon Kant's dualistic antitheses between matter and mind, nature and reason, sense (or feeling) and thought. The original or natural human condition, he argues, is predominantly sensuous. Reason gives people the power to free themselves from the deterministic constraints of their sensual nature, but only so long as they do not succumb to the opposing and equally deterministic tendency of their intellectual nature. To be fully human, then, is to achieve harmony between one's opposing natures without suppressing either. Both are essential to the realization of full humanity.

Schiller conceives of these two opposing natures as drives or impulses,[76] either of which, if unchecked by the other, can be inimical to one's full humanity. People who indulge their lower, sensuous drives, succumbing to animal passions and appetites, relinquish their essential human freedom and dignity, becoming little more than "slaves of nature," precisely as Kant contended. Like animals, overly sensuous people merely react or respond, allowing themselves to be swept along by influences outside themselves. In this "savage" state,[77] people are driven by feelings and instincts, engaging in essentially mindless activity whose only value is the pleasure it affords.

People's formal 'drive', on the other hand, is what compels them to seek pattern, unity, and meaning among the objects of experience, to wrest order from the otherwise chaotic. It is to the formal drive we owe all ideas, principles, and concepts. And yet, if indulged to the utter exclusion of feeling and sense, the formal drive is as inimical as the sensuous, reducing people to abstract thinkers with cold hearts. Imbalance in the direction of the formal results in inaction and lethargy, in a too-extensively cerebral disposition, or worse yet, that "barbaric" state[78] wherein intellectual principles completely subdue feeling. The ivory tower intellectual is as driven by principle as the hedonist is driven by feeling. Neither is truly free. Neither is fully human.

This danger of becoming 'polarized' to the detriment of our fully human potential is exacerbated by modern society's push for specialization. Specialization encourages the fragmentation of humanity, divorcing mind from feeling, nurturing one side of our nature to the detriment of the other. It creates people with ideas but lacking in sense or compassion, or it creates practical people with narrow minds and undisciplined imaginations. In the latter case, a rampant imagination "ravages" the intellect, creating individuals who prefer to dwell in the "twilight of obscure ideas"; in the former, intellect suffocates the imaginative play to which it owes its very existence.

Such division and one-sidedness is, according to Schiller, the root of society's ills. But society can be restored to its full humanity through the aesthetic experience afforded by the arts, in a process Schiller calls the "aesthetic education" of humanity. Commerce with art promises to restore the properly human balance between feeling and thought, between pure activity and pure passivity, to free people from the obnoxious determinism of either extreme. Our two opposing natures or drives are harmonized by a third drive, a *play* drive, whose purpose it is to create an ideal balance or synthesis of sense and intellect. Art is its ideal vehicle. The free play of aesthetic experience is not achieved at the expense of either feeling or thought, but by a perfectly balanced integration of the two. By beauty, "sensuous man is led to form and thought"; and by beauty, the person of pure abstraction is "brought back to matter and restored to the world of sense."[79]

In contrast to Kant's purely subjective aesthetic experience, then, in which the scales stood even because both sides were empty (devoid of both interest and concepts), Schiller insists his "scale" balances precisely because both sides are full.[80] In aesthetic play, feeling and thought achieve ideal synthesis: feeling becomes properly cognitive, and thought becomes appropriately felt. Feelings are purged of any excessively passionate character, and reason is freed of its logically obligatory character. Schiller's aesthetic experience is at once contemplative and active, at once restful and impulsive, at once (in his words) "melting" and "energizing." The play impulse, which art nurtures like no other experience, unites people's sensuous and formal propensities in a "living form,"[81] stifling or dulling neither, restoring people to wholeness and freedom.

Schiller's 'play' is not the entertaining diversion of sport or game. Nor is it the unbridled imaginative fantasy of dream. It is a fully engaged mode of activity, pursued in absolute earnestness, and it is utterly indispensable for the realization of our full humanity. In aesthetic play, people are liberated from sensual servitude, but not yet constrained by reason and duty. This state is essential to full realization of the human condition. Indeed, Schiller urges, "man only plays when he is in the fullest sense of the word a human being, and he is only fully a human being when he plays."[82]

Equally crucial to Schiller's theory of beauty is his concept of semblance, or sheer appearance. Schiller accepted Kant's portrayal of the aesthetic experience as a wholly disinterested and unconditional appreciation. The object of aesthetic perception is a sheer appearance—not an appearance of reality, but a higher, more abstract, imaginative achievement. The capacity to entertain and be entertained by pure images without recourse to any further connections is the supremely human capacity. It is when form becomes an important source of enjoyment, when we take satisfaction in mere appearances (free from the "fetters of utility," free from the necessity of sensation, free from the compulsion of intellect and desire), that we most fully exercise our distinctively human power of abstraction. Ordinary perception employs the imagination, but in far more modest ways. Only when it "tears itself free from reality" does the formal drive attain its full potential. And when the appreciation of beautiful semblance becomes a source of significant pleasure, it cannot help but transform the inner world at the same time. In the enjoyment of semblances, people achieve their highest humanity and greatest nobility.

It is the duty of art and culture, then, to maintain balance between the sensuous and the formal drives, to liberate us from the excesses of each, and to protect each from the other. Yet at the same time, art and culture enrich human capacity for both the feeling and the thought from which play derives. At the heart of Schiller's theory lies a familiar paradox, then: the ideally free and fully human state of aesthetic play is at once the ultimate end in itself yet at the same time a way of cultivating the powers of feeling and thought. From his descriptions, it is clear he intended the aesthetic to be conceived of as the consummate human experience; but in arguing for aesthetic education, he maintains that such experience serves a further end, that of leading sensuous people to rationality—a notion strongly reminiscent both of Plotinus and of Kant's contention that art ought to serve the higher culture of mind.

Artistic beauty is not merely a valuable vehicle, one option among others, for leading humankind from sensuality to rationality. According to Schiller there is no way of "making sensuous man rational except by first making him aesthetic."[83] The way to the head is through the heart. Schiller never escapes this paradoxical ambivalence, in which the aesthetic is simultaneously valuable for the distinctive quality of the experience it affords and as a vehicle for education. Beauty's capacity to gently seduce the coarse mind to refinement, to lead men from caprice and frivolity to more noble ideas, is at least as important to Schiller as the experience itself.

In one of his few specific references to music, Schiller intimates that the *purely* aesthetic state may ultimately be unattainable, only approximated in high degree. "Even the most ethereal music," he says, "has, by virtue of its material, an even greater affinity with the senses than true aesthetic freedom really allows."[84] Furthermore, in a truly successful music, content counts for nothing and form for everything: it is "only from form that true aesthetic freedom can be looked for."[85] Thus, a 'purely' aesthetic state may, at least in music's case, be an unattainable ideal. But this did not deter Schiller's impassioned and influential contention that "Taste alone brings harmony into society, because it fosters harmony in the individual. All other forms of perception divide man, because they are founded exclusively either upon the sensuous or upon the spiritual [or intellectual] part of his being; only the aesthetic mode of perception makes of him a whole . . ."[86]

Schiller's writing is an impressive attempt to create a more vital, experientially engaged account of aesthetic experience, one with strong attachments to both the felt and the cognitive life. His simultaneous insistence upon art's sensual roots and refusal to permit its reduction to abstraction, his effort to integrate more fully artistic form and content (qualities that appeal to and excite the senses), is of great historical significance. This line of thought assumes axiomatic status in the influential work of Hegel.

Hegel: The Ascent Toward Absolute Idea

Art, Music, and Idea

Few philosophers have written so voluminously and on such a tremendously broad range of concerns as G. W. F. Hegel. His influence was vast, not only in positive terms but also in terms of the backlash his highly speculative metaphysics generated in subsequent generations of philosophers. And although his theories about art and music are probably wrong in some of their most fundamental assumptions, their impact (along with other German 'idealists') has been immense. Despite their shortcomings, Hegel's writings contain provocative insights into the human significance of art generally as well as the characters of the individual arts. His reflections on music introduced a number of assumptions that survive unaltered in much contemporary thought, particularly among those who maintain that music has essentially to do with feeling and the spiritual side of human nature. If his ideas about music are perplexing, the motivation behind them is laudable: a desire to account for its universal and profound significance in human affairs. Music, for Hegel, was among the greatest human achievements, something whose import extended well beyond the capacity of its formal designs to sustain personal pleasure.

The impetus for Hegel's philosophy of art lay in Kant's idea that the human mind structures and regulates the 'knowable', and that beyond the phenomenal lies a noumenal thing-in-itself, forever inaccessible to human cognition. Hegel vigorously contested Kant's separation of mind from the objects of its knowledge. Mind must be shown capable, he believed, of knowing reality as it is, if human experience is to be regarded as anything more than a dream. Experience and reality, phenomenon and noumenon, must be reunited. Kant also erred, believed Hegel, in assuming that all minds are structurally identical across individuals, cultures, and historical periods. Against this, Hegel proposed a historically evolutionary view of mind's progressive development.

Hegel was also less than enthralled with Kant's portrayal of aesthetic judgment as a purely subjective affair, in which beauty was largely a function of the feeling of free play among the cognitive faculties, for that seemed to say more about the subject's experience than the attributes of the beautiful object itself. Thus, where Kant had grounded his aesthetic in feeling and form, Hegel sought to portray beauty as an objective attribute and as something particular to art objects. Kantian aesthetics, he thought, had deprived art of its profound human significance by reducing aesthetic judgments to interesting, pleasant, but largely superfluous affairs. To Hegel, art was infinitely more important than that.

The key to Hegel's views on music lies in his vexatious theory of the "absolute idea," which does not yield graciously to paraphrase. Hegel maintains that the universe is not an unknowable mystery, but rather a fundamentally rational place. Accordingly, people can grasp ultimate truths, not partially or one-sidedly as Kant had held, but as they absolutely are. Reality consists in the unfolding divine truth of Spirit (or alternatively, of mind or of God). Spirit manifests itself most fully to humankind in absolute idea: comprehension of the cosmic totality of the universe, simultaneously concrete and abstract, simultaneously particular and universal. Human grasp of this absolute is at first dim and fragmentary, but becomes progressively more adequate through a long historical process in which mind (spirit) ascends toward eventual full comprehension of the whole to which it belongs.

Absolute idea is neither abstract nor subjective. Rather, it is that ultimate concrete reality toward which understanding and experience constantly strain. All of human history—indeed, the evolution of the entire universe—consists in absolute idea coming increasingly to fruition by infusing the 'material' with Spirit. Eventually, through a succession of stages of ever-increasing self-awareness, mind is destined to achieve full comprehension of the absolute unity of all that is. In absolute idea, conception and reality (thought and its objects) coalesce into a state of complete unity. Absolute idea is "not mind regarded as finite, that is, subject to the conditions and limitations of sense-perception, but the universal and *absolute* Intelligence, which, out of its own free activity, determines Truth in the profoundest signification of the term."[87]

The beauty of fine art is essential for realizing absolute idea, for comprehending the world as it fully and absolutely is. Art, as Hegel sees it, is absolute idea made manifest to sense. It is spirit or mind given sensible form; and so, music's distinctive sensory/felt character is epistemologically important, not fleeting and suspect as it had been for Kant. Hegel thinks it wrong to divide the world into wholly incommensurable phenomenal and noumenal realms. The quest for comprehensive knowledge is not some confused, misguided attempt to know an unknowable in-itself, but rather a process in which knowing gradually becomes more fully adequate to the world as it absolutely is. Knowledge by its very nature entails a move beyond the explicit or observable. As Schiller had said, one cannot know truth without venturing beyond actuality.

Misguided though Kant's noumenal-phenomenal dichotomy had been, though, it was an important step in reason's quest to grasp the absolute fully. By presenting to consciousness an antithesis between subjective thought and objective things, Kant identified polarities that demanded to be transcended through the 'dialectical' process by which, according to Hegel, all knowledge evolves. Reality and knowledge are not static but dynamic and processual, he maintained. Since a thing is what it is by virtue of not being other things, this 'otherness' is a definitive feature of everything that is. Entertaining any given conception or 'thesis' necessarily implicates its contradictory 'antithesis', what it is not. The tension between thesis and antithesis leads to a synthesis that reconciles them, but in turn becomes the thesis in another dialectical triad. Each successive synthesis represents a fuller grasp, a closer approximation of absolute idea. And so it follows, Hegel believes, that history is fundamentally progressive. The universe consists in a constant evolutionary process, a dialectical unfolding in which absolute idea becomes increasingly manifest to human awareness, and human mind draws ever closer to ultimate comprehension of divine truth. The evolution of the universe, Hegel concludes, is no less than the record of mind achieving adequate consciousness of itself through a cyclical process of alienation and higher-level reconciliation: thesis, antithesis, synthesis.

Tempting though it may be to dismiss this idea as speculation run rampant, we cannot understand Hegel's aesthetic theory without it. To Hegel, Kant's explanation of aesthetic judgment had been an important attempt to reconcile the antithesis between understanding and nature. But that attempted synthesis failed, leaving beauty a subjective affair, radically cut off from truth and reality, and leaving mind and nature profoundly alienated. Schiller, Hegel believes, had broken through the subjectivity and abstractness in Kant's aesthetic theory by "intellectually grasping the principles of unity and reconciliation as the truth, and realizing them in art."[88] Beauty, Schiller had shown, consists not in the absence of reason and of sense, but rather in their integration, harmony, and unity. Beauty synthesizes sense and reason. In the perennial human struggle for understanding, Hegel explains, reason's fondness for unity and abstraction constantly runs up against nature's particularity, diversity, and concreteness. Schiller's great achievement was to show that aesthetic experience transcends these antagonistic forces, giving "such form to inclination, sensuousness, impulse, and heart, that they may become rational in themselves," and at the same time bestowing concreteness and vitality upon rational abstraction.[89] This account of beauty unifies the rational and the sensuous, forging a synthesis that approaches ultimate reality more closely than either sense or reason alone.

Beauty brings together sense's freedom and reason's necessity, fuses abstract thought's universality and nature's particularity, unites mind and nature. This remarkable synthesis approaches absolute idea with a fullness inaccessible to sense or reason. Artistic beauty dissolves the apparent contradiction between subjective mind and inert matter. Artistic beauty is absolute idea given concrete form: it reveals "*the truth* in the form of sensuous artistic shape."[90] And since its value lies in its synthesis of the ideal and the material, it follows, Hegel believes, that artistic excellence is a function of "the grade of inwardness and unity with which Idea and Shape display themselves as fused into one."[91]

It is significant that Hegel makes this claim for specifically artistic beauty, not natural beauty as Kant tried to do. To Hegel, art is a beauty born of mind. "The mind and its products are higher than nature and its appearances . . . the beauty of art is higher than the beauty of nature. Indeed . . . even a silly fancy such as may pass through a man's head is higher than any product of nature."[92] Therefore, true beauty exists only insofar as it partakes of or is created by the human mind. Natural beauty is imperfect and incomplete, substantial only to the extent that it is perceived by the mind. It pales in comparison to that beauty in which mind recognizes its own creative achievement, through which mind attains fuller awareness and understanding of itself.

Thus, art assumes, in Hegel's accounts, a place of honor alongside religion and philosophy, whose common purpose is to bring to consciousness "the deepest interests of humanity, and the most comprehensive truths of the mind. It is in works of art that nations have deposited the profoundest intuitions and ideas of their hearts . . ."[93] Art's distinctive office is to represent "even the highest ideas in sensuous forms, thereby bringing them nearer to the character of natural phenomena, to the senses, and to feeling."[94] Artistic beauty is, in short, "the first middle term of reconciliation between pure thought and what is external, sensuous, and transitory, between nature with its finite actuality and the infinite freedom of the reason that comprehends."[95] The conception of an inner and an outer world is a cruel deception which art shatters, breaking through what Hegel calls the "hard rind of nature" to liberate "the real import of appearances from the semblance and deception of this bad and fleeting world . . ."[96]

Before we become too excited about such lofty, noble, and inspiring claims to art's value, though, it is well to note that Hegel still believes art reveals only a certain "grade of truth,"[97] a fact with significant implications for art's ultimate status in his system. In fact, it is "far from being the highest form of mind,"[98] for "[b]eyond a doubt the mode of revelation which a content attains in the realm of thought is the truest reality."[99] Art is a "living creation, in which the universal is not present as law and maxim, but acts as if one with the mood and the feelings."[100] To this extent, "the beauty of art does in fact appear in a form which is expressly contrasted with abstract thought."[101] Clearly, art remains in-

ferior to philosophy; and yet, its 'semblances' are superior to things in the natural world because they do not pretend to be real and true in themselves. Instead, art "refers us away from itself to something spiritual which it is meant to
bring before the mind's eye."[102] Ultimately, then, it is the fact that art is a creation of mind that makes it spiritual in nature. Since art "pervades what is sensuous with mind," it is always "nearer to mind and its thinking activity than is
mere external unintelligent nature."[103] In contrast to the experience of natural
beauty, "in works of art mind has to do but with its own."[104]

Still, since mind's 'own' is given sensuous form in art, it is not quite a matter of mind taking pleasure in *itself*. Art's sensuous character presents mind with
"an alienation from itself," a contrast to its essentially abstractive nature. When
experiencing art, then, "the power of the thinking spirit" comes to "recognize
itself in its alienation in the shape of feeling and the sensuous, in its other form,
by transmuting the metamorphosed thought back into definite thoughts, and so
restoring it to itself."[105] Thus the work of art, in which thought alienates itself
in the sensuous and subsequently restores itself to thought on a higher level of
self-awareness, contributes in important ways to mind's full self-realization. Its
ultimate significance is as a means to that end.

Given the potential significance of art to mind's development, it will come
as little surprise that Hegel believes neither artistic content nor artistic form
should "rove in the wildness of unfettered fancy."[106] Since art exists to bring to
consciousness the highest human interests, the profundity of its content (its
meaning) and its sensuous form must be carefully scrutinized in terms of their
adequacy to each other. Not just any form will support ideal content. To be
good art, content and form must be compatible. "[E]very definite content,"
Hegel believes, "determines a form suitable to it."[107]

As human spirituality evolves from its first vague inklings to levels of increasing self-awareness, the artistic activity adequate to its expression must
progress to increasingly sophisticated levels. Although art is an indispensable vehicle for the expression and enhancement of spiritual awareness, as that awareness grows, the kind of art adequate to that function changes. Primitive art suits
the spiritual needs of the primitive mind, but as mind grows in its compass,
drawing closer to idea, the artistic forms adequate to its expression change. Sensuous artistic modes are less and less satisfying as it ascends toward ideal abstraction. So just when art reaches the height of abstract expression in music,
mind in effect outgrows its need for art. Having seen, through art, the simultaneous concreteness and universality of absolute idea, mind renounces earthly
traces to bask in pure ideality.

Like Plotinus, then, Hegel finds it necessary to turn away from art to grasp
its ultimate significance. Like Schiller, he sees the sensuousness of artistic form
as preparing the mind for insight into higher, ideal truths. But Hegel departs decisively from the likes of Plotinus and Schiller in his historical conception of
the process, and in the ultimate ends to which he believes it leads. The ascent
to absolute idea that makes art necessary eventually necessitates its demise. For
once art elevates human mentality to the level where it can embrace the spirituality of the absolute idea, the very materiality and sensuousness that formerly

made art significant become irrelevant. Modern intellectual culture, Hegel believes, has reached a point "beyond the stage at which art is the highest mode assumed by man's consciousness of the absolute. The peculiar mode to which artistic production and works of art belong no longer satisfies our supreme need. . . . Thought and reflection have taken their flight above fine art . . ."[108]

In earlier times art met the spiritual needs of humanity by making the lawfulness of idea manifest in concrete, living forms, forms that seemed "as if one" with emotion and feeling. But having elevated humanity's spiritual awareness to new heights, art has outlived its usefulness for anything but the entertainment its forms may afford. Its former spiritual mission can now be achieved more effectively by thought itself. Art no longer satisfies. Despite its inestimable role in human destiny, it has become "a thing of the past. Herein it has further lost for us its genuine truth and life, and rather is transferred into our *ideas* than asserts its former necessity, or assumes its former place, in reality."[109]

In summary, Hegel expands the compass of knowledge as Kant had conceived it in a way that makes a serious epistemological claim for artistic beauty. Their capacity to transcend the noumenal-phenomenal schism brings art and music into the domain of knowledge, as idea made manifest to sense. Art presents truth to consciousness in a sensuous semblance. Yet, despite the considerable value of having rendered the ideal intelligible, art remains a vehicle for idea's expression. Because of its materiality, art cannot achieve absolute idea's perfect unity of content and form as effectively as philosophy. Art's significance as an expressive vehicle, then, was a historical phase that has now lost its truth to life. Its revelatory function was but a passing phase in a greater historical process. Unlike Plato, who had a provisional plan for the readmission of the muse he had banished, Hegel has no plan to restore things like music to their former prominence. Hegel's art is a sweet but transient interlude in the all-important quest for the absolute idea. Art's sensuousness is a necessary yet imperfect manifestation of the absolute, the sensible but ultimately inadequate expression of truth. Hegel's aesthetic in effect proclaims, as one scholar says, "[A]rt is dead; long live philosophy."[110]

Art's Historical Evolution: Symbolic, Classical, Romantic

Art's capacity to make idea manifest evolves over time. Early art's youthful exuberance and naiveté are not well suited to art's ultimate role in ideal revelation. But it grows and matures, gradually overcoming its inadequacies, becoming better and better suited to its ultimate purpose. Each individual art is involved in an ongoing struggle to master its medium, progressively removing impediments to completely adequate expression of idea and growing in profundity. The value of art is, then, a matter of congruence between form and content, or more specifically, of the extent to which form lends itself to the expression of spiritual content. The relation of form to content is dynamic. Within each artistic medium, stylistic changes reflect mind's unfolding grasp of itself. Therefore, the value of music and art rests on two dynamic, interrelated concerns: the capacity of the particular artistic medium to give proper form to ideal content, and the abstractness or profundity of that content. Hegel identifies three distinct "relations of the Idea to its outward shaping,"[111] three successive historical stages in artistic development: the symbolic, the classical, and the romantic.

Symbolic art emerges when objects first acquire a general sense of significance or meaning beyond themselves. Idea in art first appears as an indeterminate sense of "import,"[112] a vague sense of wonder, a sense that an immediate physical presence is somehow a manifestation of something or some power beyond itself. At this stage, idea is ambiguous, and its representation only suggestive. Symbolic art is more of a "search after a plastic portrayal than a capacity of genuine representation."[113] Form and content fail to coalesce as they ought, and matter takes precedence over ideal content. Symbolic art is constrained by physical law, is predominantly 'material', and is therefore insufficiently infused with idea. "In it the abstract Idea has its outward shape external to itself in natural sensuous matter . . ."[114] Symbolic art consists in objects left largely unshaped by mind in the creative process. Their sense of significance is more projected onto objects than inherent in them. So symbolic art suffers from a double defect. Content (idea) is too vague or obscure, and material form is too concrete or determinate. "Hence . . . the relation of the Idea to objective reality becomes a *negative* one, for the former, as in its nature inward, is unsatisfied with such an externality . . ."[115] Symbolic art fails because "in spite of all aspiration and endeavor the reciprocal inadequacy of shape and Idea remains insuperable."[116]

The art most illustrative of the symbolic stage of development is architecture. In its sense of power and permanence it conveys indistinct intuitions of the omnipotence of idea or spirit. But architecture's appeal to human sensibilities rests only on external, formal relationships among material elements. It works with 'matter itself', the physical products of inorganic nature; its forms do not depart significantly from the symmetrical relations already evident in nature. "In this material and in such forms, the ideal as concrete spirituality does not admit of being realized."[117] In short, architecture partakes too much of nature, and too little of idea.

Classical art, of which human sculpture is the highest manifestation, overcomes symbolic art's double defect by synthesizing content and form. It is "the free and adequate embodiment of the Idea in the shape that . . . is peculiarly appropriate to the Idea itself."[118] Thus, in classical art, ideal content and material form enter into unconstrained accord with each other, resulting in imaginative artifacts capable of direct expression of idea. Since the sculpted human form is at once a human creation and a clear manifestation of mind, it is well suited to ideal expression. Says Hegel, "[I]t is only in its proper body that mind is adequately revealed to sense,"[119] and in art's classical stage it is sculpture that provides this body. Unlike symbolic art, the significance of which is tied to the realm of 'mere sensuous existence', classical art, in its concern with "the existence and physical form corresponding to mind", escapes the "contingent finiteness of phenomenal existence."[120] Sculpture's form and material transcend the outer-directed, physical realm, directing mind toward an ideal state of inwardness — in effect, balancing objectivity with subjectivity. Thus, in sculpture, "the inward and spiritual are first revealed in their eternal repose and essential self-completeness."[121] By giving spirit concrete form, classical art becomes "the highest excellence of which the sensuous embodiment of art is capable."[122]

As mind continues its ascent to absolute idea, however, the reliance of classical art upon sensuous, external embodiment eventually becomes an encumbrance. The object of art, Hegel says, is mind, "the conception of which is *infinite* concrete universality—in the shape of *sensuous* concreteness."[123] Mind's growing self-awareness creates a need for more comprehensive expression of its essence; and that essence, it is increasingly recognized, is the incorporeal inner world of thought and feeling, a realm of 'infinite subjectivity', a state of "absolute inwardness."[124]

The solution to classical art's incapacity to accommodate the ever-growing idea is romantic art: painting, music, and poetry. In romantic art, material externality is increasingly contingent, giving way to expressions of "pure inwardness" better able to capture and present idea's ultimate spirituality. Classical art revealed the unity of human and divine nature in the experiential immediacy of the human image. But once mind becomes sufficiently conscious of and able to contemplate its spirituality, "the true medium for the reality of this content is no longer the sensuous immediate existence of the spiritual ... but self-conscious inward intelligence."[125]

Romantic art thus addresses the inner, spiritual self, the world of heart, mind, and feeling. In it, mind "coalesces with its object simply as though this were itself."[126] 'Subjective inwardness' triumphs over outer-directed experience, and "the sensuous appearance sinks into worthlessness."[127] This is not to say romantic art renounces materiality and form altogether, but it renders such things "transient and fugitive."[128] Romantic art sheds classical art's sense of material externality, finding its significance in the inward realm of felt experience. In so doing, says Hegel, mind is drawn closer yet to its innermost nature, revealing idea "in the medium of spirit and feelings as perfected in itself. And it is because of this higher perfection that it withdraws from any adequate union with the external element, inasmuch as it can seek and achieve its true reality and revelation nowhere but in itself."[129] The realm of romantic art is "that of divine truth artistically represented to perception and to feeling. ... It is the independent, free, and divine plasticity, which has thoroughly mastered the external elements of form and of medium, and wears them simply as a means to manifestation of itself."[130] In romantic art, then, "form and content exalt themselves to ideality."[131]

Painting is romantic because its images are free of the mechanical constraints of mass and of three-dimensional space. It liberates art "from the sensuous completeness in space which attaches to material things."[132] Music, on the other hand, liberates ideal content from matter and spatiality altogether. Its forms and patterns are predominantly mental, subjective, inward. Moreover, music is an active and dynamic thing, an "inchoate ideality of matter, which appears no longer under the form of space, but as temporal ideality." Sound is almost perfectly suited to idea's "mental inwardness," as its patterns are imaginative mental achievements. It is able, therefore, to give expression to "the heart with its whole gamut of feelings and passions."[133]

Yet just as classical art was transitional between the symbolic and the romantic, so is music transitional, a middle ground "... between abstract spatial sensuousness, such as painting employs, and the abstract spirituality of poetry."[134] Poetry represents a higher level of ideality, of pure inwardness, than music. Since it is not fettered to earth by sound as music is, poetry is the most purely ideal and the least material of all arts. It is "the universal art of the mind which has become free in its own nature, and which is not tied to find its realization in external sensuous matter, but expatiates exclusively in the inner space and inner time of the ideas and feelings."[135] Thus, romantic art, through poetry, frees the human spirit from material tethers and releases it into the world of absolute mind. In so doing, art transcends the last of its earthly (sensuous, material) tethers, passing "from the poetry of imagination into the prose of thought."[136] Precisely at its highest moment of achievement, art's human value comes to an end.

Thus, Hegel's historicized account of art incorporates both lofty claims and a gloomy prognosis. Before exploring in more detail music's place in all this, it is worth reviewing Hegel's claims regarding art's distinctive nature and value. First and foremost, art is a manifestation of human mind and spirit. As such, it is neither an irrational accident nor an act of self-indulgent entertainment, but a "meaning-laden spiritual activity."[137] It is, moreover, essential to fully human self-awareness. By stripping the external of its "stubborn foreignness,"[138] art enables humanity's discovery of its inner, spiritual nature. This account offers to correct a number of misconceptions about art. For one, it is not a matter of mere sensory arousal. It works through the senses, but that does not mean it is primarily sensual. The feelings it evokes hardly exhaust its significance. In fact, feeling is an "indefinite dull region of the mind," and things 'felt' are private affairs.[139] Taking the feelings art arouses for its content neglects art's concreteness or materiality, resulting in "vacant subjectivity" rather than artistic experience.

The idea of 'taste' is equally misleading, believes Hegel, for such judgments are superficial and dilettantish. Taste bases its judgments only upon the "external surface about which the feelings play."[140] An understanding of art is served little better by most technical scholarship, though, because it errs in the direction of excessive abstraction. Art does not address sense and thought, separably, but rather "the undivided reason and the mind in its solid vigour."[141] Art may be sensuously apprehended, but it does not cater primarily to human sensual desire. Indeed, sensuous apprehension is "[t]he lowest mode of apprehension, and that least appropriate to the mind."[142] Art's sensuousness "has a right to existence only in as far as it exists for man's mind,"[143] and experience that is purely sensual is never artistic. And yet, although art satisfies the interests of mind, it differs from intellectual activity in important ways. It is interested in its objects for their concrete individuality. Artistic contemplation does not attempt to transform its objects into "its universal thought and notion."[144] Its concern is, rather, the presentation to mind of "immediate determinateness and sensuous individuality," "the immediate appearance of objectivity."[145] In short, art "occupies the mean between what is immediately sensuous and ideal thought."[146] Its sensuous patterns are appreciated "... not simply for their own sake and for that of their immediate structure, but with the purpose of affording in that shape satisfaction to higher spiritual interests . . ."[147] Art is a sensuous material presence infused with mind, an experience in which "the spiritual and the sensuous side . . . [are] as one."[148]

Hegel is equally anxious to refute claims to the instrumental value of art: claims, for instance, to therapeutic value (as a 'tamer' of passions) or moral influence. Art is not a means to anything outside itself. Its purpose is strictly self-contained, and the fact that it occasionally accompanies the pursuit of nonartistic ends has nothing to do with its nature as art. If it is objected that Hegel's own theory portrays art as just such a vehicle for the attainment of extraneous ends, Hegel's response would likely be that the 'truth' he believes art serves to reveal is not something separable from the concrete, particular form that it bears. "[T]he work of art ought to bring a content before the mind's eye, not in its generality as such, but with this generality made absolutely individual, and sensuously particularized."[149] Thus, apparently, art is simultaneously revelational and autonomous, at once transitive yet wholly self-contained.

Art is, paradoxically, generality made particular; it is "one of the means which resolve and reduce to unity the . . . antithesis and contradiction between the abstract self-concentrated mind and actual nature, whether that of external phenomena, or the inner subjective feelings and emotions."[150] Its contradictions and paradoxes notwithstanding, Hegel's theory clearly claims for art and music a higher place in human endeavor than the mental pleasure in pattern Kant called 'aesthetic'. Art, Hegel unwaveringly believed, exists for the important purpose of making absolute idea manifest.

Music: Sounding Inwardness

The Hegelian conception of music presents a striking contrast to Kant's sensually 'agreeable' art. Where Kant approached music from the perspective of a nature-derived aesthetic theory, Hegel takes it as given that all art as a manifestation of mind and spirit, is inherently superior to natural beauty. For Hegel, as we have seen, the relative value of the arts is a function of their efficacy in elevating mind's awareness of its ideality. And since arts that are more reliant upon external, material configuration are more modest in this capacity than those that share spirit's disembodied inwardness, music enjoys a place of prominence in Hegel's view. Remarkably, this elevated conception of music derives from the very attributes Kant finds so annoying and suspect: its processual nature, its temporality, its felt character. These qualities, Hegel believes, are the very features spirit requires at a particular stage in its evolution to conceive of and express its vital essence fully. Where visual and plastic arts create external presences, concrete objects extended in space, music has the striking capacity to eradicate the distance between perceiver and perceived so prominent in visual experience. Music consists not in images of external things, a world out there, but in a field of inwardness whose felt patterns of tension and repose illuminate and nurture the soul's dialectical ascent to the freedom of idea.

Hegel's music is an art of time, one that renounces spatiality and materiality, turning consciousness away from external appearances and attuning it to the unfettered inwardness of ideality. Music's transience is not the impediment Kant believed, then, but an invaluable instrument of self-realization. All art is born of mind, but music is ideal to an exceptionally high degree since its materials are predominantly mental and its experience more inward and abstract. Music forsakes materiality, spatiality, externality, turning people immediately inward and enabling a spiritually enriched self-awareness that eludes visually reliant art. This is, to be sure, only a passing phase in spirit's ascent to absolute idea. Yet it is a distinctive and bold claim for music, one that ascribes to it a character and capacity unique among the arts. Music is not sensual titillation, not mental entertainment, but a vehicle for human growth and self-realization. We now undertake to examine in greater detail why and how Hegel found music so distinctive and important. If some of his ideas sound lavishly speculative—as they are bound to in an era where metaphysics are no longer philosophically fashionable—many of them will at the same time sound remarkably familiar. For such was Hegel's influence that even in a period generally impatient with "idealism" his ideas remain prominent reference points for many accounts of music's nature and value.

As Hegel sees it, the 'inner life' is both music's content and its form; and that makes it uniquely suited to expressing the ideality of conscious life. The world of the ear is "more ideal than sight,"[151] in part because it does not rely upon the "tranquil relation of juxtaposition"[152] that typifies visual experience. Music is special in its capacity to "give resonant reflection, not to objectivity in its ordinary material sense," but rather to soul's inner motions: to "subjective life and ideality."[153] Because it establishes "direct contact with the most intimate ideality of conscious life," it is "more than any other the art of the soul."[154] Since it "inevitably disappears precisely at the point of . . . becoming externality," eschewing the "objective mode of spatial persistency," music's content is "part of our own personal life."[155] The instant of perception leaves behind ideal traces of actual sound that resound "in the depths of the soul, which are thereby seized upon in their ideal substance, and suffused with emotion."[156] In short, where visual experience concerns itself with stable relationships among external, seemingly objective things, musical experience is profoundly inward and subjective, infused with "the melodic chime of emotions."[157]

Music's inward, emotional quality makes it an "entirely artistic expression of a wholly different type from that we find in painting and sculpture . . ."[158] Yet to be emotional is not, in music's case at any rate, to be irrational. On the contrary, music's harmonic and rhythmic relationships answer to exacting rules, by virtue of which music constitutes at once the "profoundest ideality and soul" and "the most rigorous rationality."[159] Music's "swiftly evanescent world of tones" penetrates directly "to the depths of [the human] soul, attuning the same in concordant emotional sympathy."[160] Thus, like Pythagorean theories of which Hegel's is in some ways reminiscent, there is an strong link between music's harmonious character and the soul's attunement. The experience of music is at once "formal ideality, in other words pure tones," and "a retreat into the free life of [one's] own soul, a voyage of discovery."[161] By affording "liberation of the soul . . . from constraint and restriction," music delivers humanity "to the final summit of that ascent to freedom."[162]

Visual art cannot extend such freedom, since its objects and images are tied to something which "already floats before the mind."[163] Music's significance, on the other hand, is "almost wholly determined within the sphere of tone itself."[164] Since its meaning is exhausted in its presentation to inward sense, it needs no content beyond its 'emotional chime'. Music's abstract inwardness promises to acquaint people with the inner soul-life, while at the same time enriching and vitalizing it through its immediacy, vividness, and intimacy.

However, this distinctive power is not without risk. Because music lacks the constraints of materiality and concreteness, there is danger a composer "may progress just as he likes, and by what by-paths he likes," using "the full force of his personality and caprice to pass at every point into more or less important digressions, to let spontaneous ideas travel hither and thither as they please, to lay stress for the moment on this or that motive, and then once more to drown it in an overwhelming torrent."[165] These concerns about compositional caprice and indulgence point to an important underlying ambivalence in Hegel. To realize its potential, music must be free; but under such conditions, music may degenerate into self-indulgence or trivial play of pattern. "In recent times especially, the art of music, by its wresting itself from all content that is independently lucid, has withdrawn into the depths of its own medium . . . [On] this very account and to this extent it has lost its compelling power over the soul, inasmuch as the enjoyment . . . is only applicable to . . . the purely musical characteristics of the composition and its artistic dexterity, an aspect which wholly concerns the musical expert, and is less connected with the universal human interest in art."[166] Thus, Hegel complains, "independent music" suffers from composers' propensities for asserting "practically unrestrained mastery in every sort of conceit, caprice, interlude, inspiriting drollery, startling suspension, rapid transition, lightning flashes, extraordinary surprises and effects."[167] Plato's disdain for self-indulgence and vulgarity was little more extreme.

Music that is purely musical, then, the very music one might expect to find at the "summit of the ascent to freedom," is often 'merely' musical. If it affords entertainment, diversion, and stimulation, it risks doing so at the expense of its broader human significance: music without "spiritual content and expression" is "not really genuine music at all."[168] Thus, music that is wholly autonomous is 'only' musical, and therefore deficient in spiritual value. Craftsmanship without spiritual or emotional content is not truly musical.

So music should be free, but apparently not too free. It must assert its independence from external constraint, but not at the expense of its spiritual obligations. Sound has an inherent relation to the soul, "an alliance which is consonant with its spiritual movement," a kind of "sympathetic relation which is always of an indefinite character."[169] This relation makes sound "the most immediately vital expression of soul-conditions and feelings, the ah and oh of soul."[170] Music builds upon this inherent resonance between sound and soul, only in an abstract, indefinite manner. This indefiniteness is the source of music's distinctive strength, but it is its undoing as well: poetry can render concretely and directly what music can only render abstractly. Poetry may lack some of music's 'spiritual intimacy', some of its capacity for 'speechless apprehension of the soul-life', but it can express "emotions, perceptions, and ideas as they are."[171] Music's intimacy and indefiniteness enable it to purvey "soul-impressions,"[172] no small feat in its own historical moment; but where music only suggests, poetry discloses.

Still, in its historically favored moment, music is of paramount importance, an art that does at least some things no other art can. It is wholly unique in its capacity to make content "a living thing in the sphere of the personal soul" such that soul's "essentially veiled life and inweaved motion ring forth through the independent texture of tones."[173] Since the 'inner personal life' is both music's form and its content, music is uniquely capable of revealing to mind and soul their innermost nature, a nature that would otherwise forever elude people. Because of its distinctive congruence to spirit's inner character, music reveals soul to itself. Its sensory impact is thus strictly secondary to its capacity to reveal soul to itself "under the veils of emotional movement."[174] Music offers insight into an otherwise unfathomable inner life.

Thus, the felt character of musical experience imparts firsthand awareness of soul's "abstract inwardness."[175] It is important to note, though, that this inwardness is abstract: the 'feeling' music imparts is not the definite kind encountered in everyday experience, feeling as felt. Music addresses itself, says Hegel, to an "ego . . . void of externality,"[176] to the indefinite inner life of feeling—not to its particular manifestations. This abstract inward field encompasses all specific emotion, "every shade of joyfulness, merriment, jest, caprice, jubilation and laughter of the soul, every gradation of anguish, trouble, melancholy, lament, sorrow, pain, longing and the like, no less than . . . reverence, adoration, and love . . ."[177] In short, music is "the expression of the personal life of soul"; no "purely natural outcry of emotion but the articulate artistic expression of the same."[178] It is no mere venting or emotional discharge, but an ordering of emotions "into tone relations of definite structure" in a way that weans them from wildness or unruliness.[179] Music transforms feeling in the raw, conferring upon it the kind of orderly regularity befitting the ideal.

Musical tones are "capable of disuniting and uniting themselves in the most varied kinds of immediate concords, essential discords, oppositions and transitions," in dynamic patterns of tension and resolution that have varying degrees of affinity to the ideal aspects of emotion, thereby enabling music to "disclose the animated expression of that which is present to Spirit as definable content."[180] This is not the static realm of spatiality but the dynamic ideal realm of temporality, one shared equally by "the form of the feeling . . ."[181] Since music and feeling are both temporal phenomena, and since in musical experience "the time of tone is likewise that of the conscious subject," music "penetrates into the self of the conscious life . . . and places the Ego in movement . . ." At the same time, the "other configuration of tones, as the expression of emotions, brings yet further a more definite material to enrich the unity of consciousness, a wealth by which it is at once affected and carried forward."[182] As a temporal art whose kinetic patterns are congruent to those of feeling, music makes spirit's inner essence conceivable. This, Hegel believes, explains music's "unrivaled power" over a soul otherwise "accustomed to live within the ideal range and secluded depths of pure emotion."[183] Its content is no less than "the inward life itself, the ideal significance of fact and emotion . . ."; enabling it to penetrate directly "the ideal habitat of all the fluctuations of soul-life."[184] Music "seizes" consciousness without confronting it with objects, and "whirls it away" in a "flood of tones."

Organic Unity and Profundity

So long as musical expression remains "steeped in soul,"[185] it is apparently acceptable for consciousness to whirl along in a tonal torrent. But music must never become a "purely indefinite rustle and sound,"[186] an "unregulated rambling."[187] Sound only becomes musical when tones enter into organic temporal relations with each other. Only then do they become manifestations of mind. It would be equally wrong, however, to regard music as a dispassionately intellectual matter of ordering sound. A sonorous creation that fails to touch "the innermost heart" is not real music, only the "skill of an expert in its laboured production."[188] Without emotional profundity, sound and craftsmanship cannot be musical. Only when sound is imbued with a sense of emotional and formal necessity does music transform the inner world by giving shape to the inchoate, order to freedom.

   To attain true profundity music must engage opposing forces in "a battle waged between freedom and necessity."[189] To this end it employs "the most discordant contrasts and disclose[s] its unique power amid the tumult . . . wholly confident in its ability to celebrate finally the grateful triumph of melodic tranquillity."[190] Though contrasting patterns of tension and repose are a primary link between music and spirit, it is axiomatic for Hegel that contrast must not become excessively discordant or extreme. He approves of Mozart's symphonies precisely because they avoid dramatic excess: "[I]n the most graceful fashion we . . . get a kind of conversation of appeal and response, which has its beginning, advance and consummation."[191] Excess poses a threat to music's sense of being "beyond all doubt rounded off and secure," a sense that is essential if it is to "reflect the free self-subsistency of the subjective life."[192] Only music that restores spirit to tranquil equilibrium yields a vision of the inner life that is properly 'exalted' and 'untarnished'. While at its best music permits spirit and soul to "ring forth in their untrammeled immediacy, and derive satisfaction in this record of their self-knowledge,"[193] restraint is essential. Expression must not be "whirled away in bacchantic thunder and tumult, or be left in the distraction of despair, but retain the blessed freedom of its deliverance in the extremity of sorrow . . ."[194] In truly great music, "the luminous sense of proportion never breaks down in extremes: everything finds its due place knit together in the whole; joy is never suffered to degenerate into unseemly uproar and even lamentation carries with it the most benign repose."[195] Although Beethoven is not explicitly criticized, his name is conspicuously absent from Hegel's list of exemplary composers: Palestrina, Pergolesi, Gluck, Haydn and Mozart.

To ensure that its ideal content is lucid and untarnished, music should assert throughout its course "one fundamental progression of emotion," so that it is "primarily one chord of the soul that it emphasizes."[196] Music suited to spirit reflects ideal unity rather than fragmentation, abrupt change, stark contrast, or excessive agitation. Overly dramatic music fails to unify contrasting passions, resulting in little more than "a fine uproar" that "tumble[s] us from one side to another, without any principle of union."[197] Abrupt juxtapositions and violent contrasts are incompatible with spiritual unity. Genuine musical beauty requires that the same "fundamental tone of beauty" pervade the entire piece in order to reflect what Hegel calls the "coalescing and suffusing principle of life."[198]

Among the musical facts with which Hegel's philosophy had to come to grips was the ascendancy of 'absolute' or 'pure' music—music wholly without text or program. The importance of 'indefiniteness' in his accounts seems to reflect that trend. And yet, such indefiniteness can, particularly in absolute music, threaten coherence, clarity, and unity. Text or libretto can serve as a kind of ballast or balance to the potential excesses of abstractness. Collaboration between word and music, Hegel writes, "compels the attention to forsake that field of more visionary emotion destitute of distinct idea, in which we are permitted to range without interruption, and are not forced to abandon our licence to receive from pure music whatever chance impression or wave of emotion it may arouse."[199] Since organic unity of form and content is crucial, though, it is equally important that music not dominate or disregard text. Italian composers, it seems, are especially guilty of violating this latter principle. Rossini, for instance, "says goodbye to his libretto, and gives free vent to his melodies, precisely as his mood dictates, so that we have nothing left us but the alternative either to stick to the subject matter and grumble over the music that is indifferent to it, or abandon the former and take our hearty delight in the inspired irrelevances of the composer and the soul which they reveal."[200]

Music like Rossini's undeniably stimulates the senses, arouses emotions. But what is significant about music is not "the progression of determinate emotion such as we indicate by the words love, yearning, jollity, and so forth," but rather "that inward sense which presides over it, which expatiates in its suffering no less than its delight."[201] It is important, in other words, to distinguish between specific feelings music may arouse and the more indeterminate field of inwardness which is its true spiritual content. Music that caters to the former gives us entertaining diversions of 'mere melodious sound', art that is decorative or distractive, without depth or profundity. Music adequate to its deeper spiritual mission is no mere sonic stimulus, but an experience in which "we are admitted to the most intimate conception of ideal blessedness and attuned spirits."[202] Since this "purely emotional grasp" of soul's "intrinsic nature" is not a matter of specifically aroused feelings, it is crucial that we differentiate between music's "specific content . . . and the more ideal or intimate life of which it seeks to reflect in its harmonies."[203] Apparently, particular feelings—feelings felt—are not music's true spiritual content. In its deepest and most profoundly spiritual moments, music renders comprehensible an entire field of inwardness, the universal nature of ideal life.

The supreme governing principle of music for Hegel, then, is soul's ideality: "the subjective state in its bare simplicity . . . defined by no assured content, and for this reason not forced into motion either one way or another, but reposing on its unity in unfettered freedom."[204] And to realize this principle to its fullest, music must ultimately renounce the security it might otherwise achieve through alliances with text, master its content using exclusively its own resources. "If music is to be nothing but music simply, it must . . . detach itself absolutely from the definite substance of language. Thus alone it becomes entirely free."[205] Clearly there is some tension here, for this wholly independent music seems to be the very music Hegel denigrates elsewhere for its inspired irrelevancy. Music that is not supported by independent ideas deals abstractly with indefinite content. To this end, music resorts to things like variations in motion, "the ups and downs of the harmony or melody, the stream of sound through its degrees of opposition, preponderance, emphasis, acuteness or vivacity, the elaboration of a melodic phrase . . ."[206] Such is the nature of this abstract, indefinite realm that not everyone is equally equipped to gauge music's significance. The preferences and experiences of ordinary people differ in important ways from those of musical experts. Ordinary people prefer music whose emotional or expressive content is immediately apparent, whereas experts find satisfaction in the intricacies and complexities of abstract musical pattern. "A complete satisfaction of this kind [in purely absolute music] comes rarely to the mere amateur. He is seized with the vain desire to master this apparently phantomnal process of music . . . in the sound that invades him," yet finds "little beyond mysterious problems that vanish in the moment they are propounded, which baffle his powers of solution and in general are capable of a variety of interpretations."[207]

While some musicians are properly attentive to music's spiritual content, a great many are indifferent to it, devoting themselves instead to problems of structure or demonstrations of skill. But intellect and technical prowess do not in themselves assure true musicality. In fact, music that relies on such capacities "readily tends to become defective both in the range of its conception and emotional quality, and as a rule does not imply any profound cultivation of mind or taste in other respects."[208] Musical talent, for instance, often emerges well before people show any real evidence of maturity in judgment and taste. And many mature composers remain "men of the poorest and most impoverished intellectual faculty in other directions."[209] Clearly, Hegel believes, the capacity for achieving the kind of ideal balance between form and expressive content befitting music's spiritual mission comes from something deeper than intellect, more substantial than virtuosic skill: a spiritual depth or "penetration of character" that is a relatively rare commodity, even among musicians. In a word, genius. It is, he concludes, a "riddle of riddles" that "a mere piece of mechanical craft can become an instrument one with our life, [an instrument] which enables us to follow, as though through a flash of lightning, a power of ideal conception

... by virtue of which the imagination of genius penetrates to the core of life as instantaneously as it vanishes therefrom."[210]

Taking Stock of Hegel

Hegel's thought was an important philosophical watershed that inspired both devout allegiances and fierce opposition. His metaphysical speculation strained philosophy to its very limits, eventually precipitating a backlash that profoundly altered philosophical inquiry. His conflation of the real and the ideal; his application of propositional thought's dialectical-synthetic process to history; his notion of a universe inexorably progressing toward ultimate spiritual self-awareness—each of these considerably exceeds the sphere of philosophical inquiry as it has come to be understood since Hegel's time. On the other hand, ideas developed in his musical aesthetics have struck resonant chords in the imaginations of many. Though modified in significant ways, many of his ideas about music have proven quite persuasive, resilient, and long-lived.

Many of Hegel's basic philosophical tenets were quite sound, of course. He was certainly right to insist that ideas are genuinely influential 'actors' in the world, even though he probably attempted to extend the implications of that point much too far. And although it is easy to see the Western bias in his belief in inevitable and inexorable progress, at least some human endeavors do proceed dialectically. It is probably safe to say, however, that Hegel's notion of a monolithic, absolute truth is an historical relic that has long since yielded to conceptions of multiple perspectives, and of knowledge as a function of belief.

It is to Hegel's credit, many arts advocates might urge, that he conceived of art and music as important forces in understanding ourselves and the world. Idea was for Hegel no coolly intellectual phenomenon, something purely cerebral or analytical. There is far more to human ideality, he believed, than intellect. Mind is not merely brain, it is spiritual. And spirit is not merely personal, it is culturally collective. Music, then, plays an essential role in human understanding. It is an important way of being in the world which broadens and deepens our humanity by challenging mind to ever more adequate self-awareness. One need embrace neither Hegel's notion of the inevitability of historical progress nor his notion of the absolute idea as its inevitable realization to appreciate the limited sense in which his observations are valid. That human thought proceeds by positing contradictory polarities and subsequently wrestling to resolve them can scarcely be denied. Arguably, something of this very process lies at the heart of musical expression and stylistic evolution, in which musical 'theses'—whether motives, conventions, or stylistic traditions—precipitate searches for creative alternatives and resolutions, which spawn, in turn, renewed searches for innovative, expressive, more satisfying solutions. Also, the 'historicity' of his theory, its assumption that musical (and other) values are historically relative rather than universal and timeless, has come to characterize a broad range of contemporary philosophical thought.

Although many of Hegel's specific claims about music seem specious, his music philosophy is not without important insights. As we have seen, Hegel believes music's infusion with mind means it must be regarded as something markedly different than instances of 'natural beauty'. Music is not 'natural': it is a profound manifestation of human spirituality. Indeed, it is one of the most spiritual of the arts, since even the raw materials from which it is forged are human creations. Music is no empty sounding, insists Hegel, no fleeting illusion, but a vital expression of what it is to be human. The musical attributes Kant found so troubling became conspicuous strengths in Hegel's account. Music is the least tangible, the most perishable and processual of the arts, but as an art of time, its great value derives from precisely these characteristics. As well, since the distinctive medium of each art was a central concern to Hegel, music is what it is, does what it does, in virtue of its sonorous, temporal medium. The unique qualities of sound are not defects but sources of integrity and value. A fundamental feature, and perhaps the most valid aspect of his music philosophy, is thus the inwardness of musical experience. Vision is outward and analytical; hearing is inward, intimate, synthetic. Music, then, stands to reveal truths about the world (or, as Hegel would have it, idea) which are accessible by no other experience. Taking their inspiration from Hegel, others have argued that music can show us the inner nature of human sentience, put us face to face with the 'felt life' with a vividness and immediacy only partially attainable through other perceptual or conceptual endeavors. Where so much other experience turns us outward, music directs us ever inward.

The most troubling aspects of Hegel's musical aesthetics arise at this very same point, though. The concept of music's inwardness as its primary value determinant leads straightaway to a host of intractable dualistic polarities or dichotomies: inward and outward, subjectivity and objectivity, material and ideal, form and content. Kant's formalism, recall, led music philosophy to struggle with a number of important questions: Do music's patterns and forms exhaust its human value? Can they alone account for music's ubiquity in every known human society? for its centrality in such an immense range of significant human endeavor? Does music have the capacity to 'mean' as well as to 'be'? If so, in what sense? Hegel's position on these matters hardly requires reiteration at this point. In the end, it is difficult to avoid the conclusion that Hegel's efforts to bridge this form-content dichotomy were less than successful. In fact, his attempts to keep both form and content in music often appear halfhearted, and he sometimes appears to regard the possibility that music can achieve a true synthesis of the two unlikely. It is poetry's superiority in this regard that makes it music's necessary successor in the historic progression toward absolute idea. Despite his claims to the contrary, musical form and musical content never quite achieve promised unity. The capacity for deriving spiritual content from formal configurations is apparently, in Hegel's view, a gift not widely shared: artists and connoisseurs of high art music have it, but the masses do not—particularly when it comes to abstract or absolute ('independent') music. The synthesis of ideal content, pleasing pattern, and formal unity in such music is apparently quite precarious. Yet, formal excellence in itself can lay only the flimsiest and most superficial of claims to artistic excellence: the musical and the more broadly human value of music are not the same. Music without spiritual content is not yet music.

Because form alone cannot attain music's ideal, humanizing mission, Hegel is critical of 'independent' music's tendencies to excess. And ultimately, this is what prompts him to pronounce the death or obsolescence of musical art. As one scholar puts it, Hegel's philosophy of art is, in effect, "a long, eloquent, epitaph upon art."[211] So, too, was his philosophy of music a long, though not always eloquent, epitaph upon music. His idealistic presuppositions and the apparent priority of his metaphysics over his aesthetics led him to deny to music the 'intrinsic value' many might wish to claim for it; and in the end, he appears to hold music to standards and expectations to which only ideas can conform.

Hegel's conviction that dramatic contrast is inimical to musical expression is only marginally less conservative than Plato's, a position that clearly favors tradition and convention. And the priority he assigned ideal or spiritual content yields only the most elusive of critical bases for assessing musical value. Indeed, Hegel resembles Plotinus in his conviction that music's higher value consists in the turn inward—away, that is, from the sensible phenomenon itself. Ideality's inwardness is for Hegel the essential source of music's import. Having turned one inward, having shown one the inner richness of human spirituality, music has fulfilled its mission. Music supposedly makes conceivable something that otherwise eludes human awareness, a 'something' that is neither quite emotion, nor quite music, nor yet quite idea. But the inaccessibility of such abstract inwardness without music is among the many things Hegel asserts rather than demonstrates.

It can be tempting to make more of the seemingly noble claim to music's inwardness than Hegel may have intended. For music is ultimately unable to escape the sensuousness of its tonal medium, and poetry's superiority derives from the fact that its sound is all but dispensable. Music may be a sensuous embodiment of idea, but the dialectical foundation of Hegel's thought necessitates music's obsolescence. Music may be an indispensable stage in the ascent to absolute idea, but it is one whose moment has passed. Music's sounding inwardness, its evocative emotional content, is not the ultimate inwardness. Indeed, concludes Hegel, it "no longer satisfies" because it lacks the pure and free self-consciousness by Spirit of itself which only philosophy can achieve.

Schopenhauer: Lifting the Rational Veil

The World as Will

Many of the basic tenets of Arthur Schopenhauer's philosophy resemble those of Kant and Plato, from whom he drew his primary inspiration. Their systems were correct, he thought, as far as they had gone. Yet each required certain strategic 'corrections' which he undertook to make. Behind the phenomenal representations given to human consciousness, he held with Kant, lies a noumenal essence. But this essence is neither the absolutely unknowable thing-in-itself Kant had postulated nor Plato's archetypal Idea. It is, rather, what Schopenhauer calls 'Will'.

As much as he respected Kant and Plato, Schopenhauer detested Hegelian idealism. His doctrine of the Will diametrically opposed it at virtually every turn. Yet, the accounts of music which emerge from Schopenhauer's and Hegel's theories parallel each other in several noteworthy respects that warrant recognition at the outset. Specifically, both found music unique among the arts, and highly privileged in comparison to her 'sister' arts. For Schopenhauer, like Hegel, this privileged status was a result of music's capacity to mediate something beyond itself, although they could scarcely have disagreed more profoundly about what that 'something' was. Also, Schopenhauer attributed to music something akin to what Hegel called its 'inwardness'.

If idealism is defined narrowly, the label fits Schopenhauer crudely. He strenuously rejected Hegel's arbitrary identification of the real with the ideal, and significantly modified both Kant and Plato. The essence of reality, Schopenhauer maintained, is not ideal or rational but rather something blindly irrational: an incessant striving, an inanimate and obnoxiously deterministic force, of which everything that exists is a manifestation in some sense or other. Art and music are important because they offer sweet interludes of relief from the grip of Will, temporary releases from the day-to-day pressures of practical and intellectual activity, precious escapes from desiring and striving after ultimately insatiable wants and needs. Schopenhauer thus shared little of idealism's buoyant optimistic belief in the inherent goodness of mind and spirit, and his dark, pessimistic views often presage twentieth-century existentialism more strongly than they reflect the period in which he wrote.

The essential features of Schopenhauer's system are encapsulated with deceptive simplicity in the title of his *The World as Will and Representation*.[212] And yet, both 'will' and 'representation' have been widely misunderstood and misrepresented. The last term in this title (*vorstellung*) has been translated into English as 'idea' rather than 'representation' despite the presence in his theory of something very different that goes by that same name. Designating two distinct concepts ('ideas' and 'representations') with a single term ('idea') has caused what one scholar describes as "confusion on a profligate scale."[213] Indeed, Schopenhauer emphatically rejects the primacy of ideas, insisting that thought, understanding, and reason always answer to 'will'. The term 'will' is probably even more poorly understood, only in this case the fault is strictly Schopenhauer's: he uses a single term to designate two very different concepts. Thus, the distinctions between idea and representation and between two senses of 'will' are crucial to understanding Schopenhauer.

The doctrine of 'will' builds upon Kant's unknowable thing-in-itself. Recall once more that for Kant reality consisted of the noumenal world—the world untouched and unfathomable by human consciousness—and a phenomenal realm, extensively shaped by the cognitive schemata that mediate perception and conception. This dualistic account of things is essentially correct, believes Schopenhauer, only Kant was wrong to insist that the noumenon is absolutely unknowable. The heart of Schopenhauer's philosophical quest is an effort to show how the thing-in-itself can be at least indirectly known, and to describe its nature. Although the noumenon cannot be known as it 'absolutely' is, enough of it manages to filter through the veil of appearances (our mental representations of things) in certain kinds of experience that we can at least sense what kind of thing it is.

This 'Will', the inner essence of everything that is, consists of an undifferentiated, unitary, universal, and indestructible force. Will is "absence of all aim, of all limits . . . an endless striving,"[214] a "blind, irresistible urge."[215] It is manifest both in inorganic forces like gravity and in animate beings as an unceasing quest for survival,[216] and it manifests itself in human experience (phenomenally) as yearning or desire—things which, in contrast to Will, always have some object or goal. And yet, Schopenhauer names this blind, aimless force after something which, in human experience, is never blind or aimless. Human 'willing' invariably entails awareness or consciousness, and is always directed toward some further object or state of affairs. So although they share the same name, the phenomenal and the noumenal 'wills' are clearly very different things. The noumenal 'will' (here we will call it 'Will') is the force behind not only human 'willing,' but things like avalanches and earthquakes as well. In other words, Will is a blind, undifferentiated, unconscious force that drives and determines everything in the universe: what modern physics calls 'energy'. And Schopenhauer chooses to name this force after what he thinks is its most intimate, immediate manifestation in the phenomenal world of human experience. But Will is never given to human experience, only its phenomenal *representation*: Will as given to and shaped by consciousness. Unlike human will, noumenal Will is "a striving devoid of knowledge."[217] It is a force common to the motion of the cosmos, imperceptible subatomic activity, and human existence. In Schopenhauer's words, "[T]he [W]ill-without-knowledge . . . is the foundation of the reality of things . . ."[218]

Schopenhauer cautions repeatedly against confusing the noumenal Will with its phenomenal manifestation: "The [W]ill as thing-in-itself is quite different from its phenomenon . . ."[219] Or more specifically, "Without the object, without the representation, I am not knowing subject but mere, blind [W]ill . . . In itself, that is to say outside the representation, this will is one and the same with mine; only in the world of representation . . . are [subject and object] separated out as known and knowing individual. As soon as knowledge, the world as representation, is abolished, nothing in general is left but mere [W]ill, blind impulse."[220] But as one prominent scholar observes, "the damage has been done. . . . In choosing the word 'will' to denote a noumenon whose essential nature is not conative at all but is through and through non-human and impersonal, without consciousness, without inner sense, without aim and . . . without life. . . . he has ensured that all but close students of his work are bound to take him to be saying something else."[221]

With these caveats in mind, the essential features of Schopenhauer's worldview can be outlined. Beneath it all and without the mediation of human consciousness, the world is a blind, inanimate, impersonal force: Will. Consciousness affords phenomenal representations of Will, human striving and desire notable among them. Since human 'willing' is the representation which "lies nearest to us,"[222] it affords us our most immediate sense of the unknowable essence of the universe. While world exists as Will and its representations, strictly speaking people can only 'know' only the latter. Human willing is the representation of Will in which "the thing-in-itself is manifested under the lightest of all veils . . ."[223]

So pure blind energy is the essence of the universe. When we perceive or conceive of anything, we represent it in a particular way: in terms, for instance, of functions, relationships, causes, time, space, and so on. But these are not characteristics of the world in-and-of-itself; rather, they are the residues of human acts of apprehension. Independent of its representations, Will is pure, impersonal, universal, indestructible force. But if Will is utterly beyond all human comprehension, it is just Kant's noumenon given a new name. So, according to Schopenhauer, human striving and desire share certain of Will's attributes— most notably its perpetual yearning. Will cannot be known, but apparently its character is implicit in human will. "[T]he act of will is . . . the nearest and clearest phenomenon of the thing-in-itself . . ."[224]

In contrast to Hegel, then, the essence of the universe is not reason, not idea, but blind, irrational Will. The intellect cannot know it. Indeed, ideal activity is extensively determined by it. Logic and reason are merely phenomenal, driven like the entire universe by Will's blind irrationality. The world and human existence are ultimately pointless, devoid of the meanings mental representations seem to achieve. It is precisely because of these gloomy facts, however, that art is extraordinarily valuable. For it affords a temporary reprieve from the perpetual yearning and obnoxiously deterministic influence of willing. It makes temporary sense of the senseless, bringing temporary peace. Kant's 'disinterestedness' thus figures centrally in art's capacity to deliver people from the grip of practical desire. Once one recognizes the illusory nature of representations and the ultimate pointlessness of human striving, one can renounce it, attaining a Nirvana-like unity with Will's unconscious aimlessness.

Will and Platonic Ideas

Especially in light of their views on music, Schopenhauer's indebtedness to Kant and Plato is rather startling. But it is their metaphysics more than their accounts of music that interest Schopenhauer. According to him, the "inner meaning of both [Kant's and Plato's] doctrines is wholly the same . . . [B]oth declare the visible world to be a phenomenon which is in itself void and empty, and which has meaning and borrowed reality only through the thing that expresses itself in it (the thing-in-itself in the one case, the Idea in the other)."[225] By splicing Plato onto his Kantian system, Schopenhauer transforms both significantly. Plato's theory of archetypal ideas, the universals of which experience and observations give partial, often illusory information, is right in one important respect, believes Schopenhauer. Platonic Ideas are abstract universals whose nature is never fully manifest in experience and must therefore be inferred from particular instances. But at the same time, Plato requires some correcting because Ideas are not the ultimate 'stuff' of reality: Will is. Ideas can not attain Will's absolute universality, because they are always differentiated from one another. They cannot be truly universal because they are plural. Neither is the independence of ideas from the phenomenal world's particularity absolute, for ideas always pertain to the spatiotemporal world. Ideas forge unity from change and particularity, as Plato maintains; but they are ultimately situated on the phenomenal side of the noumenal-phenomenal dichotomy. Thus, Platonic Ideas are not ultimate but intermediate. Ideas are phenomenal manifestations of Will.

At the same time, Platonic Ideas are not the same as other of Will's representations. They are what Schopenhauer calls Will's "adequate objectifications": what one might call a high grade of Will's manifestation to human consciousness. Although ideas never quite penetrate the veil separating human experience from Will, neither are they mere illusions. Thus, Platonic Ideas occupy a substantial yet precarious epistemological position as intermediaries between Will and representation. They do not give us the Will itself, because as representations they inevitably transform the thing-in-itself. And by itself, Will simply is. But as high grades of Will's objectification, their role in the world of representations is one with important implications for nonmusical art, as we shall see shortly.

Schopenhauer's remarkable worldview is thus a kind of Hegelian idealism in retrograde inversion. Since the human mind has evolved in service of phenomenal existence, Schopenhauer believes, it is quite unsuited for anything more. Therefore, metaphysical speculation (or at any rate, any but his own) is a misguided and ultimately absurd exercise, a vain attempt to speak the unspeakable, to conceptualize the inconceivable. Will simply cannot be known by reason. In this sense, all philosophy before him had "completely reversed the truth":[226] Mind or idea is not what is primal in the universe, but rather the sheer blind striving of Will. In its eagerness to distance mankind from animal existence, philosophy (and Christian philosophy in particular) has fabricated notions like spirituality, soul, and the like, all rooted in a naive belief in freedom and supremacy of mind. But mind is controlled by Will, so that thinking is always distorted in some degree by willing. "Love and hatred entirely falsify our judgment," Schopenhauer says, and "A hypothesis . . . makes us lynx-eyed for everything that confirms it, and blind to everything that contradicts it. . . . What opposes the heart is not admitted by the head. . . . Thus is our intellect daily befooled and corrupted by the deceptions of inclination and liking."[227] Mind distorts and transforms virtually everything it touches, as though it were "intentionally designed to lead us into error."[228]

The true nature of the ultimate can be comprehended only by "shaking off the world."[229] Will's primacy makes human faith in the ultimacy of rational truths absurd, and the true nature of existence almost horrifyingly vacuous. Human existence is pointless and empty, a state of futile, anxious striving driven by likes and dislikes. Indeed, human love of life and determination to survive only seek to sustain "an existence which is full of want, misery, trouble, pain, anxiety, and then again full of boredom, and which, were it pondered over and considered purely objectively, [people] would of necessity abhor."[230] The world is inherently undesirable and inescapably evil. The human mind ever deludes people into attributing purpose and meaning to what is at base pointlessness. "[T]he futility and fruitlessness of the struggle of the whole phenomenon are more read-ily grasped in the simple and easily observable life of animals," Schopenhauer says, for in them can clearly be seen "the absence of any lasting final aim," the "momentary gratification, fleeting pleasure conditioned by wants, much and long suffering, constant struggle . . ."[231] Before proceeding to his account of art and music it is well worth noting, however, that what Schopenhauer seems to abhor is the phenomenal will, rather than Will itself. For in itself, Will is nei-ther good nor evil, it only exists. Human striving may be painful and futile, but Will simply is.

Art and Ideas

As noted earlier, Schopenhauer's Platonic Ideas have a rather precarious status within his system: neither ultimate nor illusory, neither noumenal nor merely phenomenal. They are, however, central to Schopenhauer's claims to the uniqueness and import of art. For art enables the direct and immediate appre-hension of Platonic Ideas without distraction by the irrelevant clutter that ob-scures them in everyday experience. Art distills the essential from the apparent, separates the necessary from the contingent, and thereby enables the perception of pure ideas: ideas purged of all that is superfluous or accidental.

On Schopenhauer's account, art is an essentially cognitive affair in which universality is discerned in the particular. This rare capacity and the ability to communicate such insights through artistic creations are gifts of genius. Most people have this capacity in modest degree, which is what enables recognition and appreciation of art. But few have the capacity always to discern universality amidst the particular, and fewer still the ability to transform that vision into im-ages perceivable by the less-endowed. Artistic genius affords insights into Pla-tonic Ideas by rendering with vividness what is there for all to see yet few actu-ally see. Thus, in contrast to his ontological and epistemological theories, Schopenhauer's account of art is decidedly idealistic. Art is an essentially cog-nitive affair, a purveyor of insight into the ideal realm through the particularity and concreteness of perception. It is, as Kant said, conceptless. But, Schopen-hauer asserts in effect, that does not mean it is cognitively deficient: only that "knowledge of the Idea is necessarily knowledge through perception, and is not abstract."[232]

Artistic genius presents images of Ideas purely, uncluttered and undistorted by conceptual abstractness. In such representations, knowledge "tears itself free from the service of the will. . . ."[233] Thus, since the particularity and concrete-ness of experience of art enable it to avoid encumbrances with meanings and conceptual relations outside itself, it extends a state of mind in which the sub-ject is temporarily freed from willing. Schopenhauer summarizes: "If, therefore, the object has to such an extent passed out of all relation to something outside it, and the subject has passed out of all relation to the will, what is thus known is no longer the individual thing as such, but the Idea, the eternal form. . . . [A]t the same time, the person who is involved in this perception is no longer an in-dividual, for in such perception the individual has lost himself; he is pure will-less, painless, timeless subject of knowledge."[234] Object loses its externality and subject its internality, perceived and perceiver become as one. In this way, people "relinquish the ordinary way of considering things," achieving a state of being in which "we no longer consider the where, the when, the why, and the whither in things, but simply and solely the what. Further, we do not let abstract thought . . . take possession of our consciousness, but instead . . . devote the whole power of our mind to perception, sink ourselves completely therein, and let our whole consciousness be filled by the calm contemplation of the natural object actually present. . . . We lose ourselves entirely in this object . . . in other words, we forget our individuality, our will, and continue to exist only as pure subject, as clear mirror of the object, so that . . . we are no longer able to separate the perceiver from the perception. . . ."[235] In contemplating the Idea, the entirety of one's consciousness becomes "nothing more than [the object's] most distinct image," because in that moment "subject and object reciprocally fill and penetrate each other completely."[236] Although one does not behold the thing-in-itself in aesthetic contemplation of Ideas, Schopenhauer clearly believes the experience brings one remarkably close. In his words, "Without the object, without the representation, I am not knowing subject, but mere, blind [W]ill; in just the same way, without me as subject of knowledge, the thing known is not object, but mere [W]ill, blind impulse."[237] In short, the respite from willing afforded by experience with art comes very close to the experience of the noumenal Will as it might be without phenomenal encumbrances.

This description is provocative and highly original, and one that anticipates the experiential emphases of phenomenological approaches to art as well. The insight art affords is fundamentally perceptual, immediate, experiential, and nontranslatable: direct awareness of Ideas. Art communicates Ideas, those points where phenomenal and noumenal reality touch. While the Platonic Idea is not the thing-in-itself, it approaches it more closely than virtually anything else in the phenomenal world. Such experience communicates an awareness more potent and pure than any mediated by the intellect. Says Schopenhauer, "If the world as representation is only the visibility of the [W]ill, then art is the elucidation of this visibility."[238]

On this view, art purveys a kind of nonconceptual cognition. The experience of being 'pure will-less subject' gratifies far more deeply and profoundly than abstract, conceptual understanding. And yet, art's pleasures are not affairs of particular feeling, for feelings are attributes of the willing whose absence Schopenhauer extols in aesthetic perception. Instead of emotions, art affords release from the tyranny of the phenomenal will. In the fleeting moment of direct contact with the Idea, "we are delivered from the miserable pressure of the will."[239] Particular feelings and emotions are peripheral to Platonic Ideas, and what art seems to promise is deliverance from the intensity of feelings actually felt, emotions actually undergone.

Not unlike Hegel's belief that the various arts had different degrees of adequacy for the expression of absolute idea, Schopenhauer believed Will is objectified in four ascending "grades": inorganic matter, then plant, animal, and human life. Since inorganic matter is Will's lowest grade of objectification, inanimate art is best suited to communication of Ideas like mass and weight. Like Hegel, Schopenhauer finds architecture best suited to such ends. The beauty of plant life is best captured in painting; animal life in sculpture; and human life in verbal arts. If music is conspicuous by its absence from Schopenhauer's hierarchy, that is because it is so completely different from other arts that it requires a theory all its own. Music does not elucidate Platonic Ideas but is itself the Will's direct copy.

Music: Copy of the Will

Communicating the Incommunicable

Schopenhauer offers not one theory of art, but two, because music differs too radically from the other arts to fit within a system which revolves around the elucidation of Ideas. Music "stands quite apart. . . . In it we do not recognize the copy, the repetition, of any Idea of the inner nature of the world."[240] Music's relation to the innermost essence of existence is mediated neither by images of individual things, nor by Platonic Ideas that are Will's 'adequate objectification': music's relation to Will is direct and immediate. Its impressions and effects are uniquely powerful, speaking profoundly and directly to our innermost being in an "entirely universal language, whose distinctness surpasses even that of the world of perception itself," and whose infinite truth is "instantly understood by everyone."[241]

Where other arts provide indirect intuitions of Will, music "passes over the Ideas" altogether, is "quite independent of the phenomenal world, positively ignores it, and, to a certain extent, could still exist even if there were no world at all . . ."[242] Because it is "by no means like the other arts . . . but a copy of the [W]ill itself,"[243] its effect is "much more powerful and penetrating than is that of the other arts, for these others speak only of the shadow, but music [speaks] of the essence."[244] Although Will is manifest in both Ideas and music, music penetrates the veil, casting aside Ideas' inherent plurality. Music is "as immediate an objectification of the whole [W]ill as the world itself is," and it alone is "the copy of an original that can itself never be directly represented."[245]

Schopenhauer is well aware of the striking paradox this presents. He concedes that characterizing music as "a representation to that which of its essence can never be representation" is a position whose logical demonstration is "essentially impossible."[246] Yet it satisfies him, and he remains confident that others who similarly direct their attention purely to the impressions the 'wonderful art of tones' affords, who give proper priority to the actual experience music, as (presumably) opposed to abstractions about it, will find his view persuasive. Music is, mystically, miraculously, a means for communicating the incommunicable, for speaking the ineffable, for presenting that innermost essence of the universe which cannot, by definition, be represented. A more ambitious claim for music can scarcely be imagined: an art which, solely through the impressions of its tones, affords knowledge of the unknowable. That this claim is as impossible and contradictory as it is ambitious, however, was only a minor deterrent to its endorsement by people convinced of music's supremacy and conditioned by the enormously influential Hegelian tradition to embrace the fantastic. Since echoes of Schopenhauer ring throughout the Romantic era and continue to reverberate even in a great deal of contemporary thought, his music philosophy deserves careful and detailed examination.

Music bears no overt resemblance to "the world as representation, i.e., nature," but there is between music and nature "a distinct parallelism,"[247] believes Schopenhauer. He finds in music the "analogue of the fundamental disposition of nature."[248] Music consists in a hierarchy ranging from the weighty, fundamental tones of the bass through the free lyricism of melody. Bass, tenor, alto, and soprano (analogous in Schopenhauer's view to the root, third, fifth, and octave) correspond in their interrelationships to those of Will's objectification in the mineral, plant, animal, and human domains. The distance between inorganic matter and the lowest form of life is analogous to the construction of a chord, which is always "more powerful and beautiful" in open than closed voicing.[249] Moreover, the bass moves slowly and ponderously in contrast to the soprano line's lyrical freedom, a fact which also parallels the contrast between crude, inorganic mass and the freedom of Will's higher representations. The bass lacks the "sequence and continuity of progress which belong only to the upper voice that sings the melody."[250] "[M]elody alone has significant and intentional connexion from beginning to end."[251] But just as organic life is reliant upon the inorganic realm for its existence, so too is melody's apparent freedom always reliant upon the harmonious support of its supporting voices, the bass being the indispensable foundation.

These analogies are scarcely less extravagant than the Hegelian excesses Schopenhauer despised. He says, for instance, that in chordal harmony, "I recognize the whole gradation of the Ideas in which the [W]ill objectifies itself. Those [voices] nearer to the bass are the lower of those grades, namely the still inorganic bodies manifesting themselves. . . . The definite intervals of the scale are parallel to the definite grades of the [W]ill's objectification, the definite species in nature."[252] And finally, in melody, "I recognize the highest grade of the [W]ill's objectification, the intellectual life and endeavour of man."[253] What Schopenhauer describes as analogy clearly aspires to more.

Melody and Rhythm, Tension and Tranquillity

Novel and interesting as these claims are, they are not the most influential and enduring aspect of Schopenhauer's musical philosophy. It is in his remarks on melody that his influence can most clearly be seen. Melody, he asserts, "relates the most secret history of the intellectually enlightened [W]ill, portrays every agitation, every effort, every movement of the [W]ill, everything which the faculty of reason summarizes under the wide and negative concept of feeling. . . . Thus it has always been said that music is the language of feeling and of passion, just as words are the language of reason."[254] Language is to reason as music is to feeling. Its sonorous images help to shape, structure, and make comprehensible an otherwise amorphous realm. And melody has a distinctive capacity to elucidate human experience's alternating patterns of yearning and satisfaction. Melody is "a constant digression and deviation from the keynote in a thousand

ways ... [expressing] the many different forms of [W]ill's efforts, but also its satisfaction by ultimately finding again a harmonious interval, and still more the
keynote."[255] More specifically yet, melody seems to reflect dramatically the powerful reciprocal attraction between these dialectically opposed experiential states.
"[T]he non-appearance of satisfaction is suffering," writes Schopenhauer, and
"the empty longing for a new desire is languor, boredom."[256]

Music's alternating patterns of tension and release, discord and concord, are
analogous to the patterns of human willing and satisfaction. As human pleasure
is marked by the relatively rapid and effortless satisfaction of desire, so too "rapid
melodies without great deviations are cheerful."[257] On the other hand, "melodies
that strike painful discords and wind back to the keynote only through many
bars, are sad, on the analogy of delayed and hard-won satisfaction."[258] Feelings
of deepest satisfaction and release "can follow only the most pressing desire."[259]
Therefore, light, quick phrases "speak only of ordinary happiness which is easy
of attainment,"[260] whereas longer phrases and more protracted deviations be-
speak "nobler effort towards a distant goal."[261] Adagio, for instance, "speaks of
the suffering of a great and noble endeavor that disdains all trifling happiness",
and "in the minor key reaches the expression of the keenest pain ..."[262] This
early effort to explore music from its 'inside', to illuminate something of the
manner in which melody's convergence and divergence from tonal center is
linked to the phenomenal experience of life's ebb and flow, is a remarkable step
forward in the description of music. So, too, its attempt to account for the depth
or profundity of the experience.

But melody's tonal motion is not the whole story. Its qualitative, tonal
component is complemented in crucial ways by a quantitative, rhythmic one.
"Rhythm is in time what symmetry is in space, namely division into equal parts
... that are again divisible into smaller parts subordinate to the former."[263]
The horizontal, spatial aspects of tonal relations are always experienced against
the 'vertical' impact of its rhythms. And although of pitch and rhythm, rhythm
is the more fundamental since it can by itself "present a kind of melody,"[264]
interaction between pitch and rhythm is fundamental to melodic effect. When
pitch and rhythm move disjunctively, the effect can be "disquieting,"[265] and
without proper rhythmic reinforcement a melodic return to tonic cannot affect a full sense of closure. Furthermore, "we see in this procedure of the
melody a condition to a certain extent inward (the harmonious) meet with an
outward condition (the rhythmical)": a situation which portrays in musical
terms "the meeting of our desires with the favourable external circumstances
independent of them, and is thus the picture of happiness."[266] Thus does
Schopenhauer describe the way music's kinetic patterns of discord and reconciliation derive from the interaction of tonal and rhythmic patterns, from
anticipation and appreciation of the particular ways they pursue their complementary courses. Music, like human willing, alternates between desires and
their satisfaction, now separating inside from outside, and now bringing them
together to create a temporary sense of unity and tranquillity. Music is a "constant succession of chords more or less disquieting ... with chords more or
less quieting and satisfying; just as the life of the heart (the will) is a constant

succession of greater or lesser disquietude through desire or fear with composure in degrees just as varied."[267]

Due to the extent of its influence on succeeding generations of thinkers, this line of thought does not require elaboration. Here in Schopenhauer can be seen the ancestry of Langer's assertion that music is the "tonal analogue of the emotive life": a sonorous parallel to the cyclical ebb and flow of human sentience. And here in rudimentary form can also be seen the beginnings of the effort to trace the felt aspects of music to specific formal determinants.

The Inner Kernel of Being

Schopenhauer is insistent, though, that what he is describing are only analogies and no more. "[M]usic has no direct relation to [feelings themselves], but only an indirect one; for it never expresses the phenomenon, but only the inner nature, the in-itself of every phenomenon, the [W]ill itself. Therefore music does not express this or that particular and definite pleasure, this or that affliction, pain, sorrow, horror, gaiety, merriment, peace of mind . . . [but rather] their essential nature, without any accessories, and also without the motives for them."[268] Music's significance, then, has nothing to do with particular feelings—the kind that resides in the phenomenal realm—but only with the inner essence of feeling. Imagination, stirred by its recognition of the unspeakable Will, inevitably tries to give it a concreteness, "to clothe it with flesh and bone, and thus to embody it in an analogous example."[269] Yet music bespeaks human passions and emotions "only in the abstract, without any particularization . . . their mere form without the material . . ."[270] Music presents the form of feeling, the abstracted inner nature of feeling, and not feelings per se. The need to relate this copy of the indescribable Will to something familiar, to associate it with fundamentally different things from the phenomenal realm, is a perfectly natural tendency, but it is nonetheless misguided: it neither promotes nor enhances enjoyment of what is fundamentally musical, "but rather gives it a strange and arbitrary addition. It is therefore better to interpret it purely and in its immediacy."[271]

Music must not be construed as a stimulus that induces or arouses feeling. For what it presents is the formal essence of the eternally striving Will, in all its innumerable nuances and degrees of satisfaction and dissatisfaction. This explains why music "never cause us actual suffering, but still remains pleasant even in its most painful chords."[272] In musical experience, Schopenhauer claims, we actually take pleasure in "the secret history of our will and of all its stirrings and strivings with their many different delays, postponements, hindrances, and afflictions . . ."[273] In everyday life, "our will itself is that which is roused and tormented," and "we ourselves are now the vibrating string that is stretched and plucked." Musical experience, on the other hand, is a function of "tones and their numerical relations".[274] What it conveys, it conveys always and only "in mere tones."[275] Thus, the difference between feelings felt and musical 'feeling' is easily explained, believes Schopenhauer: "The inexpressible depth of all music, by virtue of which it floats past us as a paradise quite familiar and yet eternally remote, and is so easy to understand and yet so inexplicable, is due to the fact that it reproduces all the emotions of our innermost being, but entirely with-out reality and remote from its pain."[276]

Using materials and a language uniquely its own, music "expresses only the quintessence of life and of its events, never these themselves . . ."[277] Melody's "constantly renewed discord and reconciliation of its rhythmical with its har-monious element"[278] present what the imagination takes to be feeling. But mu-sic speaks with a universality of which mind is incapable, a universality known only to Will itself. Music's is not the "empty universality of abstraction,"[279] but a universality which is "united with thorough and unmistakable distinctness."[280] Thus does the significance of Schopenhauer's having posited Will rather than Ideas as primal make its significance fully manifest: music, as copy of the Will, has a deeper universality than reason or idea can ever attain. It requires noth-ing from the phenomenal world of Ideas, concepts, or words, speaking a lan-guage completely its own. It speaks a truth which is truer to reality than any con-cept or verbal proposition can ever attain. Indeed, were music to attempt portrayal of phenomenal things and events, it must be judged defective for fail-ing to speak its own language. Where Hegel had faulted Rossini for failing to remain true to the ideal content of his text, Schopenhauer praises him for hav-ing avoided that temptation: "his music speaks its own language so distinctly and purely that it requires no words at all, and therefore produces its full effect even when rendered by instruments alone."[281]

In this contrast between Hegel and Schopenhauer can be seen vividly the transition between the conception of music as a supporter of text and the con-ception of music as a truly autonomous art. Music is, in Schopenhauer's view, no ornamental support for poetry, but a wholly independent art: "in fact, it is the most powerful of all the arts, and therefore attains its ends entirely from its own resources."[282] When words and music collaborate, the musical tones in-variably take the upper hand: "[W]ords are and remain for the music a foreign extra of secondary value, as the effect of the tones is incomparably more pow-erful, more infallible, and more rapid than that of the words."[283] Words give only the "stripped-off outer shell of things," whereas music gives us the inner-most "kernel."[284] And the human voice, which Hegel had declared the most musically favored 'instrument' in virtue of its capacity to directly convey ideal content, is "originally and essentially nothing but a modified tone, just like that of an instrument."[285] Music itself is utterly and completely indifferent to text and ideal content. Indeed, "like God, it sees only the heart."[286] Purely instru-mental music is not inferior as Hegel claimed, then, but music most true to it-self. This explains the seemingly ironic capacity of a Beethoven symphony to present us "with the greatest confusion which yet has the most perfect order as its foundation; with the most vehement conflict which is transformed the next moment into the most beautiful harmony. It is . . . a true and complete picture of the nature of the world, which rolls on in the boundless confusion of innu-merable forms, and maintains itself by constant destruction."[287]

Music cannot, as music, be the imitation of anything consciously known, for in that case it fails to express Will's inner nature, and "merely imitates its phenomenon inadequately."[288] Nor, by extension, can the composer consciously set out to compose a piece whose expressive aim is fully known: the composer's achievement must arise "from the immediate knowledge of the inner nature of the world unknown to his faculty of reason . . ."[289] Imitative music that draws its inspiration and content from or imitates the (phenomenal) world of perception should be "entirely rejected."[290]

Given Schopenhauer's lofty claims for music, it is easy to overlook the fact that beneath them lies a dark and pessimistic metaphysics. In the end, whatever pleasures music affords must be transient, because satisfaction is momentary and fleeting, striving eternal. Perfect harmony is impossible, even in music: "a perfectly pure harmonious system of tones is impossible, not only physically, but even arithmetically."[291] The imperfections and compromises necessary for the equal temperament system are proof that "a perfectly correct music cannot even be conceived, much less worked out; and for this reason all possible music deviates from perfect purity. It can merely conceal the discords essential to it by dividing these among all the notes, i.e., by temperament."[292] Music's pleasant episodes, then, afford but temporary escape from Will's perpetual striving. The high value of art is its capacity to console in the face of an essentially meaningless existence, to transfigure ordinary experience by providing momentary freedom from Will's tyranny. In this limited sense, art is rightly regarded as "the flower of life."[293] But what remains when the bloom withers and fades is "the in-itself of life, the will . . . a constant suffering [which is] partly woeful, partly fearful."[294] The contemplation of musical beauty is no absolute "quieter of the will," for "it does not deliver [us] from life for ever, but only for a few moments."[295] However it may seem to "exalt our minds," to "speak of worlds different from and better than ours," it ultimately "flatters only the will-to-live" by giving a distorted, "glowing account of its successes."[296] In the end, it seems, music's chief value is its capacity to lighten the burden of pointless, ceaseless striving. The distinctive status of music as copy of the Will does not alter the fundamental fact of life's inherent meaninglessness and Will's blind striving.

Schopenhauer in Review

Its enigmatic metaphysical assumptions notwithstanding, Schopenhauer's treatment of music is in many respects strikingly original. The extent of its influence can hardly be overstated. Schopenhauer saw music as a kind of concrete perceptual knowing which stood in contrast to the 'emptiness' of conceptual abstraction. Music delivers insights deeper than those mediated by thought and ideas: a direct, immediate awareness, whose roots penetrate deeply into human nature and the ineffable nature of the universe in a way no other experience can claim. Music is a face-to-face encounter with the innermost nature of existence.

Music's deep significance arises neither from feelings it portrays, nor from feelings aroused, undergone, or 'felt'. It only reminds us of these because of an analogous relation to phenomenal feeling. Music gives us feeling without its object, the innermost "kernel" of which our worldly strivings and satisfactions are but an "outer shell." The stirring power of music derives from its ever-evolving patterns of tension and resolution; of expectation, anticipation, and desire, yielding to gratification, satisfaction, and momentary peace. Because music copies the universal Will, Schopenhauer metaphorically characterizes music's inner workings as a 'universal language', one linked through imagination to the phenomenal realm of feeling.

Schopenhauer articulates a powerful and historically influential argument for music's autonomy—not only from other arts, but from the natural world, and from the verbal and conceptual realms as well. Music achieves what it achieves entirely with its own resources. It is, in effect, a closed system, but is not on that count an empty, confused, or noisy diversion. Music's significance relies neither upon text nor idea. It is significant in virtue of its capacity to represent the unrepresentable in-itself of the universe, that which undergirds all human thought, all animal and plant life, and which even comprises the inner essence of inorganic matter. It is somehow congruent with, and thereby the mirror of, the blind force that is the indestructible essence of all that is.

At the same time, Schopenhauer presents a powerfully influential argument for music's fundamental reliance upon feeling. Despite his insistence that Will and human willing are two different things, he calls them both by the same name and mixes descriptions of the two, thus conflating music's elucidation of Will with understanding of the phenomenal will. To remain wholly consistent with his metaphysics, Schopenhauer would need to maintain that music illuminates no more and no less than the otherwise unknowable pointlessness of existence. This is at least implicit in his assertion that the pleasure music affords, its capacity to transfigure everyday experience, merely 'flatters' the human will to live, imparting a delusory sense of meaning and purposiveness to the inherently repulsive truth of Will's aimlessness. At the heart of his theory, then, lies a deeply troubling paradox: that this wonderfully stirring copy of the Will (the 'picture of happiness', the 'flower of existence') is the copy of something one must, having recognized it as inherently chaotic, miserable, and repugnant, ultimately renounce. By renouncing the material world and all personal wants, saints and Buddhist monks apparently achieve something far more real and enduring than music can ever deliver.

Concluding Remarks

This examination of Kant, Schiller, Hegel, and Schopenhauer has introduced an extraordinarily broad range of philosophical thought. Nineteenth-century idealism arose from the intellectual ferment created by two opposing elements of Enlightenment philosophy: rationalism and empiricism. Where rationalists approached music from a belief in innate, self-evident truths, truths from which the nature and value of music could be systematically deduced, empiricists were steadfastly skeptical about the existence of any such truths. Their conviction that knowledge could only be derived inductively, from sense-based experience, led to conceptions of music more as sensory evocation and psychological response than rational activity.

Kant's demonstration of the impossibility of pure rationality and a pure empirically derived knowledge profoundly and permanently changed the face of philosophy, and with it conceptions of music. Most of the musical doctrines of nineteenth-century idealistic thought (and many in the twentieth) can be traced directly to arguments set forth in his critiques. His extensively formalistic account of aesthetic experience sowed the seeds from which musical idealism's preoccupation with both form and expression grew. Having posited the human mind as the shaper of all phenomenal experience, Kant's philosophy prompted questions about how the mental activity involved in musical judgments might relate to rational and moral judgments. His tenets of conceptlessness and disinterestedness reverberate through all subsequent idealistic speculation. If music is conceptless, yet still the work of mind, what sense is to be made of such cognitive activity? If not concepts, what kind of insights does music afford? If it is divorced from practical interests and unrelated to practical ends, precisely what is music good for? If it is not primarily a matter of sensory gratification, what is to be made of music's distinctive pleasure, of the feelings it disposes? And perhaps most fundamentally, how does music escape being a mere noisy diversion, an irrational aberration in a human mind otherwise given to wresting coherence from the 'data' given it?

Kant's solution to the problem of judgments of taste, although he believed it only modestly applicable to music,[297] lay in form and pattern. The enjoyment of beauty derives from the playful resonance of imagination and understanding in the presence of elegant structure or design. The value of aesthetic experience for Kant consisted primarily in the contemplative delight it afforded, in the free play of our mental powers as they seize their object in its pure individuality.

For Schiller, human nature consisted of two fundamentally opposed polarities or drives, one formal and the other sensual; one conceptual, and the other given to gratification of desire; one cerebral, and the other more physical in character. The indulgence of either to the exclusion of the other threatened the full realization of human potential through free, playful integration of form and sense, abstraction and concreteness, intellect and feeling. The high purpose of art, in his view, was self-realization and self-integration: the achievement of organic wholeness through 'aesthetic education'. This integration of mind and feeling was at once an end state and a means to richer and more elevated understanding of the human condition: simultaneously an end in itself and a means to higher knowledge.

For Hegel, art and music were essential means to ideal/spiritual elevation. Art was at once a manifestation of mind and an important sign of mental possibilities. The notion of art as pleasantly entertaining pattern was spiritually bankrupt, an irresponsible belief that ignored the deeper significance Schiller had shown. Art was a sensuously concrete way of knowing, and as such, a uniquely revelatory vehicle. In fact, music was blessed with a distinctive inwardness that promised to advance human awareness in crucial ways of which nothing else was capable. Music's felt nature was not diametrically opposed to idea, but was among its essential features. Music was uniquely able to show the crucial role of emotion in cognition. Music enabled the spiritual elevation of mind to a level it could never achieve on its own. Yet, having performed this essential mission, music guaranteed its own obsolescence.

In addition to inwardness and outwardness, Hegel's philosophy was also influential in articulating polarities between form and content, and between art and craft. Since pattern alone was insufficient to account for music's spiritual and ideal mission, there had to be a further 'something', a content, born of form. What was distinctive about musical content, the feature in light of which it promised to enrich ideal awareness, was its distinctive expressiveness. And since music's conceptlessness precluded its generation by rules, it was essential to distinguish musical craft from art. Craft was predominantly concerned with the technical execution of preconceived, concrete ends, whereas musical art was a deeper matter of exploring spirituality and ideality through the medium of sound. For Hegel, music's nature and value were fundamentally expressive; and without expressive content, music was a mere empty sounding.

Schopenhauer turned most of the Hegelian system upside down, and found in purely autonomous music a reflection of what he took to be universal—not Idea or anything remotely rational, but blind, irrational Will. And yet, even on this account autonomous music owes its significance to a revelational capacity, a capacity to provide insight or access into something otherwise unfathomable. At the heart of Schopenhauer's musical theory is still a cognitive claim of sorts, one that involves a distinctly perceptual kind of knowledge, an awareness deeper and more profound than thought. Music presents a world inaccessible to ideas and only indirectly given to phenomenal experience. Thus, a metaphysically transcendental awareness figures as centrally in Schopenhauer's theory as Hegel's, as music penetrates the phenomenal veil to put people face to face with the inner essence of all that is. Like the Hegelian system he so despised, Schopenhauer took as given that music consisted in a fundamentally inner, felt realm of experience.

To the idealist, the human mind is fundamentally given to structuring and shaping, to transforming whatever it is given by the senses. As a product of such activity, music must therefore be essentially mindful. Further, as an achievement of mind, music must amount to a kind of knowing. Yet it must be knowing of a very distinctive kind. Kant had serious misgivings about music in this regard, since it was more 'agreeable' than 'fine'. Hegel, on the other hand, found music particularly well suited (at least for one stage in historical evolution toward absolute idea) to knowing of a particular kind. Schopenhauer, too, conceived of music as affording a distinctive kind of awareness, although it was cognitive in a curiously paradoxical sense: in its capacity to afford insight into the unknowable realm of noumenal Will. Idealism is thus concerned with establishing that music is more than an object impinging upon the senses, or a mere matter of diversion and entertainment. Music is a unique mode of cognition or awareness whose significance extends beyond its material presentation. It is not knowledge in a conceptual sense, but neither is it purely sensuous experience. The idealist is typically concerned with showing what is 'known' in musical experience: mind and idea are the standards by which music's worth must be gauged.

Although musical experience must not be reduced to purely sensuous experience, its deep involvement with feeling and emotional life are impossible to ignore. Thus, another of idealism's concerns is how music's felt character relates to mind, awareness, and consciousness. The generally favored answer is that musical feeling is not so much aroused, evoked, or undergone, but rather mentally apprehended and contemplated. Kant found it rather annoying and troublesome that music was so transient and intrusive. Hegel claimed its concreteness and emotional character could enrich the awareness of idea's concrete, felt essence. Schopenhauer found in music a copy of the Will's perpetual yearning, somehow freed of the constraints of everyday feeling and practical desire. Music, emotion, and expression are thus intimately linked.

Idealistic accounts of music often invoke a number of seemingly paradoxical notions as well. Chief among these is the idea that music somehow invokes awareness of something beyond itself, a 'something', however, that does not exist independently of the music. Music consists in something known, yet it is not quite knowledge. Music is felt, yet what is felt is not quite feeling in the normal sense. Music achieves and presents a mysterious unity of inside and outside, of self and other; a meaning without anything that is concretely meant. Although these enigmatic notions are variously described, the term of choice is most often 'expression'. One of the most distinctive and troublesome problems of musical idealism is thus to describe how music is expressive yet expresses nothing that can be named or unambiguously described, how expression is both something music 'has' and 'does'. Although musical expression is 'of' something, that something is utterly ineffable, existing nowhere outside the musical experience itself. This tension between the notion of expression as both transitive function and intransitive possession figures centrally in most idealistic accounts of music.

Put slightly differently, idealism often attributes to music extraordinary significance as a surrogate for something beyond its own phenomenal existence. As a result, music is at once autonomous and heteronomous; important for what it is and for what it reveals; expressive without expressing anything definite; feelingful, yet not concerned with feelings-felt. Music is not a referential or a representational affair, yet it affords intuitions or insights of profound transcendental significance. Music is at once an end in itself and a means to spiritual elevation, at once fundamentally mindful and fundamentally felt.

The attraction of idealism hardly ended with the close of the nineteenth century. It has found eloquent and persuasive twentieth-century advocates in Croce, Collingwood, Langer, and numerous others. Cognitive activity, Croce urged, takes two basic forms: logical and intuitive. Art deals in the intuitive experience of particular images whose cogency and coherence are functions solely of the feelings they embody or express. Collingwood argued that unlike craft, art is not rule governed and therefore has no 'technique'. Accordingly, "a work of art may be completely created when it has been created as a thing whose only place is in the artist's mind";[298] or more strongly yet, "The work of art proper is something not seen or heard, but something imagined."[299] Langer, whose theories are examined in more detail later, maintains that music is concerned not so much with feelings-felt as with the form of feeling. Music is not so much matter, or action, or sensation, as it is idea.

Clearly, musical 'idealism' is not an orderly or neatly delineated body of thought, but a constellation of doctrines generally concerned with establishing the mindful or spiritual significance of music and musical experience. And although the central tenets of particular theories vary substantially depending upon what a given philosopher singles out for criticism, idealists do share some general tendencies or predilections that warrant brief consideration here.

While most philosophy has its binary oppositions, idealism is noteworthy both for the abundance of its dualistic categories and for their presumed mutual exclusivity. The dualistic oppositions between sense and mind, mind and body, subjectivity and objectivity, and inner life and the outer world are distinctively idealistic preoccupations. Among other things, these dichotomies reflect the tendency of idealism to conceive of knowledge and experience as things that exist within and are bounded by an insular 'self'. On this view, knowledge and feeling alike tend to be construed as personal, psychological states whose linkage to the material world is problematic. The quest for accurate knowledge of a world perceived by an isolated subject is thus a recurrent idealistic theme. And it is a typically idealistic claim that music and musical experience are somehow uniquely able to penetrate and reveal the innermost nature of the world and human experience.

Idealism is also noteworthy for an orderly systematicity made possible by the presumed existence of universals and absolutes. It favors grand metaphysical explanations that claim to transcend time and circumstance and escape the contingencies, transience, and contextual relativity of human experience. Thus, for instance, even though Hegel's is a strongly historicized philosophy, its ultimate destination is the static, abstract domain of absolute idea. The purpose of philosophy is thus to describe 'reality' from a perspective outside all human experience, and the idealist typically has little use for accounts of music that are pluralistic or relative, or see music as a multiple, constantly changing phenomenon.

Just as idealistic philosophy's focus on the relationship between a solitary knower and an absolute known tends subtly to marginalize other kinds of philosophical discourses, it invariably privileges certain musics while trivializing others. Much of the German idealism examined in this chapter, for instance, privileges 'inwardness' as a universal basis for valuation of music. Musics that conform to this ideal are more inherently musical and valuable. On this view, there is a single (essential) way it is best for music to be, in whose light all musics and musical practices can be evaluated. In other words, idealism subtly rationalizes its preferred musics and attendant spheres of influence in light of their supposed capacity to afford privileged information or insight. It is fond of constructing normative value hierarchies based upon the presumed adequacy of various musics to an ideal standard. In short, idealistic claims to one essential musical nature and value divert attention from the cultural relativity and multiplicity of musical practices, and obscure their own ideological biases as to whose musical practices are most desirable. While the German idealists examined in this chapter are hardly the only philosophers to show these tendencies, they do illustrate clearly some of the advantages and disadvantages of conceiving of music as idea.

DISCUSSION QUESTIONS

1. The mind-body problem is one with which music philosophy must deal in one way or other. Having seen the difficulties idealism creates by construing mind and body as mutually exclusive and hierarchically ordered (body being denigrated and mind venerated), how might you go about reintegrating them? How might the idea of embodied cognition recast our conceptions of music's nature and value?

2. The need to show that music constitutes a kind of 'knowing' rather than a merely sensory response has been one of music philosophy's perennial concerns. These endeavors often proceed, however, as if what 'knowing' means were perfectly clear and unproblematic, with the result that intellectual abstraction becomes the norm by which music's cognitive adequacy must be assessed. Might music's human significance and value be substantiated without recourse to knowledge claims? How?

3. Idealistic philosophy's dualistic roots create a host of binary oppositions— conceptual pairs in which the former term is valued over the latter: mind/body, objective/subjective, inward/outward, universal/particular, knowing/feeling, culture/nature, restraint/indulgence, cognition/sensation, truth/belief, fact/fancy, order/chaos, etc. Is it possible to deconstruct binaries like these without succumbing to complete relativism?

4. The 'aesthetic' experience is most often described in terms of what it is not: it is not technical, not intellectual, not sensual, not practical or instrumental, and so on. Positive definitions most often stress its contemplative nature and distinctively felt quality (thus, feelingful cognition, cognized feeling). Can you identify instances of such experience in your musical involvements? When, where, and with what music? Can you think of genuinely musical experiences that seem emphatically non-'aesthetic'? When, where, and with what music?

5. Many people use the terms 'aesthetic', 'artistic', and 'musical' interchangeably. Are there important differences between musical value and aesthetic value? between aesthetic and artistic qualities? What does your answer imply about the object of musical instruction? musical analysis? musical composition?

6. Idealistic music philosophy has a difficult time finding value in the making or doing of music, emphasizing instead its status as an object of contemplative, perceptual experience; in short, listening is the presumed norm for musical experience. Why is this so? Is it justified? Why or why not? What kind of revisions might idealism require if music making or participation were regarded as the quintessential musical experience?

7. Are there grounds for disputing matters of 'taste'? Put differently, are there any reliable or defensible grounds for asserting that 'this' music is better than 'that'? If not, how do we justify imposing musical values in the process of education?

8. Schiller's notion of play suggests that music situates itself between the determinisms of sense and reason, that the best music is that which achieves and maintains an ideal balance between these two polarities. In your experience, is it true that music which is either too visceral or too cerebral tends to atrophy as music? Illustrate your answer with specific musical examples.

9. Does music progress, advance, or evolve toward some higher, more sophisticated level, or does it rather just change? Does music's stylistic evolution represent or reflect an advance in human intelligence or self-understanding?

10. Do you think that 'art' music has outlived its time, as Hegel implies? Does art music serve a need we may have in some sense outgrown? Is the music of 'high culture' becoming irrelevant or obsolete? Has it lost its 'truth to life'? If so, what might be done to change this? Or is that possible? If not, how do you account for declines in support for the Western canon and the organizations dedicated to its preservation?

11. It is often alleged idealistic thought's metaphors of heart and mind lead to the neglect of sociocultural, political, and ethical issues: issues, for instance, of economic, racial, and sexual power and privilege. Can musical discourse be confined to such a realm, or is it so fundamentally social that to ignore issues like these is to miss what music in fact is?

12. Much idealistic thought treats musical meaning and value as universals and essences. Although Hegel's absolutes remain 'absolute', he does historicize and to that extent relativize music's value. Do you believe there is an 'essential' substrate of music, something durable, foundational, and universal?

13. Many of idealistic philosophy's dualisms can be traced back to Plato. Discuss the points of convergence and divergence among the music philosophies of Plato, Kant, Hegel, and Schopenhauer.

14. Hegel's theory points to the phenomenally distinctive characteristics of sonorous experience—its inwardness, its eradication of boundary, its transience—and suggests in effect that because of these, music affords a distinctive kind of self-knowledge attainable through no other human experience. How might these insights be developed into a viable defense of music's educational value in modern society?

15. Expression, spirituality, or profundity are, for Hegel, requisites of truly great music. What do these terms mean? Does music have to have each of these in order to be 'great'? Are any of them expendable? Are the terms

'expressive', 'spiritual', 'profound', and 'great' just honorific terms applied to music that is highly esteemed?

16. The idea of 'inwardness' often directs attention to a presumed relation between music's tonal-rhythmic configurations and the responses to them (between form, that is, and feeling). This is often achieved at the expense of awareness of music's intersubjective meanings, its social embeddedness. Does inwardness implicate a withdrawal from the public and political realms? Why or why not?

17. For Hegel, emotion contemplated or 'infused with idea' (and thereby given order) is more valuable than emotion felt. Is this distinction a viable one in your estimation? Can you illustrate the difference by referring to a specific piece? How might one teach in order to assure that the 'proper' kind of experience occurs?

18. A central tenet of Buddhist philosophy is that clinging to the idea of 'self' is a source of human suffering and pain. This view, implicit in Schopenhauer's thought as we have seen, appears to be at odds with convictions that the primary value of musical or artistic experience is increased self-awareness, self-realization, self-growth. Which view do you find more persuasive and why?

Music as Autonomous Form

In this chapter we examine what might be regarded as the other side of ideal-ism's dualistic currency: the belief that an understanding of music's nature and value is not to be found in its effects, the insights it affords, the feelings it arouses, or indeed, its connections with anything outside itself. Its value, on this view, is strictly its own, strictly intrinsic, located wholly within a purely musical realm. Interesting and important though people's subjective musical experiences may be, it is the 'objective' cause of those experiences that interests philosophers who prefer formalistic perspectives. Not just any response to music is musically relevant: only the response that ensues from perception of qualities that are 'out there', in the 'work' or the music itself. The genuinely musical experience, then, is a response to objective features—and more specifically, to features ordered or structured. So where the idealist of expressionistic persuasions finds music's sig-nificance in the distinctively inner stirrings associated with its experience, the formalist prefers to look 'outward' to the sonorous event that causes such stir-rings. Both, note, tend to accept the mutual exclusivity of the subjective and ob-jective realms, of mind and matter, of the 'inner' and 'outer'. As we explore sev-eral of the best known formalistic accounts of music, it will be well to keep in mind this presumed split between the inner and outer realms, the 'ideal' and the 'real' we might call them, tracing the way it weaves through their accounts.

It may also be helpful to bear in mind that 'formalism' is often a pejorative label, applied to philosophical positions by their detractors rather than their ad-herents. The alleged 'elitism' of musical formalists and the notion that they ab-solutely reject feeling are likewise misrepresentations of the views we actually often find on closer examination. The advocate of what is sometimes called struc-tural hearing does not usually maintain that it is a capacity given only to a se-lect few, and most so-called formalists are not so much anxious to deny the ex-istence of the felt musical response as to stress its uniqueness and the importance of its material or structural source. Most of the perspectives to be explored here posit a range of felt response to music that is strictly and purely musical—a range of feeling which is therefore unlike any other, existent only as a function of full and adequate perception of music 'itself'. At the same time, they illustrate vividly the problems that attend the noble quest to define a range of value strictly music's own, the most severe of which is utter irrelevance.

After examining several ancient precursors to the conception of music as autonomous form, we will turn to the views of **Eduard Hanslick** (1825–1904). In a highly polemical and provocative treatise, Hanslick wrote what many consider to be the 'classic' defense of music's purely musical value. He mounts a stinging critique of efforts to portray music as a bridge to something beyond itself, and seeks to define a musical realm that is wholly and uniquely musical. He attempts to bring together musical form and musical content in the beauty of what he calls music's "tonally moving forms." Not feeling, he passionately argues, but beautifully patterned sound is what music is about. Music's moving forms are its content, and not anything outside music itself. In particular and most pointedly, what music is has nothing to do with 'feeling' in any sense of the word. The notion that feeling is the locus of musical value, he argues, turns people inward and away from the sensible source of musical experience—the very thing to which they should be attending. Emoting over music is the neophyte's or the novice's mode of engagement, not the musician's. Hanslick emphatically rejects claims that music arouses, represents, or expresses feeling. The truly musical mode of engagement consists in a kind of rapt, vigilant, contemplative hearing which is strictly auditory; pleasure that is properly musical consists in the mental alertness associated with such hearing, not some diffuse, emotional experience. So stinging are his denunciations of people who believe music's worth has to do with feeling, so entertaining his unflattering descriptions of people who mistake self-indulgence for musical experience, that his primary point is easily missed: music's worth, Hanslick believes, is a purely musical matter, something that can only be gauged by one who fully perceives music as it objectively presents itself. Musical beauty is a beauty like no other, and its source is none other than tonally moving forms.

Vivid and memorable though Hanslick's arguments are, they do not achieve (or attempt) close philosophical analysis. In contrast, the music philosophy of **Edmund Gurney** (1847–1888) is remarkably even-handed, devoting meticulous attention to detail. Gurney makes a number of important distinctions that help refine and advance the formalistic perspective. He carefully explores the differences between what he calls the lower and the higher senses, between visual and musical form, between representation and presentation, between expression and impression, between expression and 'expressiveness', and between physical and musical motion. On their most fundamental points, Hanslick and Gurney are in full accord: music and musical experience are wholly unique, and extraneous comparisons are deeply detrimental to our understanding of it. In fact, Gurney goes so far as to insist that it is mediated by a special mental or cognitive 'faculty', a claim that resonates in certain respects with more recent claims to the existence of a distinct 'musical intelligence'. Gurney's primary strategy is to show that all supposed similarities between music and other things are spurious and misleading, a strategy he employs with remarkable ingenuity and persuasiveness. He shows quite effectively the inadequacy of visual metaphors like 'line' or 'contour' to music. He explores the profound differences between music's distinctive motion and physical motion—musical motion being one in which nothing really moves or changes place. He mounts cogent arguments against the doctrine of musical expression, drawing an important distinction between 'expressing' and 'being expressive', and insisting that there exists a voluminous body of impressive music from which expression is notably absent. And although he considers music 'form addressed to the ear', he is insistent that what musical form shares with nonmusical form is trivial compared to its distinctive qualities: its progressive, temporal character, for instance, and its presentational immediacy. He is steadfast in his belief that the world of beauty is pre-eminently one of form: the perception is no mere feat of auditory acuity; not sound, but sound patterned and forged by mind's musical faculty into 'ideal motion' is the essence of musical experience.

The contemporary theories of **Leonard Meyer** (b. 1918) elaborate the formalistic perspective with highly sophisticated philosophical and musical expertise. Meyer offers a subtly nuanced account of how distinctly intramusical meanings arise and are sustained by a sonorous musical source, or 'stimulus'. Although its specific details resist concise summary, his theory's basic premise is that for listeners conversant in a musical style, musical patterns or 'events' tend to suggest or imply more or less likely modes of continuation and elaboration. These modes of continuation (other musical events that are more or less likely to ensue) are what musical events 'mean', or 'refer to'. This range of meaning is not extramusical but wholly intramusical, contained within the music's own materials, events, and patterns. And there exists, accordingly, a specific, rather circumscribed range of feeling or 'affect' which is genuinely and purely musical: one that comes of having one's musical expectations variously fulfilled, pleasantly surprised, and so forth. It is important to note that Meyer's theory is a highly elaborate version of the formalistic effort to ground feeling in auditory perception of pattern, structure, or form. Music is, in his view, primarily a formal, mental affair, grounded in perception of sonorous relationships. Thus, as we shall see, Meyer's arguments carry forward three cardinal formalist principles: first, that truly musical meaning is limited to and demarcated by things objectively 'there' in the music; second, that truly musical experience is fundamentally reliant upon the detection of patterns or form; and third, that music is less a matter of sense than of mind. In the end, Meyer's theories are better suited to explaining 'absolute' music in the Western 'art' tradition than other musics. That, however, is neither coincidental nor surprising, since creating music 'most itself', music most 'purely musical', is what that tradition has long presumed to do. Such music is precisely what the formalistic perspective seeks most often to explain and describe.

Ancient Precursors: Aristoxenus, Philodemus, Sextus

Although the prevalent view of music in ancient Greek times was as an imitative or representative phenomenon, unanimity of opinion was no more characteristic of their times than it is of ours. This chapter's survey of formalistic accounts of music begins, then, with several ancient thinkers who disagreed, sometimes vehemently, with the musical theories of their day—theories which attributed social, political, moral, or mathematical significance to music. The fact that these are not, strictly speaking, 'formalistic' accounts points to the need for several important preliminary distinctions. First, arguing that music is a realm with concerns all its own does not necessarily commit one to a further claim that its meaning and value are functions of form or structure. A claim to music's autonomy, in other words, might conceivably be rooted in things other than form. Second, rejecting claims to music's heteronomous value is not quite the same as endorsing the existence of a range of value all music's own. Saying 'what music is not' leaves open the question of what it is; and indeed, denying music's connection to certain values does not preclude the more extreme position that it is wholly without value. It is a good idea, then, to distinguish rejections of heteronomy from endorsements of musical autonomy. What we find in these dissenting, critical voices from ancient Greece are the former. They challenge the idea that music contributes in significant ways to things like human character, but without mounting a further claim to formal musical self-sufficiency. Not until the emergence of so-called absolute music centuries later could a true 'formalism' begin to emerge. In short, those who reject heteronomous accounts of music do not necessarily do so with the intent of establishing music's autonomy. In fact, many an apparent formalist is not so much interested in denying all possibility of heteronomous musical connections as exploring what music seems to be and do on its own.

One of the earliest voices to challenge the prevalent accounts of music in ancient Greek times was that of **Aristoxenus of Tarentum**, son of a fourth-century-B.C. musician, and a student of Aristotle. Before Aristoxenus, declares one authority, "the limits of Musical Science had been wholly misconceived."[1] The fault for this lay partly with practicing musicians and partly with philosophers. Musicians were too preoccupied making music to contribute anything of real substance to its understanding. Although they should have been well suited to that task, musicians were guilty of "dispensing with reason and demonstration" to such an extent that they had nothing to contribute but "isolated dogmatic statements."[2] Those who were theoretically inclined had strayed too far in the opposite direction: due to extensive Pythagorean influence, their accounts had more to do with mathematics than with music as actually practiced and experienced. As Aristoxenus saw things, musicians were engaged in unreflective practice, and philosophers were lost in theory; music's practitioners were "musicians without science," writes Macran, while philosophers were "men of science without music."[3]

Thus, Aristoxenus sought to create a theoretical account of music that was grounded in the way music was actually perceived, instead of things like number and ratio. He strenuously insisted that the ear was indispensable to understanding music; yet for him, such understanding clearly required theoretical inquiry as well. "Some," he writes, "consider Harmonic a sublime science, and expect a course of it to make them musicians; nay some even conceive it will exalt their moral nature. . . . Then on the other hand there are persons who regard Harmonic as quite a thing of no importance, and actually prefer to remain totally unacquainted even with its nature and aim. Neither of these views is correct. On the one hand the science is no proper object of contempt to the man of intelligence . . . nor on the other hand has it the quality of all-sufficiency, as some imagine."[4]

So far as Aristoxenus was concerned, a musical science worthy of the name must rest in the final analysis upon "the two faculties of hearing and intellect. By the former we judge the magnitudes of the intervals, by the latter we contemplate the functions of the notes."[5] Both faculties, the perceptual and the conceptual, must be deployed; but should there be a discrepancy between ear and intellect, the ear is the final arbiter. Unlike such disciplines as geometry, where reasoning is more important than perceiving, "for the student of musical science accuracy of sense perception is a fundamental requirement."[6] Since everything else in music ultimately rests upon accurate hearing, anything not demonstrable to sense perception "cannot stand as a fundamental principle."[7]

Ear and mind, sense and intellect, are thus united in Aristoxenus's approach to music. Music's apprehension is fundamentally reliant upon the cooperation of sense perception and memory, "for we must perceive the sound that is present, and remember that which is past. In no other way can we follow the phenomena of music."[8] The role of the intellect in Aristoxenus's view is, in strong contrast to Pythagorean theories, specifically and concretely musical. "Mere knowledge of magnitudes," he writes, "does not enlighten one as to the functions of the tetrachords . . . or the modes of melodic construction, or indeed anything else of the kind."[9] Nor do Pythagorean acoustical insights enable one to distinguish a "tuneful melody" from one that is utterly unmusical.[10] In short, the Pythagorean fascination with number and ratio had created an excessively cerebral orientation that had lost contact with what it presumed to explain. Pythagoreans "introduced extraneous reasoning, and rejecting the senses as inaccurate fabricated rational principles, asserting that height and depth of pitch consist in certain numerical ratios and relative rates of vibration—a theory utterly extraneous to the subject and quite at variance with the phenomena. . . ."[11]

Although it is not crucial to examine this Aristoxenian-Pythagorean debate in detail, one issue is illuminating. Pythagoreans defined the interval of the whole tone as the difference between the ratios for the intervals of the fourth and fifth. However, when whole tones in this system were divided into semitones, the resulting ratios were what we call irrational numbers. This in turn led to practical problems, since twelve such semitones exceed the perfect octave. Against this Pythagorean account, Aristoxenus suggested the semitone be derived simply from equally partitioning the octave. Not only was this 'neater', leaving no embarrassing residue at the octave, it was perfectly acceptable to the ear. So in contrast to a Pythagorean system awkwardly encumbered by theoretical baggage, Aristoxenus proposed a pragmatic, perceptually based alternative, one in which the octave is simply a continuum in which each successive pitch merges gradually with the next.

Although 'The Musician', as Aristoxenus was often called, left no comprehensive account of music's nature and value, it is his fundamental orientation that is of interest here. Attend to the sounds, he urged: music's significance must be explained in terms of these sounds, their relationships, their functions within a musical system—not extramusical affairs like mathematical proportions. Music consists, he argued in effect, not in isolated acoustical 'data', but in tendencies, connections, and functions within a musical system. A truly musical theory cannot be built from acoustical information about discrete tones or intervals, but must address the ways these function within musical practices. Neither can a truly musical theory ignore what the ear hears, regarding it as somehow deceitful or dispensable to its accounts: for the musical world is always and unavoidably a world of the ear. The ancient Pythagoreans, concludes one scholar, "missed the true formal notion of music which is ever present to Aristoxenus, that of a system or organic whole of sounds, each member of which is essentially what it does, and in which a sound cannot become a member because merely there is room for it, but only if there is a function which it can discharge. . . . [that of] a science of music which will accept its materials from the ear, and carry its analysis no further than the ear can follow . . ."[12] Aristoxenus was adamant that musical theory not be permitted to "transgress the limits of the sensible,"[13] a concern of paramount importance to those who insist the ultimate grounds for music's nature and value are to be found in the perception of its sonorous patterns.

Philodemus of Gadara, an Epicurean of the first century B.C., caustically denounced most of the claims about music we have explored through Plato and Aristotle. Music's connection to the soul, its capacity to shape character, its importance to education—all these ideas are wholly without merit, according to Philodemus. Epicureans tended to equate perception with sensation, a belief that made them rather dubious about music's potential cognitive or moral significance. As sensory experience, music gives pleasure—no small achievement, perhaps—yet it does little more than that. Its value is simply a function of its capacity to give us enjoyment. It is a natural, harmless source of pleasure, but there is no particular point in studying or engaging in it beyond that.

Philodemus's work is philosophical in only the loosest sense of that term. In the opinion of one scholar, his writing consists largely of "irrational tirades" with only a "modicum of real or supposed musical-historical fact."[14] He was, to be sure, hardly a model of rational deliberation. He argued simply from what he no doubt regarded as the plain, 'common sense' point of view, one that was highly impatient with what it took to be excessive speculation and theorizing. According to Philodemus, "[N]o melody, *qua* melody, being irrational, either rouses the soul from a state of tranquillity and repose and leads it to the condition which belongs naturally to its character, or soothes and quietens it when it is aroused. . . . For music is not an imitatory art, as some people fondly imagine, nor does it . . . express . . . magnificence, humbleness, courage, cowardice, orderliness and violence—any more than cookery."[15] Music does not, according to Philodemus, cause a "shift of emotions in virtue of which . . . and through which a given type of character is imputed to us."[16] If, indeed, music ever really succeeds in changing or improving character, it does so only because of the influence of its words. In itself, it is powerless to influence character, and "[a]s for those who say that music makes us gentle, softening our spirit and taking away its savageness, one must consider them utter fools; for it is only the instruction of reason which accomplishes this."[17] The idea of musical ethos is apparently a figment of the imagination: "[Some people] allege that one kind of music is solemn, noble, single-natured, and pure, and that another is unmanly, vulgar, and illiberal; others term one severe and imperious, another gentle and persuasive. In either case they . . . attribute to music what is not there. . . . And certainly it is evident that music, though it may show the greatest variety of form . . . has never in itself made ethos manifest."[18]

It is also sometimes alleged, relates Philodemus, that setting texts to music adds emotional force and that this constitutes evidence of music's emotional or expressive power. However, he counters, "as far as impressiveness and the reasoning faculty are concerned music does not change a single thing but merely adds listening pleasure."[19] Expressiveness and ethetic influence are simply not facts of musical perception. That music is pleasant Philodemus does not contest: indeed, he concedes, music's capacity to lull babies to sleep is clear evidence of some unlearned human affinity for it.[20] But its significance extends no further than the pleasure it affords. For Philodemus, music apparently consists in nothing more than pleasant patterns of sound. Although many contemporary supporters for this position could doubtless be found, severing music's connections to everything but pleasure has serious and far-reaching consequences—consequences with which those who advocate music's autonomy must somehow contend.

Sextus Empiricus, a Skeptic of the second century A.D., argued many of these same points, though with a different end in mind. Sextus thought it impossible to comprehend such things as 'ideals' or 'essences', and hence foolish to make assertions one way or the other about music's essential nature. The skeptic's method was to show that for any given argument, an equally plausible opposing position was possible. Confronted with plausible yet contradictory explanations, one presumably had no alternative but simply to suspend judgment. The point in refuting a position was not so much to substantiate an alternative as to establish the pointlessness of holding tenaciously to any position at all. Furthermore, since perception is always shaped and influenced by the sense organ doing the perceiving, sense perception cannot be a reliable source of insight. The skeptical 'tropes' in Sextus's book *Against the Musicians* stress variously that people's temperaments and moods influence and distort perception; that different sense organs can give contradictory impressions of the same object, that pleasant things in excess become harmful, that perspective and orientation influence perception; and that the idea of 'the' definitive account of anything is impossible.

Sextus directs his tropes against what he takes to be the primary argument favoring musical study: the belief that music's nature and value extend beyond a 'strictly musical' realm. He acknowledges that Pythagoras supposedly used music to calm drunken youths, that the Spartans apparently used music to fire their spirits for battle, and that Achilles used music to assuage his anger. But, he claims, ". . . it is not because it has the power of discretion that [music] restrains the heart, but rather because it has the power of distraction. . . . [T]hus, a certain type of melos does not restrain a grief-stricken soul or a heart agitated by anger but—if it does anything at all—distracts them."[21]

Music's supposed influence upon character is likewise delusory, for it is "disposed by nature only to give delight."[22] Infants can be put to sleep by "emmelic cooing," and the most irrational of the animals can be "charmed by the aulos and syrinx," yet neither infants nor animals truly experience or conceive of music.[23] Thus, education is quite unnecessary for music to exert its affective influences, its powers of distraction. And while trained musicians may "apprehend technically better than the common person . . . they gain nothing more of the pleasant passion."[24]

Like Philodemus, Sextus believed that the feelings music disposes contribute nothing to human character or education. ". . . [E]very theory of melody according to the musicians does not have its substance in any other thing except in the notes," he writes. "And because of this, if they are abolished, music will be nothing."[25] Again, music's value extends no further than its capacity to please or distract. Although for different reasons, Aristoxenus, Philodemus, and Sextus Empiricus were each suspicious of philosophical attempts to link music to what they regarded as extramusical affairs. Stick with what is given to the ear—with 'the musical facts'—each argued, in effect. Clearly, none envisioned an intrinsically musical range of value, but only sought to narrow the range of musical relevance to exclude things that in their view had nothing to do with music. However, by denying music's connection with human concerns, one risks making it ineffectual, useless, and ultimately irrelevant: for 'value' is always value for some purpose. To argue that music has no significance beyond itself, then, is precariously close to arguing that it has no significance, period.

Hanslick: Tonally Moving Forms

While Eduard Hanslick was one of the most influential Viennese music critics of the nineteenth century, he is best remembered today for the little book he published in 1854, early in his career. Despite Hanslick's modest intentions in writing it, *Vom Musikalisch-Schönen*, or *On the Musically Beautiful*, has come to be regarded as one of the most important (or to some, infamous) treatises on the nature and value of music ever written. The classic 'manifesto' for musical formalism, it has seen publication in more than twenty editions and has influenced philosophical debate in music beyond all proportion to its modest length. At least part of its enduring attraction is probably due to its tone: Hanslick's derisory treatment of the 'feeling theories' he wishes to discredit is at least as entertaining as it is insightful. Whether, with the editor of the book's 1957 English version one finds it a "devastating critique of unsupportable views,"[26] or rather regards it as largely polemical, there is no denying its influence or its importance as a landmark in music philosophy.

Hanslick is a good deal more lucid about what he opposes than about what he proposes. The greatest part of his book consists of scathing indictments of various "feeling theories," on which music's value is presumed to reside in its capacity to represent, portray, express, or arouse emotion. His negative thesis—that musical beauty has nothing whatsoever to do with feeling—is expressed in a remarkable barrage of criticisms directed at the aesthetic theories of his day. Although it is often obscured by his histrionics and combative style, Hanslick has a positive purpose and a positive thesis as well: to restore the integrity of specifically musical beauty, as against idealized, general concepts of beauty which presume to bring all instances under a universal. More specifically, Hanslick seeks to emancipate musical beauty from "servile dependence" upon a "supreme metaphysical principle of general aesthetics,"[27] redirecting attention to the beauty inherent in music's own internal structures—music's "tonally moving forms."[28]

Music's autonomy is Hanslick's paramount concern. But autonomy from what? His book offers numerous and various impassioned responses to this question, each of which involves showing the error in linking music's nature and value to 'feeling'. Besides their misguided preoccupation with feeling, the theories Hanslick detests share two additional important features, he suggests: naive sentimentality and falsehood.

Hanslick is determined to replace 'feeling theory' with an account of musical beauty that is more scientifically oriented, one that illuminates "whatever among our thousand fold flickering impressions and feelings may be enduring and objective."[29] And of one thing Hanslick is unwaveringly certain: such enduring objectivity will not be found among the feelings that adventitiously accompany musical experience. Objective musical beauty is beauty whether a listener is emotionally aroused or not. Indeed, objective musical beauty remains beauty even if the music is "neither perceived nor thought."[30] Emotional arousal, then, is wholly irrelevant to musical beauty. But emoting over music is no mere naively harmless activity: for it turns people inward, away from the sonorous phenomenon that should be engaging their attention. Most of the feelings music is supposed to elicit can be aroused more consistently and effectively by nonmusical means, asserts Hanslick, and attempts to link musical beauty to feeling have yielded "not a single musical law."[31]

Feeling is neither sufficient nor necessary to musical beauty. A piece of music is always "music first and foremost, objective structure."[32] The experience of musical beauty, if, that is, it is truly musical, never rests in any significant way on features outside this structure—as feeling must. What determines the worth or significance of a piece of music is its own distinctive beauty, never its "arbitrary effects" on the audience.[33] Although musical experience may of course be feelingful, such feeling is neither the source of musical beauty, nor is it music's content. Nor, for that matter, has music's purpose anything to do with feeling: all feeling adds to an otherwise objective account musical beauty is "guesswork or fantasy."[34]

If his quest for something more enduring or trustworthy than 'flickering impressions' sounds reminiscent of Plato's and Kant's worries, Hanslick has no intent of turning to some metaphysical Ideal realm for anchorage. The root of his beauty is not ideal, but sensible. Obviously, then, Hanslick regards sensation and feeling as two very different things. Sensation, he says, involves "perception of a specific sense quality," whereas feeling consists in an awareness of a mental state "with regard to its furtherance or inhibition, thus of well-being or distress."[35]

Sensation is simple and direct. It may, if taken by a perceiver as a stimulus for subjective introspection, dispose feeling. But in the presence of musical beauty, sensation is part of an outwardly directed, contemplative experience, a specifically and uniquely musical pleasure. The difference between merely sensual pleasure and musical pleasure, then, is that music "first of all puts something beautiful before us. It is not by means of feeling that we become aware of beauty . . ."[36] Despite a common source in sensation, then, feeling and musical pleasure depart from the sensible in opposite directions: feeling in the direction of internally subjective musings, and musical experience toward a beautiful, sonorous 'object'.

What governs pure musical contemplation is imagination. Imagination cannot be reduced to either understanding or feeling, the two concepts which have unfortunately dominated aesthetic accounts of music. Instead, it stands directly between them.[37] Contemplative experience of a predominantly intellectual bent is "logical" rather than imaginative, whereas contemplative experience that succumbs to feeling is "pathological."[38] Accordingly, imagination, never intellect and (certainly) never feeling, is the supreme aesthetic authority. Imagination strikes an appropriate balance between the polar extremes of the intellectual and the emotive, the logical and the pathological, its product being neither quite reason nor yet quite feeling.

What Music Is Not

This nicely balanced account of imagination as the organ of musical beauty, partaking of both understanding and feeling but yielding to neither, fairly represents a certain strain of Hanslick's argument, but not its overall tone. So obsessed is he with purging musical aesthetics of aberrant feeling that the balanced view he suggests is often rather elusive. Feeling is "nothing more than a secondary effect,"[39] he asserts. But more often he leaves the more extreme impression that even the slightest feelingful tinge is a contaminant and defiler of musical beauty, that feeling has positively nothing to contribute to an objective concept of musical beauty. Looking to feeling for clues about the nature of music is like trying to ascertain "the real nature of wine by getting drunk," says he.[40] When it comes to musical beauty, the tendency to 'pathological' excesses is clearly far more worrisome than the tendency to logical ones.

Hanslick's account cautiously opens the door to a number of important philosophical insights into music; yet, whenever he senses feeling lurking there, he hastily slams it shut. Thus, while he intends to establish that feeling does not play a definitive role in musical beauty, he comes precipitously close to denying its relevance under any circumstances. The object of his concern is Plato's honeyed muse, the seductive side of music Augustine thought one might take in so long as one is not taken in. It is the cheap, the easy, the self-indulgent, the merely sensuous, the transient, as opposed to the true and the enduring. Unlike his philosophical predecessors, though, Hanslick offers no plan for reconciliation. Musical experience may well involve feelings, but they have no place in an account of musical beauty.

Suppose one were to concede to Hanslick that aroused feelings or feeling-felt have nothing to do with musical beauty, that musical beauty is specifically and exclusively musical. Perhaps instead of arousing feeling, music somehow represents, imitates, or expresses it. Might feeling be the content or subject matter of music—what it is about, as opposed to what it evokes? Does music present images of feeling, or of feeling's salient features? Does music tell or express something about feeling or convey insight into the nature of 'felt' life? Hanslick believes these claims to be just as perverse and insidious as arousal theories. Like arousal theories, they divert attention away from music instead of deepening engagement with it. They nurture the delusion that what music is 'about', what it 'means', is feelings rather than melodies and harmonies. But there is an even deeper problem for representation and expression theories: "[T]he representation of a specific feeling or emotional state is not at all among the characteristic powers of music."[41] What makes any feeling a feeling, what differentiates it from others, is something music is completely incapable of portraying. What specifies or designates a feeling ('love', for instance) is not some vague sense of mental agitation, but its "conceptual core, its real, historical content . . ."[42] Without some kind of cognitive appraisal, without a conceptual or objective focus, there can be no such thing as a feeling. Love cannot be conceived or felt without an object, situation, or individual toward which it is directed. "[M]usic is incapable of expressing definite feelings; indeed, the definiteness of feelings lies precisely in their conceptual essence."[43]

What of the contention that music represents not specific feelings, but indefinite feeling? Or what of the claim that music and feeling share a kind of 'indefiniteness' that makes music ideally suited to represent feeling in the abstract? This is equally impossible, responds Hanslick, because the very terms "unspecific" and "representation" are fundamentally contradictory.[44] "[E]very artistic activity consists in individualizing, in impressing the specific upon the unspecific, the particular upon the universal. The 'unspecific feeling' theory insists upon the exact opposite."[45] Music is far too particular and concrete to represent or portray feeling in the abstract.

If music is fundamentally nonrepresentational, how might Hanslick account for the abundance of music that specifically purports to be representational: musical drama, vocal music, 'program' music, tone poems, and the like? He turns to this issue with particular relish, taking as his ideal instrumental music, since it alone "is music purely and absolutely."[46] Instrumental music is music by and for itself, and "what instrumental music cannot do, it ought never be said that music can do . . ."[47] To differentiate between vocal and instrumental music with regard to their nature or value is to engage in mere "dilettantish dogmatism," since musical meaning or content has nothing whatever to do with words, titles, or program. "Union with poetry," insists Hanslick, "extends the power of music, but not its boundaries."[48] The beauty of the music always takes precedence over associated text. "The most tawdry poem, set to beautiful music, is powerless to diminish our pleasure in it; but the greatest poetical masterpiece cannot prop up a sagging musical work."[49] So the idea that text or plot is a kind of black-and-white sketch to which music adds color is completely fallacious. Music is itself both design and color.

For conclusive proof that efforts to fit music to text or program succeed "in inverse proportion to the autonomous beauty of the music,"[50] Hanslick says, one need only consider recitative, where music most perfectly supports its text. Subordination to text inevitably means a loss of both musical autonomy and beauty. Thus, as he sees it, opera is no blissful marriage of music and word but "a constant struggle between the principle of dramatic realism and that of musical beauty, with endless compromises between the two."[51]

Hanslick's ultimate goal is simply to "transfer the beauty of music to tonal forms."[52] Music can still lay claim to sense and logic, then, but musical sense and logic are wholly and exclusively musical, an untranslatable musical language with a 'center of gravity' all its own. Unlike speech, in which sound is a transparent conveyor of meanings, musical sounds are ends in themselves.[53] So diametrically opposed are the preeminence of sound in music's autonomous beauty and the subservience of sound to thought in spoken language that a completely successful combination of the two is "a logical impossibility."[54] And the transition from singing to speech, Hanslick declares, "is always a descent."[55]

A visitation of Hanslick would be incomplete without a brief inventory of his caustic characterizations of the naive proponents of feeling theories—music 'enthusiasts'. Such people enjoy 'wallowing' in feeling, he says, 'merrily rattling the chains' in which their fuller human potential is bound by their self-indulgence. What musical people hear, he insists, the naive musical 'enthusiast' only feels,[56] floating along in a "constant twilight" of reverie, a "fuzzy state of supersensuously sensuous agitation." Music enthusiasts slouch in their seats, he claims, variously dozing, brooding, or swaying to the music. What engages their attention (if, in fact, anything may be truly said to be engaged) is the "noisy cheerfulness" a piece shares with countless others, never what is distinctive to a particular piece or performance. "[F]or all they would know, a fine cigar or a piquant delicacy or a warm bath produces the same effect as a symphony."[57] The "effortless suppression of awareness" they so seem to enjoy could as easily be accomplished, he suggests, by the use of drugs.

In Hanslick's estimation, then, all heteronomous accounts of music degrade it to mere natural force that somehow 'works on' a human perceiver. But this completely overlooks the profound distinction between music and sound. "To undergo unmotivated, aimless, and casual emotional disturbances through a power that is not *en rapport* with our willing and thinking is unworthy of the human spirit," he asserts.[58] After all, music apparently 'moves' animals, "[b]ut is it really so commendable to be a music lover in such company?"[59] When, in experiencing music, people surrender themselves to mere elemental gratification, that is hardly to that music's credit; and still less is it to the credit of people who so indulge themselves.

What Music Is

Ascribing to music power over feeling is the single most significant impediment to the development of musical aesthetics, insists Hanslick.[60] But given the depth of this conviction and the force with which he so often asserts it, what is to be

made of assurances like, "Far be it from us to want to underestimate the authority of feeling over music"?[61] or of passages in which he claims no desire to trivialize the "intense feelings which music awakens in us," the "otherworldly stirrings" music elicits "by the grace of God"?[62] Indeed, what of the fact that Hanslick's own musical criticism makes very extensive use of feeling-language?[63] And yet again, what is to be made of his claim in the preface to the eighth edition of his book to bewilderment at accusations that he has argued the complete irrelevance of feeling to musical experience? Is Hanslick being disingenuous, or contradictory?

Apparently, neither. When Hanslick occasionally lets down his guard, it is clear he does not intend to denigrate feeling, however admirably he succeeds in doing so. Indeed, feeling appears to be prominent among his personal reasons for valuing musical experience. The point he so urgently wishes to establish is that music's fundamental nature and the feeling it may dispose in a listener are two distinct matters. At the same time, however, he wants to establish that musical feeling is utterly unique. One commentator observes, "Musical pleasure was, to him, very potent and very much a matter of feeling. But it was, he insisted, a feeling like no other."[64] In other words, Hanslick accepts feeling in music, indeed even embraces it at times. But there can be no place for it in an account of music's objective beauty. Feeling, he apparently believes, is an attribute of people rather than music, and music's beauty is beautiful regardless of how (or even whether) it makes someone feel. And even if feeling were something music had or possessed, it would not follow that music thereby represents feeling. "The rose is fragrant," grants Hanslick, "but we do not say that its content is the representation of fragrance; the forest diffuses shady coolness, but it does not represent the feeling of shady coolness."[65]

That Hanslick believes the nature of musical beauty is not concerned with feeling is abundantly clear. But what precisely is the nature of this autonomous musical beauty for which Hanslick has gone to such lengths to create a place? "The primordial stuff of music," he declares, "is regular and pleasing sound": "Unconsumed and inexhaustible, melody holds sway over all, as the basic form of musical beauty. Harmony, with its thousandfold transformations, inversions, and augmentations, provides always new foundations. The two combined are animated by rhythm, the artery which carries life to music, and they are enhanced by the charm of a diversity of timbres."[66] Music consists in purely musical, wholly self-subsistent ideas: in its "tonally moving forms."[67] Its meaning and value are wholly and specifically musical, neither conceptual, moral, emotional, nor anything else extramusical. "If the musically beautiful is missing, it will never be compensated for by cooking up some great meaning. And such meaning is superfluous if the musically beautiful is present."[68] Music's power is no mystical or metaphysical affair, but "the inevitable result of musical factors which are at work in the melody . . ."[69] Autonomous musical beauty is an objective thing that resides for Hanslick in the motions of music's tonal system.

Musical beauty is heard, not conceptual, and not ideal. Hanslick is quite critical of idealism's "undervaluation of the sensuous,"[70] and of the moralistic persuasions of 'older' aesthetic theories. In an effort to distinguish his accounts from such misguided theories, Hanslick is insistent that music's 'tonally moving forms' are not the skeletal structures often designated by the term 'form'. Musical beauty is concrete, immediate, sensuous, and alive. It is no "mere acoustical beauty or symmetry of proportion," he says: "forms which construct themselves out of tones are not empty but filled; they are not mere contours of a vacuum but mind giving shape to itself from within."[71] In hearing music, the musical imagination "enjoys conscious sensuousness in the sounding shapes, the self-constructing tones, and dwells in free and immediate contemplation of them."[72]

Given Hanslick's considerable pains to rid musical philosophy of its representational delusions, it is a little surprising to learn that music can, "with its very own resources, represent most amply a certain range of ideas."[73] Since music moves tonally, its forms are quite capable of representing dynamic or kinetic qualities, such things as expansion and diminution, advancement and attenuation, acceleration and slowing. The shapes and motions of music are congruent to those of feeling. But congruence or similarity of shape cannot represent specific feelings, only the kinetic qualities of feeling in general. "Music has no other means of fulfilling its alleged purpose than the analogy between motion and the symbolism of the tones."[74] Music may represent the dynamic qualities of feeling, then, but not feelings as such.

Note Hanslick's assumption that the basis of representation is structural similarity or correspondence. On this view (sometimes called the 'copy' theory), the possession of similar attributes is what enables representation. So music's possession of dynamic formal qualities that resemble those of feeling make it representational, at least in a restricted sense. Yet music needs to represent qualities it has no more than the rose must represent fragrance, and as we have seen, Hanslick was resolutely unwilling to concede the latter. Furthermore, if possessing a quality were enough to establish representation, Hanslick would need to concede that music potentially represents not only the dynamic qualities of feeling, but of any and all moving things. Still more troubling, if this principle of imitation or structural similarity indeed obtained, not only would music represent feeling (and other moving things), feeling (and other moving things) would represent music—a proposition seriously entertained by no one.

Thus, Hanslick's attribution of limited representational capacity to music, one that is at odds with his staunchly autonomist position, is a concession he need not necessarily have made. But in any event, this designative or referential capacity is something he apparently regards as rather indirect and incidental—not sufficiently significant to implicate feeling in judgments of musical beauty. This abstract relationship does, however, help to explain and justify the judicious metaphorical use of 'feeling' terms in musical description. Hanslick does not seriously intend that musical experience or descriptive language be strictly clinical, analytical, and cerebral. The use of emotion words is perfectly legitimate so long as their fundamentally metaphorical nature is recognized. Music can connote certain aspects of feeling, but does not denote feelings. Music may suggest "varying accompanying adjectives," says Hanslick, but never des-

ignate substantives.[75] Apparently then, expressive language may be useful and even necessary in descriptions of music. "But this feeling, which in fact to a greater or lesser degree unites itself with pure contemplation, can only be regarded as artistic," according to Hanslick, "when it remains aware of its aesthetic origin, i.e., the pleasure in just this one particular beauty."[76] Given this, it is clear that Hanslick's pronouncements about the aesthetic irrelevance of feeling were not intended to be utterly absolute and unqualified.

Still, conceding the musical legitimacy of feeling that 'unites itself with pure contemplation' is hardly an unqualified endorsement of feeling. It allows for only a limited range of felt pleasure, evidence for which Hanslick finds in the differences between the importance accorded feeling by musicians and non-musicians. Musical novices are most likely to 'feel' music, he says, and artists least likely. The former tend to ask whether a piece is cheerful or sad, while the latter are far more concerned with whether it is good or bad.[77] The properly musical listener attends to what is distinctive and self-subsistent in the work, finding "its similar or dissimilar impressions upon the feelings to be of trifling significance."[78] In the properly contemplative stance, then, music's individuality and particularity predominate. Imagination is engaged by its tonally moving object to an extent that "paralyses music's elemental influence."[79] Not feeling, but contemplation is what music appropriately engages: "[C]ontemplative hearing is the only artistic, true form; the raw emotion of savages and the gushing of the music enthusiast can be lumped together in a single category contrary to it. To the beautiful corresponds an enjoying, not an undergoing. . . ."[80] The "worthiest, the wholesomest . . . manner of listening to music" is one in which one takes pleasure primarily in "one's own mental alertness."[81]

What precisely is this contemplative pleasure, this feeling not quite feeling, this imaginative experience that so enriches experience yet apparently eludes so many? "It is the mental satisfaction which the listener finds in continuously following and anticipating the composer's designs, here to be confirmed in his expectations, there to be agreeably led astray."[82] As Weitz summarizes, ". . . listening to music ought to be a painstaking attending to the unfolding of the tonal combinations, much more an intellectual and an imaginative procedure than an emotional one. The enjoyment or disappointment derived from understanding the progression of sounds are the only legitimate emotional accompaniments of proper musical response."[83]

This process of 'mental streaming' directed by a musical 'object', present in high degree in musical perceivers but largely lacking in others, is the foundation of the theory Meyer develops a century later. It is the sense in which music is most often held to mean nothing but itself. Music consists, Hanslick insisted, of tonally moving forms. These forms are music's only true content. "[M]usic speaks not merely by means of tones, it speaks only tones,"[84] proof of which can be readily seen in the fact that the only reliable way to indicate specifically music's content is to sing or play it.[85] This is precisely where musical beauty departs from all other kinds of beauty: its form and content comprise a profoundly inseparable unity. It has no subject matter apart from its tonally moving forms. It means nothing and yet it is meaningful. For its content, its subject matter, and its meaning are wholly, specifically, and only musical.

Conclusions

Hanslick's combative little treatise is no philosophical masterpiece, but of course it was never intended to be. Although it sparked heated and continuous controversy throughout his life, Hanslick never bothered to revise it, devoting his time instead to music and music criticism. Whatever their difficulties, his claims about the relationship of music to feeling are directly and forcefully articulated. The same cannot be said, however, for the beliefs and assumptions that frame his arguments. His assumptions about what musical aesthetics should be, what it means to be 'scientific', and about the nature of 'subjectivity' and 'objectivity' orient his thought in important but implicit ways. Hanslick accepts without reservation the idealistic dichotomy between subjectivity and objectivity, as well as the notion that science is utterly objective, and any 'nonscientific' residue strictly subjective. Because sciences deal in objective truth, no self-respecting musical science can ever allow that musical beauty relates in any significant way to subjective feeling states. Musical beauty is an objective, public thing, while feeling is personal and private. If musical aesthetics aspires to anything like scientific status, as Hanslick clearly believes it must, it has little choice but to renounce feeling. Beauty is something music has, feelings are not. Music does not feel, people do. "Scientific investigation," writes Hanslick, "should never ascribe to or presuppose of music any other concept than the aesthetical, unless we abandon all hope of ever establishing this tenuous science on a firm basis."[86]

But what kind of 'aesthetical' concept do these assumptions privilege? Obviously, one in which music is tainted by association with anything other than its own tonally moving forms, and one to which anything that threatens to break music's contemplative spell or disrupt perceptual vigilance is inimical. Hanslick's commitment to musical autonomy has deep roots in dualistic thought that pervade virtually every aspect of his aesthetic theory. He accepts a set of opposed polarities (outer/inner, control/indulgence, intellect/sensuality, artistic/primitive, contemplative/mundane, human/animal) whose nature makes the renunciation of feeling virtually a foregone conclusion.

This conception of musical beauty relegates to the status of primitivity or sub-musicality a great deal of music and musical experience that is neither primitive nor submusical. At the same time, it privileges and confers the highest status to musics of a particular kind. If 'pure contemplation' is the archetypal musical activity, it requires music that is well suited to sustaining that contemplative attitude: music that is orderly and well behaved, music that foregoes all relations to other things, music whose formal integrity is unimpeachable. Not surprisingly, the musical achievements Hanslick regards as most exalted, whose tonally moving forms have musical beauty to the highest degree, are those of the Western tonal tradition from Mozart to Brahms. Musics that violate the principle of tonal congruity are deemed inferior, as are those that violate tonal primacy by catering to baser, more bodily effects (rhythm and timbre, for instance) or abdicate their

autonomy for nonmusical ends. Accordingly, the music of South Sea islanders should not really be regarded as music at all, but only as unintelligible "wailing" accompanied by rhythmic "banging" on "bits of metal and wooden staves."[87] And a charming Strauss waltz ceases to be music the moment it is used for dancing.[88]

Another manifestation of Hanslick's idealism and dualism is a determined distinction between musical beauty and common, everyday experience. To remain wholly and specifically musical, music's pleasure must stand in marked contrast to the pleasures associated with the quotidian world. However, his insistence that the feelings associated with musical beauty are wholly unlike any other seems to remove music to a rarefied realm uninhabited by normal human beings. It is tempting, then, to characterize Hanslick as an elitist whose lofty conception of musical experience is inaccessible to any but a chosen few; and his indiscriminately contemptuous tone does little to alleviate that impression. Yet, it is important to bear in mind that his 'tonally moving forms' and the 'otherworldly stirrings' they awaken are there for all to perceive, if they will only assume the proper (contemplative) stance toward music. Hanslick's considerable disdain for musical 'enthusiasts' does not appear to stem from their incapacity but from their disinclination to listen musically. And his contempt is directed less to the average person than to the philosopher, the critic, and the composer: people who should know better yet persist in deluding an unsuspecting public with their ill-conceived theories.

Whatever the shortcomings of Hanslick's arguments, his fundamental conviction that not just anything constitutes musical beauty was on the mark. His insistence upon a more substantial basis for musical judgments than personal likes and preferences, and his determination to situate music at the center of musical experience and discourse, are likewise laudable. Hanslick makes a compelling case for a concrete perceptual focus in musical experience at the same time he seeks to articulate a middle ground between reductions of music to crass sensation and the vaporous extravagances of idealistic metaphysics.

Hanslick also draws distinctions, albeit rudimentary ones, among various ways feeling is often held to relate to music: as arousal, as representation, as expression. Though acutely sensitive to music's felt nature, and though willing to concede music's capacity to represent certain aspects of felt experience, he is insistent that designating or expressing particular feelings is quite beyond music's powers. Emotion-talk, then, is convenient and economical, a kind of metaphorical shorthand which, taken literally, leads to unfortunate confusion between purely musical and extramusical feeling. Hanslick never seriously questions music's capacity to arouse feeling, only the musical significance of feelings so aroused. He does not suggest that feeling never accompanies musical experience. What he insists, however, is that feeling not lure people away from the audible patterns of tonal motion that are the source of genuinely musical pleasure and the essence of musical beauty. Whatever is felt in the musical experience must have music as its object. On this Hanslick is always perfectly clear. And the best way to assure this, he seems to have been convinced, is to insist that feeling is altogether beside the point in the experience of music.

Hanslick's fundamental preoccupation was to demarcate a domain of beauty that was music's and music's alone. The uniqueness of music could not be accounted for, he believed, in theories that presume to conflate musical beauty with natural beauty or even with that of other so-called arts. The autonomy of which he thought music capable illustrated a degree of independence unparalleled by any other product of human endeavor. Such independence entailed an entirely intrinsic beauty, exemplified, he believed, in the 'absolute' music of his day. Hanslick was consumed by the desire to substantiate music's autonomy, even while he accepted the assumption that it had (somehow) to have a 'content', something it was 'about'. Since its value could not be a function of its relation to anything but itself, he concluded, music had to be 'about' itself. Its content was its form. But this entirely self-subsistent musical beauty, dependent for its existence on nothing but itself, more often appears in Hanslick's treatment as 'freedom from' than 'freedom to', leaving the unfortunate impression that music is not only autonomous, but utterly insular.

The quest for the inherently and uniquely musical led Hanslick to locate musical beauty in tonally moving forms, the sonorous unfolding of music's tonal configurations, and the pleasure of anticipating and following music's designs "here to be confirmed in [one's] expectations, there to be agreeably led astray."[89] His 'forms' were not empty abstractions, but concrete, vital, and moving, and the experience they engendered was rich and stirring.

However, it is one thing to hold that, in certain musics, there is a range of musical meanings and values that inhere in internal relationships, and quite another to insist that this range is the only valid one, rejecting all other meanings and values as spurious and trivial. Hanslick begins with an essentially positive declaration that music has beauty, meaning, and value all its own, but proceeds to buttress that claim by renouncing music's linkage with anything outside itself, feeling in particular. His claims of music's utter and complete autonomy are only forcefully asserted, not demonstrated—for the simple reason that the idea of purely intrinsic or inherent value cannot be sustained. Thus, as Scruton has charged, Hanslick's characterization of music as an 'absolute' art is "as unwarranted as the theories which he used it to attack."[90]

Despite large gaps in his arguments and an extraordinarily polemical tone, Hanslick remains one of the most influential voices in the history of musical philosophy. The intemperateness of his arguments creates philosophical difficulties, but the entertainment it affords is also an important factor in his enduring notoriety. It is the positive message behind his caustic denunciations that is Hanslick's primary philosophical legacy, however. Historical perspective shows clearly that Hanslick's arguments opened important new conceptual territory, however crudely they may have charted it. Subsequent exploration of this territory was taken up by Edmund Gurney, who approached the task with determination, tenacity, and—unlike Hanslick—patience.

Gurney: The Power of Sound

Twenty-six years after Hanslick's treatise was first published, Edmund Gurney published *The Power of Sound*, a book in which he outlined his own influential formalist conception of music. Despite the care and cogency of his work—

or perhaps because of it—his project never attained anything approaching the notoriety of Hanslick's polemical little book. Yet, the questions he posed and the manner in which he set about answering them are very much in the spirit of modern philosophy, and many of his observations and insights are as illuminating today as they must have been in 1880. Like Hanslick, Gurney set out to show what was distinctive about musical beauty. In a sense, though, he took that project a step further: for where Hanslick had argued that musical beauty was unlike beauties given to other senses, Gurney insisted that music was in important ways unlike even the experience of sound. So wholly unique is musical beauty, in his view, that a special faculty of mind is required to gauge its rightness. A more apt title might thus have been *The Power of Music*, since music does not share its definitive 'ideal motion' even with sound. Musical beauty defies all explanation and necessarily eludes attempts to account for it by general principle: any such principle one might propose, Gurney ingeniously demonstrates again and again, can as easily generate trivial melodies as beautiful ones.

Higher and Lower Senses

Gurney begins his philosophical project with a distinction between 'lower' and 'higher' senses. The higher senses, vision and hearing, differ from lower senses like taste and smell in their capacity for perception of form. They can discriminate discrete units that in turn enable combination and coordination into larger patterns, configurations, and structures. Ear and eye far surpass the "slow-acting and rest-needing" lower senses[91] both in this relational, constructive capacity, and in the speed and voraciousness with which they execute it. Not only do higher senses make fine, complex discriminations of which lower senses are incapable, they further engage in a kind of formal, combinatory play that makes purely sensual activity an exceedingly rare occurrence for eye and ear. Thus, the higher senses have the power to group and combine sensa, an apparently inherent need to do so, and are distinctive for the pleasure they take in perceiving form.

There exist two quite different kinds of human perceptual experience, according to Gurney. What he calls 'character discrimination' is qualitative in nature—the detection of differences in intensity. 'Position discrimination', on the other hand, involves spatial or temporal location. While lower senses are restricted to qualitative (character) discriminations, higher senses discriminate both character and position. Since eye and ear engage in perception that is at once qualitative and quantitative, they are higher, more comprehensive, more mindful. They take in qualitative attributes like color and timbre, but also pattern and form. Such formal perception yields impressions that are "wholly unique"[92] because they draw upon both feeling and intellect.

Beyond this common capacity to discern discrete elements and subtle relations, eye and ear differ a great deal. In practical everyday use, eye's relational and constructive capacities probably exceed the ear's, because vision begets distinct, external objects, whereas sounds "present no certain group having the character of an object."[93] Sounds are one thing, however, and music another. For when sounds are given form as music, they leave the realm of mere sense for the higher realm of beauty. "The world of Beauty," Gurney pronounces, "is pre-eminently the world of Form."[94]

There is a crucial difference, then, between the "simple and unformed sense-impressions"[95] of nonmusical auditory experience and the experience of musical beauty. Music consists of distinct and differentiated pitches and rhythms not present in the natural soundscape, and musical listening therefore consists of much more than mere auditory acuity. Necessary though such acuity may be, it is not sufficient to musical perception. Only when hearing extends beyond "unformed sound" to concern itself with form does it encounter true beauty.[96] Form is the eye's everyday concern, but the ear encounters beauty only in musical form. Everyday visual experience and the perception of visual beauty are both formal in nature, whereas the perception of sound and of music are so different that they demand wholly different ways of attending. People listen to sound with primary concern for its non-sonorous implications; they listen to music in total disregard for anything but the "otherwise unimaginable world" presented in its patterns.[97]

Representational and Presentational Art

Gurney postulates two basic categories of art: arts of representation and of presentation. In the representational arts of poetry, sculpture, and painting, the subject matter "exists externally to and independently of" the work itself.[98] Since what they are about lies outside the work, their form is, though not dictated by it, "implied in" that subject matter. Since the subject matter of presentational art, of architecture and of music, is not external to the work as such, its forms are not constrained by imitative or representational obligation. In other words, representational arts convey or portray a subject matter, while presentational arts constitute it.[99] The content of presentational arts is, as Hanslick said, their form: what they are 'about' is internal properties and configurations.

Because of their inherent abstractness, then, the presentational arts of architecture and music have greater autonomy from the everyday world than do poetry, sculpture, or painting. But there are crucial distinctions between the two presentational arts as well. Architecture's subject matter is "visible forms and arrangements of form," and its basic aims are utilitarian. Although its forms consist of "abstract lines and surfaces and their proportional arrangements,"[100] these configurations serve an external purpose. In contrast, music's subject matter is "auditory forms, i.e. series and combinations of sounds, wholly independent both of external phenomena and external utility, and having no existence independent of art."[101] Music's 'auditory forms' exist nowhere but the world of music. And even sound, in and of itself, is not properly speaking the material from which music is constructed. Rather, music is built from a "system of notes."[102] Music's subject matter is auditory forms. Its raw material is a system of notes. And its form is comprised of "abstract proportions of time and pitch."[103] Therefore, concludes Gurney, neither music nor any of its constituent elements exist anywhere but in musical activity.

In Gurney's theory, then, music is wholly unique and autonomous. Like Hanslick, he grants that the ascription of external subject matter (textual meanings, for instance, or feelings) is "convenient" and "natural." But it is nonetheless a "fatal" mistake. Texts and feelings are only things with which music is sometimes associated. Verbal descriptions of a piece's musical content may seriously mislead, because music does not have 'subject matter', it has musical 'subjects'. What titles and verbal descriptions designate is "strictly and essentially the subject of the words, and only loosely and accidentally the subject of the music."[104] Asked to guess a title for an unknown piece, Gurney suggests, "a hundred auditors . . . would originate a hundred new ones."[105] As Hanslick urged, the only way to refer with precision to music's subject matter is to sing or play it.

Musical and Visual Forms

Despite their 'presentational' kinship, the relation of architecture, a visual art, to music, an auditory one, is "chiefly one of contrast." "The saying that 'Architecture is frozen Music', is, for all its prettiness, exceptionally misleading."[106] Comparisons between music and visual art are facile and pernicious. Music, 'abstract form addressed to the ear', is wholly unique, something to which visual terms apply in only the most indirect metaphorical way. Characterizing musical beauty in terms of 'symmetry', 'line', 'mass', or 'color', for instance, has considerable potential for distortion, since what these terms mean in musical contexts is profoundly different from what they mean visually. Visual metaphors are convenient, but seriously misrepresent the facts of musical experience. Even the concept of harmony has quite limited applicability to music, since it purports to describe notes in simultaneous combination with one another, and simultaneity, according to Gurney, is the distinctive feature of visual rather than musical experience. It is, simply, "Melody or notes in succession, which is the prime and essential element in Music."[107] And there is no visual analog to melody, Gurney declares. 'Line' comes close, perhaps; yet visual line has none of melody's moment-by-moment transience. Nor does it have melody's distinctive emotional coloration. Visual line has a continuous, unbroken quality, whereas each "note-unit" in a melody "has definite relations of time and pitch to its neighbours," such that a "proportional element indubitably enters at every single note."[108] Melodic line, unlike visual line, is notable for the proportional arrangements and relationships among its constituent components (notes). And melody is a fundamentally processual phenomenon with none of visual line's characteristic "simultaneity," its "impression of conspiring parts all there at once."[109]

Another striking contrast between visual and musical line is melody's resistance to alteration. Given a tune "on which the mind has dwelt with pleasure, any conceivable change will be resented"[110] as an intrusion or disfiguration. The reason, Gurney believes, is that melodic form has a greater "definiteness"[111] than visual form. Melody has a temporal urgency or immediacy quite unlike the perception of visual line wherein the eye "wanders at its own pace over the parts of objects."[112] And finally, in contrast to visual line, melodic line is comprised of discrete pitches, each with its own intonational requirements. The musical ear shares very little of the eye's characteristic latitude.

It follows from the particularity or individuality of musical (melodic) forms "that they present nothing analogous to an outline or skeleton of lines, capable of being presented or imagined alone,"[113] except their sonorous and temporal particularity. Even the idea of melodic contour fails to capture the essential "proportional relationships" among successive parts of melody, and neglects the fact that in a genuinely beautiful melody no pitch can be less important than another. Representing a melody by its supposedly essential notes, Gurney asserts, gives one "not an imperfect notion, but no notion of the actual form,"[114] just as giving a face a new nose makes "not so much a new nose as a new face."[115]

In visual forms, parts are subordinate to wholes. In musical forms, on the contrary, the parts are "more important and primary than the whole; for the whole being a combination of parts successively (and many of them to a great extent independently) enjoyed, can only be impressive so far as the parts are impressive; and the impressiveness can only be perceived by focussing the attention on each of the parts in turn. . . ."[116] Music exists, then, more as a constellation of local, individual effects than is typically true of the visible world. There is no musical whole apart from passage through each successive part of the melodic surface. So what is mere ornamentation in visual form is essence in music, as one's hearing "is concentrated on the special bit of form then and there passing . . ."[117] Melodic forms do not owe their beauty to their place in a larger whole. "[T]here are no necessities and conditions external to the essential nature of [music] itself, whose forms in their free progress know no control save 'Duty/To the law of their own beauty'."[118]

Obviously, Gurney's conception of music's form differs significantly from the architectonic sense, the sense in which 'rondo' or 'sonata' are forms. Pieces that share common 'form' in this sense have kinship of only "the most external and nominal kind."[119] This 'form' is an abstract, skeletal affair that "has no beauty or meaning for us, no ideal place in our imagination. . . . little essential connection with the individual beauty of the forms which it embraces and unites."[120] Whether a piece is a rondo or minuet has little to do with its beauty. In fact, these are not "distinct concrete forms at all . . . but only certain abstract conditions for introducing and making the most of [genuinely musical] forms."[121] The architectonic sense of 'form' implies something durable and temporally transcendent, whereas music "makes only occasional and temporary appearances on the earth, and builds there no permanent habitations or temples; being literally the 'queen of the air'."[122]

Of the 'motions' which figured centrally in Hanslick's account, Gurney is rather cautious. A term imported from the spatial realm, 'motion' is rather an awkward fit to music: neither music's resemblances to physical motion nor its "impulse to move"[123] can account for melodic beauty—its force perhaps, or its power, but not its beauty. More strongly yet, "physical movement is not a characteristic of the differentiated senses at all, and à fortiori not of the two preeminently artistic senses."[124] Music can and does suggest some features of motion outside ourselves, "motion of the sort that we realise by seeing."[125] Only, sound "does not give us a picture of events, but only leads us to infer they are happening: our true channel for knowledge of the outside world . . . is sight, not hearing."[126] Music's motion, then, is not literal or physical, but strictly musical. Music has "powerful though vague and remote"[127] associations with visually perceived physical motion, but in it "no material object or event is in the dimmest way represented (unless it be through conscious subjective fancy)."[128] Music can capture or present only a very limited range of motion's aspects.

Thus, Gurney ultimately insists, describing musical beauty with visual terminology or its objective correlates is a "ludicrous" practice.[129] Liking a melody, he claims, is no more explicable than enjoying sugar.[130] But while they are both inexplicable, musical pleasure and sugary sweetness are strikingly different kinds of pleasure: in contrast to thinking about the taste of sugar, going over a beautiful melody in one's mind is itself a pleasant experience. Musical experience partakes of both mind and sense, and so, is 'ideal'.

Ideal Motion

Gurney's musical form is unlike any other, one with pleasures and satisfactions all its own. It is not imitative, not representative, and has no supernatural link to a noumenal world. It is simply a phenomenal presentation. Unlike visual pattern, music is processual, temporal, "perceived by continuous advance."[131] It 'moves', then, but in a sense wholly unlike physical motion. Musical forms, concludes Gurney, "cannot be abstracted from the continuous process by which alone we perceive them, or rather which constitutes our perception of them. I can think of no better term to express this unique musical process than Ideal Motion."[132]

Gurney is aware that this phrase Ideal Motion has tremendous potential for misinterpretation. He intends 'ideal' in only a special and limited sense, and he means by motion something very unlike the motion that occurs outside music. Ideal motion is "an absolutely unique beauty perceived by an absolutely unique faculty," having "no parallel outside Music,"[133] and whose contrast with physical motion is striking. Since any comparison must amount by definition to a distortion, Gurney's self-imposed task is no less than describing the indescribable. But rather than attempt the impossible, Gurney resorts to another strategy—by revealing the spuriousness of all possible analogies or comparisons, the possibility for any but a wholly unique musical motion is systematically eliminated. Music moves, but temporally rather than spatially. Both its form and its motion are manifestations of mind, and are, to that extent, 'ideal'.

In developing his claim to music's utter uniqueness, Gurney turns first to its materials, insisting that music can never be reduced to anything existing outside the musical realm. Sound—even pitched or rhythmic sound—extends pleasure of only "a rudimentary kind, insusceptible of large variety or of development."[134] Musical form is melodic form, and melody cannot be reduce to either its linear (spatial) or rhythmic (temporal) components. It consists, rather, in an 'indissoluble union' of rhythm and pitch.[135] It is the "resultant of two quite different proportional series," "the product of two lines of perfectly heterogeneous impressions, each empty and insignificant alone," yet "absolutely interpenetrative" when melodically integrated.[136] Melodic form cannot survive dismemberment into pitched or rhythmic components.

As evidence of the inability of rhythm to account for musical beauty, Gurney points out that both captivating and utterly trivial melodies can share the same rhythmic structure. Nor, he continues, is melodic beauty possible without the distinctive vitality contributed by rhythm. It is profoundly shortsighted, then, to construe pitch or rhythm as "framework[s] or mould[s] to be separately appraised . . . [or] for the meaning to be poured into . . ."[137] or as ". . . a set of suitable mechanical pegs for hanging the form out on. . . ." They are not containers or supports for musical/melodic form: rather, together they *constitute* it, ". . . just as 5 multiplied by 6 constitutes 30."[138]

Changing the rhythm of a beautiful melody is as destructive of its beauty as substituting different pitches. The melodic union of rhythm and pitch is indispensable to the ear's "cardinal expectations," to music's capacity for "getting into the blood and clinging to the memory."[139] In music that is truly beautiful, "this definiteness of time is . . . as truly essential as variety of pitch . . . [W]ithout it a prolonged succession of the most beautiful sounds is no more melody than a block of Parian marble is a statue."[140] "[I]n all impressive melodic form the rhythm is not something superposed, or more or less consciously suggested or referred to, but is essentially there."[141] Rhythm is no pleasant but dispensable musical option, but an utterly essential component of ideal motion. Harmony is another matter, however. Despite the support its patterns of consonance and dissonance lend to ideal motion, harmony is not essential. Rhythm is more primal, with roots that extend deeply into human instinct. Without rhythm, music would appeal only to an elite few with "peculiar exquisiteness of sensibility."[142] It is rhythm's primacy, believes Gurney, that accounts for musical sensibility being so widespread. Because music is conceivable without harmony but not without rhythm, harmony is a secondary trait.

The indissoluble union of pitch and rhythm in music begets, as we have seen, a uniquely musical phenomenon that neither requires nor admits any content outside itself. And importantly, it moves, although its motion is one in which nothing moves physically—an ideal motion. Gurney's cautions against the temptation to regard form and motion as different things, for in ideal motion they are one. Music's motion is ideal not in the sense of being a distillation or idealization of something already known—an "idealised quintessence" of physical motion, for instance—but rather in the sense of "yielding a form." "The common use of the term idea, in relation to Music, to express some special bit of striking form is thus entirely accurate," says Gurney, "in spite of the extraordinary bungling to which it often leads, as though the idea were one thing and the music another."[143] In a musical idea, idea, form, and motion are one, and ideal motion's significance is entirely exhausted in that union.

Gurney's description of the process by which people follow ideal motion's continuous advance is so vivid it warrants quotation at length. Musical form presses forward, he says, "through a sweetly yielding resistance to a gradually foreseen climax; whence again fresh expectation is bred, perhaps for another excursion . . . round the same centre but with a bolder and freer sweep, perhaps for a fresh differentiation whereof in turn the tendency is surmised and followed, to a point where again the motive is suspended on another temporary goal; till after a certain number of such involutions and evolutions, and of delicately poised leanings and reluctances and yieldings . . . the sense of potential and coming integration which has underlain all our provisional adjustments of expectation is triumphantly justified."[144] The notions of anticipating the tendencies of musical form, of delighting in excursions and returns, presages in important ways the ideas of Meyer that we will examine shortly.

Also distinctive to melodic form, to ideal motion, is the way it creates a "sense of entire oneness with it, of its being . . . a mode of our own life."[145] It has objective character to the extent "we instinctively recognise that it has for others the same permanent possibilities of impression as for ourselves," and yet its experience is not that of an external, objective presence so much as "something evolved within ourselves by a special activity of our own."[146] Thus, the experience of music is at once objective and subjective: an experience in which body and spirit, the corporeal and the incorporeal, achieve unity.

Necessary though ideal motion is to an adequate account of musical beauty, it is not sufficient. It does not determine and cannot assure beauty. Motion can no more account for musical beauty, Gurney cautions, than the possession of a nose and a mouth and two eyes can account for the beauty of a face.[147] Sensitivity to motion does not enhance appreciation of the "differentia" or "unique proportions" crucial to musical beauty,[148] nor is the amount of motion an indication of musical greatness. Though necessary, ideal motion does not guarantee or constitute musical beauty.

Finally, ideal motion is "progressive": it is a form that creates a sense of continuous anticipation and expectation. Like speech, which shares its auditory-temporal character, it has the sense "of being *something said*, an utterance of imperative significance."[149] Yet, for all its similarities to other things, music's forms "so far as they are impressive, are each new and unique things, not like new expressions or postures, or alterations and reminiscences, of known things: each fresh melodic presentation which is profoundly felt is felt as till then wholly unknown."[150] So completely irreducible is music to any of its constituent aspects, feels Gurney, and so utterly distinct is music from any other experiential domain, that it can only be the achievement of a "uniquely isolated faculty, whose decisions can no more be justified than they can be impugned by any law or from any standpoint external to the impression in each case."[151] Not only is music unique, but each particular piece is unique as well. Judgments of musical beauty, therefore, are inexplicable in any but musical terms—in terms of anything but the rightness or impressiveness of a particular musical presence.

Music's Essential Form

From all that has been said thus far, it is evident that ideal motion is the kind of affair that cannot be brought under any set of general rules. In fact, argues

Gurney, any rules one might propose can as easily generate "weak," "twaddling," or "dreary" melodies as beautiful ones. One must not turn to general formal structures for an understanding of music, but rather to the musical foreground: the way each successive "bit" enters into "organic union with the one next to it"[152] with an air of "divinely ordained necessity."[153] Musical beauty is a function of melody's "cogency of sequence at each point."[154] There exists a kind of 'relational' beauty, in the ingenuity of music's relation to stylistic conventions, or the way an individual piece plays with familiar configurations, for instance. But musical beauty consists more essentially in particular episodes or motives, in "actual bits of form which moment after moment engross the ear."[155] Such beauty is not relational but wholly self-subsistent. It consists in "complete unities ... tested by the ear's strongly and instinctively resenting any change or omission."[156] Abstract structural configurations do not bear the sense of "strictly vital independence" so crucial to musical beauty. Truly essential form is to be found in the intimate bond between a note and its neighbors in the "moment when we are thinking through the form," not in some abstract resemblance to "further parts of the chain."[157] Music's temporal, processual nature demands that formal priority be given to the unfolding foreground. "The scheme," in short, "has no value apart from the bits."[158]

Music's essential form, then, entails the "entire mutual interdependence of elements,"[159] a principle of "close coherence at a very large number of points."[160] It is to be found in successions of notes "as they turn up moment after moment, throughout any piece of music which is keenly ... enjoyed."[161] It is only in "enjoyment of the parts, one after another, that [the] quality of close and vital organism takes effect. . . . [and] the whole has no meaning except as expressing the sum of our enjoyments from moment to moment; a sum which will be increased in proportion as the organic principle pervades the whole."[162] This organic interdependence of successive parts in cogent musical ideas is the essence of musical beauty; and it is most compellingly evident in melody, when each and every note necessitates the other. Extended sections draw on this sense for their beauty, though they manifest it more diffusely; and on the broadest, most extended level, formal descriptions become no more than barren generalities, devoid of beauty and vitality. Architectonic formal descriptions are as applicable to the dreary as the beautiful, as descriptive of the dead as the living.[163]

Wherever music's forms "present recurrences and imitations and variations and amplifications ... they still do this by dint of being just what they are, note after note, bar after bar, not by dint of carrying out any pre-existent or separable 'design'."[164] Beethoven's genius, then, lay not in his capacity to conceive 'grand schemes', but rather in "the extraordinary manner in which one bit of form acted in his mind as a germ for new but related forms."[165] Because the structure of a piece has neither meaning nor value apart from the 'bits' from which it is created, music's essential form is not something supported by its parts or 'bits' — rather, it resides in them and in the way they cohere. "The strictly essential 'proportions' in Music are none other than those of time and pitch,"[166] features whose beauty is their sole reason for being. Therefore, the further descriptions of music stray from these essential temporal/tonal relationships, the more uninstructive and misleading they become. Musical beauty has cogency, a sense of divinely ordained necessity in each passing moment. It can be described but never explained. Musical considerations like repetition, contrast, melodic contour, modulation, or rhythmic pace and force can be found in "wretched" pieces as often as masterful ones: they can never account for "the sustained beauty and individuality of essential form."[167]

Clearly, Gurney's stress on the individuality of musical beauty makes it highly particularistic: for not only is musical beauty unlike other beauty, the beauty of any given piece a beauty all its own. It requires "motives of individuality," such that "of music more truly than of anything else may we say with Bacon 'there is no excellent Beauty that hath not some strangenesse in the proportion'."[168] The beautiful melody is one that has "some special rarity in the Ideal Motion, any substitute for which seems banal and charmless."[169] One thing and one thing alone can render a musical composition more beautiful: "new and beautiful themes."[170]

But beautiful melodies cannot be conjured up at will, or derived rationally, by formula. The intuitive, sensory character of mind's musical faculty keeps it on a "much shorter tether than the free intellectual faculty."[171] When intellect oversteps the bounds of musicality, the result is "a loss of feeling for true unity and sequence of development" in which melody is reduced to "complicated patterns and ingenious mazes," or worse yet "a formless chaos of flying fragments."[172] Rather than being "centres of growth," melodies become mere "parts of a medley."[173] Music that substitutes rational complexity for musically "impressive themes" fails to attain "noble and loving development" or indeed anything "sufficiently arresting to be particularly worth remembering."[174] Intellect begets "uninspired ingenuity, which may produce a thousand series of showy fragments, but never a single piece of first-class form."[175] Beautiful melodies are not so much rational accomplishments as rare and precious "jewels . . . which must often be long and diligently searched for."[176] So intellectual rules and general principles are no substitute for the musical faculty's distinctive sense of rightness or cogency. Music that ignores that faculty's intuitions risks losing "the popular element which is the mainstay of its existence, and . . . becom[ing] the ingenious amusement of a clique."[177] The acceptance of "strange and cloying sequences of tone in place of definitely organic and apprehensible form," says Gurney, betrays a "feverish craving for novelties which is a sure sign of disease."[178] Fortunately, however, mind's musical faculty is instinctive enough that "the musical perceptions of the majority are incapable of being permanently warped."[179]

The Primacy of Form

Gurney's effort to delineate the centrality of form to music necessitates, in his view, a further distinction between music's primary (formal) attributes and those that are secondary: in particular, its tone-color or timbre. This contrast between primary and secondary musical parameters was anticipated to some extent in his distinction between the higher and lower senses, where the prominence of mind was the deciding factor. While music answers to the higher sense of hearing, it consists of both ideal and sensory elements: a matter of some moment for Gurney's account. Not only is music's tone color separable from its form, "its distinction from musical form is absolute."[180] Color is a quality that musical tone has secondarily, not fundamentally: more what it 'has' than 'is'.

As Gurney sees it, qualitative discrimination is primarily a sensual matter, whereas formal perception—discernment of discrete degrees—is quantitative, a function of mind. It is, he says, "a law of our being that in the apprehension of form we find a sense of active grasp and self-realisation entirely distinct from sensuous enjoyment."[181] The fixed degrees and proportions essential to formal perception are "the individualising element[s] by which things are known and recognised."[182] Such fixed degrees and proportions are, however, wholly absent from timbral perception. The color qualities of music's sonorous material are "as entirely distinct from musical form, as the redness of a cherry is distinct from its spherical shape."[183]

It might seem, Gurney says, since "there is no means of presenting forms to the ear absolutely without timbre of some sort, that the colour-quality of musical forms would be less liable to be abstracted in the mind than that of visible forms."[184] But precisely the opposite is true. Timbre plays nowhere near the role in musical memory that color does in visual images: in fact, musical recall occurs "with perpetual elimination of distinct colour-qualities."[185] For that reason, people invariably seem to take greater pleasure humming or whistling a tune than in silently imagining it.[186]

Gurney finds further evidence of timbre's secondary status in the fact that timbres can be altered or substituted for one another without changing a piece's identity. "*God Save the Queen*," he reasons, "is *God Save the Queen* whether played on an organ or a Jew's-harp."[187] As well, a composer may write music without stipulating its instrumentation or timbre; but a composition devoid of form is unfathomable. If music's forms "are weak and empty," Gurney concludes, "no amount of attention to their coloured investiture will give them importance or individuality."[188] Attempting to compensate for formal deficiency with timbral color is a futile effort to "persuade men's ears that the garment is the reality."[189]

Since "the structure of an elaborate movement, with 'subjects' and 'workings out' and episodes and all the rest, is not always immediately obvious,"[190] people often first hear it in a fragmentary way. In such instances, a generalized, sensual response to music's secondary characteristics permits access until familiarity enables fully musical (formal) perception. It is perfectly understandable, thinks Gurney, that amateurs take relatively little satisfaction in a "single chance hearing" of a complex piece of music: perceiving essential form is more musically demanding than responding to sensory qualities. It is easy to marvel at "kaleidoscopic effects," to "be dazzled over the boundary, in Music so dangerously indefinite, between sense and nonsense."[191] Yet there is a profound difference between music and "finely-toned noise,"[192] a difference rooted in formal perception.

There are two different ways of hearing music, Gurney reasons. One, the 'definite' way, attends to individuality or particularity of what is heard. The 'indefinite' way of hearing is more vague and general, "involving merely the perception of successions of agreeably-toned and harmonious sound."[193] Since musical experience often involves both, Gurney is reluctant to call them musical and nonmusical; and yet, it is the case that many people who can neither sing nor recognize melodies "often derive extreme pleasure of a vague kind"[194] from music—particularly if it is rapid or forceful. In such experience, sound stimulates or soothes, acting "as a congenial background for . . . subjective trains of thought and emotion," such that "it is a matter of indifference what is being played or sung, as long as the volume of tone is full and the quality agreeable."[195] Indefinite hearing is predominantly sensual, and therefore inferior, following as it does from "the nearly universal nervous susceptibility to the effect of rich and powerful sound."[196]

In fairness, adds Gurney, the indefinite response to music is "rarely or never a matter of purely sensuous impression (like the quite unintelligent enjoyment of taste or smell)," because vaguely perceived though they may be, "tangible fragments" of musical form are always there.[197] Indefinite musical hearing is seldom as wholly formless as "a summer-evening or a dose of opium," concedes Gurney. But "whatever their value . . . such effects are obviously very indirect, quasi-accidental, and subjective; they are not the composer's message; they cannot be presented to the inward ear when the orchestra has vanished, and though combinable with perception of form they can never replace it."[198] Indefinite hearing cannot be refined or educated, and is clearly inferior to "the mode of hearing which follows and distinguishes the motives as they pass."[199] But this is not so much because of incapacity as insufficient opportunity. Indefinite hearing is not so much due to the average ear's inability to comprehend essential form as its inability to do so "at a glance."[200] Few people perceive the true individuality of music without benefit of repeated hearings. And even among those who hear definitely, "when once the element of individual form ceases to be definitely and engrossingly attended to, nothing is left to the account of less definite impression than so much moving and coloured sound."[201]

Musical Expression and Impression

Some kind of musical formalism almost invariably follows from convictions that music's value is distinctive and self-contained rather than referential or heteronomous. Gurney's account is notable for its success in keeping its positive points at the fore. And yet, like other formalists, Gurney has a negative thesis, the case against heteronomist or expressionist accounts of music. The main points of his argument are easily grasped: that expression is neither necessary nor sufficient to the ideal motion that is the locus of musical beauty; that music is a completely self-sufficient domain to which expression relates as subjective effect; and that there is a fundamental difference between what music 'is' and what it adventitiously resembles.

In elaborating his views on expression, Gurney first observes that people use the term 'express' in two subtle but decisively different ways. It is one thing to say that music is expressive—that it is expression-like—and quite another to say that music (or a composer, or a performer) expresses something. Expression in the latter sense is something music rarely achieves with any clarity; and while music may often be expressive (the former sense), that is not a matter of 'expression' as such. Expression proper necessarily "involves two things, one which is expressed by the other," observes Gurney.[202] Further, a thing is always restricted in its range of expression to "occasional attributes": it can never 'express' the essential attributes of its class.[203] To speak of something expressing its own essential attributes is a confused way of talking. A flower, for instance, does not express its beauty or its fragrance. These are qualities it has, essential parts of what it is.

Properly speaking, then, expression consists in a transitive relationship between two separate things. Accordingly, musical expression occurs "when a particular feeling in ourselves is identified with a particular character in a particular bit of music."[204] Since music cannot 'have' feelings, musical expression necessarily entails some relation between music and human feeling. Music can express things outside itself, but not its own qualities: things like speed or loudness. Music can also possess and display—though not 'express'—qualities like 'simplicity', which have nothing to do with a listener's 'feeling simple'.[205] The other meaning of 'express', the sense in which music is held to be expressive without expressing something definable, applies to musical experience in a manner somewhat different than is commonly assumed. 'Expressiveness' which does not implicate a distinct thing 'expressed' most often indicates a heightened sense of interest or arousal, as when people "call great music significant, or talk of its import . . . without being able . . . to connect these general terms with anything expressed or signified."[206]

There is an important difference, then, "between music which is expressive in the sense of definitely suggesting or inspiring images, ideas, qualities, or feelings belonging to the region of the known outside music,"[207] and music whose 'expressiveness' is held to be intransitive and intangible. The key to unraveling this philosophical knot lies in a distinction between music's *expressiveness* and its *impressiveness*. To be expressive, music must first be impressive: "no music is really expressive in any valuable way which does not also impress us as having the essential character of musical beauty."[208] However, to be impressive, music need not be expressive. Indeed, expression "is either absent or only slightly present in an immense amount of impressive music."[209] So it must be conceded that the expression of "describable images, qualities, or feelings, known in connection with other experiences, however frequent a characteristic of Music, makes up no inseparable or essential part of its function."[210] Impressive music may be expressive, but it need not be. Impressiveness is always a characteristic of beautiful music; expressiveness is not. When music gives rise to verbalization, the utterance is more apt to take the form "How beautiful!" or "How indescribable!" than to designate connections to other things. Moreover, the feelings associated with music most often defy articulation. They are complexes of feeling ("fused . . . as in the colours in a ray of white light")[211] that elude verbal description, and whose "essential magic seems to lie at an infinite distance behind them all."[212] By contrast, the music itself, the thing that actually impresses, has none of this sense of vagueness or "subjective jumble," being instead a "perfectly distinct object, productive (in a thousand minds it may be at once) of a perfectly distinct though unique and undefinable affection."[213] And where more focused perception yields a more distinct "affection," it is if anything less amenable to description. Nameable feelings are general things; musical affect is concrete, specific, particular, and unique to each presentation.

Because the emotions or feelings associated with musical impression are strictly unknown outside the musical realm, and because each presentation is wholly unique, they defy all description. Musical expression, on the other hand, necessarily involves identifiable connections between points in the musical form and extramusical emotional states. Yet, even where such expression occurs, it has nothing to do with musical beauty: ". . . a tune is no more constituted beautiful by an expression . . . than a face is."[214] Beauty and expression are distinct affairs, and the former does not require the latter. The common belief that beauty requires expression involves a logical lapse like this:

- Because individual pieces of music are often highly impressive, and

- Because some of these correspond to aspects of emotional experience,

- All music expresses extramusical emotional experience.[215]

The error is in mistaking an occasional occurrence for a universal one. But it is beyond the power of music's timbre, harmony, dynamics, meter, or mode to consistently elicit or express any nameable affection. And since music cannot 'express' characteristics it possesses (these being attributes it *has*), things like animation, agitation, and tranquillity are not things music, properly speaking, expresses. Furthermore, if the music is not first impressive, if, that is, its ideal motion "is not satisfactory or striking, no amount of accenting of its rhythmic outline will redeem its poverty, or make it seem expressive of any emotional quality."[216]

When a melody is said to express a yearning quality, then, "we are yearning, not for inexpressible things, but for the next note, or at all events for some foreseen [musical] point beyond."[217] Musical experience resembles expression in its "gesture and attitude of straining, of stretching out towards a thing,"[218] but what it typically strains or stretches toward are not events or mental states of an extramusical sort, but simply other musical occurrences whose inexplicability is simply a function of their purely musical nature. None of the supposed sources of musical expression (rhythm, mode, timbre, etc.) has any emotional or expressive capacity if the essential form is not first of all "musically delightful," nor can such elements convey to someone unfamiliar with a given melody "the slightest shadow of its rare and individual beauty."[219] One only needs to attempt to describe or catalogue the emotional states supposedly expressed by such features to become painfully aware "how transient and uncertain they often are; how little they sum up the substance of the thing which is actually delighting us."[220] "[I]n hundreds of the most emotional instrumental [pieces], the effect is rarely, even for so much as a few bars, the suggestion of a recognisable emotion, and is never essentially that, but rather like a revelation of self-evident and wholly untranslatable import."[221]

Expression proper, then, is "remote from the essential effects of Music."[222] And expression of the mysteriously intransitive type is perfectly explicable in purely musical terms, in terms of the "wholly untranslatable import" of music's essential form: it is not a matter of expression, but of being impressive. As Hanslick implied, then, it may be reasonable enough to resort to figurative description of musical effects so long as one remembers that such descriptions are not literally true. "In poor music," Gurney explains, "note after note and phrase after phrase seem to present themselves trivially and pointlessly; but in music we enjoy, as we progressively grasp the form, the sense of absolute possession, of oneness with it; the cogent and unalterable rightness of every step in our progress, may produce the most vivid impression of triumphal advance."[223] To say this music expresses triumph, though, is not quite right: for triumphal character is something the music has, not what it expresses. And whatever the feelings music arouses, one must "recognise that the particular sense of excitement belongs to a state of consciousness known only in the realisation of music, and not essentially referable to any mode or exhibition of feeling belonging to times when music is not being realised."[224]

The upshot of this is that "The definitely expressive element is far less constant and essential than is usually imagined," and that the essential effect of music lies not in expression, but in music's "independently impressive aspect."[225] This impressiveness stems from a beauty that is particular to every piece of music, that affords in every occurrence a "new source of otherwise unknown delight" as, in each experience, "our attention is centred on forms which are for us the unique inhabitants of a perfectly unique world."[226] "We can yearn, triumph, and so on in purely musical regions,"[227] concludes Gurney. "[T]here is a sense," he concedes, "in which Music may be truly considered a reflection of the inner life"; and yet, that sense is "most general and indefinite," very different from any "definable expression."[228] "[I]f the following and realising of music be regarded as itself one complete domain of inner life, we may then perceive that it is large and various enough, full enough of change and crisis and contrast, of expectation, memory, and comparison, of general forms of perception which have been employed in other connections by the same mind, for the course of musical experience . . . to present a dim affinity to the external course of emotional life. In this way we may feel, at the end of a musical movement, that we have been living an engrossing piece of life which . . . has certain qualities belonging to any series of full and changing emotions. . . ."[229]

But even granting the possibility that a musical passage's "successions of intensity and relaxation, the expectation perpetually bred and perpetually satisfied, the constant direction of the motion to new points, and constant evolution of part from part. . . . may project on the mind faint intangible images of extra-musical impulse and endeavor"[230]—and even granting it the occasional power to present truly "describable affinities"[231]—the fundamental fact remains that it is first and foremost musical. Music's "matchless structures stand out to the musical sense as unalterably right and coherent, and any one who musically appreciates them knows as much and can tell as little of their secret as Beethoven himself."[232] The manifold musical misconceptions to whose elimination Gurney's book is devoted "all point to the same figment of the necessary pre-existence of some extraneous and independent feeling or idea for which notes have to be found."[233] However striking the resemblance between musical impressions and extramusical emotion may at times be, the feeling one encounters in a given piece invariably bears a stronger resemblance to what one feels in other compositions by the same composer than anything else.[234] Since the musical 'faculty' is part of the same mind that mediates all human awareness and sentient experience, it is not surprising to find occasional "dim affinities" between the sense that mind finds in music and other life experience. But musical experience is a completely self-subsistent domain, and the emotions implicated by definite hearing are purely musical. Speculating over music's associations with other things may be pleasant and amusing, but it is "distinctly detrimental to the musical perception and education of many hearers to have this obvious stage of extraneous comparison to take refuge in."[235]

Conclusions

Although Kant and Gurney reached strikingly different conclusions about music, Gurney's debt to Kant's idealism is apparent in many aspects of his theory. His insistence upon the ultimate inexplicability of musical beauty can be traced to Kant's tenets of the conceptlessness of aesthetic judgments and reason's incapacity to account for them. His insistence upon the particularity of musical beauty likewise resonates with Kant's assertion that beauty embodies rules that cannot be articulated. Gurney's notion of a distinct musical 'faculty' of mind has certain affinities to the imaginative faculty Kant thought mediated aesthetic judgments. Gurney's characterization of music as an 'art of presentation' is strongly reminiscent of Kant's description of imagination as a 'faculty of presentation', and like Kant, he maintains that judgments of beauty are first and foremost functions of the capacity of such presentations to 'impress'. Gurney's 'beauty' is, like Kant's, a matter of taking pleasure in form rather than sensation, and his distinction between primary and secondary attributes is presaged by Kant's contrast between the agreeable and the beautiful.

Gurney's debts to Hanslick are conspicuous enough that they require little elaboration. Unlike Hanslick's, however, Gurney's rhetoric is even-handed and his assertions well-supported by musical examples. Both Gurney and Hanslick struggled to situate music between the untenable polarities of intellectual abstraction and sensual indulgence. Just as Hanslick located music between the 'logical' and the 'pathological', in the imaginative enjoyment of tonally moving forms, Gurney advanced his concept of 'ideal motion' as neither purely ideal nor physical, neither strictly rational nor strictly sensual. Like Hanslick, Gurney rejected claims to musical expression because of music's incapacity for definite representation. Both argued in their own ways that feeling is a secondary musical effect, more a response to music than what music is. Both maintained that music is not 'about' a subject matter, but that its content was its form; and that this 'form' was no mere abstract structure but a vital, moving thing. And finally, both believed that although the properly musical experience was more predominantly object than feeling focused, music implicated a range of feeling that was purely musical.

Admittedly, Gurney's account leaves many troublesome issues unresolved. His insistence that only pitched and rhythmic sound can be musical and his relegation of tone quality to secondary status severely narrow the range of potentially musical sonorous materials. His insistence that music's 'essential' form lies on the musical surface, in the organic unity created by note-to-note successions, neglects the formal role played by other musical parameters. Gurney needs a multifaceted scheme that more fully integrates his many perceptive insights, one that shows how multiple musical parameters interact rather than pitting one against the other in quest of the 'most essentially' musical. And finally, Gurney's relentless insistence upon the absolute uniqueness of music comes precipitously close to the kind of radical particularism that regards each piece's beauty as something utterly unique and wholly unrelated to any other—a state of affairs which, if true, would negate all possibility for comparative activity, and indeed, education. Despite these shortcomings, however, Gurney's descriptive insights and method of argument represent significant advances over the formalism he inherited from his predecessors.

Leonard B. Meyer: Expectation, Emotion, and Musical Meaning

The theories of Leonard Meyer offer a highly nuanced and sophisticated version of musical formalism strikingly congruent in many respects with the views of Hanslick and Gurney. Like them, Meyer holds that the musical experience is, at least potentially, unique and autonomous; like them, he is convinced that something roughly akin to tonally moving forms are where musical significance is ultimately to be found; like them, he believes there is a felt response to music that is specifically musical and doubts the genuinely musical relevance of extensively sensuous or associative responses; like them, he believes truly musical experience is predominantly contemplative with an 'objective' focus; and like them, he posits a significant place for mental satisfaction of a purely musical nature, one that comes of following or anticipating the music's designs, and of having those anticipations variously confirmed or 'agreeably led astray'. Like Gurney and unlike Hanslick, Meyer is more concerned with illuminating the nature of the specifically musical experience than with denigrating what it is not. Where Hanslick's denunciations of feeling were so caustic he left the unfortunate impression that he thought feeling entirely irrelevant to music, Meyer makes a concerted effort to bring feeling back into the fold by reconciling feeling and structure.

On the fundamental point that music's meaning or significance may be accounted for entirely in intramusical terms—without recourse to extramusical notions like expression, reference, representation, or symbolism—Meyer, Gurney, and Hanslick are largely in agreement. Meyer patiently explores the ways musical forms and processes engage the imagination, in a concerted effort to render explicit what it is the "competent listener" tacitly does in the genuinely musical experience, to show how a musical "stimulus" facilitates and directs such experience, and thereby to remove musical criticism and aesthetics from the "realms of whim, fancy, and prejudice."[236]

If Meyer's ideas are sometimes obscured by psychological jargon, an equally significant impediment is the extent to which his theory and its terminology evolved over time. Since Meyer is often best known for positions on musical emotion, expectation, and meaning which his later work significantly modified, it is important to explore and compare both his early and later theory. One central thesis has remained more or less constant over the years: that truly musical experience always occurs within the context of stylistic norms. Musical 'events' are comprehended and evaluated in terms of stylistic conventions with roots in the nature of human mental activity. In Meyer's view, striving to resolve ambiguity and to structure the disorderly are fundamental human needs or tendencies. Musical styles are important outcomes of this basic tendency. They consist in musical pattern types, or "universes of discourse," that enable people to estimate the ways particular musical sequences, once initiated, are likely to proceed. As people follow music's unfolding patterns, their convergence and divergence from these stylistic templates or schemata arouse feeling, or "affect." Since this particular range of affect has a specifically musical 'stimulus', it is uniquely musical in nature. Music is not a semantic art then, but a closed system, syntactical, processive, and formal in nature. It is meaningful, yet means nothing beyond itself. Its distinctive pleasure derives from mental delight taken in patterning and structuring the musical world: a contemplative pleasure, at once formal and kinetic in nature; a profoundly entertaining experience comprised of our perception of and participation in the processive unfolding of musical patterns.

The Early Theory

Meyer's early theory of musical meaning originates in an effort to resolve the idealistic dilemma created by a supposedly dichotic relationship between feeling and form in music. Emotional-affective and cognitive-formal accounts of musical meaning are not the mutually exclusive affairs their advocates portray them to be, argues Meyer. Feeling and cognition are simply different ways of experiencing the same thing. Advocates of musical autonomy, or "absolutists" as Meyer calls them, urge that genuinely musical experience derives exclusively from the apprehension of formal relationships. "Referentialists," on the other hand, accuse absolutists of unjustifiably isolating musical experience from other life experience, and assert that to "mean" anything requires that there be something "meant": the idea of musical meaning necessitates a connection between music and the broader world. Absolutists hold to an 'intrinsic' interpretation of music's nature and value, while referentialists maintain that such an insular notion is powerless to account for the rich expressiveness of musical experience.

Although absolutism and referentialism appear mutually exclusive, Meyer suggests that all expression need not be referential, and that there exists a range of feeling evoked specifically and exclusively by music which is therefore absolute. Meyer's "absolute expressionism" purports to describe a middle position between an (absolute) formalism and a (referential) expressionism.

Absolute expressionism's critical problem is to explain how sound patterns with no fixed reference achieve "meaning" and become experienced as feeling. Clearly, not all felt response is musically relevant: a given musical event cannot implicate just any meaning or feeling. For Meyer, nonmusical meanings or responses are of essentially two kinds: the extramusical (associational) and the pre-musical (purely sensual or physiological). All such responses are personal and subjective, requiring no particular musical competence. Meanings that are genuinely musical are the kind found in musically conversant listeners, people who are fluent in the given style and whose feelings arise directly and exclusively from the perception of events and processes objectively 'there', in the music. But how precisely does this happen?

Meyer's original explanation was built upon what he calls "the psychological theory of emotions"[237] and his theory of expectation, both of which proved highly problematic. According to these theories, experience may well be emotional, yet within it exist no discrete, distinguishable entities called emotions. Meyer's 'emotions' are thus quite distinct from what common language conceives them to be; so distinct in fact that the term emotion might well be avoided in favor of one with fewer misleading connotations—"affect", emotion's 'felt' quality. Experience may have more or less affect, varying degrees of affective intensity, but affect itself is qualitatively undifferentiated. Emotional experiences are distinct from one another and become describable entities only in terms of the objects or events in which they are implicated. It is only through their attendant circumstances that feelings like love, hate, joy, or sadness become discrete emotions. There is no 'love' without a specific object or situation. There are, so to speak, no feeling-universals. There are no pleasant and unpleasant emotions, only pleasant or unpleasant emotional experiences. Affect itself is precognitive and therefore undifferentiated; emotions or affective experiences are postcognitive and differentiated.

Although this sounds like an extraordinarily convoluted way of putting Hanslick's point that music cannot represent "substantives," Meyer's intent is somewhat more ambitious: in distinguishing affect from emotions, in holding that affect is itself undifferentiated while affective experiences entail further awareness of "stimulus situations," Meyer hopes to establish the way in which a certain range of affective musical experience may be properly considered absolutely and genuinely musical. To the extent attention is focused upon the musical object, the 'feelings' accompanying its perception will be specifically musical. Affect is affect ... is affect. The distinction between musical and nonmusical feeling, then, is that the former is aroused solely by perception of a musical 'stimulus'. As Gurney and Hanslick urged, musical emotions are distinctly musical. Beneath these 'emotions', adds Meyer, lies an undifferentiated range of affect.

To explain the precise nature of the connection between music and its proper feelings, Meyer's early thought invokes another rather curious doctrine: "affect is aroused when a tendency to respond is arrested or inhibited."[238] Affective arousal follows from conflict, a situation in which an instinctive or habitual reaction meets with resistance. Meyer's example is the inveterate smoker who routinely (without affect, presumably) reaches for a cigarette, finding none. Affect is aroused. This particular experience is unpleasant (for the smoker at any rate), but inhibited response tendencies need not invariably be so, provided one believes the conflict will eventually be resolved.

Musical experience, then, is a function of response 'tendencies' in the perceiver: more- or less-conscious 'expectations' for how a given musical idea, once initiated, will likely work itself out. An 'antecedent' or 'stimulus' event thus carries with it, by virtue of previously experienced stylistic conventions, a set of possible 'consequents', of resolutions or continuations, each accompanied by some estimate of the likelihood of its occurrence. The greater the clarity and specificity of the antecedent, the more clearly implicated a particular consequent becomes. Should an anticipated musical event occur precisely as expected, affective arousal will be minimal. If, on the other hand, the event happens in a novel or surprising manner, affect is piqued. Where the situation is ambiguous and a number of consequent musical events each seems equiprobable, suspense and tension occurs, and is sustained until eventual resolution provides closure.

Again, for Meyer, humans are fundamentally predicting, patterning, structuring creatures, with an inherent passion for coherence and an abhorrence of ambiguity. Music, like all human mental activity, is a quest for cognitive orientation. In short, "the customary or expected progression of sounds can be considered as a norm, which from a stylistic point of view it is; and alteration in the expected progression can be considered as a deviation. Hence, deviations can be regarded as emotional or affective stimuli."[239] Musical expression is a function of deviation from expectations, and expectations are in turn products of stylistic familiarity. Thus, given listeners who have developed stylistically appropriate expectations, the structure of the affective experience will be identical to the musical events that cause it. The subjective musical response can be observed 'objectively' through analysis of the events in the 'stimulus' (the music) that cause it.

Intramusical Meaning

It remains to be shown how Meyer feels these ideas pertain to the problem of musical meaning. Since most attempts to deal with the issue suffer, Meyer feels, from confusion about the meaning of meaning, he offers a definition: meaning arises, he believes, when something "is connected with, or indicates, or refers to something beyond itself."[240] This formulation is significant in its implication that meaning does not inhere in things, is not a property of things, but consists in a relationship between a 'stimulus' and its referent. Meaning is of two basic kinds. Designative meaning occurs when the signified is different in kind from that which signifies, as when words designate objects. Embodied meaning is designation where sign and signified are of the same kind: when, for instance, "a dim light on the eastern horizon heralds the coming of day."[241] Recognizing that musical meaning is meaning of the embodied kind will, he thinks, resolve the confusion and controversy surrounding the subject.

Musical experience includes both designative (or loosely, "extramusical") meanings and embodied (intramusical) ones, but the former are not as directly implicated by music's patterns as the latter. Meyer's interest lies with those 'embodied' meanings that attend our musical expectations: whose basis lies in the way musical 'stimuli' point to, or lead the listener to expect, "other musical events which are about to happen."[242]

These distinctions promise to clarify many seemingly nonsensical claims about musical meaning: that, for instance, music is meaningless, or that it means itself. Autonomists or absolutists use the term primarily in its embodied sense, the sense in which music is internally coherent and purposive, its structural and syntactical relationships intelligible and therefore seemingly significant. Meaning in the designative sense is another matter: a semantic or referential affair, a matter of association with things extramusical. Compared to its embodied meaning, music's designative meanings are indefinite and indirect. Much of the rancor over musical meaning stems from the indiscriminate use of the same term to describe both designative and embodied relationships, both semantic and syntactical functions. In identifying the manner in which syntactical relationships comprise intramusical meaning, Meyer claims to show how music can 'mean' without implicating the extramusical world.

Meyer identifies three discrete stages of embodied musical meaning: the 'hypothetical', the 'evident', and the 'determinate'. Hypothetical meanings are predictions, intuitive musical hunches about pattern continuation before an actual outcome is known. Evident meanings are those attributed to 'antecedent gestures' as their actual relationships to subsequent events become more fully apparent. Finally, determinate meanings are those retrospectively attributed to the work as a whole when it has become "timeless in memory"[243] and all its relationships are grasped fully.

In short, music becomes meaningful only when it deviates in some respect from a projected course (conflict, inhibited tendency), and musical meanings are always functions of (which is to say, relative to) musical style. Styles are "complex systems of probability relationships,"[244] such that the meaning of any given 'sound event' is a function of its potential relationships with others in that system. Departure from the expected, from stylistic norms, creates imbalance or conflict which in turn creates affective arousal. This process, though often the result of unconscious perceptual habits, need not be so. For some people, particularly those with more extensive musical training, awareness of pattern continuation and deviation is conscious and even intellectually mediated. Thus, felt and intellectual responses to music are "not different processes, but different ways of experiencing the same process. Whether a piece of music gives rise to affective experience or to intellectual experience depends upon the disposition and training of the listener."[245] Both kinds of experience involve the same fundamental process wherein delays, deviations, and unanticipated turns create uncertainty, suspense, surprise, gratification, and so forth.

Meyer's theory, then, can be seen as developing a point Hanslick and Gurney conceded without much elaboration: there exists a certain range of feeling that may be considered genuinely musical. As well, like Hanslick and Gurney before him, Meyer seeks to define musical pattern as a dynamic, processual affair rather than as a static, 'objective' thing. What is vital to genuinely musical experience is not so much a structural understanding as the capacity to engage appropriate perceptual habits and expectations. Objective or conceptual knowledge is itself insufficient to this capacity, since to be truly musical it must attain "the status of an instinctive mental and motor response, a felt urgency . . ."[246] These efforts to accommodate the felt and processual character of musical experience are important modifications to the formalistic position.

Meyer's theory departs from Hanslick's and Gurney's in one very significant respect: its relativity. While his theory still holds tightly to the conviction that there exist universal explanatory principles for musical meaning, it allows for a plurality of ways those principles may be realized in actual experience. Because embodied meaning is always relative to stylistic contexts, music can be no universal language. It consists, rather, of a multiplicity of styles and idioms, each with different norms and probabilities, and each presumably implicating different 'expectational habits'. Styles are cultural (which is to say, learned) constructions that employ different and often contrasting dialects. And since deviation from stylistic norms is the source of both musical expression and vitality, styles evolve. Deviations from stylistic norms are expressive, in Meyer's view, because they are novel and unexpected. With increasing use and familiarity, deviations lose their expressive impact, much as the richness of linguistic metaphor fades with use, eventually becoming 'literal'. Styles change, expressive devices become norms and, in turn, govern future expectations. Yet not all is flux. There are constants to which the process must adhere: the psychological principles governing human pattern perception, "the ways in which the mind, operating within the framework of a learned style, selects and organizes the sense data presented to it."[247]

Nonsyntactical Meaning

Meyer is primarily interested in 'embodied', syntactical relationships and the intramusical meaning they generate, not the 'designative' remainder. Since he has so little to say about designative meaning, it is tempting to dismiss it as a nonmusical aberration, a phenomenon that lies outside the domain he calls 'absolute expression'. Meyer is reluctant to dismiss them quite so cursorily, though. To be sure, his basic thesis is that when the "forces" shaping intramusical affective experience are "purely" musical, "the form of the affective experience will be similar to the form of the musical work which brought it into being."[248] Yet there may be affective responses indirectly linked to the musical object but still able to lay at least a marginal claim to the 'objective' basis Meyer espouses. He allows that "image processes," while by nature associational, are not invariably or absolutely nonmusical. Some are indeed strictly private, personal, and subjective; yet others are intracultural affairs that are widely shared by particular interpretive communities. Not all associational 'image processes' are necessarily nonmusical.

Although private, personal images may be present to some degree in most musical experience, they are products of the individual psyche rather than the 'objective situation' itself. Nothing in such images has a necessary relationship to the music "which presumably activated them," says Meyer: the "real stimulus is not the progressive unfolding of the musical structure but the subjective content of the listener's mind."[249] Private associations thus constitute "tremendous temptations toward extramusical diversion."[250] "Group image processes," on the other hand, are somewhat more "standardized," more widely shared by members of a cultural community. These loose, collective associations that Meyer calls "musical connotations" can be accounted for in terms of either contiguity or similarity. "Connotations by contiguity" consist of conventional yet conditioned associations between musical phenomena and contiguous extramusical happenings, just as Pavlov's bell triggered a salivation response in his dogs. Connotations by contiguity are responses to actual musical 'stimuli', but they are culturally specific and arbitrary: the link between the music and what it connotes is not objective, only psychological.

"Connotations by similarity" are associations that follow from some structural congruence between musical qualities and aspects of extramusical phenomena: between, for instance, music's patterns of tension and repose and those of nonmusical sentient experience. These are the structural and kinetic similarities that Hanslick thought might permit music to represent a certain restricted range of feeling, the 'common logical form' that Langer believes to be the basis for music's symbolic capacity. Meyer is considerably more circumspect, however. Similarity implicates neither representation nor symbolism, and connotations are at root associative. Therefore, connotations are "not necessary concomitants of musical experience."[251] Whether they are aroused "depends to a great extent upon the disposition and training of the individual listener,"[252] and the presence of cues to which people are conditioned to respond. The relationship between the "musical materials and their organization and the connotations evoked" is stronger for similarity than contiguity because, "[h]ad the musical organization been different, the connotation would also have been different."[253] Yet since the music is not a sufficient cause for such responses, their meaning is of a distinctly lower order than affective musical experiences that are "objectively-determined." Meyer explains, "Since musical affective stimuli are obviously different from the referential stimuli of real life, there will always be a generic difference between musical affective experience and the experiences of everyday life. From this point of view, a musical experience is unique."[254] A great many of the qualities people claim to value most in musical experience, however, seem to dangle rather precariously between the referential and the uniquely musical, between musical irrelevance and objective determination.

It becomes increasingly clear that to be consistent, Meyer's "absolute expressionism" must hold, with Gurney, that all expression is in some sense referential, but further, that expression as commonly conceived of is beyond music's powers. For Meyer, music is an objective 'stimulus' whose felt significance is a function of its capacity to evoke or arouse rather than communicate, characterize, represent, or portray anything beyond itself. In his early writing, Meyer is reluctant to take this stance. He writes, for instance: "Music may be meaningful because it refers to things outside itself, evoking associations and connotations relative to the world of ideas, sentiments, and physical objects. Such designative meanings are often less precise and specific than those arising in linguistic communication. This does not, however, make them less forceful or significant."[255] While designative and embodied meaning are logically separable, he continues, "there is in practice an intimate interaction between them."[256] Elsewhere, he asserts still more strongly that "the syntactical and characterizing [i.e., the embodied and the designative] facets of musical communication are inextricably linked."[257] How a range of meanings can be inextricably linked to genuinely musical experience yet neither necessary nor sufficient to it is a troublesome issue for Meyer's early theory.

Information and Musical Value

Shortly after his 1956 publication Meyer became intrigued by "striking parallels—indeed equivalents"[258] between his theoretical perspective and 'information theory'. Although he eventually rejected it as "simple-minded counting,"[259] his explorations help illuminate otherwise implicit assumptions in his theory. Meyer was drawn to information theory by his conception of musical style as a system of probabilities and of the predictive nature of musical listening. Given a musical event within a certain style, its relationships to ensuing musical events can be conceived of in terms of the mathematical probability of their occurrence, he reasoned. A highly probable event carries little "information," and conversely, a highly unpredictable event is replete with informational value. The totally predictable tells us nothing new, while the totally unexpected or highly ambiguous are highly "informative." Perception remains largely habitual and unconscious until it encounters something that cannot be accommodated by habitual means. New "information" (deviation) compels reassessment of present and preceding situations.

At the same time, Meyer equates meaning with conscious awareness. Habitual experience, experience not consciously scrutinized, lacks meaning or is "meaning-neutral". Since meaning is possible only when unconscious cognitive or perceptual habits are disturbed, musical events that unfold precisely as expected have little meaning. Conversely, musical events which challenge expectations either with surprise or ambiguity are highly meaningful. Meaning is a function of novelty or uncertainty. Modifying his original definition, Meyer says meaning arises "when an antecedent situation, requiring an estimate of the probable modes of pattern continuation, produces uncertainty about the temporal-tonal nature of the expected consequent."[260] From this he believes it follows that "as a musical event . . . unfolds and the probability of a particular conclusion increases, uncertainty, information, and meaning will necessarily decrease."[261] This in turn implies that deviations are most meaningful and most affectively arousing when they occur in places where pattern closure seems likely.

Although habitual processes are low in meaning, they are not totally devoid of musical significance. Pattern consists, by definition, of repetition, and pure novelty is incomprehensible: therefore, musical "redundancy" fulfills an important role. Furthermore, since any given musical "signal" is attended by some "noise" (to continue the strained metaphor), redundancy permits the listener time to 'coast', taking stock of what has happened and speculating about where it may lead. Yet, from the perspective of information theory, "something without meaning or information is . . . valueless (indeed what we mean by 'trite' or 'banal' is the most probable means of achieving the most probable end)," and "valuations, evaluations, and perhaps values as well arise only as the result of the uncertainties involved . . . in predicting alternative antecedent-consequent probabilities."[262]

Beyond the troublesome language, these remarks point to a fundamental paradox in Meyer's theory. As one critic observes, "If the theory were correct, the first hearing of a work should reek with meaning and send emotional tingles to the tips of the toes; but with subsequent hearings the significance and emotional impact of a work ought to decline rapidly as the unexpected becomes the expected, as expectation becomes replaced by recollection and anticipation. . . . Meyer's theory seems to be incompatible with the ordinary conviction that fine music can be reheard and re-enjoyed many, many times."[263] Another is considerably less charitable: "Meyer suggests that if 'A leads one to expect B', he is more aware of his expectation if something intervenes to frustrate it or make it less certain; and this somehow makes the relationship between A and B more 'meaningful' (to quote the dread word). So . . . 'thunder means rain', but it really means rain only if you're not sure it does (because, say, in the meantime the sun has come out)."[264]

In communication, concerned as it is with the transmission of information, the more novel the message, the more 'meaning' is conveyed. Meaning increases with novelty and diminishes with familiarity. But in music the situation is more often just the reverse: meaning increases with familiarity and decreases with novelty; people find most meaningful music they have been heard repeatedly and know well.

Meyer explores six potential resolutions to this 'rehearing' paradox. First, music functions on many levels, and only after repeated hearings do people begin to discern broader patterns or relationships. Only after foreground gestures like melodic phrases become familiar do people begin to appreciate their role in broader structural or textural configurations. Second, early hearings miss subtle detail that familiarity makes more fully apparent. Third, 'stylistic schemata' are not static but dynamic. Since musical experience always modifies the schemata that mediate what is heard, rehearings are perceived against a different interpretive grid than early hearings. Fourth, performances and interpretations of a work may differ in many respects (an explanation, note, that sidesteps the issue of re-hearing). Fifth, the phenomenal nature of musical listening is such that later hearings feel like first encounters. And finally, rehearing is tolerable "precisely because listening is not taking place,"[265] because people indulge in sensuous-associative responses instead of attending to syntactically based implications. Clearly, the pleasure people take in re-hearing directly challenges some of Meyer's most fundamental tenets. Indeed, Meyer concedes that if the listener still finds rehearing a rewarding experience once the work is so familiar that all deviations are fully comprehended, his theory must be mistaken.[266] It is crucial to his theory that music not sustain competent re-hearing (hearing that is focused upon syntactical relations and deviations) indefinitely.

Musical value is reduced, Meyer believes, if any of three conditions obtain: (1) no expectations or tendencies are established; (2) a probable goal is met in an immediate and direct way; or (3) the goal is never reached, or reached "too late" relative to the perceiver's expectations, frustrating attention. On the other hand, "what creates or increases the information contained in a piece of music increases its value"; and "greater uncertainty and greater information go hand in hand."[267] Thus, the greater the ambiguity and unpredictability, the greater the value. How do such seemingly negative characteristics as ambiguity and unpredictability dispose positive musical value? Meyer's answer is that just as it is a mark of maturity to forego immediate gratification in deference to long-term goals, so it is a mark of musical maturity to defer the resolution of aroused expectations. Music that caters to immediate pleasure is less valuable than music involving uncertainty and deviation.[268] Musical value is syntactical value, residing in "the intricate and subtle interconnections between musical events" which create the resistance and uncertainty characteristic of a complex work.[269] A piece's capacity to sustain interest through repeated listening comes of its complexity. And ultimately, "it seems probable that the charm of simplicity as such is associative."[270]

If musical value is ultimately formal or syntactical, and musical charm is at root associative, how would Meyer account for complex works that are musically pedestrian? And more importantly, is there no more to musical 'greatness' than complexity? "[T]he greatest works," Meyer curiously (in light of the basic tenets of his theory) concludes, are "those which embody value of the highest order with the most profound . . . content."[271]

Meyer's early exploration of the relations among emotion and meaning attracted considerable attention, attention that brought to light many contradictions and inconsistencies. With these in mind Meyer extensively revised and refined his theory in subsequent years. Before turning to that revised theory, however, a more detailed examination of several problems in his early theory may be helpful.

Problems With the Early Theory

The contention that 'affect' is undifferentiated is of pivotal importance to Meyer's theory, since it is the mechanism that purportedly allows for the structural equivalence of musical pattern and the feeling it disposes. Since affect in itself, "emotion-felt," is undifferentiated (or more precisely, differentiated only in terms of intensity), it is possible, Meyer believes, to identify a range of 'expressive' musical experiences that are in no way referential or parasitic upon nonmusical 'feelings'. Feeling (as opposed to particular, identifiable feelings) has to do with degree of arousal. Accordingly, whatever differentiation exists among felt musical experiences is created by objective patterns within the music itself. It follows that a profile of genuinely musical expression can be obtained from hardheaded analysis of the musical 'stimulus'.

But unfortunately for Meyer's theory, the idea that affect is undifferentiated is far from uncontroversial. A great deal of contemporary psychological literature contends precisely the opposite. The theory of nondifferentiation conceives of affect purely in quantitative terms. But as Hillman aptly observes, "Irritation and fury are not to be conceived as points on a scale reading from apathy to manic seizures, like degrees of temperature; they are rather individual conditions of the personality as a whole."[272] An adequate account of emotion requires a qualitative as well as a quantitative criterion, and Meyer's arousal-plus-context formula fails to account satisfactorily for the qualitative distinctions among emotions people identify with remarkable consistency.[273] That emotion is differentiated and multidimensional is a conviction shared by a significant segment of the psychological community.[274]

That joy and sadness differ from one another only in terms of excitement level, tinged by cognitive awareness of attendant circumstances and perhaps by belief that the situation may or may not continue, is intuitively quite difficult. Similarly, it seems intuitively obvious that fear and anger are far more similar to one another than are, say, joy and sadness, and that these similarities or differences involve a good deal more than mere arousal accompanied by situational awareness. It is intuitively quite difficult to conceive of affect as though its existence were independent of context or experience. It is likely that Meyer's 'affect' is but one dimension of emotion or feeling, and that emotion experience is both richer and more complex than the arousal-plus-context model allows. The same may be said of the account of musical experience that supposedly follows from it: it is considerably richer than his arousal theory admits.

The "conflict theory" of emotion on which Meyer's early theory rests has its difficulties as well. As the idea of undifferentiated affect reduces emotion to arousal, so too the conflict theory attributes arousal almost exclusively to inhibited response tendencies. Where music unfolds precisely as anticipated, without disturbance, deviation, or novelty, there can be no affect. However, critics counter, conflict is neither necessary nor sufficient to emotion: there is emotion that is not caused by conflict, and conflict that does not generate emotion.

Perhaps the most serious challenge to conflict-based emotion theories is, as Elliott relates, the fact that "affect is a continuous aspect of consciousness."[275] Meyer maintains that cognitive and perceptual processes are essentially devoid of affect unless they are somehow disturbed or impeded. But it is meaningless to speak of consciousness without affect, since some kind affective quality is an attribute of all cognition and perception, even that which is utterly routine and habitual. That people sometimes act or perceive without full consciousness or explicit awareness in no way establishes that such processes are devoid of affect. Indeed, affect often plays a profound role in shaping and directing such activities, as Meyer's own analysis implies: for it is affect that both alerts people to perceptual/conceptual discrepancies and signifies when they have been satisfactorily resolved. Even the seemingly effortless pleasure that attends following or doing things that proceed precisely as anticipated has its own distinctive affective tone or character, which is presumably a significant part of the reason people continue to engage in highly refined skills and activities.

Confined to psychological theories, these disputes may seem largely innocuous. But recall that for Meyer affect and meaning (and ultimately, 'information' and value as well) are but different aspects of the same basic phenomenon. What is true of the affect, then, must be equally true for all meaning and value: without novelty and ambiguity they are "neutral." Since in information theory it is axiomatic that predictability and 'information' vary inversely, the least redundant situation bears the most information and (potentially at least) the greatest value. Applied to music, this means that the most perceptually complex music, that with the least repetition, that which permits the least habitual kinds of response, has the greatest musical value. And conversely, when all musical relationships have been discovered and no new 'information' can be extracted from the musical object, musical meaning and value are nil. What Meyer called music's "determinate meaning," in other words, is meaningless. To make sense of this "Babylonian muddle," as one critic describes it[276]—of the idea that the greater the disorder of a situation, the more information it conveys—one must distinguish extremely carefully between "information theory information" and information in its ordinary sense. Information theory is concerned with the transmission of 'information', and not with whether what is transmitted is ultimately intelligible. In ordinary language, something is generally considered information only if it is informative.

There may, of course, be certain truths to be gleaned from Meyer's excursion into information theory. Rich musical experience involves an optimal blend of novelty and familiarity. Musical experience devoid of freshness is by definition trite and banal. There may even be some validity in Meyer's observation that the experience of musical 'conflict' is colored in important ways by the assumption that it will eventually be amicably resolved. But music's value does not reduce to an experience of conflict. As another critic concludes, "It takes but a moment's reflection to realize that compliance with a norm is no less 'meaningful' than non-compliance."[277]

An adequate account of music's nature, then, must also account for the overwhelmingly predominant kind of musical experience in which conflict plays no discernible part, in which people take delight in hearing the music do again precisely what they knew it would. Indeed, it has been argued that among the most distinctively human attributes is the ability to savor a present moment for its pure quality, without conflict or relationship to anything else. That people are sensitive to conflict, ambiguity, or perceptual-cognitive 'dissonance', and take pleasure in its resolution, does not establish that such things determine all felt responses to music. Indeed, for the vast majority of listeners, the most profoundly moving musical experience involves music which is most familiar, known so deeply 'by heart' that the notions of uncertainty or conflict are wholly useless. The relevance of a smoker's frustration to musical pleasure is highly questionable.

There is something quite appealing in the idea that ingenious deviations from expected modes of pattern continuation are important sources of musical enjoyment. But at the same time there is something peculiar about the proposition that this pleasure is essentially dependent upon how a given listener expects music to proceed. At least some of this awkwardness comes from Meyer's ambivalence about the location of conflict, expectations, and meanings: whether they are experiential attributes of the perceiving subject or qualities of the musical object. It often seems that musical experience is objectively governed, strictly guided by and subservient to a musical 'stimulus'. Yet almost as often it seems an intrasubjective process, something generated by a given listener's expectations and anticipations. Under 'absolute expressionism' these two kinds of process are supposed to be equivalent—two different ways of looking at the same thing. But they clearly differ in crucial ways. A listener's will does not change what objectively transpires. Moreover, not all listeners' (subjective) expectations are equally musical, equally relevant to what objectively transpires in Meyer's musical 'stimulus'. A listener's expectation may, and arguably often does have little to do with the way the music actually progresses on a syntactically objective level. In a particularly penetrating analysis of this problem, Hansen shows that Meyer's failure to write a major role in his script for an 'ideal listener' leaves him without a mechanism for discriminating appropriate expectations from silly ones.[278] The musically relevant expectation occurs only in listeners who are fluent, who know the 'rules of the game', who have learned to rivet their attention to the right musical 'events'.

It would be convenient for Meyer's argument if musical experience consisted in a direct mechanical relationship between objective musical stimulus and subjective response, as he often suggests. However, it clearly does not. Indeed, that was presumably one of the reasons that prompted Meyer to develop his account in the first place: if an objective musical stimulus evoked a given range of subjective response with any kind of consistency and reliability, there would be no need to distinguish properly musical responses from premusical or extramusical ones. What all this seems to suggest is that the musical 'stimulus' is not a proper stimulus at all, but, in a fundamental sense, always already some kind of 'response'.

Moreover, as we have just observed, the fact that musical patterns, gaps, and deviations occur in the music is no guarantee of their occurrence in a listener's mind. Such phenomena are not products of just any listeners' psychological dispositions: they are realized only by an ideal auditor, one who grasps and appreciates their (objective) implications. Ironically, Hansen shows, this ideal auditor does not seem to be quite the 'absolute expressionist' with whom Meyer began his study, since "instead of having only feeling-responses . . . [this listener] constantly makes judgments concerning the musical process."[279] However extensively feeling-responses may color ideal listeners' judgments, predictions, and comparisons, their ultimate concern is not feeling but its causes. The 'absolute expressionist' feels, but is not particularly interested in the reasons for such feelings. The 'formalist', on the other hand, is constantly concerned with explaining the felt response, comprehending how the music worked as it did.[280] It is the latter position that Meyer really holds, as his detailed analyses show. The circumstances under which the music's patterns and the listener's responses will most closely approximate each other involve an intellectually oriented listener whose attention is focused exclusively upon the piece's syntactical relationships.

One of the most vexing problems in Meyer's early theory is the multiplicity of concerns he conflates under the rubric "meaning." The term is used to denote both objective relationships and subjective processes, both semantic relationships and syntactical ones. So broad is its application that meaning risks meaninglessness. Meyer's basic distinction between designative and embodied meaning pretends to be rather more clear than it actually is, and the introduction of hypothetical, evident, and determinate meanings clouds the waters still further. 'Designative' meaning is a conventional and familiar sense of the term. 'Embodied' meaning, however, is meaning where the designated and designator are alike in kind, as when light 'means' the approach of day or clouds 'mean' approaching rain. But these natural signs, when they so function, do so because of their frequency of association,[281] not because they are alike in kind. Clouds and rain neither resemble each other nor are they essentially alike. Nor is there any apparent basis for generalizing the relationship of clouds to rain to the musical domain. Musical antecedents and consequents are alike in that they both consist of sonorous materials. But words designate other words or word-sequences in much the same way, and 'syntax' is the relatively clear term for such relationships. Substituting 'syntactical relationships' for 'meaning' resolves many of the difficulties in Meyer's early theory.

In Meyer's account, music's expressiveness and much of its value derive from the relative novelty of particular musical 'events', and from a kind of forward-projecting mental activity that estimates probable modes of pattern continuation. Subjectively, this entails a kind of 'speculation' in which listeners strive to make structural sense of the music. Objectively, Meyer's concern is syntactical relationships among musical events, and the ways events interact within stylistic 'probability systems' to imply more or less satisfactory modes of continuation. For the most part, expectation and syntax are presumed to be the exclusive sources of musical significance (except for pesky connotative tendencies that have no real objective status). Thus, genuinely musical experience is a projective and predictive experience in which, if 'now' counts, it is only as it relates to the future. Moreover, syntactical meaning consists in relationships among more or less discrete musical events: what Gurney called music's quantitative or definite parameters.

Issues that lie outside of any theory's basic interpretive framework tend to be glossed over or marginalized, and Meyer's theory is no exception. Its focus upon form and syntax leads it to relegate to secondary status musical parameters that defy quantification and notation, and experience that is dynamic, corporeal, and above all, qualitative. Elements that do not serve syntactical ends are merely sensuous, and sensuous qualities can evoke only associative responses. Syntactical relationships, on the other hand, beget understanding. It is thus important, according to Meyer, to distinguish between "what is pleasurable and what is good."[282] More directly, "The sensuous-associative [response] is of minor importance in the consideration of value. Music must be evaluated syntactically."[283] Or yet more extensively, "[T]he syntactical response is more valuable than those responses in which the ego is dissolved, losing its identity in voluptuous sensation or in the reverie of daydreams."[284] Thus, Meyer apparently believes, like many notorious idealists before him, that musical experience consists in two mutually exclusive alternatives: syntactical understanding or mindless sensuousness.

As Titchener and Broyles observe, however, the syntactical account fails to differentiate satisfactorily between knowing music and experiencing it.[285] It is one thing to know, for instance, that in a particular setting the leading tone resolves to the tonic, but that knowledge and the actual experience of such resolution, even for the hundredth time, are profoundly different. Even the ideal listener—a composer or musicologist, likely—who has ascended to the heights of fully determinate meaning does not renounce the hearing of the music in order to savor soundless syntactical relationships. To imply as Meyer does that sensuous qualities pertain primarily to the musical response, while syntax is the stuff of music itself, reduces the dynamic-kinetic character of musical experience to a predominantly contemplative affair. And since nonsyntactical parameters have more to do with response than with music proper, temporal and timbral affairs should make little difference for musical value: a given pattern may be fast or slow, scored for flute or electric guitar, without altering its primary, syntactical configurations.

The syntactical account of music privileges musics that prioritize syntax, and demeans or trivializes those that do not. Meyer recognizes this bias, but apparently not its extent. His discussions of antiteleological music face frankly the limitations of his theory for such music, yet at the same time subtly imply that the limitations of his theory and the limitations of human perceptual capacity are one: to be without syntax is to be without meaning and value. John Cage aside, it is clear that a model like Meyer's legitimates the musics from which it is primarily derived, and that even the music of, say, Debussy would fare relatively poorly against a purely syntactical criterion.

As Keil aptly observes, Meyer's theory "implies not only a one-to-one relationship between syntactic form and expression but a weighting in favor of the former factor to the detriment of the latter."[286] In view of the inadequacy of syntax alone to account for the primacy of activity, vitality, and immediacy in many musics (Keil mentions jazz, but the argument is more broadly applicable), Keil proposes a complement to Meyer's syntactic domain: a "processual" dimension. This processual dimension consists of the direct, immediate, quasi-physical qualities of musical experience, the 'feel' of textures, timbres, gestures, and rhythmic flow: felt qualities as contrasted to the cognitively mediated feelings which attend syntactical contemplation. Its attendant musical parameters, because they are continuous and qualitative, defy discrete categorical articulation. The values that distinguish music's processual dimension are not the unity and control that subtly underlie Meyer's syntactical theory, but individuality and transience. Its sources are not resistance and conflict but the joy of unimpeded activity.

Meyer's early theory contains provocative insights into how music's structures and processes (loosely, its formal properties) enter into the musical experience of an informed and sensitive listener. As an exploration of the syntactical workings of certain musics, it is extraordinarily nuanced and illuminating. However, many of the assumptions upon which Meyer bases his argument that feeling and intellectual responses to music are but the same phenomenon viewed from different perspectives prove very problematic. His effort to articulate an 'absolute' account of expression, an objective account of music that remains sympathetic to 'feeling', invariably gravitates more toward the subjective pole than his deeper convictions can tolerate. Thus, though claiming to accommodate both rational and felt musical meanings, the most prominent place in his theory is reserved for the former.

The Theory Revised

In order to clarify his theory and address many of these criticisms, Meyer made extensive modifications to his theory. Although he claims his 'basic' way of viewing and explaining music has not changed,[287] his revisions often diverge substantially from the fundamental assumptions of his earlier writing. The issues of musical 'emotion' and 'meaning' that figured so prominently in his earlier work (and proved so problematic) become more peripheral concerns, as his interest seems to turn from the subjective toward the objective, from listener's affective states to attributes of a musical 'object'. His later writing is far less concerned with purported parallels between music and listeners' psychological propensities, and far more frankly interested in music 'itself'. The listener in Meyer's revised theory is stylistically fluent, one whose attention is always directed to 'properly' musical attributes and whose affective responses are presumably beside the musical point. Positing an ideally competent listener allows Meyer to focus almost exclusively upon structures, events, and patterns objectively within the music: the 'stimuli' to which truly competent listeners respond. Meyer's interest in "expectations" and "tendencies" shifts to music's "implications," and talk of "meanings" is subtly redirected toward musical "relationships." The later theory is more concerned with issues of criticism than of psychology. Criticism cannot explain the idiosyncrasies of the individual human psyche, but that is not where its interests really lie. Criticism, Meyer asserts, "endeavors to understand and explain the relationships among and between musical events, not the responses of individual listeners."[288] It is not that people's affective responses to music are wholly irrelevant; but such responses are little help when it comes to explaining music per se.

In Meyer's later theory, then, his interests become unabashedly 'objective' and formal, and his method extensively analytical. In explanation, he offers that "conceptualization precedes and qualifies affective experience."[289] Feeling 'responses', as he argued earlier, ensue from and become differentiated only given cognitive appraisal. Better, Meyer apparently believes, to examine music's objective "causes" than its subjective "effects." In one particularly revealing passage, he states that he "dispute[s] vehemently the notion that an intellectual response to works of art . . . is inhuman or undesirable. Quite the opposite. . . . [T]o entertain ideas—to see pattern and structure in the world—and to be entertained by ideas is both the most human and the most humane condition to which man can aspire."[290]

This is not, however, to suggest that all valid or genuine musical experience is necessarily intellectual. Systematic accounts of musical relationships do not purport to account exhaustively for the experience they dispose, Meyer allows. Explanations of music are not experiential prescriptions. 'Competent listening' is a matter of correctly acquired habits, not theoretical understanding. It is more, one might say, a knowing-how than a knowing-that. The musical relationships revealed by criticism, then, may influence musical experience in ways other than conscious mediation. However, Meyer appears to believe, these objectively verifiable relationships do fundamentally constrain competent listening.

Listeners, Archetypes, and Choices

Many of Meyer's central tenets do remain unchanged in his later writings. He continues to maintain that all musical events are grounded in and relative to stylistic 'universes of discourse', and that music is an essentially probabilistic affair in which, given certain stylistic constraints and propensities, some modes of pattern continuation and elaboration are more likely than others. Although such stylistic 'probabilities' are not deterministic, neither can they be accounted for in terms of purely personal or individual dispositions. Music is not just whatever a listener's subjective musings might like it to be. What saves music from the profound relativity of individual, idiosyncratic 'expectations' is the objectivity of stylistic frameworks and the competence of the ideal listener. In all goal-directed (teleological) music, patterns and sequences enable the mind to get its bearings by making 'events' of what would otherwise be mere sonorous succession. Exposure to and experience with the patterns and sequences typical of given styles leads to highly stable perceptual habits, estimates of the way events of a particular type 'behave' in particular contexts. Among truly competent listeners, those whose stylistic fluency assures that only appropriate 'expectations' direct the musical response, there is considerable agreement about the significance of pattern continuations, deviations, and so on. In fact, because the expectations of 'competent' listeners converge so strongly, Meyer apparently feels they can be treated as objective attributes of the music: that is, as musical 'implications'.

That such patternings are constrained by psychological laws governing human perceptual and cognitive activity (chief among them the principles of Gestalt psychology) also contributes significantly to their regularity and predictability. Meyer offers the following examples: "proximity between stimuli or events tends to produce connection; disjunction usually creates separation; once begun, a regular process generally implies continuation to a point of relative stability; a return to patterns previously presented tends to enhance closure; the more some parameters change, the more likely it is that others will be relatively constant; regular patterns are . . . more readily comprehended and remembered than irregular ones."[291]

Given a musical style in which they are conversant, fluent ("competent") listeners, perceive and tacitly evaluate what they hear against archetypal models of what music of 'this kind' might typically be expected to 'do' in such a situation. These archetypes are not ideal Platonic affairs, but products of habitual associations within particular styles, the result of frequently replicated formal plans and processes synthesized by the listener into a general awareness of tendencies, functions, and relationships within the style at hand.

Thus, musical events are always understood in light of normative stylistic schemata. Competent musical listening gauges the compliance and divergence between phenomenon and principle, between what is heard and an archetypal pattern to which it is appropriately related. Although intrapersonal matters like familiarity and novelty are important features in such experience, Meyer's later work focuses upon the music itself, upon objective relationships among objective events. Understanding that is properly musical always involves appreciation and evaluation of the relationships (plural) between an actual occurrence and what might have happened given the circumstances: an appraisal of the ingenuity or aptness or triteness of a particular 'solution' to a particular implicative 'problem'.

Genuinely musical appreciation requires tacit awareness of the range of possible alternatives that attend a particular event, the nature and range of choices available to the composer or performer. Notably, then, whether a certain event is actually expected is not the issue it was in Meyer's early theory. One need not actually 'expect' an event to occur in order to appreciate its ingenuity. Therefore, given an understanding of the constraints and choices pertinent to a situation, one can marvel at the beauty of a certain turn of phrase again and again, and come to appreciate its profundity more fully with each subsequent exposure. "[W]hat audiences enjoy and appreciate is neither the successions of stimuli *per se*, nor general principles *per se*, but the relationship between them as actualized in a specific work of art."[292] Musical pleasure consists in enjoying the choices a work embodies in light of the options potentially available. And musical value is a function of the ingenuity of choices.

Implicative Relationships

By replacing 'expectations' with 'implications', and 'embodied meanings' with 'implicative relationships' Meyer sidesteps the subjectivism of his earlier theoretical formulations and evades the complex problems that attended his earlier efforts to account for musical 'meaning'. Music is, Meyer states directly and unequivocally, a 'nonsemantic art',[293] a matter of "goalless mental play"[294] rather than of meaning in the transitive sense. The shift from expectation to implication clearly represents more than a mere modification of terminology. Unlike expectation, which was conceived as an essentially unidimensional and forward-directed affair, "musical events imply one another in different ways, to different degrees, and on different hierarchic levels. . . . [They] may not act in concert— may not support one another—in the articulation of structure and process. At any particular moment, disparate, or even contradictory, goals may be implied by a complex musical event."[295] To say, for instance, that a passage's harmonic and rhythmic patterns dispose a simultaneous 'expectation' of closure and continuation is contradictory; but to say that a musical event implies closure on one level while implying continuation on the other is both a reasonable explanation and a relatively common experience.[296] In musical implication, an event "is patterned in such a way that reasonable inferences can be made both about its connections with preceding events and about how the event itself might be continued and perhaps reach closure and stability."[297] A given musical event may thus imply multiple patterns of continuation, a set of potential modes of continuation that range from the highly probable to the improbable.

Meyer believes this revision improves upon his expectation theory in at least four ways. First, implications may be plural in a way expectations cannot. Second, since implications are 'concrete signs' objectively embodied in musical style, situations structured in certain ways can be held to "imply" regardless of whether the implication is realized, and regardless of whether a given individual (say, one to whom the passage in question is extremely familiar) actually 'expects' a particular outcome.[298] Third, unlike expectation, implication is at once prospective and retrospective, drawing at once upon awareness of what might have happened and what has. And finally, deviation or surprise is but one possible outcome of implicative relationships, rather than the paradigmatic one. What makes implication and implicative inferences possible are orderly patternings. Novelty, conflict, and surprise are not deterministic "rules" governing musical response, but specific instances of the way the broader implicative process works.

Implications always include various and multiple alternatives, the value of the 'actual' always being a function of its relationship to the 'possible' and the 'likely'. Appreciation of the particular aptness of a road taken is always relative to the fluent listener's recognition of others that were not. And, highly important for Meyer's theory, such appreciation does not diminish with familiarity, since the ingenuity of a particularly remarkable solution will only become more enjoyable as its ingenuity and implicational richness (on a variety of levels) becomes increasingly apparent.

Conformant Relationships

Although Meyer's conviction that pattern is the essence of music remains unchanged, his later theory distinguishes between two basic kinds of musical patterning: the formal and the processive. This distinction is essential in order to account for both the kinetic processes by which music temporally unfolds and its more architectonic, structural aspects. As Meyer observes, "musical enjoyment lies as much, if not more, in the act of traveling as in the fact of arriving."[299] Hence, an adequate account of musical pattern must attend to the manner in which formal and processive relationships complement and reinforce one another.

Relationships between events taken out of time and considered as entities Meyer labels conformant relationships. Before musical events may become elements in any larger-scale pattern or process, they must be perceived as discrete entities. For pattern to exist there must be perceived repetition. Conformant relationships are simply those in which discrete musical events are recognized as similar to one another—seen to be common members of some class of musical events. In Meyer's words, "conformance . . . fosters coherence and provides the constancy in terms of which change can be comprehended."[300] Musical motives display foreground conformance, alternating sections in rondo form have higher-level formal conformance, and so forth. Conformant relationships are the ways in which musical components structurally 'go together'.

Conformance is a function not only of the similarity of musical events, but also of their contiguity: the more remote they are from one another the more difficult it becomes to recognize conformance. Other features may obscure conformance as well. For instance, contrasts in register, timbre, dynamics and the like (parameters Meyer calls "secondary") can conceal or camouflage an otherwise strong degree of similarity between two melodic sequences. The more disparate two events become with regard to one parameter, the more "conservatively" the other parameters must behave in order for conformance to be perceived. "Because the amount of information which the human mind can comprehend at one time is limited, the more information one parameter carries, the more redundant others must be if musical relationships are to be perceived."[301]

This represents a significant refinement of Meyer's early unidimensional conception of musical information and redundancy, in which musical complexity and musical value covaried so directly that they seemed virtually synonymous. The revised theory acknowledges the limitations of perceptual complexity, thresholds of 'informational' complexity beyond which musical experience can only revert to noise. Moreover, since the complexity of any single parameter is always qualified by its interaction with others, the apparently simple can be often remarkably complex. A 'simple' melody can be an extraordinarily complex musical event.

According to Meyer, conformant relationships "create foreground coherence while at the same time allowing attention to be directed to higher-level syntactic processes, contribute to the formal articulation of musical structure on all hierarchical levels, and also provide the satisfaction of return, thereby enhancing the impression of closure."[302] But conformance alone cannot account for the distinctive sense of organic unity and motion Hanslick and Gurney believed central to music. What happens between and among conformant events, the ways they interrelate, are matters of paramount importance. As Meyer puts it, "Conformant relationships create the strongest impression of unity when they are embodied in some sort of functional process."[303]

Processive Relationships

Processive relationships are functional, dynamic affairs, supporting goal-directed music's distinctive sense of temporal motion. Music's senses of mobility and closure are made possible by the interaction of two different types of musical parameters, Meyer believes: those that demarcate structure (the quantitative, or proportional parameters, as Gurney would have it), and those that sustain its sensuous quality; "primary" (syntactical) parameters, and "secondary" (or 'statistical') ones.

Primary musical parameters demarcate the beginnings and ends of sections and create rhythmic, harmonic, and melodic closure. They are "primary" because without them relationships among musical 'stimuli' would dissolve into perpetual presentness. Primary parameters perform their shaping functions because they can be divided into qualitatively discrete units—rhythmic patterns, pitches, chords, and so on. This categorical discreteness, as Gurney observed, is what that enables their combination into larger structures and configurations. Such parameters are thus "primary" in Meyer's theory for the same reasons they constituted "essential form" in Gurney's.

Not all musical parameters lend themselves to discrete, categorical perception. While the pitch continuum, for example, readily accepts division into whole steps and half steps that may be combined to create distinct intervals and harmonies with significant implicative power, secondary musical parameters cannot be so segmented and combined. Meyer explains, "[D]ynamics may become louder or softer, tempi may be faster or slower, sonorities thicker or thinner, timbres brighter or duller. But because they cannot be segmented into perceptually discrete entities, there are no specific closural states for such parameters."[304] Where primary parameters articulate forms and processes, secondary parameters serve primarily to reinforce or sustain what the primary parameters initiate. They are modes of activity, and their role in the implicative process is restricted to their tendency to imply their own continuation once established. Since they present themselves as degrees rather than patterns they lack syntactical power. They contribute most directly and forcefully to music's intensity, its "apotheosis," its "more physical attributes."[305]

While parameters that support the syntactical relationships so important in goal-directed musics may reasonably be designated 'primary', the term 'secondary' carries unfortunately negative connotations that detract from their indispensability, and that compromise the description of musics in which such 'secondary' parameters are in fact primary bearers of significance. Recognition of 'secondary' parameters and their role in processive musical relationships helps counter the syntactical exclusivity of Meyer's early theory. However, Meyer continues to underestimate the significance of timbre, texture, and other purportedly qualitative parameters to music.

Hierarchical Relationships

Meyer's distinction between form and process rests upon a further assumption that music is fundamentally a hierarchical phenomenon. If, Meyer reasons, "musical stimuli . . . did not form brief, but partially completed events . . . , and if these did not in turn combine with one another to form more extended, higher-order patterns, all relationships would be local and transient—in the note-to-note foreground."[306] The subsumption of foreground events under broader perceptual-conceptual categories or archetypes, and the enjoyment of such relationships, is essential to Meyer's conception of music. To a nonsemantic and nonrepresentative art, hierarchical relationships are utterly indispensable, for they are what permit absolute music's "separable parts" to "combine into intelligible wholes."[307]

For atomistic 'stimuli' to form the larger-scale 'events' Meyer believes constitute the foundation for higher-order processive and formal relationships, it is essential they exhibit closure. While closure is extensively the achievement of 'primary' parameters, hierarchical interactions make it possible for parameters to function either congruently (signaling closure on multiple levels at once) or noncongruently (where some parameters signal closure while others imply continuation). Congruently defined closures create more distinctly demarcated 'events' and thus figure more decisively into the articulation of higher level shapes and structures. Those that are not congruently defined figure more importantly in creating and sustaining the sense of motion and continuation.

The role specific parameters play in articulating structure depends upon the style, but can also vary on distinct hierarchical levels: ". . . as one moves from one level to another, there is always an alternation of functional significance. What is processive on one level (for instance the note-to-note relationships within the first measure of the theme) becomes formal (a motive) on the next; what is formal on one level tends to become processive on the next."[308] Meyer appears to mean that music's conformant and processive relationships, though distinct, complement each other hierarchically. Lower-level, foreground processes (Gurney's cogent sequences or essential form) may, on a higher level, function as events that enter into conformant relationships, and in turn become bases for still further processive implications.

These points clearly reveal Meyer's decisive departure from information theory's overly simple emphasis on complexity. Earlier, he had written of the need to ground musical value in a principle of "psychic economy" that would weigh musical "results" against apparent effort and distinguish the pretentiousness of needless complexity from complexity worth its while.[309] The applicability of information theory to music, Meyer came to conclude, was "much more restricted" than he had previously estimated: for it addresses only "foreground successions, not extended higher level relationships."[310] Seemingly simple and predictable musical events often involve higher-level relationships that are rich, elegant, and complex. When potential interactions between note-to-note successions and higher-order implications are taken into consideration, it is evident that musical complexity is profoundly multidimensional.

One of the notable accomplishments of the hierarchical account of music is its illumination of the abundant "relational richness" to which seemingly simple musical ideas can give rise. Although complexity thus remains an important underlying determinant of value, "richness" is different from foreground complexity, and is "in no way incompatible with simplicity of musical vocabulary and grammar."[311]

Ethos and "Ethetic Relationships"

Because it is "difficult to describe and problematic to explain the effective [*sic*] experiences evoked by works of art,"[312] Meyer has less and less to say in his later work about feeling responses to music. Still, he believes, there are two different sorts of musical experience which are appropriately described as 'affective': the processive/implicative, and the "ethetic." The former consists of responses that unfold along with the music's "intricate patternings of anticipation and tension, delay and denial, fulfillment and release."[313] They are directly evoked by cognition of conformant, processive, and hierarchical relationships. Ethos on the other hand "refers to those aspects of the affective experience which remain relatively constant over time and which are the basis for the characterization of all or part of a composition."[314] Ethos is the music's "character," its feeling-tone, and is a function of the fluent listener's "empathetic identification" with music. Since fluent listeners respond to music with their "total being," ethos is "quite literally felt, and it can be felt without the mediation of extramusical concepts or images."[315]

Ethos is more abstract and general than the moment-to-moment experience of music's unfolding patterns, yet curiously, they arise from the same fundamental source. Beneath it all, "ethetic relationships are inseparable from implicative and hierarchic ones."[316] Secondary musical parameters, those foreground qualities associated with constancy and activity, directly influence music's ethos, permitting the characterization of moderate, steady music as calm or even idyllic. And by the same token, syntactical development and high-level formal structure may quite literally be "regular or sporadic, balanced or asymmetrical, predictable or capricious." "Broadly speaking," says Meyer, "ethos is delineated both by the disposition of relatively stable parameters (e.g., tempo and register, dynamic level and mode) and by foreground grammatical/syntactic organization"; yet "if ethos is to 'ring true', it must be justified by the larger syntactic structure. 'Empty bombast' is emphatic insistence without relational support."[317]

Meyer's earlier writing implied ethos was exclusively associative, the result of similarities between the musical processes and those in everyday life. In his later thought, though, ethos is linked to processive and formal relationships. Thus, he seems to imply, even though musical experience and responses cannot be neatly segregated from the nonmusical, for the truly competent listener even ethetic responses are rooted in music's objective patterns.

The Values of Musical Formalism

In musical formalism's long history, Leonard Meyer's work is probably the most articulate, systematic, and balanced account yet attempted. His is a relatively plausible and self-consistent defense of music as a "closed system," one that employs "no signs or symbols referring to the non-musical world of objects, concepts, and human desires."[318] Because of its detail and scope, Meyer's theory is well suited to an exploration of the advantages and disadvantages, the strengths and weaknesses, of formalism in general.

Efforts to define and defend the formalist position repeatedly encounter at least four basic issues. First, there is the apparent difficulty of stating an essentially positive conviction in negative terms. Second, the world of musical form is often held to be so distinctive or unique that access seems limited to the select or the specially endowed. Third, formalism is often undergirded by a subject-object dualism that tends to denigrate the role of the listener[319] in comparison to the putative concreteness and objectivity of music's structures. Finally, structural/formal accounts of music are often hard put to accommodate music's phenomenal movement, its profoundly processual character. Weaving its way through each of these issues in turn is the more fundamental question about the relative significance of sense, emotion, imagination, rationality, and their many cognates to music.

Meyer confronts these problems with varying degrees of success. His extensive efforts to describe the nature and value of music in positive terms are far more successful than those of his predecessors. The results of his effort to unravel the subject-object dichotomy and to reconcile music, emotion, and meaning are more uneven, however. His 'objective stimulus, subjective response' paradigm, though significantly modified over time, creates dilemmas that may be insurmountable for musical formalism. The fact that his valiant efforts to reconcile music, emotion, and meaning eventually gave way to descriptions of objective works and their 'implications' for 'competent listeners' suggests that, beneath it all, formalism's foundational assumptions may be hard-pressed to accommodate the full range of musical experience and musical value.

Meyer's basic beliefs about music's nature and value emerge with clarity and consistency despite changes in terminology and subtle shifts in rationale. Music's nature and value are inextricably wed to its patterns, and to the experience that accompanies discrimination and appreciation of intelligible internal relationships. Music may sometimes refer, sometimes express, sometimes assume social significance, Meyer concedes. Yet music is none of these things essentially. Furthermore, although music is undeniably sensuous, it is "directed, not *to* the senses, but *through* the senses, and *to the mind.*"[320] It is to the perceptual capacities of that mind, to the objective nature of the musical patterns it delights in perceiving, to what Meyer designates 'the presentational facts' that all genuinely musical affairs must ultimately be referred. These, Meyer believes, stand in stark contrast to "realms of whim, fancy, and prejudice,"[321] to "voluptuous sensation or . . . the reverie of daydreams,"[322] and to the "vagaries of subjective interpretation" characteristic of nonformalist perspectives. "If one directs attention to the materials and their organizations," Meyer concludes, "meanings . . . will . . . take care of themselves."[323]

Whatever music's emotional appeal, Meyer ultimately finds that such pleasures are "of a lesser order."[324] In fact, he characterizes his early efforts to articulate a central place for affect in music as "Romanticism in quasi-empirical garb."[325] Musical emotion and meaning, he appears to have decided, are secondary to the conscious cognitive appraisal of objective structures and processes. Genuinely musical affective responses are, after all, consequences of cognition.[326] The pleasure of listening to music is first and foremost a cognitive, contemplative pleasure linked to pattern and implication, to the mental comparison of the possible, the probable, and the actual. Its pleasure is not innate, immediate, and direct, but follows from the perception of a particular musical 'event' relative to an appropriate stylistic 'universe of discourse', and an appreciation of its particular ingenuity or relational richness. Pleasure and affective experience are musically relevant, but only for the 'competent' listener in whom all feeling is the direct result of having perceived the objective structural and processive relationships Meyer's theory explicates. And Meyer's ideal listener is not the 'absolute expressionist' who, as Hansen points out, is more interested in feeling music than understanding its rationale, but rather the formalist who "struggles to explain feelings which result from deviation, delay, surprise, etc. in the music."[327]

The fact that awareness of relations is constitutive of genuinely musical experience admittedly means that consciousness transforms or alters the sensually given. But music is not unusual in this regard. After all, some kind of conceptualization "takes place whenever one attends intelligently to the world. It is the only way in which we can cope with the buzzing, booming confusion which everywhere surrounds us."[328] If the ground Meyer appropriates for himself and his theory favors conscious awareness over intuitive immediacy, it is because, in his view, the conscious response is superior to unconscious feeling. Hansen defends Meyer's position: "If intellectual activity in and about musical listening is not *better* than intuitive musical response," he asks, "why ever study music?"[329] It is only by resort to formalist analysis that the legitimacy of any felt response to music can be substantiated. Competent listeners, Hansen continues, are listeners who "feel uncertain where the music is ambiguous . . . [or] feel relief at a resolution."[330] And the only truly reliable way to verify that such feeling has anything to do with music is to subject the music that supposedly evokes the felt responses to close examination and conscious scrutiny.

Just as consciousness is more valuable than intuition, so too are the musical parameters that enable perception and retention of pattern more valuable than those that do not. Since pattern consists in relations among discrete components, musical parameters that can be discretely perceived and related are primary. Other musical parameters, those that contribute more predominantly to qualitative intensity or activity for instance, are, by default, secondary. But this is not intended to imply that things like dynamics and timbre are dispensable. Indeed, Meyer allows that statistical parameters are "more universal," "more natural," and less conventional in their operations than their syntactical counterparts.[331] But because they function by perceptual 'law' rather than conventional rule, their effects are more immediate and direct. They are 'secondary', then, because they sustain activity and continuation instead of delineating structure and articulating form. As qualitative, instinctively apprehended parameters, they are less inherently 'conceptual' in nature, and are therefore as accessible to naive listeners as competent ones. They play an important role in sustaining 'processive relationships', but Meyer's theory favors form and pattern over action and process. Thus, what began as a defense of 'absolute expressionism' ends in formalism.

Among the attractive features of formalism, according to Meyer, is its ideological and cultural neutrality, its descriptive rather than prescriptive nature, and its resultant compatibility with relativism and pluralism. Modern society, he maintains, has renounced monistic and absolutistic orientations for markedly more relativistic and pluralistic ones. Convictions that all reality, all art, and all music are cut from essentially the same fabric have lost their persuasiveness. The long history of attempts to bring music under a single, 'essential', or 'absolute' banner has given way to recognition that music consists in numerous, diverse styles. Because it takes its descriptive cues exclusively from music's objective presence, according to Meyer, formalism is value neutral, capable of representing without distortion the "presentational facts"[332] about music. Formalistic criticism, he believes, is the mode of criticism best suited to understanding stylistic diversity.

Meyer discusses two untenable alternatives to formalism: "traditionalism" and "transcendental particularism." Traditional aesthetics and criticism bifurcate music into instrumental ends and material means. From the traditional perspective, music's value consists in its capacity to imitate, represent, express, communicate, symbolize, socialize, and so on. Whether couched in utilitarian, spiritual, or semantic terms, music is a fundamentally transitive phenomenon whose understanding requires finding what it is "about." Such segregation of subject matter from materials (of content from form) is no longer convincing, Meyer argues: "It is not that art no longer represents, it often does; or that it is no longer expressive, it frequently is; or that it has ceased to be socially relevant, at times it may well be so. Rather it is that . . . content and meaning are no longer considered to be definable and explicable apart from the specific materials of a work of art and their formal structuring in that work."[333] Contemporary musical thought renounces "willful interpretation," rejects "blatant and flatulent criticism" in favor of objectivity, rigor, and the 'presentational facts':[334] the specialties, he believes, of formalism.

At the other end of the means-ends continuum lies 'transcendental particularism', which claims exclusive interest in materials as materials, in sound as sound. The locus of value lies in the particularity of "this discrete sound" rather than meanings, relationships, or abstractions. Particularists want to shatter the interpretive lenses that mediate and therefore distort perception, to return people to a state of naive, unmediated innocence—to the beauty of sound purely in itself. Particularists want to embrace the "true and natural" world of flux rather than trying to conquer it or impose human will upon it. Their "method" consists in the denial of pattern and relationships, the abolition of discernible structure, and the achievement of radical novelty: a purely sensuous 'aesthetic'.

Although novelty clearly figures prominently in Meyer's account, it always operates within style instead of against it, in an effort to destroy it. The particularist's radical version of novelty shuns stylistic norms, hoping to "present the concrete particularity of sense experience, unstructured by habit and unguided by known schemata."[335] It embraces novelty "not because it expands the categorical sensibilities . . . but because it destroys them altogether."[336] But according to Meyer, particularism is psychologically untenable because people abhor uncertainty and find nothing more poignant and disturbing than not knowing.[337] Moreover, perception without conceptualization is simply impossible: "even unique particulars are experienced categorically."[338]

Meyer's descriptions of traditionalism and particularism are clearly undertaken with the intent of establishing formalism as the reasoned middle ground between two untenable extremes. Formalism is an "objective, neutral method."[339] It evaluates music not in terms of absolutes but in terms of its "consistency, precision, and ingenuity,"[340] concerns always relative to stylistic 'universes of discourse'. Where traditionalists hold that music represents reality and particularists that it presents reality, formalists maintain that music creates a reality.[341] The formalist's primary concern, then, is to understand and enjoy how such 'realities' are created and treated in each instance. The formalist's criteria of musical value are "elegance of design and ingenuity of process, precision of rhetoric and impersonality of craft, rather than emphasis upon individual self-expression or social significance. The arts [should] be valued not because they purify the soul or promote social good, but because they involve the fun and fascination of exercising that faculty which is most peculiarly ours: namely the human mind."[342]

Meyer's claim that formalism is flexible, relativistic, and capable of providing illuminating insights into multiple and diverse musics may well be true. And that formalism tends to be less doctrinaire, reserving a more central place for music's own voice than certain other philosophical programs, may also be a defensible claim. However, Meyer's formalism is not value neutral, nor is it as pluralistic as he maintains. The idea of a perspectiveless perspective is itself subtly ideological, and the claim that formalism is value neutral only serves to hide certain biases. Among Meyer's central convictions is a belief in the inherent desirability of pluralism. "An educated person," according to Meyer, "is one to whom a broad spectrum of ideas and works of art are meaningful."[343] And the kind of society to which he thinks such education should lead is a secular, humanistic one that "delight[s] in diversity and dig[s] differences."[344] But whether formalism is inherently and fundamentally pluralistic remains to be seen. Despite his formalistic persuasions, Hanslick for instance is not conspicuously pluralistic. More to the point, Meyer's theory is itself laden with often-implicit assumptions as to what music should be and do. The diversity in which it 'delights' is not unlimited, and it 'digs' certain differences quite a bit more than others.

Felt responses to music are invariably secondary to cognitive ones in Meyer's theory. Like the 'absolute formalist' described in *Emotion and Meaning in Music*, he appears to believe that "the meaning of music lies in the perception and understanding of the musical relationships set forth in the work of art, and that meaning in music is primarily intellectual."[345] Complexity—or more properly, syntactical complexity—is also clearly among the criteria for musical value favored by Meyer's formalism. Although he denounces information theory's 'simple-minded counting', the multidimensional "relational richness" he prefers in later writings is at bottom a highly nuanced kind of complexity. Formalism does not regard syntactical simplicity as a musical virtue. And the fact that Meyer's brilliant musical analyses are invariably drawn from the Western European canon of 'learned' musics is no coincidence.

Just as more complex is better, so is the delayed gratification demanded by complex formal configurations inherently better than the joy of the moment. Formal perception requires mindful effort and time. The best music is music whose implications become fully evident only with many repeated hearings. The enjoyment of music's sensuous surfaces, the 'secondary' parameters that supposedly support them, and musics that extensively employ such parameters are less valuable than their formally sophisticated counterparts. The kind of indulgence to which they appeal is like "getting . . . drunk on the green wine of immediacy"[346]—obviously, for Meyer, no proper way to experience music.

In short, structure, syntax, and the 'mindful' relationships they implicate are more valuable than the particular, the immediate, and the sensuous. So, too, is music characterized by "impersonality of craft" better than music closely linked to the individuality and idiosyncrasies of those who make or perform it. The personal and the particular intrude upon and divert attention from the universal and the objective. This account clearly favors certain musical traditions over others. For some musics—those, for instance, that are composed rather than improvised, hierarchically structured and intended for perception by a fundamentally reflective act rather than created on the spot—this approach may work relatively well. For others, such assumptions distort and trivialize attributes that are constitutive: personality of expression, joy in the moment, the richness of the sensuous surface itself, the exquisite sense of presence, and temporal passage. Thus, formalism's claims to 'value neutrality' are not only inaccurate, they hide biases and tacit assumptions that privilege some musics and marginalize others.

One of the more striking features of Meyer's theory is its continuity with idealistic philosophical traditions. Just beneath its 'modern' surface lies a conviction at least as old as Plato that 'merely' sensory experience is of a lower order of reality and value than experience mediated by mind, and a belief in the possibility of descriptive neutrality and objectivity. True musical value resides in patterns and relationships that carry the definitive human trait of rationality. Meyer departs markedly from many idealist predecessors in his advocacy of pluralism and relativism, his belief that the twentieth-century world is one "without scientific, metaphysical or aesthetic absolutes."[347] Yet his relativism and pluralism only extend so far: they do not extend to formalism's own foundational assumptions. In Meyer's view, perception of objective structure enables musical experience to transcend private and personal experience and engage the most elevated of human capacities, rationality, in goalless play.

In summary, while musical formalism represents a beneficial reaction against the metaphysical excesses of idealistic theory, many of its own assumptions and priorities are subtly ideological as well. These assumptions and priorities privilege certain musical 'voices' and effectively marginalize—even silence—others. Formalism's preoccupation with what it designates 'intramusical' clearly devalues the 'extramusical' remainder. Its interest in system and structure may devalue personal expression and activity. Its interest in contemplation and reception may devalue action and agency. Its interest in 'objectivity' may devalue parameters and experiences that tend to be more personal and subjective. Its interest in the uniqueness of musical experience risks severing music from realms of humanly significant endeavor. Yet these are contingent rather than necessary features of musical formalism, and a great deal is owed to those who have insisted that musical philosophy ground itself in the phenomena it purports to explain. To be fully understood, fully felt, or fully experienced, the musical formalist insists, music must first be fully perceived.

Concluding Remarks

As we have seen, formalism has historically been somewhat clearer about what it opposes than what it proposes, more successful in clearly articulating what music is not than what it is. Its most passionate criticisms have been leveled at the idea of 'musical expression' and related doctrines which portray music's meaning and value in a heteronomist light, as affairs that are somehow referential or instrumental in nature. Music's beauty, its essential nature, and its highest value are things that are music's and music's alone, the musical formalist insists. Understandably, then, the formalist is intent upon discrediting theories that neglect music's uniqueness by subsuming it under some other banner, thereby reducing it to an instance of something not music. As a result, the formalist argument frequently states its positive thesis in negative terms, a tendency well exemplified in Stravinsky's pronouncement, "I consider that music is, by its very nature, essentially powerless to *express* anything at all. . . ."[348] It is not altogether surprising, then, to find the term 'formalism' used more often by detractors as an epithet of abuse than by adherents as a term that accurately describes views they hold. 'Formalism' is a rather pejorative label for convictions regarded as essentially positive by those who hold them.

In this chapter we have explored from a number of perspectives what might be called music's 'demarcation problem': What counts as 'musical' and what does not? Where does one draw the line between musical and extramusical value? These were contentious matters, we have seen, even in ancient Greek times. But it was the advent of 'absolute', instrumental music in Europe and the attendant idea of musical autonomy that brought urgency to these issues for Hanslick and Gurney. They found metaphysical philosophy's solution to the form-content problem wholly unacceptable. In their eagerness to elucidate music's contribution to mind, such theories had focused on its resemblances to idea and feeling to the detriment of the distinctly and purely musical. Hanslick attempted to set the record straight by insisting that people's sensual responses and emotional associations not be mistaken for its content—for such notions turn people away from the very phenomenon they presume to be explaining. Music's form (albeit, tonally moving form) is its content, argued Hanslick. Properly musical meaning resides in a closed system, a domain that is wholly and exclusively musical. Gurney took up this argument, maintaining that musical beauty is so utterly and wholly unique that it can only truly be accounted for by the existence of a strictly musical mental faculty. His patient, thorough analyses are unwaveringly devoted to showing that music is a kind of form, of experience, of movement like none in any other human realm—facts that require a definite kind of hearing capable of grasping music's individuality and particularity, not the vague, fuzzy, 'indefinite' hearing of the kind so easily diverted by superficial (extramusical) connections and resemblances. In particular, like Hanslick, Gurney is skeptical of heteronomist claims to expression: music may at times be expressive, he shows, but this in no way establishes that expression is its inner nature. A piece of music resembles nothing so closely as other pieces of music, and music simply lacks the definite representational capacity required for it to designate or express emotion and feeling.

Meyer's contemporary accounts advance an explanation of music and feeling with which both Hanslick and Gurney would likely concur: there is a properly musical range of felt experience, but it is exclusively and uniquely musical. Meyer allows for the musical relevance of only a relatively restricted range of feeling: that which arises as a direct result of the perception and cognition of sonorous ('intramusical') patterns and relationships. We have also seen that he believes music's intramusical relationships are objective and stable enough to warrant the label 'implications'. He, like Hanslick and Gurney, regards emotional or subjective responses as being of a lesser order than those objectively linked to (or caused by) auditory-cognitive processes. We have already observed how these convictions manifest themselves for Meyer in an apparent hierarchical superiority for structural musical parameters over processual or experiential ones, and how this may compromise his claim to formalism's value neutrality. Since belief in the existence of a wholly and strictly musical domain is explicit in the views of Hanslick and Gurney and at least implicit in Meyer's, we would do well to note once more that the formalist point of view cannot be a point of view without point of view (or, in other words, 'value neutral'). For in addition to formalism's preference for pattern over process, mental experience is more valued than bodily experience, cognition more than sociality or intersubjectivity, and listening—rapt, vigilant listening—more than other modes of musical engagement and agency. Mindful listening is musical formalism's most exemplary and exalted mode of musical involvement: contemplative attention to temporally emergent patterns of sound. This view has been, and remains, enormously influential. Indeed, the neatness of its demarcation of the 'properly musical' makes it very appealing and useful in disciplines ranging from music instruction to cognitive science. From the points of view of many whose views will be explored in the chapters ahead, however, formalism seriously underestimates what music is and tragically undervalues its broader human significance. Whether something appropriately called formalism is ultimately capable of accounting for the full range of music's potentialities thus becomes an issue that cannot be taken lightly.

DISCUSSION QUESTIONS

1. The distinction between 'primary' and 'secondary' musical parameters closely parallels the distinction between cognition and sensation, subtly implying that musics in which secondary ('felt' as 'quality') parameters predominate is somehow baser or of lesser cognitive value. In other words, knowing is the measure of musical worth, and the corporeal a separate, inferior kind of musical engagement. Identify and listen to (or better still, play or perform) a music in which so-called secondary parameters are predominant. Discuss this contrast in light of your experience.

2. Gurney's distinction between expression and expressive ('impressive') music suggests that the felt response to music has no necessary connection to a realm of extramusical feeling, and that 'expression' is not a necessary function of music. Apply this distinction to a piece of music you regard as highly expressive and to one you regard as inexpressive.

3. Aristoxenus's concern that philosophers often generate theory without musical grounding is one for which support is not difficult to find. What

of his complaint that performers are oblivious to philosophical/theoretical concerns? In your estimation does this accurately describe the situation today? Why should practicing musicians be conversant in the philosophical issues in their field of endeavor?

4. How would you respond to Philodemus's assertion that music no more contributes to human character than cookery? to Sextus's claim that music's power is mainly one of distraction? Is music merely a 'decorative' art, a diversion? If so, how can its study be justified? If not, what does music offer that makes it more than an entertainment?

5. Hanslick's contrast between logical and pathological responses to music—what Gurney characterizes as the definite and indefinite ways of hearing—is rooted in a conviction that not all musical responses are equally musical. Hanslick might well have argued that music's 'enthusiasts' do not so much know what they like as they like what they know. Is this position elitist? Why or why not?

6. It is easy to take issue with Hanslick's comparison of the 'enthusiast's' musical experience to warm baths and cigars, or Gurney's comparison to opium-induced reverie. How might you characterize the musical experience of a hypothetical listener who has not yet developed the capacity to detect and follow music's tonal or ideal motions? Presumably, this is the way all of us experience musics with which we are wholly unfamiliar. How well do your classically honed, Western, musical perceptual skills serve you when listening to music in a tradition with which you are wholly unfamiliar? What in your experience (if anything) might serve to distinguish it from the mindless indulgence in sheer sound Hanslick and Gurney seem to have in mind?

7. Many of the intractable problems associated with idealistic accounts of music stem from its dualistic foundations. Can you identify viable alternatives to the disposition that separates musical stimulus from response, feeling from thought, body from mind? Specifically how would such alternatives reorient idealism's approach to questions of music's nature and value?

8. The distinction between possession and expression, between things music can express and characteristics it has, is an important logical point that Nelson Goodman will refine in the next chapter of this book. Can you explore this distinction, referring to specific pieces of music?

9. Do you think it possible for humans to listen to music on a purely sensual level? Or should such listening be regarded as by definition premusical? Do you think it possible to perceive music on an exclusively musical level as described by the philosophers discussed in this chapter—purging from experience everything not objectively and empirically there in the sound? Why or why not?

10. What do you make of Meyer's claim that the formalist and the expressionist are simply attending to the same thing in different ways?

11. Discuss the difference between conceiving of music syntactically (or as it is sometimes described, as a 'meta-language') and semantically. Which do you find more persuasive? Why?

12. What significance do you attribute to the fact that formalist accounts of music appear to assume that listening rather than participating or performing lies at the heart of 'the musical experience'? to the fact that they appear to arise from 'literate' rather than 'aural' cultures?

13. Discuss Meyer's contrast between the musically 'referential' and the 'absolute'. Under this latter heading, Meyer posits 'absolute formalism' and 'absolute expressionism'. What is the basis for these distinctions? Can there be expression that is not referential? How so or why not?

14. Prominent among Meyer's reasons for endorsing formalism is its resistance to what he describes as 'willful interpretation', its capacity to keep speculation on a relatively short leash. Meyer sometimes appears to believe, however, not just that the leash is shorter but that there is no leash at all: that attending to formal concerns assures a kind of descriptive neutrality capable of even-handedly describing all musics as they objectively are. Is the formalistic perspective value- or bias-free, capable of description without interpretation? Why or why not?

15. Steven Feld criticizes Meyer's theories for approaching musical meaning purely as a psychological problem, neglecting "the social character of the musical communication process: the listener is implicated as a socially and historically situated being, not just as the bearer of organs that receive and respond to stimuli. . . . [L]istening is not just a juxtaposition of a musical object and a listener." It is, rather, a dialectical entangling of ". . . mental and material, individual and social, formal and expressive. . . ."[349] Explore the challenges music's social and material dimensions present to Meyer's psychological perspective. How might the idea of musical listening as a dialectical process help resolve some of the tensions in Meyer's account?

Music as Symbol

Interest in the ways people formulate and share meanings with each other has led in the twentieth century to close analysis of the way things come to signify, refer to, or stand for other things in human cognitive experience. Theories that seek to explain these processes of meaning construction have sometimes been generally described as symbol theories, while the rigorous discipline devoted to illuminating the systems and processes that underlie the human use of signs and symbols, and the way these mediate cognitive activity, is known as semiotics. In this chapter we undertake an examination of several noteworthy attempts to bring music under the rubric of symbol, and to situate music within semiotic theory.

Much of the pioneering work in this field was concerned primarily with realms of discourse and language—indeed, the great majority of it still is. Accordingly, much of this work makes the implicit assumption that the limits of discourse and of rational meaning are one and the same—and that whatever lies outside the domain of propositional discourse must be, by default, irrational. Clearly, assumptions like these create a rather inauspicious situation for undertakings like music and 'the arts'. Those convinced that things like music play crucial roles in the construction of meanings and ideas have thus argued strenuously that it should be recognized as symbolic activity, as an instance of semiosis. Accepting the premise that cognition is mediated by signs, symbols, and the kinds of referring to which they give rise, an effort is made to show how music and the arts partake of these processes. An adequate account of the human use of signs and symbols for constructing and interpreting the world, they maintain, must include a place of prominence for the arts.

Not surprisingly, though, beyond commitment to this fundamental principle, accounts of what it means to call music a sign or symbol diverge rather dramatically. Precisely what the terms 'sign' and 'symbol' should designate and how they function are by no means universally agreed upon. Nor, in fact, do all adherents of semiotic theory even purport to study 'symbolism' per se: for that word has accumulated a diverse and bewildering range of meanings which many adherents of semiotic theory would prefer to avoid. Yet, references to the 'musical symbol' have become quite commonplace, and an understanding of what this symbolic claim entails is clearly of philosophical importance.

The idea that music is in some sense symbolic has philosophical roots that probably extend at least as far back in history as the ancient doctrines of mimesis and ethos—the belief that music imitates and shapes attributes of human character. The influence of idealism is also quite often evident in symbolic theories, since its quest to secure a place for music in the realm of cognitively significant activity yielded so many inspiring descriptions of music's distinctive felt and rational attributes. Also, since symbolic accounts generally entail the conviction that music's significance is a function of its capacity to signify, point to, or represent something other than itself, familiar tensions between expression and autonomy (between referential capacity and presentational immediacy) often lie very near the surface. Thus, symbolic accounts of music occasionally resonate deeply with idealistic philosophical orientations of formalistic or expressionistic persuasions, orientations to which they are in certain respects related.

Explaining how music is symbolic is dauntingly difficult. Yet, the idea that music is a distinctive kind of symbol situation with its own musically unique semantic devices and revelatory capacity is one that inspires intense loyalty. In a world bewitched by scientific knowledge and technology, establishing music's status as 'intelligence' and explaining the mechanisms responsible for its mindfulness have become an urgent project in the minds of many. Knowledge has become the measure of musical worth, and showing how music contributes to people's representations and understanding of the world has become key to its being taken seriously.

We begin this chapter with the extraordinarily influential work of **Susanne Langer** (1895–1985), whose life-long quest to construct a theory of human mind that recognizes the cognitive significance of artistic engagement convinced generations of musical scholars that music was fundamentally symbolic. Although the strong influence of German idealism is often apparent in her ideas, her unwavering conviction that music is in fact an important vehicle by which humans construct their conceptions of 'reality' led her to forge an inspiring account of music as a special kind of intelligence. In Langer's view, music is a provider of profoundly important human insights attainable in no other way, and specifically, a means of gaining insight into and understanding of the nature of human feeling.

At the heart of her theory lies a very distinctive definition of 'symbol': a vehicle for the conception of reality. By this Langer means that symbols are the things with which we wrest entities and events from 'raw' sense data and the flow of undifferentiated presence—things with which we forge pattern and meaning from randomness and confusion. We cannot know the world as it 'really' is, believes Langer, only those aspects that get refracted for us by symbols and are thus rendered conceivable. What music does, in this view, is enable conception. This act of coherence making is, furthermore, the common foundation of thought and music; this achievement of coherence, not the logical operations by which it is subsequently manipulated and ordered, is the root of humankind's distinctive mental power. In other words, thought and music are each ways—albeit contrasting ways—of 'transforming reality symbolically'.

These two ways of symbolization Langer designates 'discursive' (after 'discourse') and 'presentational'. The former, obviously, is what language employs, while the latter is exemplified by music and the arts. As symbolic modes, both function in accordance with the same underlying principle: perception of common logical form between symbol and symbolized. So the patterns inherent in verbal expression make it well suited to certain kinds of conceptions and insights, while those in music are specially suited to others. Langer claims variously that music makes change perceivable, makes time audible, and creates a 'sonorous image of passage'; but it is music's special relationship to feeling that is its most significant value. Music should be regarded neither as a symptom nor as the cause of feeling, she urges, but rather as the logical symbolic expression of the inner, felt life. Music is structurally analogous to the realm of human sentience and thereby an important vehicle for the conception, and indeed even the 'education', of the life of feeling. Music does for feeling what language does for thought.

Nelson Goodman (b. 1906) offers sophisticated technical analyses of the ways symbols and symbol systems work. Goodman's conviction that humans symbolically construct their worlds resembles Langer's thesis on a general level; but his close explorations of the 'logic' of symbolic functioning clarify many issues that remained cloudy in Langer's accounts, and correct points on which it appears she was probably mistaken. Many details of Goodman's account and some of his most basic philosophical assumptions diverge substantially from the theory advanced by Langer. For Goodman, symbols are not so much purveyors of insight into otherwise inaccessible realms of experience as tools with which people construct or create their worlds. Nor are Goodman's art symbols go-betweens for mind and feeling, vehicles that mediate a cognitive grasp of the 'felt world'. Music's relation to feeling is more a function of the way symbols work: in musical experience emotions function cognitively, in service of infinitely fine interpretive judgments and executive decisions. Where Langer's views were idealistic, Goodman's are nominalistic: that is, he believes general terms and universals are just names, without objective reference. Words and other symbols, thus, must not be viewed as proxies for a 'reality' to which they refer, nor vehicles for its conception. There is no way the world is, believes Goodman, only various ways it may be. Symbols are simply tools we employ for the important human business of 'world making'.

As Goodman sees it, the difference between 'art' and 'non-art' symbols, or what Langer called discursive and presentational symbols, is not a function of whether they refer or not: all symbol situations are referential; all symbols, by definition, refer. Nor do these differences have anything interesting to do with structural similarity between symbol and symbolized, for symbols do not work that way. Their functions are more arbitrary, more conventional; matters of habit, rather than of fact. Thus, for Goodman, symbolic activity is never a process of neutrally representing, mirroring, or 'conceiving' an external reality as it 'really' is. All representation is representation-as, interpretation, and hence reality construction.

If the distinctive character of art or music symbols, their felt immediacy for instance, is not a function of reference or similarity, though, how do we account for it? Goodman's answer is disarmingly simple and direct. The 'expressiveness' of such symbols is explained by their being instances of exemplification, a symbol situation in which what a symbol refers to are features it actually possesses. Music expresses melancholy, for instance, when it both refers to and has that quality. Although this is not yet the place to engage in the detailed explanation this point requires, it is important to anticipate where it eventually leads us. Determining which of the features a symbol refers to it also possesses is, Goodman maintains, a matter of infinitely fine cognitive adjustments. And thus, the mysterious realm known for two hundred years as the 'aesthetic' is after all a matter of symbolic cognitive activity. We will conclude our consideration of Goodman, by examining an intriguing debate between him and aesthetician-philosopher **Monroe Beardsley** (1915–1985) that highlights some of the tensions between the aesthetic and semiotic paradigms.

The semiology of **Jean-Jacques Nattiez** (b.1945) takes the fluidity, polyvalence, and plurivocality implicit in Goodman's account further yet, examining the relations among sound, production, and interpretive stance in musical experience. In his theory it becomes evident just how decisively semiotic accounts of music have departed from the idealistic propensities evident in Langer's influential work. Nattiez's theory rejects the idea of one-to-one correspondences between signifiers (symbols) and signifieds (symbolized). Like Goodman, Nattiez emphatically rejects the notion that music is an element in a direct, transitive process where meanings are somehow 'read off' a musical 'text' in a structurally determined way—the kind of interpretive process formalists often appear to have in mind. Rather, insists Nattiez, music is whatever people choose to recognize as such, and its meanings are constituted by an open-ended interpretive process constrained only by sounds and the lived experiences of those engaged with them. Thus, while music figures importantly in the construction of meanings, the range of those meanings is potentially infinite, and the 'referring' process that generates them is always indeterminate. Music is thus plural and dynamic, and its meanings are relative to a potentially infinite range of interpretive variables.

This point of view presents sharp contrasts to those advanced by Hanslick, Gurney, and Meyer. For in this view, musical meaning (indeed, what music 'is', and even *when* it is) is not a stable, or indeed, a unidimensional thing—it cannot be accounted for in perception of patterned sound alone. Musical meanings are not structurally determined or defined. They arise and are sustained in cultural context, and are enmeshed in webs of interpretants; and thus, there is no definitively musical meaning for any musical event or sign situation. Musical meanings are multiple, fluid, and dynamic—perhaps, we might say, like a ship being perpetually rebuilt while at sea.

The upshot of all this is that structure is blind to musical meaning, a point that raises profound questions about the adequacy of musical theory and analysis which restrict themselves to the level of auditory pattern. Music is always polysemic; and the difference between music and non-music cannot be determined by attending to sound alone. In should be clear, then, that this stance raises provocative and important questions about the 'relativity' of music—about whether the pursuit of a single, unitary nature or value of music is advisable, and indeed, whether the centered, unitary idea of 'music' is but an empty abstraction.

Despite the marked contrasts and profound differences among the three accounts examined here, each is concerned in its own way with the ways this thing called music (or, these things called musics) come to 'mean', and with what they mean. Each theory seeks in its own distinctive way to show how music enters into and mediates the cognitive connections that form and inform a human world.

Langer: Conceiving the Patterns of Sentience

Susanne Langer's theories about music and the arts are part of an ambitious effort to articulate a theory of mind that encompasses the wealth of human mental powers beyond the narrow bounds staked out by such "scientific" orientations as positivism and behaviorism. Such orientations privilege human undertakings congruent with their conceptual frameworks, but trivialize or ignore those whose nature makes for a more awkward fit. Typically, they divide reality and human experience hierarchically: into the observable, objective, and rationally explicable on the one hand, and the subjective, ineffable, and irrational on the other. In other words, outside the objective world amenable to rational discourse and scientific analysis lies a mysterious, mindless realm dominated by feeling and intuition. It is to this latter realm that artistic endeavor is presumed to belong. Langer passionately rejects this apotheosis of 'objectivity' that construes music and the arts as irrational aberrations, or the mistakes of an otherwise perfectly rational mind. Like discourse, Langer argues, art is intelligent; like language, works of art are vehicles for understanding: they are symbols. Humans use symbols to wrest images of the world from the ongoing flow of perpetual presence, in effect making it hold still so it can be comprehended. Because music no less than language is a vehicle for the conception of reality, musical experiences are important instances of knowing.

As we have seen, this conviction that music has cognitive value has ancient roots, and is a conspicuous presence throughout the recorded history of reflection on music. Like all cognitive theories, Langer's takes knowledge as the measure of humanity. And like most, hers gravitates toward the historically prevalent heteronomist view that music's meaning and value lie somewhere outside the music itself. What distinguishes Langer's approach from its many predecessors is its attempt to establish music's cognitive significance by stressing its symbolic nature. But bringing music under the umbrella of symbolic activity inevitably raises questions about what music symbolizes, and how. Langer's treatment of these issues has the vigor and vitality (as well as some of the naiveté) characteristic of any early exploration of uncharted waters. Despite inevitable shortcomings, Langer's portrayal of music as a symbol and of musical activity as fundamentally rational are an important historical link between nineteenth-century idealism and contemporary semiotic accounts of music.

Langer's theories built on the work of **Ernst Cassirer** (1874–1945), pioneer in the philosophy of language. Cassirer contended, in the Kantian tradition, that all knowledge and experience of the world are shaped by the categories we impose upon them, the schemata by which we conceive them. We cannot know reality independent of our means for conceiving it. Linguistic symbols transform sense data, meaningless in themselves, into things, relationships, and events. As mediators of perception and conception, they determine what we can think or know. Language is no neutral conveyor of information about preexistent reality, truth, or meanings. It gives such things shape and in so doing determines what the world can be. We cannot know prereflective reality (reality as it "really" is), only various cognitive refractions afforded by symbols. Before the refinement of reason and propositional thought, people knew their reality metaphorically. Language and logic offer powerful alternatives and extensions to metaphorical thought, but have not replaced it. The foundation for all propositional thought and discourse, these ancient, imaginative powers remain viable today and are exercised extensively in artistic endeavors. So language and art share a common function, as symbolic systems: mediating our grasp of reality.

Both Langer and Cassirer share an intriguing ambivalence about whether symbols reveal reality or construct it. Do symbols afford insight into something already there, or actually create something new? To deal with this issue and show how music is doing in its distinctive way what language does in its own, Langer developed the enigmatic idea of music as a special kind of symbol, one whose referential function is "unconsummated." Music is symbolic, but exercises its symbolic function quite differently from what she occasionally calls "genuine" symbols.[1] To bring music within the realm of symbols, then, Langer found it necessary to maintain that signifying and referring are not essential symbolic functions. What symbols do, rather, is enable conception—of the world, of 'reality', of the realm of human sentience and feeling. Thus, as we shall see, at the heart of her theory lies a deep and unresolved tension between revelation and creation, between conception and reference.

Symbolic Transformation

In her first book, Langer set forth the basic thesis (a new philosophical "key") whose elaboration became her life's work. For all of science's impressive accomplishments, Langer says, it has utterly failed to elucidate the important area of human mentality. In fact, wherever science's methods have been directed to understanding human mental life, they have succeeded only in obscuring it: science, she claims, has proven itself "bootless for the study of mental phenomena."[2] By contrast, she finds growing recognition of the role of symbolism in human experience and intellection a tremendously exciting generative idea, one that is full of promise for illuminating what science has left a muddle. Its central theme: human consciousness is not passive, but constructive.[3]

In stark contrast to animals', human mentality is through-and-through bound up with symbols that transform mere experience into something conceptual. Despite their continuities and similarities, symbolic capacity is a point of radical divergence between human and animal intelligence. It is a profound error, argues Langer, to construe human behavior as an extension of the stimulus-response reflex arc, to portray human thought as an elaboration of capacities shared in some modest way by animals. Symbolism radically transforms conscious experience, changing the merest act of perception from animal sensation into a process of formation. The process of symbolization enables people to abstract things like objects, events, and relationships from their constant bombardment by sensory stimuli. The power of symbolization creates a distinctively human world of thought, with a past, a present, and a future.

But is symbolization truly unique to humans, Langer wonders? For instance, animals can be taught to use signals to refer to things in their immediate surroundings. Such signaling activity is not symbolic, but symptomatic, reasons Langer, its use restricted to immediate wants and things physically present. Symbols on the other hand are tools that enable us to deal with things not present, to bring things to mind. They transform sensory impressions into things, events, ideas, and values. The human mind incessantly and automatically transforms sensory input into something new, something no animal has: conceptions that endure beyond the experiential data that give rise to them.

This transformational process is the definitive characteristic of symbolization as Langer conceives it: not the more systematic act of thought that it subsequently enables. Thought follows from symbolic activity but is not coextensive with it. "[I]t is not the essential act of thought that is symbolization," declares Langer, "but an act *essential to thought*, and prior to it. Symbolization is the essential act of mind; and mind takes in more than what is commonly called thought."[4] Achievements like signification and reference are relational functions into which symbols may enter, but such functions require prior completion of the act that is truly symbolic: the transformational process that patterns the given, rendering it perceivable and conceivable. Since Langer's symbols are vehicles for conceiving reality,[5] the essential work of symbolization is complete before any of its products are logically, relationally, or propositionally employed.

Recognizing that this formative symbolic process is the essential foundation of all cognitive activity has profoundly important implications for the arts and music, Langer believes, for it establishes that these uniquely human interests are fundamentally cognitive in nature. Although art symbols may be "pre-rationative" in the sense that they are not yet incorporated into systematic thought, they are not "pre-rational."[6] Human perception is a rational achievement, a transformation of fleeting sense data into meaningful images and situations. This being the case, music warrants recognition as a symbol, and its experience warrants recognition as a rational, cognitive achievement.

Since contemporary semiotics generally maintains that both symbols and signs are instances of referring, it is important to understand precisely how Langer's account differs. In her view, referring is essential to the function of signs or "signals," but not to symbols. Signs are of two kinds, natural or conventional. 'Natural signs', explains Langer, contain actual symptoms of what they designate, while the relationship between 'conventional signs' what they signify is largely arbitrary. This distinction, however, is undergirded by a common logical or functional foundation, a relationship between something accessible yet inherently less uninteresting (a sign) and something interesting but less accessible (the signified).[7] Signs signal, "announce" the presence of, or point to their objects: they are instruments of action. Symbols, on the other hand, are instruments of thought: their purpose, says Langer, is not to bring things into our hands, but to bring them to mind.[8]

The link between signs or signals and their referents is a direct one. By contrast, symbols refer to or mean their objects indirectly, through the crucial process of conception. Where signals consist of relatively simple, three-term relations among signal, object, and perceiver, the symbol situation is more complex. In symbolism, the link is not between sign and object, but between symbol and conception: the connection of symbol to symbolized is always mediated by a conception. Where signals are part of a three-term relation (subject-signal-object), symbolism involves a four-term relationship among subject, symbol, conception, and object.[9]

This four-term logical structure is the basis of Langer's important distinction between denotative (literal, or "dictionary") meaning and connotative meanings. In denotation, one associates a symbol with a broad, personal conception, and subsequently determines what it conveys, choosing from the array of objects, events, or situations compatible with the conception. Connotation is the first stage in this process: the correlation of the symbol with a conception. Denotation, then, involves the further matter of determining which, from among the many things a given symbol connotes, a particular context actually implies.[10] Similarly, what we know as concepts are actually inferred from 'constellations of connotations':[11] a concept, says Langer, is "[t]hat which all adequate conceptions . . . must have in common."[12] Thus, in effect, successful communication is a function of the accuracy with which the parties involved identify which among the many connotations associated with a particular symbol situation are appropriate and relevant to the business at hand. The fact that everyday discourse achieves these inferences quickly and effortlessly makes it easy to overlook their underlying complexity and indeterminacy, the remarkably fine discriminations which underlie all concepts and meaning.

This 'conception' that distinguishes signification from symbolization is the common foundation of all human mental processes. Propositional thought and pre-propositional, imaginative experience (music, for instance) appear radically different until one appreciates that they are both manifestations of this fundamentally human tendency to transform symbolically what is given to experience. Since both imaginative and rational activity grow from the same symbolic root, Langer argues, it is clear that human intelligence and knowledge extend well beyond the limits of language. Things like music may not partake of the "rationative" intellectual processes characteristic of propositional thought, but to say that something is "pre-rationative" is not to say that it is "pre-rational." The root of rationality is the formative symbolic process that is already fully manifest in non-propositional cognitive undertakings like music. The act of symbolically transforming sense data into meaningful gestalts is a rational event, a feat of intelligence.

The verbal symbols used in linguistic systems (discourse) Langer calls *discursive* symbols. These discursive symbols and the particular kinds of meaning they purvey, she believes, represent only a small part of the symbolic activity of which humans are capable. The assumption that symbolism extends no further than this discursive realm overlooks a powerful symbolic device every bit as essential to the human mind: a symbol without assigned reference, a "purely connotational semantic."[13] There is, in other words, a symbolic situation in which a symbol is linked to a conception but to no determinate object beyond it. Thus, while the discursive symbolism underlying propositional meanings is much more complicated and indeterminate than is generally assumed, nondiscursive imaginative experience is far from unstructured and mindless. Linguistic representations of 'reality' are not our only ways of knowing. The difference between perception and logical thought in humans is only a matter of degree, not a fundamental difference in kind. Both are, after all, forms of symbolic activity.

However, this is not quite the whole story. According to Langer, symbolic activity is possible because of recognizable formal congruence between a symbol and what it symbolizes. We conceive what sentences convey, for instance, because their (discursive) structure parallels or fits the structure of the events they symbolically represent. The truth or falsity of a sentence, she says, depends on "whether the pattern of things . . . denoted is analogous to the syntactical pattern of the complex symbol."[14] That is, since "words have a linear, discrete, successive order; they are strung one after another like beads on a rosary,"[15] the referential range of discursive symbols is restricted to things which are themselves linear, discrete, and successive. Things not amenable to this particular mode of 'logical projection' are ineffable, incommunicable by words, and indeed, unthinkable.[16]

So sentences are symbolically successful to the extent their syntactical structures parallel the structures of what they convey. Says Langer, whenever discursive thought "seizes on any material—sensations, memories, fantasies, reflections—it puts its seal of fixity, categorical divisions, oppositions, exclusions, on every emerging idea, and automatically makes entities out of any elements that will take the stamp of denotative words."[17] Not every cognitive experience is amenable to discursive form's constraints, though. For instance, "an idea that contains too many minute yet closely related parts, too many relations within relations . . . is too subtle for speech."[18] Since Langer's symbolic functions require an iconic resemblance between the symbol and symbolized, language is quite limited in the range of experience it can symbolize.

Positivistic philosophers, Langer protests, have quite wrongly mistaken the limitations of discursive symbolism for the limits of the knowable. In their accounts, the knowable is "a clearly defined field, governed by the requirement of discursive projectability. Outside this domain is the inexpressible realm of feeling, of formless desires and satisfactions, immediate experience, forever incognito and incommunicando."[19] But for Langer, the fact that a domain of experience is incompatible with language's logical devices does not necessarily make it utterly irrational and inexpressible. There exists a "genuine semantic beyond the limits of discursive language."[20] In fact, nondiscursive symbols are vehicles par excellence for the conception of the vast ranges of experience that elude discursive forms. "[T]he limits of language are not the last limits of experience, and things inaccessible to language may have their own forms of conception, that is to say, their own symbolic devices."[21]

As we indicated earlier, nondiscursive symbols differ from their discursive counterparts in that they lack assigned and conventional reference. In other words, they do not denote, only connote. Speaking "directly to sense," such devices are "first and foremost a direct *presentation* of an individual object."[22] Accordingly, Langer designates them 'presentational' symbols. The presentational symbol does not signify, it only articulates and presents. It has neither a fixed vocabulary nor syntactical rules. It cannot be translated or even paraphrased without radically altering what it conveys. Indeed, it has no meaning apart from its particular mode of presentation. Its import is specific rather than general. Its reference is only to 'this', not to 'this kind'. It is not, says Langer, exemplary but unique.[23] Presentational symbols are formal abstractions made directly by the ear and the eye, "our most primitive instruments of intelligence."[24] But they are primitive only in the sense of being 'foundational', not in the sense of being defective or crude. Indeed, presentational symbols comprise the enabling base for intellect's "higher" achievements. All "so-called 'repeated' experiences are really *analogous* occurrences, all fitting a form that was abstracted on the first occasion."[25]

Unlike the presentational symbol, "a genuine symbol, such as a word, is only a sign; in appreciating its meaning our interest reaches beyond it to the concept. The word is just an instrument. Its meaning lies elsewhere, and once we have grasped its connotation or identified something as its denotation we do not need the word any more."[26] So the verbal symbol is a transparent, transitive affair, a kind of conduit through which we attend to something else. And that function is seriously compromised where the symbol itself becomes too interesting. The meaning or significance of presentational symbols, on the other hand, is direct and immediate. They show rather than tell, demonstrate rather than designate. Their meanings are inseparable from their form and must be grasped either intuitively or not at all. The presentational symbol's significance is not gleaned by attending through it, but attending to it. It is not so much transparent as iridescent.[27]

Langer argues strenuously that ineffability and nontranslatability do not make this 'purely connotative semantic' a second class symbol. Indeed, it has the capacity to formulate and present to conception (to make 'knowable') things that will forever evade language. Without presentational symbols, for instance, we might never know the "ever-moving patterns, the ambivalences and intricacies of inner experience."[28] Language itself is possible only because of the prior human capacity to transform experience conceptually, to "see reality symbolically"—and that is precisely the office of presentational symbols. They are, in short, "genuine symbolic materials, media of understanding, by whose office we apprehend a world of *things*."[29]

Given her emphasis upon the contrasts between discursive and presentational symbolism, it is a little ironic that Langer turns to language for a demonstration of its action. Yet, in metaphor she finds what she believes to be a vivid illustration of the way presentational symbolism works, as well as evidence that the limits of logical reasoning are not coextensive with the limits of verbal meaning. A metaphor, though literally false, is a potent cognitive vehicle, a source of meaning and knowledge. Metaphorical expression is no mere linguistic coloration or ornamentation, rather, it articulates new ideas and insights, and with an economy and precision that eludes literal discourse. Metaphors are not, as the logical positivist would have it, symptoms of confused or ill-formed thought. They are simultaneously illogical and highly rational. Indeed, metaphor is the very source of linguistic novelty and vitality. Despite the logical impossibility of metaphor (brooks cannot laugh, nor pines whisper), apt metaphorical meanings are grasped immediately, intuitively, and no amount of explanation can compensate if that intuitive achievement fails. And importantly for Langer's theory, metaphorical meaning rests upon the spontaneous recognition of formal similarity, not the logical-sequential processes of discursive thought.

The immediacy and effortlessness of metaphorical expression shows "how natural the perception of common form is,"[30] declares Langer. In metaphorical expression, "an image of the literal meaning is our symbol for the figurative meaning, the thing that has no name of its own,"[31] and our grasp of that figurative meaning rests upon prereflective recognition of the structural similarity between the two. This perception of common form is a new meaning, a meaning presented directly to imagination rather than logically deduced. As particularly apt metaphors are used repeatedly, they gradually become conventions and acquire literal meaning. Their (presentational) iridescence fades to (discursive) transparency.

The power of language, then, has its roots in the inauspicious kind of symbolic functions epitomized in perceptual images. Somewhere along the way, the presentational symbol acquires conventional meaning which liberates it from the immediacy of the moment. Once this occurs, its symbolic efficacy depends upon our ability to attend through it to what it designates—unlike the presentational symbol whose utility is a function of the intrinsic quality of its surface. Yet, "the parent stock of both conceptual types . . . is the basic human act of symbolic transformation. The root is the same, only the flower is different."[32] Behind the striking contrasts between discursive and presentational symbols lies a shared symbolic mission: the process of symbolic transformation that brings things to our minds and enables us to keep them there. "[T]he greatest intellectual value and . . . the prime office of symbols," writes Langer, is "their power of formulating experience, and presenting it objectively for contemplation, logical intuition, recognition, understanding. That is articulation."[33]

The human capacity to apprehend common logical form lies at the heart of Langer's theory, a capacity rooted in imagery and the imagination. Images comprise the core of symbolic activity as Langer conceives it. Indeed, it appears intelligence is essentially a kind of 'imagic' fluency, a capacity to discern subtle differences and similarities among images. In the press of everyday life this capacity is put to predominantly practical use: people attend to images only long enough to assess their significance or utility for further ends. But that utility leads us to overlook the more profound value of images: their power to "hold us to a conception."[34] The vivid, memorable image is the source of all rational cognition, and not, as we are often asked to believe, the processes of formal reasoning. "[O]ur primitive intellectual equipment is largely a fund of images. . . . [W]e apprehend everything which comes to us as impact from the world by imposing some image on it that stresses its salient features and shapes it for recognition and memory."[35] More directly still, "the process of seeing things as exemplifications of subjectively created images gives us the original, objective phenomena that theoretical reasoning seeks to understand,"[36] and "[a]ll thinking begins with *seeing*; not necessarily through the eye, but with some basic formulations of sense perception. . . . For all thinking is conceptual, and conception begins with the comprehension of *Gestalt*."[37]

Cognition and perception are not fundamentally different types of activity. Imagination, a way with images, is our basic cognitive process, the essential foundation of propositional thought. And imagination functions intuitively, guided more by feeling than by logic. If this is granted, Langer believes, cognition can no longer be construed as a purely logical, cerebral process. Thought "passes from insight to insight not only by the recognized [logical] processes, but as often as not by short cuts and personal, incommunicable means. The measure of its validity is the possibility of arriving at the same results by . . . demonstrating formal connections. But a measure of validity is not a ground of validity. Logic is one thing, and thinking is another. . . . the wide discrepancy between reason and feeling may be unreal; it is not improbable that intellect is a high form of feeling—a specialized, intensive feeling about intuitions."[38]

The Musical 'Symbol'

Although as we have observed, Langer's musical philosophy has deep roots in nineteenth-century idealism; so too, she maintains, does "practically all serious and penetrating philosophy of art."[39] It was the idealists, she explains, who took the relationship between art and mind seriously, and paved the way for a conception of music as a rational, symbolic activity. Thus Langer sees her theory as emergent from but an improvement on idealistic accounts of music.

For instance, although idealists were essentially right to connect music with feeling, clearly it will not do to confuse that feeling with immediate sensual gratification—a state of arousal that is an unmediated response to a stimulus. If music were that kind of thing, Langer reasons, great music would appeal to "the untutored as well as to the cultured."[40] And although the Freudian insight that human consciousness is undergirded by a symbolic dynamic is richly suggestive, if music were only a matter of releasing pent-up desire, music's formal excellence would not matter the way it does. Then too, important though formalism's emphasis on autonomy is, it leaves unexplained why and how such a purely autonomous music should have the broadly human appeal it does. Then there is the idea of self-expression which, although it rightly focuses on music's distinctive felt quality, tends to portray music making as a symptom of emotional upheaval and listening as a kind of voyeuristic eavesdropping on other people's experience. What is frequently meant by self-expression, Langer explains, might better be called emotional discharge or self-exposure: hardly the kinds of things that attract most people to music. In fact, the more 'self'-expressive something is, the less musical it is likely to be.

Music, Langer is convinced, is not about exposing, discharging, or expressing feeling; and yet, it is clearly related to feeling in some important way. How might that be? Simply, music is a presentational symbol; and as such it is neither a stimulus nor a symptom of feeling: it is "not the cause or the cure of feelings, but their logical expression."[41] Music comes by its emotional 'content' the same way language comes by its intellectual content: symbolically.[42] Music is not a signal though, the kind of thing that points to what it means; it is a symbol that enables conception of its object.[43] Thus, its emotive significance is not a function of feelings felt, evoked, or aroused, but of insight into the form of feeling. The images of feeling with which music presents us invite "not emotional response, but insight."[44] In short, "[M]usic is not self-expression, but formulation and representation of emotions, moods, mental tensions and resolutions—a 'logical picture' of sentient, responsive life, a source of insight, not a plea for sympathy."[45]

Since this point is crucial to Langer's thesis, she articulates it in quite a number of overlapping and subtly different ways that warrant careful consideration here. "There are certain aspects of the so-called 'inner life'," she explains, "which have formal properties similar to those of music—patterns of motion and rest, of tension and release, of agreement and disagreement, preparation, fulfillment, excitation, sudden change, etc."[46] Since similarity of logical form is the basis for her 'purely connotative semantic', and since music and the 'inner life' share logical forms music and discourse do not, it follows, Langer believes, that "music articulates forms which language cannot set forth."[47] So the difficulty of describing musical feeling is the perfectly reasonable consequence of the fact that "the forms of human feeling are much more congruent with musical forms than with the forms of language."[48] If words could convey what music does, we would not need music.

Note that, consistent with the sentiments of idealism, this explanation imputes a kind of controlled rationality to the way feeling is encountered in music. Thus, music can be a felt phenomenon, yet since it is not concerned with actual, particular feelings but with feeling in general, it is not a dangerously or sensually indulgent affair. Music is not about feelings-felt, but rather the "morphology of feeling."[49] What music gives us is not so much feelings themselves, but something more abstract, a "knowledge of 'how feelings go'."[50] In other words, music is a symbolic presentation of the form of feeling.

Unlike conventional symbols whose significance lies in what they point or refer to, this musical symbol wears its significance 'on its face', so to speak. Its function is fulfilled not by attending through it, but by attending to it. In other words, as a presentational symbol music is a "a significant form without conventional significance,"[51] an "unconsummated symbol."[52] It has "all the earmarks of a true symbolism, except . . . an assigned connotation."[53] What it gives us are articulations or formulations of vital, sentient experience—things that would pass undetected and unknown were it not for music. Music's noble mission is thus to convey a "wordless knowledge . . . of emotional and organic experience, of vital impulse, balance, conflict, the ways of living and dying and feeling."[54] In musical experience, we engage in a mental experience attainable in no other way, in "unconventionalized, unverbalized freedom of thought."[55]

Because music's and feeling's forms are so structurally similar, and because "certain effects of music are so much *like* feeling,"[56] it is understandable that people would mistake particular feelings for music's content. But that is a mistake, nonetheless. For what people take for moods and emotions in music are not really moods and emotions at all: "They merely *sound* the way moods *feel*."[57] Again, music does not arouse or evoke emotion; it articulates a form that is congruent with ("isomophic" to) and capable of exemplifying the salient formal characteristics of a vast range of human feeling. It is "a tonal analogue of emotive life."[58] Its analogous relationship to the patterns of feeling enables it to function symbolically, as a vehicle for the conception of the patterns of human sentience. Yet, because it has no assigned reference, it is an 'unconsummated' symbol.

Criticisms and misunderstandings of her theory led Langer to modify her terminology in important ways over the years. Since, for instance, the idea of 'meaning' is so deeply enmeshed in discourse about conventional symbols (and since meaning for conventional symbols is a function of the act of referring rather than an inherent property of the symbol), she found it necessary to distinguish music's meaning from the common sense of the term: "Just as music is only loosely and inexactly called a language," she writes, "so its symbolic function is only loosely called meaning, because the factor of conventional reference is missing from it."[59] Instead of 'meaning', then, 'vital import' is what the musical symbol conveys. Likewise, because her special account of how symbols function was so widely misunderstood, she found it necessary to stress that the music 'symbol' was quite different from 'true' or 'genuine' symbols. Unlike "true symbols," she explains, music only "formulates and objectifies experience for direct intellectual perception, or intuition," and is thus a symbol only "in a special and derivative sense."[60] Music objectifies sentient experience, making it comprehensible. "In this way, and in no other essential way, [music] is a symbol."[61]

The primary themes articulated in Langer's early work changed remarkably little over the years. Throughout a long and prolific philosophical career, Langer continued to challenge accounts of music as either a symptom or cause of feeling, insisting that notions like these portrayed musical emotion as a purely subjective affair in a way that undermined the possibility of critical judgments. Music's purpose is not so much to provide pleasure as to acquaint the listener "with something he has not known before."[62] It presents feelings for conception, not for enjoyment; for knowledge, not experience. It "negotiates insight, not reference."[63] Music is indeed intimately related to feeling, but not at all in the way most people believe. It shows us, in effect, what feeling might sound like were it the kind of thing we could hear. Because of the close relationship between music's dynamically moving forms and those of feeling, music affords unique and important insight into the patterns of human sentience.

The Sonorous Image of Passage

Langer's determined effort to show music's distinctiveness as a symbol some-times left the unfortunate impression that music was doing in a vague and con-voluted way what 'proper' symbols do straightforwardly and unambiguously. So as 'vital import' took the place of 'meaning' in discussions of music, the term 'symbol' gave way to characterizations of music as an 'expressive form'. Crucial to expressive forms is the sense of otherness, the "air of illusion" they convey.[64] Thus, music puts before us a "virtual" object, a special image or 'semblance' that transcends the materially or physically given. Like rainbows, expressive forms are only given to perception.

Like the presentational symbol, the expressive form has significance as a function of its structural congruence with salient features of felt experience. In contrast to other symbol situations, though, there are no fixed conventions for determining which among the many features apparent in the music semblance should 'count' in determining its import. Potentially, at least, everything counts: "*all* the relationships of its elements to one another, all similarities and differ-ences of quality."[65] Accordingly, musically expressive form's significance cannot be "logically discriminated" but must be "felt as a quality."[66] In other words, ap-prehension of musical import is an intuitive and immediate achievement, not a matter of reflection and interpretation. It can "only be exhibited, not demon-strated to any one to whom the art symbol is not lucid."[67] One either 'gets' the image intuitively or does not.[68]

And yet, Langer urges, it would be a profound mistake to regard this intu-itive foundation as evidence of irrationality. Intuition is, after all, "the same sort of insight that makes language more than a stream of little squeaks . . ."[69] In-deed, intuition is the foundational human intellectual activity, what people do whenever they perceive unity amidst difference. In this view, reason is not the paradigmatic rational power, just "a systematic means of getting from one intu-ition to another."[70] The difference between insight achieved by reason and the insight conveyed in the musical 'illusion' is only the difference between putting intuitions to logical use on the one hand, and engaging in them prereflectively on the other.

Each art has its own distinctive illusion, affords its own distinctive insights into life's vital essence. Although music is comprised of sonorous material, what is important about it is not sound, but an "illusion begotten by sounds."[71] The essential feature of the musical illusion is its motion, a motion in which noth-ing moves: not change of place, but "change made perceivable."[72] It is the mu-sician's task to generate and sustain this illusion of motion, setting it off clearly from the material or physical world of sound, and assuring that its articulated form "coincides unmistakably with forms of feeling and living,"[73] thereby cre-ating "an irresistible appearance of livingness and feeling."[74]

Although motion is not unique to music, musical motion uniquely consists of pure durations or temporality. Music's primary illusion, then, is "an order of virtual time, in which its sonorous forms move in relation to each other—always and only to each other, for nothing else exists there."[75] In this way, "Music makes time audible, and its form and continuity sensible."[76] It "spreads out time for our direct and complete apprehension,"[77] transforming everyday clock time (a "one-dimensional, infinite succession of moments"[78]) into lived time, into felt time consisting in a "dense fabric of concurrent tensions." It acquaints us with time's true richness, a richness profoundly absent from nonmusical temporal experience. Music is thus no less than "the sonorous image of passage."[79] In rendering the richness of temporal passage conceivable, music achieves its primary symbolic mission, presenting us with a rich, nondiscursive image of sentient and emotional reality.

The idea that music is the sonorous image of passage is a universal claim, so any sonorous experience that sustains a sense of flowing organic tension and resolution must be considered musical. "Anything that helps concentration and sustains the illusion," says Langer, "be it inward singing, following a half-comprehended score, or dreaming in dramatic images—may be one's personal way to understanding."[80] Indeed, whatever enters into and helps sustain the primary musical illusion becomes part of the music itself. Music's remarkable power to transform, assimilate, and absorb into its fabric things with which it is associated means that quite a broad range of phenomena may be reasonably considered musical—so long as they support and sustain active engagement in music's primary illusion of temporal passage.

Feeling and Its 'Education'

Calling music an image rather than a symbol does seem to alleviate some of the confusion created by Langer's unconventional definition of what symbols do. And saying that music's meaning or import is inseparable from its form seems a reasonable articulation of the autonomist account of musical value. But despite these adjustments and clarifications, Langer's remains at root a heteronomist stance: this expressive musical form, this sonorous image of passage, is only significant to the extent it implicates something beyond music itself. While it is intuitively and immediately perceived, the significance of the musical image always derives from what it shows us of the quality of motion, of passage, of felt time, and most importantly, of feeling.

It is in Langer's efforts to illuminate the relation between music and feeling that the enigmatic nature of her idea that music yields insight without referring becomes most pronounced. The crux of her argument is that what musical images offer is a "way of conceiving emotion," and that what they convey about feeling is "not 'communicated', but revealed."[81] The composer, then, "is not saying anything, not even about the nature of feeling; he is *showing*. He is showing us the appearance of feeling, in a perceptible symbolic projection; but he does not refer to a public object, such as a generally known 'sort' of feeling, outside his work."[82] What music gives are not feelings per se, but 'articulations of feeling', "forms of life and feeling, activity, suffering, selfhood—whereby we conceive these realities, which otherwise we can but blindly undergo."[83] Music articulates differences in otherwise undifferentiated consciousness, and each piece uniquely articulates its own unique feeling complex.[84]

Music does not arouse or evoke actual moods or emotions. Instead it formulates conceptions of feeling, revealing to us important qualities of inner life. At the same time, "it shapes our imagination of external reality according to the rhythmic forms of life and sentience, and so impregnates the world with aesthetic value."[85] It presents us with images that shape and differentiate consciousness in unique ways, ways which subsequently reorient the way we perceive the world. Simultaneously, then, music subjectifies the world and objectifies our felt existence—which would otherwise (lacking objective, logical form) collapse into "a condensed and foreshortened memory almost as fast as the experience passes."[86] For these reasons, musical experience amounts in Langer's view to "the education of feeling, as our usual schooling in factual subjects . . . is the education of thought."[87] Music gives perceptible shape to people's subjective worlds: "It is their school of feeling, and their defense against outer and inner chaos."[88] Our musical engagements teach us something very significant, and not in spite of, but precisely because of music's ineffable nature. Music is a vehicle for conception; or perhaps more precisely, music articulates for perception a vital image with tensions and rhythms commensurate with the form of feeling. In this way, musical experience serves the important end of educating human feeling.

The nature of 'feeling'—that which it is music's distinguished office to 'educate'— evolves in subtle but significant ways in Langer's writing. In her earlier work feeling is largely synonymous with emotion; but its scope expands dramatically as her theory evolves, until eventually it includes "forms of growth and of attenuation, flowing and stowing, conflict and resolution, speed, arrest, terrific excitement, calm, or subtle activation and dreamy lapses—not joy and sorrow perhaps, but the poignancy of either and both—the greatness and brevity and eternal passing of *everything vitally felt*."[89] 'Feeling' encompasses "whatever is felt in any way, as sensory stimulus or inward tension, pain, emotion or intent";[90] it includes "the sensibility of very low animals and the whole realm of human awareness and thought, the sense of absurdity, the sense of justice, the perception of meaning as well as emotion and sensation";[91] it is an essential element of "impression, emotion, overt action, thought, dream, or even obscure organic process";[92] it includes "the feeling of rational thought, which the discursive record of rational order has to omit";[93] it includes, indeed, utterly everything "from the diffused somatic tonus of vital sense to the highest intensities of mental and emotional experience."[94]

Thus, this 'feeling' realm is something dramatically broader than mere mood or emotion—the things generally designated 'feelings'. It includes the intuitive 'sense of rightness' and 'sense of wrongness' which are "the ultimate criteria whereby we judge the validity of logical relations,"[95] and thus constitutes the very foundation of intellect. Feeling is essential to both subjective experience ("whatever is felt as action") and to objective experience ("whatever is felt as impact").[96] The images with which music presents us, the differences it carves into our consciousness, are not emotions, but wordless conceptions of "what life feels like."[97] What these conceptions convey are not the kind of things words can designate, since "no name such as 'sorrow' or 'joy' fits any actual feeling throughout its course. Feeling is a dynamic pattern of tremendous complexity."[98] Music's articulate transience deals not in discrete feelings, not in particular emotions, but in the form of our inner experience: "the mere feeling of vitality, energy, or somnolence, or the sense of quietness, or of concentration, or any of the countless inward actions and conditions which are felt in . . . mental life";[99] even "how a small fright, or 'startle', terminates, how the tensions of boredom increase or give way to self-entertainment, how daydreaming weaves in and out of realistic thought, how the feeling of a place, a time of day, an ordinary situation is built up . . ."[100]

What Langer apparently hopes to accomplish in defining 'feeling' so remarkably broadly and inclusively is that there is something all felt experiences have in common, some dynamic, vital nature that human consciousness finds extraordinarily elusive. What music does is render this 'something' conceivable. Because music presents us with vital images, it is an image of vitality: an image that reveals to us the otherwise hidden truth about how feeling feels. Music is a "semblance of organism,"[101] a "semblance of becoming, of something constantly emerging."[102] The musical image is itself a 'living form', which, in its dynamic unfolding, helps us grasp the subtle intricacies of feeling's form.

And yet, it might be argued, what music seems to render conceivable in this account is not so much the *form of feeling* as the *felt qualities* of experience—how feelings feel. And to complicate matters further, these insights music purveys are not, in the end, insights into feeling as commonly understood. For what Langer means by feeling are not what we call feelings or emotions, but rather the 'felt' qualities of any and all human feeling experience—propositional thought apparently included. What music does is present us with a form that is "subtly but entirely congruent with forms of mentality and vital experience, which we recognize intuitively as *something very much like feeling.*"[103]

Criticisms and Difficulties

One way to summarize Langer's basic thesis is that symbols are the means by which humans wrest 'conceptions' from the flow of perpetual presence: they are abstractive vehicles that enable transformation of sense data into things and events. In this view, rationality is a mechanism that transports us from insight to insight; but it owes its lofty achievements to the more fundamental act of symbolic transformation. Also on this view, images are symbols: the perceptual coherence and unity they evince manifests this symbolic transformation of particularity into conceivable generality. Such images, music obviously among them, are symbols that do not signify but only 'present', significant forms, bearers of vital import without denotative significance.

Langer's efforts to illuminate music's symbolic function were motivated by a deep conviction that music performs a crucially important cognitive role, one related in some crucial way to the felt nature of human experience. Music has a symbolic mission, she feels, by virtue of which its significance is much more profound than the capacity of its sonorous patterns to afford pleasure. But can this symbolic claim be sustained? How might it be verified or substantiated? Is music genuinely symbolic, or does it only resemble symbols in certain interesting respects?[104] Is structural similarity the mechanism by which symbols work? Does music have to be 'symbolic' to have cognitive value? Can music be symbolic without referring, purvey insight into feeling by drawing on nothing but its own inner resources?

In the following sections we turn to a number of criticisms that have been leveled at Langer's account—criticisms that have proven quite important in subsequent efforts to show how music is involved in constructing our conceptions of the worlds we inhabit.

Signification and Similarity

As we have seen, Langer's theory rests on the assumption that perception of common logical form (or resemblance) is the essential mechanism for all symbolic activity. She claims, for instance, that a "*proposition is a picture of a structure— the structure of a state of affairs,*"[105] and that for a proposition to be true, its structure must mirror salient structural relations in what it describes. So linguistic symbols' range of reference is restricted to things whose forms are compatible with the linearity and sequentiality of discourse. At least in the case of language, however, it appears she was badly mistaken. This 'correspondence' or 'copy' theory of language, a throwback to the ancient doctrine of mimesis, has been largely discredited. As Welsh points out, word order can be altered within extraordinarily generous limits without seriously impairing comprehension of a sentence's meaning.[106] Languages can describe a given event with a tremendous diversity of grammatical patterns. Langer holds that since discourse proceeds by means of sequences of discrete utterances (or words on pages) everything thought discursively must either share these structural attributes or else be ineffable. Yet if this were the case, people's thoughts would probably be restricted to the structural pattern of the discourses in which they are embedded. Langer herself speaks eloquently against this possibility in insisting that the limits of language are not the limits of thought. And against the logical positivists, she warns not to conflate logic with thought or to mistake methods of formal verification for the essential processes of thought.

And yet, the positivist's misportrayal of discursive knowledge ("whatever can be thought at all can be thought clearly") is strategically advantageous to her argument; for if discourse were capable of representing more than sequences of atomistic events, that would seriously undermine the need for a 'presentational' symbol. Only if an important range of "logical forms" resist linguistic portrayal is a presentational symbolism required.

Surely one of the notable accomplishments of her analysis should be recognition of the extent to which discursive meanings are profoundly indebted to imaginative, intuitive achievements, a recognition that helps close the tremendous gulf which so often appears to separate her discursive and presentational symbols. But maintaining a severely attenuated picture of the powers of language is useful when arguing for the existence of a cognitive void which demands to be filled by a symbol of a different kind. As Welsh observes, if one grants to language the impressive range of things it can in fact do (particularly if one acknowledges expressive devices like inflections, contours, accent, rhythm, and the like—which Langer neglects), the need for a "second kind of symbolism which shall do what language already does" appears far less urgent.[107]

Langer's misrepresentation of discursive symbolism is motivated as least in part by a desire to rescue music from the status of a pleasing but trivial art by showing how it helps compensate for the gross deficiencies of language. Only, language is not restricted to the kind of beads-on-a-rosary occurrences Langer suggests it is. The fact that verbal utterance is successive does not mean that what it designates or symbolizes must be so—as Langer's own discussion of metaphor appears to establish. As Weitz comments, language is not the 'mirror' of reality the classical theory conceives it to be, but "an enormous toolbox, full of the most diversified sorts of tools, practically all of which resemble not at all those things in the world they may be applied to."[108]

In other words, the doctrine of a syntactically iconic relationship between statements and events cannot be sustained. Making a sentence 'picture' what it describes reduces the difference between discourse and presentational symbolism to a difference in what they respectively portray, rather than in symbolic function. And finally, if there were such a thing as a 'discursive' symbol as Langer has described it, it seems likely that music itself would be one: successive and sequential phenomenon that it is, music meets these criteria remarkably well.[109]

Music as Icon

Sentences, then, need not resemble what they symbolize. But some situations clearly do display this isomorphic relation that Langer stresses. Pictures, for instance, often strongly resemble at least some aspects of what they represent. Is it still possible, then, that music is a kind of symbol that works as it does because of its structural resemblance to feeling—even if sentences are not? An effort to verify this would encounter a number of stubborn obstacles: first, establishing what the forms of feeling may be (especially since they seem to be infinite in number); second, showing that (and how, and where) music and feeling are in fact isomorphic; and third, showing that the similarity between the two is sufficient to be immediately and intuitively grasped.

Even if these considerations were all met and an unquestionable resemblance granted, however, it would still have to be established that music actually symbolizes feeling. If similarity of pattern were sufficient to establish music as a symbol, we would be obliged to say music symbolizes any number of things it resembles—including many that have little to do with music or symbolization. And the idea that closer resemblance makes for better symbolic capacity is troublesome as well, since a photograph is hardly a better symbol than a drawing or painting despite its truth to its subject. Many highly effective symbols resemble what they symbolize hardly at all.

We may well agree with Langer (and Hegel, and Schopenhauer, and Hanslick, and numerous others), then, that music seems to sound something (or perhaps even a great deal) like feelings feel, and that, for instance, they have in common recurrent patterns of tension and release. Only, similarity is not symbolism, and almost anything can be found to resemble anything in some way. Even where one thing resembles another so strikingly we cannot help but be reminded of it, the relationship between them need not be symbolic. Similarity is neither sufficient nor necessary to symbolism. Perhaps, then, as philosopher Monroe Beardsley argues, there are no particularly compelling reasons to hold this symbolic/semiotic theory of music, and some rather compelling reasons not to. It is doubtful, he concludes, "if we can find any good reason for saying that music is an iconic *sign* . . . though it can be iconic."[110]

Had she spoken directly to these criticisms, Langer might have offered several defenses. First, her critics miss her fundamental point that the essential symbolic function lies in articulation, not signification. Beardsley's criticisms of what he designates "signification theory" would be far more telling if signification were something she attributes to music. But Langer herself insists music does not signify. Second, she might respond that it is not specific feelings but the form of feeling that music presents. To object, for instance, that it is not at all apparent from simply hearing music what feeling it symbolizes (and how) misses the point that what music symbolizes are not particular feelings, but rather the form of feeling. An abstract form of feeling may articulate and sustain any feeling congruent with it.

If Langer's theory is less vulnerable than it appears at first gloss, that may be at least partly because her particular definitions lend themselves readily to evasive action. The security of her thesis draws extensively on its grounding in the "forms of feeling," and the difficulty, indeed the impossibility, of saying with any precision what such forms might be. If they are opaque to discursive symbols (words and sentences), and if the only way they can be adequately grasped is through musical symbols, the argument seems inescapably circular.

Images as Symbols

Let us turn next to Langer's claim that, as vehicles for the conception of reality, symbols exist wherever particularity is transformed into something conceivable — that things serve us as symbols whenever they enable conception, and as such, images should be considered symbols. What critics find vexing in this claim is that images need not be, and indeed, often are not, symbolic. Moreover, since it is also the case that in this 'presentational' situation a symbol seems to be showing qualities it has in itself, it seems the symbol and the symbolized are one and the same — in which case little is added by designating the situation 'symbolic' except confusion. What Langer's 'presentational symbol' brings to our attention is not something it means, but something it has, and is. Symbols are symbols by virtue of their capacity to mediate, continues this line of criticism, and a mediating device that does not mediate, a significant form that does not signify, an expressive form that does not express, a symbol that does not symbolize — each of these are deeply troubling notions. Images play a fundamental role in defining and organizing experience, to be sure; but images are not symbols.

Langer's insistence that the presentational symbol is at once intransitive and a purveyor of insight is one of the most persistent and unresolved tensions in her theory. Yet it is clear why the problem arises, for this is precisely the same tension encountered in the idealistic philosophical tradition upon which her theory builds. To secure the claim that music is cognitive, she feels she must show what it is 'cognitive of', yet without conceding that music's meaning and value rely on anything in the nonmusical world. One of the most damaging criticisms leveled at Langer's theory is that something cannot be symbolic until its significance extends beyond itself. The presentational symbol is one whose significance simultaneously does yet does not reach beyond its presentation. If the musical image is an image 'of', that directs attention away from the bearer of significance, converts 'aesthetic' properties into semantic functions. This thorny problem has led more than one scholar to conclude that 'presentational symbol' is the name not of a proposition but a contradiction.

Music and 'Feeling'

It might reasonably be expected that, having set out to elucidate the essential relationship between music and feeling, Langer would define 'feeling' explicitly and unambiguously. Since she criticized psychology for inadequately conceptualizing its mental and emotional subject matter, and since in her view music is a kind of 'school for feeling', a clear and consistent concept of feeling seems a key requirement for Langer's theory. It is, unfortunately, a missing key.

As we observed earlier, the meaning of 'feeling' in her work grows ever more broad and inclusive, until it eventually comes to encompass utterly everything that is or can be felt. Thus, Langer maintains, music has the capacity to reveal feeling ranging "from a fleeting small experience to the subjective pattern of a whole human life."[111] Philosopher Forest Hansen's thoughtful analysis of the range of concerns subsumed by 'feeling' in Langer's writing identifies three very different kinds of feeling that are conflated in her analysis: feeling as sensation; feeling as emotion; and feeling as consciousness, thought included.[112] That sensation, emotion, and thought are each 'felt' in some way is a defensible position. But this also masks important contrasts. Sensation, Hansen points out, is intensified by focused attention, whereas emotional 'feeling' is usually diminished by subjecting it to such scrutiny. The feeling of thought is something different still, ranging in intensity from so-called intellectual passions to coolly detached calculation. Langer's inclusion of corporeal, emotional, and intellectual states under 'feeling' gives the term (not unintentionally) the most abstract sense imaginable.

The idea of music as an 'educator of feeling' is difficult enough; but with feeling extended to include sensation, emotion, perception, cognition, and indeed, the patterns of any and all human sentience, it becomes rather difficult to distinguish between education and awareness, or simply experience at large. It is hard to identify the specific sense in which music is educational here, what is known as a result of having had it, what might count as evidence of its having occurred, and perhaps most importantly, what its ultimate value might be. It is difficult to say in what way understanding of a pinprick or a headache might be enhanced or informed by copious musical experience. It is even more difficult to determine whether, since thought is also felt, this should be taken to imply that intuitive perception of music's formal configurations educates thought processes. Even if the definition of feeling is not confined to emotion ("art can express other feeling than emotion"[113]), suggesting that music's significance lies in its capacity to educate feeling seems to shift attention from the agent of such education (music) to its product (elevated awareness of something-not-music). Like the presentational symbol, the idea of music as a teacher of feeling struggles to maintain a precarious balance between heteronomous and autonomous value. Langer's strategic solution to this problem—that what music confers is insight not into feelings, but rather the form of feeling—creates problems reminiscent of Schopenhauer's entangled 'will' and 'Will'.

Several additional issues encumber the claim that music's cognitive value is "[s]elf-knowledge, insight into all phases of life and mind."[114] First, it sounds very much as though what is being claimed is that music is of value primarily to the extent it helps us grasp what is already ubiquitously given to experience. It is not entirely clear that music is either essential or uniquely endowed with the capacity to provide such self-knowledge. Moreover, to the extent music is held to be a vehicle, to mediate insight, it must relinquish its claim to autonomy, yielding to the referential or heteronomous account of its nature and value Langer so wishes to avoid. Notably, then, this conception of music's value subtly but persistently diverts attention away from what the music is, toward what it resembles, facilitates, and educates.

Equally troublesome is Langer's contention that a society which neglects the education of feeling through art "gives itself up to formless emotion. Bad art is corruption of feeling. This is a large factor in the irrationalism which dictators and demagogues exploit."[115] Here, then, is further indication of what music's education of feeling may mean. It educates feeling by objectifying it, transforming what is otherwise "formless emotion" into a more comprehensible, more controllable, and ultimately more disciplined thing. It is noteworthy, though, that this is the office of good music. Bad music, after all corrupts, a capacity that presumably makes exposure to bad music at least as undesirable as no musical exposure at all. It is difficult to understand why, given music's potential for corruption, Langer can justify leaving musical value so loosely defined, grounded ultimately in intuition and feeling.

Intuition

We have seen that intuition figures prominently in Langer's account of symbols. Indeed, it is the primary way their significance is apprehended. On her account, intuition is no irrational, mystical affair, but "an act of understanding, mediated by a single symbol"[116] whose meaning or import is inextricably bound up in the form that conveys it. We perceive relations, forms, and significance all at once, or else not at all. "The entire qualification one must have for understanding art is responsiveness. That is primarily a natural gift. . . . Since it is intuitive, it cannot be taught."[117] And although its felt quality is a distinctive feature of intuition, there is "not much to say about the feeling in question except that it is an index of good art." Still, urges Langer this intuitive achievement must not be regarded as either rare or exotic. Indeed, intuition is the very source of all insight and discovery. To discount intuition for its inscrutability or ineffability, Langer claims, is to discount cognition at the same time, since the intuitive apprehension of the form is the foundation upon which rationality is built.

But intuition's inscrutability presents significant challenges to a theory that purports to establish cognitive import and educational value for music. Intuition defies verbal elaboration and analysis. As a fundamentally synthetic achievement of the imagination, analysis, explanation, or interpretation necessarily distort intuition. Either one 'gets it', then, or one does not. An observation by Beardsley delivers us to the heart of an apparent philosophical impasse: "In so far as something is believed intuitively, that is, because of an immediate feeling of truth, it is not yet knowledge, but a hypothesis to be investigated."[118] For Langer, anything which is conceived is known. For Beardsley and others, what is intuited remains a kind of preknowledge until it is put to some further use: until, that is, one can say or show what is known by it.

As an intuitive account, it is clear that Langer's theory, for all its perspicacity, provides little by way of a critical basis for music, no particularly reliable way of distinguishing musical triumphs from disasters, the musically profound from the pedestrian and the banal. What matters in the end is whether, for a given individual, the "musical illusion" is achieved. Weitz has argued that Langer speaks as if all people invariably respond in musically appropriate ways, as if bringing the proper attitudes into play is something people do normally and naturally.[119] There is little evidence for this, and, in fact, a good deal to the contrary. The problem the theory faces is that, given an improper intuitive response, virtually all one can do is back up and have another go. Should that fail, one is left lamenting the inexplicability of tastes. Whether a good musical symbol is necessarily good music is an issue intuition seems ill suited to address.

Revelation and Creation

Among the most vexatious aspects of Langer's theory is its ambivalence over the question of what it is music does. There are several ways of stating her thesis that bring this ambivalence into clear focus. Langer claims that music should be the exclusive focus of the musical experience, yet at the same time music's definitive 'illusion' necessarily implicates more than music. In such a case, Rudner observes, "the art work is no longer the aesthetic object."[120] While what is distinctive about the presentational symbol is its immediacy, it must at the same time mediate, even educate, yielding insight into feeling. On the one hand, music helps us grasp the 'true' patterns of sentience, revealing something that exists beyond the immediacy of the perceptual moment. On the other hand, indeed at the same time, music is held to formulate knowledge. In Langer's words, "Music is . . . formulation and representation of emotions, moods, mental tensions and resolutions . . ."[121]

But formulation and representation are two very different functions, one implying the creation or construction of something new, the other implying reference to a pre-existent order. Langer wishes to avoid the idealistic extreme that maintains minds make the world: "[T]o see in certain forms is not to create their contents."[122] And yet this remains a thread that weaves its way through most of her writing. What eventually emerges as the label of choice is 'articulation'. Music's symbolic forms articulate the form of feeling, the patterns of sentience. Only, this masks the tension instead of resolving it.

This tension underlies many of the fragile dualisms with which Langer labors so diligently: signification and articulation, presentation and transformation, immediacy and mediacy, discovery and construction, meaning and significance, revelation and creation. Even the most defensible statement of her thesis takes two forms which, despite their apparent similarity at first gloss, imply diametrically opposed positions on the issue raised here: is music a 'vital image', or an 'image of vitality'?

In proposing that music's significance must be immediately apprehended while at the same time negotiating insight into something not itself, Langer claims music simultaneously does two mutually exclusive things. As Rudner puts it, "To include direct apprehension of an object or property within semiosis as an exemplification of that case in which an object or property is a sign of itself would have as a consequence that any experience of anything would be an experience of a sign; everything becomes, at least, its own icon."[123] In experiencing one thing, people sometimes take account of something else. But to call such occurrences symbolic seems to deny any meaningful distinction between symbolic activity and experience in general. If every experience in which we take account of something is symbolic, it is difficult to see what the notion of symbolism adds to the concept of experience, or why it should be needed at all. There is a difference between experience and symbolic experience, continues the argument, and that difference lies in the definitive symbolic function of mediation, signification, or reference; and that is an incontrovertibly transitive or heteronomous state of affairs. To say that a piece of music is a symbol, yet bespeaks nothing other than itself, is to speak in riddles and paradoxes. Either music conveys or represents to consciousness something important about the world 'out there', or it creates (formulates) a difference in consciousness where otherwise there is none. Insisting upon both raises as many issues as it resolves.

When pressed, Langer most often comes down on the side of revelation. In other words, while claiming transformation, Langer more often argues revelation. This revelation thesis appears in many forms, but one of the more convincing ways of putting it is this: A piece of music presents us with a particular image, one that exemplifies a *universal*, a form—in this case, that of 'feeling'. Music-heard and feeling-felt both have formal characteristics and qualities that can be traced to a universal form. The musical image makes manifest a universal, acquainting us with it—not by telling about it, but simply by showing. By this acquaintance, we acquire insight into 'the way feelings go'. What is apparently distinctive about music, rendering it more valuable as a revelatory vehicle than other perceptual experience, is the fact that it is more saturated with these qualities and has them in greater purity. Thus it discloses subtle patterns, qualities, and ranges of sentient experience that otherwise elude us. By so doing, music transforms and enriches our perception of reality, helping us more fully realize our uniquely human potential.

And yet this transformation, to the extent it 'articulates' a difference in an otherwise undifferentiated consciousness, must be creative. If consciousness is in itself a "no-thing,"[124] if consciousness 'is' only what it is 'of', then musical experience constructs consciousness and hence reality in some significant way. Langer seems to imply this constructive capacity by maintaining that music's cognitive value is a function of its capacity to yield self-knowledge. Yet she wants at the same time to be able to say that music negotiates a conception of 'what feeling is like'—something outside itself that music reveals or points to. Thus, the theory contains a deep, unresolved tension between the heteronomist claim that music is revelatory, a purveyor of insight, and the autonomist claim that music transforms, articulates, or in some sense creates a reality.

Music, Universals, and Qualities

Langer's account of music as revelatory faces yet another challenge, one that is disarmingly direct and forceful: that it derives from the deposed theory that knowledge consists in somehow tapping into 'essences'. But there are no such things as essences, no 'forms of feeling' apart from the experience of feelings themselves. No characteristics are in themselves essential attributes of anything, except for purposes of classifying. What is 'essential' is thus a function of one's purposes and perspective, not absolute. In Beardsley's words, "There is no essential characteristic of trees or of passionate longing for the creative artist to abstract, intensify, and embody in his work."[125]

Moreover, the "difference in consciousness" Langer believes music articulates is not cognitive but precognitive. However interesting and important it may be, it is not yet knowing. It does not follow from the fact that something 'has' a particular quality, that in having perceived that quality, it becomes 'known'. Knowledge by acquaintance, pronounces Beardsley, is "not knowledge but just acquaintance."[126] Here then is the crux of the argument, the issue on which Langer's thesis appears to hinge. Where she argues music is 'pre-rationative' yet not 'pre-rational', her challengers contend that the pre-rationative is pre-rational by definition, a conviction Beardsley states with precision: "[The semiotic thesis] is right in saying that the qualities presented by aesthetic objects may become the data for future knowings, and that aesthetic objects are connected with knowledge in this way. It is wrong in saying that the presentation, or the reception, of such qualities itself constitutes an act of knowledge."[127]

Langer's argument, her paradoxical accounts of unfelt feeling and of patterns of sentience music reveals to us without our experiencing them, appears to neglect an important distinction between experience and knowledge. Acknowledging that music is 'feelingful', or that its felt qualities are salient features of such experience, hardly establishes that understanding or knowledge of such qualities is its primary mission. The value of signs and symbols must ultimately be assessed in terms of their clarity and lucidity, and the value of knowledge by its capacity to sustain rational activity. If music's images transform experience, shaping it and imbuing it with qualities nothing else can, perhaps, some would argue, we need look no further for its value. Perhaps the particular qualities it imparts to experience are more important than anything it can be shown to reveal. Perhaps, in other words, that fact that music presents us with unmistakably vital images does not necessarily make it an image or 'symbol' of vitality.

Again, the presence of difficulties in Langer's theories does not negate her basic conviction that music is fundamentally mindful, that it plays an important formative role in human mental life. The effort to illuminate music as rational and mindful continues unabated today, with ever more sophisticated conceptual tools being brought to the task of understanding the mechanisms involved in musical cognition—thanks in no small part to Langer's important pioneering work.

Goodman: Music and World Making

While some areas of scholarly inquiry have been profoundly altered by semiotic theory, its impact on philosophical accounts of art and music has been relatively modest. And yet, the conception of music as symbol has been extensively refined and reformulated, and the philosophical tools brought to that task have become ever more sophisticated. The effort of Nelson Goodman to show how 'aesthetic experience' should be considered a kind of cognitive activity is a case in point. His logically incisive work clarifies many of the issues that troubled Langer's theory and offers rigorous explanations in their place. Because of their 'aesthetic' orientation, Goodman's theories address the arts inclusively rather than music in particular; but their philosophical rigor and thoroughness greatly assists in bringing into clear focus the advantages and difficulties associated with the idea of music as a symbolic or semiotic affair.

While Goodman shares Langer's basic conviction that music is symbolic, their approaches and conclusions diverge sharply. Langer's work was firmly rooted in speculative philosophical traditions, and shared their fondness for grand theory. Goodman, too, is a theory builder, but one whose frame of reference is contemporary analytical philosophy. More important, while Langer worked from an idealistic base, Goodman's approach is thoroughly nominalistic: flatly rejecting notions like essences and universals, and embracing the belief that human 'reality' is a human construction. He has little use for the kind of philosophy designed to reveal the way 'reality' essentially 'is', and little interest in pursuits that presume to explain once and for all what all music everywhere means or reveals. From his perspective, music's value is not its capacity to provide insight into ultimate reality, sentient or otherwise. For Goodman, music's primary function is formulative and creative rather than revelatory. Symbolic activity is reality construction. And engaging in musical undertakings, like all semiotic activity, is an act of 'worldmaking'.[128]

In place of Langer's enigmatic idea of music as presentational symbol, Goodman offers a logically rigorous account of 'exemplification' that traces music's immediacy and intransitive character to the simple fact that samples possess what they symbolize. Like Langer, Goodman maintains the existence of two rather distinct symbolic modes; but his accounts of denotation and exemplification reject isomorphism or structural similarity. Assigned reference and iconic similarity are not distinguishing features of symbolic modes. In Goodman's account, reference is a definitive aspect of all symbolic situations. Symbols differ not in terms of whether they refer or not, but rather in terms of the direction of reference. These ideas will be explored in more detail shortly.

His effort to subsume 'aesthetic experience' under cognition has not gone unchallenged, though. Those who believe that the kind of heightened perceptual awareness afforded by works of art is distinctive and unique—that what this kind of experience shares with so-called cognitive activity is less important than its particular 'aesthetic' quality—take issue with Goodman's claims that aesthetic experience is best regarded as a cognitive process and that its value should be judged by cognitive standards. Because this debate over mediation and immediacy raises important questions about the meaning of 'cognition' and the existence of a uniquely 'aesthetic' range of experience, we shall take advantage of Goodman's arguments to explore those intriguing issues. But first, Goodman's theory.

Denoting

One of the most intriguing aspects of Langer's symbolic account of music was its determination to describe the workings of a kind of symbol that did not do what, according to her critics, all symbols must do by definition: that is, refer. Goodman's theory does not attempt so radical a reconstruction of the definition and function of symbols. Like Langer, Goodman believes there are significantly different kinds of symbols; but those differences have nothing to do with the presence or absence of reference (what Langer sometimes called "consummation"). For Goodman, all symbolic activity involves reference. Langer's theory of music as a kind of nonreferential or intransitive symbol cannot stand, then, because to be symbolic, music must refer. However, Goodman shows, reference is a far more complex and richly varied process than commonly assumed. It works in a number of ways, practically none of which are quite as they appear at first gloss. Relatively few 'common sense' notions about symbolism survive Goodman's analysis without substantial alteration and refinement. He rejects the idea of one largely undifferentiated, generic symbolic process in favor of an intricate and highly nuanced system of symbolic modes: each distinctive in logical structure, and each making its unique contribution to the essential symbolic mission of creating reality, of making worlds.

There is no way the world ultimately 'is', argues Goodman, only various and diverse ways it may be found. Each of these is perspectival and partial. Symbols create various worlds or 'realities' by acting as lenses that emphasize certain features while they blur or neglect others. Symbols powerfully mediate perception and conception, profoundly shaping the kinds of 'reality' people apprehend. Thus, they are a fundamental means of creating our actual and possible worlds. Obviously, this position poses serious trouble for the classical 'copy theory' encountered in Langer's theory, where symbolism is a function of structural resemblance and symbols capture the aspects of 'reality' most structurally congruent with them. For Langer, as we have seen, language bore an iconic relation to logical reality, as did music to felt reality or sentience; and that resemblance was what enabled discursive and nondiscursive symbols to reveal the logical and felt aspects of reality, respectively. Among the first tasks to which Goodman directs his attention is purging the concept of representation of "perverted ideas of it as an idiosyncratic physical process like mirroring."[129]

Representation and description, pictures and words, are closely related, Goodman allows, only not at all in the way Langer and others maintain. Both representing and describing are instances of the same logical function, but resemblance has nothing to do with either. Representing and describing are ways of denoting. Denoting means standing for, referring to, but in a particular way. That is, when one describes or depicts something, one applies a label to it, characterizing it in one way rather than another. The crucial point is that both describing and depicting perform this same function, and perception of formal similarity has nothing essential to do with either. The belief that either depiction or discourse work by iconicity or copying is, in Goodman's view, a "grave misconception."[130]

Several of the arguments Goodman employs in support of this claim have already been considered in the context of Langer's theory. First, despite their perfect 'resemblance' to themselves, people never take things as their own representations. Even the relationship between a picture and what it depicts challenges the resemblance theory, because resemblance is always a symmetrical affair in which the depicted and picture are as similar as are the picture and the depicted. If resemblance were essential to representation people would encounter difficulty distinguishing the represented from the representation. Further, if resemblance were sufficient to representation, people would be forever mistaking as representative things that are not, since virtually anything can be found to resemble anything else in some way. A great many things that resemble each other to a high degree are never taken as representations. Since even striking resemblance does not make something a representation, and since practically anything may represent something else, resemblance is neither necessary nor sufficient to representation.

Which among an object's infinite aspects must a good imitation portray? Which are contingent and which are essential? If the actual object consists as it must of the totality of such aspects, how can an adequate representation portray anything short of that totality? And would not such an absolutely perfect portrayal, if it were possible, cease to be distinct from the object portrayed? The fact is, Goodman believes, the notion that realism is achieved by eliminating interpretation (by using an innocent or 'mindless' eye to copy the given neutrally) is impossibly absurd. The eye "is a dutiful member of a complex and capricious organism," says he. "Not only how but what it sees is regulated by need and prejudice. It selects, rejects, organizes, discriminates, associates, classifies, analyzes, constructs. It does not so much mirror as take and make."[131] Any attempt to purge representation of "comment" takes crucial content along with it, because representations always characterize: represent-as.

If neutral perception is impossible, the copy theory is in dire difficulty; for what, precisely, is to be copied? The plain truth, we are told, is that the most realistic and the most fanciful representations only differ in degree from one another. No depiction, however literal we take it to be, can ever accomplish unbiased or neutral transmission. All depiction interprets, characterizes, represents in a certain way. How realistic or literal a picture is depends upon people's acquired facility for 'reading' representational conventions. In short, 'realism' is "a matter of habit."[132] How it characterizes what it represents is crucial to understanding any given representation: depicting and describing are interpretive, not imitative.

Since representation both denotes and characterizes (both refers and interprets), it is important to distinguish these two functions in any representation situation: to ask both what a given representation denotes, and how it characterizes or interprets it. Put differently, there are two independent concerns in any representation: what is represented, and what kind of representation it is. Denotation both classifies and characterizes.[133] The point is that reality is not a ready-made thing, there for the taking, but the product of particular ways of organizing, classifying, and characterizing. Description and representation are indispensable tools to that end. And both work in the same fundamental way, affecting realignment of the structures and events which comprise our world. "That nature imitates art is too timid a dictum," Goodman concludes: "Nature is a product of art and discourse."[134]

Aside from the need to distinguish between what is described (depicted) and the kind of description (depiction) it is, several interesting points emerge from this treatment of representation. For Goodman, things like pictures, music, and talk are symbolic means by which people construct worlds and realities. This being the case, it is wrong headed to talk about, say, a musical symbol providing insight into the way feelings (or anything else) 'really' are, because there is no way feelings 'really' are apart from our feeling or symbolically portraying them. And it is even more misguided to conceive symbolic representation as a kind of servile copying or mechanical resemblance. It is always, inescapably, a matter of constructing, shaping, characterizing.

Exemplifying

The terms 'reference' and 'expression' are both subject to abundant confusion in discourse about art and music. Reference is often aligned with language, and expression with feeling. Reference is often conceived as a transitive or mediating function, to which expression's immediacy is presumed opposite. As well, expression is often construed as a kind of emotional arousal, while reference is cool and calculated. For Goodman, however, expression is not an inherently emotional phenomenon; or at least it is not appreciably different from other symbolic functions on that count. Nor is it the polar opposite of reference. In fact, expression is itself a particular mode of reference whose workings can be quite satisfactorily illuminated by careful analysis of symbolic processes.

According to Goodman, expression belongs to the symbolic-referential mode of exemplification. Symbols that exemplify differ from denotative symbols in one primary way. They possess that to which they refer. Thus, exemplificational symbols actually present samples of what they symbolize, demonstrate or put forward qualities that they themselves have. Symbols that function exemplificationally exhibit and refer to certain of their own features. If in representational modes of symbolization, then, one is properly concerned with what the symbol denotes and how, in the exemplificational mode the question is what the symbol is denoted by. In other words, the appropriate questions are What kinds of labels may be applied to it? And which, among those that may, actually do apply?

What a symbol can exemplify is restricted to properties or qualities it possesses, yet reference remains its basic function. After all, referring is what symbols do. The differences between exemplification and the modes of reference discussed above are two: possession, and the direction of reference. Where representational reference runs from a symbol to what it denotes, in exemplification reference runs to a symbol from what it is denoted by. Something red can exemplify (serve as a sample of and refer to) redness because it has a quality appropriately denoted by the word 'red'.

Exemplification is thus a distinct symbolic domain characterized by both reference and possession, neither being sufficient in itself. "To have without symbolizing [referring] is merely to possess, while to symbolize [refer] without having is to refer in some other way than by exemplifying," says Goodman.[135] Things possess numerous qualities or properties of which they need not serve as examples, so having a property or quality leads to exemplification only if that property or quality is referred to. Whereas denotation involves reference between two elements in one direction, "exemplification implies reference between the two in both directions."[136] In the abstract, this seems arcane. But it is really only to say that here, in exemplification, a symbol has some of what it refers to, so that it both refers and shows at the same time. The color on the lid of a paint can, for instance, both refers to and presents a sample of its content.

Goodman's analyses offer some very helpful correctives to Langer's account, not least by showing how symbols may present (or show) and refer at the same time. The relevance of these points for a symbolic account of music, however, remains somewhat remote until one recalls that Goodman considers expression a species of exemplification. Musical expression, then, has the double constraints (reference and possession) just discussed. But it has a few more, because expression is metaphorical exemplification: what music expresses are attributes it possesses not literally, but metaphorically. What it expresses, it has, but has acquired elsewhere.

Saying that expression is metaphorical rather than literal by no means implies expression is make-believe, less substantial, or less efficacious than other symbolic modes, cautions Goodman. Metaphorical possession is every bit as 'actual' as literal possession: "Calling a picture sad and calling it gray are simply different ways of classifying it."[137] Therefore, judging the aptness of a particular metaphorical label for an expressive quality is not all that different than estimating the goodness of fit between literal labels and what they designate. Asking why a metaphor is successful is much the same as asking why literal labels are appropriate or adequate to the tasks we set for them. "And if we have no good answer in either case, perhaps that is because there is no real question."[138]

Goodman has plenty to say about the 'logic' of metaphors, however. Metaphors involve the transfer of a label from one domain to another, in what might be considered a kind of "calculated category-mistake."[139] Since the transferred label brings along from its home realm an entire interpretive schema and attendant semantic baggage, its entry into a new domain is not a mechanical, matter-of-fact occasion. Goodman characterizes this act variously as an 'invasion' of 'territory',[140] "teaching an old word new tricks,"[141] a "happy and revitalizing, even if bigamous, second marriage."[142] Two conditions are essential: attraction and resistance. Successful metaphors require both conflict, the presence of differences, and the possibility of amicable resolution. Unless there is contradiction, a label applies literally; if these differences or tensions cannot be resolved, the label is false. In short, metaphors occur when "a term with an extension established by habit is applied elsewhere under the influence of that habit; there is both departure from and deference to precedent."[143]

Notably, Goodman's account of metaphors relies not on structural similarity, but on habits or conventions, and their disruption. Metaphors force reorganization, realignment, and reconstruction within their new conceptual realms. Over time, the once-compelling metaphor demands less radical adjustment, becomes less invasive. Its novelty cools until it eventually freezes as an alternative literal meaning. Since both metaphorical and literal meanings are at root matters of labeling, sorting, and conceptual alignments, their primary difference is the degree of cognitive adjustment each demands.

Given a musical passage expressive of joy, then, 'joy' is both referred to by and metaphorically denotes the music in question. The passage is not literally joyful, for only sentient beings can literally experience joy. It is none the less actually joyful, to the extent joyful properties are among those it has appropriated elsewhere. If joy were an attribute the passage literally possessed, it could exemplify (or offer a sample of) joyfulness but not express it. As Gurney argued, music cannot 'express' qualities it (literally) has.

Metaphorical possession is only expression, however, if exemplification occurs: that is, joyfulness must not only be possessed, it must also be referred to, "exhibited, typified, shown forth."[144] Of the innumerable properties possessed by every sonorous configuration experienced as music, some are literal possessions and some metaphorical. Literal possessions cannot be expressed, only exemplified. The attributes a passage possesses metaphorically may or not be expressed (shown forth). Only those which are shown forth or referred to are expressed. All reference depends upon "singling out certain properties for attention,"[145] a process of selecting from among a multitude of potential properties and relationships with utmost sensitivity. Although expression is clearly constrained by the necessity for possession, boundaries between the metaphorical and the literal are "ephemeral"[146] never fixed, permanent, or absolute. Therefore, distinguishing between properties an object has literally and those it has metaphorically is at root a "matter of habit—a matter of fact rather than fiat."[147]

Despite the distinctions between and among these various symbolic modes—description, representation, exemplification, and expression—each partakes of a common referential function. This analysis shows that the differences between linguistic and nonlinguistic reference are not as radical as commonly assumed. On the one hand, there is far more (or depending upon one's perspective, far less) to denotation than is generally assumed. It is not so precise and fixed a function as habit makes it seem. On the other hand, exemplification and expression "are symptomatic neither of uncontrolled caprice nor of impenetrable mystery but of exploration and discovery."[148] Thus, musical expression neither resides in some nether world of the "sacredly occult" nor is it "hopelessly obscure."[149] Expression is continuous with other symbolic activity and a vital participant in the fundamentally human business of world making.

Symbolic Systems

Goodman's description of symbolic modes is prefatory to an exploration of the ways symbols combine to form systems, or 'languages', each with distinctive syntactical and semantic requirements, and each making its own distinctive contribution to the semiotic process of world making. Although Goodman's analysis of symbol systems is rather technical and unwieldy, a passing familiarity with his main points is crucial to understanding how he situates music within semiotic activity.

Goodman describes three kinds of symbol systems: digital, discursive, and analog. Of these, digital systems have the greatest referential precision, allowing the least interpretive latitude. Although he considerably overestimates its prescriptive capacity, Goodman believes musical notation is a good example of a digital scheme. Scores, he reasons, provide the authoritative, definitive basis for identification of a piece, independent of its history of production—something talk and pictures cannot do. Definitions and pictures allow a range of potential reference that the musical score simply does not tolerate. Only the precise notes and rhythms prescribed in the score are correct: all others are mistakes.

Goodman attributes the precision and invariance of notational ("digital") schemes to five basic conditions, two syntactical and three semantic. The first syntactical requirement is *character-invariance*.[150] All instances or inscriptions of, say, 'middle C' must be precise replicas of each other, such that it cannot be mistaken for or become on some future occasion a 'B' or a 'C-sharp'. Similarly, eighth notes must invariably have one beam rather than two or some indeterminate number. In other words, all instances of a particular character in a notational scheme must be true copies of each other. Second, characters in notational schemes are *finitely differentiated*, such that all characters are clearly different from each other and have no inscriptions in common. Where a symbol scheme meets both these syntactic conditions, when its characters are distinct and discrete, it is syntactically *articulate*. If, by contrast, a scheme were to allow that between any two given characters there might always be a third (so that even the most minute differences would influence how the symbol is to be 'read') such a scheme would be syntactically *dense*.

In symbol systems a symbolic scheme is associated with something it refers to: its *compliance class*:[151] The association of symbolic scheme with compliance class is the semantic relationship. The first semantic requirement of a digital system is that reference be *unambiguous*.[152] Second, reference must be *semantically disjoint* so that every character stands for a distinct compliance class and no two characters share the same compliant. Finally, reference must be *semantically differentiated*, so that compliance is utterly unequivocal. Obviously, systems that conform to each of these conditions are quite rare. Even musical notation fits only if one takes a very narrow view of what the score refers to.

If these general ideas of articulateness and density are understood, a more detailed analysis is not essential for present purposes. The distinguishing feature of digital systems is that they are both syntactically and semantically articulate. Both their symbol schemes and their compliance relationships are differentiated, discrete, discontinuous. Analog systems, on the other hand, have precisely the opposite characteristics. Since they are syntactically and semantically dense, characters are not conspicuously differentiated, and exceedingly subtle differences have important syntactical and semantic implications. This contrast can be illustrated by comparing analog and digital clocks. Since on an analog clock any hand motion, however slight, indicates actual passage of time, it designates the time more precisely. Only, since there can be no firm rules for distinguishing significant from insignificant movement, 'error' is introduced into the system: two different observers may report two different times. Digital clocks report the time unequivocally, such that it is either 2:00 or 2:01 and not some indeterminate time in between. Where the analog clock registers absolute position on a completely saturated (dense) continuum, its digital counterpart is articulate: it counts discrete and differentiated events. Thus, digital systems have the virtues of invariance, definiteness, and repeatability, but at the expense of absolute precision. Symbol systems with syntactical and semantic density record and represent with greater precision, but lack clearly demarcated margins for error. Therefore interpretation relies upon extremely fine discriminations and judgments, increasing referential and semantic variability.

These distinctions are useful in completing the discussion of distinctions between description and depiction begun earlier. Discursive systems are typically syntactically articulate, and semantically dense. They employ discrete and differentiated characters to denote compliance classes that may be dense and overlapping. Representational systems, on the other hand, are both syntactically and semantically dense, deploying 'analog' schemes for both syntactic and semantic referring. In a line drawing, for instance, each minute difference in a line's thickness, sharpness, or curvature has both structural and semantic significance. There are few conventions for distinguishing aspects which may be taken as contingent from those which must be considered constitutive.[153] Representations vary in degree of density, with diagrams and paintings lying at opposite ends of what one might call a density continuum. Diagrams are more *attenuative*, having relatively fewer aspects which must be taken as constitutive, while paintings are *replete*.

The important point is that the distinction between descriptions and representations has nothing to do with degree of resemblance, as the iconic theory maintains. It depends, rather, upon what kind of symbol system is employed, and whether that system tends more to attenuation or to repleteness. "A picture in one system may be a description in another; and whether a denoting symbol is representational depends not upon whether it resembles what it denotes but upon its own relationships to other symbols in a given system."[154] What is being symbolized and its internal structure matter not at all. Thus, remarkably, the distinction between icons and other signs "becomes transient and trivial."[155] This is so not because all signs are in some degree iconic, as Langer believes, but because resemblance or iconicity is simply not a requirement for signification.

Predictably, exemplificational systems are more complex yet. In the first place, discerning what properties a musical passage exemplifies or expresses demands the utmost in sensitivity. Add to that demand the task of describing or verbalizing, and the situation becomes more intricate and labyrinthine yet. In fact, Goodman concludes, verbally stipulating what a musical passage exemplifies "is a matter of fitting the right words from a syntactically unlimited and semantically dense language"; like "measuring with no set tolerances."[156] Expression demands "maximal sensitivity," and entails an unending quest for accurate adjustment between the symbol and the symbolized.[157] In stark contrast to the relationship between a score and its compliance class of performances, a musical performance's exemplification or expression of anything not explicitly prescribed by its score entails "reference in a semantically dense system and a matter of infinitely fine adjustment."[158]

Aesthetic Value as Cognitive Value

In many respects, Goodman's ultimate stance is the polar opposite of Langer's. Goodman wants no part of an account of music that is at once a presentational immediacy and a symbol. Nor does he believe that symbols mysteriously unveil, or yield insight into, some essential 'reality'. Nor, apparently, does he find anything persuasive in accounts of music's capacity to provide pleasure of a predominantly emotional sort. Notions that music either simulates or imitates emotion mistakenly assume (like the deposed copy theory of representation) that music is but a reality surrogate. The theory of special 'aesthetic emotion' succeeds only by arguing in circles and begging questions: "No doubt aesthetic emotions have the property that makes them aesthetic," writes Goodman. "No doubt things that burn are combustible. The theory of aesthetic phlogiston explains everything and nothing."[159]

Both traditional difficulties accounting for music's emotional character and reluctance to concede music's cognitive status arise from the fundamental failure to recognize that in so-called aesthetic experience "the *emotions function cognitively*," being the "means of discerning what properties a work has and expresses."[160] Music consists in "making delicate discriminations and discerning subtle relationships, identifying symbol systems and characters within these systems and what these characters denote and exemplify, interpreting works and reorganizing the world in terms of works and works in terms of the world."[161] As such, the restless, searching character of musical experience is "less attitude than action: creation and re-creation."[162]

On this view, musical experience should be judged not in terms of emotional intensity, but by cognitive criteria: the emotions are relevant only to the extent they support and facilitate an essentially cognitive task. Indeed, "finding that a work expresses little or no emotion can be as significant aesthetically as finding that it expresses much."[163] The perennial failure of efforts to sort experience into two discrete classes, the aesthetic and the nonaesthetic, shows the need for a more rigorous attack and a different perspective on the problem, one that denies the temptation to become diverted by talk of emotions, quality of experience, and the like. 'The aesthetic' can be defined quite adequately by resorting to nothing more than the characteristics typical of the symbolic devices employed in its service, believes Goodman. These characteristics are not necessary nor sufficient conditions for the aesthetic, not 'criteria', but rather "symptoms" or "earmarks" that tend to be present when music is encountered 'aesthetically'. They do not define the aesthetic, then, but are simply clues to it: "the patient may have the symptoms without the disease, or the disease without the symptoms."[164]

Goodman lists five symptoms of the aesthetic: both syntactical and semantic density; repleteness, where many features of a symbol 'count' in its interpretation, and few can be ignored; exemplification (including the special exemplificational case of expression); and "multiple and complex reference, where a symbol performs several integrated and interacting referential functions."[165] In other words, where nonaesthetic experience employs symbols that are predominantly articulate and attenuated, the characteristics typical of symbols that mediate 'aesthetic' experience are density, repleteness, exemplificationality, and extremely subtle interrelations. Accordingly, such experience demands exceedingly fine discriminations and cognitive adjustments. The ineffability of musical experience reduces, then, to "density rather than mystery" and its immediacy is accounted for in terms of "exemplification rather than of intimacy—a function of direction rather than of distance."[166] Further, music's nontransparency or 'intransitiveness', its tendency to arrest rather than direct attention, does not negate its symbolic function. That too is simply a feature of the modes and systems of symbolization music employs.

Only, why, particularly given the demands such interpretive activities place upon an already taxed mind, would people engage in them? 'Aesthetic pleasure' is not an explanation Goodman is willing to entertain, since he finds the proposition circular. We seek out musical experience neither for the sheer fun of it, nor for purposes of communication, nor with the intent of enhancing our imaginative or intellectual capacity. What motivates the use of musical symbols is not practical need, but pure understanding. "[W]hat compels is the urge to know, what delights is discovery. . . . The primary purpose is cognition in and for itself."[167] Music's attraction is essentially the same as that of any symbolic activity: intellectual curiosity. Musical experience is a form of cognition. And it is to be judged, ultimately, by how faithfully it serves that function: ". . . by the delicacy of its discriminations and the aptness of its allusions; by the way it works in grasping, exploring, and informing the world; by how it analyzes, sorts, orders, and organizes; by how it participates in the making, manipulation, retention, and transformation of knowledge. Considerations of simplicity and subtlety, power and precision, scope and selectivity, familiarity and freshness, are all relevant. . . ."[168] The value of symbolic activity, music included, lies in its cognitive efficacy. Accordingly, Goodman urges rejection of the "myth of the insularity of aesthetic experience,"[169] which maintains musical experience is *sui generis*. Distinctive though musical cognition may be in many respects, it is not sufficiently unique from Goodman's perspective to warrant the introduction of a discrete, aesthetic category of experience. Music, like all symbolic experience, is a way of world making. And if this perspective yields relatively few concrete criteria for evaluations of musical excellence, thinks Goodman, so much the better: for that kind of activity only deters us from the kind of inquiry most appropriate to music. "[W]orks of art are not race-horses, and picking a winner is not the primary goal. . . . Judging the excellence of works of art or the goodness of people is not the best way of understanding them."[170]

Cognitive Versus Aesthetic Value

It is hardly surprising that music, especially music that purports to be non-referential, presents major challenges to those who seek to portray the arts as symbolic. And yet there are many who remain convinced that, despite its complexity and difficulty, the project is essential. Clearly, the idea that music is a symbolic phenomenon is tenacious and resilient. One reason may be the substantiality 'symbolic' status seemingly confers, its promise of cognitive credibility to something often considered inconsequential and insubstantial. On the other hand, there are those who believe that all meaning or significance is a function of cognitive connections, and music is no exception, no matter the difficulties of explaining precisely how that is so. Goodman's rigorous theory promises to salvage the cognitive thesis with a semiotic explanation of unparalleled subtlety and complexity. There is no disputing that Goodman has done a great deal to illuminate the remarkable intricacy and diversity of symbolic functioning. But its impressive precision notwithstanding, how persuasive is Goodman's claim that music is language like, cognitive in nature, a fundamentally semantic affair? It is one thing to demonstrate that certain aspects of music lend themselves well to description in terms of symbol systems, but does that make music symbolic? And if so, does that really help us better understand actual music and musical activities? This section explores a few of the interesting issues raised by Goodman's theory, focusing primarily on the claim that musical value is a subset of cognitive value.

Although it is not an insuperable obstacle to Goodman's theory, it is interesting to note how a cognitive account like this must value knowledge over mere experience. That is, music's worth is a function of how effectively it participates in the making, manipulation, retention, and transformation of knowledge. Some 'cognitive realignment', to use Goodman's phrase, is essential if the claim to cognitive efficacy is to be sustained. However, it may be that this places a far greater emphasis upon new and different musical experience than many people seem to seek out. As was observed within the context of Leonard Meyer's theory, a great deal of musical experience tends to entail not so much discovery as rediscovery, to be more a matter of renewing friendships than making new acquaintances. To be sure, Goodman's theory accommodates both familiarity and novelty. But basing a claim to music's worth on its contribution to cognitive growth places more emphasis upon 'expeditions abroad' and new discoveries than is often the case in musical experience. Or, to put it slightly differently, the fact that music can contribute to cognitive growth may not necessarily implicate the further claim that it does so necessarily or even typically.

Further, Goodman's subsumption of music by reference and cognition tends to divert attention from what some would argue is the distinctive character of musical experience. If music is symbolic, it is symbolic in specifically musical ways, a point Goodman would certainly grant. But because referring is what symbols do, his account tends to gravitate toward what may be known as a consequence of musical experience rather than what the particular quality of that experience may be. His 'languages' orientation is more revealing of what 'musical symbols' do and how they do it than of what is most interesting and distinctive about our experience of them.

This may be inevitable in a theory that urges replacing aesthetic experience with cognitive experience, but if music is to be properly regarded as a languagelike system that begets distinctive ways of knowing, perhaps more should be said about what specifically this language says and what is known in specifically musical cognition. Since the cognitive realignments generated by music demand infinitely fine sensitivity and consist in unpredictable and even undetectable transfers, perhaps it is ultimately as inscrutable as Langer's intuition. While Goodman suggests that debate over the relative aesthetic merits of pieces is pointless, his theory offers nothing more substantial in its place. On seemingly crucial questions of specifically musical value, then, Goodman's theory is silent. Since music's primary value is cognitive, there is little to be said about the relative worth of specific pieces or experiences. Apparently, if they affect conceptual realignments, they are desirable; if not, they are worthless. But this is a very relativistic, even particularistic stance that radically individualizes questions of musical value and seems to deny all possibility for critical comparisons.

One of the primary issues symbolic accounts of music must confront is the mediacy-immediacy problem. Langer's solution was to deny that all symbols refer and to posit a class of symbols that only present. Goodman shows that symbols can present and refer at the same time, so that music's expressive power and sense of felt immediacy are not at odds with what he believes to be its symbolic function. Although this offers to resolve certain issues, it raises others. For Goodman is not only interested in establishing that music can be conceived as symbolic; he is saying further that the sense of perceptual immediacy called aesthetic can be accounted for quite adequately by semiotic theory. Thus, there is no need for a special aesthetic realm marked by special dispositions and feelings, lying outside the domain of symbols and cognitive activity. He wants nothing to do with "the tradition that associates the aesthetic with the immediate and nontransparent and so insists that the aesthetic object be taken for what it is in itself rather than as signifying anything else."[171] Exemplification is very different from this notion of aesthetic intrinsicality, since exemplifying is a kind of referring. "[E]xemplification, like denotation, relates a symbol to a referent, and the distance from a symbol to what . . . is exemplified by it is no less than the distance to what it . . . denotes."[172] Immediacy or nontransparency are not matters of distance, but simply features of the way different symbolic modes work.

There are those, however, who find this response troubling. There is an important difference, Smith maintains for instance, in the "cognitive range" of aesthetic and cognitive experience, respectively.[173] While some musical experience probably brings about cognitive growth of the kind Goodman claims, not all music does. Often, musical experience is primarily concerned with attending to and savoring the qualities of an unfolding musical surface, or features that are already quite familiar and therefore, presumably, well understood. This appreciative experience is, Smith suggests, more closely akin to 'awareness' than to the normal meaning of 'understanding'. Since Goodman's argument maintains that the value of all symbolic experience is cognitive, the merest act of noticing must somehow stand as an instance of cognitive growth.

Put in slightly different terms, the problem with exemplification theory is this. Since reference is the common core of symbolism, and since music is symbolic, music must, even in exemplifying and expressing, refer. This poses problems for that significant body of music which seems, at any rate, to refer to nothing. Goodman avoids this difficulty by using the word 'refer' in a very broad sense, one that includes any instance in which a property is "presented for apprehension," "shown forth," or "made manifest."[174] This is how a symbol can symbolize something that does not lie outside itself. But does music, in exemplifying, necessarily refer?

In instances where a property is simply displayed and perceived (the so-called aesthetic experience), does the term 'reference' belong in the formula 'exemplification-equals-possession-plus-reference'? Monroe Beardsley insists there is nothing to be gained, and perhaps a good deal to be lost, in the additional notion of reference. What music "shows forth," it possesses, he maintains, but that is not a matter of referring: "It is not easy to think of musical compositions . . . as though the composer had something to sell besides the work itself."[175] Rather than exemplifying (at least as Goodman has defined the term), music only 'exhibits'. Calling a Beethoven finale triumphant may indeed be to say it 'has' or 'serves as a sample of' triumph, concedes Beardsley. But this is not to say that it also refers to the quality of triumph. The Beethoven finale is "triumph-music rather than music-referring-to-triumph."[176]

What is it, Beardsley persists, that "converts mere possession of a metaphorical label into exemplification of it?"[177] How is it some things are merely possessed while others are exemplified, shown forth? All manner of characteristics may be possessed without being 'exemplified', why not musical ones as well? In short, Beardsley wants to retain an account in which musical compositions "have qualities describable by metaphorical predicates, which they present for our apprehension but do not refer to."[178]

Music can refer to properties it possesses. A piece can serve, for instance, as an example of rondo form. But music does not always function this way. In fact it probably does so neither the majority of the time nor for the majority of its properties. Although Goodman allows that not every property possessed is necessarily referred to, properties exemplified are more important than properties only possessed. Only exemplified properties are symbolic, and therefore have cognitive significance. The challenge Beardsley presents to Goodman is that, in musical experience, reference seldom seems to matter as much as qualities shown forth, possessed, made manifest, exhibited—and no more. In short, music need not be a symbol to possess, either literally or metaphorically. Nor need it be symbolic to be of cognitive value.

Placing cognitive efficacy above all else has at least one further serious consequence that was noted earlier in passing, a dismissive stance toward judgments and debate over the musical merits of specific pieces. "To say a work of art is good . . . does not after all provide much information . . . Works of art are not race horses, and picking a winner is not the primary goal," Goodman asserts, and "Estimates of excellence are among the minor aids to insight."[179] But it would seem such 'minor aids to insight' might be of considerable value when they are grounded in musical perception and supported by reasons that serve to focus and refine musical experience. Under such circumstances critical discourse might be not just a minor but a major aid to insight. Beardsley takes Goodman to task on this issue as well, arguing that exemption from judgment is no "inalienable right,"[180] and that, indeed, every act of choosing implies a judgment. Pleas for exemption from judgment should only be honored where probable harm can be shown to ensue. Judgments as such pose no threat to music, concludes Beardsley, only "unfair judgments or unreasonable judgments."[181]

If the claim that music's value derives from cognition in-and-for-itself has these disadvantages, what of the 'aesthetic' alternative proposed by Beardsley? From an aesthetic perspective, according to Beardsley, music's value lies in its capacity to impart, through apprehension of its qualities and relations (including its semantic ones, if any) "a marked aesthetic character to experience."[182] Saying one piece is better (more valuable) than another amounts to observing that it has greater capacity to confer experience that is aesthetic in character. Music may well serve other purposes as well, but is best understood and appraised in light of the distinctive way it fulfills this aesthetic purpose. But as Goodman has complained, saying aesthetic value derives from a capacity to sustain experience with aesthetic character is a circular claim. In an effort to meet this criticism, Beardsley proposes a definition of aesthetic experience which, like Goodman's symptomatic account, is "compound and disjunctive." Experience that is aesthetic in character tends to exhibit five symptoms, says Beardsley: a sense of object-directedness, a sense of felt freedom, a sense of detached affect, a sense of active discovery, and a sense of wholeness.[183] Aesthetic musical experience has at least four of these symptoms, including the first, and aesthetic value is a function of music's capacity to confer or sustain experience in which such qualities predominate.

Note that Beardsley is not claiming intrinsic value for aesthetic musical experience. Music's worth is not, as Goodman has it, a matter of its contribution to knowledge; but neither is it something music just "has." Musical value is a function of its capacity to confer aesthetic quality upon experience. Music's distinctive value comes not from what we know of it, or with it, or through it, but rather from its remarkable capacity to remind us deeply and vividly, as nothing else can, of "the possibilities of living fully."[184]

On the other hand, a symbol whose fundamental mission is cognition is compromised when it attracts and rewards attention to itself: when the kind or quality of experience it affords becomes more noteworthy than its capacity to convey understanding. Goodman acknowledges this tendency of art and music to draw attention to themselves, but declares that "far from involving denial or disregard of symbolic functions, [this tendency] derives from certain character-istics of a work as a symbol."[185] Beardsley's point is that although Goodman has shown how the sense of musical 'immediacy' can derive from characteristics of the work, the words "as a symbol" are a needless appendage.

Perhaps the most persuasive way of putting the symbolic argument is one that downplays the 'knowing' aspect of the cognitive claim in favor of mere awareness, or of an articulated difference in consciousness. This perspective ap-pears to rest extensively upon what phenomenology calls the 'intentionality' of consciousness, the fact that consciousness 'is' what consciousness is 'of'. Con-sciousness without an object is an impossible contradiction. In the merest act of perception, then, whether of music or anything else in the world, the object of that perception actually constitutes consciousness in important respects—sets up a difference where before there was none. If every discriminable aspect of the perceived thus begets a difference in consciousness, and if music is a dis-tinctive kind of perceptual object, musical consciousness takes on the music's qualities—whether coarse or subtle. In effect, consciousness becomes what con-sciousness perceives. Since conception and reality (subject and object, perceiver and perceived) do not simply run along parallel to each other in their respec-tive realms, with perception serving to span the chasm between them, musical perception is a profound shaper, a creator of 'worlds' of consciousness, of possi-ble modes of existence. Musical experience, as Langer argued, humanizes the natural world and shapes consciousness in ways nothing else does. The more subtle, the more elegant, the more ingenious the music, the more so is human consciousness.

Nattiez: Signs, Reference, and Infinite Musical Interpretants

Controversy over the applicability of semiotics to music is hardly confined to the cognitive-aesthetic debate discussed above. Indeed, the very nature of the field, its methods, and its purview have themselves been the topic of vigorous debate in recent years. Given the lack of consensus on the precise nature of semiotics, it is not at all surprising that assessments of its applicability to music should run the gamut from enthusiasm to skepticism. As an example of the lat-ter, Henry Orlov warns that the mere fact that music lends itself to description in semiotic terms "does not necessarily mean that the terminology and theory of semiotics will help us to understand music better."[186] And Joseph Margolis concludes a close philosophical analysis with the blunt assertion that "evidence favoring a . . . regular discipline of semiotics—particularly fitted to nonlinguis-tic phenomena—is extremely weak . . ."[187]

Musicologist Jean-Jacques Nattiez is perhaps foremost among musical theorists who currently employ the terminology and conceptual framework of semiotics, although, for reasons that will become more fully apparent in due course, he prefers the term 'semiology' to 'semiotics'. The conceptual ground that separates Margolis's skepticism from the advocacy of Nattiez can be grasped most directly in the contrasting ways each characterizes semiotics. For Margolis, musical semiotics seeks to place music within the context of "the study of languages, or of language-governed or language-like communicative systems . . ."[188] Nattiez, on the other hand, declares that although the most conspicuous activity and progress has occurred in the area of language study, "*Semiology is not the science of communication.*"[189] Indeed, the notion that semiology is fundamentally and essentially concerned with communication is, in his estimation, a "myth."[190] This is conceptual ground that needs to be cleared before we proceed further.

At issue is whether a language-focused semiotic science can accommodate music in a way that is meaningful and helpful. Margolis and Nattiez would agree it cannot, though for different reasons. Where they diverge is on the issues of whether language is the paradigmatic instance of symbolic activity and whether the field's structuralist history is a continuing impediment to its fruitful application to music. Margolis appears to answer both questions in the affirmative, while Nattiez firmly rejects both assumptions. It all depends, it seems, on how one construes the basic aims and methods of semiotics.

Modern semiotics originated in the structuralist theories of **Ferdinand de Saussure** (1857–1913), which construed semiotics as a discipline devoted to elucidating relationships between signs and what they signify (between 'signifiers' and 'signifieds'). The structuralism he espoused amounted to a closed syntactical system whose relationship to semantic 'meanings' was more or less deterministic, invariant, and exhaustive—perhaps not unlike Goodman's description of 'digital' schemes. Accordingly, it tended to priorize syntactical relationships and the meanings they engender over meanings that arise in other (nonsyntactical, non-'structural') ways. Many of Margolis's reservations about musical semiotics seem to follow from its structuralist heritage, and what he sees as an inherent emphasis upon idealized systematicity. In particular, he believes the slipperiness and the sheer multiplicity of musical meanings defy the kind of systematicity required by semiotic science. On Margolis's view, musical meanings are contingent, culturally relative, and culturally emergent in ways that make them unlikely candidates for study from the systematic purview of semiotic science. Pointing to Wittgenstein's conception of language games as extensively improvisational, fluid, and unpredictable affairs, Margolis believes meanings are contingent and consensual phenomena. They are deeply embedded in the various and ever-evolving social practices that give rise to them. In short, the rigorous aspirations and rule-governed nature of semiotics is ill suited to the ambiguity, the multiplicity of potential meanings, the indefinite variability, and the diversity of musical phenomena and practices. If, says Margolis, "one thinks of music as a practice generated within a 'form of life' . . . then improvisation (like natural speech itself) is more the 'rule' than ornament. . . . The failure of [semiotic accounts of music] lies, precisely in their incapacity to make intelligible at all the phenomenon of natural musical invention and the correspondingly enlarged (and instantly self-adjusting) listening to what is thus genuinely emergent. . . ."[191] For a science of semiotics to accommodate the slipperiness and polyvalence of musical meanings, it would have to meet conditions Margolis thinks are largely incompatible with the basic instincts and dispositions of the field. A semiotics capable of accounting for musical activity would need to regard rules as strictly provisional arrangements, and to respect the highly improvisational character of the cultural practices to which such 'rules' are applied. It would need to replace its presumptions of orderliness and lawlike systematicity with a willingness to accept disorderliness and contextual relativity. It would have to replace the ideal of a closed system with an open-ended one with radical possibilities for cultural emergence. It would have to give up its presumption of syntactical priority. And it would have to renounce its implicit but pervasive conviction that language is the paradigmatic instance of semiosis.[192] Add to this music's significant potential for inscrutability, and the challenges for a 'science of signs' are indeed daunting.

Margolis does not deny music's capacity to exhibit semiotic features, features like quotation, allusion, the kind of implicative relationships elucidated by Leonard Meyer, and so forth. Only, since these features never exhaust the rich possibilities for musical meaning, and since such meaning as music has can be functionally specified only within living communicative practices, he doubts the capacity of a systematically oriented science to engage in much more than empirical observation and counting in a particular set of circumstances, at a given point in time. Compared to semiotics' espoused interest in studying and illuminating "language-like communicative systems," that seems a rather modest achievement.

Although the subtitle of Nattiez's book is tantalizingly equivocal on the possibility of a full blown semiology of music ("*Toward* a Semiology . . ."), it is clear he conceives of its basic objectives and concerns quite differently than Margolis. Fully sensitive to the shortcomings of structuralism, Nattiez remains confident that a nonstructuralist or poststructuralist semiology is potentially both viable and fruitful. He articulates his basic thesis this way: "[T]he musical work is not merely what we used to call the 'text': it is not merely a whole composed of 'structures'. . . . Rather, the work is also constituted by the procedures that have engendered it . . . and the procedures to which it gives rise: acts of interpretation and perception."[193] By renouncing communication as a definitive characteristic of semiotics, and by rejecting a structuralist approach in favor of one that endeavors to accommodate generative, perceptual, and interpretive practices, Nattiez's semiological account of music offers to successfully confront many of the challenges posed by Margolis.

Like all semiological theories, Nattiez's begins with a definition of the sign, of the kind of referring that obtains between signifiers and signifieds, and of the kind(s) of meaning(s) to which such referring gives rise. Given his rejection of 'communication' as a satisfactory label for these meanings, Nattiez's preference for semiology to semiotics is reasonable. The latter still strongly connotes the structuralist penchant for a scientifically explicable system, whereas semiology is descriptive of the broader range of potential meanings Nattiez wishes to address. The shortcomings of Saussurean structuralism enumerated by Margolis are perfectly clear to Nattiez. Most notably, it was imperative to structuralist accounts that the signifier-signified relationship be stable and invariant: a static state of affairs that, unfortunately, obtains in neither linguistic nor musical situations. As Margolis rightly claims, it is inconceivable for historically and contingently placed humans to construct the kind of totalized system Saussure envisioned.[194] Moreover, common human experience shows that this kind of invariance in the relation between signifier and signified is indeed rare, even in the case of language. Instead of taking his lead from Saussure, though, Nattiez draws his account of 'referring' from the writings of Charles Sanders Peirce. According to Peirce, a sign is something that becomes connected to something else (another sign, its 'object') in such a way that it draws a third element (the 'interpretant') into a relationship with that same object. But the signifier-signified-interpretant relationship is not a simple, closed system; its meaning is never exhausted in that three-way connection. For the interpretant also functions as a sign, mediated by still other potential interpretants that relate to the object in still different ways, and so forth, ad infinitum.[195] In short, construing the relationship between signifier and signified as a straightforward, unidimensional affair fails to account for the richness and polyvalence of the meanings signs engender. As Nattiez says, "the process of referring effected by the sign is *infinite*."[196]

This implies, further, that since the relationship between signifier and signified is mediated by potentially infinite interpretants, the 'object' to which a given sign refers cannot be wholly or strictly 'objective', that its meaning is not totally explicable without recourse to an infinite web of interpretants. The object referred to by a sign is always "virtual," says Nattiez: it "does not exist except within and through the infinite multiplicity of interpretants, by means of which the person *using* the sign seeks to *allude to* the object."[197] Thus, signs do not implicate particular references by virtue of static or stable functions within a closed system. Rather, what signs refer to are always "contained within the *lived experience*" of those who use them.[198] With this historically and culturally relative definition of the sign in place, one that is always tied to a potentially infinite range of dynamic interpretants, Nattiez reformulates Cassirer's (and Langer's) definition of the symbolic form. It is, quite simply, "a sign, or a collection of signs, to which an infinite complex of interpretants is linked."[199]

So for Nattiez, semiology is the broad study of things that (for someone, in a particular set of circumstances, at a particular time) refer to something. It is not a science concerned with revealing invariant structural foundations of communication, nor does it have as its object the illumination of absolute, invariant relationships between (say) a given sonorous form and universal characteristics of reality. The matter of meaning is clearly of pivotal import to his semiology, however. Meaning is not to be construed along the lines of message transmission or communication (modeled, that is, after the particular situation of language). Meaning is a slippery and transient affair that arises among the dynamically related sites within Peirce's web of interpretants. Meanings are not idealized, timeless entities that arise from static signifier-signified relationships. Meaning is engendered, Nattiez says, any time an individual places "an object of any kind" in relation to his or her lived experience: "that is, in relation to a collection of other [virtual] objects that belong to his or her experience of the world." More succinctly still, "meaning exists when an object is situated in re- lation to a horizon."[200] Since this is a world of virtual objects and multiple hori- zons, Nattiez's semiological project may be characterized as the attempt to elu- cidate the many, perhaps infinite, kinds of referring and meaning to which symbolic forms (defined as Nattiez has stipulated) give rise.

The Tripartition

Given his explicit recognition of contingency, historicity, perspectival situated- ness, and dynamism, it is clear from the outset that Nattiez's semiology will not sanction the idealistic pursuit of musical universals. He acknowledges only one absolute condition: sound. Beyond that, his semiological explorations strive to expose the impossibility of being everywhere at once, of assuming a perspective that is itself beyond all perspective. This is made particularly poignant in his commentary on the communication myth. The classic schematization for com- munication is one in which a producer's message is transmitted by someone and received with minimal distortion by someone else. But this wrongly construes the message or the word or the piece of music as a middle term in an act of largely mechanical transmission between producer and receiver. When all is functioning with minimal resistance, as often seems to be the case in everyday discourse, for instance, this simple model appears adequate. But the seeming ease of successful linguistic communication masks a far more complex process that consists in the interaction of three different levels or dimensions. The in- teraction between the producer and the object is a constructive process, one in which something material is brought into existence by someone who produces it. This Nattiez (after Molino) calls the *poietic* process. What is thus created has a level of materiality, an existence that bears the "traces" of the poietic process that brought it into being: the *immanent* (or alternatively, the *neutral*) level. Where the communication model errs is in presuming that the trace is trans- parent, or that it serves as a conduit for transmitting the meaning or intentions of its producer. On the contrary, the relation of the perceiver to the trace is, like the producer's, a constructive one. This act of apprehending, interpreting, and giving meaning to the trace, of bringing the trace into various possible relations with the perceiver's horizon, Nattiez calls the *esthesic* process.

Failure to distinguish clearly among the attributes of the poietic process, the esthesic process, and the neutral materiality of the trace, together with the presumption that the linkage between them is direct and automatic, leads to all manner of confusion regarding the nature of semiology—and of music as an ob- ject of semiological analysis in particular. The poietic process is concerned with making, with forging materials into particular empirical configurations, be they words, pictures, objects, gestures, or pieces of music. These materials, so ma- nipulated and so organized, may bear traces of the poietic process and may, to varying degrees, provide clues as to the operations that went into their making, the intentions of the maker, and so forth. However, these clues are just that and no more. They are at most suggestive, not directive. They are incapable of dictating, prescribing, or exhaustively determining the range of relevant interpretation. Only when maker and perceiver share an identical universe of discourse could the esthesic process constitute a perfect complement to the poietic, and this is rarely the case. On the poietic side, the maker can never dictate the particular horizons in relation to which the trace acquires meaning for the perceiver. On the esthesic side, a perceiver may respond to features of the trace unknown and unintended by the maker, and bring to bear a range of interpretants so vast no maker could possibly envision them in the poietic act. Since the potential linkages that engender meaning are infinite, there can be no single definitive meaning of any sign situation. It is impossible to scrutinize any symbolic form from all three partitional perspectives simultaneously, and none is capable of accounting for all meaning.

Attempts to construe music as a linguistic-communicative affair are fundamentally misguided. "A given type of music should not be condemned because its poietic strategies can never be captured by our perceptive strategies. In fact, a perfect balance between [them] seems to be the rarest of birds in the history of music. . . ."[201] The very possibility of stylistic evolution depends upon defying and exceeding current perceptual habits: upon a disjunction between the poietic and the esthesic.

The upshot of this threefold or tripartitional model in which multiple and dynamic interpretants give rise to manifold meanings is that it construes communication as a distinctive yet nonparadigmatic instance of a broader process of symbolic activity. Communication is "only one of the possible results of the symbolic process,"[202] not its definitive case. There are multiple modes of potential interaction among the poietic, the immanent, and the esthesic levels, and multiple horizons to which any given sign may refer. Thus there is always potential for slippage, and sometimes potential for incommensurability among the various players in a symbol game. There are no guarantees that the producer's intentions will be captured in the trace and conveyed to the perceiver. It is not possible, even in seemingly straightforward acts of verbal communication, to determine which of the potentially relevant features of the trace will be taken up by the esthesic process. Nor is it possible to assure that different perceivers will bring the same features of the trace to bear on contiguous or similar experiential horizons. Although people are fond of believing that for any given symbol or any given instance of signification there is a "hard kernel" of objective meaning that stands in stark contrast to its "dust cloud of personal and affective associations,"[203] Nattiez maintains this is not the case at all: "[W]hat we ordinarily call denotation designates a constellation of interpretants that are common to the poietic and the esthesic."[204] Thus, whether meaning is connotative or denotative is not formal but conventional: it depends strictly upon the extent of overlap among patterns of interpretants, so that there can be no a priori distinction between denotation and connotation. In other words, the meaning of semiological events, even the most seemingly unequivocal, is always open. It is "never guaranteed that the webs of interpretants will be the same for each and every person . . ."[205] This being the case, the meaning of any given or signifier or symbol can differ greatly among perceivers, and between producer and perceiver as well. There is, then, in the material trace, a neutral level, or as Eco puts it, an "empty form, to which one can attribute many possible meanings."[206] Attention to structure alone is always blind to meaning. It is only in the poietic and esthesic perspectives that immanent structure becomes meaningful.

One great advance of this poststructuralist semiological orientation over those associated with structuralism, and one with enormous potential for our conception of music, is its determination to turn us "away from the immanent, in order to rediscover the author and the reader."[207] It tells us not to seek an 'all' of music or an 'all' of musical meaning unless that 'all' attempts to remain both plural and diverse at the same time. Much of traditional 'aesthetic' theory, for instance, has focused upon Nattiez's 'esthesic' processes and their presumed implications at the neutral level, taking them as the ultimate measures of musical worth, and taking that musical perspective as the one with the most inherent worth in accounting for the nature and the value of music. What Nattiez's tripartitional model begins to do is show that music's nature and values are plural, dynamic, and relative.

We need to be clear, however, that it is emphatically not Nattiez's intent to dismiss the significance of the neutral level, the level of immanent configurations. Structuralism's failure was to have presumed its sufficiency in accounting for music's meaning and its value. But among its significant achievements was establishing that symbolic forms cannot be reduced to either biographical or social phenomena. Symbols, writes Nattiez, "manifest a level of specific organization, that must be described. But this level is not sufficient: the poietic lurks under the surface of the immanent; the immanent is the spring-board for the esthesic."[208] The challenge for a semiology of music, then, is to resist the temptation to reduce its tripartitional symbolic system to any one of its integrally related dimensions. Properly construed, then, musical analysis consists in a recurrent "dialectical oscillation among the three dimensions of the object,"[209] none of which is dispensable. While immanent configurations or structures are incapable of accounting for musical meaning, they are none the less essential for elucidating a "unity that might be overlooked by purely poietic or purely esthesic analysis."[210] The neutral level is not static, but dynamic. It is "perpetually subverted"[211] and reshaped as it is related to new interpretive horizons, whether poietic or esthesic.

The great benefit of Molino's tripartitional model, then, is its attribution to symbolic systems of a distinctive organizational composition, one that differentiates them from other social systems: the bio-social, the ecological-economic, and the socio-political among them. And yet, despite this distinctive organizational character and its descriptive methodological utility, Nattiez states emphatically that "[s]emiology does not exist."[212] Apparently he means as well that it cannot exist, at least if by semiology is meant the general science of signs and languagelike systems Margolis claims that semiotics aspires to be. There is, Nattiez concludes, "no collection of concepts, methods, and rules that permit analysis of the symbolic, in whatever domain it may exist."[213] Accordingly, we are left—or so it seems—to conduct specific investigations of particular symbolic situations in light of whatever information can be brought to bear upon them one by one. Given the perspectival nature, the relativity, the partiality of all musical meanings, Nattiez appears to imply, the agenda of establishing a global semiology is not a particularly promising one.

That, however, is not to suggest that generalization about the symbol situation is wholly impossible. The symbolic process, Nattiez offers, is a constructive and dynamic process that consists in a process of referring; meanings engendered in symbolic activity are not necessarily discernible in the trace that gives rise to them; the symbolic is an autonomous domain, distinct from the social, the psychological, the economic; and the symbolic is a tool that modifies and transforms our worlds. But above all, symbolism's tripartitional nature and its deployment of infinite interpretants demand that music be recognized as a profoundly polysemic affair. For Nattiez, calling music a symbol system simply means that it shares with all symbolic activity the capacity in its various referential valences to "give rise to a complex and infinite web of interpretants."[214] Thus, Nattiez's semiology does not attempt a typology of signs, only a general account of the nature of symbols which acknowledges "the polysemiousness of any [symbolic] expression, and . . . [the] infinite exegesis that carves out that expression's meanings."[215] Its provision for infinite interpretants roughly parallels the complexity and multiplicity of referential relations that underlie Goodman's theory. Likewise, Nattiez's conviction that symbols mediate the construction of a distinctive and autonomous domain within human experience resembles Cassirer's and Langer's thesis that symbol use creates perceptual and conceptual universes, and Goodman's account of symbolic world making. Nattiez's belief in the infinity of potential relations among interpretants, however, is for him not a resting place but a point of departure in explicating the ways that tripartitional interactions illuminate specific musical and philosophical problems. The line of inquiry most immediately relevant to the survey being undertaken here is the theory's implications for the thorny question of the fundamental nature, meaning, and value of music.

The Meaning(s) of Music

Common parlance would have it that the concept of music, what music is, is self-evident. On the contrary, says Nattiez, not only does the notion of a universal, culturally invariant concept of music fail to square with global anthropological facts, but even within a given society "there is never a single, culturally dominant conception of music; rather, we see a whole spectrum of conceptions."[216] Therefore, he concludes, "music is whatever people choose to recognize as such, [and] noise is whatever is recognized as disturbing, unpleasant, or both."[217] The distinction between music and noise is always a socio-cultural achievement, and rarely is there consensus over where the border between the two should be drawn. The provocative conclusion to which this leads Nattiez is strongly reminiscent of Goodman's nominalistic conviction that there is no way the world 'is', only different ways the 'world' may be construed: "There is not a music, but many musics . . ."[218]

Even within the seemingly homogeneous framework of Western art music, what is considered salient about music can vary considerably, depending upon the relative emphasis placed upon poietic, immanent, or esthesic factors. Poietic orientations locate 'music' in generative or reproductive acts, regarding it as an art concerned with the creation and manipulation of sonorous material. Immanent accounts gravitate toward music's 'intrinsic' features, the sound object's intramusical relations and sonorous properties. Esthesic orientations see perceptual pleasure and displeasure as music's definitive characteristic, focusing on the way music is experienced. That is, conditions of production, conditions within the sonorous object, and conditions affecting reception each lead to distinctive, divergent, and sometimes incommensurable conceptions of what music is, what distinguishes better specimens from worse. Nattiez goes still further than this, though. Since "[t]here is no limit to the number or the genre of variables that might intervene in a definition of the musical,"[219] apparently all definitions of music are partial, perspectival, relative to a particular era and culture. Any particular definition of music invariably selects and privileges certain attributes while ignoring, marginalizing, or neglecting others.

The interpretants potentially implicated in musical activity are not only infinite, they are mobile as well, a fact that does not bode well for efforts to achieve an invariant, all-inclusive account of music's 'essential' conditions. Even seemingly uncontroversial attempts to make sound music's definitive characteristic must contend with the elusive boundary between noise and music, the relation between sound and silence, and the inclusion by many if not most cultures of more than sound under the heading 'musicality'. The boundary between noise and music has migrated considerably throughout history, and there is no empirical basis for a universally applicable distinction even today. In some instances, such non-sonorous features as physical gesture or spontaneous interaction among participants figure centrally in the conception of the musical. Even the social, affective, and referential components the Hanslickian tradition regards as contaminants to music proper often figure centrally into what certain groups consider music. The breadth of the ancient Greeks' conception of music, then, is probably not as unusual or exceptional as is often presumed. Music is a label applied to an essentially open conceptual, behavioral, and experiential range.

In Nattiez's view, then, what constitutes music for a given culture or subculture is never determined at the level of sonorous configurations. Accounts of 'the musical' must embrace poietic and esthesic processes, the social and cultural interactions in which all music-like actions are embedded. Without such openness, calling something 'music' threatens to force together practices that other cultures keep separate, or to separate out aspects of the phenomenon that are inextricably linked. There is a broad continuum of terms that may enter singly or in combination into various conceptions of "the musical": Nattiez suggests noise, music, language, game, dance, and social action.[220] If the range of potentially relevant interpretants is indeed infinite, and if the domain of 'esthesic' processes is elastic enough to accommodate the "entire lived experience" of participants as Nattiez suggests,[221] even this list may be quite narrow.

The situation Nattiez portrays is ironic. While on the one hand, activities we find convenient to describe as musical occur in every known human society, on the other, there is no characteristic they all share, no essential common nature, no single job they all do. Thus, the semiology toward which Nattiez's efforts are directed cannot be the universally explanatory semiotic science envisioned by many. It is a relativized, even particularized undertaking that regards all symbolic activity as culturally relative. Nattiez himself is reluctant to concede that this rules out all possibility of musical universals, though. Universals should not be sought at the level of immanent structures, he writes, "but in more profound realities."[222] If musical universals are to be identified, they must be sought not in static or culturally transcendent structures, but rather in the "behaviors associated with sound phenomena."[223]

Music has one irreducible 'given': sound. However, the difference between sounds that are musical and sounds that are not can never be determined by attending to the sounds themselves. It is in what people do by making and using sound that musical universals should be sought. And since "there are no a priori limits on the numbers of different interpretants that producers or interpreters might associate with a given sound complex,"[224] the project of musical semiology cannot be conducted without attention to the sociocultural contexts in which all poietic and esthesic processes are embedded. Nattiez believes it is possible to construe music as a symbolic system (or perhaps more appropriately, as a constellation of symbolic systems). But it becomes abundantly clear that when "symbol system" is construed to accommodate the polysemious character of something like music, it must relinquish all pretensions that the signifier-signified relationship is a direct or fundamentally transitive affair. The meanings the 'musical symbol' engenders are not structurally determined, but are instead social constructions whose 'musicality' is always relative to cultural habit and the ways people use them. If this sounds more like anthropology or sociology than semiology, we have to recall that in Nattiez's view what is distinctive about semiology is its persistent effort to elucidate the relationships between the constructive and functional features of music and its materiality. Semiology as he apparently conceives it is fundamentally devoted to revealing the multidimensional webs of meaning to which the basic act of referring can give rise.

Plurality and Relativism

As we have seen, Nattiez conceives of musics as symbolic systems: that is, as complex sonorous configurations with the potential to refer to vast, diverse, perhaps innumerable horizons, to implicate potentially infinite webs of interpretants. These webs are expansive and heterogeneous enough to accommodate both internal and external kinds of referring, what others have called absolute and referential meanings. Where Nattiez seems to depart from those others, and what sets his theory apart from those that are language and communication based, is his willingness to acknowledge both as instances of semiosis. An adequate account of musical meaning, in his view, must accommodate all possible forms of musical referring. The 'intrinsic' or internal referring of the aesthetic/absolutist tradition is one such form. It embraces both intramusical referring—the syntactical/implicative relationships which Leonard Meyer and others have explored in such detail—and intermusical referring, the situation of particular musics within certain styles and conventions. Extrinsic referring, that which is semantic in character, implicates experience that is spatiotemporal, kinetic, and broadly affective in character. But "intraversive" and "extroversive" semioses, as he calls them, are not discrete processes or domains. They are both processes of referring, and in actual musical experience they are always tightly intertwined. Indeed, one of the most distinctive qualitative features of much musical experience is the state of instability and dynamic fluidity that exists between these two modes of referring.

Since for Nattiez there is no simple one-to-one correspondence between musical signifiers and signifieds, and since on his view music does not aspire to conceptual clarity and logical articulation the way language does, his semiology necessarily encompasses all instances of referring or association to which musics give rise. Any and all instances of interpretation and meaning to which sounds give rise may be instances of music and thus objects of musical semiology. Such inclusiveness and pluralism raises important issues, though. Is Nattiez's belief in the existence of universals warranted? Or has he, in having renounced a structural foundation for music, created an account that is so open, inclusive, and pluralistic that relativism ensues?

Let us briefly revisit some of the seemingly relativistic features of this account. First, and most obviously, there is Peirce's idea that signs are linked to infinite and dynamic complexes of interpretants. Then there is Molino's tripartitional explanation of semiology, in which poietic, immanent, and esthesic dimensions need not correspond: where, indeed, ambiguity and slippage are the rule rather than the exception.[225] While Nattiez concedes that the structuralist library need not be burned,[226] it is central to his position that accounts of musics and their values recognize that structural configurations constitute but one kind of referring to which musical sounds give rise, one kind of activity in which they are implicated. If interpretants are potentially infinite and always dynamic, and if the three perspectives that comprise the tripartition are potentially mutually exclusive, relativism of some kind seems the unavoidable outcome.

Moreover, Nattiez asserts that music is whatever people choose to recognize as such, and that what counts as music or noise is "always culturally defined."[227] 'The musical' is "*nothing more than* the sonorities accepted as 'music' by an *individual*, group, or culture,"[228] writes Nattiez in a statement that seems willing to set aside even intersubjective consensus as a criterion of 'the musical'. The mobility of interpretants over time; the fact that they may differ profoundly for different people in different eras and in different situations (perhaps even on different days?); the fact that what one group (or culture, or individual?) recognizes as relevant to "the musical facts" is not temporally or culturally invariant: each of these bespeaks a relativistic orientation. All three dimensions of the tripartition are valid or legitimate in their own way, Nattiez suggests. And "... there is never *only one valid* musical analysis for any given work."[229] Nor is the 'view from inside' necessarily more valid than the 'view from outside'. "A culture is nothing other than a style: a style of beliefs, customs, behaviors."[230]

And yet, despite his historicism, his perspectivism, his insistence on the plurality of legitimate views, Nattiez maintains that "excessive culturalism should not prevent us from recognizing, from accepting, the existence of *facts* and *truths*."[231] But how, if all perspectives (all interpretations, all performances, all analyses) are necessarily partial, can the ideas of truth and facts be sustained? How can Nattiez continue to hold out hope for musical universals, even at the poietic or esthesic level, if all such processes are conventions relative to the cultures (and individuals) who hold them in common? In having rejected the elusive security of structuralism, have Nattiez and other poststructuralists renounced any claim to rights and wrongs? In having extended the semiological agenda to embrace any and all instances of referring to which the musical phenomena may give rise, have all musical meanings been equally authorized and all value claims been rendered equally (in)valid?

Such is the postmodern, poststructural dilemma. Nattiez's response is, if not wholly satisfying, at least illustrative of one promising direction. The kind of facts and truths to which Nattiez aspires are not the timeless, abstract entities of the idealistic tradition. They are, apparently, provisional truths, or as some might prefer, beliefs that seem warranted given currently available information. There is a multiplicity of sources that can and should inform our understanding of the meanings borne by musical symbols, some more persuasive (or, in traditional terminology, more valid) than others, and others equally legitimate despite their incompatibility. Although the quest for a universal explanation intrigues Nattiez, he seems to sense its futility. In its place, he proposes a rich descriptive and interpretive process that attempts to examine the "total musical fact" (as he is fond of calling it) from as many perspectives as possible. "It is important," he writes, "that we help our students understand the how and why of these different approaches, and their divergences in dealing with the same object. This divergence . . . [is no] institutional scandal. It is, instead, the inevitable result of the symbolic nature of musical and analytical facts . . . the fact that we are presented with a very large latitude of choice between all possible interpretants. . . ."[232]

Apparently, if such a thing as a musical totality exists, it is not to be found in a theoretical quest for universal generalities and truths, but in a constellation of perspectives at the local level. The proper challenge for musical semiology, then, is to explore the interrelationships among various modes of musical being and, presumably, to weigh the relative persuasiveness of their claims to legitimacy; or as Nattiez puts it elsewhere, "to show how poietic and esthesic interpretants are linked with the work's material presence."[233] That these linkages are invariably multiple and necessarily partial is simply a function of the basic semiological fact of referring. The point of a semiological approach to music is not to achieve a perspective that somehow escapes all perspective. It is, rather, to help us gain access to the lived worlds (conceptual, perceptual, social, political, etc.) within which various musics and musical experiences are situated sufficient for us to grasp ever more of the myriad potential meanings they carry. The kind of investigation Nattiez describes can never attain the quasi-scientific rigor Margolis ascribes to semiotics, but neither, apparently, does it aspire to. Nattiez forthrightly acknowledges the culturally relative nature of his own remarks, offering them not as *doxa*, but as elements in an ongoing and potentially open-ended dialogue.[234]

But conceding the existence of multiple opposing (yet legitimate) perspectives and their susceptibility to change over time in light of new experience or evidence does not make of Nattiez what one might call an abject relativist. Reluctance to privilege any single perspective is not the same as conferring equal validity upon all. Within even disparate and divergent universes of musical discourse there exist descriptions, interpretations, and value claims that are more apt, persuasive, and or defensible than other contenders. Reluctance to designate any single perspective definitive or supremely authentic is not the same as saying none can be mistaken. One need not choose between universal truth on the one hand and total interpretive freedom on the other. In Nattiez's view, seriation is at least one powerful way of controlling interpretation by subjecting claims to scrutiny from the three distinctive orientations of the tripartition. If, additionally, claims to musical meaning and value are derived from explicitly acknowledged observations, assumptions, and criteria, there are grounds for holding to them provisionally, until something better comes along. And even when musical beliefs and values give way to others, the process is more often akin to erosion than earthquake. Conceding relativity does not mean renouncing something we call truth, only recognizing that "the quest for truth is asymptotic."[235]

So for Nattiez, there is a 'truth' somewhere out there, a "total" musical "fact," despite our inability to grasp it in any but a partial manner. And although it has been suggested here that his esthesic level might indeed be extended to include the entire social matrix in which musical activity occurs, Nattiez most often characterizes the esthesic as predominantly perceptual in character, the process by which interpretants establish meaningful linkages with the immanent domain of sonorous configurations. To this extent his account falls short of its implicit promise to place music within the context of the entire lived experience of those involved. For that experience has an inevitable sociopolitical side that is for the most part invisible in his treatment. As Walser observes, Nattiez appears to believe that there is a way of securing claims to musical value without confronting messy and complicated issues like social contestation, institutional prestige, and power. Against this tendency in Nattiez, Walser argues, "There is no way to decide what something means without making a political statement. Underpinning all semiotic analysis is, recognized or not, a set of assumptions about cultural practice, for ultimately music doesn't have meanings; people do. There is no essential foundational way to ground musical meaning beyond the flux of social existence. Ultimately, musical analysis can be considered credible only if it helps explain the significance of musical activities in particular social contexts."[236]

Still, it is to Nattiez's great credit that his 'semiological' project recognizes that music means different things to producers, reproducers, users, perceivers, and so on, and that music's sheer sonorous existence, its dynamic configurations, are not mere middle stages in a process of transmission. It is also to his credit that calling music a symbol or instance of semiosis does not lead him to attempt to bring all music under a single, unified banner. Nattiez's account endeavors to respect the plurality and fluidity of musical meaning. To speak of music a symbol system is, for Nattiez, simply to place it within the realm of things that are humanly constructed, that possess an artifactual presence independent of intentions or perceptual predilections, and that are given meaning by constructive and culturally influenced actions. Were his 'esthesic' processes extended to accommodate not only music's perceptual but its social, political, and economic functions, it would hold even more promise for extending the understanding of music. Whether, given such an extension in range, such exegetic and descriptive activity might any longer be considered 'semiological' is another issue.

Concluding Remarks

In this chapter we have examined three very distinctive theories, each devoted to exploring how music functions symbolically or as an instance of semiosis. For Susanne Langer, music is a vehicle for the 'conception of reality'. In her view it is exceedingly important to establish that music is mindful, and to show how it is mindful. She developed a theory of symbolism in which a common symbolic 'root' gives way to two different kinds of symbolic 'flowers': one discursive, the other presentational; one with assigned reference, the other without. In her view, symbols work by iconic resemblance or common logical form: whereas discursive symbols are a good fit for ideas that are logical and propositional, art symbols (presentational symbols) are a good fit for the form of the life of feeling—for the patterns of human sentience. Thus, what language offers to do for thought, music does for feeling: wrest pattern and meaning from sense data, enabling us to make sense or conceive of the 'real' world.

Nelson Goodman's incisive analysis represents, as we have seen, a substantial advance in symbol theory, showing that the music symbol, like all symbols, refers—only in different, more complex ways. In Goodman's view, the musical symbol is just another instance of the important cognitive business of world making, of reality construction. Symbols are not go-betweens for mind and world, or mind and feeling: rather, they are constructive tools. And music's distinctive, felt character is just the logical outcome of the cognitive role feelings play in musical expression, that being a special case of the symbolic relation of exemplification. For Goodman, then, music is no window onto the world, but one of the many important ways people build their worlds. Its meanings are not universal and absolute, but historical and conventional—products of cultural habit.

Jean-Jacques Nattiez, like Goodman, rejects the idea of a one-to-one relation between signifier and signified, stressing what we might call the slipperiness and polyvalence of musical experience, the polysemy of the musical 'sign'. His views mark a decisive renunciation of the structuralist or formalist belief that the auditory signal can contain music, and an endorsement of the view that musical semiology implicates a potentially infinite process of referring. What counts as music or noise cannot be determined without recourse to its cultural situation, the doings that bring it into being and the web of interpretants that make it meaningful.

Thus we see evidence of some rather significant shifts in semiotic accounts of music: away from a rather narrow and specific understanding of the domain of musical reference, and toward an inclusive, dynamic one; away from a conception of music as an essentially unitary and univocal affair, and toward one that is radically plural and conspicuously diverse; away from a view of symbolism as bridging a gap between the apparent and the real, and toward one that views semiosis as creating worlds of experience and possibility; and perhaps most important, away from a view of music cognition as insular and hardwired ('modular', as current cognitive science jargon would have it), and toward one that is open, porous, malleable, and pluralistic.

DISCUSSION QUESTIONS

1. Langer's 'vehicle for the conception of reality' thesis suggests that symbols are the tools by which people forge meaningful patterns from mere 'raw' sense data. This seems to bear certain resemblances to Goodman's contention that symbol systems are ways of world making. Where do the accounts of Langer and Goodman most strongly diverge? How and why?

2. Specifically how does Goodman's theory amplify, correct, or clarify Langer's concept of a 'presentational' symbol?

3. Compare Langer's and Goodman's explanations of the relation between feeling and musical experience. Include in your discussion references to feelings-felt, feeling symbolized, and feeling's role in expression.

4. Where Langer generally speaks of music in an inclusive sense, Goodman's phrase 'languages of art' leaves open the question of whether music comprises one such 'language' or whether there might be multiple musical symbolic 'languages'. Nattiez, however, states directly that there is no music, only musics. Which view do you find more persuasive? For a semiotic account of music, which do you think more important: the distinctions between musical practices or the similarities among them?

5. Do you believe, with Langer, that there is a 'reality out there' into which music gives people insight? or do you rather hold, with Goodman, that 'reality' is what we construct with musical (and other) symbols? In other words, is music something that mediates insight into an otherwise inaccessible reality, or is it rather constitutive of reality?

6. It is currently fashionable to appeal to music's status as a distinctive 'intelligence' in defense of its place in education. However, establishing its mindful nature does not show why this particular form of mindful activity

should be nurtured and cultivated. Which of the three accounts examined in this chapter offers the most compelling arguments to this end? How?

7. Compare Langer's belief that reference works by structural analogy or iconicity with Goodman's argument that reference is just a matter of habit and convention. How does this difference relate to their respective accounts of metaphor? Discuss the role and function of metaphor as outlined in these two symbol theories.

8. Discuss the similarities and differences among the terms 'self-expression', 'expression', and 'expressive' as they relate to musical experience.

9. Langer's idea of music as an educator of feeling seems to stem in part from a conviction that music somehow renders feeling more refined, controlled, and orderly. Do you agree? If you agree, do you think some musics better serve this end than others? Does the right kind of music dispose people to better moral behavior, as the ancient Greeks believed? If you disagree, how would you counter the claim that if music does not somehow make people more refined, there is little point in making or studying it?

10. Explore Beardsley's 'symptoms' of aesthetic experience using Goodman's 'symptoms' of aesthetic symbolic activity.

11. Compare and contrast Nattiez's account of music with Meyer's formalist/structuralist view. Which do you find more persuasive? Why?

12. Nattiez's semiological theory dramatically extends the musically relevant interpretive range, yet it maintains that symbolic experience is distinct from social, psychological, and economic experience. Hence, interpretive activity is still primarily concerned with understanding the 'neutral level'. Put differently, while the range of potential interpretants may be infinite, their relevance must apparently be gauged in terms of what they show about music 'itself'. If all meanings are, as Goodman contends, matters of habit and convention, and if the sociopolitical world is where such habits are developed and maintained, is it proper to regard the symbolic and sociopolitical as separate?

13. Is music really, as Nattiez contends, whatever people choose to recognize as such? Or do you believe there are limits on what people can so 'choose'? What might the nature of these limits be?

14. If there is never only one valid—or one 'best'—way to analyze a work, what might this imply for the way music is approached, understood, and taught by contemporary musicology?

Music as Experienced

The philosophical method known as phenomenology is among the twentieth century's more distinctive philosophical orientations, and one with considerable appeal for music philosophers. Its most distinctive characteristics are a distaste for theoretical distortion and excess and a determination to describe the objects of human experience in their full richness—as they are lived. Because of a methodological preference for descriptive richness over logical and theoretical 'purity', phenomenology can yield strikingly divergent results in the hands of different individuals. But despite their differences, phenomenologists share strong convictions about how philosophy should and should not be conducted. Phenomenology is critical of both empirical and rationalistic philosophical traditions for having reduced the richness and complexity of human reality to bring it into conformity with their basic tenets. By imposing preordained philosophical categories and constructs upon the given, non-phenomenological philosophy seriously distorts what it purports to describe. Phenomenology, by contrast, is the study of presences and appearances, a 'first philosophy' whose concern is to elucidate the primordial ground for human knowledge and experience before it becomes overlaid with conceptualization, systematization, abstraction, and reason. Where other philosophies seek to explain, in other words, phenomenology strives for full description.

Phenomenology has little sympathy for philosophy's historical preoccupation with grand metaphysical narratives designed to bridge a presumed gap between the 'objective', material world and its manifestation in subjective experience. Such narratives commonly treat the whole of human experience as if it consists in 'nothing but' the favored categories of their particular classificatory systems. In its insistence that sensory experience and sense data are foundational, for instance, empiricism tends to constrict the range of the philosophically relevant 'evidence', excluding things it regards as 'mentalistic'. Thus, human values and motives become private, subjective states which are deemed dispensable to an account of the world as it 'really' is. The 'empirical' world consists of nothing but sense data, data whose existence is totally independent of human experience. Similarly, rationalism's insistence upon the centrality of mind and reason tends to construe reality in purely or predominantly mental terms. Phenomenology denies the idealistic splitting of reality into subjective and objective, apparent and actual, and attempts to avoid the reduction of one pole to the other. In actual human experience, phenomenology insists, there is no gulf that requires a metaphysical bridge, no mutually exclusive relationship between knower and known.

This conviction that in actual human experience there is no fundamental distinction between the apparent and the real contrasts strikingly with the idealistic philosophical legacy. Appearances, phenomenology maintains, are not illusory and suspicious, but potent sources of foundational knowledge. In strong contrast to Kant's contention that the thing-in-itself is completely inaccessible, phenomenology maintains that by adhering to its method people can be brought face to face with the innermost essences of things. If theoretical habits, biases, and presuppositions are set aside, the mind is capable of perceiving the essential in appearances. Metaphysical conjecture generates layers of conceptual 'sedimentation' that cover over what it purports to explain. Phenomenology 'excavates' beneath these layers of distortion to reveal things as they are before the intervention of perceptual and conceptual habit. It operates on a prereflective level where distinctions between knower and known, perceiver and perceived, do not pertain. This 'lived' world phenomenology strives to uncover is no 'objective' domain onto which people project 'subjective' (qualitative, value-laden) veneers. It is, rather, a vital world replete with its own meanings and values.

As a philosophical approach to music, the phenomenological method typically resists efforts to explain what music is 'about', resembles, symbolizes, or is useful for, preferring instead to describe as richly as possible what music itself says, how music is experienced. Instead of explaining, it describes. Meaningful claims about music's nature or value can follow only from close attention to the way it is actually heard, experienced, lived through. Thus, phenomenological musical inquiry promises a 'return to beginnings'. Its concern is not so much to establish absolute or universal truths, but to help recover the richness and fullness of the experientially given.

Because phenomenology is so distinctive as a philosophical method, we begin this chapter with a short survey of its origins in the thought of **Edmund Husserl** (1859–1938), and a general introduction to the kind of assumptions and convictions that lie behind it. We will then examine the key features of the thought of **Maurice Merleau-Ponty** (1908–1961) — not for its commentary on music, since he has little to say about it directly, but because his insistence on the centrality of the body and perceptual experience is rich in musical implications taken up by others. Knowing, Merleau-Ponty believes, cannot be severed from its corporeal roots, a view which disposes a deep skepticism toward abstraction and claims to universality. Not the detached, abstractive mind, but the vital, embodied mind is our source of contact with the world.

We turn next to **Mikel Dufrenne's** (b. 1910) phenomenological examination of 'aesthetic experience', which introduces among other things the idea that such experience differs from other sense-based experience in the extent to which it deploys imagination. One important outcome of this is the 'aesthetic object's' so-called quasi-subjectivity—its humanness. Aesthetic objects, he reasons, are not encountered like other objects in the world: for they bring with them a sense of interiority, of having or being a world, not just of being in one.

Thomas Clifton's (1935–1978) exercise in what he calls 'applied' phenomenology is a richly evocative work that shows well certain of phenomenology's descriptive strengths. Drawing extensively on Merleau-Ponty's theme of corporeality or embodiment, and Dufrenne's idea of quasi-subjectivity, Clifton offers stirring accounts he hopes may help music 'speak for itself': the music is, he insists, what it says it is. His description of tonality as a 'corporeal acquisition', for instance, is illustrative of his desire to return the experiencing person—embodied, actively engaged—to center stage in accounts of music. Clifton wants to resist the kind of mind-body dualism that situates music out-there, impinging somehow on an in-here, subjective self. Music is, he declares, 'what I am when I experience it'—a phrase highly reminiscent of T. S. Eliot's vivid description of ". . . music heard so deeply/ That it is not heard at all, but you are the music/ While the music lasts."[1] Clifton's explorations of what he regards as music's four 'essences'—time, space, play, and feeling—vividly portray the fragility and exquisite sense of oneness with music that musicians know so intimately and value so deeply.

We will next turn to **David L. Burrows** (b. 1930), who explores with remarkable sensitivity the ways sound, speech, and music relate to and differ from one another. Burrows' basic thesis is an intriguing one: that the distinctiveness of the human species, including in particular the intellectual powers in which we so pride ourselves, derive from the special way we relate to and experience sound. As we follow his explorations of the uniqueness of sonorous experience and the ways it plays out in various realms of human endeavor, we will see certain similarities to some of the views advanced by Hegel, Gurney, and others. But Burrows goes further, developing a persuasive account in which sound's felt immediacy plays a crucial role both in self-development and in creating the kind of sympathetic resonance essential to community.

The chapter closes with two brief but important postscripts. First, the beginnings of a phenomenological examination of the act of making or participating in music—as distinct, notably, from more common philosophical preoccupations with listening. **Eleanor Stubley** (b. 1960) writes about the creation, in performance, of a musical field in which musical play unfolds and players engage in an ongoing 'symbiotic tuning' where self opens out onto possibilities of otherness. And finally, we will touch upon philosopher **Mark Johnson's** (b. 1949) analysis of the embodiment of mind, a theory that is both rich in its implications for music, and highly congruent with many of the aims of phenomenological pursuits.

Phenomenology: Origins and Assumptions

The speculative excesses of idealism brought about a backlash that severely eroded belief in philosophy's global explanatory power. A new empirical science of psychology began to take root in ground formerly claimed by philosophy, and much philosophical endeavor turned to the domain of logic in an effort to recover lost prestige and security. Humbled by the spectacular successes of the physical sciences and haunted by allegations that philosophical claims were, beneath it all, rationalizations of psychological dispositions or inclinations, late nineteenth- and early twentieth-century philosophy aligned itself increasingly with linguistic and logical analysis. In this shift toward the apparent rigors of positivism and behaviorism, however, matters of human subjectivity became ever more marginalized.

Edmund Husserl resolutely continued to pursue a philosophy that did not shy away from broader issues of human meaning and value. Against the rationalistic extremes of 'logical positivism', Husserl's phenomenological 'study of appearances' sought to maintain the centrality of human consciousness in philosophy. Husserl was determined to establish a method of inquiry that would avoid the reduction of philosophy to either psychology or logic, that would restore rational inquiry's claim to broad human relevance. Where positivism dramatically restricted the scope of philosophical inquiry by rejecting meanings resistant to strict 'logical' analysis, Husserl's philosophical method sought to explore without presuppositions the entire range and content of consciousness. And since Kant had so clearly shown the interdependence of structure and content in consciousness, Husserl sought a philosophical method capable of dealing not only with mind's content (as Descartes had attempted to do), but with the form of consciousness as well.

Husserl's phenomenology would not be theoretical, but purely descriptive. Instead of relying upon conceptual constructs, phenomenology would describe the way the world actually reveals or presents itself to consciousness. Rather than discarding potentially important truths because of their failure to conform to the theoretical or categorical assumptions of a given system of analysis, Husserl sought to describe experience as fully as possible. Unlike empiricism's tendency to treat consciousness as though it consisted largely of mechanical responses to sensory impressions, phenomenology would retain a central place for mind's transformational capacity. And unlike rationalism's tendency to attribute the ultimate significance of consciousness to its abstractive, constructive capacity, phenomenology would respect the particularity of the 'given'.

The key to getting behind conceptual distortions to pure appearances is an act of suspending, setting aside, or 'bracketing' all presuppositions. 'Bracketing' involves a temporary abstention from judgment in order to allow total attention to the objects and processes of consciousness as they exist in and of themselves. It does not deny the world's physical existence or attempt to dissolve it; rather, it sets questions of actuality or validity temporarily aside in order to enable full investigation of the phenomenal field. This attitude encourages openness and descriptive richness at precisely the point where other approaches impose restraints that narrow their range of investigation. By suspending beliefs about reality, utility, logical consistency, and so forth, one can examine the way experience presents itself before it is overlaid with the aftermath of mind's categorizing and abstractive activities.

Applied to the experience of time and space, for instance, the act of bracketing requires the suspension of everyday assumptions and associations so as to focus upon 'lived' time and 'lived' space. Lived time bears little resemblance to the conceptual time mediated by such things as clocks and historical narratives. Lived time consists in an infinite succession of present moments, of 'nows', rather than in a past, present, and future. The 'past' consists only of traces of previous nows, and the 'future' consists only of projections from a state of perpetual presence. Phenomenologically speaking, time is always 'now'. 'Then' (whether past or future) exists only in reflective abstraction. Likewise, the lived experience of space is one of perpetual 'here'-ness, to which everything else relates as 'there'. Thus, the phenomenological experience of 'here' and 'now' is the philosophical bedrock for any adequate conception of space and time.

Another of Husserl's important ideas concerns the 'intentionality' of all conscious experience: that consciousness is always 'consciousness of' something not itself. Accordingly, there can be no such thing as an entirely self-contained thought or idea. To think is always to think about. There can be no such thing as simple, self-contained awareness, because all thought and perception is invariably directed toward other things. The intentionality or directedness of conscious experience means that conscious states are about more than mere 'subjectivity'. Descartes's conception of mind as pure, 'thinking substance', a notion that splits reality into a mutually exclusive subject and object, is thus profoundly mistaken. The thinking "I" that Descartes believed delivered him from radical doubt ("I think, therefore I am") was empty and meaningless: a state of pure subjectivity. But, counters phenomenology, thought, perception, and feeling never exist without an intentional object: in prereflective human consciousness, subject and object always constitute an indissoluble unity.

Thus, phenomenology seeks to illuminate the world as it is lived through, unencumbered by the prejudices of things like 'common sense': to get beneath the sediment of abstractions, to ground philosophical inquiry in the concrete world as it presents itself. Philosophy's proper focus is the content of consciousness—entities, feelings, values—and its method consists in directing attention strictly to the 'essential' inner core of experience, jettisoning the peripheral, the contingent, the irrelevant. By riveting attention to the immanent, one achieves a state of pure consciousness.

Phenomenology strives to illuminate the richness of lived experience, not experience as it might appear from the perspective a disinterested, objective observer. Its concern is not with matters of general fact but rather with matters of 'essence'. Intellectual abstraction turns one away from what it seeks to interpret, overlaying the particularity of the given with conception's generality. Phenomenology, by contrast, uncovers essences within the given. The perception of essences thus entails a 'turning toward' at precisely the point critical reflection would turn away. Since essential meanings are not imposed from without, but emanate from within, they elude logic and theory. As the prelogical, pretheoretical foundation upon which logic and theories are subsequently built, essences can only be discerned by attending to the thing itself.

In summary, phenomenology contends that the ways things present themselves to perception and consciousness give valuable insights into their essential nature and value. The challenge lies in distinguishing the habitual, the easy,

and the stereotypical from the essential. To the phenomenologist, human reality is far richer and more complex than abstract theory can convey, for such theory is inherently reductionistic. It reduces thinking to the physical activity of a
brain, perception to the reception of sense data, reality to idea, feeling to hor-
monal imbalance, values to rationalizations of personal wants, and so on. The
phenomenological method offers liberation from intellectual categories, permitting the objects of consciousness to speak for themselves. In music's case,
phenomenology promises to help people set aside their tendencies to hear types
and classes, in order to experience its essentially sonorous nature. Phenomenology questions the utility of visual terms for describing this sonorous character, and works to undo the deep split that separates the lived musical experience
from intellectualization about it. It strives to restore music to its lived status as
a vital, dynamic presence that too often and too easily gets buried beneath the
inert deposits of speculative abstraction.

What phenomenology's adherents see as the method's great strengths, however, others often regard as serious flaws and weaknesses. The act of bracketing
and the metaphorically rich descriptions to which it gives rise generate stirring
accounts of music's 'non-empirical' attributes, but at considerable cost to philosophy's necessary discipline and rigor. At issue here are two strikingly divergent views of what philosophy should be. To the phenomenologist, the analytical philosophical approach is excessively positivistic: too cerebral, too occupied
with questions of logic, too stolid and somber. But to the analytical philosopher,
phenomenology is more poetic than philosophical. It is highly metaphorical,
given to fantasy, excessively intuitive: irrational, illogical, lacking in rigor. Thus,
analytical philosophy and phenomenology eye one another rather suspiciously
from opposing ends of the objective-subjective continuum.

Phenomenology need not be undisciplined, unrestrained, or self-indulgent.
It is as suspicious of metaphysical fantasy as analytical philosophy, and equally
insistent that philosophy curb its metaphysical tendencies, grounding itself in
the everyday world. But where analytical philosophy seeks its grounding in the
logical rules it believes undergird meanings, phenomenology seeks it in the
meanings it believes undergird logic. Phenomenology has little interest in analytical philosophy's specialized jargon and detailed linguistic analyses, things
that divert attention from the very things they purport to describe. Musical philosophy, the phenomenologist believes, should return its practitioners to a fuller
awareness of the lived qualities of musical experience and restore music's capacity to speak for itself.

Merleau-Ponty: The Bodily Basis of Knowing and Being

The writings of Maurice Merleau-Ponty do not speak directly to music, but they
explore and elaborate two concerns of major significance for musical phenomenology: the foundational epistemological status of perceptual experience, and
the body's status as our instrument of engagement in the world. By founding his
theory of knowledge in the sensible realm rather than upon thought, Merleau-
Ponty challenges one of the mainstays of traditional epistemology: its belief in

the possibility of purely objective knowledge. Since a perceptually derived knowledge is fundamentally a perspectively situated knowledge, it differs significantly from the idea of a purely objective, universal knowledge, valid from any and all perspectives at once. Furthermore, since a knowledge that is mediated by the body must always bear that body's indelible impression, Merleau-Ponty poses significant challenges to the assumption that knowledge is a predominantly abstract, cerebral affair that stands opposed to feeling and sense. Such ideas are fertile ground for examining the status of music's felt qualities and their relation to knowledge. That his philosophy is often described as a philosophy of irrationalism and ambiguity is not surprising, given its denial that reason is the foundation of knowledge.

Although his effort to claim epistemological status for perceptual experience may seem similar to empiricism's claim that knowledge builds upon sense-experience, Merleau-Ponty is resolutely opposed to empiricism. Empiricism errs in assuming that there is a distinction between sensing and what is sensed, between stimulus and response, sensation and its objective causes. Merleau-Ponty's phenomenology insists upon framing the sensing act along with the sensed, upon a reciprocal relationship between the perceiver and the perceived. It emphatically denies the reduction of perception to a neutral, receptive act that is largely determined by the perceived and does not shape what it takes in. On the other hand, rationalism argues from the unreliability and deceptiveness of sensation, basing its account of the world on the organizing function of the human mind, on reason. However, like empiricism, rationalism assumes the existence of a world objectively there, behind the screen of appearances it is reason's job to transcend. So both rationalist and empiricist assume the existence of a gap in need of bridging, a sharp division between consciousness and what it is conscious 'of'. But for Merleau-Ponty, there is no troublesome divide between apparent and real, between the phenomenon and the 'thing-in-itself', between the perceived and the known. For Merleau-Ponty, things are as they appear. "We see the things themselves, the world is what we see."[2] Indeed, "the world is always 'already there' before reflection begins—as an inalienable presence."[3]

Merleau-Ponty strenuously opposes the notion of a world independent of the human act of perceiving it. The mind does not engage in fundamentally discrete acts of attending and understanding. The merest act of attending entails a perceptual unity which is already a meaning, a rudimentary kind of knowledge. Reason is not solely a matter of conscious or abstractive reflection, then. It is rooted in a realm that is pre-rational, prereflective, and preobjective: the lived world of the body.

It is bodily experience rather than conscious experience that is our essential way of being in the world, maintains Merleau-Ponty. The body is never simply an object among other objects in the world, but is rather a lived object. "To say that it is always near me, always there for me, is to say that it is never really in front of me, that I cannot array it before my eyes, that it remains marginal to all my perceptions, that it is *with* me."[4] And as our primary instrument of knowledge, its perspective is an inextricable part of everything we know. It defines our point of view, and without it or the perspective it affords, we could know nothing. Thought and abstract reason are not our primary ways of knowing the world, as traditional epistemology has taught: rather, perception is. But since perception is always perspectival and partial, a matter of orientation, epistemology can never achieve its espoused goal of totally objective knowledge. If all knowledge is a personal acquisition that rests upon a perceptual/bodily foundation, pure objectivity and its promise of absolute certainty are utterly impossible. In place of the deposed objective order, Merleau-Ponty offers the world-as-perceived as the only world there is: "the *perceived world* is the always presupposed foundation of all rationality, all value, and all existence."[5]

According to Merleau-Ponty, perception's foundational status is shown by its irreducibility, its opaqueness, its refusal to yield to further penetration by reflection. Whereas it is necessary to invoke perception as the founding act of thought, there is no corresponding need in the case of perceptual experience. Moreover, in perceiving, one "lives in" the perceptual object to an extent that renders doubts as to its actuality or existence impossible. Reflective experience is radically different, though. Its objects lack the concrete fullness and nearness characteristic of perception. To perceive something is to live in it; to think about something, to hold it at a distance. Perception is attached, reflection detached. Therefore, substituting reflection for perception replaces a state of "primordial being" with an "imperfect reconstruction."[6] Perception is always bodily in a way intellectual consciousness is not. And the body is always, in perceiving, "saturated with its object"[7] to the extent that the distinction between the perceptual act and its object disappears.

In short, Merleau-Ponty maintains that perceptual objects are fully constituted in the act of perception, requiring no further contribution from a disembodied intellect. And as one interpreter observes, since it is always linked to the body, "perception is always spatially situated, is perception *from somewhere*, so that things inevitably present themselves to me in a one-sided fashion; they offer themselves to my perception by way of profiles, and I never manage to perceive a thing from everywhere simultaneously, i.e., from nowhere."[8]

But how can something be both fully constituted and yet only partially revealed in perception? What is to be made of perception's radical ambiguity, its tendency to be at once present to and absent from us? Merleau-Ponty's explanation is that the appearance of any particular profile is schema-dependent: perception does not consist of apprehending a single profile, but is always attended by awareness of other potential profiles implicit in the operative schema. Consequently, perception always transcends the particularity of a given perspective in the direction of its object. This is what enables recognition of an object's constancy when observed from different profiles, assuring that different profiles are not mistaken for different objects. This linkage among profiles is no mere mechanical feat, but an intuitive one in which perception assures that various profiles present themselves "as so many steps towards the thing itself."[9] What the act of perception adds to mere sensation, then, is a sense of depth beyond surface, a recognition that its object always consists in more than just this one presentation. Perception carries with it a sense of the inexhaustibility of ways its objects can present themselves. Recognition of this potential for infinitely extended presentations enters profoundly into perception's unique sense of 'concealed plenitude'.[10]

Since an object's properties and profiles are always perceived as an indissoluble unity, talk of various 'qualities' as though they were somehow separable from the object follows from an act of intellectual abstraction. Such abstractions do not enhance perception, though. When thought segregates features like color, smell, texture, or shape, the perceptually constituted object is invariably reduced to something whose nature is profoundly different. As Merleau-Ponty suggests, "this red would literally not be the same if it were not the 'woolly red' of a carpet,"[11] and "a thing would not have this color had it not also this shape, these tactile properties, this resonance, this odor."[12] The perceptual object, then, is a unique integration, with its own inherent configurations and connections that are essential aspects of the given. Analytical reflection can never achieve what perception fails to accomplish. Perception is no mere extrapolation from sense data, nor do perceived entities "line up" behind their appearances. Rather, "The significance of a thing inhabits that thing as the soul inhabits the body."[13] The prereflective relation between consciousness and its objects always consists in a sense of lived unity that defies reduction to either (mindful) thought or (corporeal) feeling.

The upshot of these observations is, once more, that perception is in no way subservient to reflective thought. Perception has an activity, a vitality, a richness all its own. As such, Merleau-Ponty insists, "The world is not what I think, but what I live through."[14] Human knowledge is deeply rooted in perceptual/ bodily experience that constitutes its pre-rational foundation. Because of the contingency of this perceptual foundation, belief in an absolutely objective knowledge is unfounded. And innocuous though it may seem, the idea of a purely objective knowledge, absolute, timeless, perspectiveless, and untainted by human subjectivity, trivializes and demeans whatever fails to measure up to its impossibly austere standards. To grant Merleau-Ponty's fundamental premise of perception's primacy is thus to restore the world to its full humanness and deny that humans can ever relate to the world as detached, impartial spectators.

Against the possibility of a wholly explicit, wholly scrutable knowledge, Merleau-Ponty observes, "If it were possible to lay bare and unfold all the presuppositions in what I call my reason or my ideas at each moment, we should always find experiences which have not been made explicit . . . a whole 'sedimentary history' which is not only relevant to the *genesis* of my thought, but which determines its *significance*. . . . [W]hatever I think or decide, it is always against the background of what I have previously believed or done."[15] In short, all knowledge is situated, perspectival, partial. Indeed, "Truth is another name for sedimentation."[16] Does this undermine all claims to 'truth' and 'certainty', replacing knowledge with mere belief? Merleau-Ponty responds, "whatever truth we may have is to be gotten not in spite of but through our historical inherence. Superficially considered, our inherence destroys all truth; considered radically, it founds a new idea of truth. As long as I cling to the idea of an absolute spectator, of knowledge with no point of view, I can see my situation as nothing but a source of error. But if I have once recognized that through it I am grafted onto every action and all knowledge which can have a meaning for me, and that step by step it contains everything which can *exist* for me, then my contact with the social in the finitude of my situation is revealed to me as the point of origin of all truth, including scientific truth."[17]

In short, a pure, noncorporeal consciousness presumed simultaneously capable of all points of view is actually no point of view at all. Far from defining a wholly explicit knowledge, it yields no knowledge. A wholly objective knowledge is knowledge of a barren world, completely uninhabited by and irrelevant to human beings.

Does human involvement in knowing necessarily undermine claims to its universality or absoluteness? Can the partiality of human access to 'truth' be conceded without relinquishing its claims to objectivity and absolute authority? Apparently not, for as Merleau-Ponty asks, "What is this eternally true that no one possesses? What is this thing expressed which lies beyond all expression . . . ?"[18] What people call absolutes are only convergences of opinion, or consensus. Calling things absolute, or universal, or 'true', is only an indication of agreement. From Merleau-Ponty's perspective, belief in absolutes is not just pointless, but destructive, for they obscure people's lived, bodily sense of the world. In Merleau-Ponty's powerful words, "there is no vision without the screen; the ideas we are speaking of would not be better known to us if we had no body and no sensibility; it is then that they would be inaccessible to us."[19]

Thus, Merleau-Ponty replaces the Cartesian "I think," and Kant's ideal of a detached, critical, reflective consciousness, with the idea of a corporeally appropriated knowledge and a world that is what it is by virtue of human participation. The defining ground of knowledge is not abstract reason, but rather perceptual experience. And the point of origin of human perceptual experience is always the body. Humans are not contemplative, subjective spectators of an inert, objective world, Merleau-Ponty appears to conclude, but indispensable participants in the creation of a vital and dynamic world.

The implications for music philosophy, though Merleau-Ponty did not state them as such, are obvious. Contrary to the claims of the metaphysician, music's meaning is inextricably and irreducibly perceptual: inseparable from its sonorous presences, and undetachable from its sensible surfaces. To be understood fully, things must be perceived fully, and musical understanding cannot be separated from musical perception. Analysis and abstraction can never supplant the rich, embodied meanings that inhere in the perceived musical surface. Just as importantly, in Merleau-Ponty's account of knowledge, musical meanings are not less substantial because of their untranslatable, bodily nature. For all knowledge ultimately rests upon the same perceptual and bodily foundation. With this as background, it will be instructive to turn to several phenomenologies that are specifically musical, and in which Merleau-Ponty's voice often resonates clearly.

Dufrenne: The Musical 'Quasi-Subject'

Although there were earlier efforts to explore 'aesthetic experience' phenomenologically, it was Mikel Dufrenne's work that sparked broad philosophical and artistic interest in the method. Dufrenne's treatment of music is a small part of a much broader project concerned with the 'aesthetic experience', but it introduces both the 'flavor' of the method and the controversies it often spawns.

Before venturing too far into Dufrenne's accounts, it is important to acknowledge a particular criticism leveled against them. It has been argued[20] that Dufrenne's work violates some of the most fundamental tenets of phenomenological method by using phenomenology as a springboard for metaphysical speculation rather than as a tool for exploring the world of concrete human realities. The kind of classification and generalization in which Dufrenne engages, it is claimed, is not properly phenomenological. More specifically, it is alleged that by taking an inherently abstract and general notion like "aesthetic experience" as his object of study, Dufrenne has failed to engage the concrete things of experience. In other words, instead of describing the concreteness and particularity of individual things and experiences, Dufrenne begins with the general and the abstract: those characteristics supposedly shared by all genuinely aesthetic experience. Rather than describing the uniqueness of individual presences, he examines a general category of experience.

Dufrenne accepts Merleau-Ponty's basic notion that music's physical presence is something experienced prereflectively, bodily. He argues, for instance, that aesthetic experience cannot be a purely contemplative phenomenon because its object is a "sensuous thing which is realized only in perception."[21] Its meaning is only fully realized in a fundamentally sensuous experience. Unlike Merleau-Ponty, however, Dufrenne consistently treats the aesthetic 'object' or musical 'work' and its experience as different things. Where Merleau-Ponty insisted that perceptual experience need not extend beyond the sensuous surface, Dufrenne believes the notion of 'the bodily' is insufficient to account for the "thickening" of this surface, for its "depth" of expression. The expressive domain, he holds, is mind's contribution. Instead of a single-leveled account, Dufrenne's consists of three tiers. Its foundation is concrete, bodily presence, but since he thinks this cannot provide an adequate account of expression, Dufrenne posits a middle term, imagination, that transforms physical presence into a special, 'aesthetic feeling' under the guidance of the object. It is on the level of feeling or affect that the object and its experience are reconciled. In strong contrast to Merleau-Ponty, then, who argued for a single and simultaneously presented unity, Dufrenne believes that sheer presence cannot account for aesthetic feeling and that imagination provides a necessary link. His theory's idealistic assumptions require a transcendental imagination to achieve experiential unity.

According to Dufrenne, what is most distinctive about aesthetic experiences of art is their "apotheosis of the sensuous."[22] The sensuousness associated with art is unlike the "brute sensuousness" of everyday things and experiences. Aesthetically sensuous objects assert "sovereign imperialism"[23] over other things in the phenomenal field, demanding that perceivers submit to their "magnificent presence."[24] But how is mere 'brute' sensuousness transformed into the more 'imperious' kind? By the imaginative deployment of temporal and spatial schemata whose interaction constitutes the work's internal world. Instead of being just another object in the world, then, the object comes to have a world of

its own. It presents an internal complexity and coherence that is otherwise encountered only in people. Accordingly, the aesthetic object is not so much an
object as what Dufrenne calls a "quasi subject." It is an object whose mode of
presence is very much like that of another person. Like encounters with actual
human subjects, the quasi subject invokes and invites exploration of its "interiority." This experience consists of "a sort of communion between the object and
myself"[25] in which the object and perceiving self become one.

It is in the realm of feeling or affect that experience and object join together,
for "the sensuous is an act common both to sensing being and to what is
sensed."[26] Through feeling or expression one becomes fully present to the aesthetic object. It is this expressive quality that confers unity on the object's diversity and complexity, establishing its difference from the world of brute sensuousness. Since they are not so much 'in the world' as they 'are a world', things
like music do not occur in space and time. Rather, space and time occur within
music: they are "internal to the [aesthetic] object and assumed by it. It is they
that make it a quasi subject capable of a world which it expresses."[27]

The definitive characteristic of aesthetic experience, then, is the quasi-
subjectivity or expressiveness of the aesthetic object and its distinctive sense of
"bewitchment."[28] Because of these qualities, it commands of us total perceptual
engagement, an involvement in which we do "nothing but perceive."[29] Yet, to
perceive the aesthetic object in its "ultimate form"[30] as an inherently expressive
thing requires perceptual experience that is also imaginative and tinged with
feeling. "It is entirely possible that feeling is what is given first and that all perception begins in feeling, since it may be true that we perceive forms first and
that feeling is the soul of form."[31]

What musical insights follow from this somewhat obscure and surprisingly
abstract phenomenology of the 'aesthetic'? Dufrenne offers a number of tanta-
lizing suggestions. "Music unveils," he says, "a world invisible to the eye, un-
demonstrable to the intellect. Yet this world can be expressed only by music, for
it is a world which vanishes once the music ends. It exists in the music insofar
as it is perceived, and nowhere else."[32] Moreover, music presents itself in a "gradual unfolding of the sensuous—the sensuous being both the means and the end
of the work, its matter and its final result."[33] As sound, Dufrenne says, music is
"apparent first to the ear, then to the rest of the body."[34] Music has no apparent subject matter in the conventional sense, being simply a discourse or interplay among sounds, although it does contain "something like a 'subject'."[35]

More specifically, Dufrenne identifies three essential "schemata" whose operations distinguish music from brute sound: harmony, rhythm, and melody.
Harmony, for Dufrenne, is an "ideal space"[36] between a composition and the
environment in which it is realized. Harmony's distinctive way of organizing this
ideal space "makes sound into a graspable reality—as opposed to noise, which
startles us initially but fails to hold our attention." According to Dufrenne, "All
music is harmonious, because harmony is the primary condition of musical being."[37] To call music harmonious, then, is somewhat redundant, since if it were
not harmonious it could not attract and engage properly 'musical' perception in
the first place. Harmony is a precondition for any musical perception, the ideal,

spatial field within which the patterns and relationships occur that make music "an authentic object which can be grasped as such."[38]

On the other hand, rhythm is the "very movement which animates the work,"[39] the work's "heartbeat" or "secret law of its internal development."[40] As the essential source of music's distinctive sense of "self-movement," rhythm's animation and dynamism are never things that are projected onto an otherwise complete and unified musical object. Since it "espouses and expresses the very being of [music],"[41] rhythm is musically essential. Music's rhythmic vitality, its patterns of tension and repose, are not mere sensations or 'subjective' associations. Rather, rhythm is music's very being, "the reality of the musical object, which by its very nature is known only through impressions."[42] Its temporality is not the kind that contains music, but "the time which it is, the internal becoming which constitutes it."[43] Rhythm is the means by which the music "organizes its own future development."[44]

Rhythmic musical experience invokes pre-rational schemata for movement that we "imitate . . . deep within ourselves in order to grasp it in the object."[45] Such schemata "objectify" and "order" movement, enabling musical apprehension, yet they are fundamentally bodily affairs rather than matters of understanding. "Schematizing is an art deeply hidden within the human body," says Dufrenne, a way of "finding oneself within the musical object."[46] Rhythmic schemata "present themselves as an invitation for us to make the necessary inner movement to place ourselves on the level of the musical object."[47] This is confirmed, he believes, by rhythm's remarkable capacity to close the distance between music and self, magically transforming what might otherwise be alienating sound into an intimate friend. At the same time, music whose rhythms are repetitious and persistent can distance and alienate people. Rhythmic vitality, then, is our point of access into music's 'inner life', while overly repetitious rhythm can destroy that life by addressing only the 'brute senses' of the body. In short, rhythmic schemata "stimulate imagination and put us in accord with the musical object. These schemata allow us to move in step with the musical object, to participate in the same adventure."[48]

No matter how free it impresses us as being, musical rhythm must always display perceptible pattern. It must display evidence of its construction, of its fabrication, or vanish into noise and nonsense. Rhythm's freedom "must be earned and exercised in terms of a rule . . . [Its] structure must be supported by schemata or else risk annihilation."[49] The presentation of perceptible time, moreover, is fundamentally reliant upon a sense of 'spatialization' conferred by rhythmic schemata because "time cannot be measured except by movements in space."[50] By conferring spatiality upon succession or duration, musical rhythm renders time perceptible. To the extent music exists in time, it appears as an object. By creating its own time, however, music is "the origin of its own becoming and is animated by its own self-propelled movement."[51] By so doing it commands recognition as subject rather than object.

Melody, according to Dufrenne, is the profoundly irreducible thing that "appears spontaneously in the work when we yield to it, when we sit back and let it sing."[52] Its meaning is ineffable, but is meaning nonetheless. Melody is what the music "says," what makes music musical, rather than an "incoherent succession of sounds."[53] In short, "Melody is expressive, and conversely, expression is melody."[54] Although both harmony and rhythm "dissolve" in melody, melody cannot be reduced to either. Therefore, reasons Dufrenne, although harmony and rhythm are properties of music, "melody alone is music."[55] Harmony and rhythm may account for the singularity of a work, but never its musicality.[56] Since melody is that within which "all music fulfills itself,"[57] unmelodic music simply cannot be: melody is the essential aspect of music's being.

The 'theme' is melody's "nucleus of meaning," that which serves to "guarantee the presence of spatiality, without which the musical object (though not itself spatial) would have no objectivity and would thus risk complete disintegration."[58] Not only do themes operate as generative devices, they are also primary musical 'characters' in the work's physiognomy. Unlike harmony and rhythm, then, melodic themes refuse to fade into the more general musical fabric, and insist on remaining in the foreground. The theme "participates in the final triumph of the melody which it produced and which it continues to animate."[59] Melody has its own spatial character as well, a volume that can fill concert halls and can penetrate our bodies. The roots of this spatiality lie in the "depths of the imagination," realized "in and through the body."[60]

If the results of Dufrenne's awkward effort to balance music's sensuous (bodily) nature and Kantian categories of mind are not entirely satisfying, it does help to clarify more fully some of phenomenology's fundamental tenets. Rather than maintaining the indissoluble linkage between consciousness and its objects, Dufrenne resorts to dualistic constructs (aesthetic sensuousness vs. brute sensuousness, cognitive schemata vs. physical presence, objective materiality vs. aesthetic feeling) and theoretical speculation that are at odds with phenomenology as it is now widely conceived. However, his notion of music as acquaintance, as friend, and as quasi subject point to dimensions of the lived musical experience upon which subsequent phenomenologists have built more successfully, as we shall see.

Clifton: The Geometry of Musical Experience

In *Music as Heard*,[61] Thomas Clifton undertakes a study in what he calls "applied phenomenology," a study of how music presents itself to experience, buttressed by concrete musical examples. Determined to remain true to the phenomenological tenet of object-directedness and to avoid idealistic dualisms, Clifton carefully balances description and reflection, experience and explanation, ever wary of mistaking theoretical satisfaction for musical insight. The challenge phenomenology poses to the musician is, in his words, "to listen carefully to what is given, making sure that what is given is the music itself."[62] Clifton's efforts admirably illustrate the distinctive musical insights this often enigmatic philosophical method can yield.

Music, Clifton offers in a preliminary, working definition, is "the actualization of the possibility of any sound whatever to present to some human being a meaning which he experiences with his body—that is to say, with his mind, his feelings, his senses, his will, and his metabolism."[63] Several things are immediately apparent in this statement. First, it tries to resist the kind of abstractive or general presumptions that mark the point of departure for many philosophical investigations of music. It carefully avoids characterizing music as inherently symbolic, or associative, or representational. It acknowledges the importance of sound, yet resists the temptation to reduce music to sonorous materials or form. Rather than seeking a fixed, foundational explanation in the extramusical world, and insisting upon its universality, Clifton wants to let the music speak for itself, to let it be heard simply for what it is and what it has to say. The key to understanding what music is lies in the way its sounds are experienced, the way music is lived. It is not simply a thing in the world, but a humanly meaningful way of being, of lived experience that lies at the nexus between a human being and sound. Most importantly, music is a bodily experience in the fullest sense: a richly corporeal mode of being that integrates mind, emotion, all the senses, an entire person.

Sound is not music, cautions Clifton. Although "the musically behaving person experiences musical significance by means of, or through, the sounds,"[64] in sonorous experience that is musical, sounds become transparent. Sounds are the materials that bear music, then, but music is not reducible to them. Lived musical experience is constitutively human, and it makes little sense to speak of music as though it were somehow comprehensible apart from human experience. It follows that music can never be "factually in the world the way trees and mountains are,"[65] but is always a meaning for someone. Without the presence and complicity of a person, there simply is no music. The relation between the music and the 'musicing' person is, Clifton believes, always reciprocal. Neither element in this relationship is dispensable: "[p]erception is a two-way street. We are not the passive receivers of uninterpreted sense data, nor are we the cause of an object's properties. . . . Thus, while it is true that a sonata by Mozart exists independently of me, it has significance *for* me to the extent that I perceive it adequately."[66] Since musical meaning is a function of perceptual adequacy and that in turn is a function of personal orientation or perspective, Clifton finds the idea of 'objective' aesthetic standards "pedantic" and "patronizing."[67] "What right have I," he asks, "to demand that a person experience a piece of music exactly the way I do?"[68] In short, to avoid reducing music either an objective or subjective affair, Clifton grounds its nature and value in the lived experience of people who reside in a fundamentally human world. The result is a distinctly and laudably pluralistic account of music. Whether it can avoid relativism as well is an issue on which we may want to reserve judgment until we have examined his position more closely.

Clifton's project is guided by two closely related concerns: that the music be allowed to speak for itself, revealing its own order and meaning; and that the distorting potential of habitual or 'logical' presuppositions be avoided. The essential needs to be separated from the apparent, the foundational from the contingent. What, then, are music's essential modes of being from a phenomenological point of view? What are its essences, its "basic strata"? What is truly basic in lived musical experience? A number of seemingly commonsense answers can be eliminated. For instance, traditional music analysis takes things like pitch and interval as basic substances to which features like timbre, dynamics, and expressive qualities somehow adhere as 'attributes'. "Do we really hear *col legno* as something simply attached to the primary substance of pitch?" asks Clifton. "If a French horn prolongs an open E, and then quickly mutes it, is it the same E? Logically, yes; but in terms of musical behavior, I think not."[69] The so-called basic materials or elements of music are not basic to lived musical experience. When the sedimentation of learning and habit is cleared away to reveal music's self-givenness, Clifton suggests, "what counts as lived musical experiences are such intuited essences as the grace of a minuet by Mozart, the drama of a symphony by Mahler, or the agony of Coltrane's jazz. If we hear the music at all, it is because we hear the grace, the drama, and the agony as essential constituents of . . . the music itself. It is not even accurate enough to say that these constituents are what the music is *about*: rather they *are* the music. . . . What the music says is what it is."[70]

At the heart of Clifton's phenomenology lie four essential musical strata, four fundamental constituents of meaningful musical experience: time, space, play, and feeling. But before turning to these, let us briefly survey his reasons for rejecting the foundational status of conventional categories of music analysis. That pitch is not essential or foundational is obviously demonstrated by its minor role in some musics. But even if this were not the case, it would still be wrong to regard pitch as essential: for in experience that is musical (as opposed to analytical) one does not attend to pitch; rather, one attends through pitch to music. Were pitches per se to become the perceptual focus, the lived sense of musical experience would fly apart. Pitch may function as medium, something through which one encounters music, but it is not a basic stratum, not an essence. In fact, it becomes musical only when drawn into deeper currents of spatiotemporal activity by rising and falling, advancing and receding, intensifying and relaxing.

Distance between successive pitches, or interval, is musically meaningful only as gesture. And "to try to define precisely the locus of this gesture by reducing it to a certain interval is to turn away from the phenomenon."[71] In actual musical context, intervals are absorbed into musical flow, and to isolate discrete intervals within that flow is to "ignore particular situations in favor of general concepts."[72] Nor are intervals geographical boundaries that 'contain' other intervals. "[W]hen I hear an 'octave'," says Clifton, "I hear nothing so complicated as 'a diapason divisible by eight'. I do not even hear a diapason. . . . I hear a form of musical space, experienced either as a thickening of a single line . . . or as the stratification of an otherwise undifferentiated space . . ."[73] What is musically significant about a given musical interval is not determined by referring to other musical intervals, because the intervallic experience is fundamentally temporal and spatial. Similarly, harmony, consonance, and dissonance are not foundational: they become musically meaningful only to the extent pitches coalesce to create a "homogeneity of space."[74] Tones achieve harmony with other tones by adhering to a common space, inhabiting the same spatial world. Thus, harmony is an experiential field that attracts consonant tones and repels dissonant ones, but such attractions and repulsions are conventional, not essential. Scales are not musical essences either, but "collection[s] of pitch classes"[75] divorced from lived musical experience. Music is not comprised of scales but of melodies.

Despite its experiential immediacy, tonality is not foundational either. "If I did not already have a prior understanding of motion in time, of 'toward' and 'away from', rest and tension, beginning and ending, anticipation and fulfillment, how would I ever recognize in myself the power to appropriate precisely these tones, through the medium of which a certain kind of motion, etc., called 'tonality', is particularized?"[76] Since the experience of musical tonality is founded on prior spatiotemporal experience, it should not be regarded as a thing in the world, but as a human 'aptitude' that follows from "the way my body behaves in its presence."[77] Tonality is a "corporeal acquisition," the achievement of a body that "knows how to behave in a tonal situation."[78] And the sense of tonal movement is animated by feeling, by a sense of mutual possession between self and music: without that, gestures and motions become mechanical, music an external object. It is no accident that descriptions of tonality are replete with feeling-words, for "I am at the center, and these tones which I perceive as swirling around this center have significance because of my presence which sustains them."[79]

Symbolic accounts of music are also quite problematic from Clifton's phenomenological perspective. Despite Langer's provision for music's 'presentational' character, for instance, her theory is rooted in idealistic presuppositions that phenomenology cannot countenance. Distinctions between virtual and actual, between what music is and what it means, between musical form and the form of feeling it somehow reveals, make the idea of music as a symbol "perilously dichotomous." The idea that music's significance consists in a relationship between music and something-not-music which it resembles seriously violates phenomenology's commitment to describing only what is immanent in the given. Despite impressive efforts to the contrary, symbolic accounts of music appear unable to avoid diverting attention away from music itself. In Clifton's view, the key to avoiding such diversions and misconceptions is to recognize that music is a fundamentally bodily phenomenon, and not one in which music refers to or stands for something bodily. Music is an experience of the body. 'Vigor' or 'elegance' or 'liveliness' are "not what a particular melody has or depicts, but what it *is*."[80] When the rational proposition that subject and object are mutually exclusive is neutralized, it becomes apparent that " 'lively' is not an invented *relation* between musical and bodily pace, but rather an experienced *unity*. The meaning that we find in 'lively' is not primordially a meaning of similarity but rather one of necessity. That is, 'lively' expresses an essential aspect of the piece's character, and one which is immanent in the piece itself."[81]

Clifton's phenomenology seeks to describe music as it is lived, to return the "experiencing person to center stage," and to restore appreciation of the full "geometry" and richness of musical experience.[82] Music is a humanly constructed meaning, a meaning constructed not by a mind but by an embodied mind. Viewed from a lived, bodily informed perspective, what is essential to music are its temporal, spatial, playful, and felt dimensions.

Musical Time

Clifton's description of music's temporal foundation draws extensively on the work of Edmund Husserl,[83] arguing against the idea of 'objective' time as a serially ordered, "transitive succession of discrete nows,"[84] and urging that human events like music do not so much exist in time as carry their own time within themselves.

The notion of time as an objective affair is an abstraction, the verbal representation of an experientially immediate event whose lived quality eludes words. Experientially, time is not a unidirectional, uniform flow. Unpleasant events prolong time, impede its passage. When one is up against something that insists on dictating experience on its terms, time passes haltingly and disjunctly. In striking contrast, pleasant experience flows along smoothly and seamlessly: both "we and it move in the same direction deliberately, desiringly, and possessingly."[85] In the first case, time's 'presentness' is constricted while past or future (anywhere but here!) are enlarged. In the second case, the present is dilated or enlarged while past and future recede sharply into the distance. These temporal experiences are not aberrations, suggests Clifton, but the way time presentationally is. Time is never experienced as a homogeneous temporal river with a continuous, uniform flow. There exists no experientially-independent time into which experience somehow gets inserted. Instead, experience contains and constitutes time. Clocks are useful things, but "tell us nothing about time itself."[86] 'Past', 'present', and 'future' are not different places or even discrete temporal states. They are crude labels for complex interrelationships between people and events. Time is not an objective envelope into which human events are inserted. Says Clifton, "It is events, as lived through by people, which define time."[87] There is no time 'out there', flowing evenly and inexorably from future through present and on to past. Time is "the experience of human consciousness in contact with change."[88] The idea of time as a succession of discrete 'nows' artificially separates past, present, and future, "fragmenting experience and provoking an unsuccessful search for a quantifiable present."[89]

Instead of conceiving time as a discrete chronological succession that leaves us struggling to situate an elusive 'now' between not-quite-yet and just-was, Clifton advocates that time be regarded as a temporal field, dilating and constricting. Instead of fixed borders, this field of presence has flexible, permeable 'horizons' that permit its integration with futures and pasts to which it is always phenomenally linked. The idea of temporal horizons enlarges and enriches the present, acknowledges important connections to past and future, and accommodates their interpenetrating, overlapping character. Present is no longer hermetically isolated from future or past. In Clifton's words, "the identity of the present is established by what the past and future 'see' of it."[90]

Applied to musical experience, the idea of temporal horizons helps account for tones' extension beyond their immediate duration, their influence on newly 'present' tones even when past, and the way the character of past tones continues to be modified as melody unfolds. Although there is an immediate 'now' in all temporal experience, the experience of melody per se is possible only when one can "push back the borders of the present to include itself, as a singular event, in a single present."[91] As a mere succession of tones, melody would fail to achieve its definitive coherence, each tone occupying the 'present' only momentarily before vanishing into the past. Melody requires the fusion of present with past and future. As a result, Ferrara explains, each musical tone has a distinctive "temporal density," such that it is "both now and retained (undergoing continuous modification) in our consciousness."[92] This temporal density also extends toward the future as musical expectation. When music dilates the present, one is carried along by the inflections of a 'moving' passage. When music broadens presence in the direction of the past (as when vividly recalling and reliving a musical experience) it squeezes 'real' presence and future to one side, making past present again.[93] In musical anticipation, the present is dilated in the direction of the future. Experience that is truly musical does not emerge from a completely indeterminate future or vanish into an irretrievably and immediately forgotten past. The temporal experience of music occurs not in flat chronological time but in experientially overlapping and simultaneous past, present, and future.

The phenomenological terms 'retention' and 'protention' describe the enlargement of temporal horizons toward the past and future respectively, the analogous term for the present being '*at*tention'. Retention, Clifton says, "clings to events happening now, qualifying the real now with a wider, phenomenal now."[94] Unlike its more deliberative counterpart, recollection (an experience in which memories of events remain experientially past), in retention the past and the present articulate with and engage each other. In Merleau-Ponty's words, "If the past were available to us only in the form of express recollections, we should be continually tempted to recall it in order to verify its existence. . . . whereas in fact we feel it behind us as an incontestable acquisition."[95] Retention is essential to musical experience, since without this sense of a "past which has been . . . but has not gone by"[96] we would never experience music, only meaningless successions of sonic bits. On the other hand, protention enlarges the present toward a future anticipated, as opposed to one merely awaited.[97] Protention, says Clifton, is an "irreducible necessity"[98] for musical experience, the means by which previously experienced pieces—the great majority of those to which we listen—are "reopened" or "renewed *as* future."[99]

Time as it is experienced, as it is lived by one's self, is simply not comprised of an 'earlier than' past and a 'later than' future; for 'now' always reaches into and informs the future and the past, just as future and past reciprocally inform the present. Thus, Clifton maintains, the time music 'takes' is a contingent affair, whereas the time music 'has' or 'is' is an essential or fundamental aspect of musical experience. The time in music is musically critical, while the time music is in is incidental. The fluidity and mobility of music's temporal horizons enable it to present us a future anticipated, not just awaited; a past retained, not just remembered; a present lived, not just encountered.

Musical time is time opened out into and richly resonant with lived human experience.

Musical Space

The extraordinary difficulty of describing music's temporal character without spatial terms shows that musical time and space are experientially inseparable. Yet even if it is not discrete, space is an essential foundation of musical experience, Clifton believes. Like Merleau-Ponty, he holds that all perceptual acts are situated, presuming some spatial orientation or perspective. 'To be' is always to be located or situated somewhere, spatially: "to be here or there, near or far, present or absent, under or above, high or low."[100] However, music's spaces are very unlike the 'objective' spaces we ascribe to visual, physical, or geometrical forms. Music's spaces are phenomenal spaces, spaces that move without going anywhere, change while staying the same. But above all, they are spaces given to a conscious body, which experiences them not just with the ear, but synesthetically. Spatiality is possible only because of human bodily experience. What, then, is musical space—or as Clifton prefers to ask, how does music "speak to us of space?"[101]

According to Clifton, one of the keys to understanding the foundational role of space in musical experience is the marked difference between musical and 'acoustical' space: the experience of musical space is never strictly auditory. Musical space is a field of action, and the human body our instrument of musical comprehension. The body is a "synergetic system which responds to a musical situation addressed to tactile and visual, as well as auditory, functions."[102] Accordingly, music is no mere auditory stimulus onto which people project a veneer of human qualities. Its perception is fundamentally synesthetic, the achievement of a whole human body. As Merleau-Ponty pointed out, 'scientific' realignments to people's experiential 'center of gravity' have dulled our awareness of perception's synaesthetic basis: ". . . we have unlearned how to see, hear and generally speaking, feel, in order to deduce, from our bodily organization and the world as the physicist conceives it, what we are to see, hear, and feel."[103]

The bodily and gestural vocabulary that pervades descriptions of musical space is not the clumsy result of a need to describe economically vaguely sensed similarities between music's patterns and human behavior. People do not encounter mere sounds, then overlay them with qualities, or gestures, or location. Spatial, gestural, and expressive characteristics are not imagined resemblances, but emergent realities, inseparable from the body's comprehension of music. Synesthetic comprehension is foundational to musical experience, the source of all musical knowledge. Tone quality, for instance, is not a stimulus but a bodily fact, and a bodily achievement: according to Clifton, "It is my body which produces its effects on tone quality, and it is only because of my body that there can be any talk of quality at all."[104] Lochhead articulates the same point this way: "[Musical] perception is not the mechanistic process of registering the properties of an independently existing world or . . . of interpreting the data of sensory input, but rather it is a *bodily enaction of meaning*. . . . I meet the sounds with my body and through it enact the melody as a felt significance."[105]

Music's fundamental sense of spatiality is a function of one's bodily experience of a phenomenal field. It is active, not contemplative; synesthetic, not merely aural. Music does not consist of essential sound plus contingent qualities. Without its spatial qualities, this highness or lowness, this nearness or remoteness, this sense of containing or being contained, music would not be present to us as music in the first place. In musical experience, we take up music's space, dwelling in it. The distance between 'it' and us is closed and our spaces become one: our very being becomes musical. "Ultimately, musical space has significance because a person finds himself there, as a place to take up a temporary habitation," writes Clifton.[106] Since this act requires the simultaneous deployment of all one's faculties, it is wrong to regard a violin's velvety tone, an organum's mood, or the seductiveness of a particular melodic turn as contingent aspects of musical experience: "'Seductiveness' might very well be the essence of that line, the main reason for its value."[107]

Musical space is a fundamentally textural affair: "Texture — or space — is what we experience when we hear durations, registers, intensities, and tone qualities."[108] The simplest conceivable instance of musical space is a single sustained tone which, permitted to "expand its own space" by moving up and down, or advancing and receding, begets 'line'. Line, Clifton observes, may be variously smooth, spiky, continuous, or broken. It may climb steeply, fall abruptly, glide gently, float above, lurk beneath, pass through other lines, and even change color.[109] A seemingly simple musical line is thus experientially rich and complex. A single, monophonic line creates its space through its "gestural activity."[110] Since melody occurs in both time and space, its spaces are never experienced in terms of spatial thickness or thinness alone. The auditory counterpart of visual pattern, Clifton seems to suggest, is gesture. "The retentions and protentions accompanying the thinness of the tone now being heard tend to give to that tone more presence than its merely acoustical volume possesses."[111] This expanded presence opens line out into multidimensional musical space. In the experience of Gregorian chant, for instance, Clifton illustrates that vowel sounds vary a line's width and phenomenal distance.[112] Thickness and distance in turn interact to modify line's solidity and intensity. Melodic and verbal accent interact to add yet another experiential dimension to linear motion. So while chant seems to speak simply on an acoustic level, experientially it embodies "at least five parameters: contour, width, distance, timbre, and rhythmic level."[113] And as musical lines thicken and interact they demarcate boundaries and coalesce into surfaces with varying degrees of relief, opacity, and translucence; and indeed, even into three dimensional masses that may be penetrated, carved, and sculpted by silences.

In short, in Clifton's view musical experience always takes place in a multidimensional field of action and motion. The experience of music is always marked by a sense of phenomenal location, of being in musical space. That space is fundamentally textural and its experience richly synesthetic. Thus, tonality is a sensuous rather than a syntactical affair. Its center is not pitch, but one's body: a body that moves in space and whose fund of spatio-temporal experience ('toward' or 'away from'; inside and outside; center or periphery) is what enables one to experience tonally in the first place. "[T]onality is a movement of my body,"[114] and music a corporeal action in musical space.

Musical Play

In asserting that play is a musical essence, Clifton is not just suggesting that play is a common psychological accompaniment to musical experience. Rather, he claims, its status is ontological: play is utterly constitutive of music, and music is something which is played. Without the stratum of play, sonorous experience is simply not music. "[M]usic is unthinkable without its ludic foundation . . ."[115]

It should be noted that by 'play' Clifton is not designating music a frivolous activity, opposed to seriousness, or a make-believe activity, opposed to reality: because dualisms like these are a poor fit for phenomenological orientation, but also because play can be and often is very serious, earnest, and real. Although he is clear on these points, he unfortunately offers no clear, succinct definition. Still, several of the senses in which he believes play constitutes music can be inferred from his discussion of the ritualistic and heuristic character he maintains music and play share. Ritual consists in formalized behaviors that ensure a desired activity is sustained or continued. People engaged in ritual are not simply 'going through motions'; their actions are purposeful, aimed at initiating and sustaining a desired state of mind. Ritual's stylized behaviors and its special settings serve to assure continuation and minimize the possibility of interruption. Music's rituals are often played out in carefully designed settings like concert halls, where adherence to codes of conduct help enhance and sustain appropriately musical states of mind and minimize distractions. Musical experience is thus rendered possible by engaging in deliberate, purposeful actions in specially designed contexts and settings. Moreover, because its existence as music is always the result of a personal investment, a personal acquisition, musical experience is seldom regarded as merely arbitrary, as a take-it-or-leave-it affair.[116] Music is a purposeful, intentional undertaking, carefully sustained, in which lightness and seriousness are fused together in an experiential unity. In ritual, one plays at work and works at play. In musical activity, "we 'play' a composition which is a 'work' of art."[117]

Moreover, like ritual, music's route and destination are generally known in advance. Rarely is the music people choose to play or listen to completely novel. Yet, although the general procedure and outcome may be clear, the quality of the particular experience is constituted anew each time. The importance of the musical experience lies, like a game, in the way it is played, something that may never be the same way twice. So even though the music may be well known, the manner in which one 'lives through' the experience may differ significantly from one occasion to another. One knows, and yet does not know, how musical events will unfold in a familiar musical situation. The possibility that it may 'fly apart' is ever present, and it is precisely ritual's job to minimize the chances of this happening.

According to Clifton, music created in sonata form exemplifies music's ritualistic character in its dialectical interactions between formal and elaborative

features, in the interplay between its structural scheme and the 'rhetorical devices' that flesh it out. Sonata's interplay between structure and rhetoric, form
and inflection, is a ritualization of the dialectic between freedom and control.
The way rhetorical gesture plays with and against structural constraint is thus
essential to sonata as experienced. A development section, for instance, undermines the "tonal authority" of its musical theme: it "weakens, dismembers, and
otherwise puts upon" that authority. But such elaboration is not mere decorative elaboration or diversion. The tension of its interplay with theme's tonal authority is precisely what enables the recapitulation to be experienced as it is: development's rhetorical devices are "an ordeal from which [the main structural
supports] return with greater tonal authority."[118] What Clifton is apparently anxious to establish is the ritualistic character of this reciprocity between control
and freedom, between centered stability and flying apart, and the fact that neither rhetorical gesture nor stabilizing structure could exist, one without the other,
as its essential dialectical complement. The status of rhetoric, he urges, is not
mere "superficial dross hanging from the essential structure."[119]

Another dimension of musical play can be seen in its heuristic character:
the fact that it always carries with it a sense of discovery. Wondering how music may unfold and wondering at the manner it eventually does are fundamental aspects of the musical experience. Because of this processual character, even
a piece known intimately is experienced with uncertainty. Musical experience
is at once known and unknowable. Sonorous experience can only become musical by our assent, but we cannot will just anything to be music. Thus, musical experience is always "a dialogue among equals."[120] Since one can never be
certain how it will unfold (and seldom does it unfold precisely as anticipated),
musical experience always carries an element of discovery. Music is always capable of revealing some previously unknown side, and the possibility always exists that something unforeseen may shatter it into sonic fragments, reducing a
musical 'thou' to a non-musical 'it'.

Besides its ritualistic and heuristic dimensions, musical play has what Clifton
calls an aleatoric or 'chance' dimension, which has already begun to emerge in
the above paragraphs. What Clifton wants to establish here is that because all
music has this chance character on an experiential level, it is misleading to construe aleatoric music as an opposite to 'composed' music on that count. Experientially, highly structured music and music generated by chance procedures
can be difficult to distinguish, because there is little in the experience of 'chance
music' that identifies it as such: one must be told. Its unrepeatability does not
really differentiate it from other musical experience, either, since strictly speaking, no music is repeatable. Even if a recording preserves acoustic identity, each
listening experience will still be unique. Thus, unrepeatability "is an essential
feature of *every* piece, not just demonstrably aleatoric ones."[121] And as for
aleatoric music's supposed 'irrationality', only compositional choices may be irrational, but never musical experience, never music experienced musically. Let
composers resort to irrational practices if they choose, says Clifton, but they cannot share that irrationality musically[122]—for irrationality is wholly incompatible
with the nature of music's experiential meaning. In fact, even at its most comic

and frivolous, music is not mindlessly irrational. Music's comical play is fundamentally rational in nature, requiring familiarity and subtle understanding of
musical norms.

In summary, Clifton believes the stratum of rational and serious play is fundamental to musical experience. Its dialectical tensions between structural
scheme and rhetorical gesture, between freedom and control, between known
and unknown, are universal and essential elements of music.

The Bodily Stratum: Feeling

Clifton's claim that 'feeling' is a musical essence is more than an observation
that all musical experience is accompanied by feeling. Feeling is no mere affective accompaniment, but part of music's innermost core. "[p]erhaps the most
important part of the way in which musical time and space arise as meanings,"
says Clifton, is "the kind of feeling infusing them."[123] Of the entire range of felt
experience that pervades music, however, one is utterly foundational: the feeling of 'mutual possession' underlies and enables all musical meaning. Possession is a reciprocal relation, running both ways between music and listener.
Without possession, sound is simply not music. Before music can be anything
else, Clifton declares, it must first be ours: "something through which we live,
something which, in a certain sense, we become. [It] has value because I possess it, and it possesses me."[124]

Possession is intimately related to belief, to a willingness to experience
sounds musically. No necessary or automatic connection can assure that given
sets or sequences of sounds, even those regarded as artistic masterpieces, become
music for us. On the contrary, music is the product of an intentional act, of a
personal belief that a given event is musical. This is not the product of logical
deliberation, but an act of personal commitment concurrent with music's unfolding. And it is a dynamic process, subject to continuous revision and requiring constant renewal. Where belief falters and possession ceases, music slips
back into sound, becoming just a sonorous thing 'out there' in the world. Music is only music to the extent it remains music for oneself. But this cannot be
achieved simply at will, whenever and wherever one feels the inclination. Belief and possession must be directed toward present objects and events with care
and concern. Put simply, "Sounds become music when they become meaningful to me. . . . [T]he Being of music is sustained, consented to, acted upon—
all operations of a will motivated by care."[125]

Sounds that attempt to enter one's world without one's consent, belief, and
care are quite another matter, however. Such sonorous intrusions may have all
the external trappings of music; they may even be music to someone else (or to
one's self under different circumstances). But unwanted 'background' music or
the sounds blaring from an automobile's sound system are not music-for-me: I
neither consent to their presence nor am I inclined to share my personal space
with them or permit them to dominate mine. Sounds in such situations are
"signs or indications of activities that are being engaged in somewhere else at
this moment," says Clifton. "We observe them as we would inanimate objects

which, for that reason, remain at a distance . . . [W]e are pierced by these un-wanted tones the way a sadist sticks pins into an insect."[126] An encounter with unwanted sound is an invasion resulting in a nonconsensual loss of personal freedom. Rather than the feeling of mutual possession characteristic of musical indwelling, one only feels next to, up against, a foreign object. "A raw sound event," writes Clifton, "is experienced as such when an involuntary proximity of sounds is felt as closing in. . . . On the other hand, music is experienced as such when a voluntary proximity of sounds is felt as opening toward: a condition *toward* which we use our freedom to effect the closure between ourselves and mu-sic."[127] Since this closure is a bodily experience, the difference between music and mere sound is the sense of "bodily complicity" in the former[128] and its ab-sence in the latter.

Among the greatest mistakes of traditional aesthetics, Clifton thinks, are its misguided portrayals of music as a metaphor or symbol, and its efforts to estab-lish the objectivity of value judgments. Both errors can be traced to the mis-taken belief that attributes that belong to music and those supplied by the hu-man perceiver are distinct and separate: a too-hasty demarcation between what is inside music and what is outside, the intramusical and the extramusical. Mu-sic does not consist of the barren physical entities described by acoustical sci-ence onto which a human perceiver projects things like feeling. Rather, feelings are qualities the music actually has. Calling Tamino's first aria in *The Magic Flute* "tender and dignified," Clifton urges, is no more metaphorical or sym-bolic than calling it tonal.[129] Tonality and tenderness are both immanent mu-sical qualities, verified by their bodily sense on the experiential level. There can be no music without a "'music-ing' self,"[130] insists Clifton. Upon entering mu-sic's distinctive space, music ceases to be an objective thing in the world (like mountains and trees), whose only significant attributes are physically objective. Rather than an "it," music is experienced as a "thou," with an internal world like our own—or perhaps more precisely, with an internal world that is ours in common. Accordingly, "If I become tender and dignified, it is because the mu-sic is tender and dignified; if I am tonal, the music exhibits the pull and ten-sion of tonality. In the presence of music, I qualify my own ontology: I *am* ten-der and dignified; I *am* tonal."[131]

To treat such expressions as metaphors wrongly suggests that there is some-thing objective and distinct in the melody that somehow resembles strictly hu-man attributes of tenderness or dignity. Worse still, it suggests that melody might somehow enjoy an 'objective' existence, independent of one's "complicity" with it. Clifton's position, by contrast, is that "melody is a fragile thing, that it need not appear, but, once having appeared, requires sustenance if it is not to slip back into mere sound. To say that a melody is tender, dignified, etc., is . . . to qualify the very Being of these sounds as melody."[132] Segregating music's sup-posed 'insides' from its 'outsides' is responsible for another serious distortion as well: conferral of extramusical status on musically presented phenomena like parades, or the crucifixion, or the sea. "But," asserts Clifton, "Debussy's con-ception of the ocean is not 'outside of' *La Mer*; the essence of the ocean shares in the essence of the music. It is not music which is adulterated by exposure to other natural or cultural phenomena, it is these phenomena which have become musicalized."[133]

Musical experience is indeed extraordinarily fragile. We slip out of it with disconcerting ease. Because of this fragility, Clifton is highly suspicious of musical value judgments based on technical or formal concerns. Such judgments err in "substituting a causal 'why' for an experiential 'how'."[134] They attribute musical success or failure to objective causes rather than the lived experience that is the locus of all musical meaning and value. Since music is a personal achievement, the validity of musical value judgments must address that achievement. From this bodily, experiential perspective, 'bad music' is a profoundly contradictory phrase. For bad or repellent music is in fact not music at all. It may well have music's trappings, but it fails to achieve the bodily complicity essential to music. So the phrase "bad music" is an oxymoron, a pathetically imprecise description of a state of affairs where music's "attempt to emerge from its earthly sound source"[135] is thwarted. Even if a little music somehow manages to 'get through', since "meaningless data . . . prevail over the assertions of music itself," instead of 'music' one encounters only a "physical opacity" with a "fractured mood."[136] Instead of creating a space where bodily consciousness is free to savor its musical unity, a space that eradicates boundaries between us and it, inside and outside, "bad" music thwarts possession and erects barriers. Bad music is, in short, "the unsuccessful attempt of good music to come into being."[137] Thus, Clifton says, there is "no such thing as bad music . . . only bad situations."[138] In the lived musical experience, music is not a physically objective thing but an event that engages one's entire body. One either experiences music ("good" by definition) or one encounters something not music (something therefore inappropriately called "bad music"). When we live in music's time and space, music surrounds and envelopes us. It fills consciousness completely, leaving no room either for self-consciousness or for the kind of dualistic thinking that pervades our everyday lives. Clifton paraphrases Merleau-Ponty: ". . . [M]usic is first of all an event which grips my body, and this grip circumscribes the area of significance to which it has reference. The music [word] is then indistinguishable from the attitude which it induces."[139]

In short, "music has meaning because it is ours,"[140] and not the other way around. It is not a sonic object 'out there', but a presence in which one dwells. Accordingly, concludes Clifton, "Music is what I am when I experience it."[141] Music appears when "the commonsense meanings of 'outside', 'inside', 'self', and 'other' become effaced by the meaning of something possessed"; and on this level, feeling is "not so much a matter of what the subject *has*, as what the object *is*."[142] Music is not something a person can 'have', Clifton seems to say: it is a collaborative experience in which possession is always mutual.

Although on this view feeling is essential to music, it is not the kind of feeling Hanslick called 'pathological'. There is an important distinction for Clifton between "receiving" or authentic feeling, and (inauthentic) "responding." In receiving, one is fully present to the work, while in mere responding, one only drifts along in 'hedonistic mists'. "[A]uthentic feeling has an ontological, not a psychological, function. It brings the meaning of the artwork into being."[143] Human feelings are not simply something we have, they constitute our very being. So too for music: feelings are not things it refers to, stimulates, or simply has; they are essential to music's very being, a fundamental and inextricable part of what music is.

Commentary

Clifton's is a moving and in many respects compelling description of what music is and what it may mean in human experience. His acknowledgment of the indispensable place of the human subject's role in an adequate account of music, his recognition that there is never a known without a knower, is a vitally important point for music philosophy. Indeed, coming to grips with the full significance of that truth may well be one of the greatest challenges confronting contemporary music philosophy, undermining as it does the tenacious objectivistic conviction that notes and structures are the locus of music's ultimate significance. That music is no simple fact, but a meaning invariably constituted by embodied human beings, is an insight whose consequences are far-reaching.

Clifton's account raises many provocative questions, the most obvious of which have to do with the strata he designates as musical essences, and their 'essential' status. As essences, the bedrock foundations or innermost cores of musical experience, Clifton is clearly claiming universal status for these four strata. But whether they are invariant substrates of musical experience is a matter that warrants close examination. It might be maintained, for instance, that this appeal to universals constitutes a reliance on the very presuppositions phenomenology presumes to set aside. Are Clifton's 'essences' truly essential, then — constitutive of every experience that is genuinely musical? Or do they rather constitute interesting and important yet contingent aspects of musical experience: ways it often is but need not always be? Might we acknowledge the value of Clifton's insights as correctives to disembodied, objectivist accounts that neglect the ways musical meanings are constituted, but still resist the notion that they are necessarily universal, essential, and definitive of such meanings in each and every instance? In short, are these essences in fact essences?

Or to raise a slightly different issue, is it possible that Clifton is right to insist that the perspective of the experiencing self is necessary to an understanding of music, yet wrong to imply that it is sufficient? It may be fairly objected, for instance, that his account neglects the social and political nature of musical experience; and that his idea of the bodily basis of musical meaning errs in neglecting sexual and gender issues; and further still, that the listener's perspective should not be taken as the paradigmatic stance, the most quintessentially musical. In other words, whether these four strata exhaust the foundations of musical experience is an issue that begs careful examination. Are music's foundations determinate in number (four, to be precise), or are they potentially infinite?

Clifton's descriptions of each respective stratum also raise a number of intriguing issues. In his accounts of music's temporal and spatial strata, for instance, he contrasts musical time, time that is in the music, with the chronological time music is in. Although musical time is profoundly different from ordinary time, Clifton apparently believes it somehow 'speaks of time' in a way that is informative and valuable. The temporal experience music presents apparently serves to teach us something about temporality at the same time. Only this seems to run counter to Clifton's rejection of music's symbolic nature, as well as to generate occasional confusion about which 'time' Clifton is referring to: the time within it, or the time it is about. Clifton's descriptions of the play and feeling strata raise still more difficult issues. Although his accounts of various dimensions of musical play are intriguing, Clifton offers a much clearer explanation of what play 'is not' than of what it is. While he describes ways music may be playlike, he leaves us without an explanation of the nature and character of this 'play' his various examples are intended to illuminate. And finally, although Clifton assures us that 'feeling' is essential to all musical experience, his analysis focuses predominantly on a general feeling called 'possession', one that "underlies and prepares for more recognizable feelings."[144] The case for this 'possession' feeling and its bodily basis are persuasively argued, and Clifton makes a compelling case that musical time and space arise as meanings only because of "the kind of feeling infusing them."[145] Beyond this, however, Clifton has surprisingly little to say about actual feelings, and although that hardly negates his argument for feeling's essential status, neither does it strongly support it.

Probably the most far-reaching issues raised by Clifton's project concern his success evading the subject-object dualism rejected by his phenomenological convictions. Ferrara makes the telling point, for instance, that Clifton's constant resort to the first person (I, me, mine) betrays a subject-centered orientation that seriously—perhaps fatally—neglects the intersubjective (we, us, ours), socially constructed nature of all meanings, musical or otherwise.[146] For Clifton, says Ferrara, the notion of music as 'mine' positions an isolated subject at the center of things. Instead of a cultural being, concretely situated in particular social and historical circumstances, then, Clifton's musical listener is an isolated individual, curiously detached from the rest of the world. Thus, Clifton's account "does not appear to follow a basic shift in phenomenology from subjectivism into 'intersubjectivism' in which man exists within an onto-historical situation marked by interaction."[147]

One of the reasons for Clifton's subjectivism can be traced to the particular 'brand' of phenomenology to which he subscribes, and its belief that once presuppositions are put aside, what remains is music as it purely 'is'. But this belief that phenomenological bracketing enables a pure description capable of evading all distortion is highly questionable. In the first place, it carries deep within it a belief that there is a way music ultimately and immediately 'is', in itself, and that by eliminating all presuppositions, music will present itself to us as it 'really' is. On this view, as we have seen, phenomenology deals in descriptions, not interpretations or explanations. But as Ferrara rightly observes, the idea of describing music 'purely as it is', music as it purely 'presents itself', conceals a kind of "obscured objectivism."[148] The idea of pure description made possible by immediate perception wrongly assumes it is possible to step completely outside all tradition, culture, habit. As Ferrara cautions, "Try as one may, the full, pure, or absolute suspension of one's tradition is impossible. We live and think in and through forms of knowledge and being that are inextricably rooted in our tradition. If one can never be fully theory-less, value-less, or without tradition, the promise of a method that enables [one] to perform pure description fails . . ."[149]

The idea of phenomenological inquiry as a suspension of all presuppositions, then, appears to rest on a very significant unexamined presupposition of its own: that phenomenological description is not itself an interpretation. It seems to fancy itself a description that is not itself situated, perspectival, and partial. But all descriptions, like all perceptions and all knowledge, are situated and therefore both mediated and partial. All descriptions are themselves interpretations. There can be no view from nowhere. Paradoxically, then, the phenomenological suspension of prejudgment seems intended to permit a stance that, to the extent its description is pure, is ultimate, irrefutable, and in at least some limited sense, objective. The idea of an insular, autonomous subject (an 'I') contains deep within itself belief in the possibility of a music 'in itself'. Both are problematic. Phenomenology's determination to explore music from an experiential perspective is far from misguided or fruitless, but it may be over-hasty to presume its perspective more authentic, ultimate, definitive, and to that extent more 'objective' than all other contenders.

The suggestion that instead of foundations we may have only perspectives, that instead of absolute truth we may have only temporary agreement or consensus, that Clifton's phenomenology may reveal not so much the innermost essences of music as some of the important ways people sometimes constitute its meaning, leads logically and unavoidably to the question of relativism—just as Merleau-Ponty's perceptual knowing invited charges of irrationalism. What precisely is Clifton's stand on music's nature and value? Presumably, that it is a spatiotemporal object constituted in lived experience by an embodied person; and that musical experience is playlike and feelingful in important respects. Only, certain of Clifton's claims seem very much at odds with the idea of anything foundational or substantial that might ground one's claims to music's nature and value. Assertions like "Music is what I am when I experience it," and questions like "What right have I to demand that a person experience a piece of music exactly the way I do?" suggest he believes music's value is (again) very much a personal or individual matter. If music is always relative to "my" experience of it, what grounds, if any, might there be for asserting that 'this is good music' or even 'this is music' for anyone but "myself"? What if someone else experiences it differently? If her point of reference is her (bodily) experience, what common ground might we have for discussion? What grounds might I have for selecting one kind of music for instruction instead of another? Is music whatever I say it is? Clifton's insistence upon the mutuality of possession makes it clear that his response to this last query would be an emphatic 'no'. After all, music is 'what I am' because it requires one's bodily complicity to become truly musical. Clifton does not suggest music is what I am and nothing more, even if he does occasionally seem to wish to restrict the range of musically relevant experience to a listener's body. But neither does he directly address the question of the musical relevance of a person's experience. Perhaps Hanslick's slouching, brooding, swaying enthusiast's musical experience is every bit as valid as any other?

Suggesting that Clifton's success at neutralizing subject-object dualism is mixed is neither to declare it a complete failure nor to dismiss the significance of his project, only to point out its elusive character and the precariousness of the balancing act it seems to require. Certainly his effort to illuminate music's constructed, intentional nature, to urge its basis in human bodily experience, to blur comfortable conceptual boundaries between the intrinsic and the extrinsic, and to return the experiencing person to philosophical center stage are laudable. Construing music a field of human action is a view fecund with philosophical possibilities. The possibility that it may offer 'a' way of viewing music rather than 'the' definitive one changes none of this.

Burrows: Sonorously Experiencing the World

In *Sound, Speech, and Music*,[150] David Burrows undertakes a wide-ranging exploration of the experience of sound, drawing on provocative phenomenological insights to argue the distinctive character of the human experience of sound, a unique mode of awareness he thinks constitutes the foundation for musical expression and thought alike. The way we experience sound has played an enormously important role in human evolution, he believes, freeing us from the tethers of the material, physical world, and making possible distinctively human ways of thinking, communicating, and expressing. At the same time, the experience of sound offers humans a unique sense of connection to and unity with the world. Therefore, an appreciation of the way we experience sound is fundamental to understanding both music's distinctive power and the human capacity for thought and reason: the very things that make us most distinctive as a species. Burrows states his primary thesis this way: ". . . the distinctiveness of human beings as a species—in particular their capacity for free-wheeling and wide-ranging thought—is to a great extent an outgrowth of the distinctiveness of the way they use sound, itself distinctive in a number of ways among the senses."[151]

Key to Burrows' argument is the point that in human experience the living body is the center to which everything else in the world relates as periphery, as 'other'. Life is radiation around this center, influenced by experiential forces that are characteristically either centrifugal or centripetal: pulling away from or drawing in toward center. 'Self', Burrows explains, "is defined whenever the force of its centrifugally radiating energies encounters the resistance of the 'other'. The self is the other than other."[152] So, too, in social experience: 'we' consists of overlapping individual center/periphery schemes, defined by our common, collective differences from others. Thus, the tension between center and periphery, between self and other, is fundamental to human experience and identity, both individually and collectively. And since the further the center radiates or extends itself and the more inclusive it becomes, the more secure it feels, this dialectical self–other interaction is basic both to human evolution and to personal identity and sense of well-being.

This center/periphery scheme manifests itself in three different experiential fields of action, according to Burrows. 'Field 1' is physical space, the material world in which the body resides, a field of action given primarily to the senses—vision chief among those. The world of the 'here and now', Field 1 is fundamentally concerned with physical constraints, boundaries, and proximities, with connections and separations. 'Field 2' is meta-sensory, mental space. Although this field of action is still rooted in the body, mind takes the concrete immediacy of the here-and-now and opens it out "to include past, future, elsewhere."[153] The entities at play in Field 2, then, are not sense data but images and concepts: the synthetic, immaterial stuff of which memories, plans, and expectations are made. This mental field of action is free from the concrete, material tethers of physical space. Its boundaries and limitations are not physical, but consensual ones: negotiated standards of logic, coherence, and clarity that are mutually endorsed. 'Field 3' is the field of spirit, understood as the "sense of self as diffused through the full range of awareness."[154] Field 3 is an unbounded space in which center is everywhere, the world of newborns and mystics. In short, "In Field 1 the view is the view from here; in Field 2, the view from anywhere you can name or imagine; in Field 3 the view from everywhere, of an undifferentiated everywhere."[155] Each successive field thus enlarges the sphere of human awareness and being in the world.

The significance of all this lies in Burrows' contention that what historically made humans' distinctive mental and spiritual life possible is the way they experience sound. Sight and sound are both crucially important means by which humans convey and transmit information across distances, but sound is much more lightly tethered to the physical, sensory realm of 'Field 1' than vision, says Burrows. Because of its 'radical detachment' from the world of enduring, physical entities, sonorous experience is the most likely point of entry to the metasensory, mental realm that distinguishes humans from other animals. Sound's phenomenal characteristics make speech the ideal vehicle for formulating human mental life. Thought may be inspired by the ideal of permanence and fixity, of the control, clarity, and stability characteristic of visual experience; but thinking is fundamentally a kind of movement. Sound's capacity to detach itself from the world of stationary objects and things, its fundamentally dynamic, processual character, is what enabled human entry into the distinctively human field of mental life. At the same time, sound is centrally implicated in spiritual awareness, that experience in which people transcend not only the physical world given them by their senses, but also the dualistic world given them by their ideas.

Sound

Burrows undertakes to document the marked phenomenal contrasts between visual and aural encounters with the world. Consider, he suggests, the differences between seeing a bell and hearing it ring. In contrast to the "cool constancy" of its sight, the bell's ringing is experienced as "a series of sharp explosions followed by tremulous dyings-away," a process of continual change and renewal.[156] Visual experience has a sense of solidity, distinctness, and objectivity, characteristics conspicuously absent in aural experience. Sight is of things and objects out-there, reaching us with a sense of durability and clarity. Hearing is more inward than outward, more about process than things, and largely indifferent to the kind of distinctions vision constantly strives to achieve. Seeing and hearing are strik-ingly different senses, each putting us in the world in radically different ways.

Visual experience is of objects and things whose outsides we perceive when light reflects from their surfaces. Because these reflections always come from outside and elsewhere, the visual world is one experienced at a distance from our lived human center: it is a world of surfaces, spatial relations, and objects. And since it is also a world of proximity, configuration, arrangement, and loca-tion, sight likes its objects and spaces discrete, distinct, and clear. The world given us by visual perception, then, is phenomenally objective and categorical, one that brings with it the impression of fixity, reliability, and solidity. Sight brings us objective 'things' that claim to exist at a distance from our subjective selves. "Vision sorts things out in space, putting them in their places in relation to each other and to us," says Burrows.[157] Sight is thus an experience of sepa-ration, of reaching outward to touch the seen.[158]

Furthermore, visual experience is fundamentally unambiguous. Sight re-lentlessly seeks the twin Cartesian ideals of clarity and distinctness. Because of its special aptitude for sorting, arranging, and detecting or conferring structure, vision is a highly 'trustworthy' sense. And because of this, ". . . for most purposes we must give it first place. Far more often we look around because of something we have heard than we listen because of something we have seen."[159] Seeing, the saying goes, is believing; and "[p]eople speak of the light—but not of the sound—of reason."[160] It is not coincidental, then, that intellectual insight is so often referred to as illumination or enlightenment, and that the most common epistemological metaphors are visual.[161] For vision extends the sense of fixity and stability required of absolutes like truth and certainty.

If vision gives us facts, asserts Burrows, hearing gives us rumors; and if see-ing is believing, hearing is more a matter of "guessing and hoping."[162] The ex-perience of sound is fundamentally equivocal, polyvalent, uncertain. In contrast to the clear orderliness and predictability shared by vision and 'Field 1', the ex-perience of listening "shades over into one in which different and shifting den-sities, textures, and intensities of activity coexist in varying degrees of interpen-etration."[163] Hearing has little of vision's sense of cool control, of durable constancy, of reliability and objectivity. Sound comes and goes as it pleases, and cannot be ignored by facing away or averting one's eyes. And because it sur-rounds us and approaches us from all directions, sound lacks vision's clear sense of spatial location. Thus its experience seldom has the 'out there-ness' so famil-iar in visual experience. Unlike the seemingly straight path between eye and vi-sual object, sound "moves in shock waves that balloon out invisibly around some source of disturbance, filling in around objects in its path as does its carrier, the air. Air is all around us, and consequently sound is too . . ."[164] Sound consists in "an emanation from the bodies producing it that leaves their materiality and concentrated localization behind."[165] Sound moves in many directions at once, freely mixes with itself, comes into and passes out of being without our bidding, and consists in a state of seemingly perpetual change. Its range of activity "is rarely tied in any inherent and necessary way to what matters about the size and shape of its source."[166] Thus, in contrast to the eye's promise of clarity and distinctness, the ear's world offers us ambiguity and mystery. Hearing, Burrows remarks, is "the dark first-born sibling of sight."[167]

This ambiguity or vagueness is due at least in part to sound's profoundly processual nature. As noted above, sonorous objects only exist by a process of continuous, moment-by-moment renewal. Where sight gives us physical entities, the heard world is phenomenally evanescent, relentlessly moving, ever changing. Says Burrows, "We see the world as a noun and hear it as a verb."[168] Rather than lining up in space like visual objects—next to, behind, above or below, nearer or further—sounds emanate and reverberate in all directions at once, intermingling, coalescing, penetrating and even passing through each other. Simultaneous perception of superimposed images is exceptional in vision, but the rule for hearing. Moreover, "Sounds flow over and through each other and jut up in one another's midst in ways that bear no resemblance to the ways their sources relate in space."[169] Given its locational vagueness and constant movement, sound could hardly be expected to conform to vision's discrete, categorical, objective norms. In fact, sound "tells us nothing at all about the finer details of spatial disposition we call appearance."[170]

But hearing has norms and standards of its own that wholly elude sight. Perhaps the most salient of these is sound's sense of inwardness, of intimacy. Says Burrows, "Sight draws me out, sound finds me here. And sound goes beyond touch, which respects the perimeter of my skin, and beyond its degree of intimacy in seeming to be going on within me as much as around me."[171] Unlike vision's sense of touching things out-there, at a distance from one's lived center, sonorous experience is a corporeal one, of events happening in-here at that center. If separation and distance characterize visual experience, sonorous experience is close and connected. "Seeing is like touching, hearing like being touched; except that the touch of sound does not stop at the skin. It seems to reach inside and to attenuate, along with the distinction . . . between here and there, the . . . one between within and without. In this way sound can ease some of the tension that goes with the duality of the organic condition."[172] Because it is more experientially subjective, more inward and personal than vision, the experience of sound also has a sense of urgency and insistence unparalleled in visual experience. The immediacy of sound's inward touch may be soothing and intoxicating, or it may be violent and invasive. Thus, the sonorous world is characteristically more urgent and engaging, and our relationship to it more vulnerable than is typically the case in visual experience. "[T]o hear a sound," Burrows explains, "is to be involved: detachment comes more easily to seeing than to hearing. The difference between signaling an intention to pass on the highway by flashing headlights . . . or blowing the horn is the difference between a request and a demand. To hear is to be touched, moved perhaps, or even driven . . ."[173]

Thus, the experience of sound contributes profoundly to our sense of being alive to the world. It affirms our bond with the world, and at the same time confirms its unity. It is primarily through sound that we transcend the insularity of selfhood, the I—it duality of visual experience. Sounds nurture our sense of being-in-the-world by neutralizing the opposition between the in-here and the out-there. Sounds temporalize and vivify the static inertness of the unheard world. As Burrows says, sounds run through us "like a vital current of belief, molding us into a living interior that is proof against the unbelieving emptiness that lies around."[174] Because its spatial vagueness tends to draw the listener toward its source, because of its peremptory demands to be taken in and that one adapt to it, and because of its extraordinarily transitory nature, the experience of sound requires a relationship of openness and empathy rarely experienced in visual experience. "[L]istening is necessarily participation, stressing commonality with the source rather than difference from it," writes Burrows.[175] Sound reaches us as "a sign of something out there, outside my own delimited and contingent being, with some of the same surge and flux I know in myself. I am not alone in being under way, growing and fading, pausing, then starting up again, and I feel confirmed."[176] Sonorous experience tells us we are not alone in our transitoriness and contingency. Hearing, Burrows reminds, is the way we are first present to the world: long before we become viewers in an illuminated world, we are listeners in the darkness of the womb.[177] Sonorous experience unifies and generates feelings of oneness. Vision is an experience of separateness and duality, hearing of connection and unity.

If sound contributes so substantially to experience, it is hardly surprising that its absence might be unsettling. In fact, says Burrows, silence is experienced not so much as a void as a 'negative presence': "So important to us is sound in all its variety that its absence comprises a whole richly textured anti-world."[178] Silence is death, and background sound is something people need, "a kind of protodiscourse whose message is that we are not alone . . . that the world is a place where a dialogue of vitality can be established."[179] The need for silence is more properly considered a respite from noise: sound that is intrusive, untimely, chaotic, or perversely ordered.[180] The very qualities that give sound its unequaled power to soothe, center, and console also give it the power to startle, alarm, and offend. Noise is sound that imposes, interferes, intrudes, forcing us (since one cannot turn away from sound) to experience the uninvited and unwanted. Our "auditory defenselessness casts us often in the role of victim, our privacy invaded by someone else's stereo or car horn."[181] Thus, the inwardness and corporeality that figure so prominently and favorably in the experience of welcomed sound make the experience of noise range from minor nuisance to violent imposition: an uninvited intrusion into one's personal space, a violation of one's very self. If we are the music while it lasts, one might say, so too are we the noise while it lasts. Sound matters to us, at least in part because it enters us, makes us resonate along with it for good or ill, becoming in that process not so much something we have as are.

Sound, then, is an utterly unique mode of construing and constructing the world. Sound's "peremptory immediacy,"[182] its ambiguity, its diffuseness, its vital transience—each imparts to human existence qualitative experiential dimensions unparalleled in any other realm, unknowable in any other way. Since sounds enter so deeply and profoundly into hearing people's experience, it is vastly more than a biological orienting mechanism. Furthermore, sound's experiential power helps explain the ubiquity and import of music. Rarely are people casual or indifferent about their musics. Music matters so much because of sound's immediacy, perfusiveness, and inwardness: its capacity to touch the vital center of our being—who we are—and induce a kind of resonance with itself. Both the intensity with which we embrace music and the repugnance we feel toward noisy impostors are functions of the distinctive way sound mediates human experience.

Voice

Burrows' conception of life as radiation from a bodily center is integrated with his understanding of sound in an exploration of the basic form of personally emitted sound: the human voice, itself an emanation from a center. People are present to each other visually and vocally, but because of the characteristics of sound discussed above, voice is by far the more intimately social of the two. Not only are we drawn closely to people's voices, experiencing them as connections, but variations in vocal volume, pitch, and resonance are the basis for crucial judgments about a speaker's mood, veracity, and character. We infer a great deal about people from their vocal presence alone. There is a 'truth in timbre' that enables understanding even when the language spoken is not fully grasped. The "inarticulate, preverbal music of mood and intent is a constant undercurrent of speech," one whose melody we instinctively submit to "a kind of instantaneous musical analysis. Affect is deduced by assessing the balance of force and resistance expressed in timbre, on a scale from breathiness to strangulation."[183]

This is possible, Burrows believes, because voice exists precisely at the threshold between self and world, center and periphery. And as such, "Anything at all . . . that has bearing on the relationship between self and other can be reflected in the vocal representation of the threshold between them."[184] Voice is always a window on the vocalizer's life situation, "a freely manipulable representation and advertisement of the life that underlies it."[185] At the same time, says Burrows, voice's sound initiates a kind of "power play" wherein the tension between self and other is transformed into a "ludic performance" of the interface between self and world.[186] So one's voice always "strikes out beyond the way things are; it is always a performance reaching beyond the self-evident, a manifestation of will and intention. Even indifference becomes a performance when it is voiced."[187]

Because vocalization plays with the tension between self and other, an important part of the satisfaction it affords is a result of "the illusory sense of control it gives us over what it stands proxy for, our situation in life. . . . The vocal threshold is right there at our disposal; the vicissitudes of life are not."[188] And yet, this ludic performance of control presents only half the story, the other half of which is hearing the sound of one's voice. In hearing one's voice one is returned to oneself, re-encountering oneself in the immateriality of sound. This completes a self-confirming loop, "a closed circuit in which kinesthetic and auditory sensations confirm each other."[189] This sonic loop generates "a sustaining sense of inviolable self-sufficiency" and of "self-celebration" that accounts for the distinctive pleasure people find in singing, humming, or chanting. Humming divides one into two 'I's—I the sound producer, and I the listener. And two, comments Burrows, "is company."[190] Thus, "People who sing to themselves . . . are self-enfolded in resonance that leaves appearance and location behind. They sense themselves as a diffused happening that does not depend for its validation on this or that outside event or object or consideration, a flow with no pronounced sense of before or after, of first this and then that. . . . [p]eople who hum or whistle to themselves can achieve a temporary omniscience, since they are provisionally both self and other . . . [They attain a consciousness in which] no division is made between within and without and the world is the resonance of self."[191]

The sense of control that attends vocalization operates on a social level as well. As voice radiates outward to others, it invites, even insists that they attend to and participate in it and the life it represents. Vocally sounding oneself is thus an important way of disseminating one's presence throughout one's surroundings. And since the existence and duration of a voice's space are matters of the will and discretion of the person who sets them in vibratory motion, voice always stakes out a kind of territorial claim for its owner. That is one of the primary functions of bird song, observes Burrows, and perhaps also of the portable stereo carried down a city street.[192] At the same time, hearing involves "entering into an ambient process and perceptually moving along with it, and the social use of the voice invites others to this kind of sympathetic involvement in our lives."[193] In this way, the experience of humanly generated sound transforms the dualistic threshold between individual self and an outside world into "a new front of shared concerns," with a new, collective frame of reference: 'We'. "Partners in conversation," says Burrows, "are at once apart . . . and together in a new synthetic place, the location of their sympathetic resonance in common."[194]

Words and Music

The most distinctive initiative of the human species, as Burrows sees it, is its "massive colonization" of the territory of sound, linguistically and musically. The world of concept and thought—'Field 2'—became possible only because of speech's sonorous nature. Sonorous experience in the form of spoken words pushes back the horizons of the here and now to include elsewhere, past, and future; speech's sound has remarkable power to make the absent forcefully present. Indeed, the fact that reality extends beyond the apparent is verified in first-hand experience every time we speak. The move to representing physical objects with sounds, then, marks a momentous shift from a world of stable spatial configurations to one of invisible movement. Because of their invisibility, sounds can stand for "anything in space, or for any place, or for everywhere or nowhere."[195] Thinking and hearing are far more alike than thinking and seeing, sharing an invisible fluidity that cares little for fixed spatial coordinates and freely enters into novel combinations with itself. Accordingly, "the sound of the human voice in its lability and linguability is the best patron thought has."[196]

The impulse to preserve and systematize, however, motivates the creation of a visual record of thought's processes. Since the written word "leaches the voice out of articulated thought," it achieves an aura of "oracular impersonality" the sound world of speech never has: an air of impartial authority sustained by the absence of spoken words' sensuous particularity, their attachment to the personal world. The remoteness and stability of visual experience gives speech's written record a sense of finality and absoluteness, such that people are always in "greater danger of believing everything they read than everything they pick up as hearsay."[197] Whether spoken or written, however, Burrows maintains that the force of language is always centrifugal in character: in its designation of significances beyond itself, its vectoral direction is always away from our lived human center. Speech has a "centrifugal thrust that dilates the shared present of speakers and has them taking their bearings by what once purportedly was the case, or what is the case (according to someone) but someplace else, or what they hope or fear may or may not eventually happen."[198] But the cost of being a talking, thinking, and perhaps especially, a writing animal—of extending our grasp beyond the reach of sense—is a loss of "innocence, the primitive sense of being unconditionally here, and right, the source from which the world takes any meaning it has."[199]

That elusive sense is precisely what musical experience offers to restore and sustain: for unlike the centrifugal character of speech-mediated experience, musical engagement is fundamentally centripetal in nature. Music is centered awareness, the sense of "self as world,"[200] of being "centered in the synthetic sensuous actuality of the moment."[201] Accordingly, says Burrows, while we talk our way out of innocence, we can sing our way back in. Musical experience "gives the participants a sense of themselves as individuals with a central responsibility for the creation of their own provisional worlds," worlds of "self-validating, nondualistic . . . presence in, and through movement."[202] In such experience, people find temporary freedom from deterministic forces, release from the presence of otherness: that "out-there oppositional world," about which they somehow feel an obligation to do something.[203] While musical participants form a duality with their music, "to attend deeply to this other is to merge with it,"[204] such that awareness is centered, and everything in awareness becomes a function of that center. In short, while musically engaged, participants "feel continuous with whatever matters," sustaining the "healing illusion of their noncontingent presence at that center which is everywhere."[205] As in the experience of sound, musical experience carries no awareness of inside and outside, of here and there. Such awareness is wholly incidental to musical experience's "incantatory resonance, [its] sense of vibrant swelling stillness that brings its participants a conviction of their unconditional presence in the world."[206]

Speech and music, grafted to the same sonorous root, grow in opposite directions, into radically different experiential realms, each uniquely and vitally human. Moving along with a temporally unfolding sound signal, where one enters centrifugally into the dualistic field of thought and concept, the other moves centripetally into the field of unitary spirituality, undifferentiated awareness, and unconditional presence.

The fact that words and music are such close neighbors physiologically and perceptually, yet so profoundly different experientially, leads Burrows to reflect upon the nature of the gap between sonorous experience—inherently processual, invisible, fleeting, ambiguous, and therefore radically resistant to representation—and various ways of representing it. These reflections offer, among other things, to explore the adequacy of verbal descriptions, explanations, and interpretations of music: issues of direct significance to the enterprise of music philosophy. The problem is not just that music slips through the net of language, Burrows notes: after all, everything does to some extent. There are, however, "few gaps between an experience and its representation wider than the one between music and its analyses and descriptions."[207] Musical scores and diagrams are inescapably selective and partial in what they convey of music because, in representing, they also denature and transform. But so do all representations. Since representation is inherently reductive, suppressing detail deemed dispensable for particular purposes, what is important is to acknowledge what is being reduced and how much. Gesture, for instance, comes the closest to representing music of any nonauditory modality. But while it succeeds in capturing things like rhythm, volume, and expressivity, it neglects melodic, harmonic, and timbral detail, and is quite incapable of representing things as fine grained as sixty-fourth notes. Musical scores offer a detailed visual record of melody and harmony, but designate rhythm only approximately and generally; and they are wholly unable to convey the lived, processual sense of music's unfolding, or the sensual, tactile sense of timbre and texture. Scores are "coldly detailed and inert. . . . [and] above all silent."[208] Verbal accounts—the stuff of philosophy—endeavor to explore both music's acoustic and experiential dimensions, yet encounter an immense gap when they encounter music's dynamic, processual character. Music, remarks Burrows, is like "an ongoing experiment in pushing change as far as it can coherently be taken": a fact that invariably frustrates the human need to fix and locate things.[209] Because of the enormous gap between fixity and flow, discourse about music resembles what it purports to describe scarcely at all: it is 'lumpy' and 'granular', 'engorged with syllables and meaning', while music exists in a domain of 'relentless emergence.'[210]

Reflections and Queries

Burrows' explorations of the profound contrasts between the worlds of the eye and the ear; of the relations among the experiences of sound, speech, noise, and music; of thought's debt to the spatial ambiguity and temporal fluidity of sound; and of langauge's close alliance with the visual ideals of fixity and objectivity are each extraordinarily valuable reminders that the worlds of the ear have been crucial in human evolution and continue to play major and distinctive roles in the formation of human identity. His eloquent descriptions are important reminders that the human ear is far more than an orienting device or aural receptacle for acoustic signals, and that the importance of sonorous experience extends far beyond its acoustic properties. Situating sound, particularly, voice, at the nexus of self, other, fixity, and permanence is an insight with potentially far-reaching consequences for the conception of musical experience.

Among the benefits that attend Burrows' description of the gaps between verbally and musically mediated experience is a balanced appreciation of the inherent shortcomings and potential benefits of representations of music. While he concedes, for instance, that language—philosophy's most basic tool—moves experientially in a direction opposite music, it does not appear to follow that all efforts at representation are futile. Language may well be incapable of representing music as it is experienced, and indeed, experience that is musical may occur in a radically different field of action than does nonmusical thought. But acknowledging these profound differences does not establish that words and music are wholly incommensurable, only that they can never be coextensive. That linguistic representations of music can never be more than partial is a claim equally valid for any representation of music, whether by verbal description, analytical diagram, gesture, or score. In other words, the difficulty is not so much that linguistic description cannot definitively represent music as lived, but that, because of the distinctive kind of 'thing' it is, music cannot accommodate definitive representations. Its radically temporal character, its polyvalence, and its corporeality mean that efforts to explain, interpret, describe, analyze, or represent it must be inherently reductive. But that does not establish that they are pointless, or that we have no philosophical recourse but to retreat to mysticism. Different representations offer different perspectives, each inescapably partial, each with its blind spots, yet each with potential insights as well. Although Burrows does not make the point explicitly, his demonstration of the inherent partiality of all representations of music—scores, gestures, and words—seems to extend the possibility that description and analysis, description and interpretation, and gesture and score offer potentially complementary insights that collectively promise to enhance understanding of music. The key seems to be acknowledging the partiality and fallibility of each, resisting the visual-conceptual need to claim ultimacy.

Perhaps the most fecund aspect of Burrows' project is its phenomenal account of 'voice'. Voice's location at the threshold between self and other, and its ludic, performative character, may be useful in understanding quite a broad range of musical experiences and values. If voice were metaphorically extended to embrace things like musical instruments, for instance, and if conversation were extended to collective musical engagement, Burrows' accounts might have considerable potential for conceptualizing the distinctive nature and value of music making. The parallels are intriguing. Like vocalization, music making is experienced as emanation from a bodily center, and like voice, musical participation occurs in a unique field of action. Also like voice, musical performance may be viewed as at once a dissemination of oneself and an invitation to sympathetic participation by others. Music making, like vocalization, takes us out of the here and now, and pushes back spatial and temporal boundaries to establish a dynamic, flexible field of bodily engagement, opening up an experiential realm that effaces self's insularity. Making music is, like vocalization, a ludic engagement in which sound is simultaneously experienced as sonic other and a manifestation of oneself. That experience, while it is sustained, is one of wholeness, of integration and integrity, of self-sufficiency. If this is so, musical performance cannot be solely a matter of executing 'the music' but is always also the enactment of a resonant field where self and other are one, where two experiences of self—as producer and listener—fuse into a nondualistic, centered experience of wholeness.

Stubley: The Transformative Power of Musical Performance

These speculative remarks point in a direction that Burrow's account of voice might perhaps take, yet does not. For the most part, Burrows (like most philosophers) speaks as if musical listening were the quintessential musical activity, and as though the body were engaged similarly in all musical experience. There are those, however, who maintain that engagement in the making or 'performance' of music constitutes a fundamentally different manner of being, with special philosophical problems of its own. Although it is not specifically indebted to Burrows, it will be instructive to examine briefly an account of musical performance that invokes some of the phenomenological insights explored in this chapter and extends them to the actual act of music making.

In an effort to establish the "transformative powers of musical performance" and show its distinctive experiential basis, Eleanor Stubley[211] explores how body and music inform each other in the act of music making. It is a major philosophical mistake, Stubley believes, to regard musical performance either as the kind of physical feat where a body mechanically executes the musical directives of mind or as a simple interpretive act in which players seek to discover and reproduce the music encoded in a score. The reasons are closely related: both seriously neglect the fundamental importance of the body in making music. The body's role in musical performance is more than physical execution; and in performing, players are not just trying to find the sense of the music, but rather "to get a sense of who they are in relationship to this music."[212] Music making situates the body in a musical field, and the way the music-making body moves and orients itself within the musical field is crucial to a full appreciation of such experience. In this musical field, the music's movement and that of the musically behaving body are experienced as one. To be sure, the bodily sense is crucial to all musical experience; but in music making, the link is more direct and profound. Musical participants, Stubley observes, are "so immersed in their bodies that their movements seem to define their total sense of being or self-awareness."[213] And yet, what occupies their attention is not movements as movements, but rather the way these movements "feel and define their sense of being as the [musical] play unfolds."[214] What it actually means to engage in music making cannot be determined by looking in from the outside: for as Merleau-Ponty maintained, 'the world' is not what one thinks, but what one lives through. A true understanding of the significance of musical performance, then, requires that we get inside the field where the action occurs, a field that is at once physical, mental, and spiritual.

One of the most striking features of this musical field is the "symbiotic tuning" by which it is sustained: tunings between and among body, mind, instrument, sound, and the musical actions of other musicians. In musical performance, music is not simply given to or executed by the body; rather, the musical performance is "something done through and with the body."[215] And collectively, musical participants engage in a similar tuning process: they are "driven by a movement of mind which enables the musicians to reach through their bodily actions and experience the outer edge of the sounds," sounds encountered not so much as physical actualities, but as musical possibilities.[216] This musical field has a distinctly dilated sense of the present as well as a marked sense of forward extension. Its dilated presence and forward extension are one with the ongoing tuning process, a constant regeneration that "lets each moment circle back on itself and become an ever-developing present."[217]

The musical field's boundaries are not tangible or material. They are encountered as resistances, felt as otherness—in pitch deviations, in rhythmic asynchronies, in timbral distortions—perhaps the kind of phenomena one scholar calls "participatory discrepancies."[218] Yet, under favorable circumstances, voice, style, and trust manage to prevail, collectively sustaining this fragile, dynamic field, ensuring its vital continuity, preventing its collapse.[219] Voice is one's way of being in the sound, a kind of force that exists precisely and only at the 'body-sound interface'. Voice's freedom interacts dialectically with constraints inherent in various stylistic conventions and rituals. And ultimately, the field's formal integrity is maintained by an attitude of trust, a sense of "being apart together"[220] which gives the field elasticity, freedom, and variation. Thus, voice, style, and trust interact to generate a sense of constant renewal—the sense that gives the musical field its qualities of searching and discovery, of freshness and vitality, as if the music were being heard for the first time.[221]

At the heart of music making, then, is a sense of play which consists in a distinctive experience of self. Playing music, Stubley writes, is "an on-going tuning process in which the self is experienced as an *identity in the making*."[222] Each moment in that process is directed by outward attention to opportunities or demands for deployment of the player's manifold skills and proficiencies, by a keen sensitivity to possibility and otherness that keeps awareness riveted at the player-action interface. The player both fills and is filled by the unfolding action, resulting in an "empathic bonding in which the other is experienced . . . as a potential I."[223] The experiential field thus created is an open and ever-expanding space in which one feels "larger than life, as if I am two Is at the same time, me and a significant other."[224]

When musical performance falters, this empathic bond is broken, the sense of deep connection severed. Temporal flow freezes, and the field collapses with a shock to the body. The senses of self-other unity and identity-in-making are shattered. An adequate understanding of musical performance thus requires, according to Stubley, recognition of "the sense in which *engenders a meeting of 'Is' at the body-sound interface*."[225] Only from the outside is skillful performing a matter of mere technical execution, or of reconstructing a work. From the inside, as played, skillful music making is "a matter of learning to experience the self as an *identity in the making*, of learning to reach out and create a playful space in which the self is open to the possibilities of an other."[226] In Stubley's view, musical performance occurs in an experiential field marked by unique ways of being in the body and being in the sound: a field where self and music are ever engaged in vital processes of mutual formulation and reformulation.

Music as Embodied Experience: The Body in the Mind

Because of their commitment to grounded description rather than abstraction and interpretation, the philosophical accounts of music generated by phenomenology can sometimes sound idiosyncratic and personal, and occasionally even appear to lie outside the realm of philosophical discourse. If, for instance, what one purports to be describing is one's own embodied sense of music, how can that possibly be right or wrong? If, after all, Clifton tells us music is what he is when he experiences it, then presumably we must take his word for it. Only, how is that philosophical? Although what phenomenologists attempt to describe is admittedly personal, it seems clear they do not regard it as utterly and profoundly private, either. Personal experience, the phenomenologist would remind us, is after all what validates all truths, including those that purport to be absolute, objective, and eternal. Meanings are things people construct, not find.

Phenomenology's frequent resort to first-person accounts and commitment to grounding itself in personal experience contrast strongly with philosophical approaches that presume to speak for everyone, everywhere, for all times. But that does not mean it is a solipsistic, purely introspective affair. In the first place, it is apparent that phenomenological inquiry strives to identify what is foundational, and thus, broadly given to experience. Its findings, then, should be at least potentially shareable by anyone willing to approach experience with the proper (phenomenological) attitude. Furthermore, the convergence of various phenomenological accounts suggests the existence of intersubjective common ground. Phenomenological accounts of music clearly differ, but they are not private musings. The phenomenological method's openness to diversity, multiplicity, and complexity makes it extraordinarily well suited to dealing with a broad range of music's 'experiential facts', and its determination to ground itself in firsthand musical experience is in many respects a welcome alternative to the metaphysical flights of fantasy in which philosophy has too often been known to engage.

At the same time, there probably is some validity to the charge that phenomenologists are rather too quick to construe musical experience as an individual rather than a social affair: to dissolve the subject-object dilemma in the direction of a self-sufficient, insular 'I', instead of a socially situated subject whose experiences and meanings are always both personal and intersubjective. While these issues, together with phenomenology's doubtful claim to the kind of utter immediacy that completely avoids presuppositions, are cause for concern, they should be weighed against the many rich insights achieved by working against the grain of conventional philosophical method.

For a method that aspires to bring philosophical discourse back down to earth, though, the extent of phenomenology's penchant for the poetic sometimes conveys the impression that metaphysical indulgences may have been exchanged for lavishly metaphorical ones. Especially for those who see the distinction between music and its effects, what it is and what it does, as among the more important advances in our understanding of music, phenomenology's preoccupation with the body is troublesome. On this view, people's bodies have little if anything to do with music as it objectively is—only with the way it is received subjectively, by the senses. From this perspective, phenomenology's appeals to the body are not just extravagant; they are not particularly useful philosophically. But is this insistence on music's bodily basis only metaphorical? Does body's significance to music extend no further than its ability to receive and register sensation, and transmit them to the musical mind?

Phenomenologists are not alone in arguing the body's complicity in cognitive experience. Recent philosophical work by Mark Johnson explores the body's crucial role in even the most seemingly cerebral of cognitive activity, providing a solid analytical validation of phenomenology's insistence on music's corporeal roots. As Johnson sees things, it is profoundly wrong to regard the human body as a mere container for mind, because bodily experience plays a constitutive role in even the most abstract, rational achievements: the body is in the mind.[227] Johnson believes that failure to recognize the crucial role of imagination in human cognition has led current scientific and philosophical accounts of mind to a fundamental impasse. In these "objectivist" accounts, knowledge is best advanced by setting personal experience aside, as if the world somehow has a rational structure independent of the way people construe it. The best knowledge, then, is that which has freed itself of the distortions of personal perspective, attaining a vantage point from which reality is known just as it is in itself. But this objectivist vantage point is a point of view without a perspective: a mythical stance only a god could achieve.

The objectivist ideal of a god's-eye view and an experience of reality that somehow avoids perspectival situatedness and partiality is not just a perverse piece of logic; it fails miserably to account for the richness and multivalence of meanings, and the importance of discovering or creating new ones. A knowledge without a knower would not be a human knowledge at all. Human knowledge is never a mirror image of some free-standing, 'external' reality, but something that is constantly being constructed and modified. Sense and imagination sort, organize, and interpret new experience in light of past experience. By ignoring the way imagination generates meaning, objectivism overlooks the processes that lie at the very heart of human knowledge. Says Johnson, "any adequate account of meaning and rationality must give a central place to embodied and imaginative structures of understanding by which we grasp our world."[228]

Because the objectivist sees rationality as a rule-governed process consisting simply of logical linkages between concepts or propositions and the external structure of reality, imagination is not just dispensable but an impediment to reliable knowledge. Interesting and useful though it may be in certain circumstances, imagination is undisciplined, unruly, idiosyncratic, personal, and therefore fundamentally at odds with knowledge. In Johnson's view, however, imaginative processes constitute the fundamental core of human reason, the foundation without which nothing worthwhile could be known. Although imagination may well be pre-conceptual, it is hardly undisciplined, impulsive, or private. Its fund of images is what enables us to find order and structure in human experience. And our bodily experience is among the most vital and important sources of those image patterns. Johnson explains, "Our reality is shaped by the patterns of our bodily movement, the contours of our spatial and temporal orientation, and the forms of our interactions with objects. It is never merely a matter of abstract conceptualization and propositional judgments."[229] In short, our lived experience of our bodies gives rise to image schemata, "recurring, dynamic pattern[s] of our perceptual interactions and motor programs,"[230] and it is by means of these that we find coherence and pattern in what we would otherwise only experience as chaos. Were it not for recurring patterns in the physical and perceptual activity of our bodies, cognitive meanings and rationality as we know them could not exist. The structure we find in abstract domains is only meaningful because we experience structure in bodily movements and interactions with our environment, and metaphorically map those patterns onto experience in other spheres, interpreting it in their light. This metaphorical mapping of pattern from one experiential domain onto another is the source of all rational powers. "Image schemata and metaphorical projections are experiential structures of meaning that are essential to most of our abstract understanding and reasoning,"[231] Johnson explains. And because those structures originate in and remain tied to our bodily experience, the body is always and necessarily in the mind: the body is the ineliminable source of human rationality.

These metaphorical mappings do not happen just willy-nilly, but are themselves "highly constrained by other aspects of our bodily functioning and experience."[232] Experience is not the mere reception of sense impressions, but a complex interaction among "perceptual, motor-program, emotional, historical, social, and linguistic dimensions," drawing upon "everything that makes us human."[233] Nor is the body's contribution some passing, formative phase which 'pure' reason eventually casts aside. It remains the deep-seated basis of the most advanced and seemingly pure intellection. The body is no subjective contaminant of rationality, but the very thing that makes it possible. In short, rationality is possible because of our imaginative ability to recognize and project into novel domains the basic structure of our bodily actions and experiences. Abstract reason is a refinement of patterns of bodily experience. Sensory experience is not separable from rationality, then, because rationality is itself built from the image schemata derived from sensory experience. Image schemata are not backgrounds against which meaning emerges, they are part of that meaning.

Although space does not permit detailed recounting of Johnson's fascinating evidence for these claims here, a brief example may help. The experience of containment, or boundedness, is one of the most pervasive features of bodily experience, explains Johnson. Our *in–out* orientations result from our intimate awareness of our bodies as three-dimensional containers into which we put things, and out of which things emerge. From the very beginning, physical containment pervades our interaction with our surroundings as we move in and out of places and situations, or put things into and remove them from containers.

Each such experience has repeatable spatial and temporal structures, or schemata. "The experiential basis for *in–out* orientation is that of spatial boundedness," explains Johnson: of "being limited or held within some three-dimensional enclosure, such as a womb, a crib, or a room."[234] These recurring experiential image-schematic structures entail things like protection/resistance to external forces, sense of restraint, fixity of location, amenability to observation, and transitivity (such that if one is in bed and one's bed is in a room, one is also in the room). Two significant points become immediately apparent. First, the origin of these schemata, what gives rise to and gives sense to them, is our bodily experience of center-periphery and in-out. Second, these very spatial, temporal, and vectoral schemata are what we use to organize and make sense of all experience: "You wake *out* of a deep sleep and peer *out* from beneath the covers *into* your room. You gradually emerge *out* of your stupor, pull yourself *out* from under the covers, climb *into* your robe, stretch *out* your limbs, and walk *in* a daze *out* of the bedroom and *into* the bathroom. You look *in* the mirror and see your face staring *out* at you . . . Once you are more awake you might even get lost *in* the newspaper, might enter *into* a conversation, which leads to your speaking *out* on some topic."[235]

While some of these senses are clear-cut physical orientations in space, others are not: waking out of a sleep, speaking out, entering into conversation. Add to these relational dimensions experiences like up-down, near-far, left-right, front-back, toward-away, and so on, and the profound extent of our dependency upon such experiential structures becomes quite apparent. As Johnson goes on to show, the containment metaphor is one of our most common conceptual structurings. We enter into arguments. We back out of agreements. Indeed, the categorical sense that underlies concepts, propositions, and the principle of negation, is itself guided by containment experience: we understand categories as containers, such that what is appropriate to a category lies within it, and what is not lies outside. "Because schemata are so central to meaning structure, they influence the ways in which we can make sense of things and reason about them,"[236] says Johnson. And because we are animals, "it is only natural that our inferential patterns would emerge from our activities at the embodied level."[237]

The repercussions of exposing the concrete, corporeal roots of abstract thought are sweeping and dramatic. An embodied account of meaning does not require that concepts be utterly clear, logical entities with discrete boundaries. Since it can account for cognitive activity with something other than discrete, distinct concepts, it can accommodate ambiguity, shades of grey, multiplicity and variousness of meaning, and provide for such crucial cognitive events as intuitive hunches, discovery, and creativity. Image schemata derived from bodily action and experience have the dynamic, fluid character and polyvalence characteristic of human understanding. Perhaps most important for our purposes here, by illuminating the structural basis of cross-modal experience, it establishes the cognitive legitimacy of metaphorical descriptions of music, so that tactile, kinesthetic, gestural, and perhaps even gendered attributions assume a credibility denied them under objectivist accounts—where 'the notes' can mean nothing but themselves.

Revealing the bodily basis of mind enables us not only to assert, but to show how music is at once a cerebral and a bodily competence. It provides a helpful balance to disembodied accounts of 'music cognition' in which musical experience consists primarily of the detection and contemplation of abstract patterns of sound. Musical experience, both in its overtly active 'performative' mode and in its covertly active listening mode, consists of distinctive ways of being in the body. Unlike objectivism, this orientation is not awkwardly embarrassed by the presence of conspicuously corporeal features in music, or the suggestion that physical movement and gesture are musically significant. The body that experiences music is not just a hearing body, but the corporeal center that integrates the entire range of human experience. Accordingly, musical balance, musical force, even music's perennial patterns of ebb and flow, tension and release, 'in' and 'out' of tune, are not simply formal qualities addressed to an appreciative, disembodied mind. They are experiential structures learned by the body and recognized in other embodied experience that is similarly structured. Moreover, the bodily basis of musical meaning offers to explain how emotion or affect are integral to the experience of music, not mere postperceptual or extramusical associations. Indeed, the basic imaginative capacity of mapping structural similarities across experiential domains offers a powerful explanation for the extraordinary intermingling in musical experience of characteristics objectivist theory can only conceive as logically discrete, incompatible, and hence, irrational: the synesthetic blending that seems more the rule than the exception in music.

By integrating mind and body in experience, Johnson's theory also offers to explain the crucial significance of life experience to musical production, performance, and listening. The life experiences of the embodied mind are, on Johnson's theory, not separable from its musical ones. Since the structures of such experience become integral parts of the imaginative and interpretive powers deployed in musical experience, it is only reasonable that some musics seem to withhold their deepest meanings until people have lived and experienced more deeply, that suffering is sometimes regarded as an essential prerequisite for artistic achievement, or that the dazzling technical proficiency of a prodigy can so often seem to lack 'spiritual depth'. Necessary though they obviously are, highly refined technique and sophisticated formal knowledge cannot compensate for the richer, more complex interpretive schemata that come only from life experience and maturity.

Recovering mind's bodily basis undermines the presumed opposition between subject and object, form and content, process and product, and a whole range of troublesome binaries, revealing their continuity and showing how they partake of one another. At the same time, the polyvalence and multiplicity of embodied experience pluralizes music, replacing a singular objective entity, a 'piece' of music, with a striking range of potentially relevant interpretations. Musical meaning, no less than any other, is a perspectival affair. Among the comfortable categorical distinctions this account also undermines is the one between the musical and the social. For if experience is an important source of the image schemata by which we organize and make sense of our worlds, and if human experience is fundamentally social, our shared experiences are vitally important to music's meaning. How we relate to and interact with one another becomes part of music's fabric. And just as important, the patterns and relations in musical experience are integrated into and reflective of the structures by which we relate to one another socially. Thus, music and society are not discrete concerns, but reciprocally related and profoundly interactive. Music is a form of social discourse, a form of social reasoning, playing a vitally important role in the construction and maintenance of human society, and a valuable reflection of our patterns of social relatedness. And if the musical, the bodily, and the social are in fact coextensive, the idea of 'pure' music, of 'music itself', cannot stand.

If the body is in the mind, it is in music as well. And if it is in music, many of our most cherished and comfortable convictions about music's nature and value must be carefully reconsidered. Thus, we might well conclude, although phenomenology is indeed metaphorical, there is nothing 'mere' about metaphor. Whatever its potential shortcomings, phenomenology's success in persuading musical scholars of the import of speaking about music in ways that respect and reveal its bodily basis immensely benefits music philosophy.

Concluding Remarks

In this chapter we have explored a variety of theories that employ to some degree the philosophical method known as phenomenology. Devoted to the study of presences, phenomenological accounts attempt to get beneath the sedimentation of abstractions, to resist temptations to indulge in metaphysical theory building, in order to return us to beginnings, to music as it is actually lived or experienced.

In Merleau-Ponty's work, we saw a determined effort to found knowing not in ungrounded abstraction but in perception: bodily engagement with the world. This paves the way for accounts of music more fully capable of accommodating its tactile, gestural, and other bodily mediated dimensions. It also serves as an important reminder to those involved in music theorizing not to neglect the corporeal roots without which the idea of music would make little sense.

Dufrenne's accounts highlighted the quasi-subjectivity of music, the fact that music is not simply an object in the world the way things like mountains and trees are. Rather, it is experienced as something with interiority and depth — more like the way we relate to other people than to other objects.

Clifton's stirring descriptions of lived musical experience make it easy to understand the attraction phenomenology holds for many musicians. His effort to keep the experiencing subject center stage — the locus of meaning and value — is in many ways quite appealing, as are his perceptive accounts of the ways space, time, play, and feeling manifest themselves musically.

Burrows' ingenious investigation of the important role that sound — and, by extension, music — plays in human experience likewise raises intriguing issues for our consideration. As the "first, dark-born sibling of sight," hearing puts us in the world in ways profoundly different from any other experience. Hearing, as Hegel observed, is a bodily, inward, transient sense, radically unlike the clarity, stability, and cool inertness of the visual world. To hear, Burrows reminds, is to be touched, and to be involved. Thus, experience with music affirms our bond with the world and our 'aliveness' as few experiences can. Burrows' account of voice as the threshold between self and world, and of the music-making experience as a momentary omniscient state in which inner and outer (self and other) fuse as one, is richly descriptive of what many musicians consider the essence of musical experience.

We concluded this chapter's consideration of phenomenology with Stubley's inquiry into the transformative power of musical performance, and with a cursory examination of Johnson's evocative philosophical analysis of the bodily roots of cognition: reminders that the social and the bodily are important, many would say definitive, musical dimensions. Taken together, the theorists whose views we have surveyed in this chapter prove remarkably successful at revitalizing our views of music's nature and value, at bringing back into the musical fold qualities and attributes frequently dismissed as mere response, or mere context—and therefore extramusical.

Musical phenomenology's success at defusing the dualisms typical of idealistic thought has been, we must probably conclude, uneven. For as we have seen, musical phenomenology sometimes gravitates to an apparent extreme subjectivism which, on close examination, seems to impute subtly to music an objectivity at odds with phenomenological tenets. The belief that music can be, even approached phenomenologically, 'purely itself' is probably naive, as is the idea of a perceptual position that somehow steps outside of and avoids the supposed distortions of cultural situatedness. These concerns, however, do not wholly negate the method, nor do they alter its potential value for uncovering important musical truths obscured by habit and abstraction.

DISCUSSION QUESTIONS

1. Discuss how description relates to interpretation. How might the ideas of social situatedness, intersubjectivity, and consensus offer to resolve the dilemma presented by the impossibility of 'pure' musical description? What specific implications do these issues bear for musical analysis? for musical learning and instruction?

2. Merleau-Ponty's insistence that perception is an act of knowing, his denial of a world independent of that given to the senses (and therefore, the body), begets an account of cognition that is rich, corporeally informed, and inescapably 'partial'—that is, context-specific and context-relative. Is there a difference between truth, habit, and belief? Is it possible to study music alone, music as it is in itself? Or is music so inextricably intertwined with things like meanings, uses, and values that to study it without explicitly addressing such 'contextual' concerns is to distort it seriously?

3. How is the idea of knowing as an invariably bodily acquisition significant for music philosophy? For instance, how might you develop an argument that the sensuousness which has so troubled philosophers is in fact a con-

spicuous 'plus' for music, since its corporeal roots lie so near the surface, providing a more authentically human way of being in the world? How might this relate to Schiller's version of 'aesthetic' experience?

4. Dufrenne's idea of a 'quasi subject' suggests that we never experience music the way we do natural or material objects: that to experience musically is to engage a sonorous presence as we would another person. Explore this idea using an actual piece of music, distinguishing between the contributions of 'brute' sensuousness and imagination.

5. In one sense, Clifton's phrase 'applied phenomenology' is a tautology. Discuss how this might be so. How do music philosophy and music criticism converge in musical phenomenology and why?

6. Do Clifton's doubts about his right to demand that others experience music exactly as he does, and his claim that there is no such thing as 'bad music', mean that any and all ways of experiencing music are equally valid? Does this make all claims to musical value, all judgments of musical worth, strictly and profoundly personal? Why or why not? Do these convictions reduce all instruction to indoctrination?

7. To call something a musical 'essence' is to suggest it obtains universally, for all musics everywhere. Explore the applicability of Clifton's four essential substrates to a piece of popular music, and then to a piece of music from a non-Western tradition. What do you conclude about their claims to essential status?

8. Explore the body's role in perception of tonality and timbre. Is it possible to account for motions away from and toward tonal centers without invoking bodily engagement? Is it possible to describe tone quality without implicating the body? Explain.

9. How does the body mediate perception of musical 'gesture'? Is it possible to experience music as music without this bodily sense?

10. Discuss how Burrows attributes humankind's mental and spiritual life to the ways people experience sound and music. In your estimation, has Burrows succeeded in establishing that sonorous experience is a unique and necessary part of human experience? With these insights in mind, discuss what it might be like to be congenitally deaf.

11. If hearing is the "dark first-born sibling of sight," a fact seemingly supported by the preponderance of visual metaphors for trustworthy knowledge, how is it that sonorous experience plays so important a role in opening up 'Field 2'? In other words, how does something so ambiguous, fleeting, and processual help create a conceptual realm whose significance is defined by the opposite qualities?

12. Watch part of a television show without sound, then without picture. How do sound and sight differ in constructing the experience? Which do

you think contributes more substantially to the notorious seductiveness and hypnotic effects of the medium? Why?

13. Explore the way the sound track contributes to and shapes the mood or character of a movie, and the way background music enhances (or detracts from) a shopping or dining experience. In what ways does sound function as more than sonic wallpaper? Does this raise any potentially ethical issues for you?

14. Burrows situates voice at the nexus of self and other, center and periphery, and places 'self' in an experiential field that constantly dilates and contracts. Do you think there is a durable substrate of 'self', or is one's identity always in a state of flux as Burrows' accounts seem to suggest? Of what significance is this question to music philosophy?

15. What does the radical difference between visual and aural experience suggest about the status of things like scores and of activities like analysis in the study of music?

16. Stubley's and Burrows' accounts both seem to suggest that music making consists in a reciprocal, reflexive process of discovering and creating both music and oneself: in an exploration of the interface between self and other. Can you build on this idea to create a defense of musical performance's distinctive educational significance? Can musical performance develop 'character'? How so?

17. Listen several times to a passage of music you find deeply meaningful. How is the body involved? Specifically how and where does the experience build on image schemata derived from bodily actions? Might that experience differ if you had a different body—say, a congenitally paraplegic one, or one of a different sex? How?

18. How does musicianship, proficiency and fluency as a performer, alter the way you hear music? Is it possible to set this aside in listening? How does the listening experience of the nonmusician likely differ from that of someone who has extensively engaged in music making?

Music as Social and Political Force

The views we explore in this chapter grow out of convictions that whatever else it may be, music is fundamentally social. It is a cultural phenomenon, and not just incidentally or parenthetically. 'The social' does not relate to music as 'context', a container into which music proper is somehow inserted, a background against which 'music itself' is perceived. The social is an inextricable part of what music *is*, and accounts that presume it can be understood apart from that sociocultural situatedness err, and err profoundly. The theories examined here take the seemingly innocuous fact of music's social status and use it to effect provocative, dramatic transformations of the way music is conceived—views that challenge above all the belief that there exists a level on which music is inherently and exclusively musical, wholly uninvolved with anything outside itself.

Those who espouse the social view of music maintain that music is always and fundamentally a mode of human activity, something people do with or for each other. As such, its true nature cannot be adequately grasped by looking inward, as phenomenology and psychology often seem inclined to do, or 'outward', as formalists sometimes seem to do. Music is socially constructed, socially embedded, and its nature and value are inherently social. Musical practices are not the kind of things that have a fixed, durable, objective 'essence' or inner core; they are constituted by collective human actions. The notion of a music in-itself, of 'music alone', is one that not only impedes and distorts understanding, it is deeply pernicious because it encourages people to overlook what may in fact be most important about music: the ways it shapes and defines human society. Music is not something that occasionally and tangentially serves social ends, then: it is itself social, always and already.

Such convictions significantly complicate discussions of music by situating it, for instance, amidst struggles for power and influence, and by insisting upon the musical relevance of the kinds of social relatedness music reflects, represents, reinforces, or generates. But from a social perspective, music is never a 'pure', self-contained thing, however convenient and reassuring that may be to believe. It is cultural, and culture is constantly being created, recreated, modified, contested, and negotiated. As well, music's sociocultural facts pose significant challenges to ideas like musical autonomy and the existence of culturally invariant musical universals. As sociocultural constructions, musical values and functions are not 'absolute', but relative: culturally specific, and as fluid, various, diverse, and unstable as culture itself. From the perspective of the views it undermines, these may sound like negative claims. But for those who advance the social view of music, they are vivifying ideas: convictions that promise to confer upon music renewed senses of potency and force, of relevance and import wrongly taken from music by the misguided doctrine of musical autonomy.

This chapter begins with the an examination of the thought of **Theodor Adorno** (1903–1969), whose theories pose radical challenges to the traditional philosophical assumption that music can be understood apart from its sociocultural roots. In his view, music interacts with and shapes social consciousness, and not casually or optionally. Truly great music has a fundamental social obligation to advance human consciousness and thereby social progress. On the other hand, cheap, tawdry music which panders to mass taste is hardly a harmless diversion: its mind-numbing nature shapes consciousness, too, only in a purely negative, regressive way. Guided by these deep convictions, Adorno creates a strongly normative, hierarchical account of musical value, in which the distinguishing characteristic of truly 'modern' music is its capacity to confront and challenge consciousness or awareness, and to undermine 'false consciousness' rooted in stereotype and habit. Such 'false consciousness' is, however, precisely popular music's stock in trade. Created by a commercial culture industry for mass consumption, popular music reinforces and perpetuates mindless perception, 'thought' that is critically unaware. Even though this strongly normative, hierarchical conception of musical value no longer has much currency among theorists who interpret music socially, Adorno's influence has been and continues to be immense. By wrenching music from the realm of autonomous, aesthetic insularity, Adorno paved the way for explanations of music's nature and value that challenge some of music philosophy's most cherished and time-honored beliefs. As something that is fundamentally and invariably social, music is never innocent, never pure. In fact, myths of purity and innocence themselves serve the sociopolitical end of masking music's social complicity, sustaining the social status quo while going unacknowledged, unexamined, and unchallenged.

For Adorno, the best (the most modern) music is music that resists soporific consumption, challenging people's expectations and habitual modes of musical perception, thereby helping to resist society's deeply troubling drift toward unthinking conformity, unconscious passivity, and capitulation to the dehumanizing forces of monopoly capitalism. Music that caters to easy consumption or to a communal sense of togetherness is ideological: it dulls people's awareness of the individual, of difference, and of particularity, creating an all-is-well state of mind which facilitates a kind of collective brainwashing, an uncritical consciousness totally determined by outside forces. Good music resists comfortable consumption and popularity: it attacks the law of the marketplace. By contrast, inferior music—light music, easy-listening music, popular music—actually serves to maim consciousness. Thus, in Adorno's view, good (modern) music plays a crucial redemptive social function by refusing to capitulate to commercialism and conformity, keeping alive some small remnant of mental and social independence. And bad (regressive) music serves the social end of reinforcing passivity and conformity, making the dehumanizing influences and depravities of capitalism seem not only natural and inevitable, but pleasant.

Like Adorno, **Jacques Attali** (b. 1943) finds music a potent social force, something whose roots extend directly and deeply into some of humankind's most pressing concerns. In his view, not only is music a social fact, it is deeply implicated in the construction of socioeconomic and sociopolitical relations. In fact, musical practices reflect such relations directly, immediately, and with remarkable accuracy. Accordingly, music registers and indicates changes in sociopolitical and socioeconomic relations long before they become apparent elsewhere, and can even be read as a kind of barometer of sociopolitical change.

The human experience of sound, Attali suggests, is a fundamentally threatening and disorderly affair; and how societies control and order it in musical practices affords valuable insights into how they structure political power and accommodate differences. From this, Attali creates an account of music's historical development that contrasts strikingly with those to which most musicians are accustomed. Music is, Attali maintains, among our most important tools for creating and consolidating community, a potent force linking power to its subjects. This force he attributes to the distinctive way humans experience sound. A primordial sign of the presence of danger, sound is experienced immediately, directly, powerfully: it is unsurpassed in its capacity to startle and to demand attention. Sound is also a fundamentally abstract and ambiguous sense. Because of all this, noise represents threat or violence, and its control is a clear manifestation of power. Thus, music's regulation of sound amounts to a powerful ritual enactment of power, and music is an important agent of social control. Indeed, suggests Attali, the history of music can be read as the history of the effort to get people to believe in and accept consensual social order. Different ways of making or engaging in music should be seen, then, as reinforcing different modes of social relatedness, different ways of structuring the relationship between the individual and the collective, different ways of conceiving and modeling 'appropriate' relations to power.

On the views we will examine in this chapter and the next, music is not just influenced by social circumstance; human social orders are constructed and sustained in vitally important ways by their musical practices. And as a powerful shaper of human consciousness, identity, and social order, music becomes the locus of radical and wide-ranging critique and contestation. As a sociopolitical force, then, music emerges from the realm of marginal human interests to resume a place of pivotal influence and profound significance in the human world.

Adorno: The Critical Social Function of Music

Theodor W. Adorno was a fiercely individualistic intellectual whose ideas stubbornly and deliberately defy summary and paraphrase. Translators have in fact described his work as untranslatable.[1] One authority calls him "cryptic," "paratactical," and "eccentric,"[2] while others choose words like "labyrinthine," "obscure," "dense," "arcane," and "contradictory," and still another remarks that Adorno sometimes reads like "a jaggedly compiled aggregate missing a host of internal connections."[3] Adorno himself would probably be appalled at attempts to render his ideas more easily accessible, observes one commentator.[4] Indeed, he might well have considered a clear and orderly exposition of his ideas proof positive they had been misunderstood. Adorno's notorious difficulty is hardly accidental. Rose Subotnik explains, "Adorno's esoteric effect is in large measure a by-product of the great care Adorno takes to define and preserve a concept of individual integrity through his use of words, by choosing each word with precision, refusing (like the twelve-tone composer in the musical medium) to augment his words with redundant explanations or appositives, and giving the impression that every decision . . . every detail, and every connection in a highly individualized entity matters in the extreme, so that no element can be adequately duplicated, replaced or summarized."[5] Most would agree that if this was Adorno's intent, he was highly successful. Yet despite their stubborn resistance to summary, his ideas are far too significant, provocative, and influential to escape the effort.

The concern for the integrity of the individual to which Subotnik refers is among the most recurrent themes in Adorno's philosophy. In a near-perfect inversion of idealism, Adorno's principle of 'non-identity' maintains that individuality and particularity are more fundamental than generality and similarity. For Kant, recall, what made knowledge possible was a kind of congruence between the objects of consciousness and the a priori structures governing them. Knowing and perceiving, then, were functions of the compatibility between particular things and events and the interpretive schemata that mediated their grasp. For Adorno, however, to know something only as an example or instance of something else is to neglect what is distinctive and different about it: to miss what it *is*. Authentic knowing or perceiving is not so much about similarity as difference, not a matter of identity but of non-identity.

Thus Adorno strenuously resists what he regards as the tyranny of generalization, all universalizing or 'totalizing' agendas, all attempts to smooth over discontinuity, distinctness, and difference. He is resolutely unwilling to participate in the kind of distortion introduced when abstraction lumps together things that are individual and particular. Conceptual and perceptual habit, he seems to believe, is a potent instrument of false consciousness. Such habits cover over the cracks and fissures of particular reality with slick veneers of sameness. Thought and perception that are not sufficiently critical make people mindless followers and acquiescent consumers—not in control of their own destinies, but the unwitting victims of ideology. So Adorno wants nothing to do with the idealist's a priori truths, timeless absolutes, and universals. Instead, he espouses a critical consciousness rooted in awareness of individuality, multiplicity, and change, one that renounces the neatness and comfort of habitual modes of awareness for the messiness, difficulty, and complexity of non-identity.

Adorno's writing is remarkably consistent with these convictions. Rather than use logical analysis leading to generalization, he sets up dialectical tensions and leaves them deliberately unresolved: 'constellations' or 'force fields' of opposing ideas whose contradictoriness is crucial to their meaning. Instead of transforming particularity and difference into sameness, he works to honor what makes them distinct. Since in order to do that he must subvert convention, stereotype, and habit, his ideas seem to defy paraphrase as a matter of fundamental principle.

These convictions are central features of his philosophical accounts of music, too, for like good philosophy, he believes, good music should defy effortless consumption. Awareness that is truly critical or authentic is not, he believes, like a warm, cozy bed, all prepared and waiting for us to snuggle in. His disdain for the easily accessible led Adorno to deprecate (often indiscriminately) music designed for facile consumption by the masses. It also led him to develop a philosophy of 'modern' music, in which music has a fundamental obligation to challenge consciousness critically and thereby advance society. Like philosophy, music should complicate the easy, undermine the habitual, and challenge the status quo, thereby creating critical awareness of the problems and contradictions, the alienation and suffering, inherent in modern life. These convictions and his deep suspicion of totalizing claims thus led Adorno to wrestle with two extraordinarily complex issues that, as it turns out, have become matters of paramount concern for twenty-first-century music philosophy: "the problem of how to philosophize in the absence of ontological 'givens', and how to write an aesthetics after the destruction of aesthetic norms."[6]

Raised in a rich musical environment, Adorno's early passion for philosophical inquiry grew hand in hand with conspicuous musical talents and interests. His early circle of acquaintances included an impressive array of seminal artists, critics, and philosophers who shared his interest in art's capacity to shape and modify social consciousness. Eventually, he became associated with the Institute for Social Research in Frankfurt (the so-called 'Frankfurt school'), an interdisciplinary group of leftist intellectuals who were the architects of 'critical theory', a program devoted to exploring the relations between mass and individual consciousness, with particular attention to the effects of propaganda and culture. During the Second World War Adorno lived in exile in the United States, an experience that freed him from "culture-bound naivety," as he put it, and significantly enhanced his "ability to see culture from the outside."[7] Adorno's 'outsider' perspective manifests itself both in a kind of melancholy pessimism and in a remarkable capacity to defamiliarize the familiar. It is also undoubtedly an important factor in the independent perspective from which he launched his devastating critiques of uncritical compliance. In the years after the war,

Adorno and his fellow critical theorists brought intense scrutiny to bear on 'totalizing tendencies' in political, intellectual, and cultural life — not only in totalitarian regimes, but in capitalistic democracies as well. Adorno was deeply concerned about people's vulnerability to sociopolitical influence, the kind of passivity that enabled fascist and totalitarian regimes to flourish and made atrocities like Auschwitz possible. The obvious fact of totalitarian group-think, and Adorno's recognition that capitalist democracies were no less disposed to unthinking conformity, made him deeply suspicious toward all 'totalizing' claims, and convinced him that critical awareness was utterly essential for social progress.

Adorno was far too intellectually independent to be regarded simply as a Marxist. He was nothing *simply*. And yet, critical theory's neo-Marxist lineage is essential to an adequate grasp of his thought. Adorno and the critical theorists saw both the alarming spread of Nazi and Stalinist power and the rapid growth of capitalism as clear indications that socialism had failed. Clearly, Marx had been mistaken in predicting the overthrow of bourgeois oppression by a revolutionary proletariat. His basic impulses and intuitions were correct, but changes in society and consciousness Marx simply could not have foreseen meant that his theories required revision and refinement. Critical theory thus undertook to reconstruct and refine Marx's critiques of exploitation and oppression, showing how social and cultural institutions perpetuate the false consciousness that protects existing power structures from critical scrutiny by mystifying sources of oppression. It sought to understand how the consciousness of the proletariat had become so highly susceptible to manipulation, and to better understand how to nurture the kind of authentic consciousness that might reverse society's alarming acceptance of political and social domination.

One of Marx's primary philosophical concerns had been to reconcile the subject-object relationship so radically polarized by idealism. Idealists of an objective bent (Kant, for instance) had treated reality as a 'given', somehow separate from the knowing mind, while those of a subjective bent (like Hegel) had reduced all reality to consciousness. Against these two untenable extremes, Marx maintained that reality is neither objectively 'given' nor the creation of a subjective consciousness. The relation between subject and object is not one in which mind passively contemplates sense data, nor is reality whatever people's minds make it. Consciousness is, rather, a fundamentally social construction, shaped and directed by the social, material, and economic conditions in which it occurs.

Because economic, material, and social forces shape consciousness, it follows that different sociopolitical arrangements give rise to distinctive kinds of consciousness. In capitalist societies, specialized production and division of labor have profoundly alienated people from what they produce. As the link between human agency and what it produces is weakened and obscured, the world is viewed increasingly in terms of relationships among things, rather than people. Even ideas assume the status of objects or natural things, seemingly free of social and economic influences. Thus, as the economic and social origins of thought are obscured, ideas take on the appearance of inevitability and immutability. An ideological superstructure develops, one that effaces historical and social context, and self-servingly portrays ideas as objective, universal, natural, and necessary.

As Marx saw it, maintaining this ideological superstructure is crucial to those who wield power: it assures that people regard the existing order as something inevitable. However, that consciousness is false and distorted: it is an ideological deception that serves to legitimate and perpetuate inequitable, exploitative economic and political arrangements. Idealism's claims to universality, then, are at root political. By severing ideas from the power relationships that give rise to them, idealism convinces people to impute autonomy and absoluteness to things that are really contingent and historical constructions, thereby rationalizing the relationships that sustain the ruling class's power. Ideology thus consists of vested sociocultural interests which claim accord with natural laws. To the extent these values are acritically accepted, they undermine critical awareness; they legitimate the status quo by making things appear natural, enduring, and nonnegotiable when they are not.

At the same time, capitalistic societies' preoccupation with producing commodities leads people to value things less for their immediate consumption or use than for their status as abstract units for potential exchange: 'use value' becomes less important than 'exchange value'. So although labor is the source of whatever value exchangeable commodities have, capitalist ideology mystifies and obscures the relationship between labor and value. Products become fetishes, impersonal things with values apparently all their own. As a result, commodity production transforms relations between people into relations between things, and people's lives become increasingly defined by the exchangeability of the commodities they produce. Because of commodity fetishism, things assume higher value than humans, and social relations deteriorate into mere exchange relations.

Lukacs' application of Marxist economic and political principles to the area of culture was an immensely important influence on Adorno and the Frankfurt School. Where orthodox Marxists treated commodity fetishism as an economic phenomenon, Lukacs extended it to the broader domain of class consciousness. In his view, idealism's mystification of its sociohistorical roots shared a common source with capitalism's obfuscation of the link between products and the labor which produced them. This commodity problem permeated virtually every aspect of class consciousness. To Marx's ideas, Lukacs also added the concept of 'reification', in which abstract values come to be treated as material 'things', amenable to exchange and consumption. Reification operates in cultural spheres as well, as cultural artifacts and practices with abstract values come to be treated as commodities demanding superstitious and sometimes extravagant devotion. Reification, commodification, and fetishization thus conspire to erode awareness of the fact of human agency. In so doing, they create and sustain the illusion that the system of commodity production is immutable, and the 'use value' of cultural artifacts gradually degenerates into mere 'exchange value'.

Reification has the social effect of reducing people from active agents to passive spectators, witnesses to processes over which they feel no sense of control. People become powerless cogs in the capitalistic machine. Lukacs writes,

". . . as the capitalist system continuously produces and reproduces itself economically on higher and higher levels, the structure of reification progressively
sinks more deeply, more fatefully and more definitively into the consciousness
of man."[8] Thus, the class situation mediates not only economic processes, but
cognitive and cultural ones as well. And one way to understand Adorno's work
is as an attempt to demystify this commodity fetishization: to show how it serves
the forces of domination by desensitizing people and making appear impersonal,
natural, universal, and inevitable things that are in fact particular and contingent.

This difficult task was complicated enormously by the extent to which the
proletariat had already succumbed to capitalistic ideology, as well as by the consolidation of political and economic power in 'state capitalism'. Even Western
democracies thus increasingly resembled what Adorno frequently calls the "totally administered society." His critical philosophy strives to expose and undermine the social structures that make people vulnerable to domination, whether
in capitalistic democracies or overtly totalitarian regimes. Only through critical
awareness, he believed, could false consciousness be undone, emancipating people from the tenacious grip of totalizing ideology.

Thus, Adorno's critical perspective stresses the integrity of the particular (the
nonidentical), refusing to sacrifice the individual to the inherent distortions of
generalization and abstraction. In this quest, Adorno's unresolved dialectical constellations are one of his primary tools. The other is radical modern art. The role
of each within his critique of ideology lies precisely in its capacity to undermine
the habitual, stereotypical modes of thought and perception that serve the 'administered world' and the forces of domination.

Music's Social Significance

With this as background, we are in a position to begin more specific examination of Adorno's ideas about art and music. As we have seen, Adorno thought art
and philosophy shared a common cognitive purpose, or more accurately, obligation: to shock, or jar, exposing contradictions in a way that undermines false or
ideological consciousness. Knowledge molded by conceptual categories falsifies
its object. Systematization betrays difference by imposing unity upon the multiply distinct, similarity upon the individual. Authentic knowledge is knowledge
that breaks the mold of conventionality and familiarity, entering more fully (more
authentically) into the objects of consciousness. Efforts to totalize knowledge and
experience, to represent it as being the same for everyone, undermine authentic
experience and individual autonomy. In an increasingly administered society, the
problems of reification and domination converge, and the uniqueness of both
things and ideas is falsified by the category. Thus, 'common sense' ideas and art
created for effortless consumption by the masses fail to fulfill their social (cognitive) obligation. Worse yet, they dull critical awareness, nurturing passive reception and paving the way for domination. Popular or mass culture thus contributes
directly to the reification of consciousness by substituting a kind of standardized
pseudoexperience for the authentic experience of autonomous individuals.

For Adorno, acquiescence to such conventional modes of thought and perception seriously erodes the individual's capacity for free choice, creating a false sense of uniformity that in turn leads to resigned acceptance of standardization. In such a society, consumers come to mistake superficial fashion for genuine novelty, consensus for truth, popularity for value. A society placated by pseudonovelty is lulled into a lazy sense of unwarranted complacency, an attitude that vitiates all possibility for genuine social change or progress. Thus Adorno's commitment to restoring individual autonomy and critical awareness, exposing how vested interests masquerade as natural or universal laws.

One of the most distinctive features of Adorno's critical philosophy is the pivotal role it assigns to modern art, or more specifically, to music. In orthodox Marxist accounts, all music functions ideologically to perpetuate bourgeois consciousness. But in Adorno's view, that is not necessarily or invariably the case. As producer and laborer, the musician—particularly the composer of autonomous music—can take up the subversive task of which the proletariat is apparently no longer capable. In its forms, its dissonances, and its discontinuities, truly 'modern' music has the capacity to undermine the sense of organic wholeness that lulls people into the false belief that all is well. Thus, though music often functions ideologically, it can also function redemptively. It may function as an instrument of propaganda or as a bearer of truth (if only by resisting propaganda). Music can serve the status quo, but it can also resist it. Music, Adorno insists, is "never purely natural material, but rather a social and historical product . . ."[9] Since it "recognizes no natural law,"[10] its nature and value are not immutable or invariant. Music in modern society is situated between two dialectically opposite poles: as a commodity, it perpetuates false consciousness; as social critique, it subverts ideology and serves authentic consciousness. Whether a music is good or bad can never be determined by examining purely intrinsic qualities: that is mystification, a smoke screen. A music's value can only be determined in light of critically evaluated social and historical facts. The most salient of these facts for Adorno, however, were rather gloomy. "The role of music in the social process," he asserts, "is exclusively that of a commodity; its value is that determined by the market."[11]

Although music would seem, particularly because of its particularity and ability to avoid the totalizing tendencies of language, ideally suited to Adorno's critical agenda, its commodification greatly complicates matters. Since music's positive potential is achieved only where it resists capitalism's transformation of all values into easily consumed commodities, modern music must resist the seductive lure of accessibility and communicability. It must challenge convention and easy reception.

Among the musics that best exemplify these qualities, in Adorno's view, was the early atonal work of Schoenberg. By subverting traditional and habitual modes of (tonal) musical perception, Schoenberg's music showed that the apparent naturalness and necessity of tonality was really only contingent. By resisting convention, it revealed the historicity and arbitrariness of tonality, undermining its domination. At the same time, by refusing to cater to easy consumption such music staunchly defied the forces of reification and fetishism.

In their internal structures and relations, then, Schoenberg's works challenged and contradicted totalizing influences. By undermining society's tendency to cover over difference with similarity, they serve to awaken people to particularity and difference. By subverting the habitual, modern music advances consciousness.

So despite the pervasiveness of commodification, it appears at least some music manages to evade the invidious influence of ideology, thereby performing a social function of inestimable importance. Only, since in order to do this music has to resist easy communicability, 'modern' music faces quite a dilemma. To fulfill its social obligation music must be autonomous; but the very cohesiveness that makes its autonomy possible must be resisted in order to fulfill its social obligation.

In "On the Social Situation of Music," Adorno sets out to show how various musics subvert and enhance consciousness in contemporary society. Music can be read, he believes, as a kind of social text. It is capable of revealing with utmost clarity "the contradictions and flaws which cut through present-day society."[12] And yet, music and contemporary society have also become profoundly alienated from each other by the petrifying effects of commodification. People today seldom grasp anything but music's "ruins and external remains."[13] It no longer fulfills the genuine human needs it once did. Its once-conspicuous social and participatory character have been crushed by capitalism's relentless embrace of commodity exchange. Music has become less a social process, less a mode of human action and interaction, and more an article for consumption.

A powerful "culture industry" has extended its control even into the intimate and meaningful musical sphere of domestic music making, until, rather than making music together, people now prefer to have it made for themselves by others. Music so produced and disseminated has lost both its individuality and its sense of immediacy. "Through the total absorption of both musical production and consumption by the capitalistic process," Adorno asserts, "the alienation of music from man has become complete."[14] The forces of reification that elevated sociomusical practice to the status of 'art' have now "taken music from man and left him with only an illusion . . . thereof."[15] If not all music has succumbed equally to these forces, certainly none has escaped their influence. Music that resists reification and commodification, refusing to relinquish its individuality, is, however, largely incomprehensible to most people in contemporary society. It is marginalized, cut off, compelled to exist in exile. Profoundly alienated and seemingly irrelevant, music that most tries to meet its social responsibilities is least able to do so.

Because music is itself a social fact, it cannot directly resolve the problem of its own alienation. The most it can do is "portray within its own structure the social antinomies which are also responsible for its own isolation."[16] This critical portrayal or revelation is, Adorno believes, music's social function today. Music "fulfills its social function more precisely when it presents social problems through its own material and according to its own formal laws—problems which music contains within itself in the innermost cells of its technique."[17] Socially responsible music thus attempts to do intramusically what critical social theory attempts to do in its own sphere: to confront false consciousness. To neglect this critical task would be to capitulate to fetishism, thereby perpetuating "the major difficulty and most basic problem"[18] that today's music needs to portray. So under no conditions must music be regarded as "a 'spiritual' phenomenon, abstract and far removed from actual social conditions."[19] The only way it can maintain its right to exist is to resist the gravitational pull of fetishization and reification that lies behind appeals to spirituality. 'Modern' music does this by challenging easy consumption, by demanding critical perception, and by denying society's fetishistic tendency to shroud it in mystery and reverence. 'Modern' music, like critical philosophy, is obliged to attempt to transform "the current consciousness of the masses."[20] To do this it must both engage and extend that consciousness.

Music that caters to familiarity, comfort, and easy communication unwittingly aggravates the problem of its own alienation by capitulating to the forces of fetishization. On the other hand, music that wholly renounces communication for the esoteric and the private lends credence to the misguided notion that musical tastes and preferences are just matters of "primitive musical immediacy," a belief that legitimates and licenses uninformed, narrow-minded judgments. Such beliefs, Adorno thinks, have been promoted "to the point of neurotic stupidity" precisely to keep awareness naive and critically unaware.[21] Although music must extend and refine people's consciousness, music which pursues that obligation by subordinating its own integrity to utilitarian ends errs as well, for that instrumentality plays once again to the forces of commodification.

The 'most advanced' modern music, then, is music that pursues its social obligation not by attempting social 'relevance', not by pursuing popularity or utility, but rather "by developing within music itself . . . those elements whose objective is the overcoming of class domination."[22] Music fulfills its social role best when it presents social problems in its own materials and forms. Any music that, as Adorno puts it, wants to preserve its 'right to exist' must, through its formal configurations, present challenges to mind; it must give 'clear form' to the problems immanent in its materials, which are never 'natural' but always sociohistorical products. Thus, authentically 'modern' music's solutions to its dilemma have the same critical status as philosophy. As a fundamentally social phenomenon, distinctions between music's musical and social value are completely spurious: music's socially critical function is exercised within its own formal language and technique.

Although the 'most advanced' music does not capitulate to the demands of the marketplace or the forces of commodity fetishism, that is hardly true of most music. A few musics resist, but most are unwittingly complicitous. What Adorno wants to show is the difference between the "quantitatively dominant"[23] music which reaffirms the status quo by catering to passive consumption, and music that, by refusing to conform to trend and fashion, "expresses alienation"— not programatically, but within its formal and structural configurations. So far as he is concerned, the vast majority of music in modern society unfortunately falls within the category of consumer music, 'use' music, or 'light' music—popular music, jazz, and so on. By catering to immediate needs, light music acts as kind of soothing salve, a seemingly innocuous diversion from social misery, a distraction. Light music trivializes consciousness, yet evades critical exposure in two ways. "First of all, it is looked upon as harmless—as a minor happiness of which man must not be robbed. Further, it is viewed as lacking in seriousness and unworthy of educated consideration."[24] But Adorno emphatically rejects the notion that light music is ideologically neutral: indeed, "as pure commodity, it is most alien of all music to society."[25] Belief in its harmlessness helps keep its ideological effects invisible. And as Adorno rightly observes, "Organized scholarship has paid no attention to any of this."[26]

It would be a mistake, however, to reduce the contrast between critically responsible and ideological music to one between 'serious' and 'light' music: for much of what is commonly regarded as 'serious' music, says Adorno, is equally guilty of pandering to popular tastes. Many of the 'classics' portray harmonious, unalienated conditions that no longer pertain to the modern social situation, and cater primarily to nostalgia—at considerable cost to critical awareness. Once part of the canon, they become museum pieces with the same fetishized commodity character as entertainment music. The classical 'pops' are objects for fashionable consumption, diversions rather than vehicles for refining critical awareness. Thus, 'serious' music of the past functions as a kind of upper-class hit parade with patterns of marketing, distribution, and consumption that are virtually indistinguishable from those of light music. Because they dull rather than sharpen consciousness, light music and use music serve as propaganda for the forces of domination.

"Objectivist" composers (Stravinsky is Adorno's favorite example) may recognize the problem of alienation, but judging from their compositions they apparently do not fully appreciate how profound that problem actually is. Unlike the music of the Second Viennese School, in which awareness of total alienation is everywhere apparent, the compositional practices of objectivist composers betray the misguided assumption that alienation can be fixed by ignoring it. Rather than confronting the problem, they retreat to styles and forms of the past, wrongly believing that these forms have a timelessness (an "objectivity") that can somehow evade modern life's ubiquitous alienation. However, says Adorno, "such forms cannot be reconstituted within a completely changed society and through completely changed musical material."[27] Objectivists wrongly attribute to past musical forms the capacity to transcend their time and place, to unify what modern life has torn asunder; they attempt to "evoke the image of a non-existent 'objective' society or . . . 'fellowship'."[28] They naively assume that pre-bourgeois musical forms can resurrect what they nostalgically regard as music's "original natural state."[29] But it is fundamentally mistaken to believe that nonmodern music has the kind of objective timelessness that permits it to speak to the radically different social conditions of today. Today's sociohistorical (cultural) circumstances are profoundly changed. Eternal modes of expression and timeless truths are ideological smoke screens, Adorno thinks, and efforts to return music to its former state of innocence are hopelessly naive and regressive. The belief that worn-out solutions of the past can be revitalized or recycled shows that objectivist composers like Stravinsky profoundly underestimate the severity of the problems facing modern music and modern society.

The sense of organic wholeness objectivists pursue in their music is illusory, and they are socially naive to conceive alienation as a merely intramusical or stylistic problem. In fact, when efforts to overcome alienation are confined to the level of artistic imagery, "alienation is permitted to continue unchanged in reality ... [because the] audience is already too far removed from music to place central importance upon such configurations."[30] By failing to recognize the social dimension of musical alienation and failing to appreciate the dimensions of the problem, objectivists' music actually insults society.

Music deliberately crafted to foster a sense of community is closely related to objectivist music in its belief that music can overcome social alienation through its own materials and practices. Like objectivism, communal music diverts attention from social conditions rather than confronting them. "It attempts to make the individual believe that he is not lonely, but rather close to all others in a relationship portrayed for him by music without defining its own social function."[31] However, in capitalist societies, this ideal of a "human state of togetherness" is only "a fiction."[32] Both objectivist and communal music are thus purveyors of illusory and false consciousness. They erode people's critical awareness, lulling them into sleepy complacency. Because they attempt to evade alienation rather than come to terms with it, such musics are nothing but "aesthetically elevated 'use' music."[33]

Adorno's concern over this regression to outmoded forms, and over naive attempts to restore community, extends well beyond the musical practices themselves, though: the broader issue is the way such practices encourage society's increasing acquiescence to administration. At the heart of the "estate-corporative organization" of industrial capitalism is an image of conformity, he believes. In it, "the sovereign composer stands in free control of the supposed musical organism, in much the same way that in fascism a 'leadership elite' ... appears to be in control, while in truth power over the social 'organism' lies in the hands of monopoly capitalism."[34] Thus, implicit in the objectivists' conception of the relation between composer and music is a disturbing, even potentially fascistic tendency, wherein musical decisions are guided not so much by the demands of the musical material as by the arbitrary will of the composer. Rather than a process that arises out of respect for the integrity of music's immanent meaning, composition consists in the imposition of personal taste.

In addition to the blatantly commercial 'use music' and the 'aesthetically elevated use music' discussed above, Adorno describes yet another kind of use music. The "surrealist" composer, as Adorno calls Kurt Weill, is "socially more alert than the objectivist and recognizes the solutions offered by his [objectivist] colleague as illusions. He denies himself a positive solution and contents himself with permitting social flaws to manifest themselves ... with no attempt at camouflage through attempts at an aesthetic totality."[35] The surrealist composer combines or juxtaposes the conventions of bourgeois music with the stereotypes of crass consumer music to create a self-consciously artificial montage whose fractured surface negates pretenses to aesthetic wholeness. Recognizing that the objectivist's way of dealing with alienation is a pseudosolution, the surrealist resists the false comfort of an apparently affirmative stance. The surrealist composer thus forgoes objectivism's quest for smooth 'organic' wholeness, and instead creates compositions out of "rubble and fragment," out of "falsehood and illusion."[36] Showing people their own 'use' music through the "distorting mirror" of surrealistic method confronts them with the fact of its commodity character. Thus, surrealistic music defamiliarizes the familiar in a way that reveals the triteness and ideological character that escape detection in habitual musical experience. In Adorno's vivid words, it "overexposes common compositional means, unmasking them as ghosts, expresses alarm about the society within which they have their origin and, at the same time [negates] the possibility of a positive communal music, which collapses in the laughter of devilish vulgar music, as which true use music is exposed."[37]

Adorno's characterizations of objectivist, communal, and surrealist music provide a context from which the full social significance of Schoenberg's musical achievements can now be more fully appreciated. Schoenberg understands and confronts the problem of alienation. Unlike the objectivist, he does not retreat to the false comfort of pre-existent forms and conventions. Rather than cater to listeners' needs for reassurance, he takes his directions strictly from the internal demands of his musical material. Indeed, Schoenberg seems to have created a music free of overt social function, one which "severs the last communication with the listener."[38] Because his music is unsurpassed in terms of "immanently musical quality" and "dialectical clarification of its material," it presents "such a perfected and rational total organization that it cannot possibly be compatible with the present social constitution."[39]

In this incompatibility, this refusal to subordinate itself to the laws of consumption and the market place, are the seeds both of music's autonomy and its capacity to elevate critical consciousness. Schoenberg's music is one that, "without consciousness of its social location or out of indifference toward it, presents and crystallizes its problems . . . in a merely immanent manner."[40] Schoenberg refrains from imposing his "subjective intentions upon heterogenous material in an authoritarian and inconsiderate manner."[41] By resisting the temptation to shape the music from the outside, willfully, in accordance with his private tastes, he assures that his interventions are always solutions to problems that arise inside music. And yet, since music's materials are never purely natural but always social and historical products, his musical solutions are not strictly musical either. Indeed, they "stand equal to theories."[42] Schoenberg refuses to retreat from alienation, pursuing it rather to its logical conclusion. And because it demands critical perception, his music furthers the cause of critical consciousness. Thus, Schoenberg's music expresses social alienation immanently, within its own forms and structures.

Adorno vehemently rejects the kind of "consumer consciousness" which seeks protection from music's true cognitive force by retreating to music that "conceal[s] reality through dream, intoxication, and inward contemplation."[43] Such music is ideological in that it supports "a form of satisfaction which accepts and stabilizes the existing consciousness, rather than revealing through its own form social contradictions, translating them into form and cognition regarding the structure of society."[44] The basic law of bourgeois musical practice, concludes Adorno, is "the relation between the satisfaction of needs and ideological obscurement."[45] The sedative listening to which such music caters replaces critical awareness with mere feeling, a fact that leads inexorably to musical fetishization.

Fetishization and Regressive Hearing

Concern over the erosion of individual integrity by the forces of domination and administration permeates every aspect of Adorno's philosophy. Because of his belief in music's redemptive potential, he abhors the effects of reification and commodity fetishism on music's situation in modern society. Society's capacity to hear music is actually deteriorating—profoundly so—and that fact has implications that are far-reaching and ominous. Since music's value is not a function of people's preferences but rather of its capacity to advance consciousness and thereby assure social progress, erosion of the capacity to listen is at once a loss in critical consciousness and evidence of society's continuing drift toward total domination. "The liquidation of the individual," says Adorno, "is the real signature of the new musical situation."[46]

But Adorno is adamantly opposed to the possibility that this deterioration simply reflects a change or shift in people's musical tastes.[47] The notion of taste is in fact wholly inappropriate to music's modern dilemma, because the term 'taste' connotes awareness or engagement with music. People today are unaware, and their consumption of music is not guided by conscious judgment, so to speak in terms of 'likes' and 'dislikes' seriously misconstrues how most people currently relate to music. So complete is the culture industry's domination of music that talk of value judgments is nothing but a "fiction for the person who finds himself hemmed in by standardized musical goods."[48] The kind of music generated, supported, and disseminated by capitalistic powers is so utterly lacking in individuality, so completely identical, that people's espoused preferences are wholly accounted for by private, nonmusical associations. "The familiarity of the piece is a surrogate for the quality ascribed to it," writes Adorno.[49] People no longer know what they like, they only like what they know.

The ascent of entertainment music in modern society has reduced people's relationship to music to one of silent, passive, and largely mindless consumption. Formerly a mode of human behavior, interaction, and engagement, music has atrophied to such an extent that it is now only a soothing sonic background for human activity. Music in modern society "inhabits the pockets of silence that develop between people . . ."[50]

The ubiquity and ever-sameness of commercial music has conditioned people to such a degree of inattentiveness that even music's most anarchic, Dionysian impulses have become neutralized. Thus, what was formerly a source of defiant opposition to authoritarian domination has been co-opted by the "authority of commercial success." Adorno says, "The delight in the moment and the gay facade becomes an excuse for absolving the listener from . . . proper listening. The listener is converted, along his line of least resistance, into the acquiescent purchaser. No longer do the partial moments serve as a critique of that whole; instead, they suspend the critique which the successful esthetic totality exerts against the flawed one of society."[51] Music has been drained of any "insubordinate character" it formerly had, and with that character has gone its critical power as well. Its primary function is now only diversionary, ideological.

Music's ability to rekindle people's sense of (and sensitivity to) individuality is lost. Music's potent experiential immediacy has been replaced by the dull monotony of sameness and familiarity. Its true power "survives only where the forces of denial are strongest: in the dissonance which rejects belief in the illusion of the existing harmony."[52] Only dissonance and contradiction have the power to overcome the mindless banality of listening which has been overtaken by musical fetishism, Adorno believes. Thus, dissonant music "records negatively just that possibility of happiness which the only partially positive anticipation of happiness ruinously confronts today. All 'light' and pleasant art has become illusory and mendacious."[53]

The sole ray of hope, the only source of opposition to this pathetic and deplorable situation is that "advanced product" that resists consumption and commodity character. All other serious music has been "delivered over to consumption for the price of its wages. It succumbs to commodity listening. The differences in the reception of official 'classical' music and light music no longer have any real significance."[54] Like the popular or commercial music audience, the serious music audience really only attends concerts for purposes of self-confirmation. So infatuated have people become with 'star' composers, performers, and pieces that their responses "have no relation to the playing of the music."[55] In modern society, the "most familiar is the most successful and is therefore played again and again and made still more familiar."[56]

It appears that Marx's doctrine of commodity fetishism, in which the products of human labor become transformed into mysteriously venerated objects valued primarily for consumption and exchange, describes these musical facts very well. The act of consuming music has become more important than what music is being consumed. Exchange value (the very "cement" that "holds the world of commodities together"[57]) has now altogether replaced music's use value. Pieces of music have become mere "cultural goods," their former value destroyed by "irrelevant consumption." As they are recycled again and again, these musical goods become increasingly worn out. Their internal structures come to be experienced as mere successions of disconnected, random bits, as "conglomeration[s] of irruptions."[58] Listening has thus become quite infantile and primitive. Only, insists Adorno, this particular primitivism is much less a matter of underdevelopment than of forced retardation.[59]

This process of musical fetishization deprives people not only of their capacity for concentrated musical listening, but of their freedom of choice and sense of responsibility as well. Indeed, so thoroughly has it done its work that people now doubt even the possibility of perception, choice, and responsibility. Listening has regressed to the point that "nothing is left for the consciousness but to capitulate before the superior power of the advertised stuff and purchase spiritual peace by making the imposed goods literally its own thing."[60] Regressive listening demands "standardized products, hopelessly like one another," pieces that, if people really listened, would be totally unbearable. Since regressive listeners can no longer tolerate the strain real listening requires, they accept whatever is given them, provided it presents no challenges. Musical fetishism creates a public which makes no real demands of music save that it not disturb, a public that arrogantly and ignorantly rejects everything unfamiliar. Regressive listeners, says Adorno, are like children who "[a]gain and again and with stubborn malice . . . demand the one dish they have once been served."[61] Such habits and attitudes are "a growing and merciless enemy not only to museum cultural goods."[62] They threaten people's critical awareness, sense of responsibility, and ultimately even their capacity to choose. Modern art music's redemptive mission is thus one of the utmost urgency: to keep alive the "anxiety," the "terror," and the "insight into the catastrophic situation" that regressive listening seeks to evade and most musics seek to cover over.[63]

Types of Listening

Adorno's polemical criticism of fetishism and regression can leave the distinct impression that all listening is uniformly vacuous and concentrated listening is on the verge of extinction. Elsewhere in his writing, however, he allows for the existence of a variety of musical listening types that vary in terms of their adequacy. As we have seen, Adorno believes personal tastes and preferences have nothing to do with musical value. Pieces of music are, rather, "objectively structured things and meaningful in themselves, things that invite analysis and can be perceived and experienced with different degrees of accuracy."[64] Although there is no musical experience without an experiencing subject, the constructive role of perception must always take its directions strictly from the music itself. Neither personal experience nor consensus among experts can establish whether listening is adequate or not. The final court of appeal is none other than the work's inner structure. Adorno's ideally competent listener is one who is fully conscious, who "tends to miss nothing and at the same time, at each moment, accounts to himself for what he has heard."[65] It is a listening that fully grasps the concrete reality of the music. Adorno calls it "structural hearing."[66]

To expect expert listening beyond a relatively small circle of professionals is, Adorno concedes, unrealistically utopian. And yet there are "good" listeners who, while they many not be entirely aware of technical and structural concerns, do at least hear more than isolated bits. Although they may lack explicit technical knowledge, good listeners make connections among musical events and evaluate music by truly musical criteria. Because of mass production and distribution and the demise of amateur music making, Adorno believes good listeners are becoming increasingly rare. "[T]oday one tends to understand either everything or nothing."[67] Thus, while modern music's capacity to break through the veil of familiarity is more important than ever before, the number of people who can actually hear it is smaller than ever.

As active musical engagement deteriorates into the consumption of commercial commodities, the class of good musical listeners is being replaced by a group Adorno labels culture consumers. The culture consumer is a "copious, sometimes a voracious listener, well-informed, a collector of records," but someone for whom music is primarily a cultural asset. The primary point of being musically conversant for the culture consumer is social standing. Rather than musical knowledge, the culture consumer has extensive knowledge about music, and a familiarity that enables recognition of well-known themes. Unlike professional and good listeners, though, culture consumers' hearing is predominantly fetishistic. It is intermittent rather than continuously engaged. Their pleasure has more to do with what music can offer than what it demands of them. Their tastes are conventional and conservative. And although small in number, this group of listeners fills the ranks of the official music establishment, exerting considerable influence on concert programming. The culture consumer is notable for a "reified taste which wrongly deems itself superior to that of the culture industry. More and more of the musical cultural commodities administered by this type are transformed into commodities of manipulated consumption."[68]

The class of "emotional listeners" uses music primarily as an excuse to vent the "instinctual stirrings otherwise tamed or repressed by norms of civilization."[69] For them, music represents a kind of safe haven for irrationality in an excessively rational world, one whose ultimate value is its capacity to keep feeling alive in a feelingless world. Emotional listeners are easily moved to tears, and while Adorno does not question the sincerity of their responses, he doubts that the actual music serves as much more than a trigger for the response. What is more, the emotional listener "fiercely resists all attempts to make him listen structurally—more fiercely, perhaps, than the culture consumer who for culture's sake might put up even with that."[70] In short, emotional listeners display a troubling anti-intellectualism and use music predominantly as an excuse for extramusical emoting.

Adorno's class of "resentment listeners" is less descriptively labeled than others. These are people who vigorously reject the romanticized excess of emotional listening. But rather than attempting to move beyond it, into the kind of critical awareness engendered by authentically modern music, they naively retreat to the music of periods which they believe (wrongly) to be safe havens from the forces of reification and the predominantly commodity character of music. Apparently Adorno believes their resentment is well placed, but their solution is wrong. For in their rigid attempts to reconstruct the past authentically, they engender the very reification they believe they are avoiding. Typified by highly specialized devotees of Bach, "[t]he consciousness of people of this type is preformed by the goals of their organizations, most of which follow crassly reactionary ideologies, and by their historicism. . . . If the emotional type tends to corn, the resentment listener tends to a spurious rigor . . ."[71] The most troublesome feature of such listeners, believes Adorno, is their puritanical desire to save music from its sensual and differentiating characteristics. This repressive attitude he attributes to an apparent need to restore a secure sense of community among themselves, a sense of collectivity that distinguishes them from the undisciplined, the less cultured, the 'unrefined'.

The overwhelming majority of listeners in modern times are people to whom *"music is entertainment* and no more."[72] This is precisely the kind of listener the culture industry exists to serve. Whether the industry creates the group or the listener type creates the industry is an issue on which Adorno claims he would rather not speculate, but in light of his Marxist roots, industrial forces probably deserve the upper hand. Entertainment listeners resemble culture consumers in that in neither case is listening specifically or concretely engaged with music. Rather, individuating features are "flattened as by a steamroller, leveled by the need for music as a comfortable distraction."[73] Even calling this kind of orientation to music "listening" may be granting it too much, Adorno apparently believes. Like smokers and other victims of addictions that pass unnoticed until their source is withdrawn, entertainment listeners are most aware of music when it stops. Entertainment listeners are scarcely aware of the music or any demands it might make of them. They are quite content merely to "[splash] along with the idiomatic current."[74]

Perhaps the most striking manifestation of the bankruptcy of entertainment listening is the individual who plays the radio while working. Such absent-minded 'listening' is particularly well suited to the vacuity of the music provided by the culture industry. But just as disturbing to Adorno as this unconscious passivity is the entertainment listener's defiance of any other orientation to music. The entertainment listener "is a self-conscious low brow who makes a virtue of his own mediocrity. . . . His specific mode of listening is that of distraction and deconcentration, albeit interrupted by sudden bursts of attention and recognition . . ."[75] Lacking a strong ego, entertainment listeners are the kind of compliant people who applaud enthusiastically in response to the applause signs. They are as incapable of criticizing what they hear as they are of expending any effort in order to comprehend it. The entertainment listener "is skeptical only of what takes self-reflection . . . [and is] obstinately bonded to the facade of society that grins at him from magazine covers."[76]

Although it is a little hard to believe him, Adorno claims he does not really fault people for listening one way rather than another. Nor, he says, does the blame for the bleak situation he describes lie wholly with a culture industry "that buttresses the state of mind of people so as to be better able to exploit it."[77] The real source of the problem is in the contradictions and fissures that underlie modern life, and in the all-pervasive influence of false consciousness. And although he recognizes that "the right consciousness in the wrong world is impossible,"[78] he seems unable to avoid the gloomy conclusion that culture has failed humankind.[79]

Popular Music

Adorno's analyses of listening tendencies and listener types come together with full force in his critique of light or 'popular' music. Light music is custom tailored to the inclinations of entertainment listeners and the economic interests of the music industry. Created largely according to formula, light music's most salient features are its standardization, its predictability, and its lack of progress. Its only novelty is entirely superficial, executed so as to leave completely untouched its primitive structural foundations. Beneath a thin veneer of apparent novelty, for instance, lies the same trite, unchanging formula (the AABA 32-bar song form, for instance; or perhaps the 12-bar formula for the blues). Because of its nonprogressive character, music that commercial interests promote as 'exceptional' quickly grows old. Indeed, "the festivities to which light music permanently summons its adherents, under the name of feasts for the ears, are dismal everyday fare."[80] Nothing really new is permitted in the popular song, Adorno claims, "nothing but calculated effects that add some spice to the ever-sameness without imperiling it."[81]

Popular music amounts to commercial seduction cloaked in pseudoindividualization. Its primary audience consists of the lonely and the immature, for whom the hits function as "purveyors of an ersatz for feelings" they think they are supposed to have. But it is carefully controlled banality that imparts to popular music the vulgarity that Adorno believes to be its most distinctive trait.[82] In artistic music, each detail is indispensable and none is interchangeable with any other. In popular music, details are almost always interchangeable. The composer of popular music faces a twofold and highly contradictory task: "He must write something impressive enough to be remembered and at the same time well-known enough to be banal."[83]

As we observed earlier, banality and superficiality are not just musical deficiencies, but concerns with significant political, moral, and social ramifications. In Adorno's estimation, the popular music system is no less than "a training in a passivity that will probably spread to [people's] thought and social conduct. The befogging effect which Nietzsche dreaded in Wagner's music has been taken up and socialized by the popular one."[84] The inevitable outcome of commodification then is a commercial music that functions just like advertising, creating a demand to which production can subsequently claim to respond. Commercial music affirms life and society as they are. It is a "tautological tribute . . . to the socially dominant power concentrated in industry," and those who maintain its innocence are primarily those whose power popular music helps consolidate. "Popular music is objectively untrue and helps to maim the consciousness of those exposed to it. . . . [p]opular music undermines the autonomy and independence of judgment—qualities which a society of free men would require—while a withdrawal of that music would presumably outrage the majorities of all nations as an undemocratic invasion of inalienable rights."[85]

Music's Function

Given the seemingly overwhelming force of reification and fetishism, the regression of listening, and society's apparent incapacity to relate to music as anything but diversion and entertainment, Adorno seems to have painted himself into a corner. What possible good is the right music in the wrong time? What good can come of a musical cultural life that has become so perversely distorted that is scarcely warrants being called a 'life'? How can autonomous music redeem a society that no longer has the capacity to relate to such music? Or as Adorno himself asks, "What is the social significance of a phenomenon that in fact cannot get through to society at all?"[86]

That listeners do not understand is just part of the problem, the more serious issue is that they are no longer capable of recognizing or accepting their lack of understanding. So thoroughly ideological has their consciousness become that they would far rather splash along with the current than swim against it. To the culture industry, music's apparent functionlessness makes it fertile ground for the cultivation of fetishism: it is "sealed and superfluous to the people on whom it is foisted."[87] The notion of music for music's sake, of loving music for no other reason than because it exists, "is the consequence of obeying the extant, the inescapable."[88] The affirmative character of popular music performs a vital ideological function. It provides an "inexhaustible occasion of irresponsible and inconsequential entertainment," one that keeps people from thinking about themselves and their world, at the same time persuading them "that since this world provides such an abundance of enjoyable things it must be in good shape."[89]

An important part of music's seductive ideological power lies in its distinctive acoustic capacity to surround people and to create among them a sense of community. "By circling people, by enveloping them . . . and turning them as listeners into participants, it contributes ideologically to the integration which modern society never tires of achieving in reality. It leaves no room for conceptual reflection . . . and so it creates an illusion of immediacy . . . of proximity between strangers, of warmth for those who come to feel the chill of the unmitigated struggle of all against all."[90] Thus, people use music to escape from their sense of alienation, and to pretend that they are still capable of feeling really alive to the world. Music's "color of the inner sense, the bright, detailed imagery of the flow of time, assures [people] that within the monotony of universal comparability there is still something particular."[91] In a society dominated by choking, numbing repetition, people use musical experience to help keep alive the sense that "something is happening at all, that anything changes."[92] Music's distinctive senses of immediacy and engagement thus seem to remind people of the vitality and agency of which the determinisms of modern life have robbed them.

Adorno is quick to counter this emergent glimmer of hope, however. For to the extent musical experience offers people fulfillment, it prepares them for compliance and consent. Such satiation serves a status quo that can only be changed "by people who, instead of confirming themselves and the world, would reflect critically on the world and on themselves."[93] Thus, affirmative music only "furthers the delusion that the world itself is not yet wholly rationalized," and sustains the unfortunate belief that irrationality need not have undesirable social consequences.[94] Music cultivates the passive, receptive state of mind that is fertile ground for ideological persuasion: it "trains the unconscious for conditioned reflexes."[95] Its primary value, then, is as a kind of perverse index of how much "planned idiocy" people will tolerate, of what "threadbare, noncommittal intellectual contents" can be foisted upon them.[96] The present musical circumstances vividly illustrate the utter impotence and vulnerability of uncritical consciousness.

The Status of Music in Society: Musical Life

The serious musical life in modern capitalist society is, as Adorno sees things, an extraordinarily precarious affair, for there is an excruciating tension between modern art music and the society it seeks to redeem. In fact, the world in which serious music is forced to exist is in fundamental conflict with virtually everything that music stands for. Music, Adorno believes, must challenge and confront, it must interrogate consciousness, and people must be fully present to music. Serious music must challenge society and society must make critical demands of music. The modern world, however, is an extraordinarily hostile place for serious music. People continue to prefer music that entertains, diverts, uplifts, or sentimentally affirms the goodness of life; however, the "developed art of music has long moved light-years away from the expression of a joy that became unattainable in reality."[97] Serious music, particularly since Auschwitz, is no longer about smoothing over alienation and contradiction. The only real way music can improve the world is to make people confront it as it is.

Despite this, the basis of 'official' or institutionalized musical life remains the nineteenth-century forms and practices which cater to a passive contemplation, offering few real challenges to perception. Musical institutions exist primarily "to administer accumulated treasures"[98] of the traditional canon. As the wear of frequent repetition takes its toll, attention shifts from the work itself to its reproduction or recording: from what is produced to how it is presented for consumption. This, in conjunction with the spectacle of the star/virtuoso system, helps to obscure the underlying ever-sameness of the official musical world. "Artists are rounded up like acts for a monstrous circus. Performances are illusionary apotheoses. What is sensually pleasing and takes an errorless, undisturbed course comes to replace a meaningful presentation," observes Adorno.[99] The art music establishment thus "drives any divergent productive force and legitimate critique into a sectarian and severed stance that weakens the objectively legitimate."[100] That is, the establishment marginalizes any music that threatens people's undisturbed interiors, banishing the best (most 'modern', most 'advanced') music to the periphery of musical life. Music that makes genuinely critical demands upon the listener, refusing to cater to comfortable consumption or conform to popular preference, has no place in a musical world given over to commodity consumption. Indeed, the genuine work of art "always attacks the law of the marketplace . . ."[101]

Another hostile feature of the social milieu in which serious music must try to survive is the misguided application of egalitarian principles to matters of musical value. "There is no peaceable social atlas of musical life, no more than there is one of society," Adorno insists.[102] Music is simply not the kind of thing toward which one should assume a pluralistically tolerant stance: music's various functions are emphatically not of equal value. To suggest that different musics each simply perform different functions, and that each might thus be regarded as good in its own kind or beautiful in its own way, is utter anathema to Adorno. Musical value is an objective affair, and not all musics have equal worth. Nor do all musical perspectives carry equal weight. There is no place in the musical world for something like social egalitarianism. If there were, one would have to accord the same status to a "backwoods zither player" as to those who listen with understanding to complex modern works, a concession that "not only suppresses qualitative differences but the music's own claim to be true."[103] Designating personal or popular taste a valid criterion of musical worth deprives great music of "the only thing that makes it great and valid."[104] Degrade music to a mere consumer commodity whose popularity is the gauge of its value, and it loses precisely what makes it worth listening to or engaging in.[105]

Since affirmation is no longer an appropriate musical function, and since musical value is an objective, intramusical affair, the musical avant-garde is obliged to oppose society's crass tastes and habits. Otherwise, it is only an ideological servant of the status quo. And yet, turning its back on society places serious music at considerable risk of writing and playing only for itself. The apparently inverse relationship between popular appeal and musical value threatens to cut truly serious, authentic, modern music off from society altogether. "The lack of an art's relation to things outside it, to the part of it that is not art itself, threatens its inner composition."[106]

On the other hand, the desire to 'socialize' or domesticate modern music, to cure it or save it from its insularity, "does inalienable damage to the best of it: to its independence, its consistency, its integrity."[107] To 'communicate', music has to seek to accommodate its audience, to find a common ground. Only where this principle of communication is violated, Adorno believes, can music perform its critical mission and maintain its truth to its own intramusical value.[108]

"[T]he more purely a society is organized according to the exchange principle, the less will the organizers listen to the spokesmen of an autonomous culture and the less relevant will expertise be for the guidance of musical life," writes Adorno.[109] Autonomous music threatens the smoothly running capitalistic machine by refusing to behave as a proper product, refusing to conform to popular demand, and refusing to concede that its value is no more authentic than, say, that of entertainment music.

The mass media and technology of the culture industry have also left an indelible mark on the society in which serious music is forced to seek its survival. Not only does recording shift attention from the work to its consumable reproduction, but the capacity for frequent easy repetition fundamentally alters the relation between people and music. "Music is no longer exceptional, as at feudal and absolutist festivities and in the bourgeois concert."[110] The formerly exceptional has been devalued to the commonplace, a process that replaces difference and individuality with ever-sameness. And at the same time, easy access and repeatability create habits of passivity and effortlessness that are inimical to structural listening. The "home delivery system" has relieved listeners of any need for personal activity, so that domestic music making, "the humus of musicality in the grand style,"[111] is becoming increasingly rare. Hopes of reviving it are so much wishful thinking, insists Adorno, because "once authentic interpretations are available on records . . . home music [making] no longer has a point . . . [It] becomes a private repetition of acts which . . . can better and more meaningfully performed in other ways."[112] In principle of course, recordings abolish privilege and extend musical access to all who want it, a fact, it might be thought, that would help offset at least some of Adorno's concerns. But the costs to serious music are just too high. Records "have to pay their social dues in the form of material selection and also of quality of reproduction. Program policy must be sales oriented . . . [and the] principle governing choices is largely that of prominence, of great works that have 'arrived' and of 'name' interpreters."[113]

Adorno's descriptions of the profound alienation modern music faces are vivid and disturbing. The life of serious music in modern capitalistic society, he maintains, only superficially resembles a 'real' life. The cost of its integration into that society is its very seriousness.[114] Social integration hollows music out. The masses of entertainment listeners spurn modern music precisely because of its "socially desperate effort" to maintain its seriousness, because of the kind of concentrated listening it demands. The social context in which modern music is forced to make its way is one where music has become the very epitome of cultural commodity production, where musical value is completely determined by popular consumer demand. Modern society is thus totally incapable of hearing anything that serious modern music has to say. As Adorno says, "The life of music is not a life for music."[115]

Modern Music

Given Adorno's pessimistic account of things, it is easy to lose sight of the fact that his disparaging words always seem to assume the possibility of something better. Compromised though our capacity to perceive and experience the authentic or legitimate has become—ideological though our consciousness may be—there remains some possibility of resistance. Redemption may be a remote and slim possibility, yet there is, in modern music, at least a ray of hope.

Before examining further the particulars of Adorno's theory of modern music, a brief review of its context may be helpful. Adorno was vehemently opposed to false consciousness and ideology in all their manifestations. Ideology served the forces of domination that were bringing the world ever closer to a state of 'total administration', in which freedom and truth would be completely replaced by determinism. In capitalistic society, the forces of reification had usurped all but the faint memory of real freedom. Official Marxism had betrayed Marx's basic insights by banning critical thought and expression. The roots of fascism had found fertile soil in many countries throughout the world. The world's apparent drift toward total administration, together with the unspeakable horror of Auschwitz, quite understandably left Adorno with the conviction that society was, to say the very least, not at all well. The pursuit of "the good life" has lapsed into a state, as he says, of total neglect. "What the philosophers once knew as life has become the sphere of private existence and now of mere consumption, dragged along as an appendage of the process of material production, without autonomy or substance of its own. He who wishes to know the truth about life in its immediacy must scrutinize its estranged form . . ."[116]

Adorno thus sought to redeem thought and art as potential repositories of truth, to liberate human consciousness, to reawaken it to alternatives to the determinism of modern life. In that effort, modern music figured centrally, as perhaps the last toe-hold in the effort to shatter the illusion that 'all is well'. Music's redemptive function can only be realized to the extent it exposes the fissures and contradictions behind the slick facade.

As we have seen, Adorno does not believe all modern music is capable of this important task. Successful music is music that strenuously asserts and maintains its autonomy, refusing assimilation by the culture industry and thoughtless consumption by entertainment listeners. It vehemently opposes the "all powerful culture industry," offering instead "an ever-sharper contrast to [the culture industry's] false clarity."[117] This it accomplishes by defying the comfort of convention, by maintaining a social distance that is not compromised by utility or purpose. Avant-garde music alone can accomplish this, because it is "cut off from official culture."[118]

It is also necessary that successful music be dissonant, in order to help counter the seamless, glossy, all-is-well qualities that cloak and preserve ideology in modern society. The abrasiveness of dissonance, Adorno apparently believes, forces us to confront authentically the anguish and fragmentation of modern social life; it refuses to cooperate in the creation of the reassuring, sonorous veneers that are the stuff of false consciousness.[119] Music fulfills its redemptive function, then, in a primarily adversarial manner, by refusing to cater to effortless consumption or to capitulate to the ideological machinery of capitalism. But it must exert its resistance using only its own resources, within the 'cells' of its own technique—otherwise, it becomes just another useful commodity, losing its critical moment and entering into the functional matrix it must, to be true, oppose. In order to exercise its full subversive power, music must stubbornly maintain its dissonance, foregoing temptations of easy resolution and illusory moments of affirmation.

Avant-garde music works to counter the reduction of difference and individuality to ever-sameness. It awakens people from half-conscious slumber, countering the tendency to hear music as a generality, a mere example of something already there. It re-establishes the capacity for direct experience. And in so doing, it cuts individual strands of the ever-expanding administrative web in which the world is increasingly ensnared. To that extent, all successful music is socially critical, forcing people to confront what ideology deprives them of the ability to see.

As we have seen, Adorno believes that most music has abdicated its critical capacity. Works are no longer so much composed as generated by formula. Materials both obsolete and trivial are endlessly recycled until, as Adorno points out, familiarity replaces substance as the source of presumed musical meaning. A small handful of experts are the only ones any longer capable of adequately hearing the music, of delivering us from our pathetic situation; and the insights of those experts are, by Adorno's own estimation, not widely respected.

All the same, Adorno is convinced that Schoenberg's atonal music meets these critical criteria. It demands "active and concentrated participation . . . the renunciation of the customary crutches of a listening which always knows what to expect, the intensive perception of the unique and specific. . . . It requires the listener spontaneously to compose its inner movement and demands of him not mere contemplation but praxis. In this . . . Schoenberg blasphemes against the expectation . . . that music will present the comfortable listener with a series of pleasurable sensations."[120] Additionally, Schoenberg "steadfastly [rejects] the notion of 'style', in the sense of a category existing prior to the subject matter . . ."[121] He does not seek the soothing reassurance of clichés and formulas. He takes his lead from the internal implications of the musical material itself, following its inner logic rather than some general principle. The truth of his work is thus in no way dependent upon audience reception: it is musically objective.

Adorno's philosophy of music intentionally leaves us with a host of contradictory, unresolved truths. The primary polarities of this force field are the facts of music's social significance and the simultaneous necessity of its autonomy from social forces. In rejecting the idealistic notion that music is an immutable thing, Adorno also denies the existence of a single mission it is music's duty to perform for all time. As a socially and historically situated phenomenon whose very materials change through time, no era can rest on the insights, achievements, and values of another.

The conception of music as a socially situated phenomenon pulls Adorno in one direction, and his location of the redemptive potential of his era's music in its autonomy pulls him in the other. Avant-garde music presents social critique within its forms and structures, and to do so it must avoid yielding to the forces it would criticize. Reification is such a pervasive influence today that the only way for music to counter that influence and avoid contamination is to reject traditional structure, style, and convention. Modern music's claims to integrity, authenticity, and truth require that it be independent. It must reject the seductive comfort of a secure place within the institutionalized social matrix, as well as the modes of perception and thought that comprise its foundation. In short, the only way for music to be true to its self is to sever all ties to others.

The inevitable result of this rejection of the indulgent, the regressive, and the recycled, however, is profound alienation. Modern music becomes isolated and ineffectual. In order to fulfill its emancipatory potential, music must assert its radical autonomy, an assertion that neutralizes its import to the society to which it purports to speak. Autonomy means alienation and loss of communicative capacity; it severs the ties that enable what music says to be heard. Yet, to sacrifice its autonomy would mean being co-opted by the very forces it is obligated to resist. In short, modern music's alienation is such that, while it alone has the capacity to speak the truth through its immediacy and particularity, that voice goes unheard. The very autonomy that enables its critical resistance makes it all but impossible for that critical resistance to make a difference. Thus, Adorno leaves us with two seemingly irreconcilable truths, succinctly expressed by

Zuidervaart this way: "[A] work's autonomy has a social character, and a work's social character is itself autonomous."[122] "[Modern music's] social function is to be socially dysfunctional . . ."[123]

Commentary

The breadth and complexity of Adorno's thought, together with his negative dialectical method, leave us with a bewildering array of ideas and assertions that refuse to congeal into a neat or orderly system. That, of course, is entirely consistent with his intentions, but some of his ideas show more signs of strain than others. Let us attempt a brief assessment of Adorno's insights and enigmas.

Particularly notable among Adorno's accomplishments is his exposure of the social and historical nature of music's materials and practices. As we have seen, Adorno believed that by shattering the illusion that tonality constituted a natural and universal musical law, Schoenberg showed music's materials to be products of particular practices by particular people under particular circumstances: they are socially and historically relative, not immutable or absolute. Music's supposedly natural foundations, then, are not natural after all, only conventional. By defying tonality's claim to natural law, atonal music refused domination by all-encompassing absolutes. And by resisting the authority of the principles that formerly permitted all music to be heard as one,[124] musical value and meaning were shown to be contingent. Music is not a natural whole, but a collection of human practices without any essential core. Thus, Adorno shows the difficulty of treating all music as a single unified thing, pursuing the same ends, with the same essential priorities and values. He says, in effect, that one cannot subsume the disparate historical facts of music under one ontological essence: there is no universal concept that can accommodate the plurality of music. In Adorno's own words, "The concept of art balks at being defined, for it is a historically changing constellation of moments."[125]

Despite his suspicion of absolutes and belief in the social and historical relativity of musical materials, Adorno does not pursue these to what might seem their logical conclusion: that there are a variety of ways for music to exercise its properly critical function. On the contrary, Adorno attributes true critical power to only one music. In any given sociohistoric period, he apparently believes, there can be but one music that is truly "historically advanced." Since musics of earlier periods inevitably relinquish their critical moment to perceptual habit, it is imperative that music be 'modern' and up-to-date. Such currency can only be attained by eschewing the worn-out materials of the past. In stark contrast to the self-consciously contemporary practices of modern music, most musics consist of little more than recycled musical waste.

Thus Adorno seems to open the door to a broad range of possible musics only to close it again. Since his modernism requires that music be progressive, that it challenge what precedes it, only a relatively narrow set of musical practices can be adequate to social development at any given time. Adorno apparently thinks that redemption of individuality and particularity can be achieved only by pieces that assert their independence from stylistic norms and renounce the comfortable sameness of the culture industry. Thus, music that acquiesces to existing stylistic practices is illegitimate and ideological. Only music that challenges stylistic tradition and perceptual habit has the progressive, cognitive, and social potential Adorno considers so important. He pluralizes music, but is unable or unwilling to recognize a plurality of musical means to his critical ends. Music must be modern, but cannot be so in multiple ways. The obvious difficulty with Adorno's modernism is, as Zuidervaart observes, that modern music is considerably "more variegated than Adorno's concept of artistic material suggests."[126]

Adorno's conception of popular or commercial music is even narrower than his conception of properly modern music. Despite his criticisms of Stravinsky's neoclassicism, for instance, Adorno at least acknowledges it as one among a number of different approaches to the creation of serious music. His treatment of the music of the culture industry acknowledges no such plurality. All popular music is cut from the same cloth, comprised of endlessly recycled trite materials given only the superficial appearance of novelty. Nowhere is his subsumption of the entirety of non-'serious' music under a single banner more clear than in his short-sighted equation of jazz, popular, and commercial music. Because Adorno completely failed to comprehend the distinctive nature and traditions of jazz, he was unable to distinguish it from any other culture industry product. His caustic denunciations make for entertaining reading, but seriously detract from otherwise valid insights. Adorno injudiciously applies the values of composed, notated musics to musical traditions that are fundamentally aural and improvisational in nature.[127] This disposes him to seek syntactical and formal complexity in musics whose priorities are fundamentally processual in nature and, finding none, to declare such musics valueless. Thus, unfortunately, Adorno neglects the critical potential of an enormous range of musical practice.

Adorno's remarkable deconstructive effort, his revelation of the social significance that lies beneath the surface of musical experience, extends only so far. He retains a stubbornly monolithic view of musical value, one that seems out of place in someone so insistent about the historical and social contingency of musical meanings and materials. Although music's nature may change over time, at any given historical point in its evolution only one music can be fully adequate to its redemptive purpose, and that music constitutes the norm by which the worth of others must be gauged. In strong contrast to the post-avant-garde or postmodern philosophical viewpoint which recognizes a broad array of musical possibilities while conceding priority to none, Adorno sees music's task at any given time as single and best met by one particular kind of music.

This narrowness must be balanced against his insistence upon the social and political (and, by extension, the moral and humane) significance of music. Although he attributes it to a small and highly esoteric body of music, it is noteworthy that Adorno finds utopian and redemptive potential in music. In the right hands and under the proper circumstances, music has the remarkable capacity to break through the veil of familiarity, helping deliver people from the deterministic, totalizing forces that impinge on life in modern society. By demanding that it be experienced strictly on its own terms, music can combat the unthinking compliance that begets total administration. It can help deliver people from the tyranny of generality and restore awareness of the integrity of the particular. Music has the remarkable capacity to show things about our social situation that nothing else can. Music's particularity and immediacy can, under the proper circumstances, be truer than philosophy.

For one who, perhaps more than any other single individual, has drawn attention to the social situatedness and significance of musical endeavor, it is remarkable how little Adorno has to say about music's empirically social functions. Adorno's social philosophy does not present the kind of empirical analysis that sociology normally brings to mind. Because of his refusal to separate music's social and musical import, his discussions invariably center around questions of ideology rather than function. Or put differently, music's ideological function interests him far more than any other. On the other hand, Adorno denies that music has a social function: "[I]f any social function can be ascribed to [art works] at all," he writes, "it is . . . to have no function."[128] He often leaves the distinct impression that the only function all music shares is its decadent commodity character and attendant falsification of consciousness. The only social function of music that really interests Adorno, then, is its capacity to advance critical awareness. And that, he believes, requires musical autonomy: freedom from functional constraint.

Although belief in the importance of musical autonomy is hardly unique to Adorno, it seems curiously out of place in a theory committed to illuminating music's social significance. On most accounts, self-containedness and autonomy would seem to preclude performance of a social function. Apparently, Adorno does not intend to imply that music's autonomy be utter and complete, only that it be free from domination by institutions that might compromise its musical-social capacity for realigning consciousness. His insistence upon music's autonomy is intended to ensure its ability to defy domination and crude social determination, to establish for modern music the freedom to exercise its critical function without interference.

The question that remains is whether autonomy (even in this more attenuated sense Goehr calls "freedom from"[129]) is necessary for music to function critically, as Adorno claims it is. This is a matter of considerable import, for if Adorno is wrong, whether music is functional or autonomous is irrelevant to its critical potential. Even nonautonomous music might have critical value. Must music be autonomous in order to challenge the status quo? Does instrumental use necessarily impede this challenge? It is difficult to see why. Indeed, Adorno himself seems to concede that music's social significance depends on things 'outside' as well as 'inside' music, since social significance itself changes over time. If autonomy is not essential, though, Adorno would need to grant potential critical power to a host of musics regardless of their claim to modernity or autonomy. This he is clearly not prepared to do.

Although he would acknowledge that modernity and autonomy are in themselves no guarantees of successful critical resistance, Adorno clearly believes each is necessary. So ubiquitous and powerful are the forces of reification and commodification that the only way for music to counter them is to reject traditional structure and convention, and to eschew the security and comfort of a place in art's social matrix. The only way to be true to its individuality is apparently to renounce all ties to other. This then is the central dilemma Adorno's theory creates for modern music. To exercise its emancipatory potential it must be autonomous. But autonomy leads to isolation and ultimately the inability to reach the very people it must in order to realize its potential. The result is a rupture of the relationship between musical structure and meaning. In short, the cost of self-evident structure (autonomous individual integrity) is meaninglessness (absence of social validation). The cost of meaning, on the other hand, would be submission to the very forces modern music exists to subvert. By pursuing the only course Adorno can envisage for it, modern music loses its capacity to engage and challenge society. Music and society become like ships silently passing in the night. There is no place for modern music to go, no way out. Thus Adorno's philosophy of the individual leads inexorably to radical particularism, to utter isolation, because the autonomy music requires to perform its social-critical job assures that what it has to say will be heard and understood by virtually no one.

The idea of structurally autonomous music is, as Subotnik has concluded, a fiction rooted in a "notion of abstract, ahistorical, metaphysical truth ... the post-Kantian West has long acknowledged as inaccessible."[130] The corollary of this idea of a self-contained, self-validated, self-evident structure is Adorno's structural listening. But this too is a myth: a kind of listening defined by vigilant attention to autonomously unfolding forms that wrongly discounts crucial personal and cultural differences. The effects of subscription to such myths and fictions are nothing short of devastating. Their espousal by composers, performers, and audiences lead not to the kind of elevated critical awareness Adorno envisaged, but to utter irrelevance. In Subotnik's words, "The musical habit that contemporary music has established is not structural listening but no listening at all."[131]

However wrong he may have been about structural autonomy, though, Adorno's concerns about the commodification and fetishization of music are in large part persuasive. Musics do have the capacity to dull people's awareness of their powerlessness in an increasingly administered society. The culture industry does indeed create a sense of ever-sameness and inevitability that makes people passive participants in recycled experience at some expense to authentic individuality. Music does have the capacity to desensitize people to their situations, to numb them and make them acritically accept existences less fully lived than those of which they might otherwise be capable. Music is fundamentally social, and as such, always has an ideological or sociopolitical dimension. Music has lost much of its emancipatory power as it has deteriorated from a mode of human action and interaction into a thing, an object for exchange. Much music has indeed lost its individuality and particularity, having been leveled by the bulldozing effects of commodity fetishism and market exchange. Music's ever-sameness can exert the narcotic effect that Adorno worried about. Surface or pretended change can make people think they are experiencing authentically, when in fact they are being duped. Recycled music, whether popular hits or the upper-class hits of the classical canon, probably does help perpetuate acquiescence to the status quo by its illusory reassurance that all is well with the world.

In the end, it is important to remember that Adorno believes that music can make the world a better place, or at least a less terrible one. Perhaps the utopian impulse of his critical theory can be sustained by distributing it across a variety of musical styles and practices. In fact, given his deep distrust of totalizing agendas, it is a little surprising Adorno himself did not pursue a more pluralistic solution: one that acknowledges the existence of critical potential within a variety of musics; one that concedes that engagement and communication are necessary to social transformation and that they need not invariably reduce to pandering; one that seeks to articulate a critical dimension in popular, contemporary, and historical music alike.

Even if his solutions are sometimes rather crude, many of his basic instincts were remarkably prescient. Adorno leaves little room for doubt that music is and always must be a socially significant enterprise, that musics (all musics) are influenced by the forces of reification and commodification in today's world, and that musics are invariably undertakings with profound moral significance. Whatever his shortcomings, it must be conceded that he defines with unforgettable vividness the two extremes that deprive all music of meaning: absence of individuality, and radical individuality. Perhaps most important, Adorno shows that music has many purposes and functions, many of them beyond what is immediately apparent: that music is never 'just' music. In this light, we can conclude with Zuidervaart that the crucial question is not whether music has social functions, but rather "which purposes the work's functions are fulfilling, and whether these purposes are desirable."[132]

Attali: The Political Economy of Music

Adorno's portrayal of music's transformation into commodity and his demonstration of its social power are achievements whose resonance has extended to disciplines well beyond traditional musicology and music philosophy. Pursuing Adorno's lead, French economist Jacques Attali has articulated a highly speculative but provocative account of music's 'political economy', one that attributes to sound and music such extraordinary influence that they must be recognized as nothing less than instruments of sociopolitical power. Although his descriptions are often sketchy and metaphorical, they present a strikingly different way of conceptualizing music's nature and value, one that undermines comfortable assumptions and stereotypes, stubbornly defying conventional wisdom.

Underlying all Attali's speculations is a conviction that sound is never a benign aspect of the human environment, but a force with extraordinary power, one that is definitive of an entirely distinctive way of being in and relating to the world and each other. Sound, or as Attali more often calls it, noise, is uniquely powerful, defining patterns of human relatedness in ways of which traditional descriptions of music's nature and value are scarcely aware. Throughout its entire history, Western thought has construed the world and reality in visual terms, with visual ideals like the clarity and distinctness Descartes felt were the prerequisites to any trustworthy knowledge. Sound constitutes a backdrop, an occasional punctuation for a world that is first and foremost given to the eye. However, the world so construed is eerily silent, sterile, and lifeless, a mere shadow of the one people actually inhabit. The soundless world is abstract, an out-there whose most characteristic inhabitants are objects and things.

Attali adds his voice to the many who have urged that this ideal of silent mental abstraction, buttressed by an immense vocabulary of visual metaphors for knowledge, is profoundly deficient. Preoccupation with looking leads to the near-total neglect of what the noises of the world are saying to us, of how they shape our perception of the world and our place within it. This is no minor oversight, for sound is utterly crucial to our experience and knowledge of the world. Hearing is an utterly unique way of being in the world, and the ear's world is inaccessible to any other sense. More provocatively and directly yet, Attali asserts, "the world is not for the beholding. It is for hearing."[133]

Sounds and the ways people use and relate to them are never mere background for an inherently visual-rational world. Sonorous experience's directness and immediacy make it an instrument of unparalleled political power, enabling it to instill patterns of social relatedness and indeed, according to Attali, to announce shifts in social relations long before they become manifest elsewhere. Listening to the world, examining sounds and ways people use and interact with them, can actually perform an important prophetic function: it can show us where "the folly of men and their calculations is leading us, and what hopes it is still possible to have."[134] Music is thus a tool both for creating and for understanding the social and political world, an instrument for "the creation or consolidation of a community, of a totality. It is what links a power center to its subjects . . ."[135]

These are bold claims. But Attali's broader thesis rests on a characterization of the phenomenal character of noise that is bolder still. The human experience of noise is inherently and fundamentally violent, asserts Attali. In stark contrast to the seemingly abstract objectivity of the world of the eye, sound is a fluid, intangible, ambiguous, threatening, intrusive, invasive kind of thing. One cannot control sound by averting one's ears, and its experience is always profoundly corporeal in nature. Therefore, there is always implicit in sonorous experience a threat of violence. Because of this, sound is a source and manifestation of power. Its control is always a fundamentally political concern. Sound articulates boundaries that cannot be seen, and extends one's sphere of influence and power beyond the reaches of the physical body. Sound's function as a warning of impending danger is deeply embedded in the human psyche. Its mystery and power, together with its unrivaled capacities for affecting separation and integration, make it the ideal vehicle for the articulation, identification, reinforcement, and ultimately even the subversion of social structures. Indeed, asserts Attali, "it is sounds and their arrangements that fashion societies. With noise is born disorder and its opposite: the world."[136]

Noise, it seems, is the epitome of disorderliness and irrationality. Noise is dirt, pollution, an agent of aggression and destruction. It is a potent image of violence, and a source of both acute psychological and physical pain.[137] In fact,

Attali claims, the experience of noise is no less than an aural semblance (representation, or 'simulacrum') of murder. To encounter noise is to encounter a threat of immense proportions, and to emit noise is to commit one of the most aggressive acts of which a human being is capable. The regulation of such power is an obvious precondition for the existence of any possible human society. And the control of noise is a fundamental human preoccupation.

Among the more significant instruments for domesticating the ominous unruliness of noise is music and musical activity. Music forges cohesion from chaos, order from randomness. But in harnessing noise's inherent violence, music retains the phenomenal power and force encountered there. In Attali's formulation, "Noise is a weapon and music, primordially, is the formation, domestication, and ritualization of that weapon . . ."[138] Music channels the inherent violence of noise, and in so doing presents people with an aural semblance of sacrifice. Music thus presents people with a vivid, corporeal image that affirms the possibility of social order in which the noise of individuality is yielded to the broader, social whole.

This wresting of harmonious unity from the inherent violence of noise and dissonance is the primordial source of both music and society. By imparting form and order to noise, music consoles and reassures people. It presents them with vivid images of the transformation of general violence into something not only tolerable but pleasant. Thus, music should be considered a primary means of channeling social consciousness. Moreover, music and noise are not just tangentially or occasionally political phenomena, but essentially and always so. They are "stakes in games of power."[139]

Since music is such a potent force in people's conception of the possibility of social relatedness, its appropriation and control is crucial to any existing social order. "With music is born power," asserts Attali, and among music's primary functions is "the creation, legitimation, and maintenance of order. Its primary function is not to be sought in aesthetics . . . but in the effectiveness of its participation in social regulation."[140] While the noises, dissonances, and tensions music incorporates represent social difference and marginality, music's capacity to forge harmony, consonance, integration and balance in spite of such opposing forces is a powerful expression of social order. Because different musics tend to portray different kinds of relations between order and marginality, the regulation of musics, musicians, and musical practices is an act with far-reaching political implications. According to Attali, "The entire history of tonal music . . . amounts to an attempt to make people believe in a consensual representation of the world."[141] And central to that endeavor is always the issue of whose music should be regarded as legitimate and whose as marginal: whose tunes will be used to orchestrate sociopolitical power.

While music ensures that members of a given society under given historical and economic circumstances share a common vision of social cohesion, the specific character that belief assumes is a function of time and circumstance. Like the sounds from which it is crafted, music's reality is fundamentally fluid. Just as there are numerous ways for social structures to accommodate individual differences, so too can different musical styles reflect widely divergent structural principles. It is Attali's thesis that music's nature enables it to register shifts in the prevailing social order long before they become apparent elsewhere, a fact that makes music an important barometer of social change. In Attali's view, the history of Western music reveals three predominant historical modes of socio-musical relation, three "strategic uses of music by power,"[142] and a fourth that he believes is about to emerge. These he calls ritual, representation, and repetition, and the fourth, composition.

Ritual

Ritual is the primordial mode of sociomusical relation we began to sketch above. In ritual, music's social significance derives from participants' direct, communal involvement in wresting harmony and order from noise's violence. Ritualistic musical experience presents people with a vital affirmation of the value of sacrifice, for just as music forges order and unity from chaos, so, people come to believe, can social association provide protection from the general violence of presocial existence. Society is possible where individuality is sacrificed to social order. In ritual, music brings noise's violence, its fundamentally destructive character, its inherent threat of death, under control. By reassuringly rendering the chaotic orderly, it persuades people that social accord may be forged from disorder, and that the mode of relation we know as society is possible. In effect, ritualistic musical experience involves people in an immediate personal sacrifice of selfhood to a larger musical whole. In taming noise's violence, music provides people with a compelling model of harmonious wholes wrought from individual differences. Such experience teaches them, in effect, that just as music's magical order is sustained by merging one's individuality with the greater whole, so is the distinctive social order that is equally a part of ritual. Thus, "[p]rimordially, and not incidentally, music always serves to affirm that society is possible."[143]

   Noise, Attali believes, is the articulation of difference, whereas silence is anonymity.[144] This fundamental opposition between sound and silence becomes manifest in human experience as the antagonism between the assertion of individuality and willingness to accept others' order. As a creator of differences, sound is not a polite political phenomenon but a weapon, a site of aggression: indeed, Attali suggests, "a battlefield."[145] The very existence of any society is always predicated on its ability to accommodate or give order to fundamental individual differences. This point is axiomatic to Attali's account of political economy: "No organized society can exist without structuring differences at its core."[146]

   As the allusion to a battlefield suggests, however, this process is not inherently peaceful and rational, but the locus of struggle and resistance. Attali draws intriguing support for this particular claim from the long history of political struggles over what music (whose music) should prevail in the church. Its deep suspicion of music deemed too worldly, too indulgent, or too sensuous was prompted by its need to assure the dominance of the social order inherent in the austere sobriety that was characteristic of music it supported. The church thus went to great lengths to marginalize competing musics, to domesticate musicians, and to ensure the continued prevalence of its musics. This is not intended to denigrate the church, only to offer a convenient example of a point crucial to understanding music's true significance: there always exists a vital link between the prevalent tune and the prevalent sociopolitical order. In all social organizations, control over the articulation of difference is a fundamental political concern. Since noise is difference and other people's music is noisy, music is invariably a site of sociopolitical struggle.

If in ritual, prior to the advent of commercial exchange, music's primary function is its capacity to crystallize social organization, Attali would probably give full and enthusiastic assent to Plato's conviction that changes to music threaten to bring about changes to political and social order. Likewise, Attali is in accord with Adorno's belief that dissonance is a source of affective and political power, because of its capacity to undermine people's faith in the security of harmony. Attali thus takes his place alongside those who insist upon the fundamental ideological and political power of music, that "music is not innocent."[147] It has the capacities both to sustain and subvert the existing order. In ritual, music establishes faith in harmony by helping people escape the fear of general violence. But since it can as easily undermine that faith, music is invariably implicated in issues of power and politics.

For these reasons and more, musicians are, again as Plato so clearly believed, ambiguous and worrisome characters, wielders of remarkable power. According to Attali, musicians always perform dual roles in society, being at once "catalyzers of violence and myth."[148] They serve to reinforce the musical-political status quo, and they can seriously undermine it as well. Accordingly, when musicians pose questions or perceived threats to the existing order they quickly become outcasts and pariahs. On the other hand, when they support and honor the replication of current order, they are high priests whose creations and actions embody society's deepest values. As individuals whose creations present models for the reconciliation of sameness and difference, integration and individuality, musicians are variously regarded as superhuman and subhuman. Yet, even where a music's role in political channelization may have earned for it a place of honor as officially sanctioned institutional art, Attali believes, subversive, subterranean strains always maintain a marginal existence. Historically, such people's musics were "an instrument of the ecstatic cult, an outburst of uncensored violence. . . . At odds with the official religions and centers of power, these rites gathered marginals together in forest clearings and caves: women, slaves, expatriates. At times society tolerated them, or attempted to integrate them into the official religion; but at other times it brutally repressed them."[149] As the "quintessential mass activity," concludes Attali, music always represents a simultaneous threat and an essential source of legitimation, such that "trying to channel it is a risk that every system of power must run."[150]

In ritual, music is predominantly an activity that is nonspecialized, communal, an activity of the body undertaken and shared by all. Not yet the monopolistic domain of a musical elite, ritualistic music is so tightly woven into the fabric of daily life that it can scarcely be distinguished as a distinct entity.

Music in the relation of ritual, then, is a mode of human interaction that creates social relations by relieving people of the fear of violence. A nonspecialized collaboration among participants, it is more process than entity, its value inconceivable apart from the pleasure of being engaged in it.

Representation

Gradually, sociomusical experience becomes deritualized. Music becomes an increasingly specialized undertaking, and musicians become economically bound to powers whose legitimacy their labors are expected to affirm. Musical execution becomes the domain of skilled performing specialists, and the primary responsibility of audiences becomes silent, appreciative consumption of the musical commodities specialists produce. A deep split develops between performer and audience, producer and consumer, one that radically alters ritual's distinctive collectivity and silences many who were formerly musical participants. Where ritual had been a music of action and relation, representation is a music of commodity and spectacle. Thus, the kind of social possibilities affirmed by music undergo a radical shift.

Instead of being directly engaged in the business of channeling noise's violence, people learn to bear silent witness to compelling images of hierarchical social cohesion, enacted for them by specialists (themselves often presided over by another level of specialty, the conductor). In representation, personal action or agency ceases to be the locus of musical value it was in ritual. Musical value loses its intimate connection with musical use. Now music comes to consist of works, artifacts with a value that is supposed to be intrinsic—independent of and prior to the act of executing them. Because their value is separate from their use, they lend themselves readily and ever-increasingly to commercial consumption. Exchange value replaces and eventually destroys use value. Ritual's distinctive sense of bodily engagement and agency gives way to consumption of musical commodity. These forces of commodification so radically entrap and transform music that it no longer serves so much as an affirmation of existence as a means of producing money, as something bought and sold. Once this happens, there can no longer be any real truth to the poetic claim that music is an island of humane value in the midst of a commercial "ocean of artifice": on the contrary, music has itself become artifice.[151]

The features of music's socializing role take on a very changed character under representation as well. Representation's version of the myth of inevitable order differs substantially from that of ritual. Representational order is an order of specialized and hierarchical (superior-subordinate, bureaucratic) relationships, driven by commercial exchange. Once people begin to listen to music in passive silence and exchange it for money, its previously humane functions are replaced by "a battle for the purchase and sale of power, a *political economy*."[152] In representation, the musical weapon is for sale to the highest or cleverest bidder, a condition that transforms music into an ideological tool. Instead of consoling and providing a haven from general violence, music now performs its socializing role by making people "*believe* in the harmony of the world, that there is order in exchange and legitimacy in commercial power."[153] This it does by staging opportunities for spectators to witness the reenactment of what was formerly a human experience whose meaning was bound up in the doing of music itself. Where ritual made people forget, reassured them by directly engaging them in the creation of order, representation makes people believe in the inevitability of hierarchical order and commercial power by presenting them with spectacles that affirm the legitimacy of such order and power. Representation "replace[s] the lost ritualization of the channelization of violence with the spectacle of the absence of violence," imprinting in audiences' minds "the image of the ultimate social cohesion, achieved through commercial exchange and the progress of rational knowledge."[154]

In representation, then, music shifts from direct action and use to the theatrical presentation of commodity consumption, the "enactment of order in noise."[155] The orchestra is an ideal vehicle for this persuasive task, for in it, individual, anonymous members (their anonymity reinforced by common costume) each take a part in producing a whole, the parts of which have no meaning except for their place within that musical or orchestral whole. The orchestra can function only when individual musicians submit to the will of the conductor, the "legitimate and rational organizer of a production whose size necessitates a coordinator."[156] The bureaucratic elite readily identifies with the conductor, suggests Attali, but not all audience members do. Thus emerges an important role for yet another specialist in spectacle: the soloist. The introduction of the soloist gives the crowd someone with whom to identify, saving them "from having to choose between identifying with the anonymity of the musicians and the glory of the leader."[157] As the star system evolves, the soloist becomes a significant part of the system of commodities for sale and exchange. Eventually, even the composer capitulates to this seemingly inexorable process of producing musical commodities for profit, since having one's music heard at all requires that works cater to the sympathies of the consumer. The audience has to be groomed carefully for its new role in spectacle, as evidenced by the introduction of the claque.[158] In due time, the audience learns to accept a silent and anonymous musical role, suppressing its complicity in the performance except in approved moments when the expression of appreciation is permissible. Indeed, even the very stuff of tonal music, its alternating patterns of consonance and dissonance, participates directly and vividly in this presentation of images of order achieved through submission to rational, hierarchical power.

This world of spectacle and fetish, of silently consumed images of sacrifice, is no less than the world of "music-turned-commodity."[159] In commodity exchange, music is a means for the creation of capital and spectacle. Gradually, musicians become salaried workers, and their creations and enactments are turned into commodities and money. Musical products become distinct and alienated from the labor that creates them. Consumption replaces action. Exchange replaces use. What was formerly a collaborative affair, the common property of all, becomes in representation a mere "monologue of specialists competing in front of consumers. The artist was born, at the same time as his work went on sale."[160] Now the musical commodity is little more than a "clumsy excuse for the self-glorification of musicians and the growth of a new industrial sector."[161]

Thus, under representation, use value is replaced by exchange value, and music becomes an artifact for silent consumption. Its spectacles function ideologically, presenting and affirming the inevitability and legitimacy of hierarchical order and commercial relations. Fetishized as a commodity, it is no longer necessary that music be experienced as relation or that people directly collaborate in channeling violence to become convinced of the inevitability of order, says Attali: simply watching the spectacle of its enactment is enough.[162]

Music's transformation from ritualistic activity to consumable commodity reveals the means of and early stages in a sequence of transformation that Attali apparently believes is everywhere evident in modern capitalistic society: "deritualize a social form, repress an activity of the body, specialize its practice, sell it as a spectacle, generalize its consumption . . ."[163] As suggested earlier, Attali also maintains that these changes become apparent in music long before they are manifest elsewhere in society, and that music is therefore prophetic in nature. But in his view, representation is already largely a thing of the past. Music has gone on to foretell yet another relation, one that is increasingly evident under conditions of modern market capitalism, and one that makes Attali's rather gloomy characterization of representation seem almost optimistic by comparison: repetition. The commodification that so troubled Adorno, it seems, was but the first step in a process that leads to the mass production of semi-identical objects, an achievement that threatens not merely to further transform music's meaning, but to shatter its capacity to mean at all.

Repetition

As long as the realization of music relies upon human productive activity, even if primarily by performing specialists, its commodification remains partial. To the extent representation still entails the assembly of people in specialized venues to witness its spectacles, its music retains a social meaning of sorts, and these events are commodities in a somewhat attenuated sense. However, the capacity to record, store, and reproduce musical events by technological means changes this situation abruptly. The singularity and uniqueness of the individual musical event is shattered by objects that have the ability to capture and duplicate it without apparent limit. This capacity for repetition means that "[u]sage [is] no longer the enjoyment of present labors, but the consumption of replications."[164] Both the action of making music and the 'live' music so made are simultaneously devalued, as the recording, the repetition, becomes the locus of musical experience. Although representation's spectacles had long been drifting toward repetition, the advent of the capacity for mechanical storage and retrieval brought about a decisive and profound change. What is consumed is no longer the spectacle, but its replica. Reproduction means "the death of the original, the triumph of the copy," since in mass production the original mold "is no longer anything more than one of the factors in production . . ."[165] Just as in representation the performing specialist assumed control of the productive and reproductive role that had formerly fallen to society at large, in repetition the copy usurps the role formerly reserved for performers. Performing musicians become fabricators of products that, once produced, no longer require the performer except to help promote product sales. Creating product demand, enlarging the sphere of consumption assumes greater importance than the actual making or doing of music. Repetition transforms performance into an imitation or representation of the recording. And as listening becomes ever more removed from the trappings of live concerts and concert halls, music's distinctive collectivity atrophies. The musical product becomes ever more alienated from the human contexts to which it once owed its existence.

In economic terms, this is the inevitable outcome of music's entry into the capitalistic world of commodity exchange. For, as Attali points out, although all social organization consists in the accommodation and structuring of differences, "[n]o market economy can develop without erasing those differences in mass production."[166] The modern market economy, founded on mass production and consumption, requires that differences be "artificially recreated in the multiplication of semi-identical objects."[167] Mass production and dissemination eradicate value-generating differences. The ever-sameness, the superficial differences, and the stereotypes that Adorno associated with the culture industry, then, are for Attali inevitable features of a political economy based upon repetition. But not only are the sociopolitical implications of repetition more extreme and far-reaching than Adorno's criticisms implied, Attali holds out no hope of a 'modern', avant-garde music somehow transcending these forces. Repetition shatters the very possibility of meaning and destroys the capacity even to hear. The crisis it creates cannot be resolved from within. Only by moving beyond repetition is there hope.

Central to Attali's account of repetition is his belief that the excesses it generates actually silence music, draining it of its capacity to communicate and indeed depriving us of our very capacity to hear. As the musical product is reproduced in superabundance, and as creation of demand becomes the paramount concern of the capitalistic enterprise, sound, noise, and music come to penetrate every crack and crevice of daily life. Such superabundance not only impedes but dissolves real listening, personal engagement, and authentic communication. Excess depletes both musical and social meaning, leaving in their wake a mere "flow of noises as ersatz sociality."[168] In repetition, music loses its former socially constructive function, and even its ability (in representation) to affirm the possibility of society. Instead, it can only repeat "the memory of another society—even while culminating its liquidation—a society in which it [music] had meaning."[169]

Thus, Attali's account of the evolution of music's political economy can be completed: deritualize, specialize, sell, generalize consumption—and then, in repetition, see that music is "stockpiled until it loses its meaning."[170] Musical activity that originated as a way of organizing and articulating individual difference within the context of social relation is thus overwhelmed by economic forces that shatter all difference and individuality. Music increasingly comes to resemble Muzak, a "monologue of standardized, stereotyped music [that] accompanies and hems in a daily life in which in reality no one has the right to speak any more."[171]

Ritual made people forget. Representation made people believe. Repetition silences. It is therefore the ideal vehicle for bureaucratic, technocratic power. Massive dissemination of sound renders all potential resistance mute. It silences, censors, and ultimately deafens. Attali quotes Russolo approvingly: "[T]he machine today has created such a variety and rivalry of noises that pure sound, in its exiguity and monotony, no longer arouses any feeling."[172] John Cage would likely agree enthusiastically.

In repetition, music is no longer a collaboration among participants, no longer a collective opportunity for spectators to meet and interact, no longer, it seems, even a form of sociality at all. The consumer's relation to the 'stockpile' is now strictly an individual affair. The musical event loses its uniqueness and its social character at the same time. Since the stockpile has neither intrinsic musical nor social value, since repetition only replicates recorded representations rather than creating anything new, it generates not order but disorder. Accordingly, it must "spend increasing amounts of value to maintain order."[173] Production of the musical commodity becomes decidedly secondary to production of demand for that commodity, raising significant and disturbing questions about the role of musical education under such conditions.

In repetition, concludes Attali, "a significant portion of the surplus-value created in the production of supply must be spent to create demand; and repetition produces less and less use-value."[174] Repetition retains two limited needs for musical performance and spectacle: first, for creating molds (making recordings)—the dies from which copies are cut; and second, as advertisements for (efforts to infuse meaning into) the vast stockpiles of musical commodity. Ironically, then, the chief value of live performances comes to consist in their capacity to generate demand for recordings. Indeed, the live performance, which the recording originally set out to replicate, comes to have value primarily as an imitation of the recording. "What irony," observes Attali: "[p]eople originally intended to use the record to preserve the performance, and today the performance is only successful as a simulacrum of the record."[175]

When music undergoes the transformation from collective activity into industrial production, it loses its humanity, severs its last remaining linkage to the time when it had the capacity truly to reach and touch us. The political message inherent in this, the image of power and our relationship to it, is a chilling one. According to Attali, repetition's message is that "power is no longer incarnated in [people]. It is. Period."[176] Mass music thus honors technocratic power, and exerts a stifling social influence. It eradicates individual difference, enforces a state of absolute identity-through-consumption. In repetition, "One consumes in order to resemble and no longer, as in representation, to distinguish oneself."[177] Thus mass music is "a powerful factor in consumer integration, interclass leveling, cultural homogenization."[178] It eliminates distinctiveness, silences, anesthetizes, depersonalizes. In contemporary repetitive society, Attali concludes, it is not so much alienation as solitude that threatens people; thus, "conformity to the norm becomes the pleasure of belonging, and the acceptance of powerlessness takes root in the comfort of repetition."[179] In short, once music ceases to be an affair of the human body, once its alienation is so profound that it can no longer function as an articulation of difference, it becomes "trapped in identity and . . . dissolve[s] into noise."[180]

Unlike Adorno, Attali sees no redemptive role for 'serious' music in this situation. It may maintain the outward appearance of having evaded the clutches of repetition, of having avoided the loss of meaning to commodification, exchange, and the culture industry. However, that appearance is strictly illusory. Music produced by serious musicians has become completely abstract, "noise without meaning."[181] In truth, then, far from being guardians against the effects of repetition, serious musicians are significant agents in its continuing encroachment: for "the absence of meaning is the necessary condition for the legitimacy of a technocracy's power."[182] Indeed, modern serious composers exemplify all the essential attributes of technocracy and repetition. Their compositions operate on a level of cerebral abstraction and radical novelty that makes them remote and inaccessible. Their music is elitist, bureaucratic, and impersonal. In this, they resemble technicians and computer program designers more than creators of meaning. They have become mere mouthpieces for repetitive power, "learned minstrel[s] of the multinational apparatus . . . producer[s] of a symbolism of [technocratic] power."[183] By their complicity in the liquidation of meaning, their music confirms "the end of music and of its role as a creator of sociality."[184]

Thus, although for different reasons, modern serious music shares with popular music the definitive meaninglessness and silence of repetition. Both are purveyors of repetition's "ideology of nonsense."[185] Both are agents in the eradication of difference and meaning. These circumstances create fertile conditions for two potential outcomes: the dictatorial imposition of repetitive power on the one hand; and the outright renunciation of repetition and stockpiling on the other. Where Adorno could not have conceived the emergence of anything but a totally administered society given such circumstances, Attali's predictions are considerably more optimistic. He believes he sees evidence of the early stages of the emergence of a new kind of musical and social relation he calls composition, one that consists in "the permanent affirmation of the right to be different . . . [and] to compose one's life."[186]

Composition

Attali's images of depleted meaning, of resignation to all-pervasive technocratic power, and of a reversion to noise and violence are every bit as bleak as Adorno's, and indeed, perhaps even more so given the detail in which they are analyzed and elaborated. Since affirming personal difference and empowering individuals to compose musics and lives that are distinctly their own stand in such stark contrast to the desolation of repetition, his account of composition is particularly important. Today, he suggests, a new way of making music is on the rise, one that foretells the advent of musical and socio-political relations beyond the oppressive silence of repetition. Although it is emerging "piecemeal and with the greatest ambiguity,"[187] the clues it provides of a new, utopian reality under construction are simply too important to pass over. For composition entails the rejection of repetitive stockpiling, a renunciation of passive consumption, and a turn to direct engagement: an affirmation of the primacy of human agency. "We are all condemned to silence," he writes, "unless we create our own relation with the world and try to tie other people into the meaning we thus create. That is what composing is."[188]

Composition, for Attali, entails doing for its own sake, making music solely for the joy it brings, taking "pleasure in being instead of having."[189] It takes pleasure in producing the kind of differences that are anathema to repetitive, technocratic power. Rather than standardization and uniformity, composing celebrates originality, personal autonomy, individuality, and distinctiveness. In this it differs not only from repetition, but from spectacle and ritual as well. It is not, Attali argues, a return to any former state of socio-musical affairs but the herald of a new form of social relation. Composition eradicates the distinctions between music and its use, between worker and consumer, between doing and having. To compose is to take pleasure in actions and interactions strictly for themselves, as they occur, and not for their instrumental use toward some preordained end. Beyond music, Attali boldly contends, this new mode of relation foretells the end of specialization and of the problem of the division of labor.[190]

Composition portends the disappearance of the commercial musical site. Music will be made "not in a temple, not in a hall, not at home, but everywhere . . . in whatever way it is wished, by anyone who wants to enjoy it."[191] Although he offers scant evidence, Attali claims there is a resurgence of musics that require little study, are orally transmitted, largely improvisational, and broadly accessible. In composition, music ceases to be a product separable from the act of its creation, a fact which "shatter[s]" the commodity and reestablishes direct links between work and play, between people and their lives.[192] In this relation, "Music is no longer made to be represented or stockpiled, but for participation in collective play, in an ongoing quest for new, immediate communication, without ritual and always unstable."[193]

Composition's instability, its decentralization of power and authority, its ruggedly individualistic nature, its emphasis upon agency: all these situate composition in stark contrast to the sociomusical values and practices of repetition, representation, and ritual. Composition creates and celebrates differences instead of eradicating them through standardization and repetition. Indeed, it is nothing less than a "social form for the recreation of difference," one that is rooted in commitment to tolerance and autonomy.[194] Because of its commitment to differences, tolerance, and autonomy, composition apparently takes its chances, so to speak. Leaving the repetitive world behind is an act fraught with danger and insecurity, for it represents an endorsement of local rather than putatively universal knowledge, of a contingent rather than progressive conception of history, and of a concept of meaning that accepts fragility and temporariness as permanent and unavoidable conditions. Thus, composition is "laden with risk, disquieting, an unstable challenging, an anarchic and ominous festival . . . with an unpredictable outcome."[195] However, says Attali, it is also "the only utopia that is not a mask for pessimism."[196] If composition's instability and unpredictability arouse nostalgia for the apparent security of former times, it is imperative people recognize the ultimate impossibility of meaning in repetition. The apparent comfort of the repetitive status quo is a menacing, pernicious illusion: for "the World, by repeating itself, is dissolving into Noise and Violence."[197]

Given Adorno's contempt for jazz and popular music, it is particularly intriguing that Attali claims to find the strongest evidence of composition's break from repetition in precisely these musics. And yet, repetition's tenacity and pervasiveness must not be underestimated, as the ill-fated struggle of free jazz to break out of repetition illustrates. Attali describes the attempt of American blacks in the free jazz movement to achieve autonomy from capital by developing their own production and distribution networks. Their efforts ultimately failed because, according to Attali, they lacked the (in repetition) all important means to create and manipulate demand.[198] Unable to promote itself adequately, the voice of free jazz was unable to seize repetitive power and make itself heard. It was silenced. This failure shows both the futility of fighting repetition on its own turf, and the necessity for new modes of musical production outside the political economy of repetition. Attali claims to see evidence of the emergence of such new modes in some popular music practices: music created for enjoyment rather than money or spectacle, non-specialized music that requires no formal study and is easily and universally accessible. In these orally transmitted musics, individuals each create their own parts so that the music cannot be separated from the musician whose creation it is. "[T]he field of the commodity has been shattered," urges Attali, "and a direct relationship between man and his milieu is being reestablished."[199]

Commentary

As Susan McClary has noted, noise is both Attali's method and his subject.[200] His presentation deliberately employs the abruptness and ambiguity he attributes to noise, oftentimes at considerable expense to ('rational') consistency and clarity. But like Adorno, from whom he takes his lead, Attali apparently expects his reader to be a full participant in giving sense to his words. That he is an economist rather than a musician is often abundantly clear. But the distinctly political-economic perspective from which he speaks is at once bewildering and fresh: a point of view few beneficiaries of institutionalized musical socialization and education could be expected to imagine, let alone articulate with any cogency. Whether or not one accepts all the details of his theory, his most basic premises are both lucid and persuasive. Sound and music are indeed unique ways of relating to the world and to each other. Music indeed has significance that extends well beyond its patterns and structures. Music's import is not, and has never been, exhausted in the orderly presentation of pleasant sounds.

Attali's characterizations of noise as dirt, power, weapon, and murder startle and challenge. They force us to examine the phenomenal character of sonorous experience, the fundamental nature of the relationships between sound, the body, and the world, as well as the distinctive way sounds situate us in the physical and social worlds. His portrayals of music as an agent of power and control; as a means of integration, domestication and socialization; as an instrument for the creation of homogeneity and conformity as well as difference and subversion; as a commodity that is up for sale like virtually everything else in modern capitalistic society—all these stand in the starkest possible contrast to the prevalent view of music as an autonomous art form, insulated from and untainted by the mundane crassness of politics and economics. The idea of music's formal purity is corrupted and challenged at every turn by its involvement with money and power. In Attali's view, music is not primarily an aesthetic phenomenon. It can soothe and stimulate, but it can also disturb, persuade, silence, and deafen. It can liberate and it can indoctrinate. It can empower and it can marginalize. Among Attali's clearer points is that music has all these capacities, but none of them essentially or inherently. And yet, music is invariably a site for struggle, since what counts as music is an inescapably political question about whose voice will be heard and whose will not. Finally, Attali shows how excess sound begets silence, much as the proliferation of information generated by computers devalues the idea, leaving people better informed but less knowledgeable. Multiplication and identity destroy meaning and pave the way for technocratic rule, for Adorno's totally administered society. In all this, Attali taunts the comfort of conventional stereotypes, speaking of noise, music, and sound as though there were no necessary or essential differences among them.

Attali also undercuts the belief in music's history as a unidimensional chronology, presenting in its place a succession of fissures, ruptures, and crises that beget different kinds of musics and social relations. Although his account of music is not intended to be a historically progressive one (of inexorable progress toward some absolute good), ritual, representation, and repetition can be plausibly conceived as successive stages in a continuum of increasing silence and alienation. In ritual, people give up their strictly individual relationship to sound for the security of collectivity. Ritual's communal experience offers people safety from the fundamental threats and violence of sound. In representation, people give up the directness of personal agency for reassuring images of social cohesion achieved by adherence to hierarchical power structures. In repetition, people yield the last vestiges of individuality to the numbing machinery of bureaucracy and technocratic power. In the effort to contain sound, first noise is silenced, then people's individual voices, and finally, all meaning.

From the standpoint of the capitalistic market economy and commodity exchange, then, each of these successive stages is progressive, while from the musical or humane perspective, each consists in an increasingly regressive loss of meaning and value. In Attali's account, commodification means ever-increasing alienation from human foundations of musical meaning as human activities are reduced to mere things. It apparently means the silencing or suppression of individual integrity as well. In ritual, the individual becomes submerged in collective sacramental experience. In representation, people suppress their voices in order to permit official power to speak. In repetition, people simply coexist in anonymous, resigned solitude. The dissolution of meaning, of individual autonomy and integrity, is thus virtually complete.

Composition promises to reverse these trends, to restore people's voices. But unlike ritual, which it resembles in certain respects, it is distinctly tolerant toward and committed to the recognition of individual difference and diversity. Composition thus offers a fundamentally new social and political order that affirms the right to be one's self—or just to be. Although it promises to reverse the process of alienation, to return people to a more immediate relation to sound, and to restore their own agency, it is important to note that Attali implies this outcome is not inevitable. Its emergence is portended by certain hopeful signs, but composition is only one possible successor to repetition; its success is by no means assured. The crisis of repetition may also be "the herald of a new dictatorship of representation."[201] And given the failure of free jazz to break out of repetition despite its best efforts, this possibility is one that demands to be taken seriously.

The standardization and technocracy of repetition are among the most chilling images in Attali's account of music. Adorno's complaints about eversameness and the calculated, superficial appearance of novelty take on an even more sinister character in Attali's account of things. For where Adorno worried about falsification of consciousness, Attali sees abundant evidence of epidemic destruction of meaning and value, the eradication of difference. In repetition, he shows, the primary value of the musical event or action lies in its function in creating the mold. Consequently, making music becomes less important than creating demand for a quasi-identical 'product'. The repetitive world is one in which nothing really happens except for "artificially created pseudoevents"[202] designed to give consumers the false sense that purchasing is a meaningful act. Difference is silenced, and commodities speak instead of people.

It may be fairly objected, however, that Attali's account of the adverse impact of recording and mass distribution neglects their positive impact upon accessibility. Certainly, the possibility of listening to music from all historical periods and all parts of the world is an achievement of immense significance, one that makes the recording well suited to certain kinds of education and to enhancing the very openness and tolerance Attali attributes to composition. Perhaps, then, repetition is not wholly evil. Attali would remind, though, that repetition is a music purged of spectacle, agency, and the communal interaction that are so vital to its meaning. We need, then, to remain extraordinarily vigilant lest the glossy seamlessness and the seeming inevitability of order in the recording become mistaken for conditions of music, and lest music continue to atrophy to the condition of the mere commodity.

Given its promise of a decisive break with repetition, it is unfortunate that Attali's evidence for the advent of composition is relatively sparse. His specific examples are scant, and his descriptions are often vague. Perhaps this is because, as Attali suggests, composition belongs to a political economy that is "difficult to conceptualize."[203] Or perhaps it is too early in its emergence for its features to be heard with real precision. In any event, composition raises a number of questions worthy of pursuit, not least of which is the appropriateness of 'composition' as its label. Because of its traditional association with formal, notated structures, composition is not the most natural name for the process Attali describes under its rubric: one that is often improvised, aural, and informal in nature.

On the general conditions that favor or impede composition, Attali is clear. Composition is hindered by any tendency to treat music as an object, to assign a higher value to its usage than to its production, and by any tendency toward centralization of power. One of the most fundamental distinctions between repetition and composition, then, is that composition finds music's primary value in personal involvement and agency. Music is something to be done more than contemplated, appreciated, consumed, or exchanged. Accordingly, musical activity must not capitulate to the deterministic influence of centralized power, to overspecialization, or to the conformist forces of mass production and distribution. Composition entails a loosening of restrictions and a corresponding relaxation of order. It rejects pressures to uniformity and nurtures diversity. It is, in short, a relation that is open, tolerant, and friendly to individual difference and a plurality of musics: a postmodern political economy.

It might be argued, however, that the characteristics Attali attributes to composition are not necessarily distinctive features of a new mode of musical relation, but simply those of the maker of music, the musical agent, who has always taken pleasure in doing and being. What he identifies as composition, then, might simply be the distinctive phenomenal character of musical doing; not some new mode of musical relation, but one that has been a definitive part of music's attraction and power since its very origins. Perhaps, then, composition is simply a return to the directness and immediacy of meaningful human engagement with sound—though with an explicit wariness of the fascistic tendencies of communal participation. This does not diminish the significance of Attali's insights into the debilitating effects of repetition, commodification, and consumption, and the necessity of rejecting them. It only suggests that many if not most of the attributes he finds in composition are things that have become obscured by representation and repetition. From this view, his project involves dealing with people's alienation from sound and music, facilitating a return, perhaps, to the directness and immediacy characteristic of music before representation. Although he insists that composition is not a return to any pre-existing state of affairs, his assertion is not closely argued. Indeed, composition's emphasis upon lived experience rather than exchange, upon agency rather than commodity consumption, does sound like nostalgia for aspects of musical experience that have become covered by the sediment of representation and repetition. Of course, Attali would disagree emphatically: in his view, composing can in no way be construed as a return to ritual or spectacle: "Both are impossible, after the formidable pulverizing effected by the political economy over the past two centuries."[204]

A more difficult issue is the role of autonomy in Attali's theory, especially in light of the problems it posed for Adorno. What is most distinctive about composition is its "permanent affirmation of the right to be different . . . [and the] right to compose one's life."[205] Only, on the surface at any rate, it seems that asserting its autonomy is the very thing that deprives serious or learned music of meaning. How does Attali propose that composition avoid the dead end encountered by Adorno's modern music? The most direct answer is that composition's difference is perhaps less radical than the autonomy claimed by proponents of avant garde music. Unlike the 'learned' musics of repetition, composition does not reject communication[206]—even if it does resist convention. Composition changes rules rather than plugging into existing ones. To express oneself, Attali says, is not just to exchange messages within a system made by others; it is to create. Thus composition honors difference and creativity so long as its individuality does not become so radical as to sever all ties. Music that is too different results in incommensurability: absence of meaning, failure of communication. At times Attali comes very close to this position. He says, for instance, "Any noise, when two people decide to invest their imaginary and their desire in it, becomes a potential relationship, future order."[207] At times like this it appears he may have pushed his pluralistic and relativistic conception of music dangerously near the solipsistic precipice, implying that any noise can be music if only people will it. To suggest as Attali does that in composition "each person dream[s] up his own criteria, and at the same time his way of conforming to them,"[208] may push things too far in the direction of particularism for much of an expressive, musical, or communicative nature to happen.

To its great credit, Attali's account encourages us to think about music from a radically different perspective. Its recognition of the profoundly distinct nature of sonorous experience and the way it situates us in the world is an insight that is easily overlooked. Likewise, his historical, political, and economic insights show us that music is not so much one thing as a multiplicity of ways of relating to the world, and that to conceive of its value as a single thing is extremely shortsighted. His insights into the relations between music and power make it exceedingly difficult to continue to entertain the conception of music as a hermetically insulated realm of endeavor, placing it instead in the messy world of human interactions and struggle.

It is possible to accept Attali's insights into the political economy of music, the interrelationships between music and social structures, and the impact of the capitalist market economy on music without necessarily accepting each of the conclusions to which these lead him. Specifically, his belief in music's prophetic capacity and his conviction that composition promises to deliver society from the clutches of repetition remain highly speculative. But whether or not these ideas can be sustained, Attali has succeeded in raising a host of questions that demand serious consideration by musicians. Is it really possible for composition to break free of repetition? How is it possible for music to avoid being 'consumed' as style? How can we restore to music the meaning of which repetition and mediation deprive it? Or is increasing alienation something music is ultimately powerless to avoid?

Concluding Remarks

In this chapter we have examined in some detail two provocative and highly original theories which, despite major differences, each insist on recognizing music as a socially significant enterprise. By placing music squarely within the matrix of human sociocultural activity, socially oriented theories pose serious challenges to the view that music's nature and value are strictly musical, all its own, and confer upon musical activity significance that often proves quite elusive to other accounts. At the same time, as we have seen, such convictions raise a plethora of thorny issues: Precisely what is the nature and extent of music's social significance? Is any part of it more inherently musical than others? What happens to the idea of musical value if music's worth is gauged by its social influences? How far can the idea of music as a social phenomenon be extended before it says more about music's effects than what it is? The views we have explored here hardly offer definitive answers to such questions; nor, as the next chapter will show, does the controversy surrounding such issues show any signs of abating in the near future. One thing seems clear, however: music's sociocultural situatedness, influence, and relativity are no longer things music philosophy can justify ignoring.

Adorno's highly complex thought has been enormously influential in generating awareness and appreciation of music's important sociopolitical connections. Although his philosophy is 'social' in a highly individual sense, it nevertheless insists that music's worth be gauged in light of social obligations. And although the precise nature of those obligations is itself a cultural variable, Adorno believes that in our particular circumstances music's social duty is crystal clear: it should challenge and thereby advance critical consciousness. In contemporary capitalistic society, music is faced with two alternatives, both with important social consequences: either advance critical awareness by resisting comfortable consumption, or be a pawn of the culture industry, functioning as a regressive, mind-numbing vehicle of indoctrination. Music is thus inescapably caught up in a host of political and moral concerns, and failure to acknowledge these makes us unwitting victims of the forces of domination. Music plays an utterly crucial role in shaping people's individual and collective consciousness and assuring social progress.

Despite his insistence on music's autonomy, on the objectivity of its meanings, and on structural hearing, then, it is clear that for Adorno music is never 'just' music, and that he regards the very idea as a highly dangerous one. Under no circumstances, he believes, should music be regarded as a mystical, spiritual, affirmative affair whose significance is exhausted in its own realm. Nor should people's subjective tastes and preferences be considered trustworthy indices of musical worth, because the regression of people's critical awareness under capitalism is already so advanced that they no longer know what they like, they only like what they know. Modern music's profoundly important redemptive mission is thus to subvert the kind of hearing (and mental habits) fostered by the irresponsible, inconsequential entertainments of commercial music — music that placates and pacifies, impeding rather than advancing social progress. Music is fast becoming, Adorno warns, a consumer commodity like any other — falling increasingly short of its potential to show us our true social circumstances. To resist commodification and fulfill its redemptive potential, music must refuse easy communication and affirmation; it must, rather, confront and defy expectation and habit. Its social function is, ironically, to be dysfunctional.

In Attali's views, we find a decisive turn away from the formalist belief in musical autonomy, and an equally decisive departure from the idea that music's significance is primarily individual or psychological. The nature and value of music are neither objective nor subjective, but intersubjective: music is a cultural affair, deeply enmeshed in relations of power and control. From this perspective, to think of music as the kind of thing whose nature and value have nothing whatsoever to do with moral and political issues is to misrepresent it seriously and to grievously underestimate its significance.

Like Adorno, Attali believes people have lost their ability to hear—not just music, but sound in general—and to their distinct detriment. So wholly preoccupied have we become with vision's ideals of clarity and distinctness that the significance of the ear's world is largely lost to us. If we would but listen, Attali suggests, we would find that the world has a great deal to say. But sound is not just a vehicle for understanding our place in the world, it is also a potent instrument for defining that place: music is an important agent in the creation and maintenance of social order. In controlling sound's inherent threats of violence, music presents us with vivid images of the subordination of individuality to collectivity, of disorder yielding to ordered wholeness. In this way, music plays a crucial social regulatory role.

This regulatory role plays itself out in a number of ways as society and its modes of musical production evolve and develop. In musical ritual, participants physically enact the subordination of individuality to the greater whole, events that worked powerfully to crystallize collective social organization. In representation, most of the overt activity is transferred to performing specialists, whose demonstrations of social cohesion are silently observed by audiences. The relation here is both passive and hierarchical: its superior-subordinate (performer-percipient) structure is instrumental in the replacement of use value by exchange value. In repetition, the locus of value undergoes a still more radical shift: from the original to the copy. This completes the commodification of human musical activity, its distancing or alienation from its roots in human agency, and at the same time radically devalues originality and individuality. The resultant standardization and technocratic power create a social situation not only devoid of human meaning and significance, but highly vulnerable to manipulation.

It is well worth noting that by social standards, this commodification and dehumanization of music is a very serious matter. And evidence that these concerns may be well founded is not difficult to come by. Rather than enhancing and enriching life, music atrophies, becomes an empty shell. It loses its transformative power, decays into mere decoration, into just another commodity for consumption—or even worse, becomes part of the machinery that conspires to dehumanize society.

While not all of what Adorno and Attali have to say may be persuasive, it is difficult to deny the fundamental premise their theories share: that music is a uniquely human and uniquely socializing force; that its significance extends well beyond its patterns and structures; and that it is intimately bound up in issues of social relatedness, politics, and power. The full force of these convictions will become even more apparent in the chapter ahead.

DISCUSSION QUESTIONS

1. What are the differences between construing 'the social' as context, as adherent quality, and as musically constitutive? Why are these distinctions important? Does treating the social as a musical context or influence reveal vestiges of an assumed musical 'in-itself'?

2. While many have found Adorno's contrasts between 'serious' and 'popular' music cogent and persuasive, other scholars believe that his insistence on the ever-sameness of popular music is little different from the popular music enthusiast's insistence that all classical music is 'the same'. Do you think that linking considerations of musical value to a narrow range of musical properties and practices blinded Adorno to other potentially vital musical values? How might criteria appropriate to the evaluation of popular music differ from those of serious music?

3. Adorno apparently believed that consciousness that is highly sensitive to subtle difference, or critically aware of particularity, is essential to experience that is truly authentic—and thus to personal autonomy, empowerment, and integrity. Do you believe these are important and viable goals for music teaching and learning? To what extent do current elementary, secondary, and postsecondary educational institutions currently address such ends? What instructional practices might such goals implicate?

4. Discuss how labels, categories, types, and styles obscure particularity and individuality: how assumptions of similarity violate the integrity of the different. How do these opposites dialectically interact in the learning process? What do you conclude about the relative importance of attending to similarities and differences when learning music?

5. How might a Marxist criticize the idea of music as an 'aesthetic' experience occasioned by 'works' of art? Or more specifically, how might the idea of aesthetic value for music mystify rather than critically inform awareness? Include in your answer the ideas of fetishization, commodification, reification, and false consciousness.

6. Adorno's phrase 'culture industry' is deliberately ironic. Discuss how this is so. Do you agree that the economic interests of capitalism have co-opted culture? Can you find an example of a musical practice that has successfully resisted or evaded commodification?

7. Is there validity to Adorno's criticisms of musics that affirm, make people feel good, or do precisely what perceptual habit leads them to expect? Outline the key points in a hypothetical debate between Adorno and Aristotle on this issue.

8. Do you agree with Adorno's assessment of the regression of people's ability to hear music as it is? If not, why not? If so, to what do you attribute the problem and how might it be rectified?

9. Can people who fail to perceive, say, differences in chord quality truly be said to hear music in which such harmonic differences are definitive structural features—in, for instance, traditional jazz improvisation? Explain.

10. Compare Adorno's comments on 'surrealistic' use-music to the practice of sampling in 'rap' music. Use Adorno's claims to mount an argument for the 'redemptive' potential of rap. How does rap's co-optation of the 'culture industry's' machinery might serve as an important corrective to Adorno?

11. How does commodification replace use value with exchange value? Discuss how 'repetition' has transformed the nature of musical performance, supporting your answer with specific examples. Of what significance are these insights to musicians?

12. For Adorno, jazz was a hopelessly primitive, 'light' music. Yet the academy appears to have concluded precisely the opposite: that jazz is an art form. Discuss how a music regarded as 'light' comes to be regarded as 'serious', and thereby deserving of institutional endorsement. Can jazz be an art form and at the same time perform the social function Attali calls composition? Why or why not?

13. Discuss what the tendency to passive receptivity, nurtured for instance by television, may imply for the relative instructional significance of listening to and making music.

14. Although Adorno seems unwilling to confront it in any but a very narrow range of music, he clearly believes there is important educational and social value in what Harold Osborne once called the 'shock of the alien'. Why does Adorno think this important? How do convictions like these relate to current interests in multicultural education through music? Which do you think more musically important: the shock of the alien, or the ability to 'live into' one's own music? Why?

15. Do you agree that popularity is an inverse gauge of musical worth, that people's 'likes' say more about their habits and predilections than about music itself? Is there any musical point in studying popular musics? Why or why not?

16. One of the definitive characteristics of what is now called 'modernism' is its belief that change is progressive, an advance toward the better. Thus, Adorno is in at least one sense the quintessential modernist. Does musical change ever represent progress, or is it rather just change, just difference? If the latter, what is the point of education?

17. If the way society orders and controls sound in music reflects the way it politically structures power relations, what might 'classical' music suggest about such arrangements in Western urban society? How does this differ for African drumming? Jazz?

18. Use Attali's accounts of the nature of ritual and sound to explore the hypothesis that were it not for the distinctive ways humans relate to and through sound, a truly human society might never have emerged.

19. Marxists suggest that education in capitalist societies is a process designed to generate demand for commodities: to create consumers. One of the arguments often advanced in support of musical instruction for nonprofessionals is the need for audiences, people willing to consume the commodities generated from the labor of musicians. Are you comfortable with the idea of educating musically to create audiences? Why or why not?

20. Unlike Adorno, Attali thinks he sees musical evidence of the forces of commodification being resisted, subverted, even shattered, and of the reestablishment of a direct relation between people and their worlds. Whose prognosis for music do you find more convincing, Attali's or Adorno's? Why?

21. One of the distinguishing features of Attali's 'composition' is its tolerance toward—indeed, its desire to nurture and sustain—individual difference and diversity. How might a commitment to such ends change the way music is taught? Performed?

Contemporary Pluralist Perspectives

The quest for general, comprehensive explanations has long been considered central to philosophical inquiry. One of the hallmarks of good music philosophy, in this view, is its capacity to get beyond apparent diversity and illuminate the fundamental unity underlying all music, all experiences that are truly and properly 'musical': to transcend particular points of view and reveal the truth about music as it objectively is. In the late twentieth century, however, this notion of philosophy as a vehicle for the revelation of ultimate truth and reality appears to have lost much of its persuasiveness. Heightened awareness of the radical diversity and multiplicity of musical practices has made us keenly aware that those once presumed most inherently musical comprise but a small part of the world's musical activity. Voices once suppressed or ignored are now being heard, and what they are saying is often strikingly different from conventional accounts. It is frequently alleged that our disciplinarily sanctioned accounts of music's nature and value are shaped by particular biases and interests, and that the normative, hierarchical character of those accounts distorts our understanding of broad ranges of musical practice.

Put another way, traditional philosophy's explanations of music's nature and value have been based on implicit, unexamined assumptions about what music that is 'truly musical' should be and do. Music of a particular style or status or tradition is presumed to represent music's highest attainment; beyond it lies a large, residual body of less-than-musical practices—music that is 'other' to this norm, music which does not quite measure up. Musical philosophy, in other words, often made unarticulated assumptions about which music, whose music, was music at its best; and that most musical of musics was generally the 'high art' music of the European masters. But as technologies have brought the far corners of the globe closer together, it has become increasingly difficult to sustain the idea that music is essentially of one cloth, such that it can be hierarchically arranged in terms of its efficacy in achieving a common musical end.

356

People have become acutely sensitive to the fact that music's plurality cannot be subsumed by a single set of values, that musical differences cannot be reduced to differences in quality. Different musics serve different needs and answer to different interests. There is growing recognition that the evaluation of music by values foreign to its intent is as unjustified as colonial occupation of territory. Recognition of the integrity of diverse and divergent musics, and of the need to understand them on their own terms, has transformed the way most people engage in music philosophy today. Musics of different cultures clearly do not all conform to the same sets of concerns, cannot be judged by the same standards without distortion. 'Other', it is increasingly recognized, must not be taken for 'worse', only for 'different'.

Desirable though it might seem, then, that an introductory exploration of music philosophy close with a definitive synthesis that draws together the various strands of philosophical reflection into a neat summary formula, that will not happen here. To do so would seriously misrepresent the character of current philosophical thought. Philosophy's fascination with grand narratives has fallen into disfavor, and instead of one definitive account of music's nature and value, late-twentieth-century thought appears more inclined to offer alternatives. Where for centuries philosophy presumed its mission was to explain music—all of it, or at least all that was deserving of serious consideration—contemporary thought is far more inclined to conceive of philosophy as a perspectival undertaking whose capacity to illuminate is partial, relative to point of view and method, capable of clarifying, yet capable of obfuscating at the same time. Most contemporary music philosophy has become more cautious in its claims, more sensitive to the profound multiplicity and diversity of its subject, and less inclined to assume that music—or anything else for that matter—is unconditionally good. The Western art music canon, once presumed the apotheosis of musical achievement, is increasingly seen as one set of musical possibilities rather than the definitive one. It is increasingly recognized that efforts to 'educate' and 'elevate' tastes can be and often are destructive of vibrant, vital musical cultures. Hence, philosophy seeks increasingly to balance its traditional interest in general, comprehensive theory with respect for particularity and difference.

In short, philosophy has grown wary of universalist discourses, of accounts that purport to articulate absolute truths which obtain regardless of context. Sensitivity to the plurality, diversity, and (often) starkly divergent character of musical practices has brought about a fundamental shift away from grand theory, and toward accounts in which plurality and difference figure centrally. While this shift from static, unitary accounts to dynamic, multidimensional ones takes many forms, feminism and postmodernism are among the most provocative, representing "new paradigms of social criticism which do not rely on traditional philosophical underpinnings."[1] Decisively pluralistic in character, both strenuously resist the idea that music and musical value are fixed, singular, or uniform. Highly sensitive to the negative political and conceptual consequences of presumed neutrality and inalterability, both feminist and postmodern theorists regard knowledge and values as psychosocial constructions. Therefore, philosophy's task is not to uncover essential truths, but to illuminate how such beliefs and ideas as these have been constructed. Once deconstructed, they may be reconstructed in ways that avoid notions of fixity, permanence, and inevitability, making us more accepting of their contingency, and helping wean us from the human need apparently satisfied by ideas of universality. Doing so, it is believed, will help us conceive of things like knowledge and music in ways that are more fully human and more humane, recognizing distinctness and difference.

The trick is to avoid making an absolute of difference, or implying that differences are more inherently important than similarities. At issue is not so much whether differences among people and musics exist (they invariably do), but which among those myriad differences warrant serious consideration, and when, and for what purposes. The pluralistic perspectives sketched in this final chapter mark a decisive, perhaps radical move toward taking difference seriously, toward critically examining what differences should be taken into account, and toward more careful consideration of who makes that determination. In short, contemporary pluralist accounts of music's nature and value are deeply skeptical toward totalizing, universalist discourses, where all music properly so-called is and does basically the same kind of thing. In place of an essentially unitary 'music' concept, they posit a diverse, ever-changing field of musical practices, with values that are multiple, often competing, and occasionally even contradictory.

We will begin this chapter with an orientation to feminist issues and concerns, and then examine a number of ways in which those concerns manifest themselves in discourses about music. To the question of what it means to look at music from a feminist perspective we shall see that there is no short or easy answer—at least not that does justice to the complexity and diversity of feminist scholarship. Our strategy, then, will be to survey a relatively broad range of views in order to show some of the points of divergence and convergence among current theorists. We will first examine Heide Göttner-Abendroth's[2] effort to articulate a 'matriarchal' alternative to the dominant patriarchal aesthetic, one derived from her studies of ancient mythology and archeology. Her descriptions of a woman-centered, ecstatic ritual broadly introduce the many concerns to be explored in this chapter: women's invisibility in traditional accounts of music, the ways women's music might differ from men's, and so forth.

Since Kant's accounts of beauty and aesthetic experience have strongly influenced so many conventional assumptions about the nature of music and the arts, feminist critiques of those accounts have potentially far-reaching implications. Jane Kneller's and Mary Wiseman's resistant readings of Kant seem to suggest, for instance, that music's perennial struggle to justify itself may stem at least in part from gender-related stereotypes in which beauty, like women, is pleasant, enjoyable, civilizing, but decidedly inferior and subordinate to higher, male-identified rationality.

With Roberta Lamb, we next ask what it might mean for women to make music *as women*. The subtle insights of Suzanne Cusick show what that may sometimes mean for women performing Western classical music. By drawing attention to the capacity of beautiful, moving patterns of sound to convey hurtful messages and reinforce undesirable stereotypes, and by showing how musical performances are often performances of quite a bit more than 'just the music', Cusick underscores the need for more critically informed interpretations and more resistant renditions of music.

Susan McClary boldly and provocatively links music to matters of gender, sex, and the erotic—and not just popular, commercial music, but serious 'art' music as well. McClary is highly critical of what she sees as art music's pretentious claim to be above such mundane affairs, untainted by bodily matters. Indeed, she insists that the sensual, bodily dimensions of musical experience are chief among the things that draw people to music and make it meaningful for them. Marcia Citron concurs, and describes a number of interesting ways in which gender and sexuality are woven into art music in the symphonic tradition. Citron also advances the intriguing view that much of the music composed in that tradition may resonate with gendered processes that are more reflective of and congruent with men's experiences than women's—a possibility she thinks may account for women's conspicuous absence from the ranks of composers of such music.

John Shepherd also situates music within the social realms of gender and politics, pointing to tensions between the sensual and the rational in Western classical music, in particular its constraint and standardization of timbre, sound's 'tactile core'. The narrow range of permissible timbral variation in serious traditional music is, he believes, symptomatic of the need to control the sensual, bodily mode of engagement that timbral experience entails. Indeed, suggests Shepherd, music can be read as a kind of 'social text' with the important capacity—because of its marginal, 'feminized' status—to tell us important things about our culture that we are otherwise unwilling or unable to acknowledge.

Among the more recurrent themes to emerge in these discussions is that music plays a significant role in constructing and confirming gender ideologies—the systems of beliefs that govern patterns of inclusion and exclusion, that determine which similarities and which differences 'count' when it comes to allocating power or determining whose voice should be heeded. These sociocultural dynamics of domination and subordination, as Ellen Koskoff explains, are key to understanding women's frequent marginalization or exclusion from musical practices. But such practices and concerns are not just 'women's issues': for the ways musical practices construct 'I' and 'we', 'us' and 'them', are vitally important to all members of society. As Ruth Solie puts it, few of the meaningful differences between people are innate; rather, they are social constructions, products of socialization. Music's place as part of the 'technology of gender construction' is thus among contemporary feminism's more pressing musical concerns: for if we can better understand how music helps construct hard differences (the kind that seem to motivate acts of oppression), we will be that much closer to achieving what many advance as feminism's ultimate goal, the elimination of oppression.

The latter part of this final chapter addresses the unsettled and unsettling philosophical terrain commonly designated 'postmodern'. There we will find an orientation to music that is deeply suspicious of things like essences, absolutes, timeless truths, and universals—the very 'stuff' conventional music philosophy

has struggled so valiantly to illuminate. By rejecting the idea of an inherent musical nature toward which music is progressively advancing and by which its
worth can be gauged, by toppling hierarchies and exploding the idea of the extramusical, postmodern sentiments represent serious challenges to many if not
most of the assumptions that have formed the foundation for traditional discourses about music's nature and value. Regardless of one's disposition toward
them, then, postmodern sensibilities demand our serious attention.

Feminist Perspectives

From the perspective of many feminist theorists, philosophy's presumed neutrality and universality have a long history of advancing the views, values, and
power of men, while marginalizing, ignoring, and effectively silencing women.
All too often, voices claiming to speak for all humankind have been male voices,
and the 'universal truths' they advanced have been ideologies that secure and
preserve patterns of male control. As Biddy Martin observes, "women's silence
and exclusion from struggles over representation have been the condition of possibility for humanist thought . . ."[3] An equally significant source of feminism's
resistance to universal, inclusionary claims can be found its own recent history,
where efforts to articulate 'the' definitively and uniquely female perspective re-
sulted in theories that were largely representative of Western, formally educated,
heterosexual, able-bodied, white women. In other words, the presumption of female sameness behind these efforts and theories threatened to duplicate some
of the very transgressions feminism sought to eradicate. Because of this historically informed wariness of the distortions and injustices created when similarity
or uniformity are uncritically assumed, most contemporary feminist scholarship
is markedly pluralistic and sensitive to difference.

But besides being pluralistic, what is feminism? This seemingly straightforward question has no simple answer, at least not one that does it justice. Its theoretical orientations range from 'liberal' to 'radical', from psychoanalytic to Marxist, from relatively traditional to postmodern, and from 'black' to 'French', to
designate but a few.[4] In fact, since the very label 'feminism' suggests a unity and
uniformity that is seldom found among feminists, it is often suggested that 'fem-
inisms' would be a more descriptive term. Feminist theory is extraordinarily dynamic, interdisciplinary, and diverse. Despite widespread ideological and strategic differences, however, most feminists share a fundamental concern about the
differential power and privilege enjoyed by men and women, and a commitment to understanding and eliminating systemic oppression. Thus, understanding and transforming power relations are concerns that figure prominently in
feminist theory. It is a serious mistake, however, to assume as media accounts
frequently do that these concerns are exclusively 'women's issues': for, as one
scholar asserts, feminism seeks "nothing less than the reorganization of the world
through a commitment to eradicating ideologies of domination. . . ."[5] While
feminism is of course a 'women's movement', the ranks of feminist theorists include both men and women, and feminism seeks to transform culture in ways
that ultimately benefit everyone. And central to that effort is a fuller under-

standing of how women's situations and experiences in society differ from men's. So "while the feminist stance is not restricted to women, it is nevertheless true that feminism in both men and women grows out of reflecting upon the experiences of *women*."[6]

It is also a mistake to reduce feminism to a political movement, for that seriously underestimates its complexity and the range of issues with which it is concerned, many of which are highly philosophically significant. Although feminism is indeed often political, it is hardly the case that it is predominantly or invariably so. To the extent it seeks change, reorganization, and transformation, it is politically inclined; yet feminism is also rich in theory, embracing a multitude of issues with implications that extend well beyond politics, and promising to effect dramatic realignments in the way we think about and engage in musical activity.

Feminist critiques are often highly critical of the abstractness and dualism of patriarchal or male-dominated thought. Such thought tends to depersonalize experience and to structure reality in terms of tightly interwoven sets of binary oppositions—male/female, reason/emotion, mind/body, good/evil, culture/nature, self/other—which, Solie has suggested, usually boil down to the contrast "under control/out of control."[7] Not only do such oppositions wrongly dichotomize what is continuous and fluid, setting rigid boundaries where none exist, but they function hierarchically as well: the first term is invariably privileged over the second. Thus, the world is radically divided into the domain of the normal, trustworthy, familiar, respectable, and valuable, and the domain that is not: the domain of the different, the aberrant, the 'other'. These linked pairings, Solie observes, "create long chains of associations, virtuosic in their ready applicability, that exercise a strong and virtually subliminal influence on the ways we position and interpret groups of people, their behavior, and their works."[8] So these chained binary structures become deeply embedded conceptual habits, the mental stuff with which people organize, interpret, and unfortunately, falsify vast realms of human experience. In this process, categories of 'other'—which, of course, is where patriarchal thought locates woman—are mapped onto each other, so that 'woman' is associated with emotion rather than reason, with body rather than mind, with nature rather than culture, and is situated squarely within the category 'out-of-control'. This binary process of inclusion and exclusion, of "saming" and "othering,"[9] significantly distorts conceptions not only of women but of everything to which it is applied, including, as we shall see, music.

Because it neglects women's distinctive experience, traditional patriarchal thought and knowledge represents a view seen with only one eye, only half a picture—or so many feminist critiques maintain. But of what does the other half consist? Explanations of how and why women's experience differs from men's lead in two somewhat divergent directions: those that favor the idea that women's differences are innate and biological, and those that insist they are socially constructed. Adherents of the former view insist that there is something definitively and essentially 'female' about women's experiences and ways of knowing, such that how women feel, speak, and know is fundamentally different from the experience represented by prevailing patriarchal views of things. This appeal to a female or feminine 'essence' has been most strongly supported in France, where, as Solie explains, feminist theorists have often based their accounts on the idea of "a feminine sexuality radically different from the masculine, a sexuality that is, in some versions, fundamentally bodily. . . ."[10] However, this 'essentialism', or presumption of what we might call hard-wired differences between men and women, suggests the kind of biological determinism that seems to tie people's destinies to their sex. Rather than accept the fatalistic implications of that view, the 'constructivist' perspective prevalent in North America regards such differences as social creations: as matters of nurture rather than nature.

That they are not hard-wired, however, does not mean women's differences are imaginary or any less significant than the essentialist maintains, just that, as Solie puts it, ". . . few if any of the meaningful differences between groups of people are innate."[11] The idea of an essentially female experience may be appealing, and it is certainly understandable how it might arise as a counter to men's historical presumption that their words and ideas applied to all human beings, regardless of sex or gender. But the trouble is that belief in hard-wired differences can be used to rationalize different treatment, perpetuating the practices of domination feminists want to eliminate. If instead men's and women's identities and roles are products of socialization, if they are 'performative' rather than 'substantive',[12] then presumably they can be modified and transformed. And that is the end to which the constructivist view of gender differences is most often committed.

Although differences between men and women cannot be disputed, then, whether those differences are biological or social is an issue on which opinion is divided. One way of dealing with the issue is to insist on a clear distinction between the durable, biological categories of sex (female and male), and the socially constructed categories of gender (women and men, femininity and masculinity). Though they differ as to precisely where that line of distinction should be drawn, most contemporary feminist thinkers would insist that socialization is a far more influential factor in determining men's and women's differential identities and roles in society than their genes. As Koskoff puts it, "aside from the obvious biological differences between females and males . . . most other behaviors depend not so much on biological sex differentiation but on culturally conceived notions of gender and on prestige systems that accord value to one gender over the other."[13] Battersby puts it more strongly yet: what most distinguishes a woman, she writes, "is not her biology, but the way society categorises and treats her because of her biology."[14] On this view, most of the so-called 'natural' differences that lead to the "asymmetries of power"[15] between men and women are in fact cultural in origin. To redress those inequities, we must better understand how gender differences are socially created, performed, and maintained. And this, as we will see, is where music enters the picture: for music is, according to many feminist scholars, deeply implicated in gender relations and gender construction.

These issues can be conceptualized in terms of a cluster of questions which clearly frames their common relevance to gender, music, and issues of power:

How do we construct our ideas of sameness and difference? of 'us' and 'them'? of 'ours' and 'theirs'? How do we decide which differences should be taken seriously? and when? and for what purposes? And perhaps most importantly, who decides?

Music from Feminist Perspectives

While its place in a great many intellectual disciplines is secure and well established, feminism's entry into music scholarship has come rather belatedly. Chief among the reasons for this is a deep-rooted belief in musical autonomy, which continues to situate musical and sociocultural concerns on opposite sides of a great ontological divide. From this perspective, feminist theory and criticism attempt to politicize what is incontrovertibly unpolitical, and to locate gender and power issues where they simply cannot be: within abstract, self-sufficient patterns of musical sound. Conceding the relevance of gender issues to music, then, would diminish music's integrity, radically compromising what is perhaps most nourishing and reassuring about truly great music: its capacity to deliver and keep us at a safe distance from the troubling contingencies of the mundane world. Musically relevant theorizing must thus confine itself to 'the notes', and leave extramusical speculation to the likes of anthropologists, sociologists, and psychologists. Since convictions like these are part and parcel of the rigid disciplinarity and binary thinking many feminist theorists are committed to changing, it is hardly surprising that the feminist musical project has often encountered strenuous resistance, and is frequently characterized as a passing fad. But feminist theory is unlikely simply to go away and leave music alone. Indeed, its impact on music scholarship has already been so significant that it is simply no longer possible for an informed appreciation of the range of philosophical discourse about music to neglect feminism.

Since women's contributions are conspicuously absent from canonical lists of honored musicians, theorists, and works, one of the first tasks to which feminist scholars in music directed their efforts was compensatory in nature: identifying women whose efforts have been overlooked and ignored by male-centered scholarship, and exploring the reasons for women's underrepresentation. Since traditionally the only music believed to be of substance was that which operated in a male-dominated, public sphere, women, sequestered in a private, domestic domain, were systematically denied access to the institutions where 'important' music was made and discussed. Male institutional and disciplinary control deterred women's participation, and assured when they did participate that their status was marginal and their influence negligible. Thus, challenging the canon, interrogating its categories and value hierarchies, has been a crucial preliminary step for feminist music scholars. When feminist scholars address music's nature and value, old familiar questions are framed in radically different ways: as though women mattered.

But what might it mean if women's musical practices and contributions were taken seriously? How might women's musical voice differ from that of the historically dominant male? This phase of the feminist project Lamb characterizes as "the difficult work of discovering how we women can make musical sense collectively."[16] That work involves exploring women's situations as gendered subjects in a political-cultural world and creating authentic representations of women's musical consciousness. Key to this task is the identification of a 'women's sensibility' or a 'women's musical aesthetic'. To this end, feminist theorists frequently draw upon differences in women's and men's bodily and sexual experiences, suggesting for instance that a women's music might prefer gradual, cumulative development to the abrupt, powerful contrasts characteristic of music composed by men. According to Cox, a women's music would "deconstruct musical hierarchies and the dialectical juxtaposition and resolution of opposites, disrupt linearity, and avoid definitive closures."[17]

As Solie observes, the feminist interest in difference and distinctness implicates fundamental questions "about what pieces of music can express or reflect of the people who make and use them, and thus of the differences between and among those people."[18] Many theorists interested in these issues explore music's place in creating and reinforcing gender roles, roles integral to the power structures responsible for the long history of women's domination. Also, music is examined for representations of women that promote fear, hatred, and subordination,[19] and for harmful stereotypes of femininity and masculinity. These theorists urge critical examination of the gender messages embedded in pleasant patterns of sound, and the development of listening and performance strategies that resist such messages. Lamb cautions, "Music croons in its semiotic code those cultural myths that are no longer acceptable verbally and visually in a politely liberated society."[20]

A Matriarchal Muse

Many of the issues to which we have alluded above are exemplified in Heide Göttner-Abendroth's ambitious attempt to outline what she calls a "matriarchal aesthetic": the characteristics she thinks distinctive to women's art.[21] She bases her theory not upon essentialist assumptions about a distinctly female way of being, but on mythological and archeological evidence of ancient matriarchal societies. According to Göttner-Abendroth, evidence suggests that these societies venerated a Goddess rather than Gods. Assuring equal distribution of food, shelter, and clothing among this Goddess's children was women's responsibility. And in mythic ritual festivals, female devotees engaged in sacred, ecstatic dances that celebrated the Goddess's provision of earthly fertility and cosmic order. These were not artistic performances, but magical rituals, intimately linked to seasonal and cosmic events. In them, "dance, music, song, processions, dramatic scenes, and voluptuous revels coalesced into an indivisible totality."[22] Thus, in ancient matriarchal society, 'art' was a concrete, lived affair, inseparable from shared, social reality, and 'community' was the earthly manifestation of the Goddess's cosmic order. Organized around the moon's mysteriously recurrent patterns of growth and disappearance, these ritual dances magically enacted the forces of life and death. The link between such forces and women's experience was intimate and direct: theirs was, after all, the power to perpetuate human life; they had fertility periods that paralleled the moon's phases; they brought forth new life in precisely nine lunar months; and so on. These moon dances, then, the ancient source of everything today known as art, were women's dances. They took place on elaborately constructed, circular dancing grounds, the ancient remains of which can still be found in many places throughout the world. The dances themselves were not disciplined, regulated affairs, but ecstatic, improvisational affairs. Within the structured framework that ritual provided, "the dance was free in gesture and expression. The dancers were free to invest the framework with individual feelings, personal and social significances, and local symbols."[23] Aside from setting and occasion, then, 'art' in ancient matriarchal societies was not standardized, formalized, or constrained by disciplinary boundaries: the moon dances displayed the "[u]tmost multiplicity."[24]

With the dawning of the patriarchal age, however, these magical dances became formalized and specialized, deteriorating into empty motions, hollow imitations of the ancient matriarchal dances, with none of their former potency and magic. As Göttner-Abendroth puts it, "The ingenious fabric woven of social politics, psychology, science, and aesthetics, which the ritual dance festivals had been, was unraveled into its individual threads, which became the individual formal categories of reason that replaced the ecstatic unity. From then on, 'art' existed only as beautiful, decorative semblance. Or, where it defied categorization as mere ornamentation and retained the ancient mythic content, it was banished to the ghetto of the new society."[25] Under patriarchal order, the Goddess's ecstatic moon dances came to be replaced by Apollo's rational orderliness. The wildness of the matriarchal Muses was tamed, their madness brought under control. This 'domestication' stripped the mythic ritual festival of its immediacy, spontaneity, vitality, and vivid sense of social 'reality'. What had been experienced as a magical event atrophied into mere action. Formerly ecstatic festivals became standardized displays of hierarchical order. The Hellenic Greeks developed what Göttner-Abendroth calls "decorative state art,"[26] a highly ideological art comprised of temples, sculpture, and other flattering representations of new patriarchal aristocratic power structures.

By Plato's and Aristotle's day, matriarchal traditions had clearly become objects of derision. For Plato, myth stood opposed to truth, consisting of old wives' tales with worrisome potential for deception and confusion; and sense posed a serious threat to reason. Likewise, Göttner-Abendroth suggests, Aristotle associates 'feminine' qualities with darkness, indulgence, and disorder, both logic and science were, for him, defined by their avoidance of feminine qualities.[27] Over the centuries, musical production would become associated almost exclusively with male genius, and music itself would come to be conceived of as an autonomous affair, the product of abstract, intellectual activity. This would render illegitimate all musical practices but that very restricted range which served patriarchal order. "Art, which had once been the symbolic fulfillment of the complex social practice of an entire society, thus ultimately deteriorated into an empty cipher in the hollow space of social functionlessness."[28]

And yet, the compelling force at the heart of the ancient ecstatic festival was not entirely eradicated, only driven underground. The old magic continued to be practiced, but in the cultural margins and periphery, within the relatively uninfluential and largely invisible lower classes. In short, Göttner-Abendroth says, the matriarchal muse was banished to a cultural ghetto, where its formerly vital and vibrant practices came to be regarded as trivial folk art, mere popular entertainment. Art and true artists were those who served the needs and interests of the new patriarchal power structure; and audiences for these arts (which grew increasingly discrete and specialized) were cultivated among those privileged under patriarchal order. On the other hand, the ancient, matriarchal, "ghettoized art . . . roved about among the simple folk, where it enjoyed a wide audience but in an enclave of powerlessness."[29]

These, then, are the basic outlines of Göttner-Abendroth's theory. Art in ancient matriarchies was holistic, ecstatic, and magical; it was erotic, sensuous, spontaneous, and concrete; and it was closely linked to everyday lived reality. In contrast, patriarchal art is rational, orderly, abstract, and hierarchical: a trustworthy servant of patriarchal power. The musical rifts between serious and popular, artistic and folk, orderly and indulgent, rational and sensual, elite and common: each grow out of the patriarchal order's fundamental distrust of the magical, the sensual, and the erotic. Even folk musics, the last remnants of the matriarchal forbearer, have been transformed under patriarchal influence into trivial, commercial products, technically reproduced and mass distributed, bereft of spirituality, erotic vitality, and meaning. In short, says Göttner-Abendroth, "the ancient meanings of art . . . have entirely evaporated. The absence of content, the yawning emptiness of meaning, engendered by the tedium of arbitrary interpretability, are now merely veiled in an extravagant intellectual apparatus."[30] Since women have had virtually no voice in ideas about music, and scarcely more in its production, women who would participate in musical culture must negotiate institutional structures created and overwhelmingly controlled by men, abide by institutional constraints that distort their voices, and submit their contributions to judgment by norms inappropriate to women's experiences. Musical practices in patriarchal society require conformity to rules and values established by the suppression and domestication of the matriarchal muse.

Matriarchal art does not reside in artifacts, but in action, action that has significant power to resist and transform. It is "not a thing but a process, a praxis in which the subject speaks in actions and thereby changes the subjective and the objective world."[31] This praxis is not detached and conceptual, but immediate and bodily: matriarchal art is fundamentally sensual. These features do not constitute a strictly women's aesthetic, but they are indeed common wherever "society and art are not under the domination of men but are the creation of women."[32] Suppressed and devalued though it has been, Göttner-Abendroth believes the kind of experience once engendered by matriarchal practices is still fundamental to experience that is fully human: it has the potential to help "modern-day people—who have been fragmented, specialized, stereotyped, and controlled—to become whole again."[33]

Göttner-Abendroth sums up the matriarchal aesthetic with nine principles that may be paraphrased as follows:

1. Matriarchal art seeks to transform reality 'magically'. Unlike patriarchal art, it does not deal in the fictive, the imitative, or in 'beautiful semblances'.

2. Matriarchal art is unified, yet displays conspicuous diversity.

3. Matriarchal art is fundamentally processual, participatory, and collective.

4. Matriarchal art admits no divisions between emotion and thought, reflection and action. It demands no less than total engagement of all participants, resulting in ecstasy.

5. Matriarchal art has a dynamism and vitality that cannot be objectified, commodified, or adequately comprehended by nonparticipants.

6. Matriarchal art effaces barriers between and among artistic genres, and breaks down the barrier between art and life.

7. Matriarchal art's values are not opposite those of patriarchal art, but wholly different: subversive and revolutionary practices rooted in life and love instead of work, abstraction, and authoritative control.

8. Matriarchal art effaces the split between a formal, elitist, 'high' art and a popular, outcast art, thereby maintaining art's pivotal role in culture.

9. Matriarchal art is not 'art'. It can never be separated from social action, because it lies at the center of such action.[34]

Perhaps the most salient feature of these principles is their common commitment to vital, holistic experience: to the integration of art and life. Matriarchal art was integrative, processual, collective, participative, spontaneous, magical, spiritual, and ecstatic: characteristics that suggest intriguing questions about the kind of 'progress' many 'modern' practices truly represent in comparison to ancient and supposedly 'primitive' ones. It may be argued, of course, that experience like this is not just an ancient relic: many of the features Göttner-Abendroth designates as 'matriarchal' lie at the heart of experience variously called 'optimal', 'peak', or 'aesthetic'. Her more fundamental point, however, is the elusiveness and rarity of such experiences in a world where patriarchal values prevail.

In Göttner-Abendroth's view, matriarchal art was no entertaining diversion or escapist fantasy but was fully integrated with 'real' life, a fact which gave it the power to transform the world magically. If suggesting that music has 'magical', transformative power sounds naive or superstitious, Göttner-Abendroth thinks, that is only because we no longer truly understand what magic is. People in ancient societies were not simple-minded. In fact, their grasp of the complexities of astronomy, weather patterns, herbal medicine, and the like indicates that they were remarkably astute and sophisticated. But since their 'reality' was animate and spiritual rather than inert and objective, the world was something with which they interacted and influenced. So while, for instance, they surely understood the physical basis of illness, their magical medical practices simultaneously addressed the physical and the emotional basis of health. Knowledge integrated with emotion and spirituality was indeed magical. And experience in which intellect, emotion, action, and nature collaborated in equal measure did indeed make the world a different place. Patriarchy vilifies magic as primitive "witchcraft," and its ideals of rational control and objectivity suppress what Göttner-Abendroth believes to be a "fundamental categor[y] of human imagination."[35] In matriarchal societies such magic was a primary way of experiencing and sustaining unity, solidarity, and wholeness. A modern matriarchal art, Göttner-Abendroth therefore believes, would nurture and sustain an 'ethos of magic' with the power to "help the fragmented, specialised, stereotyped and supervised individual of today to regain her/his totality."[36]

Another conspicuous difference between matriarchal and patriarchal aesthetics according to Göttner-Abendroth is in the range of individual expression they tolerate. Matriarchal societies honor a broad range of individual expression, and are fundamentally committed to accommodating plurality, difference, and diversity. Accordingly, they might be expected to recognize the validity and value of a conspicuously greater range of musical practices than patriarchal societies. As Göttner-Abendroth puts it, "The joy of the Goddess is multiplicity, not the uniform unity to which nonconformists are sacrificed."[37] One of matriarchal music's central operative principles is, thus, "diversity in unity, in which the unity is not dogmatic, the diversity not subjective."[38]

The matriarchal aesthetic's dynamic, processual, participative nature also suggests strong contrasts to patriarchal values. Musical practices congruent with matriarchal principles[39] would not employ hierarchical productive systems where specialist composers create music for the edification of attentive audiences. Nor would they revolve around musical objects or works, because the matriarchal aesthetic values active, collective participation: the process is more important than the product. Accordingly, matriarchal practices would not maintain discrete, specialized roles for participants or require specialized institutions for music's creation, preservation, circulation, and control. Participation would be a central feature, but not 'performances' executed by artists for the appreciation of non performers. As a form of spontaneous collective expression, its outcomes are various, and fundamentally unpredictable; but that unpredictability is a crucial source of its magical power. "It is precisely this which enables matriarchal art to change reality. It is magic which is performed and experienced, and its spontaneous expressions can be so gripping that they lead to ecstasy."[40]

Like 'magic', patriarchal thought distorts and demeans ecstatic experience, again at considerable cost to the kind of musical experience that follows from matriarchal aesthetic values. Ecstasy is not an incapacitating delirium or uncontrolled madness, as patriarchal thought would have it. Rather, explains Göttner-Abendroth, ecstasy consists in a deep confluence of emotion, intellect, and activity. Words like 'inspiration' or 'intuition' hint at ecstasy's cognitive dimension, but neglect its essential emotional (affective) and erotic (active) character. And while 'erotic' points to its active dimension, it fails to capture its spiritual and intellectual dimensions. "True ecstasy unites the intellect, emotions and action in a climax where no one power is limited by another."[41] Such dynamic, integrated experience is fundamentally at odds with the detached, contemplative ideals of traditional patriarchal aesthetics. The ecstatic character of matriarchal art rejects the objectifying gaze of the spectator, and demands complete immersion in the process. Matriarchal music is not voyeuristic but fundamentally participatory: its ecstatic character is wholly inaccessible to those not engaged in its doing.

Given all this, it should be clear that the matriarchal aesthetic strenuously resists containment within the patriarchal order's conventions and boundaries. As every element in this dynamic interaction of feeling, mind, and action is bound up in an experiential whole, the result is a radically different way of living. Therefore, matriarchal art is inescapably provocative and involuntarily political: it cannot help but threaten and subvert patriarchal values because of its emphasis on wholeness, harmony, and unity instead of rigidly structured, hierarchical power relationships and rules. It enacts personal and social harmony rather than fragmenting specialization. It honors the erotic as a creative force, rather than suppressing it in deference to values like work, and discipline. Matriarchal art honors and affirms human life, not abstraction. At its center lies human relatedness and relationship: a "sense of community, motherliness and sisterly love ... and not paternal authority, dominance ... [or] egoism."[42] In summary, "Matriarchal spirituality esteems diversity, change, vitality, and a dynamism that admits of no strictures or incrustation. Matriarchal spirituality respects and promotes the union of the psychic interior ... and the physical exterior, one's well-being in the natural environment.... Matriarchal spirituality negates and neutralizes all types of dualism used by patriarchal politics throughout the millennia to secure domination ... All forms of dualism serve the principle 'divide and conquer' and are the antithesis of the radical antiestablishment politics of matriarchal spirituality."[43]

Göttner-Abendroth recognizes the difficulties involved in honoring and valuing the very things patriarchal society has "banished to the ghetto of the unreal."[44] Yet, she implies, matriarchal art's radical difference gives it extraordinary capacity for resistance to and subversion of patriarchal values, as its dynamic, ever-changing character leaves its bewildered (patriarchal) opponent "bewitched and paralysed."[45] Matriarchal art is a "complex, socially subversive praxis [that] cannot be fought with conventional weapons." By subverting patriarchal values, renouncing "specialised technique" and "exclusive know-how"[46] in favor of magic and ecstasy, matriarchal art seeks to "aestheticise the whole of society."[47]

Insights and Issues

It is not being suggested here that Göttner-Abendroth's account is the definitive feminist text on music. In the first place, hers is not, strictly speaking, an account of music but rather a theory of ritual in which music is an element. In the second place, the very notion of 'definitiveness' is fundamentally at odds with what a great deal of feminist thought has come to represent. Still, the theory is quite useful as an introductory overview of certain recurrent themes and characteristics. Most feminist theorists vigorously challenge dualistic, hierarchical accounts of music's nature and value. Their accounts often attempt to subvert disciplinary specialization and rigidity, and accommodate multiplicity, diversity, and change. Like Göttner-Abendroth, they question women's near-total exclusion from musical histories and discourses, and undertake to show how their inclusion might change things. They take very seriously the differences between women's experience and men's, sometimes pointing to the corporeal dimension as an important source of that difference in contrast to the invisibility of the body in male-centered explanations. They frequently reject abstraction, detachment, and supposed objectivity as epistemological or musical ideals, struggling to retain a position of prominence for experience that is at once concrete, corporeal, and social. And perhaps most importantly, they reject the romanticized notion that music consists in pleasing patterns of sound. A fundamental feminist conviction is that music both reflects and shapes people and social orders. It is one of the instruments by which traditional gender structures and patriarchal power are reproduced. The art music canon, traditional aesthetic theory, and the institutions in which they figure centrally serve the interests of a patriarchal order that systematically silences women's voices. Women's voices have something to say that is both different and in some sense distinctly women's. And although what they have to say may not be the kind of thing that can be neatly packaged into broad theories that claim to represent everyone, these voices must be explicitly acknowledged and heard.

The idea that music may variously support or subvert the interests of patriarchal power is a provocative one that promises (or, depending upon one's perspective, threatens) to fundamentally reorient many of the philosophical discourses outlined in the earlier chapters of this book. For instance, conceiving Plato's profound ambivalence toward music in terms of political tension between matriarchal and patriarchal values recasts his arguments in many fascinating ways. Göttner-Abendroth's claim that the magic, the ecstatic, and the erotic have been relegated to the musical periphery also introduces fascinating political dimensions to debates over the relative merits of popular and so-called serious musics. For in her view, the respectability and legitimacy attributed to elite musics and their practitioners is in no small part a function of their conspicuous orderliness, mindfulness, and cohesiveness: hence, of their conformity to and reflection of the interests of patriarchal power. Even Meyer's hierarchical designation of structuring musical parameters as 'primary' and sensuous ones as 'secondary', and his dualistic segregation of the musically objective 'stimulus' from subjective response, take on provocative new dimensions when subjected to feminist critique along lines sketched by Göttner-Abendroth. Also, the idea of conflicting patriarchal and matriarchal values suggests an interesting interpretation of the root causes for music's seemingly perennial struggle to maintain a toe-hold in formal education, and of the reasons arguments advocating musical study so often stress its 'cognitive' legitimacy above all else.[48] It also provides an intriguing basis for exploring such things as the 'pecking order' among music's subdisciplines in academic institutions, and the kinds of music deemed worthy of study there. The debates over music's inherent or intrinsic values, in this view, are invariably rooted in value systems that extend well beyond music itself.

Another noteworthy characteristic of Göttner-Abendroth's theory is its effort to break down rigid categorical boundaries and barriers: between reality and appearance, between mind and body, between emotion and thought, between art and life. Problematizing comfortable conceptual distinctions reorients thought and perception in important ways, forcing us to acknowledge their contingency, showing us that the ways they structure the world are by no means natural and inevitable. Given her determination to dissolve oppositional binaries, however, it is important to ask whether the idea of mutually exclusive matriarchal and patriarchal value systems establishes yet another of the dualisms she wants to eliminate.

The idea of a distinctly matriarchal aesthetic also permits us to pursue the issue of essentialism a bit further. As Göttner-Abendroth observes, there is significant danger that women's well-intended claims to a biological female essence will be used to cast women in "the very role patriarchy has forced upon them for millennia."[49] Claims to female essence neglect crucial differences among women and wrongly suggest a static, deterministic notion of womanhood. Göttner-Abendroth's choice of the term 'matriarchal' was made precisely because she thinks it helps "avoid the temptation to redefine women in terms of eternal characteristics."[50] Matriarchal values are not matters of biology, but complex historical facts; they are not essentially female, only associated with societies where women are not dominated by men. Significant differences exist between women and men, and significant similarities exist between and among women; but these similarities and differences are simply functions of acculturation, not of immutable biological essences.

Among the many questions raised by the idea of a matriarchal aesthetic, the most fundamental is whether matriarchal societies have ever existed. As it turns out, that depends upon what one takes the term to mean. In her examination of Göttner-Abendroth's ideas,[51] Renée Lorraine indicates that scholarly opinion on the existence of ancient matriarchies is sharply divided. Supporters point to things like art, artifacts, and elaborate burial sites as evidence that women in ancient cultures held significant status and power, and indeed, were often venerated. Furthermore, ancient mythology often attributes major cultural gifts like language and medicine to goddesses, and makes reference to prehistoric women's rule. The existence of matriarchies would be substantial historical evidence of the feasibility and viability of cultural alternatives to patriarchal order, showing that women's domination by men is no 'natural' state of affairs, and that societies can indeed exist without domination. But other feminist scholars maintain the idea of ancient matriarchies is largely speculative, resisting it at least partly because the demise of such societies might be taken as an indication of women's weakness, or that matriarchal arrangements are simply not viable. The existence of artifactual evidence does not necessarily mean women held any real power, they suggest, and ancient tales hardly constitute reliable evidence. Furthermore, societies may well recognize or even honor women without necessarily granting them any meaningful power or control.

Part of this controversy probably stems from the confused notion that matriarchal order is simply an inversion of the patriarchal: that it is one in which women dominate men. But as Lorraine reminds, matriarchal need not mean 'mother rule': it may simply describe social arrangements where women's contributions are valued, and where power is cooperatively shared. Taken this way, the matriarchal thesis becomes much easier to sustain, since the existence of such cultures is not in dispute. It is typical, for instance, to find among foraging peoples egalitarian social arrangements where women and things regarded as feminine are not trivialized or disparaged. In Lorraine's view, this is how Göttner-Abendroth's idea of 'matriarchy' must be understood: not as an inverted patriarchy but as a "nonauthoritarian culture where the status of women is high."[52] The matriarchal idea of 'goddess', writes Göttner-Abendroth, "does not mean an omnipotent, omniscient supreme Mother in Heaven, a counterpart to God the Father."[53] Rather, 'matriarchal spirituality' is grounded in "an autonomous self-confidence of women and a nonhierarchical, egalitarian relationship among women. . . ."[54] In this view, matriarchies are not social arrangements where women's values simply assume the dominant, oppressive function asserted by men's within the patriarchy. Matriarchal and patriarchal values are not opposites in a common system; they are wholly different systems.

It is an anthropological truism that societies which are collaborative in work are inclined to be collaborative in other respects. Thus, in egalitarian societies musical engagements tend to be less hierarchically structured, to be more inclusive, integrative, and participatory. Societies that recognize and value women's contributions tend to have musics that are more 'integrational' and cooperative in character—features Göttner-Abendroth has chosen to call matriarchal. While associations like these do not establish a direct causal link between women and such musical practices, Lorraine finds it plausible that societies where women are treated as equals display distinctive musical values and practices. This is a reasonable stance, so long as it is recognized that permitting women to speak does not necessarily mean that what is heard will be a distinctly or characteristically women's voice. Lorraine believes that women's activities are characteristically cooperative and integrative. And while these tendencies may be neither biologically determined nor unique to women, they appear to be more generally characteristic of women than of men. Given men's and women's social and cultural differences, the idea of gender-differentiated musical preferences and values is, she thinks, plausible.

The pivotal assumption is that in societies where women are not subject to male domination, the things they do and the musics they make are more likely to assume forms that are authentically women's. If by 'authentically women's' is meant something innate or genetically hard-wired, the idea of a women's music (even called 'matriarchal') is clearly essentialist. Writing about the musical characteristics of female and male composers within the 'classical music' genre, Marcia Citron observes that "Identifying vocabulary or syntax specifically attributable to a female rather than a male composer is a formidable challenge . . . [W]hile we might isolate certain tendencies that could be part of a female aesthetic, I have found no specific language, style, or dynamic that every woman utilizes."[55] This clearly suggests that differences and similarities between women's and men's music, where they can be identified, should be regarded as socially derived rather than manifestations of some eternal, essentially female or 'feminine' sensibility. On the other hand, where male musical culture remains the de facto norm, women's contributions, however distinctive, will only be regarded as 'other', as subsidiary, as marginal—precisely as Göttner-Abendroth insists.

Resistant Readings of Kant's Aesthetic Legacy

The attention devoted by certain feminist scholars to Kant's influential account of aesthetic judgment helps illuminate the nature of feminist critique from another perspective: the exposure of error and bias in male-developed theory. The strategy here has been to examine Kant's aesthetic theory alongside his assumptions about women and gender. While both feminist and nonfeminist scholars would probably agree that Kant subscribed to gender stereotypes that are outmoded and even silly, the tendency among non-feminists has been to regard these as fundamentally irrelevant to the validity of his philosophical accounts. After all, the hallmarks of great philosophy are logical rigor and objectivity that transcend the personal, the particular, and the situational. So what Kant may have believed about women and gender has nothing whatsoever to do with his intellectual, philosophical work.

But as we have seen in Göttner-Abendroth's theory, many feminists find belief in the supremacy of impersonal, objective knowledge highly suspect. That ideal represents a distinctly male-oriented set of values that has effectively advanced patriarchal interests while failing to empower women or make their voices audible. From a feminist point of view, the voice of universal reason is simply the voice of patriarchal power. In other words, Kant's cultural norm is explicitly male, and when he appeals to reason or speaks of 'we', he unmistakably means men. This mind-centered or logocentric ideal, the norm by which all 'reasonable' thought and action must be judged, assumes that things felt, intuited, sensed, or imagined can only be aberrant and irrational—characteristics also often ascribed, not coincidentally, to women. Universality, transcendence, and objectivity in turn implicate a conception of knowledge without a point of view, one supposedly devoid of vested personal interest. According to the implicit 'rules' of this system, women who, having been poorly served by such discourses, refuse to acknowledge their authority, are irrational, emotional, and subjective. The resulting dilemma has been described this way: "[I]f she speaks a tongue that is utterly new she cannot be heard and if she speaks the father tongue she complies with its exclusion of her."[56] Thus, the feminist critique seeks to develop resistant readings of the likes of Kant.

Wiseman's work exposes the operation of anachronistic and offensive gender stereotypes in Kant's *Observations on the Feeling of the Beautiful and Sublime*, a grand-scale taxonomic project intended to show the relationship between these two kinds of experience. Kant's account draws a strongly oppositional contrast between the beautiful and the sublime, in which beauty, when compared to the sublime, is, though undeniably pleasant, invariably identified with some form of deficit or lack. As Kant elaborates, his binarisms proliferate until what eventually seems to emerge is one fundamental, all-encompassing opposition that manifests itself in a multitude of ways, so that what is fundamental to the relationship beautiful/sublime also informs sense/reason, surface/depth, inclination/duty, emotion/principle, love/esteem, charm/profundity, passivity/activity—and most notably, woman/man. The underlying structure of this relationship is such that its terms are more or less interchangeable: beauty is charm is passive is female, while sublimity is potent is active is male. These analogies have important implications about the way Kant conceived of not only women, but knowledge, morality, and beauty as well. As Wiseman observes, 'woman' in this essay is strongly associated with "sense, inclination, and the beautiful, where these are the other side of reason, duty, and the sublime, respectively."[57]

For Kant, Wiseman shows, beauty may be associated with wit, cleverness, and artfulness, but the sublime is associated with understanding and courage. Beauty is pleasing or charming, but the sublime is profoundly moving or stirring. Accordingly, Kant believes, beauty begets love, whereas the sublime gives rise to esteem.[58] While the sublime is associated with strength, power, and privilege, beauty appears to be defined in terms of a pattern of absences: it is a passive, submissive, decorative affair. The broader significance of these assumptions becomes abundantly clear once we recognize that Kant believes women and men are related to the beautiful and the sublime biologically, in virtue of their sex—women to beauty, men to the sublime. Women's and men's ways of thinking and knowing contrast with each other along the same lines as beauty and sublimity. Women's understanding is guided by inclination, disposition, or feeling instead of logical rigor or hard fact. Men's understanding, on the other hand, is, like the sublime, principled and potent. Beauty's influence is, like women's, a function of charm and persuasion; the sublime, like male reason, carries a stronger sense of obligation or duty. Kant's own words make clear how gender is implicated in this: "The fair sex has just as much understanding as the male, but it is a beautiful understanding, whereas ours should be a deep understanding, an expression that signifies identity with the sublime. . . . Laborious learning or painful pondering, even if a woman should greatly succeed in it, destroy the merits that are proper to her sex, and because of their rarity they can make of her an object of cold admiration; but at the same time they will weaken the charms with which she exercises her great power over the other sex."[59] Wiseman summarizes, "The power of women over men is the power of the senses over reason, of inclination over duty, and no more can the senses know or the inclinations have moral worth than can the power of women be ought but resisted, contained, and constrained. Anyone who would know and do the right . . . must resist feminine, sensuous, feeling beauty."[60] Female charm thus beguiles and bewilders men, while abstract thought and reason are capacities that largely elude women. Despite their attractiveness, feminine inclinations to sympathy and meekness are no match for the potency of masculine principle and reason.

These strong differences have important moral implications as well, for Kant contends that mere inclinations, rooted in feeling instead of rational principle, cannot be considered truly virtuous. Virtue is above all principled, and "the more general [its principles] are, the more sublime and noble [virtue] becomes."[61] Virtuous conduct requires guidance by and adherence to abstract principle which is, unfortunately, foreign to women's experience. In Kant's words,

"Women will avoid the wicked not because it is unright, but only because it is ugly; and virtuous actions mean to them such as are morally beautiful. Nothing of duty, nothing of compulsion, nothing of obligation! Woman is intolerant of all commands and all morose constraint. They do something only because it pleases them, and the art consists in making only that please them which is good. I hardly believe that the fair sex is capable of principles."[62]

As Kneller demonstrates,[63] Kant's disparaging views of women also influence his later, 'critical' writings and the account of aesthetic taste developed in his third critique. Kneller identifies three important affinities between his understanding of 'taste' and of 'femininity' that suggest the former may not be as utterly unbiased as Kant might wish us to believe. First, both taste and femininity are 'civilizing', moderating influences whose value is preparatory to further ends: neither is construed as an end in itself. Second, both involve qualities which, though important, require the imposition of discipline and restraint, subordination to principled understanding. And third, these subordinate and mollifying characteristics effectively serve to bar the possibility of any but a trifling role in important moral or epistemological concerns. Clearly, then, conceiving music as an 'aesthetic' matter along Kant's lines profoundly restricts the claims one might wish to raise regarding its nature and value.

As civilizing influences, the importance of both women and taste is primarily a function of their ability to effect the kind of refinement and 'proper' decorum that makes people sociable and receptive to (principled) moral judgments. Kant tells us nature made woman "precociously shrewd in claiming gentle and courteous treatment by the male, so that he finds himself imperceptibly fettered by a child through his own generosity and led by it, if not to morality itself, at least to . . . the cultivated propriety that is the preparatory training for morality . . ."[64] Similarly, taste "has a tendency to promote morality in an external way. Making a man well-mannered as a social being falls short of forming a morally good man, but it still prepares him for it by the effort he makes, in society, to please others . . ."[65] Femininity and taste relate to morality, but only indirectly: by cultivating sociability and sensitivity, they pave the way for what is serious and important.

Recall that judgments of taste or beauty were for Kant 'disinterested' and 'conceptless', free of determination by sense or logic. In contrast to both sense and reason, the judgment of beauty was concerned with outward appearances. Taste, he remarks in the third critique, is quite different from moral thinking, for it "only plays with the objects of liking without committing itself to any of them."[66] Apparently, then, what beauty does is to assure continued engagement with the outer trappings of moral concerns, developing what might be called pre-moral habits and dispositions. Such habits, while admittedly not insignificant, are clearly secondary and insufficient, there is no mistaking their subordinate status. As Kneller sees it, Kant "contrasts the mere play of taste with the legitimate authority of the moral law . . . just as he argues that women, who, like children, beguile and cajole in order to get men to do their bidding, have no authority to shape the decisions and actions that constitute the 'objective' realm of public experience."[67] Femininity and taste make people more polite, more refined; but "for Kant, a world without 'feminine' and tasteful human beings would not necessarily be a world without morals."[68] Important they may be; yet in themselves, the value of beauty and feminine influences is only propaedeutic.

Since taste's freedom from the constraints that attend sensual and rational experience raises worries about its trustworthiness, Kant introduces the imagination, whose job it is to impart a modicum of discipline and order. Imagination's free play assures that judgments of beauty do not deteriorate into mere sensual indulgence, and that something allied with understanding is always involved. Similarly, suggests Kneller, Kant makes clear that 'the feminine' is a force in need of discipline. Consider the striking similarity between imagination's relation to understanding and Kant's prescription for marital relations: "Who, then, should have supreme command in the household? . . . [T]he woman should reign . . . and the man govern . . . ; for inclination reigns and understanding governs . . . [The man] should be like a minister to his monarch who thinks only of amusement . . . so that the monarch can do all that he wills, but on one condition: that his minister lets him know what his will is."[69] Woman is 'free' to do as she pleases, but only within her own, domestic sphere. And what she pleases, she apparently needs man to tell her. Likewise, judgments of taste partake of imagination's 'free play', yet require the restraint of imagination's affiliation with understanding to keep it on track. Judgments of taste are not absolutely free, but disciplined by an imagination that must in turn answer to reason. Kneller summarizes, "In judgments of taste the imagination resembles nothing so much as the docile wife of Kant's proper marriage: it exhibits the appearance of freedom (it 'reigns'), but it is the understanding that sets the boundaries, or 'governs' the imagination's play." Taste, Kant states, "consists in disciplining (or training) genius. It severely clips its wings, and makes it civilized, or polished; but at the same time it gives it guidance as to how far and over what it may spread while still remaining purposive."[70]

In the end, women's and imagination's domestication means their exclusion from important moral and political affairs: both are ultimately silenced, concludes Kneller. "Given Kant's account of the properly feminine woman and the properly disciplined, 'tasteful' imagination, it is understandable that he bans both from entering the moral and political realm. Children and 'wild things' are not in a position to responsibly shape moral and political reality, and I, no less than Kant, would hate to see his ideal women in positions of power and responsibility."[71] Thus, what women and Kant's conception of femininity contribute to culture are refinement, manners, and civility. They have little to contribute to the kind of abstract, universal truths that are of greatest significance to patriarchal power. Musical beauty, like female beauty, is wonderfully pleasant, yet an adornment none the less.

These analyses clearly show the oppositional and hierarchical character of Kant's conception of the relationship between women and men, and how that binary structure maps onto other relations like that between music and reason. It is difficult to imagine how a woman might find anything positive about her gender in Kant's account. And since that same conceptual framework appears to inform his representation of beauty articulated in his enormously influential *Critique of Judgment*, asking whether and how his gender stereotypes inform his analysis of taste and, by extension, of music seems not only highly appropriate, but unavoidable. The Kantian aesthetic legacy creates a conceptual framework that assures music's marginal, 'otherly' status, one in which music's productive role in culture is, like women's, strictly subordinate and secondary.

Taking Women's Music Seriously

The first steps in the process of redressing the problem of women's omission from accounts of music are relatively clear: identify women whose contributions have been overlooked and excluded, and rewrite histories to include them. Beyond that, however, the compensatory project is not as simple as might be expected. Adding women to musical discourses and practices leads to a host of difficult questions: Exactly what is being added, and to what? Is women's music distinctive in some sense? How does what is distinctive about it change the nature of accounts and practices to which it is added? Does the addition of women to the patriarchal canon substantially modify it? Or is that canon so incorrigibly patriarchal that simple additive projects are impossible? How strongly does women's music differ from men's? Are its differences really more important than the attributes the 'masterworks' have in common? Göttner-Abendroth believes, for instance, that matriarchal music is unintentionally but unavoidably subversive of patriarchal order because the values it represents are wholly different from those of the patriarchal status quo. Are women's and men's sensibilities radically different? Is the incorporation of women's music into existing practices simply a matter of 'adding and stirring'?[72] If there is something distinctive enough about it to warrant its explicit recognition, can it be incorporated into a patriarchal order without compromising its distinctness? Is the patriarchal system capable of accommodating women's musical practices without fundamentally distorting or misrepresenting them? Will its character be totally dissolved, or remain a distinctly identifiable ingredient? Might adding women create the illusion of change, leaving the root causes for women's exclusion unexposed and unexamined? Will praising the accomplishments of women who have succeeded in the "old boy system" just "[perpetuate] the patriarchal system that excludes the majority of women," as Morton suggests?[73] Might women's presence thus be reduced to an interesting footnote to unchanged, male-centered accounts, acknowledged, but with a kind of patronizing tokenism? Might the laudable project of adding women effect only superficial or cosmetic realignments, leaving patriarchal underpinnings untouched?

Under some circumstances, the solution to such a dilemma would be fairly obvious and straightforward: make a concerted effort to accommodate marginalized practices, in order to create a hybrid, synthetic practice. That is, after all, how most cultural change takes place. However, the situation faced by women appears to be considerably more complex, for as McClary points out, "There is . . . no traditional woman's voice."[74] What some might be tempted to designate 'women's music' often derives from what McClary calls "bogus" notions about "how women sound"[75]—stereotypes developed in male-dominated culture and perpetuated in the European classical music tradition. So total has been the exclusion of women in such cultures and traditions that the project of reconceptualizing and reorienting them to accommodate a voice that is authentically women's is extraordinarily elusive and complex. Male-generated stereotypes of what women's music might sound like must be replaced with something distinctively yet authentically women's. And that effort cannot succeed without simultaneously exposing and confronting the "dynamics of domination" that are the root causes of exclusion in the first place.[76]

Lamb brings these issues together with considerable force. "[G]ender," she writes, "cannot *add* to the music curriculum. Male heterosexual gender, White and exercising class privilege, *is* the music curriculum. . . . Gender cannot enrich the curriculum until women and others are present, authentically, in the music, and as musicians. . . ."[77] The pressing question is what it might mean for women to "write music *as women* or create music *as women*," developing musical practices that are "different from the malestream."[78] The answer must be sought by examining women's music "as it exists on the margins of patriarchal society [in order to] define the values that the many musics created by women contribute to musical experiences and cultures on their own aesthetic and political terms."[79] Women's colonization is an essential part of their story, but only part, observes Lamb: "[T]he master's music is not the only one experienced. There is great pleasure and solace in music for women. Music provides women with opportunity for integral time, space, and energy, wherein the contradictory becomes multi-dimensional, full with the possibility of in/corp/orated wholeness. . . . marking an area in which [they] cannot be totally colonized."[80] Women's musical practices are thus simultaneously sites of resistance (the problem is not so much "to discover who we are but to refuse who we are"[81]), of potential transformation, and of new possibilities. They reflect women's contradictory, complex situations, and are at once "self-reflexive and disruptive."[82]

Musical Performance: Resistant Musical Interpretations

The act of performing music is often regarded as musically challenging but philosophically uninteresting, and might therefore seem a rather unlikely place for feminist interventions. However, musical performance practices are often sharply divided along gender lines. Motivated by convictions that musical performance is never simply musical—that its significance always extends well beyond 'the notes'—feminist critiques of performance raise philosophical issues of far-reaching significance by insisting on a socio-cultural interpretation of what performance entails, and by calling into question the romantic ideal of obedient, 'faithful' performance.

Göttner-Abendroth's observations on the nature of musical performance, for instance, point generally to the need to resituate performance within social context, to recognize its role in shaping and reinforcing social structures. Most notably, she urges performance be construed as a collective, collaborative activity rather than a solitary task devoted to dutifully replicating musical 'works'. In contrast to the distancing, contemplative attitude associated with conventional conceptions of performance, she prefers to conceive it in terms of participation and interaction. She rejects the notion that performing is a neutral connection between composer and audience, the middle term in an essentially communicative relation; instead, she construes performance as a mode of social action with the power to interact with and change the world.

No small part of the difficulty some feminist theorists find in music performance is its character as an agent of seemingly acritical replication: its technical rather than praxical nature. Lamb puts it bluntly: "Musical performance is untheorized practice. It is not praxis; it is what we musicians do because it is what we do. Performance is very much a male-constructed model for music. The master-apprentice relationship of most professional musicians toward their students exemplifies this model. Performance is about control by a master, a conductor, usually male, usually White."[83] Given these concerns, it is easy to see how rendering performance problematic becomes an issue of some moment for feminist critique.

Beginning with the provocative question, 'just what exactly is being performed here?'[84] Cusick explores the seemingly innocuous business of performing classical music with results that are quite striking. Her findings pose serious challenges to the view that musical performance is simply an interpretive process concerned with authentically reproducing 'the music itself', whose meanings are intrinsic, residing strictly 'in the notes'. That view's romanticized notion of performance hides musical performance's role in presenting and reinforcing gender messages. No less than language, musical performance has the capacity to convey oppressive and hurtful stereotypes. No less than language, and perhaps even a good deal more: for the myth of musical autonomy cloaks stereotype and misogyny in a seductive, appealing package claiming to be something else. Assumptions of musical autonomy and purity influence musical performances in powerful ways, creating (as a poem by Adrienne Rich vividly describes them) "patterns so powerful and pure we continually fail to ask are they true for us."[85]

When hurtful or troublesome messages appear in beautiful music (Cusick points to Schumann's *Frauenliebe und -Leben*[86]), does one reject the music altogether, sacrificing its beauty along with its message, or rather does one preserve its beauty, but in so doing allow its destructive work to continue? The source of this apparent dilemma, suggests Cusick, is the mistaken belief that musical meanings are fixed, immutable things; that the musical 'work' is a kind of thing with an essential meaning whose faithful, authentic transmission is the performer's moral duty. On this view, the performer's job is to accurately complete a process of communication between composer and audience, to recreate the music's 'inherent meaning'. This "ideology of faithful performance," as Cusick describes it, serves "the same interests as the powerful and pure patterns into which Schumann once translated the ideology of gender."[87] Given the indisputable power of beautiful musical sounds, assumptions of purity and neutrality must not go uncontested; nor should we assume that what is being performed is musical only.

In Cusick's view, "the cultural work of all classical music performances . . . might be understood to be the public enactment of obedience to a culturally prescribed script,"[88] one in which both performer and audience have carefully circumscribed roles. The performer serves as the medium through which a composer's message flows in the form of a 'work'. As the connecting link between composer and audience, the performer has a fundamental ethical obligation to convey the work precisely as intended. The musical work and its meaning comprise, in other words, a closed system or fixed text with which neither performer or listener must tamper. The many elaborate rituals associated with classical performance are carefully structured to assure that what is heard is precisely the music itself.

Though it is customary to regard musical performance as an action executed for the benefit of a nonperforming audience, the audience's role is a performance as well, one that is no less governed by rules of appropriate conduct than that of the musician. "All performances," says Cusick, "are ensemble pieces involving everyone present and. . . . the actions that constitute what we call an audience's reception are every bit as performative as the actions we ordinarily call 'the performance'."[89] The classical music listener's performance ideal is one of receptivity: an attitude of quiet attentiveness, where listening predominates. Semidarkness helps listeners assume their proper role. When all goes as it is supposed to, listeners become 'all ears', suppressing other bodily awareness and vicariously experiencing a relationship with the composer whose ideas the work represents. For this to happen, listeners must not attend too closely to musicians whose primary performance is the role of medium. And to assure that the listener performs properly, attending to music rather than musician, the 'medium' must ensure the "subordination of her *persona* to the *persona* in and of 'the music'."[90] When 'properly' executed, then, the listener's performance involves the erasure both of self-awareness and of awareness of the musician, so that the music is encountered as it purely is, 'in itself', the composer's voice, pure and undistorted. It is "the composer's music, the composer's voice, which I came to hear,"[91] observes Cusick.

Thus, the pleasure of a proper listening performance comes from losing oneself in the music while, at the same time, witnessing a public display of obedience which itself involves abnegation or self-effacement. This Cusick memorably designates "the spectacle of the disappearing Self." As an audience member, "I expect to replicate [the musician performer's] subordination of *persona*, her disappearing Self, and I expect to do it as part of my performance in the recital . . . Indeed, I will perform the disappearing Self much more obviously: I will be silent; I will sit still, in semidarkness; I will become 'all ears', by which I mean I will focus all my bodily awareness on my experience of sound, and will let my consciousness be entirely filled with 'the music itself'. If, somehow, [present others] disappear, I will remember the performance we shared as . . . as ecstasy."[92] Is there beneath this exquisite, ecstatic experience a kind of ritual reaffirming obedience? Are these performances ways of teaching us the pleasure of suppressing self-interest and submitting to subtle yet profound cultural messages? Cusick asks rhetorically, "What better frame story for texts that subtly encode all sorts of prescriptions for social behavior—including gender—than a ritual of disappearing Selves?"[93]

Learning and conforming to the appropriate range of acceptable behavior is crucial to the performance of classical music. The limits of that range are carefully internalized in a sustained process of imitative apprenticeship that is a central component of musical training. As restrictions upon the latitude of permissible interpretive moves become deeply etched into the unconscious set of rules governing acceptable performance practice, performers may come to regard their performances as achievements of an autonomous, foundational 'self'. However, they are more accurately regarded as cultural constructions, the result of extensive practice and repetition. "[W]e might imagine the feelings we express to be our own, but all the ways we would know to shape a piece 'musically' would express feelings that had originated somewhere else, in someone else."[94] An 'expressive' musical performance, then, must be first and foremost an act of obedience or submission by means of which the composer's voice is brought to life: the performer's body is a surrogate for the composer's voice. Says Cusick, "[T]he composer's invasion of my body, to which I submit, makes me a medium (in both senses of the word)."[95] If the first sense of 'medium' refers to the performer's role as vehicle, the second is clearly the sense of diminished self that comes from submitting to the hand of authority, from being reductively transformed into a copy of the (genuine, authentic) original. This performance of obedience and submission, accompanied by exquisite musical pleasure, is far from benign, particularly for women. Since to be female in patriarchal society is always already to be a subordinate 'other', musically enacting obedience and self-effacement is for women doubly discomforting: first, because their subaltern status in patriarchal society implicates so many other performances of abnegation; and second, the music's beauty seems to insist the performance be experienced as pleasant. It is not just coincidental that such musical performance enacts self-negation, adds Cusick. "The mistaken belief in a relationship *original : copy* is part of the ideology I believe classical music performance is meant to uphold."[96]

The questions raised by this critique are at once discomforting and unavoidable. Asks Cusick, "I wonder what purpose is served by the comfortableness of the role 'performer' to this society's 'Others'—women, gays, people of color? I wonder if my role as performer is partly to 'perform' exactly this homology with the role of subaltern peoples. I wonder if everyone at my performances understands that one of the things I will perform will be the correct relationship of a subaltern to hegemonic power, the relationship of submission. . . . [M]ight *my* particular performance serve to make the idea of a woman's submission seem natural? Might my real work be that of demonstrating for you how submission may be most beautifully performed? Might I always be performing the role of a subaltern who knows her place?"[97]

While faithful performance does involve public demonstration of obedience to the work, that is not the end of the story as Cusick sees it. For faithful performance also requires that threats to the work's unity be suppressed. Musical performance is not just a public demonstration of obedience, but a public demonstration of the maintenance of order and control as well. In the orderly subordination of part to whole, good performance enacts suppression on a second level by controlling the distractive, the disruptive, and by suppressing whatever might threaten or compromise unity. And since unity and clarity—the strong, sure sense of where one is in the work at any given time—are marked masculine, whatever obscures that clarity or undermines that certainty is coded feminine. Thus Cusick reaches the remarkable conclusion that whether she sings the Rachmaninov *Vocalise* or a Schumann song with offensive lyrics, faithful performance invariably works to confirm and reinforce the dominance of the masculine.

Cusick's accounts of disappearing selves, bodily invasions, and spectacular enactments of submission assume, however, acquiescence to the ideology of 'faithful' performance. Her ultimate point is that people need not perform so: that performing can resist and undermine deleterious musical effects. One can perform in ways that highlight irony or playfully manipulate the music's messages. Indeed, she observes, that is precisely what many 'pop' artists already do: often, in fact, it is key to their popularity. Conversely, she speculates, classical music performance's "rigid adherence to performance rituals and standards that teach obedience might be held partly responsible for the dramatic decline in [its own] popularity over the last generation. The problem might not lie either in 'the music itself' or in the inadequately formed listening habits of the general public, but in the anachronistic social patterns so powerfully affirmed in the rituals and beliefs surrounding 'the music itself'."[98]

Although they are undeniably complex, the problems Cusick describes are not irresolvable. Ultimately, performance would need to relinquish its reverence for the work, reexamine its predilection for authenticity at all costs. Rituals might need to be reconfigured with a view to contemporary social and musical realities. Performers might be encouraged to resist and destabilize, so as to reveal fault lines and fissures. The product of such undertakings would definitely not be faithful performances, concedes Cusick; yet working against the ideology of faithful performance does not necessarily mean infidelity. Critically resistant performances are not 'faithless', but something far more complex than the binary faithful/faithless allows.[99] They take the idea of 'the music itself' at once less seriously and more so. The musical performance—especially for women—is never just a performance of music. "[W]e must listen," Cusick concludes, "a little less reverently to the patterns (so powerful and pure as to be proposed to us as timeless and true) formed by pitches and rhythms, and a little more attentively to the subtle but powerful ways those patterns may be continually transformed by the displacements of endlessly proliferating resistant performances."[100]

Gender, Sex, and the Erotic

Perhaps by now we begin to see that, compared to the complex issues to which they eventually lead, the early compensatory projects in music can seem rather tame and uncontroversial. Motivated by a nagging sense that adding women's music to the canon addressed symptoms rather than causes, feminist scholarship has ventured ever deeper into the nature of the connections between gender and music. Not surprisingly, the more closely it has approached music 'itself', the more resistance it has encountered. Compelling demonstrations of the hurtful, even vicious images of women built into the beautiful music of many (male) composers have provoked heated controversy, yet continue to be explained away, exempted from consideration in many 'serious' musical circles. Moreover, as McClary explains, "[E]ven if arguments concerning the depiction of women were granted (which typically they are not). . . . [t]o the extent that texted music is regarded as inferior, already corrupt, even 'feminine', then music itself—the hard core instrumental music that counts . . . appears to remain untouched by such analyses."[101] Probably the most stubborn obstacle encountered by feminist music scholarship is the tenacious belief that music's most fundamental values are intrinsic ones: utterly independent of (extramusical) things like programs and references, and especially of biological matters like sex and sociocultural matters like gender or power. Accordingly, for instance, while concerns about stereotypical representations of women in operatic plots may be acknowledged, the deeper issues that concern feminist scholars continue to be regarded in many quarters as fundamentally extramusical. Since music is presumed to speak for itself, it is wrongly assumed that the concerns raised by feminist scholars require relatively modest adjustments. And since, so long as musical value is regarded as an absolute, autonomous, inviolable phenomenon, feminist critique is effectively denied access to music, the possibility of a 'pure', utterly autonomous music is one that most feminist scholars simply cannot countenance. It is hardly surprising, then, that feminist theory encounters staunch resistance from those with vested interests in preserving music's purity and innocence. Feminist claims to find sex and gender issues at the very heart of music most itself, in wordless patterns of sound—hard-core instrumental music—deeply disturbs assumptions that are long-standing and foundational.

Determined to resist efforts to quarantine feminist criticism from music 'proper', feminist theories have increasingly, following McClary's courageous lead, endeavored to show "the ways in which the social organization of gender informs even the presumably value-free aspects of instrumental music and its theories."[102] Since its language purports to deal purely with music's innermost workings, the discipline of 'music theory' is a good place to begin looking for evidence of gender constructions. Eighteenth-century theorists, McClary observes, "judged major keys to be masculine (because of their natural strength) and minor keys to be feminine (because of their frailty, their dependence, their subordination to major)."[103] Nor was it uncommon even in more recent times to designate as masculine phrase endings that occur decisively, on a strong beat, creating a distinct sense of closure and as feminine those that occur on a weak beat, obscuring sense of structural clarity. Similarly, masculine themes are characterized as 'thrusting' or 'aggressive', while feminine themes are soft and passive. Thus, the masculine in music (as elsewhere) is clear, distinct, forceful, and decisive. The feminine is defined in opposition to that masculine norm: as lack, as weakness, as defect.

The pervasive operation of these constructions of masculinity as hard, rigorous, and bold, and of femininity as soft, lyrical, and passive, can be easily tested against musical examples. Renée Cox, for instance, compares Beethoven to Chopin, noting that "Beethoven is musically authoritative, definitive, conclusive; opposites are reconciled, and chaos is conquered by the light. Chopin's music seems feminine not only in its immediacy, lyricalness, gentility and sensuousness, but in its questioning, searching, inconclusive, and disruptive qualities."[104] What might the 'masculinity' and 'femininity' of such musics tell us about our conceptualizations of gender, or about the way we construct musical meaning? According to McClary, quite a bit more than many might care to admit. Unabashedly masculine music is, she suggests, a "celebration of the phallus," and listening to it "worship at the phallic shrine."[105] And she strenuously objects to the "sanctimonious pretense" that in contrast to popular music, whose corruption by things like gender, sexuality, and the body is obvious, classical music is somehow above all this. 'Serious' music is no less tainted by gender and sex than 'popular' music—just less forthright about it.

Citron suggests that masculine or feminine musical themes may be but the tip of the iceberg. Functional musical tonality and the 'sonata aesthetic'—the very systems that made the idea of pure, autonomous music possible—are themselves fundamentally gendered. "The rhetoric of sonata form," she explains, "centers on masculine metaphors, notably power, hegemony, opposition, and competition."[106] Music so constructed is comprised of contrasts between opposing forces: of patterns of struggle, conquest, and resolution; of dominance and submission; of tension, resistance, and victory. These struggles are waged through themes in contrasting keys that play against each other not as equals, but hierarchically: as dominant theme and subordinate, as primary theme and subsidiary, as masculine theme and feminine. Masculine themes occur first, and are what the movement is about. The more lyrical, feminine theme relates to the masculine as contrast, as disruption, as other. Typically, it is disruptive because of its introduction of a new key, and subordinate because it is lyrical and soft. Says Citron, "The imposition of a new tonality brings tension, even if in lyrical guise, and needs to be tamed, resolved, brought back to the original key . . . Thus, the element of Otherness is neutralized by the prevailing masculine order."[107]

So according to Citron, the sonata aesthetic presented a powerful symbol of women's subordination in society: it "became a metaphor for this gendered struggle, and once entrenched it acted to reinforce and reconstruct the gendered ideology in Western society at large."[108] But at the same time, music composed in sonata form purported to be pure and abstract, like the male 'genius' responsible for its creation. Such values and beliefs, suggests Citron, did not resonate strongly with women's experience, nor did the distanced impersonality of music created in accordance with such principles. Thus, she concludes, women's failure to compose 'absolute' music was probably not a function of their incapacity, but rather of their disinclination.[109] In this view, this most pure of musics, this music most itself, is not so pure after all. It reveals stereotypically male gender constructions, building upon hierarchical power relations fundamentally at odds with women's experience. Thus, concludes Citron, ". . . absolute music, particularly the symphony, was grounded in a gendered process reflective of one sex and alien to the other."[110]

It is important to note that this is not an essentialist argument: rather, it points to the profound significance of historically contingent constructions and representations of femininity and masculinity in music. As McClary observes, the fact that early Romantic (male) composers often embraced feminine imagination rather than masculine reason, and subjectivity rather than objectivity, clearly demonstrates the constructedness of gender differences. Yet, their status as social constructions does not diminish their influence in the least. Indeed, says McClary, "The tensions between closure-oriented norms and subversive deviations in nineteenth-century musical discourse [threw] into confusion fundamental lines of gender identity and patriarchal allegiance. The defensive masculine posturing of the nineteenth-century male artist who was colonizing what was regarded as feminine terrain is therefore not surprising—nor is the insistence that actual women not be permitted to participate."[111]

If serious music's presumed purity were not sufficiently tainted by its association with gender, McClary suggests its power to signify extends further still: to the erotic and the sexual. Indeed, she claims, "music itself often relies heavily upon the metaphorical simulation of sexual activity for its effects."[112] One of the primary agents of this metaphorical simulation in Western music is the tonal system. No more neutral or innocent than the sonata aesthetic, patterns of convergence and divergence with tonal center are laden with sexual imagery. Tonality's process of "instilling expectations and subsequently withholding promised fulfillment until climax," producing the patterns of tension and repose, resistance and fulfillment that have figured so centrally in theories from Schopenhauer to Langer to Meyer, "is the principal musical means during the period from 1600 to 1900 for arousing and channeling desire."[113] Entirely without assistance from a program or text, says McClary, "tonal compositions ranging from Bach organ fugues to Brahms symphonies whip up torrents of libidinal energy that are variously thwarted or permitted to gush."[114] Not only, then, is music a gendered narrative, it is a sexual narrative as well. Accordingly, even in a piece as supposedly purely musical as a Brahms symphony, it is appropriate to inquire, "What . . . is the listener being invited to desire and why?"[115]

Matters like these are not frivolous associations. Rather, they lie at music's very heart. Indeed, insists McClary, "Most people care about music because it resonates with experiences that otherwise go unarticulated, whether it is the flood of cathartic release that occurs at the climax of a Tchaikowsky symphony or the groove that causes one's body to dance—that is, to experience itself in a new way. Yet our music theories and notational systems do everything possible to mask those dimensions of music that are related to physical human experience and focus instead on the orderly, the rational, the cerebral."[116] These erotic, corporeal dimensions of musical experience are "perhaps the most powerful aspects of musical discourses, for they operate below the level of deliberate signification and are thus usually reproduced and transmitted without conscious intervention. They are the habits of cultural thought that guarantee the effectiveness of the music—that allow it to 'make sense'—while they remain largely invisible and apparently immutable."[117]

Like McClary, Shepherd situates music in the realm of gender politics, where patriarchal power seeks to control, subvert, and silence whatever opposes its bureaucratic world order. Focusing on the tensions between music's structural and sensual dimensions, his analysis centers around timbre: the "tactile core of sound,"[118] "the 'nature of sound itself', [its] vibratory essence . . ."[119] Before it can be or have anything else, music, as sonorous experience, is timbral. This tactile core manifests itself bodily, tactilely, rather than formally or structurally—in the way its textures rub against the body rather than in presentations of ordered pattern. Fundamental though this bodily/timbral experience is to music, though, its sensuality poses a threat to rational order. It is, one might say, at the center of the struggle Cusick finds in musical performance, wherein the prevalence of the orderly and controlled over irrational is ritually enacted. In a sense, then, music's social situation resembles that of women: carefully controlled and marginalized. Because of the sensuality of its timbral presence, music must be constrained, its threat to the dominance of rational order carefully guarded. As Shepherd sees it, both women and music are "subject to similar processes of control and domination."[120] And in fact, "the vast majority of music consumed in the Western world is concerned with articulating, in a variety of different ways, male hegemonic processes."[121]

Since its status in society is, like women's, marginalized and subordinate, music can show us important things about the way hegemonic processes create and sustain male dominance. In Shepherd's view, male hegemony is "essentially a visual hegemony."[122] In contrast to hearing and the corporeal, timbral experience that lies at music's heart, vision is a "silent and inert sensory channel which allows us not only to distance ourselves from the phenomena of the world but also to interject ourselves into the world from a distance. It is the sensory channel which allows us, from a single point of view, to order discrete objects into their uniquely structured locations in space."[123] Thus, visual experience, as phenomenologists have shown us, is an experience of distance and separation. Its contents are discrete and objective, permitting cool, contemplative scrutiny. And since vision's content lies at a comfortable distance from us, reaching us with a sense of completeness, visual experience is an experience of self-containedness. Visual experience is also voyeuristic, and the voyeur's world, as Finn points out, is one in which "there is no dialogue, no relationship, no speech, and no response, and therefore no understanding, neither of the self nor of the objects 'known'."[124] Thus, visual hegemony's power is a function of its capacity to distance, separate, objectify, and control.

Sound, on the other hand, is a fundamentally tactile sense: touching, probing, intruding, and never wholly free of bodily involvement. Since it refuses to stay at a distance, surrounding us and rubbing against us, sonorous experience is always an experience of relatedness, integration, and involvement. Says Shepherd, sound "tells us there is a world of depth surrounding us, approaching us simultaneously from all directions . . . a world which is active and constantly prodding us for a reaction."[125] Given the 'orality' of voice, and its implication of face-to-face communication, sonorous experience "cannot help . . . but emphasize the social relatedness of individual and cultural existence."[126] Further still, timbre is what "puts the world of sound in motion and reminds us that . . . we are alive, sentient and experiencing. . . ." Timbre is the "grain and the tactile quality of sound which brings the world into us and reminds us of the social relatedness of humanity . . . [and] in touching us and stroking us . . . makes us aware of our very existence."[127] Accordingly, music's sonorous condition constitutes a direct threat to the myths of objectivity and detachment that sustain visually mediated power.

Music's resistance to the ideals that sustain male domination assures for it marginal status relative to the objective matters so fundamentally important to patriarchal order. And its unruly, ambiguous, timbral core requires careful control. In Western classical music, Shepherd maintains, only a very restricted range of timbral expression is tolerated. Its timbres are highly standardized and homogeneous, and while deviations from these norms are crucial to musical expression, they are permitted only within the narrowest of bounds. Also, priority is given to the parameters (melody, harmony, rhythm) most compatible with and susceptible to control by visual representation, that is, by notation. In fact, Shepherd argues, 'classical' music renders sound's timbral core largely insensible, nearly silent: it is a music comprised of "[n]otes stripped of much of their inherent sonic possibilities . . ."[128] Just as women are rendered invisible in patriarchal discourses, so is the serious study of music "almost completely successful in avoiding any discussion of the nature of sound itself."[129] It exhibits a strong preference for abstract, structural/syntactical arrangements between and among sounds, rather than sounds themselves; an interest in organization, rather than meaning and experience. By restricting the range of admissible timbre and representing it visually, classical music confines sensuality and disorderliness to a carefully circumscribed range. Music's bodily, erotic pleasure is thus tolerated, but only in the muted terms that suit patriarchal order. In short, music becomes officially sanctioned in patriarchal society by suppressing its sensual, erotic character. Musics in which such qualities are prominent may be tolerated as entertainments or diversions; but only music that incorporates codes congruent with male hegemony (orderly, detached, restrained, and rational) can earn that elite status that is considered serious or designated 'profound'.

The theories of McClary, Citron, and Shepherd each submit the ideology of pure music to provocative criticism. There is, they suggest, a lot more going on in music than most conventional accounts of its nature and value allow. It is far more influential and deeply implicated in human sociocultural life than the theories of music's official disciplinary gatekeepers generally acknowledge; indeed, music speaks of things that notions like transcendence and intrinsic value are carefully designed to cover over. Says Shepherd in an especially suggestive passage: "It is because music is placed in a 'feminized' location in our world that it must be carefully controlled and monitored by the academy. . . . But it is also because it is placed in a feminized location that it contains the residues of what it is that our culture, publicly, does not want to communicate with itself about."[130] As McClary suggests, the things that draw most people to music and make it meaningful for them are conspicuously absent from disciplinary discourses about 'serious' music. The idea of musical autonomy bequeathed by formalist and idealistic 'aesthetic' philosophy completely misconstrues what music is, drastically underestimating its significance and potency, and rendering its sociopolitical and corporeal dimensions all but invisible. On the view that has been explored here, musical experience is a powerful agent in creating social and personal identity, and not in some general, abstract way. As Leppert has put it, "The use value of music to the lessons of gender are confirmed throughout Western history. . . . [S]onority and identity are joined at the hip. . . ."[131]

The critical response to these views is not at all difficult to anticipate: these theories attempt to locate things like gender relations, power, and sex where they simply cannot be, in pure, abstract patterns of sound. They impute to music characteristics that sonorous patterns just cannot have. Music's formal configurations represent or signify nothing outside themselves. Not only do accounts like these tell us little about music, then, they actually steer us away from it, toward matters that are properly concerns of sociology, anthropology, and psychology.

Of course feminist music theorists strenuously disagree. In fact, as Korsmeyer explains, most feminist thought has abandoned the idea that musical experience is characteristically or appropriately detached or 'disinterested', that it is divorced from all personal, practical, moral, or social concerns.[132] "Gone," she writes, "is the idea that matters of 'aesthetic' quality can be isolated from their traditional contraries: practical or instrumental value, moral significance, the exercise of political power. The answers to the questions posed from feminist perspectives are far from settled, but the framework within which they are formulated has altered the landscape of inquiry."[133]

Music, Gender, Difference, and Power

Having briefly examined several theories of how music may work to confirm or resist gender and power relationships in society, it is important to reconsider the broader context from which they emerge, the ways they are theoretically situated within recent feminist projects. After earlier (though still ongoing) compensatory projects and critiques of the canon, feminist theorists in music have increasingly turned their attention to the sociocultural dynamics responsible for women's exclusion and marginalization. Koskoff's perspective is particularly helpful here, based as it is on examinations of music cross-culturally. Since what is familiar in one's own culture can often seem natural and inevitable, cross-cultural study often reveals patterns and arrangements that would otherwise pass unnoticed. As Koskoff indicates, much of the cross-cultural work on music and gender is guided by two basic questions: "First, to what degree does a society's gender ideology and resulting gender-related behaviors affect its musical thought and practice? And second, how does music function in society to reflect or affect inter-gender relations?"[134]

'Gender ideologies', Koskoff explains, are conceptual clusters that shape people's beliefs about what gender behaviors are correct, appropriate, or natural. Unlike female-male sexual differences, gender categories are not founded in nature; they are cultural constructions, and may accordingly assume a wide variety of patterns. The relationship between sexual categories and gender categories is no one-to-one correspondence. Regardless of the particular form a society's gender ideology assumes, though, at its heart lie issues of identity and distribution of power. Most of the differences between women's and men's situations in society are not functions of sexual or biological differences but of the way socially constructed gender systems differentially allocate value and privilege to people. Although theoretically gender categories might assume practically any configuration, it is frequently the case that sexual differences (binary biological categories) are intricately linked within a society to constellations of nonbiological binaries, conceptual dualities that divide the world into same and different, better and worse. Thus, this social construction known as gender quite often takes the form of a dichotic opposition (man-woman) that functions hierarchically, conferring privilege and power upon 'man' or 'maleness', and marginalizing women and 'femininity'. Not surprisingly, contemporary feminist scholarship has had a keen interest in music's role in this constructive process.

Because they assign men and women to separate, opposing gender categories, gender ideologies also often lead to the segregation of their musical activities into two separate expressive spheres. In many societies, Koskoff explains, "a woman's identity is believed to be embedded in her sexuality: that is, she is seen (and may see herself) primarily as sexual partner, childbearer, and nurturer. Thus, one of the most common associations between women and music . . . links women's primary sexual identity and role with music performance."[135] There develop, in other words, strong ideological links between a society's constructions of gender and what that society regards as appropriate musical activity for men and women. Musical behavior, therefore, "is not only enmeshed in social concepts of sexuality, but can also serve to re-enforce and define gender identity."[136] In many societies, gender identities have traditionally been constructed so as to relegate women to a private, domestic sphere of influence, effectively barring their participation in broad ranges of (public) musical discourses and activities. Because all putatively legitimate musical activity is presumed to take place in the male-dominated public sphere, gender is not considered relevant to accounts of music's nature and value. This systematic exclusion of women from a broad range of musical discourses and practices points to the necessity for deeper analyses of the ways society's gender ideologies impinge upon musical behavior. The ways societies construct their gender ideologies, then, have important implications for their musical practices; but at the same time, their musical practices help define and reinforce those gender ideologies. Musical practices are shaped by, and in turn help shape, gender ideologies.

As suggested above, gender ideologies are invariably concerned with the distribution of power and value in societies. As Ortner and Whitehead put it, "the study of gender is inherently a study of relations of asymmetrical power and opportunity."[137] A society's gender structure, they continue, orders human relations into "patterns of deference and condescension, respect and disregard, and in many cases, command and obedience."[138] While it is certainly possible for power to be vested in women more than men, or that it be shared equally, the fact is that in most societies, dominance and privilege are accorded to men. These 'asymmetries of power' are so thoroughly internalized that they are often scarcely recognized. Yet, they may be easily observed in musical practices, says Koskoff: "Indeed, music performance provides one of the best contexts for observing and understanding the gender structure of any society. This may be so because in many societies the underlying conceptual frameworks of both gender and musical/social dynamics share an important structural feature: they both rely, to a great degree, on notions of power and control."[139]

If music is enmeshed in the construction and reinforcement of gender ideologies, and if these ideologies in turn exert potent influence on ways power, control, and opportunity are allocated, music is clearly political, and not in a trivial sense. Musical practices can and often do serve as ritual enactments of male supremacy, as spectacular celebrations of those aspects of the gender ideology that assure male domination, as confirmations of what is valuable and what is not within the established social order. And yet, Koskoff's cross-cultural studies also show that musical practices can resist, threaten, or subvert the prevalent order.[140] Because gender ideologies are constructed, they may be resisted and reconstructed in ways that are more equitable and more representative of the range of possibilities hidden by rigid, dualistic, hierarchical constructions. What is needed, Koskoff urges, is a conceptual model that integrates power, music, gender, and value, rather than construing them as discrete affairs, a model that regards each of these dimensions as continua rather than dichotomies. Such a model would examine power on a continuum from oppression to equality; musical value on a continuum between high and low; gender on a continuum between relative maleness and femaleness.[141] Such a model would be more sensitive to the complexities of the social milieu within which music always exists, and help "address the valuative role music plays in defining and reflecting established social and sexual orders and in acting as an agent in maintaining or changing such orders."[142]

Clearly, such a model would be highly sensitive to differences. It would destabilize the inclusionary and exclusionary power of conventional categories, and create alternatives to essentialist beliefs that differences are innate, oppositional, and inalterable. Since the dynamics of domination work by setting up rigid, dualistic categories without transitional shades of grey, by creating normative ideals that treat all difference as aberrance, defect, and inferiority, it is crucial that the feminist project illuminate how this business of saming and othering—this logic of 'alterity'—works. Feminist theory thus tries to take difference seriously, to offer deeper analyses of how judgments of 'sameness' and 'differentness' serve the interests of power. Differences and similarities exist everywhere, and practically anything can be found to resemble and differ from anything in some respect. But similarity and difference work by suppressing each other, and to that extent each represents a kind of distortion. 'Sameness' works by ignoring or denying difference, while 'difference' works by suppressing or overlooking possible points of similarity. In human terms, the patriarchal claim to the sameness of all 'human beings' denies the distinctness of women, just as the notion of women's common identity tends to impose categorical similarity on people that are in many ways radically dissimilar. On the other hand, claiming 'difference' is a way of denying identity with the broader category, but usually it rests on presumed similarity among those who are different. In simpler words, neither similarities nor differences are absolute. They coexist dialectically and are mutually dependent. The question is not whether, but in what ways things, musics, and people are different and alike. Since they always coexist, the fundamental issue is which differences are important to take seriously and what the consequences of failing to recognize them may be. As Solie observes, "power accrues to whoever is in the position to decide what is 'same' and what is 'different'."[143] Thus, "politically . . . difference is about power."[144]

What feminist music scholars interested in gender issues hope to show is that we can acknowledge, respect, and even honor differences without treating them like hard-wired facts. Identity categories, whether personal or conceptual, are predominantly constructed. And it is crucial to recognize that in that constructive process, broad ranges of similarities and differences are reduced to and reconfigured into binary, hierarchical arrangements where differences within the category are suppressed in order to highlight differences between the category and what lies outside it—the 'other' to which it stands opposed.[145] Binary views of culturally constructed phenomena like gender (masculine-feminine) and music (ours-theirs, good-bad) are inherently reductive; and regarding them as 'hard' or strong can "hypostatize categories in such a way that change over time becomes invisible,"[146] making them appear natural, permanent, and inevitable. By this dynamic, differences that are simply conditional conveniences get transmuted into things that are supposedly foundational, essential, innate.

But "few if any of the meaningful differences between groups of people are innate," reminds Solie.[147] They are conceptual habits, the products of nurture, not nature; of culture, not biology. If it is predominantly socialization that imparts power to men and relegates women to subaltern roles, then it is important to study the way musical expression and political power collaborate with one another. Or, as Solie puts it, "if identities are a matter of social role, we may be able to study the mechanisms—including musical ones—by which those roles are delineated, communicated, learned, and perhaps challenged."[148] Where and how does this constructive work occur? Solie indicates three mechanisms, each inviting feminist musical critique: social experience, language, and representation. Conceiving differences as social constructions emphasizes their contingency, and hence their susceptibility to transformation. Conceiving differences as linguistic constructions leads to study of the ways binary dualisms enforce normative conceptual patterns of inclusion and exclusion, as well as value hierarchies. And recognizing the ways dualistic, hierarchical stereotypes are reinforced by representation leads to study of the ways musical images confirm or undermine the status quo, establishing music as an important part of the technology of gender construction.

Of fundamental concern to feminist theory, then, is understanding "what role musics play in the construction and reinforcement of ideologies of difference and, conversely, how they may challenge or resist those ideologies."[149] And since musics are among the most treasured belongings of human civilization, it is crucial to understand how the seeming 'safeness' of the experience they offer us is a function of the way musics confirm our identities, both individually and collectively. "It matters," Solie insists, "to whom they belong and who is empowered to speak about them. It matters about whom *they* speak, and what they say."[150] Musical practices play important roles in demarcating and reinforcing identities and communities, in mediating the terrain variously organized as 'I', 'we', and 'they'. The challenge is to better understand how musics do this, and to extend the range of 'us' to include more of 'them': to create 'I's that are more fluid, 'we's that are less exclusive.

Feminist Challenges to Music Philosophy: Summary

Given the remarkable range and depth of concerns explored here, it seems clear that feminist perspectives on music's nature and value are neither marginal curiosities nor passing trends. Indeed, the heated debates and sophisticated inquiries they generate are likely to transform music scholarship in ways yet unimagined. By shattering traditional disciplinary boundaries, feminist theory profoundly challenges those for whom such boundaries have come to represent the limits of intelligible discourse. To them, feminist approaches to music philosophy are neither properly musical nor properly philosophical. But from feminist perspectives, such criticisms miss the point entirely: for the ideas of musical autonomy and of philosophy as objective, 'disinterested' discourse to which these criticisms appeal are both disciplinary constructions, and thus part of the problem at hand. Disciplinary boundaries are arbitrary constructions, carefully crafted to serve particular interests by exercising tight control over the range of admissible dialogue. As Lamb puts it, "The production of music within this ideology takes for granted the conditions of the relations of ruling, their experiences, interests, and relevancies . . ."[151] Likewise, the idea of philosophy as dispassionate pursuit of universal truths assures the continued exclusion of women's experience and concerns, and assures that power and control remain vested in the hands of those who already hold it. 'Gatekeeping' is a privilege of disciplinary authority, and allowing that authority to be challenged only within a narrowly restricted range assures that core values and assumptions remain safe and secure. Quarantining feminist critique, declaring it out of properly disciplinary bounds, is a strategy that sustains patriarchal domination. Since denying the disciplinary propriety of feminist theory is a fundamentally political act, it requires responses that are political as well. Thus, violating the musical taboo against the political is a transgression to which feminist theory is unavoidably and deeply committed.

Clearly, feminist theories and critiques challenge music philosophy in difficult, unsettling ways. Women's exclusion from most accounts of music leads many to regard masculine bias as "an integral structural element of the historic concepts of creativity, excellence, and artistic purpose,"[152] and makes them understandably suspicious toward conventional disciplinary wisdom. Most feminist theory thus rejects universal accounts of music, favoring accounts that feature diversity and multiplicity. Instead of aesthetic formalism's appeals to impersonal structural principles and detached contemplation, feminist theories valorize musical engagement that is concrete and personal. Rather than restricting properly musical experience to the narrow range of gratification afforded by vigilant attention to pattern and design, feminist theories often stress the bodily basis of musical experience, the social situatedness and processual character of musical activity, and the contextual relativity of musical meaning and value.

Feminist theories strenuously resist the objectivist view of music as structured sound (of 'music itself') to which bodily experience relates as a mere 'affective' response. In fact, the idea of music as a fundamentally embodied kind of meaning may be crucial to conceptualizing the linkage between music and gender. If bodily experience is a fundamental component of even the most abstract, cerebral experience—if, as Johnson insists, the body is always in the mind[153]—the idea that the body is a site where sex, gender, and music intersect is quite plausible. The concept of music as a bodily competence, a distinctive way of being in the body, suggests that music's patterns of ebb and flow, of resistance and submission, are experiential structures learned by the body and readily recognized in other embodied experience similarly structured.

Because of their fundamental suspicion of universalist claims, most feminist accounts of music are strikingly pluralistic and relativistic, incorporating difference and contradiction as fundamental principles. Women's extensive firsthand experience of marginalization and domination often makes them particularly vigilant toward theory's tendency to suppress particularity, the category's tendency to violate individuality. Because normative theories of music regard deviation from the norm as evidence of inferiority, feminist accounts are more inclined to stress multiplicity and difference than unity and uniformity, inclined to see differences in kind where others see differences in value. Also, the conviction that selfhood, identity, and gender are constructed and fluid leads many feminist theorists to prefer what Diamond calls "range" rather than "core."[154] In a similar vein, Godway and Finn point to a deep distrust of discourses that presume to speak inclusively, in terms of 'we',[155] and Lamb invokes the image of feminist discourses stepping "away from the unison and . . . toward the possible."[156] Convictions and suspicions like these bring to feminist musical theorizing a respect for difference, divergence, and multiplicity—characteristics that destabilize the hierarchical structures from which patriarchal power and the dynamics of domination are built. In radically pluralizing music, feminist theories undercut the idea of musical works as objective, unitary affairs that grant musical legitimacy only to a very limited interpretive range. They point out that music is not an unconditional good, and that, since none of its putative benefits accrue automatically, the vigilance music warrants must be directed to far more than pleasing sonorous patterns. They show that the apparently seamless and unitary is fractured, multifaceted, and often contradictory. They call into question the possibility of *the* act of listening, *the* authentic musical performance, and a unified phenomenon behind the name 'music'.

In place of such centered, monolithic ideas, feminist theories posit highly complex models in which personal and social histories—people's gender, racial, and other cultural differences—implicate and validate strikingly diverse interpretive moves. While such models present perplexing challenges, they also promise to reinvigorate music philosophy by showing the vital connection of music to life. Feminist theories undermine certainty, centeredness, and stability. Whether that represents a loss or a gain must be assessed in terms of its contribution to what many regard as feminism's most fundamental aim: eliminating oppression.

The Postmodern Ethos

The challenges feminist discourses pose for traditional music philosophy suggest a fundamental reorientation in the way society and its cultural achievements are conceived, an orientation rooted in experiences, assumptions, and values radically different from the ones that have generated most conventional accounts of music and its worth. In place of the idea of 'the musical' as a unitary domain of beautiful sonorous patterns, we find a multidimensional field where the personal, the political, and the moral claim genuinely musical relevance. The border between 'the musical' and 'the extramusical' has become severely eroded and difficult to patrol. The comforting belief that all music is evaluable by the same, strictly 'aesthetic' criteria has lost its persuasiveness, as has the noble vision of music as an inherently and inevitably 'humanizing' affair. The essentially musical core which 'masterworks' were once thought to represent abundantly is increasingly characterized as ideological and political subterfuge. What the term 'music' designates has become increasingly problematic, and its potential values have become radically multiple.

Feminist scholarship has been enormously influential in this trend toward pluralization and relativization; but critiques of universal claims, master narratives, and grand theory have developed elsewhere as well. Indeed, the very idea of philosophy as it has conventionally been understood appears to have undergone a rupture of wide-ranging significance. While feminists have worked to undercut patriarchal patterns of legitimation, others have mounted equally devastating critiques of the modernist ideals of progress, justice, and liberation through reason. The existence of a strong and necessary link between reason and progress has been vigorously contested from the perspective often called 'postmodern'. The postmodern, explains Lyotard, is "based fundamentally upon the perception of the existence of a modern era that dates from the time of the Enlightenment and that has now run its course: and this modern era was predicated on the notion of progress in knowledge, in the arts, in technology, and in human freedom as well, all of which was thought of as leading to a truly emancipated society: a society emancipated from poverty, despotism and ignorance."[157] At the heart of modernity's version of history, relates Bauman, was the notion of a "difficult, but eventually victorious struggle of Reason against emotions or animal instincts, science against religion and magic, truth against prejudice, correct knowledge against superstition, reflection against uncritical existence, rationality against affectivity and the rule of custom . . . [T]he modern age defined itself as, above all, the kingdom of Reason and rationality; the other forms of life were seen, accordingly, as wanting in both respects."[158] But as the prefix 'post' indicates, postmodernists see modernity as a historical period now decisively past. As Bauman puts it, "the self-ascribed attributes contained in the idea of modernity do not hold today, perhaps did not hold yesterday either."[159] Modernity is over, a "closed chapter of history."[160] Reason and rationality failed to deliver what modernity promised, and belief in their liberating potential has simply exhausted itself. Only, modernist narratives about the inexorable progress of reason, freedom, and justice were not just benign fantasies. Rather, they were stories carefully designed to sustain dominant social order and power structures. Enlightenment's inspiring promises legitimated what served the interests of a particular social order, while suppressing other ideas and practices as not just aberrant, but irrational and regressive—and as impediments, therefore, to mankind's (*sic*) progression toward liberation.

Since to postmodern sentiments, discourses about truth, knowledge, justice, and beauty are really about political power and control, the conviction that reason provides the neutral, objective machinery enabling human access to foundational or absolute truths is no longer tenable. Objective or autonomous meanings have been replaced by cultural constructions and conventions. The meaning of works of art does not reside 'behind' their sensuous or formal surfaces in some autonomous, objective realm; nor is there an absolute, autonomous realm of truth—a way things 'really' are—separated from us by a veil of appearances it is reason's job to penetrate. In postmodern discourses meanings are not stable, objective, foundational affairs, but human fabrications; things created, not found. They fluctuate in and around cultural use rather than residing in some durable substrate that simply awaits human discovery. The postmodern similarly abandons belief in a foundational 'human nature' striving throughout history to perfect itself, and even the notion of a stable, unitary 'self'. Fixity is thus replaced with change, 'the absolute' with relativity, certainty with a poignant sense of fallibility, essence with construction, foundation with contingency.

Evidence of this shift from modernity's confident security—self-assuredly grounded in essences, foundations, and progress—to postmodernism's skeptical, antifoundational stance is apparent in virtually all realms of inquiry. In the 1960s, for instance, Thomas Kuhn published an enormously influential account of the way the paradigmatic assumptions underlying scientific inquiry undergo dramatic, even revolutionary shifts, and prominent scientist Michael Polanyi proclaimed that the grounds of even the most rigorous knowledge were inescapably 'tacit'. At the same time, social and political formations once regarded as universal, objective, and in the natural order of things came to be regarded as mere constructions, arbitrary arrangements locally maintained and legitimated by concepts of truth and propriety. Intellectuals became increasingly convinced of the cultural specificity of knowledge, values, and moral and aesthetic concerns, and highly sensitive to the West's inclination to project and impose its cultural values and beliefs on others. Criticism too found itself in crisis: its judgments and pronouncements increasingly were regarded as symptoms of "an imperialist cast of mind, according to which one culture arrogates to itself the right to legislate for all other cultures whose foundations might be radically different."[161] This penchant for universalizing the particulars of the West's cultural situation, characterizing Western urban culture as progressive, advanced, and modern—always in marked contrast to supposedly backward, 'primitive' others—now bears the stigmatized name 'modernist'. 'Postmodern' is thus the general label for a remarkably broad range of antifoundationalist discourses that resist and oppose the claims of modernity.

Rather than countering modernity's arrogance with a kind of counter-arrogance that amounts to the same thing—that simply inverts modernity's presumptions of ultimacy—the postmodern assiduously avoids claims that presume to be absolute or foundational. Where modernity self-confidently ascribed its values to all 'reasonable' people, postmodern discourses make a concerted effort to acknowledge their situatedness, their relativity, their contingency, and their potential fallibility. Accordingly, the role of 'pure' reason in postmodern discourses is considerably more modest and cautious. Since reason so easily deteriorates into the kind of rationalization that finds ways to tolerate things like oppression, violence against women and children, the immense gap between wealth and poverty, wars, and a seemingly unending list of unspeakable atrocities, postmodern estimates of reason range from suspicious to skeptical. The credibility of modernity's noble promises has been shattered. However, that is not really cause for remorse: belief in reason's capacity to assure liberty and justice was not just naive, it was dangerously ideological. And so too was the idea that reason operated in an autonomous realm beyond the messy worlds of politics and power.

Again, the postmodern is a world of multiplicity, diversity, and contradiction rather than uniformity and order. Because it rejects modernity's totalizing (universalizing) discourses and colonizing attitudes, because it prefers heterogeneity and locality to homogeneity, uniformity, and universality, the postmodern is a discourse of periphery and margins, not of center. As one writer puts it, the postmodern is "a discourse which imperialism had strenuously silenced but which is now made available. It alerts the erstwhile centre to the possibility that there is not one world, but rather many worlds all being lived at different speeds, according to different rhythms, producing contradictory histories . . . [I]t releases a number of worlds which, strictly speaking, simply cannot be understood in the languages and discourse of the imperialist central power."[162] The postmodern thus rejects modernity's unwavering confidence in the superiority and universal applicability of Western rationality, morality, and aesthetic values. "Instead, it tries to reconcile itself to a life under conditions of permanent and incurable uncertainty; a life in the presence of an unlimited quantity of competing forms of life, unable to prove their claims to be grounded in anything more solid and binding than their own historically shaped conventions."[163]

If the postmodern no longer finds modernity's systems of belief and value persuasive, credible, or useful, it does not regard their passing as loss. Rather than lamenting the demise of modernity, the postmodern ethos is often surprisingly playful and capricious. This 'ludic' strain takes modernity's dissolution simply as a fait accompli, not just accepting it without grief but greeting it with apparent lightness. A more serious, 'resistant' postmodern strain, on the other hand, manifests staunchly *anti*modern overtones.[164] It often assumes a strenuously defiant attitude toward modernist ideals, vehemently renouncing totalizing regimes, master narratives, and cross-cultural generalization. Despite their strikingly different character, however, the 'ludic' and 'resistant' postmodern strains are both manifestations of skepticism toward modernist narratives, of sensitivity to the ways such stories covertly served the interests of power, control, and oppression.

This subversiveness and irreverence toward ideals and assumptions long presumed foundational destabilizes, complicates, creates nothing short of a crisis of legitimation. Indeed, it renders questionable even efforts like this to describe it: its rejection of norms and definitions makes efforts to define it contradictory. And convenient though it sometimes is, the simple addition of the suffix 'ism' to the term postmodern transforms it into something fundamentally at odds with the sensibilities it represents, imputes to it a coherence and stability it strenuously rejects. As one writer observes, postmodernism is "not a system but an ethos."[165] Another cautions that definitions of the postmodern should always be accompanied by the caveat "until further notice."[166] Slippery and elusive though it may be, however, there is no denying its potential to explode conventional views of what music is and does.

Postmodern convictions are invariably disruptive. Yet, this disruptiveness is hailed by some as a constructive force, with valuable capacity to stir up controversy and animated debate in disciplines grown stale and stagnant. The postmodern turn has given studies in the humanities, for instance, a renewed sense of significance and urgency. Postmodern orientations to music and music philosophy may also be construed positively: as efforts to rescue music from the sense of irrelevance created and perpetuated by notions like autonomy, objectivity, absolute meaning, and 'aesthetic' value. Postmodern critiques seek to knock music off its pedestal, and return it to the world where ordinary people live and breath and struggle.[167] At the same time, postmodern criticism blurs conventional disciplinary boundaries, affecting the kind of radical conceptual realignments advocates hope will destroy the various disciplinary fences that help maintain the illusion of music's autonomy and isolation. Chaos and disruption, from this perspective, can be part of a hopeful project, representing "a welcome contrast to the bad faith and delusions fostered by traditional metaphysical thinking."[168]

The postmodernist insists that music as philosophy has traditionally portrayed it—as an autonomous art form, as a unitary practice evolving in such a way as to become ever more advanced and true to itself, as an essentially humanizing influence—does not exist and probably never has. These are interesting, even inspiring ways of describing music; but to assume that they capture music's innermost essence is a fundamental mistake, and that is primarily because the idea that music has an 'essential' nature is itself dubious. In a sense, then, the postmodern is both postphilosophical and postmusical. It positions itself 'after the end' of such disciplines as they have been conceived for centuries, mounting penetrating critiques of many of their most cherished convictions. From a postmodern perspective, the philosophical agenda of modernity—of revealing a unitary reality as it 'really' is—is silly. There is no one way the world, or music for that matter, 'is': only an infinite number of ways they may be construed, each inescapably partial and temporary, useful for some purposes while useless for a great many others. The grand-scale abstractions and master narratives offered by philosophies of modernity occlude the richness, diversity, and heterogeneity of what they purport to explain. Accordingly, postmodern discourses do not presume to speak for everyone, everywhere, for all times, but strive to remain ad hoc, local, and temporary: attuned to plurality, difference,

and change. By deconstructing, destabilizing, and defamiliarizing, they paradoxically work to rehumanize and revitalize. What critics decry as a conceptual
free-fall and an intellectual meltdown, then, many postmodernists regard as a
fundamentally utopian project.

One of the issues that best exemplifies the postmodern ethos is its disposition of the idea of the unitary, stable, fixed, and centered 'self'. The postmodern identity is fluid and decentered: constantly being constructed and reconstructed in interaction with social and historical circumstances. It is mobile,
plural, and contradictory: a shifting constellation of temporary, contingent selves,
ever transitory and under realignment. It lacks, therefore, any durable 'essence',
the kind of unchanging substrate on which modernist notions of 'human nature' and personal autonomy were founded.

From a postmodern perspective, the idea of unitary, centered selfhood neglects its diversity, dynamism, and plurality, in much the same way the idea of
a uniform human nature suppresses awareness of human multiplicity and diversity, naively imputing to all human beings characteristics and values of a privileged few. Modernist thought wields and maintains its vested power, it is alleged, by radically dividing the world into that which is centered and pure (the
normal, the typical) on the one hand, and that which is peripheral and impure
(deviant, abnormal, defective, deficient, primitive) on the other. Difference is
equated with inferiority. Dominant ideologies, then, maintain power precisely
by setting up binary oppositions between normative and deviant, central and peripheral, self and other, us and them. This process of centering and 'othering',
the 'logic of alterity',[169] is the very logic that privileges a masculine norm over
feminine deviation, reason over imagination and intuition, the white race over
people of color, 'serious art' over popular diversion, and so on.

For these reasons, postmodernists regard totalizing, unifying schemes as the
machinery of hierarchical power. And the postmodern effort to 'deconstruct' that
machinery issues not so much from maliciousness as from positive commitment:
a determination to destabilize and thereby counter ideology's harmful influence.
The decentered, fragmented universe these deconstructive efforts often leave in
their wake is as difficult to restore to wholeness as Humpty Dumpty, but that of
course is precisely the postmodernist's intent: for Humpty's presumed unity was,
after all, illusory. Thus, the postmodern ethos does not so much accept its world's
fragmentation as revel in it. Its attitude is ironically playful, disrespectful of
somber authority, and indeed, often comic. It accepts and even embraces instability, fluidity, and relativity. It greets sentimental nostalgia for the unitary, ordered world—the toppled modernist order—with apparent amusement. We can
get along quite nicely without things godlike and absolute, postmodernists believe, and there are some pretty compelling reasons for learning to do just that.

In summary, the postmodern defiantly disavows absolutes and universals. It
is fragmentary and fragmenting, decentered and decentering. It prefers particularity and concreteness to universality and abstraction, the local to the global. It
renounces grand theory for personal narrative, airtight theoretical coherence for
descriptive richness. It has little use for what Haraway playfully calls the "god-
trick,"[170] the assumption of that mythically objective perspective that is some-

how supposed to escape all contingency and historicity; or with theory that presumes to transcend the particularity and concreteness of personal experience; or with supposedly autonomous masterpieces with value that is supposedly pure or intrinsic. The postmodern world is not unitary, static, and homogenous, but prismatic, refractory, dynamic, and radically plural. This world without universals, gods, or absolutes is one where personal responsibility is not mediated by abstract principle or impersonal system, one in which, as a result, people have no alternative but to acknowledge each other's particularity and individuality. And because of the awareness of the ways in which all communities suppress the interests of individuals in favor of the greater interest of community, postmodernists regard appeals to consensus or 'we-ness' with deep suspicion.

Music and the Postmodern

Since the antifoundationalist and antiessentialist convictions of postmodernism are at least partly the result of an acute sensitivity to the plurality and diversity of human values, beliefs, and practices, it is enlightening to compare it to another prominent intellectual movement spawned by this need to come to grips with plurality. Like the postmodern, the 'multicultural' orientation represents an effort to account for the multiplicity of something once regarded as unitary, an effort to acknowledge the particularity and situatedness of cultural values and norms once presumed universal. The global awareness brought about by mobility and technology has radically altered people's concepts of what music is and does. At the same time, the professional discipline of ethnomusicology has demonstrated decisively the musical legitimacy of many practices that once lay well outside what people had in mind when they spoke of music. It has thus become nearly impossible to sustain the idea that one music embodies more than others what is most musically important or valuable, that one kind of music best represents what 'music proper' should be, or does what 'music proper' should do, in contrast to a primitive, undeveloped remainder. Awareness of musical differences has relativized our understandings of music's nature and value, irreversibly pluralizing what 'music' means. As talk of music has given way to talk of 'musics', so has the idea of one 'inherently musical' value given way to recognition of diverse musical values. As Elliott puts it, "no musical practice or musical culture is innately better than any other."[171]

Recognizing that different musical practices do different things, that standards appropriate to one musical practice can be wholly inappropriate to another, poses rather significant challenges to philosophy's quest for generalizations about music as a whole. Awareness of the cultural specificity and relativity of musical practices has made musical philosophers increasingly wary of treating music as a unitary phenomenon amenable to universal descriptions. The multiculturalist response to this dilemma appears to be acknowledging the existence of multiple musical cultures and subcultures, and insisting that accounts of music's nature and value be informed by appreciation of its multiplicity and diversity. Since music is a "diverse, multicultural practice," Elliott reasons, an adequate understanding of what that term represents can only be adequately developed by encounters with diverse, unfamiliar musics. Such encounters are "musical-cultural confrontations" that challenge people to "develop the disposition to consider that what may seem natural, common, and universal to them is not."[172] Though potentially disturbing, the effect of these confrontations is ultimately liberating: "The best and perhaps the only sure way of bringing to light and revivifying . . . [our] fossilized assumptions, and of destroying their powers to cramp and confine, is by subjecting ourselves to the shock of contact with a very alien tradition."[173]

Thus, like the postmodern, the concept of music as a multicultural phenomenon works to undo the idea of music as a unitary, static thing. It insists as well that music be situated within cultural context, instead of being regarded as an autonomous affair or a 'universal language'. But at the same time, multiculturalism's understanding of musical diversity seems different from that characteristic of the postmodern. The term 'multicultural', Elliott explains, assumes (a) "the coexistence of unlike social groups in a common social system," and (b) a commitment to "exchange among different social groups to enrich all while respecting and preserving the integrity of each."[174] It both recognizes and commits to maintaining diversity and plurality, then, eschewing temptations to assimilation that might erode differences. It has, in other words, a strong commitment to maintaining the authenticity of diverse practices. In effect, the idea of a single, transcendent, universal musical practice is relaxed to make way for a number of musical practices: the idea of a single authentic practice is replaced with the idea of multiple authentic practices, such that the concern formerly directed to the integrity of the 'macroculture' is distributed among various 'microcultures'.

One might say, in other words, that multiculturalism attends to the distortive effects of lumping all musics into a single, unitary conceptual category ('music'), yet reveals a similar tendency to unwarranted generalization in its concern for intracultural authenticity—safeguarding what it regards as the centered integrity of various musical practices. While the cultural axis is treated multiply, then, musical practices in particular cultures are still regarded hierarchically, with hard distinctions drawn between the authentic and the inauthentic, the pure and the defective, the progressive and the regressive. From a hypothetically postmodern perspective, then, multicultural views of music retain belief in the normative centeredness of musical practices, thereby exercising 'colonial' or imperialist attitudes that equate deviations to defects.[175] Difference is acknowledged, but only of a limited order. The plurality of musical cultures is acknowledged, but within cultures music is still construed as essentially unitary and centered. So multiculturalism relativizes the concept of music, but seeks to limit and contain that 'relativization' and its effects. It decenters the concept of music, yet reinstates presumed centeredness in ethnically or culturally (and often, geographically) demarcated practices. It replaces one musical hierarchy with many: a single, centered 'music' with multiple, centered 'musics'. From a postmodern point of view, multiculturalism's commitment to ideals of authenticity, integrity, and stability bear a suspicious resemblance to the essentialist notions evident in modernity's Eurocentricity. In contrast, the postmodern ethos embraces a 'here and now' where new musics, musical practices, and musical meanings are currently being forged.

Put slightly differently, the multicultural orientation tends to take as given that a culture's music is sufficiently unitary and unproblematic to be comprehended fully by those within. Postmodern orientations, however, attribute significant obfuscatory power to the familiar, the conventional, and the habitual. So in addition to confronting the unfamiliar, postmodernists seek to expose and interrogate musical dimensions and meanings rendered opaque by their familiarity: to make the familiar strange. Strategically, this involves the radical alteration of musical contexts, resistance to music's claim to inscrutable autonomy, and refusal to honor or obey its pretensions of organic completeness and insularity. The postmodern thus juxtaposes incongruous images, cuts and splices, with utter disregard for issues like stylistic development, continuity, and integrity. By deconstructing our carefully constructed webs of belief—the myths designed to protect music from 'extramusical' or 'inauthentic' incursions—music's important social, cultural, and political work is revealed. In short, multiculturalism's interest in the musical 'otherness' of exotic, foreign cultures fails to address the otherness and multidimensionality of the familiar, neglecting the liberating potential of experiencing the "shock of contact with the alien" in our own musical practices. To that extent, it falls short of illuminating music's vitality, relevance, and importance.

In short, postmodern music philosophy and criticism work to subvert what is taken for granted, to undo the opaqueness of unexamined familiarity, to reconstruct human meanings in ways that highlight their humanness, their social situatedness, and their implication in power relations. They seek to show the contingency of what presents itself as necessary and inevitable, the fractures beneath apparent unity, the constructedness of the apparently natural, the transitory character of what presents itself as timeless. The postmodern rejects the idea of progression toward some distant, more advanced moment, preferring to live in the concreteness of the here and now rather than the fantasy of abstraction. It prefers fluidity and dynamism to the sober fixity created by conceptual and disciplinary boundaries. It prefers shades of grey to the black-and-whiteness of dualistic thought. It seeks to topple structural hierarchies. It seeks to reclaim indeterminacy from the determinate, to reconstruct awareness of the multiplicity and heterogeneity of cultural meaning. Its vistas are prismatic and diasporic rather than unitary and centered. As one writer puts it, "The central trope of 'white' is . . . the luxury *not* to think doubly, to see the world through the one-eyed vistas of privilege, rather than having to account for one's own identity within and against a fundamentally multiple culture."[176]

A postmodern musical 'aesthetic', then, is one that reflects the postmodern shifts in cultural forms of representation "from text to image, from linearity to simultaneity, from coherence to rupture, from argument to story, from the universal to the particular, from the 'voice of authority' to populist heteroglossia."[177] It embraces incongruous juxtaposition, fragmentation, and splicing—pastiche and collage—instead of organically unfolding unity. Its mode of engagement is the disengaged, disjunct experience typified in 'channel-' and 'net-surfing'. It is largely indifferent toward authenticity and stylistic integrity. Its interest lies not in essence, depth, or profundity, but in carnivalesque spectacle, a play of sonorous surfaces. It works to subvert the ideological work done by overdetermined coherence, renounces apparent inevitability and naturalness for unabashed performativity and conspicuous artificiality. And rather than railing against the ill effects of musical commodification, the postmodern ethos appears to regard it as acceptable, inevitable, even desirable. Not only is commodification not a valid criterion for differentiating 'serious' from vulgar music, the line between 'art' and 'popular' music can no longer be drawn with any real certainty: for that too is an ideological distinction devised to serve the interests of domination and control.

Evidence of postmodern predilections can be seen, then, in musics that embrace technology, the popular, the recycled; that juxtapose incongruous styles, idioms, and contexts; that eschew linear, progressive development and teleological models of time; and that draw seemingly at random from the 'high', the 'low', and the discarded, with utter disregard for proprietary concerns or authenticity. One of the contemporary musics that most vividly exemplifies these postmodern characteristics, urges one scholar, is "rap."[178] Given the cultural and material realities of white colonialism and slavery, Potter observes, black sensibilities were 'postmodern' long before academics and intellectuals named that territory and began exploring it. Blacks have long had abundant reason to reject modernist promises that enlightenment and reason lead inexorably to the attainment of liberty, equality, and justice. Potter puts it bluntly: blacks sensed the "fundamental rottenness of European modernism" long before the Europeans detected the first hints of indigestion.[179] Not only does black history dispose natural skepticism toward the premise of progress, but white appropriations of black musical innovations (and the elevated status that invariably seems to attend such appropriations) make blacks understandably skeptical toward ideas like inherent musical value and music's aesthetic autonomy.

Also characteristically postmodern is rap's construction of music from fragmentary resources, without regard for their authenticity or the stylistic coherence and purity of the result. Rap does not consist of stable, centered 'works of art', but rather of spectacular foreground displays. The graffiti, dance, and rap music of hip-hop culture should be recognized, Potter suggests, as "post-apocalyptic arts, scratches on the decaying surfaces of post-industrial urban America; they are not monuments to some romanticized 'human spirit', but fundamentally anti-monumental arts."[180] Rap music fractures and fragments, layers graffiti upon graffiti. It creates and resides in a temporal sense Potter describes as the "radical *now*,"[181] one utterly devoid of sentimental yearnings for wholeness or authenticity, or for times when music had the supposed power to make the world whole. In contrast to the art music institutions of modernity, then, rap consists in "localized sites and nomadic incursions, cultures of the found, the revalued, the used": it builds a distinctly postmodern culture, unapologetically and without irony or awkwardness, from the "detritus of 'pop' culture."[182]

These parallels between rap music and the postmodern ethos are not merely coincidental, though. In fact, as Huyssen points out, "Pop . . . [is] the context in which a notion of the postmodern first took shape, and from the beginning until today, the most significant trends within postmodernism have challenged modernism's relentless hostility to mass culture."[183] Moreover, the postmodern condition consists in "an ever wider dispersal and dissemination of artistic practices all working out of the ruins of the modernist edifice, raiding it for ideas, plundering its vocabulary and supplementing it with randomly chosen images and motifs from pre-modern and non-modern cultures as well as from contemporary mass culture."[184]

If postmodern influences were confined to popular or vernacular musics, perhaps they could be casually dismissed as vulgar, decadent aberrations—precisely as modernist thought has always done. However, postmodern attitudes cannot be quarantined or sequestered in a popular musical ghetto. And when they surface in accounts of classical, serious, or 'legitimate' music, their presence poses provocative challenges to deeply held beliefs about such music's nature and value, threatening its most foundational assumptions. From the standpoint of disciplinary tradition, these postmodern incursions are clear signs of decay. From the postmodern standpoint, however, they offer genuinely utopian possibilities. As Kramer explains, the status of classical music in the contemporary world is an extraordinarily precarious one. "It is no secret that . . . ['classical'] music is in trouble. It barely registers in our schools, it has neither the prestige nor the popularity of literature and visual art, and it squanders its capacities for self-renewal by clinging to an exceptionally static core repertoire. Its audience is shrinking, graying, and overly palefaced. . . . [It] holds at best an honorific place on the margins of high culture."[185]

What postmodern criticism offers, according to Kramer, what its opponents wrongly regard as a regressive threat, is to put classical music back into the real world: to rescue it from the insularity created for it by modernist myths of autonomous artistic greatness. It can help "revivify classical music by demystifying and de-idealizing it: by canceling the Faustian bargain that lofts the music beyond the contingencies, uncertainties, and malfeasances of life at the cost of utter irrelevance."[186] Strategically, this requires deconstruction of the concept of 'the extramusical',[187] created when 'form' is regarded as music's essential center. The concept of a 'music itself', a 'music' wholly accounted for in structural terms, generates a residue comprised of everything not structural: a domain located, by definition, outside music proper. But the notion of a structural musical essence to which all else is 'other' is the musical version of one of modernity's pernicious oppositional fantasies—one in which, since truth is presumed objective, pure, and devoid of the subjective, everything outside the objective realm is defiled and contaminated. Deconstructing the concept of the extramusical proceeds by undoing the idea that there exists a formal/structural core of music to which everything else implicated in musical experience relates as mere 'response' or 'context'. Contingency and situatedness, partiality and fallibility, are not contaminants, but basic conditions of all human experience and understanding.

By denying music's retreat into formal configurations that claim independence from the contingencies of personal and social experience, postmodernist theory and criticism endeavor to keep issues of meaning at the forefront and to close the immense chasm modernist thought created between 'music alone' and its experience. Modernity creates and maintains this gap, explains Kramer, by "constructing the material and expressive force of music as the other of musical form."[188] To sustain this illusion, it "brackets most living experiences of music as subjective, ineffable, or irrational in the name of a normative experience of music *qua* music . . . [and] 'takes account' of musical meaning by granting emotive descriptions, critical judgments, and indications of 'context' a small place on the fringes of discourse about style, form, structure, and technique."[189] Form is the agent of musical closure, coherence, unity: the means of containing excess and superfluity. But by opening out categories of self and other, form and context, music itself and human response, postmodern theory seeks to show that they are not first principles, only "temporary limits in a dynamic, open-ended process . . ."[190] From a postmodern perspective, in other words, self-other dualities should be recognized as "efforts to restrict a more mobile and plural play of meanings."[191] Outside this logic of alterity, asserts Kramer, "the concept of the normative is empty; observed or defied, norms are vehicles of compliance."[192] And to declare that something conforms to or deviates from a norm is one of the "strongest anti-interpretive moves available."[193] That this is so can be clearly seen by examining the constraints this logic of alterity imposes on musical discourse, the disciplinary appropriation of music's 'objectively formal' dimension as the 'inherent' source of musicality. This move "allows (some) music to become the object of (limited) disciplinary study and makes this privileged (or denatured) music available for the idealization and associated formation of a canon. Music outside this sphere can be either enjoyed or disdained as a 'lower' pleasure, appropriate for emotional or erotic stimulation but not for aesthetic contemplation."[194]

"In modernist theory," Kramer explains, "autonomy is a property of the masterpiece, the sign that the music itself has transcended all social utility and a sign into which the social as such disappears without a trace."[195] However, "[p]ersistent sightings notwithstanding, the Autonomous Artwork is as dead as Elvis."[196] We see the postmodern ethos at play in this juxtaposition of one of modernism's most revered constructs and one of popular culture's most notorious icons, and in its implication that both are cut from the same cloth. Also noteworthy is its conspicuous lack of nostalgia, and its implicit promise of liberation: "Deaf to the autonomous artwork," explains Kramer, "I can finally hear the music . . . [W]hen music 'itself' solicits my deafness, asks me to hear it as the autonomous artwork, the sound only grates on me, gravels, scores the unwalled labyrinth [of music's richly communicative, human voice] with acoustic graffiti."[197]

Problems and Possibilities

The entry of feminist and postmodern voices into philosophical discourses about music dramatically alters both the way those conversations are conducted and what they are presumed to be about.[198] To people fluent in and comfortable with the musical and philosophical languages of modernity, changes like these do not come easily. They cannot be accommodated by minor adjustments, but rather demand the reconfiguration and reconstruction of entire conceptual and disciplinary orders, and the relinquishment of many of the moorings that make modernity's hierarchical orders so apparently stable and secure. What is foundational is no longer the issue, but rather whether foundations are necessary or desirable—indeed, whether they are any longer possible. By exploding received ideas of truth and value, of what music is and of its importance in human affairs, feminist and postmodernist theories posit myriad 'musics' where one formerly kept us abundantly busy. Compared to the centered, stable, secure vantage point of modernity, feminist and postmodern critiques are disturbingly relativistic and chaotic. And they precipitate a host of thorny issues. If all musical choices are equally good, none inherently better than others, how does one choose? If there are no absolutes that can claim our common loyalty in any but an arbitrary manner, how do we avoid fascistic, willful impositions of tastes and values—the turn to raw power from rational deliberation? If there are indeed no foundations, how do postmodernists justify their deeply held conviction that pluralism and diversity are more descriptive of the way things 'really are' than unity and uniformity? If claims to philosophical reason only serve to dignify rhetorical persuasion; if all claims to 'absolutes' serve to sustain illusions of inevitability for particular sociopolitical interests; if 'truth' is only 'belief' given a fancy and influential name; if 'objectivity' is just a politically motivated cover for 'subjective' interests; then on what grounds do these voices presume their pluralistic vantage point is more adequate than those that once presumed to speak for everyone, everywhere?

An adequate treatment of these admittedly crucial issues would take us well beyond the scope of this project. However, the subtle distinction between the postmodern and the *anti*modern is probably key to resolving at least some of them. To denounce modernist claims, staunchly antimodern convictions must stand on the same discursive ground as modernist convictions they oppose. Thus, the denial that unity and uniformity are foundational slips into the counterclaim that difference and diversity are foundational. But the postmodern urges the rejection of foundations themselves, a move that appears to revoke the possibility of a defense of even its own convictions, collapsing into nihilism. Often times, the postmodern attitude toward modernity is not so much defiant as indifferent: a belief that modernity has simply spent itself. In the wake of a major paradigm shift, it seems, postmodern interests have simply moved on, moved elsewhere. They have little interest in old debates rooted in modernist conceptual frameworks. Tired of such conversations, they are increasingly determined simply to talk about other things, in other ways, to other people. Saying the postmodern is more 'after' than 'anti' modern may well be descriptive of its ethos. And yet, despite claims to the contrary it remains a foundational discourse—if in a decidedly different sense than modernism. Postmodern foundations are fluid, temporary constructions; prismatic, kaleidoscopic affairs whose rejection of binaries, boundaries, and hierarchies means that even its own convictions must admit to contingency and submit to continual reevaluation. As a nomadic orientation that seeks to confine its claims to the local and the particular, it defies definition and renders all descriptions provisional.

Whether one regards this postmodern condition as an intellectual meltdown or not, there can be no denying that it brings to a head and unflinchingly confronts tensions that show signs of becoming key issues for music philosophy in the twenty-first century. The postmodern ethos is conspicuously relativistic; but then, so is most philosophy on some level or other, and to some degree or other. Contrary to what its detractors might want us to believe, postmodern relativism is most often not the silly, anything-goes variety. While it explodes traditional understandings of music and musical value, it does not pretend its vantage point is value free or value neutral. It recognizes that the 'view from nowhere' and the 'view from everywhere' both name impossibilities. It regards situatedness and fallibility not as contaminants but as crucial characteristics of human experience. And while these convictions clearly render impossible continued subscription to modernist myths and the sociocultural orders they sustained, it does not appear to be the case that they necessarily and invariably implicate nihilism.

Whatever one's misgivings about these contemporary intellectual currents, their determination to restore relevance and vitality to our discourses about music is a laudable project. And so is their effort to account more adequately for the full range of human musical doings. Although their destruction of conventional borders and boundaries understandably generates dispute and discomfort, there may be some consolation in the realization that what is at issue is something positive: the way a postmodern world will construe music's nature and its value—the limits and grounds of 'the musical'. Both feminist and postmodern theory urge us to recognize and accept the fact of music's radical plurality and dynamic fluidity, as well as music's importance in constructing and reconstructing social and personal identities that are themselves always plural and fluid. They urge us to recognize music as an instrument of power, to divest ourselves of belief in the idea of musical autonomy that would exempt music from social criticism, and to deconstruct the elaborate system of oppositional hierarchies that idea has spawned. They urge us to deny in ourselves the totalizing tendency to represent as unitary what is fundamentally diverse. They urge greater tolerance for things like instability, change, multiplicity, and difference, while at the same time alerting us to ideological biases that can no longer be tolerated. They disrupt dreams of unity and uniformity, and expose the interests served by appeals to musical essences, absolutes, and authenticity. Perhaps most importantly, they urge that fallibility and partiality be recognized not just as ineradicable parts but as preconditions of human knowledge and understanding. In so doing, feminist and postmodernist discourses defy the institutional and ideological arrangements that isolate music from life and oppose popular/vernacular musical practices to those deemed worthy of serious study. Perhaps, then, these unsettling discourses are not corruptions of music philosophy after all, but rich opportunities to expand its relevance, its sphere of influence: provocative sources of challenges that can profitably occupy music philosophy for years to come.

Concluding Remarks

In this chapter we have noted radical mutations in accounts of music's nature and value, and indeed, in assumptions as to what philosophy is or should be. The feminist and postmodern orientations we have briefly surveyed here blur comfortable distinctions, shatter disciplinary boundaries, and are strongly suggestive of paradigmatic shifts that may profoundly and permanently alter the way we think about and experience music. Perhaps the clearest victims of these shifts are beliefs in music's purity and autonomy. Many feminist critiques regard the notion of the wholly musical, of music alone, as ideological subterfuge: in making and enjoying music, they insist, it is never *just the music* we make and enjoy. Music is a socializing influence with potent political force, an important part of the technology with which human societies generate and allocate privilege and power. Postmodern sensibilities have likewise eroded beliefs that music should be considered a centered, unitary undertaking that is inherently 'humanizing' and invariably 'good'. The normative, hierarchical accounts of which music philosophy was once predominantly comprised—accounts in which it was relatively clear what music that was 'properly musical' should be and do, and in which pure music was clearly superior to the corrupt remainder— seem to be fundamentally at odds with the pluralism and relativism typical of contemporary sensibilities.

The controversies we have examined in this chapter are profound and the philosophical challenges they present are daunting. Clearly, these are times of great upheaval. Yet, upheaval brings with it abundant opportunity for renewal and growth, and there is little doubt that our understanding of music's nature(s) and value(s) will be the richer for having seriously explored the many provocative issues posed by feminist and postmodern critiques.

DISCUSSION QUESTIONS

1. All music is alike in important ways. All music is different in important ways. Is one of these statements more important to understanding music's nature and value than the other? Why?

2. Do you believe it reasonable to claim that some musics are better, more musical, than others? If so, outline the criteria you feel might appropriately guide such judgments and demonstrate their application to two musical practices you feel clearly differ in musical value. If not, explain what guides your decisions about what music to perform or to teach.

3. It is often said that while between-practice comparisons are inappropriate, within-practice comparisons or evaluative judgments are justified and reasonable. Do you agree? If so, how do you determine whether you are in fact making comparisons within the same practice? In other words, is demarcating a boundary line for a musical practice in some sense an arbitrary act that imputes greater unity to practices than may be warranted? If you disagree that within-practice comparisons are justified, do you mean that "anything goes"? Does your position negate any possible distinction even between sound, noise, and music?

4. Shepherd suggests that because of its feminized status (and presumably, the sensuality, ambiguity, and disorder that typically attend such status), music contains the things that society does not feel comfortable commu-

nicating with itself about. What do you think those things might be? Explain.

5. The power to determine what similarities and differences 'count' is always a significant political matter. Who in Western society holds such power in musical discourses? Do you think this leads to unfairly marginalizing musical practices that may in fact be worthy of serious study? What kind of musical practices comprise the officially sanctioned canon, and what lies outside it? Why?

6. Discuss music's involvement in the logic of alterity, the process of saming and othering. Do all musics serve this function? Unavoidably? Is it desirable or possible to have a 'diasporic' musical identity, in which a music is at once 'ours' and 'theirs'? What might be gained in such a situation? Lost?

7. Traditional 'aesthetic' accounts of music assume that musics (and indeed, the 'arts') are sufficiently alike that sensitivity to the so-called aesthetic qualities of one practice transfers to others. Do you agree? Why or why not?

8. Discuss how the 'multicultural' ideal may be challenged by the emergence of transnational—indeed, global—musical hybrids and syntheses. How does commitment to authenticity conflict with the fact of cultural dynamism and change? Explain.

9. Identify a piece of music (any genre, any style) that strikes you as being particularly masculine and one that is conspicuously feminine. Discuss why you chose what you did and what this suggests about gender.

10. Charles Keil urges that music represents "our last and best source of participatory consciousness."[199] Göttner-Abendroth and Cusick describe what appear in many ways to be radically different kinds of participation. Outline what you think are the important differences between musical 'participation' and musical 'performance'.

11. Göttner-Abendroth's 'matriarchal' music is one that, though profoundly collective, still allows considerable latitude to its participants. What musical practices are most congruent with this idea? least congruent? What ideal of community do these represent?

12. While women have figured marginally in historical accounts of music, their invisibility has not been total. In what musical roles has their participation been permitted and acknowledged? Why?

13. Claims to music's educational value are usually anxious to establish its mindful character, to show it is a form of intelligence, a way of knowing. Yet some feminist critiques suggest that ideals of rationality and orderliness represent and preserve patriarchal value systems. Can you mount a defense of musical engagement that does not presume the supremacy of intellection?

14. Do you agree with Lamb that most musical performance is "untheorized practice"? Why or why not?

15. What do you think of the idea that a musical performance is always a performance of more than just the music? the idea that the contemplative audience is also always performing—self-effacement, passive acceptance, submission to authority? Attend a classical music concert and prepare an analysis of what besides 'the music' is being performed by musicians, conductor, and audience—and how. Ask yourself McClary's question: what are the listeners being invited to desire, and why?

16. How has the electronic media's capacity to juxtapose radically different 'virtual worlds' altered people's belief in the unity and uniformity of 'reality' and the continuity of time? How do these changes influence the perceptual habits and expectations people bring to music? Do you regard this as an advance, a regression, both, or neither? Explain.

17. Do you think it possible for music to achieve the magical integration of body and mind, self and other, inner and outer—the ecstatic experience of the 'here and now' so different from the obnoxious dualisms of everyday experience—described by Göttner-Abendroth? Under what circumstances? In what senses is such experience 'matriarchal'? How might preoccupation with comparison and criticism serve 'patriarchal' order?

18. McClary claims most people enjoy and engage in music because of its resonance with bodily experience, rather than the cerebral things that so concern traditional philosophers and the disciplinary gatekeepers of academia. Discuss the significance of conceiving of music as a fundamentally bodily experience. Do you agree that conventional music 'theory' masks the corporeal roots of music? Might this be avoided? How?

Notes

Chapter 1

1. Both Michael Apple and Henry Giroux develop persuasive arguments to the effect that "intensification" of labor and preoccupation with 'the practical' may effectively de-professionalize—contrary to the perceptions of those affected. See Apple's "Controlling the Work of Teachers" and Giroux's "Teachers as Transformative Intellectuals" in *Critical Social Issues in American Education*, ed. H. Svi Shapiro and David Purpel (White Plains, NY: Longman Publishing, 1993).

2. Had space and time permitted, I would particularly have liked to incorporate, as one astute reviewer suggested, the ideas of Rousseau, Kierkegaard, and Nietzsche.

3. Even on this point, philosophy is hardly unanimous. Richard Rorty, for instance, argues that philosophy is in fact a process of rhetorical persuasion. See, for instance, Rorty's *Contingency, Irony, and Solidarity* (New York: Cambridge University Press, 1989).

4. Quoted in Wayne Bowman, "Philosophy, Criticism, and Music Education: Some Tentative Steps Down a Less-Travelled Road," *Bulletin of the Council for Research in Music Education* 114 (Fall 1992): 5. The quote is taken from H. B. Redfern, "Philosophical Aesthetics and the Education of Teachers," *Journal of Aesthetic Education* 22: 2.

5. Ibid., 4.

6. These debates will not be explored here, but their general orientation will become evident in the final chapter.

7. Quoted in Bowman, "Philosophy, Criticism, and Music Education," 5. The original source is Northrop Frye's *On Education* (Markham, Ontario: Fitzhenry and Whiteside, 1988), 18.

8. Francis E. Sparshott, "Aesthetics of Music: Limits and Grounds," in *What is music?* ed. Philip Alperson (New York: Haven Press, 1987), 40. For a more free-ranging critique of the idea of 'the aesthetic', see Sparshott's "Aesthetic This and Aesthetic That," in his *The Theory of the Arts* (Princeton, NJ: Princeton University Press, 1982), 467–86.

9. Bowman, "Philosophy, Criticism, and Music Education," 9.

10. T. S. Eliot, *On Poetry and Poets* (Winchester, MA: Faber and Faber, 1957), 117.

11. I concede, and the reader should be aware, that many philosophers would strenuously contest this assertion that philosophy is not the kind of endeavor to which we

should turn for general or ultimate explanations. The view expressed here is my own, though hardly mine alone.

12. This is Northrop Frye's way of putting it. Quoted in Bowman, "Philosophy, Criticism, and Music Education," 8. Original source is Frye, *On Education* 21.

13. Although this idea has widespread currency, the memorable 'God's-eye' image is H. Putnam's.

14. In the memorable words of Ludwig Wittgenstein, "One main cause of philosophical sickness—a one-sided diet: one nourishes one's thinking with only one kind of example." *Philosophical Investigations*, transl. G. E. M. Anscombe (New York: Macmillan, 1958), §593, p. 155.

15. Richard Rorty makes this point eloquently and repeatedly, but perhaps nowhere more concisely than in Umberto Eco, *Interpretation and Overinterpretation*, ed. Stefan Collini (Cambridge: Cambridge University Press, 1992), 92: "The final stage in the Pragmatist's Progress," writes Rorty, "comes when one begins to see one's previous peripeties not as stages in the ascent toward Enlightenment, but simply as the contingent results of encounters with various books which happened to fall into one's hands. This stage is pretty hard to reach, for one is always being distracted by daydreams . . . in which the heroic pragmatist plays a Walter Mitty-like role in the immanent teleology of world history. But if the pragmatist can escape from such daydreams, he or she will eventually come to think of himself or herself as, like everything else, capable of as many descriptions as there are purposes to be served. . . . This is the stage in which all descriptions . . . are evaluated according to their efficacy as instruments for purposes, rather than by their fidelity to the object described."

16. Bowman, "Philosophy, Criticism, and Music Education," 4.

17. Ibid., 5.

18. Although his point there is not quite the same as the one being explored here, Ludwig Wittgenstein, in his *Philosophical Investigations*, writes, "We must do away with all explanation, and description alone must take its place" (§109, p. 47). Wittgenstein concludes the same section with the assertion, "Philosophy is a battle against the bewitchment of our intelligence by means of language."

19. Another formulation appears in Bowman, "Philosophy, Criticism, and Music Education," 15.

20. I take this particular term from Elizabeth Spelman, *Inessential Woman: Problems of Exclusion in Feminist Thought* (Boston: Beacon Press, 1988).

21. For more on this distinction, see Wayne Bowman, "The Values of Musical Praxialism," forthcoming in a book edited by David Elliott; Thomas McCarthy, *The Critical Theory of Jurgen Habermas* (Cambridge: MIT Press, 1978), 2–4; and Thomas A. Regelski, "Prolegomenon to a Praxial Philosophy of Music and Music Education," *Finnish Journal of Music Education* 1:1 (1996): 23–39.

Chapter 2

1. M. L. West, *Ancient Greek Music* (New York: Oxford University Press, 1994), 34

2. R. G. Collingwood, *The Principles of Art* (Oxford: Clarendon Press, 1938), 52.

3. Henry Chadwick, *Boethius* (Oxford: Clarendon Press, 1981), 91.

4. *The Republic* VII. Except where otherwise indicated, all references to Plato are drawn from *The Dialogues of Plato*, transl. Benjamin Jowett, in *Great Books of the Western World* (Chicago: Encyclopaedia Britannica, 1952). © Encyclopaedia Britannica, Inc. 1952, 1990. Reproduction of material from this volume by permission. Use beyond U.S.A. and Canada by permission of Oxford University Press.

5. *Republic* VI.

6. *Republic* VI, 510.

7. *Timaeus*, 52.

8. *Timaeus*, 51.

9. *Timaeus*, 52.

10. *Laws* III, 682.

11. *Republic* X, 602.

12. *Republic* X, 598.

13. *Republic* X, 605.

14. *Republic* X, 606.

15. *Republic* X, 607.

16. *Laws* II, 653.

17. *Laws* II, 668.

18. *Laws* II, 667–68.

19. *Laws* II, 658–59.

20. *Laws* II, 669.

21. *Laws* II, 669.

22. *Laws* III, 700.

23. *Laws* III, 701.

24. *Republic* III, 424.

25. *Laws* VIII, 829.

26. Monroe C. Beardsley, *Aesthetics from Classical Greece to the Present: A Short History* (Tuscaloosa: University of Alabama Press, 1966), 50.

27. *Laws* II, 669–70.

28. *Laws* II, 655.

29. *Laws* II, 662.

30. *Republic* III, 392.

31. *Republic* III, 398–99.

32. Warren D. Anderson, *Ethos and Education in Greek Music: The Evidence of Poetry and Philosophy* (Cambridge, MA: Harvard University Press, 1966), 29–30.

33. R. P. Winnington-Ingram, *Mode in Ancient Greek Music* (Chicago: Argonaut Publishing, 1968), 21.

34. Anderson, *Ethos and Education*, 25.

35. Ibid., 29.

36. *Timaeus*, 47.

37. *Laws* II, 659.

38. *Protagoras*, 326.

39. *Republic* III, 411–12.

40. Julius Portnoy, *The Philosopher and Music* (New York: Da Capo Press, 1980), 22.

41. *Philebus*, 51.

42. *Philebus*, 66.

43. *Republic* VII, 531.

44. *Republic* III, 401.

45. *Phaedo*, 60–61.

46. R. M. Hare, *Plato* (New York: Oxford University Press, 1982), 49.

47. *Republic* X, 619; cf. *Laws* VII, 792.

48. *Republic* III, 401.

49. *Republic* III, 401–2.

50. *Laws* II, 653.

51. *Laws* II, 659.

52. *Laws* II, 664.

53. *Laws* VII, 792.

54. *Laws* VII, 792.

55. *Republic* II, 377.

56. *Laws* VII, 802.

57. *Laws* II, 666.

58. *Republic* III, 398.

59. *Republic* III, 399.

60. Ibid.

61. *Republic* III, 400.

62. *Republic* III, 399.

63. *Republic* III, 398.

64. *Republic* III, 402.

65. *Republic* III, 411.

66. *Republic* X, 606.

67. *Republic* X, 605.

68. *Republic* X, 607.

69. John Dewey, *Democracy and Education: An Introduction to the Philosophy of Education* (New York: Macmillan, 1916), 279.

70. *Republic* X, 607.

71. Ibid.

72. Ibid.

73. *Timaeus*, 19.

74. *Republic* X, 608.

75. Julias A. Elias, *Plato's Defence of Poetry* (Albany: State University of New York Press, 1984) 214.

76. *Republic* X, 607.

77. Collingwood, *Principles of Art*.

78. Elias, *Plato's Defense*, 80.

79. *Republic* III, 401.

80. cf. J .Tate, "Plato and 'Imitation'," *Classical Quarterly* 26:3 (1932): 161–69; or Edith Schipper, "*Mimesis* in the Arts in Plato's *Laws*," *Journal of Aesthetics and Art Criticism* 22 (1963): 199–202.

81. Elias, *Plato's Defense, 233.*

82. Aristotle, *Poetics*, vii. My references to *Poetics*, *Rhetoric*, *Politics*, and *Nicomachean Ethics*, are from translations by Ingram Bywater, W. Rhys Roberts, Benjamin Jowett, and W. D. Ross, respectively, in *The Works of Aristotle* from *Great Books of the Western World* (Chicago: Encyclopaedia Britannica, 1952). © Encyclopaedia Britannica, Inc. 1952, 1990. Reproduction of material from this volume by permission. Use beyond U.S.A. and Canada by permission of Oxford University Press.

83. *Poetics*, 7.

84. *Poetics*, 9.

85. *Poetics*, 14.

86. *Poetics*, 9.

87. *Poetics*, 25.

88. See his *Metaphysics*, (985b32 and 1090a20–23), and *De Caelo* (290b21–34).

89. Anderson, *Ethos and education*, 117.

90. *Politics* VIII, 5.

91. *Poetics*, 4.

92. *Rhetoric* I, 11.

93. *Nicomachean Ethics* X, 5.

94. *Nicomachean Ethics* X, 4.

95. *Nicomachean Ethics* X, 5.

96. Ibid.

97. Ibid.

98. Ibid.

99. Ibid.

100. *Nicomachean Ethics* VII, 12.

101. *Nicomachean Ethics* X, 4.

102. *Nicomachean Ethics* III, 10.

103. *Nicomachean Ethics* X, 7.

104. Ibid.

105. cf. *Nicomachean Ethics* VII, 12.

106. *Politics* VIII, 7.

107. *Politics* VIII, 5.

108. *Politics* VIII, 7.

109. *Politics* VIII, v.

110. Ibid.

111. *Politics* VIII, 7.

112. Ibid.

113. Ibid.

114. Ibid.

115. *Politics* VIII, 5.

116. Ibid.

117. *Politics* VIII, 7.

118. *Politics* VIII, 5.

119. Ibid.

120. *Politics* VIII, 7.

121. *Politics* VIII, 5.

122. *Politics* VIII, 5.

123. *Politics* VIII, 6.

124. Ibid.

125. Ibid.

126. Ibid.

127. *Politics* VIII, 7.

128. Beardsley, *Aesthetics from Classical Greece to the Present*, 79.

129. Plotinus, *The Six Enneads*, trans. Stephen MacKenna and B. S. Page (Chicago: Encyclopaedia Britannica, 1952).

130. Fifth Ennead IX, 11.

131. Fifth Ennead VIII, 1.

132. Ibid.

133. First Ennead III, 1.

134. Ibid.

135. First Ennead VI, 1.

136. Ibid.

137. Ibid.

138. First Ennead VI, 2.

139. First Ennead VI, 5.

140. First Ennead VI, 2.

141. First Ennead VI, 3.

142. Ibid.

143. First Ennead VI, 4.

144. First Ennead VI, 5.

145. First Ennead VI, 8.

146. First Ennead VI, 8.

147. Fifth Ennead VIII, 2.

148. Fifth Ennead IX, 2.

149. Fifth Ennead IX, 11.

150. First Ennead VI, 5.

151. Henry Chadwick, *Boethius* (Oxford: Clarendon Press, 1981), 80.

152. Augustine, *On Music* VI, 12 (35), transl. Robert Catesby Taliaferro, in *Writings of Saint Augustine*, ed. Ludwig Schopp (New York: CIMA Publishing, 1947).

153. *On Music* V, 13 (28).

154. Letter VII, iii, 6, to Nebridus, cited in Beardsley, *Aesthetics from Classical Greece* 98.

155. *On Music* I, 4 (5).

156. Augustine, *Confessions* X, 33 (49), trans. Edward Bouverie Pusey. In *Writings of St. Augustine* (New York: Fathers of the Church, 1947).

157. *Confessions* X, 33 (50).

158. Ibid.

159. *On Music* I, 4 (5).

160. *On Music* I, 4 (6).

161. *On Music* I, 4 (7).

162. *On Music* VI, 17 (56).

163. In *Retractiones* I, vi.

164. Robert J. O'Connell, *Art and the Christian Intelligence in St. Augustine* (Cambridge, MA: Harvard University Press, 1978). 44.

165. Leo Schrade, "Music in the Philosophy of Boethius," *Musical Quarterly* 33 (1947): 189.

166. Boethius, *Fundamentals of Music*, trans. Calvin M. Bower, ed. Claude V. Palisca (New Haven, CT: Yale University Press, 1989), I, 2.

167. Ibid., I, 34.

168. Ibid., I, i.

169. Ibid.

170. Chadwick, *Boethius*, 101.

171. Portnoy, *The Philosopher and Music*, 58.

172. Ibid., 59.

Chapter 3

1. G. W. Leibniz, "The Principles of Nature and Grace," (1714) in *The Philosophical Works of Leibnitz*, trans. G. M. Duncan (1714; reprint, New Haven: Tuttle, Morehouse, and Taylor, 1890), 216.

2. Quoted in Monroe C. Beardsley, *Aesthetics from Classical Greece to the Present* (Tuscaloosa, AL: University of Alabama Press, 1966), 190.

3. Ibid., 191.

4. Immanuel Kant, *The Critique of Judgement*, trans. James Creed Meredith (Oxford: Oxford University Press, 1952), §5 p. 50. Reproduction of material from this volume by permission of Oxford University Press.

5. Ibid., §1, p. 42.

6. Ibid., §2, pp. 43–44.

7. Ibid., §15, p. 71.

8. Ibid., §17.

9. Ibid., §9, p. 60.

10. Ibid., §16, p. 72.

11. Ibid., §14 and §15, pp. 65–71 (quoted text is from §15, p. 69).

12. Ibid., §12, p. 64.

13. Ibid., §14, p. 67.

14. Ibid., §15, p. 70.

15. Ibid., §3, p. 45.

16. Ibid., §5, p. 49.

17. Ibid.

18. Ibid., §18, p. 81. It is, he states, neither a theoretical objective necessity, nor a practical necessity, but a necessity of a special kind that can only be termed "exemplary."

19. Ibid., §20.

20. Ibid., preface to the 1790 edition (pp. 5–6).

21. Ibid., §9, p. 58.

22. In §17, p. 76, Kant calls imagination "the faculty of presentation."

23. Ibid., §9, p. 60.

24. Ibid., §45, p. 167.

25. Ibid., §49, p. 176.

26. Ibid., §49, p. 177.

27. Harry Blocker, "Kant's Theory of the Relation of Imagination and Understanding in Aesthetic Judgements of Taste," *British Journal of Aesthetics* 5 (1965): 45.

28. Ibid.

29. Robert L. Zimmerman, "Kant: The Aesthetic Judgment," *Journal of Aesthetics and Art Criticism* 21 (1963): 337.

30. Kant, *Critique of Judgement*, §14, p. 67.

31. Ibid., §13, p. 65.

32. Ibid., §14, p. 67.

33. Ibid., §5, p. 50.

34. Ibid., §9, p. 60.

35. Ibid., §17, p. 76.

36. Ibid., §15, p. 71.

37. Ibid., §17, pp. 75–80.

38. Ibid., §18, p. 81.

39. Ibid., §22, p. 85.

40. Ibid., §22, p. 88.

41. Ibid., §46, p. 168.

42. Ibid., §46, pp. 168–69.

43. Ibid., §47, pp. 171–72.

44. Ibid., §48, pp. 172–75.

45. Ibid., §49, pp. 175–76.

46. Ibid., §49, p. 176.

47. Ibid., §44, p. 166.

48. Ibid.

49. Ibid., §51, p. 188.

50. Ibid.

51. Ibid., §53, pp. 191–92.

52. Ibid., §53, p. 192.

53. Ibid., §53, p. 193.

54. Ibid., §53, p. 194.

55. Ibid.

56. Ibid.

57. Ibid., §53, p. 195.

58. Ibid., §53, pp. 195–96.

59. Ibid., §53, p. 196.

60. Ibid.

61. Herbert M. Schueller, "Immanuel Kant and the Aesthetics of Music," *Journal of Aesthetics and Art Criticism* 14 (1955): 218–47.

62. Ibid., 226.

63. Israel Knox, *The Aesthetic Theories of Kant, Hegel, and Schopenhauer* (New York: Humanities Press, 1958), 50.

64. Carl Dalhaus, *Esthetics of Music*, trans. William W. Austin (Cambridge: Cambridge University Press, 1982), 34.

65. Schueller, "Immanuel Kant," 237.

66. Susanne K. Langer, *Feeling and Form: A Theory of Art Developed from Philosophy in a New Key* (New York: Charles Scribner's Sons, 1953), 110.

67. Ibid., 66.

68. Ibid., 113.

69. Kant, *The Critique of Judgement*, §15, pp. 69–71.

70. Ibid., §48, p. 172.

71. Ibid., §48, p. 173.

72. Ibid.

73. Dalhaus, *Esthetics of Music*, 72.

74. Ibid.

75. Ibid., 73. Alternatively, one might reason that while intellectual features may not be necessary to aesthetic experience, they are crucial to musical experience: a formulation I find more satisfying.

76. Friedrich Schiller, *On the Aesthetic Education of Man*, ed. and trans. by Elizabeth M. Wilkinson and L. A. Willoughby (Oxford: Clarendon Press, 1982), XII–XIV, pp. 79–99.

77. Ibid., IV:6, p. 21.

78. Ibid.

79. Ibid., XVIII:1, p. 123.

80. Ibid., XX:3, pp. 139–41.

81. Ibid., XV:2, p. 101.

82. Ibid., XV:9, p. 107.

83. Ibid., XXIII:2, p. 161.

84. Ibid., XXII:4, p. 155.

85. Ibid., XXII:5, p. 155.

86. Ibid., XXVII:10, p. 215.

87. G. W. F. Hegel, *The Philosophy of Fine Art*, trans. F. P. B. Osmaston (London: G. Bell & Sons, 1920), I:126.

88. G. W. F. Hegel, *The Introduction to Hegel's Philosophy of Fine Art*, trans. B. Bosanquet (London: Kegan Paul, Trench & Co., 1886), 116.

89. Ibid., 119.

90. Ibid., 105.

91. Ibid., 138.

92. Ibid., 3.

93. Ibid., 12–13.

94. Ibid., 13.

95. Ibid.

96. Ibid., 15.

97. Ibid., 17.

98. Ibid., 24.

99. Ibid., 16.

100. Ibid., 18.

101. Ibid., 21.

102. Ibid., 16.

103. Ibid., 22.

104. Ibid.

105. Ibid., 23.

106. Ibid., 24.

107. Ibid.

108. Ibid., 17.

109. Ibid., 19.

110. Knox, *The Aesthetic Theories*, 101.

111. Hegel, *Introduction to Hegel's Philosophy of Fine Art*, 145.

112. Ibid.

113. Ibid.

114. Ibid.

115. Ibid., 147.

116. Ibid., 148.

117. Ibid., 160–61.

118. Ibid., 148.

119. Ibid., 150.

120. Ibid.

121. Ibid., 163.

122. Ibid., 151.

123. Ibid.

124. Ibid., 152.

125. Ibid., 153–54.

126. Ibid., 154–55.

127. Ibid., 155.

128. Ibid.

129. Ibid., 156.

130. Ibid., 159.

131. Ibid., 167.

132. Ibid., 168.

133. Ibid., 170.

134. Ibid., 170–71.

135. Ibid., 172–73.

136. Ibid., 173.

137. Ibid., 49.

138. Ibid., 59.

139. Ibid., 61.

140. Ibid., 64.

141. Ibid.

142. Ibid., 68.

143. Ibid., 67.

144. Ibid., 71.

145. Ibid.

146. Ibid., 72.

147. Ibid., 73.

148. Ibid., 74.

149. Ibid., 97.

150. Ibid., 107.

151. Hegel, *Philosophy of Fine Art*, III, 341.

152. Ibid., 340.

153. Ibid., 342.

154. Ibid., 343.

155. Ibid.

156. Ibid., 344.

157. Ibid., 346.

158. Ibid.

159. Ibid.

160. Ibid., 347.

161. Ibid., 348.

162. Ibid., 349.

163. Ibid.

164. Ibid., 352.

165. Ibid., 351.

166. Ibid., 354.

167. Ibid., 426.

168. Ibid., 357.

169. Ibid., 354.

170. Ibid., 359.

171. Ibid., 355.

172. Ibid.

173. Ibid., 358.

174. Ibid.

175. Ibid.

176. Ibid.

177. Ibid., 359.

178. Ibid., 368.

179. Ibid., 359.

180. Ibid., 360.

181. Ibid.

182. Ibid., 365.

183. Ibid., 361.

184. Ibid., 362.

185. Ibid., 363.

186. Ibid., 368.

187. Ibid., 374.

188. Ibid., 363.

189. Ibid., 397.

190. Ibid.

191. Ibid., 384.

192. Ibid., 398.

193. Ibid., 406.

194. Ibid.

195. Ibid.

196. Ibid., 409.

197. Ibid., 417.

198. Ibid., 418.

199. Ibid., 404.

200. Ibid., 419.

201. Ibid., 407.

202. Ibid., 408.

203. Ibid.

204. Ibid., 422.

205. Ibid.

206. Ibid., 424.

207. Ibid., 424–25.

208. Ibid., 425.

209. Ibid.

210. Ibid., 430.

211. Knox, *The Aesthetic Theories*, 103.

212. Arthur Schopenhauer, *The World as Will and Representation*, trans. E. F. J. Payne (Indian Hills, CO: Falcon's Wing Press, 1958), 2 vol. (here designated I and II). Reproduction of material from these volumes by permission of Dover Publications, Inc.

213. Bryan Magee, *The Philosophy of Schopenhauer* (Oxford: Clarendon Press, 1983), 151.

214. Schopenhauer, *World as Will*, I (second book, §29), 164.

215. Ibid., I (fourth gook, §54), 275.

216. Ibid., II (supplement to second book), 299.

217. Ibid., I (second book, §27), 149.

218. Ibid., II (supplement to second book), 269.

219. Ibid., I (second book, §23), 112.

220. Ibid., I (third book, §34), 180.

221. Magee, *Philosophy of Schopenhauer*, 43–44.

222. Schopenhauer, *World as Will*, I (second book, §22), 111.

223. Ibid., II (supplement to second book), 197.

224. Ibid.

225. Ibid., I (third book, §31), 172.

226. Ibid., II (supplement to second book), 199.

227. Ibid., II (supplement to second book), 217–18.

228. Ibid., II (supplement to second book), 286.

229. Ibid., I (fourth book, §70), 405.

230. Ibid., II (supplement to second book), 359.

231. Ibid., II (supplement to second book), 354.

232. Ibid., I (third book, §36), 186.

233. Ibid., I (third book, §34), 178.

234. Ibid., I (third book, §34), 179.

235. Ibid., I (third book, §34), 178.

236. Ibid., I (third book, §34), 180.

237. Ibid.

238. Ibid., I (third book, §36), 185.

239. Ibid., I (third book, §38), 196.

240. Ibid., I (third book, §52), 256.

241. Ibid.

242. Ibid., I (third book, §52), 257.

243. Ibid.

244. Ibid.

245. Ibid.

246. Ibid.

247. Ibid., II (supplement to third book), 447.

248. Ibid.

249. Ibid.,.

250. Ibid., I (third book, §52), 259.

251. Ibid.

252. Ibid., I (third book, §52), 258.

253. Ibid., I (third book, §52), 259.

254. Ibid.

255. Ibid., I (third book, §52), 260.

256. Ibid.

257. Ibid.

258. Ibid.

259. Ibid., II (supplement to third book), 456.

260. Ibid., I (third book, §52), 261.

261. Ibid.

262. Ibid.

263. Ibid., II (supplement to third book), 453.

264. Ibid., 452.

265. Ibid., 455.

266. Ibid.

267. Ibid., 456.

268. Ibid., I (third book, §52), 261.

269. Ibid.

270. Ibid., II (supplement to third book), 450.

271. Ibid.

272. Ibid., II (supplement to third book), 451.

273. Ibid.

274. Ibid.

275. Ibid., I (third book, §52), 264.

276. Ibid.

277. Ibid., 261.

278. Ibid., II (supplement to third book), 454.

279. Ibid., I (third book, §52), 262.

280. Ibid.

281. Ibid.

282. Ibid., II (supplement to third book), 448.

283. Ibid.

284. Ibid., I (third book, §52), 263.

285. Ibid., II (supplement to third book), 448.

286. Ibid., 449.

287. Ibid., 450.

288. Ibid., I (third book, §52), 263.

289. Ibid.

290. Ibid., 264.

291. Ibid., 266.

292. Ibid.

293. Ibid.

294. Ibid., 267.

295. Ibid.

296. Ibid., II (supplement to third book), 457.

297. Kant's account of the "sublime," which I have omitted here, became a subject of major importance to late-eighteenth- and early-nineteenth-century theorists in their effort to make sense of instrumental music, and in particular the symphony.

298. R. G. Collingwood, *The Principles of Art* (Oxford: Clarendon Press, 1938), 130.

299. Ibid., 142.

Chapter 4

1. Aristoxenus, *Harmonics* ed. and trans. with an introduction by Henry S. Macran (Oxford: Clarendon Press, 1902), 87.

2. Ibid., II, §32, p. 189.

3. Ibid., 88, introduction.

4. Ibid., II, §31, p. 188.

5. Ibid., II, §33, p. 189.

6. Ibid.

7. Ibid., II, §44, p. 198.

8. Ibid., II, §39, pp. 193–94.

9. Ibid., II, §40, p. 195.

10. Ibid., I, §4, p. 167.

11. Ibid., II, §32, pp. 188–89.

12. Ibid., 89, introduction.

13. Ibid., 88.

14. Warren D. Anderson, *Ethos and Education in Greek Music: The Evidence of Poetry and Philosophy* (Cambridge, MA: Harvard University Press, 1966), 153.

15. L. P. Wilkinson, "Philodemus on *Ethos* in Music," *Classical Quarterly* 32 (1938): 176.

16. Anderson, *Ethos and Education*, 171.

17. Ibid., 168.

18. Ibid., 159.

19. Ibid., 160.

20. Ibid., 173.

21. Sextus Empiricus, *Against the Musicians*, trans. Denise Davidson Greaves (Lincoln: University of Nebraska Press, 1986), 16, p. 143.

22. Ibid., 22, p. 149.

23. Ibid., 24, p. 153.

24. Ibid., 25, p. 153.

25. Ibid., 37, p. 169.

26. See Eduard Hanslick, *The Beautiful in Music*, trans. Gustav Cohen, ed. Morris Weitz (New York: Liberal Arts Press, 1957), vii.

27. Eduard Hanslick, *On the Musically Beautiful*, trans. and ed. by Geoffrey Payzant (Indianapolis: Hackett, 1986), 2. Reproduction of material from this volume by permission of Hackett Publishing Company, Inc.

28. Ibid., 29.

29. Ibid., 1.

30. Ibid., 3.

31. Ibid., xxii.

32. Ibid., 47.

33. Ibid., 58.

34. Ibid., 56.

35. Ibid., 3.

36. Ibid., 4.

37. Ibid.

38. Ibid., 5.

39. Ibid.

40. Ibid., 6.

41. Ibid., 9.

42. Ibid.

43. Ibid.

44. Ibid., 20.

45. Ibid., 21.

46. Ibid., 15.

47. Ibid.

48. Ibid.

49. Ibid. (Here Hanslick is quoting Ferdinand Hiller.)

50. Ibid., 22.

51. Ibid., 23.

52. Ibid., 30.

53. Ibid., 42.

54. Ibid.

55. Ibid., 44.

56. Ibid., 58.

57. Ibid., 59.

58. Ibid., 61.

59. Ibid., 62.

60. Ibid., 58.

61. Ibid.

62. Ibid., 7.

63. Documented dramatically by Robert W. Hall, "On Hanslick's Supposed Formalism in Music," *Journal of Aesthetics and Art Criticism* 25 (1967): 433–36.

64. Peter Gay, *Freud, Jews, and Other Germans: Masters and Victims in Modernist Culture* (New York: Oxford University Press, 1978), 272.

65. Hanslick, *On the Musically Beautiful*, xxii.

66. Ibid., 28.

67. Ibid., 29.

68. Ibid., 36.

69. Ibid., 33.

70. Ibid., 29.

71. Ibid., 30.

72. Ibid.

73. Ibid., 10.

74. Ibid., 12.

75. Ibid., 9.

76. Ibid., 58.

77. Ibid., 65.

78. Ibid., 59.

79. Ibid., 63.

80. Ibid., 63–64.

81. Ibid., 64.

82. Ibid.

83. Morris Weitz, Introduction to Hanslick, *Beautiful in Music, xxii.*

84. Hanslick, *On the Musically Beautiful,* 78.

85. Ibid., 81.

86. Ibid., 67.

87. Ibid., 70.

88. Ibid., 66.

89. Ibid., 64.

90. Roger Scruton, *The Aesthetic Understanding: Essays in the Philosophy of Art and Culture* (London: Methuen, 1983), 34.

91. Edmund Gurney, *The Power of Sound* (New York: Basic Books, 1966), 13.

92. Ibid., 10.

93. Ibid., 12.

94. Ibid., 14.

95. Ibid., 25.

96. Ibid.

97. Ibid.

98. Ibid., 55.

99. Ibid., 54.

100. Ibid., 55.

101. Ibid.

102. Ibid.

103. Ibid.

104. Ibid., 56n.

105. Ibid.

106. Ibid., 91.

107. Ibid.

108. Ibid., 92.

109. Ibid.

110. Ibid., 93.

111. Ibid., 94.

112. Ibid.

113. Ibid., 95.

114. Ibid., 95n.

115. Ibid., 96.

116. Ibid., 97.

117. Ibid., 98.

118. Ibid., 99.

119. Ibid., 100.

120. Ibid.

121. Ibid.

122. Ibid., 101.

123. Ibid., 103.

124. Ibid., 104.

125. Ibid., 106.

126. Ibid.

127. Ibid.

128. Ibid., 107.

129. Ibid., 110.

130. Ibid., 111.

131. Ibid., 164.

132. Ibid., 165.

133. Ibid., 168.

134. Ibid., 150.

135. Ibid., 151.

136. Ibid., 150.

137. Ibid., 151.

138. Ibid., 151–52.

139. Ibid., 155.

140. Ibid.

141. Ibid., 158.

142. Ibid., 160.

143. Ibid., 165.

144. Ibid., 165–66.

145. Ibid., 166.

146. Ibid.

147. Ibid., 168.

148. Ibid., 169.

149. Ibid., 175.

150. Ibid.

151. Ibid., 177.

152. Ibid., 203–4.

153. Ibid., 217.

154. Ibid., 204.

155. Ibid., 215.

156. Ibid., 206.

157. Ibid., 207.

158. Ibid., 216.

159. Ibid., 213.

160. Ibid., 212.

161. Ibid., 214.

162. Ibid.

163. Ibid., 216.

164. Ibid., 216–17.

165. Ibid., 217.

166. Ibid.

167. Ibid., 225.

168. Ibid., 226.

169. Ibid., 226n.

170. Ibid., 228.

171. Ibid., 227.

172. Ibid., 228.

173. Ibid., 229.

174. Ibid.

175. Ibid.

176. Ibid.

177. Ibid., 228.

178. Ibid., 230.

179. Ibid.

180. Ibid., 287n.

181. Ibid., 289.

182. Ibid., 290.

183. Ibid.

184. Ibid., 296.

185. Ibid., 297.

186. Ibid., 296–97.

187. Ibid., 304.

188. Ibid., 301.

189. Ibid., 299.

190. Ibid., 302.

191. Ibid., 303.

192. Ibid.

193. Ibid., 306.

194. Ibid.

195. Ibid.

196. Ibid., 307.

197. Ibid.

198. Ibid.

199. Ibid., 311.

200. Ibid., 308.

201. Ibid., 310.

202. Ibid., 312.

203. Ibid.

204. Ibid., 313.

205. Ibid., 313n.

206. Ibid., 313.

207. Ibid., 314.

208. Ibid.

209. Ibid.

210. Ibid.

211. Ibid., 316.

212. Ibid.

213. Ibid.

214. Ibid., 317–18.

215. cf. Ibid., 322.

216. Ibid., 328.

217. Ibid., 331.

218. Ibid., 332.

219. Ibid., 333.

220. Ibid., 336.

221. Ibid., 336–37.

222. Ibid., 337.

223. Ibid.

224. Ibid., 338.

225. Ibid.

226. Ibid., 340.

227. Ibid., 346.

228. Ibid., 347.

229. Ibid.

230. Ibid., 348.

231. Ibid., 355.

232. Ibid.

233. Ibid., 358n.

234. Ibid., 359.

235. Ibid.

236. Leonard B. Meyer, *Emotion and Meaning in Music* (Chicago: University of Chicago Press, 1956), viii.

237. Ibid., 13.

238. Ibid., 14.

239. Ibid., 32.

240. Ibid., 34.

241. Ibid., 35.

242. Ibid.

243. Ibid., 38.

244. Ibid., 54.

245. Ibid., 40.

246. Ibid., 61.

247. Ibid., 73.

248. Ibid., 256.

249. Ibid., 258.

250. Ibid., 257.

251. Ibid., 266.

252. Ibid.

253. Ibid., 266.

254. Ibid., 269.

255. Leonard B. Meyer, *Music, the Arts, and Ideas: Patterns and Predictions in Twentieth-Century Culture* (Chicago: University of Chicago Press, 1967), 6. Reproduction of material from this volume by permission of the University of Chicago Press.

256. Ibid., 7.

257. Ibid., 34.

258. Ibid., 5.

259. A. Schantz, "A New Statement of Values for Music Education Based on the Writings of Dewey, Meyer, and Wolterstorff" (Ph.D. diss., University of Colorado, 1983), 203.

260. Meyer, *Music, the Arts, and Ideas*, 11.

261. Ibid., 15.

262. Ibid., 21.

263. Donald W. Sherburne, "Meaning and Music," *Journal of Aesthetics and Art Criticism* 24 (1966): 580.

264. Leon Plantinga, review of *Music, the Arts, and Ideas*, by Leonard B. Meyer, *Journal of Music Theory* 13:1 (1969): 146.

265. Meyer, *Music, the Arts, and Ideas*, 49.

266. Ibid.

267. Ibid., 27–28.

268. Ibid., 35.

269. Ibid., 36.

270. Ibid., 37.

271. Ibid., 39.

272. James Hillman, *Emotion: A Comprehensive Phenomenology of Theories and Their Meanings for Therapy* (London: Routledge and Kegan Paul, 1960), 85.

273. See, for instance, Phillip Shaver, J. Schwartz, D. Kirson, and C. O'Connor, "Emotion Knowledge: Further Exploration of a Prototype Approach," *Journal of Personality and Social Psychology* 52:6 (1987): 1061–86.

274. See Carroll Izard, *Human Emotions* (New York: Plenum Press, 1977).

275. David J. Elliott, "Structure and Feeling in Jazz: Rethinking Philosophical Foundations," *Bulletin of the Council for Research in Music Education* 95 (1987): 26.

276. Rudolph Arnheim, *Entropy and Art* (Berkeley: University of California Press, 1971), 15.

277. Vernon A. Howard, "Musical Meaning: A Logical Note," *Journal of Aesthetics and Art Criticism* 30 (1971), 217.

278. Forest W. Hansen, "Music, Feeling, and Meaning: A Study of Four Theories" (Ph.D. diss., Johns Hopkins University, 1967).

279. Ibid., 195.

280. Ibid., 201.

281. Further to this point see Howard, "Musical Meaning.".

282. Meyer, *Music, the Arts, and Ideas*, 33.

283. Ibid., 36.

284. Ibid., 35.

285. John M. Titchener and M. E. Broyles, "Meyer, Meaning and Music," *Journal of Aesthetics and Art Criticism* 22:1 (1973): 18–25.

286. Charles M. Keil, "Motion and Feeling through Music," *Journal of Aesthetics and Art Criticism* 24 (1966): 337. This article was reprinted in Charles Keil and Steven Feld's *Music Grooves* (Chicago: University of Chicago Press, 1994), along with important clarifications and extensions.

287. Leonard B. Meyer, *Explaining Music: Essays and Explorations* (Berkeley: University of California Press, 1973), 115.

288. Ibid., 4.

289. Ibid., 6.

290. Ibid.

291. Leonard B. Meyer, "Toward a Theory of Style," in *The Concept of Style*, ed. B. Lang (Ithaca, NY: Cornell University Press, 1987), 35.

292. Burton S. Rosner and Leonard B. Meyer, "Melodic Processes and the Perception of Music" in *The Psychology of Music*, ed. Diana Deutsch (New York: Academic Press, 1982), 318.

293. Meyer, "Toward a Theory," 27.

294. Leonard B. Meyer, "The dilemma of choosing: Speculations about contemporary culture," in *Value and Values in Evolution*, ed. E. A. Maziarz (New York: Gordon and Breach, 1979), 137.

295. Meyer, *Music, the Arts, and Ideas*, 8n.

296. Meyer, *Explaining Music*, 115n.

297. Ibid., 110.

298. Ibid., 111.

299. Ibid., 19.

300. Leonard B. Meyer, "Grammatical Simplicity and Relational Richness: The Trio of Mozart's g Minor Symphony," *Critical Inquiry* 2:2 (1976): 755.

301. Meyer, *Explaining Music*, 54.

302. Ibid., 65.

303. Ibid., 67.

304. Leonard B. Meyer, "Toward a Theory," 40.

305. Leonard B. Meyer, "Exploiting Limits: Creation, Archetypes, and Style Change," *Daedalus* 109:2 (1980): 189.

306. Meyer, *Explaining Music*, 80.

307. Meyer, "Grammatical Simplicity," 756.

308. Meyer, *Explaining Music*, 90.

309. Meyer, *Music, the Arts, and Ideas*, 37.

310. Meyer, "Grammatical Simplicity," 693–94.

311. Ibid., 694.

312. Ibid., 756.

313. Ibid.

314. Ibid., 757.

315. Meyer, *Explaining Music*, 242.

316. Ibid., 243.

317. Meyer, "Grammatical Simplicity," 757n.

318. Meyer, *Emotion and Meaning*, vii.

319. Note, however, that it is the act of listening rather than composing or performing that is presumed to be the definitive or most inherently musical way of relating to music.

320. Meyer, *Music, the Arts, and Ideas*, 271 (italics in original).

321. Meyer, *Emotion and Meaning*, viii.

322. Meyer, *Music, the Arts, and Ideas*, 35.

323. Ibid., 212.

324. Ibid., 35.

325. Schantz, "A New Statement of Values," 203.

326. See Meyer, "Grammatical Simplicity," 756.

327. Forest Hansen, "On Meyer's Theory of Musical Meaning," *British Journal of Aesthetics* 29:1 (Winter 1989): 18.

328. Meyer, *Explaining Music*, 5.

329. Hansen, "On Meyer's Theory," 17.

330. Ibid., 18.

331. See Meyer, "Toward a Theory of Style," 42.

332. Meyer, *Music, the Arts, and Ideas*, 212.

333. Ibid., 211.

334. Ibid., 212.

335. Ibid., 220.

336. Ibid., 220–21.

337. cf. Meyer, "Dilemma of Choosing," 119.

338. Meyer, *Music, the Arts, and Ideas*, 228.

339. Ibid., 226.

340. Ibid.

341. Ibid., 222.

342. Meyer, "Dilemma of Choosing," 139.

343. Ibid., 138.

344. Ibid., 139.

345. Meyer, *Emotion and Meaning*, 3.

346. Meyer, "Dilemma of Choosing," 138.

347. Meyer, *Music, the Arts, and Ideas*, 226.

348. Igor Stravinsky, *An Autobiography* (New York: Simon and Schuster, 1936), 83.

349. Charles Keil and Steven Feld, *Music Grooves* (Chicago: University of Chicago Press, 1994), 84.

Chapter 5

1. Susanne K. Langer, *Problems of Art: Ten Philosophical Lectures* (New York: Charles Scribner's Sons, 1957), 129.

2. Susanne K. Langer, *Philosophy in a New Key: A Study in the Symbolism of Reason, Rite, and Art* (Cambridge: Harvard University Press, 1942), 24. Reproduction of material from this volume by permission of Harvard University Press.

3. Ibid.

4. Ibid., 41.

5. Ibid., 61.

6. Ibid., 42.

7. Ibid., 53.

8. Ibid., 121.

9. Ibid., 61–64.

10. Ibid., 64.

11. Ibid., 67.

12. Ibid., 71.

13. Ibid., 101.

14. Ibid., 77.

15. Ibid., 80.

16. Ibid., 81.

17. Susanne K. Langer, *Mind: An Essay on Human Feeling, Vol. I* (Baltimore: Johns Hopkins University Press, 1967) 155. Reproduction of material from this volume by permission of the Johns Hopkins University Press.

18. Langer, *New Key*, 93.

19. Ibid., 86.

20. Ibid.

21. Ibid., 265.

22. Ibid., 96.

23. Langer, *Problems*, 177.

24. Langer, *New Key*, 92.

25. Ibid., 89.

26. Langer, *Problems*, 133.

27. Langer, *New Key*, 239.

28. Ibid., 100–101.

29. Ibid., 92.

30. Ibid., 141.

31. Ibid., 139.

32. Ibid., 143.

33. Langer, *Problems*, 132–33.

34. Langer, *Mind, Vol 1*, xviii.

35. Ibid., 59.

36. Ibid., 63–64.

37. Langer, *New Key*, 266.

38. Langer, *Mind, Vol 1*, 148–49.

39. Langer, *New Key*, vii-viii.

40. Ibid., 205.

41. Ibid., 218.

42. Ibid.

43. Ibid., 223.

44. Ibid.

45. Ibid., 222.

46. Ibid., 228.

47. Ibid., 233.

48. Ibid., 235.

49. Ibid., 238.

50. Ibid., 244.

51. Ibid., 241.

52. Ibid.

53. Ibid., 240.

54. Ibid., 244.

55. Ibid., 243.

56. Ibid., 245.

57. Ibid.

58. Susanne K. Langer, *Feeling and Form: A Theory of Art Developed from Philosophy in a New Key* (New York: Charles Scribner's Sons, 1953), 27.

59. Ibid., 31.

60. Langer, *Problems*, 139.

61. Ibid., 60.

62. Langer, *Feeling*, 19.

63. Ibid., 22.

64. Ibid., 45.

65. Ibid., 51.

66. Ibid., 32.

67. Ibid., 379.

68. Langer, *Problems*, 60.

69. Ibid., 67.

70. Ibid., 66.

71. Langer, *Feeling*, 107.

72. Ibid., 66.

73. Ibid., 68.

74. Langer, *Mind, Vol 1*, 96.

75. Langer, *Feeling*, 109.

76. Ibid., 110.

77. Ibid.

78. Ibid., 111.

79. Ibid., 113.

80. Ibid., 148.

81. Ibid., 394.

82. Ibid.

83. Ibid., 395–96.

84. Ibid., 373–74, 394–96.

85. Ibid., 399.

86. Langer, *Mind, Vol 1*, 67.

87. Langer, *Feeling*, 401.

88. Ibid., 409.

89. Langer, *Feeling*, 27 (emphasis added).

90. Langer, *Mind, Vol 1*, 4.

91. Ibid., 55.

92. Ibid., 64.

93. Ibid., 104.

94. Ibid., 115.

95. Ibid., 147.

96. Ibid., 31.

97. Langer, *Problems*, 59.

98. Langer, *Mind Vol. I*, 66.

99. Ibid., 84.

100. Ibid., 57.

101. Ibid., 209.

102. Ibid., 222.

103. Langer, *Mind, Vol 1*, 67 (emphasis added).

104. Langer conceded early on that to say music is a symbol is "certainly not true in every sense." *New Key*, 219.

105. Ibid., 68.

106. Paul Welsh, "Discursive and Presentational Symbols," *Mind* 64 (1955): 181–99.

107. Ibid., 191.

108. Morris Weitz, "Symbolism and Art," *Review of Metaphysics* 7 (1954): 470.

109. This is among the conclusions reached in James Roger Johnson, "The Primacy of Form: A Study of the Philosophical Development of Susanne K. Langer with implications for choral music" (Ph.D. diss., University of Illinois, 1988).

110. Monroe C. Beardsley, *Aesthetics: Problems in the Philosophy of Criticism* (Indianapolis, IN: Hackett, 1981), 336.

111. Langer, *Feeling*, 394.

112. Forest W. Hansen, "Music, Feeling, and Meaning: A Study of Four Theories" (Ph.D. diss., Johns Hopkins University, 1967). My treatment here draws extensively upon Hansen's analysis on pages 161–67.

113. Langer, *Mind, Vol 1*, 88.

114. Langer, *Problems*, 71.

115. Ibid., 74.

116. Ibid., 61.

117. Langer, *Feeling*, 396.

118. Beardsley, *Philosophy of Criticism*, 391.

119. Weitz, "Symbolism," 480.

120. Richard Rudner, "On Semiotic Aesthetics," *Journal of Aesthetics and Art Criticism* 10 (1951): 76.

121. Langer, *New Key*, 222.

122. Ibid., 263.

123. Rudner, "Semiotic," 71.

124. See, for instance, R. E. Innis, "Art, Symbol and Consciousness: A Polanyi Gloss on Susan [*sic*] Langer and Nelson Goodman," *International Philosophical Quarterly* 17 (1977): 466.

125. Beardsley, *Philosophy of Criticism*, 384.

126. Ibid., 383.

127. Ibid.

128. Nelson Goodman, *Ways of Worldmaking* (Hassocks, England: Harvester Press, 1978).

129. Nelson Goodman, *Languages of Art: An Approach to a Theory of Symbols* (Indianapolis, IN: Hackett, 1976), 43. Reproduction of material from this volume by permission of Hackett Publishing Company, Inc.

130. Ibid., 6.

131. Ibid., 7–8.

132. Ibid., 38.

133. Ibid., 28.

134. Ibid., 33.

135. Ibid., 53.

136. Ibid., 59.

137. Ibid., 68.

138. Ibid., 78.

139. Ibid., 73.

140. Ibid., 74.

141. Ibid., 69.

142. Ibid., 73.

143. Ibid., 71.

144. Ibid., 86.

145. Ibid., 88.

146. Ibid., 91.

147. Ibid., 89.

148. Ibid., 94.

149. Ibid.

150. Ibid., 132.

151. Ibid., 143.

152. Ibid., 148.

153. Ibid., 229. Another interesting way of exploring the digital/analog distinction might be through the phenomenon of absolute pitch. AP is not a function of (analog) aural acuity but rather of the ability to assign pitches to (digital) categories.

154. Ibid., 226.

155. Ibid., 231.

156. Ibid., 235.

157. Ibid., 236.

158. Ibid., 238.

159. Ibid., 247.

160. Ibid., 248.

161. Ibid., 241.

162. Ibid., 242.

163. Ibid., 250–251.

164. Goodman, *Worldmaking*, 68.

165. Ibid.

166. Goodman, *Languages*, 253.

167. Ibid., 258.

168. Ibid.

169. Ibid., 260.

170. Ibid., 62.

171. Ibid., 253.

172. Ibid.

173. C. M. Smith, "Symbolic Systems, Cognitive Efficacy, and Aesthetic Education," *Journal of Aesthetic Education* 3 (1969): 135.

174. Goodman, *Worldmaking*, 65; and in a letter to Monroe Beardsley, quoted in Monroe C. Beardsley, "Semiotic Aesthetics and Aesthetic Education," *Journal of Aesthetic Education* 9 (1975): 25.

175. Beardsley, "Semiotic," 12.

176. Ibid., 14.

177. Ibid., 13.

178. Ibid., 19.

179. Goodman, *Languages*, 262.

180. Monroe C. Beardsley, "In Defense of Aesthetic Value," *Proceedings and Addresses of the American Philosophical Association* 52:6 (1979): 731.

181. Ibid.

182. Ibid., 728.

183. Ibid., 741–42.

184. Ibid., 744 (this point Beardsley attributes to Dewey).

185. Goodman, *Worldmaking*, 69.

186. Quoted in Joseph Margolis, "On the Semiotics of Music," in *What is Music?* ed. Philip Alperson (New York: Haven Press, 1987), 230.

187. Ibid., 233.

188. Ibid., 213.

189. Jean-Jacques Nattiez, *Music and Discourse: Toward a Semiology of Music*, trans. Carolyn Abbate (Princeton, NJ: Princeton University Press, 1990), 15. Emphasis in the

original. Reproduction of material from this volume by permission of Princeton University Press.

190. Ibid., 18.

191. Margolis, "Semiotics," 228.

192. Ibid., 229.

193. Nattiez, *Music and Discourse*, ix.

194. Margolis, "Semiotics," 215.

195. Nattiez, *Music and Discourse*, 5–6.

196. Ibid., 7.

197. Ibid.

198. Ibid., 7–8.

199. Ibid.

200. Ibid., 9.

201. Ibid., 99.

202. Ibid., 17.

203. Ibid., 24.

204. Ibid.

205. Ibid., 11.

206. Ibid., 21.

207. Ibid., 27.

208. Ibid., 29.

209. Ibid., 32.

210. Ibid., 31.

211. Ibid.

212. Ibid., 33.

213. Ibid., 33.

214. Ibid., 37.

215. Ibid., 35.

216. Ibid., 43.

217. Ibid., 47–48.

218. Ibid., 60.

219. Ibid., 42.

220. Ibid., 58.

221. For instance, "Poietic and esthesic information brings us into contact with the entire *lived experience* of 'producers' and 'consumers' of music . . ." Ibid., 166.

222. Ibid., 65.

223. Ibid.

224. Ibid., 67.

225. Nattiez writes, "... the normal situation in musical, linguistic, or human 'communication' in general is precisely the *displacement* between compositional intentions and perceptive behaviors." Ibid., 99.

226. Ibid., 28.

227. Ibid., 48.

228. Ibid., 52 (emphasis added).

229. Ibid., 168.

230. Ibid., 195.

231. Ibid., 196.

232. Ibid., 134–35.

233. Ibid., 139.

234. Ibid., 197.

235. Ibid., 237 (see 233–37 for elaboration of these points within the specific context of musical analysis).

236. Robert Walser, in *Running with the Devil: Power, Gender, and Madness in Heavy Metal Music* (Hanover, NH: Wesleyan University Press, 1993), 31.

Chapter 6

1. T. S. Eliot, "Dry Salvages," *Four Quartets* (New York: Harcourt, Brace, Jovanovich, 1988).

2. Maurice Merleau-Ponty, *The Visible and the Invisible*, trans. Alphonso Lingis, ed. Claude Lefort (Evanston, IL: Northwestern University Press, 1968), 3.

3. Maurice Merleau-Ponty, *Phenomenology of Perception*, trans. Colin Smith (London: Routledge and Kegan Paul, 1962), vii.

4. Ibid., 90.

5. Maurice Merleau-Ponty, *The Primacy of Perception and Other Essays on Phenomenological Psychology, the Philosophy of Art History, and Politics*, ed. James M. Edie (Evanston, IL: Northwestern University Press, 1964), 13.

6. Merleau-Ponty, *Phenomenology*, 325.

7. Ibid., 215.

8. John Sallis, *Phenomenology and the Return to Beginnings* (Pittsburgh: Duquesne University Press, 1973), 36.

9. Merleau-Ponty, *Phenomenology*, 303.

10. "Concealed plentitude" (*sic*) is John Sallis's phrase. Sallis, *Phenomenology*, 77.

11. Merleau-Ponty, *Phenomenology*, 4–5.

12. Ibid., 319.

13. Ibid., 319.

14. Ibid., xvi–xvii.

15. Ibid., 395.

16. Merleau-Ponty, *Signs*, 96.

17. Ibid., 109.

18. Merleau-Ponty, *Phenomenology*, 394.

19. Merleau-Ponty, *The Visible*, 150.

20. Eugene Kaelin, *An Existentialist Aesthetic: The Theories of Sartre and Merleau-Ponty* (Madison: University of Wisconsin Press, 1962).

21. Mikel Dufrenne, *The Phenomenology of Aesthetic Experience*, trans. Edward Casey et al. (Evanston, IL: Northwestern University Press, 1973), 218. Reproduction of material from this volume by permission of Northwestern University Press.

22. Ibid., 11.

23. Ibid. "Art can express only by virtue of the sensuous and according to an operation which transforms brute sensuousness into aesthetic sensuousness" (137–38). And, "The aesthetic object exercises a sovereign imperialism. It makes the real unreal by aestheticizing it." (155).

24. Ibid., 86.

25. Ibid., 375.

26. Ibid., 48.

27. Ibid., 248.

28. Ibid., 248.

29. Ibid., 86.

30. Ibid., 142.

31. Ibid., 423.

32. Ibid., 265–66.

33. Ibid., 249.

34. Ibid., 251.

35. Ibid., 249.

36. Ibid., 256.

37. Ibid., 255.

38. Ibid., 255–56.

39. Ibid., 256.

40. Ibid., 257.

41. Ibid., 258.

42. Ibid., 261.

43. Ibid., 262.

44. Ibid.

45. Ibid., 262–63.

46. Ibid., 263.

47. Ibid.

48. Ibid.

49. Ibid., 264.

50. Ibid.

51. Ibid., 265.

52. Ibid.

53. Ibid., 266.

54. Ibid.

55. Ibid.

56. Ibid., 267.

57. Ibid., 270.

58. Ibid., 267.

59. Ibid., 269.

60. Ibid., 271.

61. Thomas Clifton, *Music as Heard: A Study in Applied Phenomenology* (New Haven, CT: Yale University Press, 1983). Reproduction of material from this volume by permission of Yale University Press.

62. Ibid., *x*..

63. Ibid., 1.

64. Ibid., 2.

65. Ibid., 3.

66. Ibid., 41.

67. Ibid., 10. Elsewhere, Clifton comments that "It is just as impossible to submit a complete listing of all the material essences of musical space, as it is to submit a universally applicable listing of criteria of aesthetic excellence—but not for the same reasons. In the former case, there are too many; in the latter, there are none." (202).

68. Ibid., 5.

69. Ibid., 6.

70. Ibid., 19.

71. Ibid., 22.

72. Ibid., 21.

73. Ibid., 22.

74. Ibid., 23.

75. Ibid., 30.

76. Ibid., 32–33.

77. Ibid., 33.

78. Ibid., 33–34.

79. Ibid., 35.

80. Ibid., 45.

81. Ibid., 47.

82. Ibid., 37.

83. See Edmund Husserl, *Phenomenology of Internal Time-Consciousness*, trans. James C. Churchill, ed. Martin Heidegger (Bloomington: Indiana University Press, 1964).

84. Clifton, *Music as Heard*, 56.

85. Ibid., 54.

86. Ibid., 51.

87. Ibid., 55.

88. Ibid., 56.

89. Ibid., 57.

90. Ibid., 57.

91. Ibid., 58.

92. Lawrence Ferrara, *Philosophy and the Analysis of Music: Bridges to Musical Sound, Form, and Reference* (New York: Greenwood Press, 1991), 148.

93. Clifton, *Music as Heard*, 58.

94. Ibid., 59.

95. Merleau-Ponty, *Phenomenology*, 418.

96. Clifton, *Music as Heard*, 60.

97. Ibid., 62.

98. Ibid., 64.

99. Ibid., 62.

100. Ibid., 137.

101. Ibid., 68.

102. Ibid., 137.

103. Merleau-Ponty, *Phenomenology*, 229 (cited in Clifton, 66).

104. Clifton, *Music as Heard*, 68.

105. Judy Lochhead, "Hearing New Music: Pedagogy from a Phenomenological Perspective," *Philosophy of Music Education Review* 3:1 (Spring 1995): 36.

106. Clifton, *Music as Heard*, 141.

107. Ibid., 142.

108. Ibid., 69.

109. Ibid.

110 Ibid., 143.

111. Ibid., 144.

112. Ibid., 145–155.

113. Ibid., 151.

114. Ibid., 34.

115. Ibid., 71.

116. Ibid., 206.

117. Ibid., 207.

118. Ibid., 216.

119. Ibid., 211.

120. Ibid., 224.

121. Ibid., 237.

122. Ibid., 238.

123. Ibid., 272.

124. Ibid., 273.

125. Ibid., 277.

126. Ibid., 278.

127. Ibid., 279.

128. Ibid.

129. Ibid., 281.

130. Ibid.

131. Ibid., 282.

132. Ibid.

133. Ibid., 227.

134. Ibid., 283.

135. Ibid.

136. Ibid.

137. Ibid., 284.

138. Ibid.

139. Ibid., 288. Merleau-Ponty actually says, "Before becoming the symbol of a concept it [the word 'hard'] is first of all an event which grips my body, and this grip circumscribes the area of significance to which it has reference. . . . The word is then indistinguishable from the attitude which it induces, and it is only when its presence is prolonged that it appears in the guise of an external image, and its meaning as a thought." *Phenomenology*, 235.

140. Ibid., 290.

141. Ibid., 297.

142. Ibid., 294.

143. Ibid., 296.

144. Ibid., 272.

145. Ibid.

146. Lawrence Ferrara, *Philosophy and the Analysis of Music*, 153.

147. Ibid., 153.

148. Ibid., 156.

149. Ibid.

150. David L. Burrows, *Sound, Speech, and Music* (Amherst: University of Massachusetts Press, 1990). Reproduction of material from the introduction and chapters two and five of this volume by permission of the University of Massachusetts Press. Reproduction of material from chapter one, which first appeared as "On Hearing Things" in *The Musical Quarterly* 66:2 (1980), used by permission of Oxford University Press.

151. Ibid., 4.

152. Ibid.

153. Ibid., 6.

154. Ibid., 8.

155. Ibid.

156. Ibid., 15.

157. Ibid., 17.

158. Ibid., 21.

159. Ibid., 17–18.

160. Ibid., 20.

161. According to some feminist literature, *visual* epistemological metaphors (seeing the light, illumination, the mind's eye, etc.) are more characteristic of men's thought than women's. Recent women's literature more often uses the metaphor of *voice* because of its emphasis upon closeness, relatedness, interaction, and subjective in-

volvement in knowing. Visual epistemological metaphors imply objective detachment and a static reality. See *Women's Ways of Knowing: The Development of Self, Voice, and Mind,* by Mary F. Belenky et al. (New York: Basic Books, 1986).

162. Burrows, *Sound,* 20.

163. Ibid., 18–19.

164. Ibid., 18.

165. Ibid., 20.

166. Ibid., 25.

167. Ibid., 17.

168. Ibid., 21.

169. Ibid., 18.

170. Ibid., 19.

171. Ibid., 16.

172. Ibid., 21.

173. Ibid., 25.

174. Ibid., 26.

175. Ibid., 29.

176. Ibid., 15.

177. Ibid., 17.

178. Ibid., 22.

179. Ibid., 23.

180. Ibid.

181. Ibid., 25.

182. Ibid., 40.

183. Ibid., 32.

184. Ibid., 31.

185. Ibid., 30.

186. Ibid., 30–31.

187. Ibid., 31.

188. Ibid., 33.

189. Ibid., 34.

190. Ibid.

191. Ibid., 35–36.

192. Ibid., 37.

193. Ibid., 36.

194. Ibid., 38.

195. Ibid., 51.

196. Ibid., 56.

197. Ibid., 58.

198. Ibid., 71.

199. Ibid., 75.

200. Ibid., 67.

201. Ibid., 75.

202. Ibid., 72.

203. Ibid., 76.

204. Ibid., 72.

205. Ibid., 77.

206. Ibid., 90.

207. Ibid., 92.

208. Ibid., 106.

209. Ibid., 98.

210. Ibid., 107.

211. Eleanor V. Stubley, "Modulating Identities: The Play of Ensemble Performance (Being in the Body, Being in the Sound)" (paper presented to the Music Educators National Conference, Kansas City, MO, spring 1966). The decision to include Stubley's ideas in close proximity to Burrows' should not be mistaken to imply that her ideas are derivative, although they do converge with his nicely.

212. Ibid., 1.

213. Ibid., 2.

214. Ibid.

215. Ibid., 4.

216. Ibid., 4.

217. Ibid., 5.

218. Charles Keil, in Charles Keil and Steven Feld, *Music Grooves* (Chicago: University of Chicago Press, 1994). Stubley does not draw this specific connection, but it seems apt.

219. Stubley, "Modulating," 5.

220. Ibid., 7. Stubley attributes the phrase "being apart together" to Johan Huizinga, in *Homo Ludens: A Study of the Play Element in Culture* (Boston: Beacon Press, 1950).

221. Ibid.

222. Ibid., 8.

223. Ibid., 9.

224. Ibid., 10.

225. Ibid., 13.

226. Ibid.

227. Mark Johnson, *The Body in the Mind: The Bodily Basis of Meaning, Imagination, and Reason* (Chicago: University of Chicago Press, 1987).

228. Ibid., xiii (italicized in the original).

229. Ibid., xix.

230. Ibid., xiv.

231. Ibid., xvi ("experiential" is italicized in the original).

232. Ibid.

233. Ibid.

234. Ibid., 21–22.

235. Ibid., 30–31.

236. Ibid., 38.

237. Ibid., 40.

Chapter 7

1. Samuel and Shierry Weber, trans., *Prisms: Cultural Criticism and Society*, by Theodor Adorno (London: Neville Spearman, 1967).

2. Max Paddison: *Adorno's Aesthetics of Music* (New York: Cambridge University Press, 1993).

3. Rose Rosengard Subotnik, *Developing Variations* (Minneapolis: University of Minnesota Press, 1991), 54.

4. Martin Jay, *Adorno* (Cambridge, MA: Harvard University Press, 1984), 11.

5. Ibid., 53–54.

6. Paddison, *Adorno's Aesthetics*, 11.

7. Adorno quoted in Paddison. Ibid., 9.

8. Georgy Lukacs: *History and Class Consciousness: Studies in Marxist Dialectics*, trans. Rodney Livingston (Cambridge, MA: MIT Press, 1971), 93.

9. Theodor Adorno, "On the Social Situation of Music," *Telos* 35 (Spring 1978): 130. Reproduction of material from this article by permission of Telos Press, Ltd.

10. Theodor Adorno, *Philosophy of Modern Music*, trans. A. G. Mitchell and W. V. Blomster (New York: Seabury Press, 1973), 32.

11. Adorno, "Social Situation," 128.

12. Ibid.

13. Ibid.

14. Ibid., 129.

15. Ibid.

16. Ibid., 130.

17. Ibid.

18. Ibid.

19. Ibid.

20. Ibid., 131.

21. Ibid.

22. Ibid.

23. Ibid., 132.

24. Ibid., 158.

25. Ibid.

26. Ibid., 159.

27. Ibid., 133.

28. Ibid.

29. Ibid., 139.

30. Ibid., 140. (The misspelled 'contral' was corrected here).

31. Ibid., 143.

32. Ibid., 144.

33. Ibid., 143.

34. Ibid., 139.

35. Ibid., 133.

36. Ibid., 144.

37. Ibid.

38. Ibid., 134.

39. Ibid.

40. Ibid., 132.

41. Ibid., 135.

42. Ibid., 130.

43. Ibid., 149.

44. Ibid., 155.

45. Ibid.

46. Theodor Adorno, "On the Fetish-Character in Music and the Regression of Listening," in *The Essential Frankfurt School Reader*, eds. Andrew Arato and Eike Gebhart (New York: Urizen Books, 1967), 276.

47. Ibid., 270–71.

48. Ibid., 271.

49. Ibid.

50. Ibid.

51. Ibid., 273.

52. Ibid., 274.

53. Ibid.

54. Ibid., 276.

55. Ibid.

56. Ibid.

57. Ibid., 279.

58. Ibid., 281.

59. Ibid., 286.

60. Ibid., 287.

61. Ibid., 290.

62. Ibid., 297.

63. Ibid., 298.

64. Theodor Adorno, "Types of Musical Conduct" in *Introduction to the Sociology of Music*, trans. E. B. Ashton (New York: Continuum, 1989), 3. Reproduction of material from this volume by permission of Continuum Publishing Company.

65. Ibid., 4.

66. Ibid., 5.

67. Ibid., 6.

68. Ibid., 8.

69. Ibid.

70. Ibid., 9.

71. Ibid., 10.

72. Ibid., 14.

73. Ibid., 15.

74. Theodor Adorno, "Function," in *Introduction to the Sociology of Music*, 39.

75. Adorno, "Types," 16.

76. Ibid., 17.

77. Ibid., 18.

78. Ibid.

79. Ibid., 20.

80. Theodor Adorno, "Popular Music," in *Introduction to the Sociology of Music*, 25.

81. Ibid., 26.

82. Ibid., 27.

83. Ibid., 31.

84. Ibid., 30.

85. Ibid., 37–38.

86. Adorno, "Function," 39.

87. Ibid., 41.

88. Ibid.

89. Ibid., 42.

90. Ibid., 46.

91. Ibid., 48.

92. Ibid., 49.

93. Ibid., 50–51.

94. Ibid., 51.

95. Ibid., 53.

96. Ibid.

97. Ibid., 43.

98. Theodor Adorno, "Musical Life," in *Introduction to the Sociology of Music*, 121.

99. Ibid., 123.

100. Ibid., 125.

101. Ibid.

102. Ibid., 119.

103. Ibid.

104. Ibid., 120.

105. Ibid.

106. Ibid.

107. Ibid.

108. Ibid.

109. Ibid., 126.

110. Ibid., 129.

111. Ibid., 132.

112. Ibid.

113. Ibid., 134.

114. Ibid., 137.

115. Ibid., 119.

116. Theodor Adorno, *Minima Moralia: Reflections from Damaged Life*, trans. E. F. W. Jephcott (London: New Left Books, 1974), 15.

117. Adorno, *Philosophy of Modern Music*, 15.

118. Ibid., 10.

119. See, for instance, ibid., 9.

120. Theodor Adorno, *Prisms: Cultural Criticism and Society*, trans. Samuel and Shierry Weber (London: Neville Spearman, 1967), 149–50.

121. Ibid., 153.

122. Lambert Zuidervaart, *Adorno's Aesthetic Theory: The Redemption of Illusion*, (Cambridge, MA: MIT Press, 1991), 88.

123. Ibid., 91.

124. For more extensive elaboration on this idea, see Subotnik's "Why is Adorno's Criticism the Way It Is?" in Subotnik, *Developing Variations*, 48–49.

125. Theodor Adorno, *Aesthetic Theory*, trans. C. Lenhardt (London: Routledge & Kegan Paul, 1984), 3.

126. Zuidervaart, *Adorno's Aesthetic Theory*, 94.

127. See, for instance, Theodore A. Gracyk, "Adorno, Jazz, and the Aesthetics of Popular Music," *Musical Quarterly* 76:4 (Winter 1992): 526–42. Gracyk is successful in defending jazz against Adorno's criticisms, but perhaps less successful in countering his indictments of popular music.

128. Adorno, *Aesthetic Theory*, 322.

129. Lydia Goehr, "Political Music and the Politics of Music," *Journal of Aesthetics and Art Criticism* 52:1 (1994): 108.

130. Rose Subotnik, "The Challenge of Contemporary Music," in *What Is Music?* ed. P. Alperson (New York: Haven Press, 1987), 362.

131. Ibid., 380.

132. Zuidervaart, *Adorno's Aesthetic Theory*, 239.

133. Jacques Attali, *Noise: The Political Economy of Music*, trans. B. Massumi (Minneapolis: University of Minnesota Press, 1985), 3. Reproduction of material from this volume by permission of the University of Minnesota Press.

134. Ibid., 3.

135. Ibid., 6.

136. Ibid.

137. Ibid., 27.

138. Ibid., 24. This passage is italicized in the original.

139. Ibid.

140. Ibid., 30.

141. Ibid., 46.

142. Ibid., 19.

143. Ibid., 31.

144. Ibid., 22.

145. Ibid., 20.

146. Ibid., 5. This passage is italicized in the original.

147. Ibid.

148. Ibid., 12.

149. Ibid., 13.

150. Ibid., 14.

151. Ibid., 36.

152. Ibid., 26.

153. Ibid., 19.

154. Ibid., 46.

155. Ibid., 57.

156. Ibid., 66.

157. Ibid., 67.

158. Ibid., 77.

159. Ibid., 81.

160. Ibid., 47.

161. Ibid., 9.

162. Ibid., 57.

163. Ibid., 5.

164. Ibid., 88.

165. Ibid., 89.

166. Ibid., 5. This phrase is italicized in the original.

167. Ibid.

168. Ibid., 111.

169. Ibid., 120.

170. Ibid., 5.

171. Ibid., 8.

172. Luigi Russolo, quoted on p.23.

173. Ibid., 33.

174. Ibid., 42. Emphasis in the original.

175. Ibid., 85.

176. Ibid., 88.

177. Ibid., 110.

178. Ibid., 111.

179. Ibid., 125.

180. Ibid., 45. Emphasis in the original.

181. Ibid., 102.

182. Ibid., 112. Emphasis in the original.

183. Ibid., 116.

184. Ibid., 117.

185. Ibid., 114.

186. Ibid., 132.

187. Ibid., 133.

188. Ibid., 134.

189. Ibid.

190. Ibid., 136.

191. Ibid., 137.

192. Ibid., 141.

193. Ibid.

194. Ibid., 145.

195. Ibid., 142 .

196. Ibid., 147.

197. Ibid., 148.

198. Ibid., 139.

199. Ibid., 141.

200. Ibid., 149 ("Afterword").

201. Ibid., 117.

202. Ibid., 90. Emphasis in the original.

203. Ibid., 144.

204. Ibid., 134.

205. Ibid., 132.

206. Ibid., 143.

207. Ibid.

208. Ibid., 145.

Chapter 8

1. Nancy Fraser and Linda J. Nicholson, "Social Criticism without Philosophy: An Encounter between Feminism and Postmodernism," in *Feminism/Postmodernism*, ed. Linda J. Nicholson (New York: Routledge, 1990), 19.

2. Since almost all the scholars cited in this chapter are contemporary, I will not continue to indicate dates of birth as in former chapters; readers interested in chronology should refer to publication dates of works cited.

3. Biddy Martin, "Feminism, Criticism, and Foucault," *New German Critique* 27 (Fall 1982): 13.

4. Roberta Lamb offers a brief overview in her "Feminism as Critique in Philosophy of Music Education," *Philosophy of Music Education Review* 2:2 (1994): 60–62. I wish again to express my gratitude to Lamb for her helpful criticisms of an early draft of this chapter.

5. Roberta Lamb, "Feminism as Critique in Philosophy of Music Education," 61. Dorothy Smith is probably the best known advocate of this position.

6. Jenefer Robinson and Stephanie Ross, "Women, Morality, and Fiction" in *Aesthetics in Feminist Perspective*, ed. Hilda Hein and Carolyn Korsmeyer (Bloomington: Indiana University Press, 1993), 112.

7. Ruth Solie, ed., *Musicology and Difference: Gender and Sexuality in Music Scholarship* (Berkeley: University of California Press, 1993), 11.

8. Ibid.

9. Naomi Schor, "This Essentialism Which is Not One: Coming to Grips with Irigaray," *differences* 1:2 (1989): 45–46. Among Schor's points: "If othering involves attributing to the objectified other a difference that serves to legitimate her oppression, saming denies the objective other the right to her difference"; "[E]xposing the logic of saming is a necessary step in toppling the universal from his/(her) pedestal"; and, "If all difference is attributed to othering, then one risks saming; if all denial of difference is viewed as resulting in saming, then one risks othering."

10. Ruth Solie, *Musicology and Difference*, 4.

11. Ibid., 8.

12. Solie observes that "No critic has been more energetic in . . . problematizing [the idea of gender categories] than Judith Butler, who argues for a performative, rather than substantive, interpretation. . . . 'There is no gender identity behind the expressions of gender', Butler says. . . ." Judith Butler's *Gender Trouble: Feminism and the Subversion of Identity* (New York: Routledge, 1990) Ibid., 18.

13. Ellen Koskoff, ed., *Women and Music in Cross-Cultural Perspective* (New York: Greenwood Press, 1987), 5.

14. Christine Battersby, *Gender and Genius: Towards a Feminist Aesthetics* (London: The Women's Press, 1989) 154.

15. Koskoff (*Women and Music*, 9) quotes Ortner and Whitehead to the effect that "the study of gender is inherently a study of relations of asymmetrical power and opportunity." Sherry B. Ortner and Harriet Whitehead (eds.) *Sexual Meanings: The Cultural Construction of Gender and Sexuality* (Cambridge: Cambridge University Press, 1981) 4.

16. Ibid 405.

17. Renée Cox, "Recovering *Jouissance*: An Introduction to Feminist Musical Aesthetics," in *Women and Music: A History*, ed. Karin Pendle (Bloomington: Indiana University Press, 1991), 334.

18. Solie, *Musicology and Difference* 3.

19. Renee Cox, "Recovering *Jouissance*," 332.

20. Roberta Lamb, "Discords: Feminist Pedagogy in Music Education," *Theory into Practice* 35:2 (1996): 127.

21. Heide Göttner-Abendroth, *The Dancing Goddess: Principles of a Matriarchal Aesthetic*, trans. Maureen T. Krause (Boston: Beacon Press, 1991).

22. Ibid., 3.

23. Ibid., 47.

24. Ibid.

25. Ibid., 47–48.

26. Ibid., 7.

27. Ibid. Some of Aristotle's more noteworthy comments on women's inferiority may be found in *On the Generation of Animals* (1.2; 2.3), and in *Politics* (1.5).

28. Ibid., 11.

29. Ibid., 6.

30. Ibid., 21.

31. Ibid., 26. Here, she acknowledges her debt to French feminist philosophers Julia Kristeva and Luce Irigaray: specifically, Kristeva's *Revolution in Poetic Language*, trans. Margaret Waller (New York: Columbia University Press, 1984), and Irigaray's *Speculum of the Other Woman*, trans. Gillian Gill (Ithaca, NY: Cornell University Press, 1985). Also influential have been Kristeva's *Desire in Language: A Semiotic Approach to Literature and Art*, trans. Thomas Gora, Alice Jardine, and Leon Roudiez, ed. Leon Roudiez (New York: Columbia University Press, 1980), and Irigaray's *This Sex Which Is Not One*, trans. Catherine Porter (Ithaca, NY: Cornell University Press, 1985).

32. Ibid. 30.

33. Ibid., 56.

34. My paraphrasing here is extensive. Göttner-Abendroth's accounts may be found both in *The Dancing Goddess*, 48–74, and in "Nine Principles of a Matriarchal Aesthetic,"

trans. Harriett Anderson, in *Feminist Aesthetics*, ed. Gisela Ecker (London: Women's Press, 1985), 81–94. The Anderson translation of this section is somewhat more accessible than the Krause.

35. Ibid., 56.

36. Göttner-Abendroth, "Nine Principles of a Matriarchal Aesthetic," 86.

37. Göttner-Abendroth, *Dancing Goddess*, 218.

38. Göttner-Abendroth, "Nine Principles of a Matriarchal Aesthetic," 82.

39. Because Göttner-Abendroth does not envision a distinctly 'musical' genre so much as an all-embracing ritual, my references to music here are not entirely consistent with her argument.

40. Ibid., 89.

41. Ibid., 90.

42. Ibid., 83.

43. Göttner-Abendroth, *Dancing Goddess*, 229.

44. Göttner-Abendroth, "Nine Principles of a Matriarchal Aesthetic," 93.

45. Ibid., 94.

46. Ibid.

47. Ibid.

48. For a detailed and insightful exploration of these and related issues, see Charlene A. Morton "The Feminized Location of School Music and the Burden of Justification" (Ed.D. diss., University of Toronto, 1996).

49. Göttner-Abendroth, *Dancing Goddess*, 223.

50. Ibid., 226.

51. Renée Lorraine, "A Gynecentric Aesthetic," in *Aesthetics in Feminist Perspective*, eds. Hilde Hein and Carolyn Korsmeyer (Bloomington: Indiana University Press, 1993), 31–52.

52. Ibid., 39.

53. Göttner-Abendroth, *Dancing Goddess*, 217.

54. Ibid., 221.

55. Marcia J. Citron, "Feminist Approaches to Musicology," in *Cecilia Reclaimed: Feminist Perspectives on Gender and Music*, eds. Susan C. Cook and Judy S. Tsou (Urbana: University of Illinois Press, 1994), 17.

56. Mary Bittner Wiseman, "Beautiful Exiles," in *Aesthetics in Feminist Perspective*, eds. Hilde Hein and Carolyn Korsmeyer (Bloomington: Indiana University Press, 1993), 175.

57. Ibid., 170.

58. Ibid., 171 (Kant makes these assertions in §47 and §51).

59. Ibid., 172 (Kant's §78).

60. Ibid., 172.

61. Ibid. (Kant's §60).

62. Ibid., 173 (Kant's §81).

63. Jane Kneller, "Discipline and Silence: Women and Imagination in Kant's Theory of Taste" in *Aesthetics in Feminist Perspective*, eds. Hilde Hein and Carolyn Korsmeyer, 179–91.

64. Ibid., 180 (quoting Kant's *Anthropology from a Pragmatic Point of View*, §306.

65. Ibid. (quoting Kant's *Anthropology*, §244).

66. Ibid., 181(quoting Kant's *Critique of Judgement*, §210).

67. Ibid. (referring to Kant's *Critique of Judgement*, §210).

68. Ibid., 182.

69. Ibid., 183 (quoting Kant's *Anthropology*, §309–10).

70.Ibid., 184 (quoting Kant's *Critique of Judgement*, §50).

71. Ibid., 185.

72. On the "add and stir" strategy for accommodation of feminist concerns, see Sandra Harding, "Is There a Feminist Method?" in *Feminism and Methodology: Social Science Issues*, ed. Sandra Harding (Bloomington: Indiana University Press, 1987); Charlene A. Morton, "Feminist Theory and the Displaced Music Curriculum: Beyond the 'Add and Stir' Projects," in *Philosophy of Music Education Review* 2:2 (Fall, 1994): 106–21; Deanne Bogden, "Pythagoras' Rib or, What Does Music Education Want?" in *Philosophy of Music Education Review* 2:2 (Fall, 1994): 122–31; and Roberta Lamb, "Aria Senza Accompagnamento," *The Quarterly Journal of Music Teaching and Learning* IV:4/V:1 (1993–94): 5–20.

73. Charlene Morton, "Feminist Theory," 107.

74. Susan McClary, *Feminine Endings: Music, Gender, and Sexuality* (Minneapolis: University of Minnesota Press, 1991), 114.

75. Ibid.

76. Charlene Morton, "Feminist Theory," 108–9.

77. Roberta Lamb, "Tone Deaf/Symphonies Singing: Sketches for a Musicale," *Gender in/forms Curriculum: From Enrichment to Transformation*, eds. Jane Gaskell and John Willinsky (New York: Teachers College Press, 1995), 111.

78. Ibid., 115.

79. Ibid.

80. Ibid., 119.

81. Susan Heald, "From Pianos to Pedagogy," in *Unsettling Relations: The University as a Site of Feminist Struggles*, eds. Himani Bannerji et al. (Toronto: Women's Press, 1991), 129, quoted in Lamb, "Tone Deaf," 117.

82. Lamb, "Tone Deaf," 111. Although Lamb uses this phrase to describe the character of her critical work, it appears equally descriptive of her conception of women's musical practices.

83. Ibid., 126.

84. Suzanne G. Cusick, "Gender and the Cultural Work of a Classical Music Performance," in *repercussions* 3:1 (Spring 1994): 77–110.

85. Ibid., 77, quoting Adrienne Rich, "The Images" in *A Wild Patience Has Taken Me This Far* New York: Norton, (1981).

86. The texts to these songs suggest among other things that woman's sole sense of worth comes from her status as lowly handmaiden to a generous husband.

87. Cusick, "Gender and the Cultural Work," 80.

88. Ibid., 80–81.

89. Ibid., 81.

90. Ibid., 82.

91. Ibid., 83.

92. Ibid., 84.

93. Ibid., 85.

94. Ibid., 87.

95. Ibid., 91.

96. Ibid., 91n.

97. Ibid., 92.

98. Ibid., 98.

99. Ibid., 108.

100. Ibid., 109–110.

101. Susan McClary, "Towards a Feminist Criticism of Music," *Canadian University Music Review* 10:2 (1990): 12.

102. Ibid.

103. Ibid.

104. Renée Cox, "Recovering *Jouissance*," 333.

105. McClary, "Towards a Feminist Criticism," 13.

106. Citron, "Feminist Approaches," 19.

107. Ibid., 21.

108. Ibid., 22.

109. Ibid., 24.

110. Ibid.

111. McClary, "Towards a Feminist Criticism," 14.

112. McClary, *Feminine Endings*, 12.

113. Ibid.

114. Ibid., 12–13.

115. Ibid., 13.

116. McClary, "Towards a Feminist Criticism," 14.

117. McClary, *Feminine Endings*, 16.

118. John Shepherd, *Music as Social Text* (Cambridge: Polity Press, 1991), 90.

119. Ibid., 159.

120. Ibid., 153.

121. Ibid., 171.

122. Ibid., 156.

123. Ibid.

124. Quoted in ibid., 157. Again, Cusick's description of the darkened concert hall comes to mind.

125. Ibid., 159.

126. Ibid.

127. Ibid.

128. Ibid., 160.

129. Ibid., 153.

130. John Shepherd, "Music and the Last Intellectuals," *Journal of Aesthetic Education* 25 (1991): 112.

131. Richard Leppert, "The Sonoric Body: Socio-Sexual Harmony—Acts of Violence," in *Compendium of the International Conference on Music, Gender, and Pedagogics* (School of Music and Musicology at the University of Göteborg, Sweden: 1996), 130.

132. Carolyn Korsmeyer, "Philosophy, Aesthetics, and Feminist Scholarship," in *Aesthetics in Feminist Perspective*, ed. Hilde Hein and Carolyn Korsmeyer, vii–xv. See also Estella Lauter's "Re-Enfranchising Art" in Hein and Korsmeyer, 21–34, for a detailed comparison of feminist aesthetic theory and traditional, formalist theory.

133. Korsmeyer, "Philosophy, Aesthetics, and Feminist Scholarship," viii.

134. Ellen Koskoff, "An Introduction to Women, Music, and Culture," in *Women and Music in Cross-Cultural Perspective*, ed. Ellen Koskoff (New York: Greenwood Press, 1987), 1.

135. Ibid., 6.

136. Ibid., 9.

137. Sherry B. Ortner and Harriet Whitehead, "Introduction: Accounting for Sexual Meanings," in *Sexual Meanings: The Cultural Construction of Gender and Sexuality*, eds. Ortner and Whitehead (Cambridge: Cambridge University Press, 1981), 4.

138. Ibid., 14.

139. Ellen Koskoff, "An Introduction to Women, Music, and Culture," 10.

140. Koskoff lists four kinds of relation between music and gender: confirmation, apparent confirmation, resistance, and threat. Ibid., 10.

141. Ibid., 15.

142. Ibid., 15–16.

143. Solie, *Musicology and Difference*, 3.

144. Ibid., 6.

145. Solie (ibid., 17) quotes Barbara Johnson: "The differences *between* entities . . . are shown to be based on a repression of differences *within* entities.".

146. Solie 15.

147. Solie 8.

148. Solie 10.

149. Solie 19.

150. Solie 20.

151. Lamb, "Tone Deaf" 126.

152. Carolyn Korsmeyer, "Philosophy, Aesthetics, and Feminist Scholarship," viii. Further, Hilde Hein writes, "Having never been the arbiters of the right, the true, and the beautiful, women have no stake in losing that status [Hein here acknowledges Sandra Harding]. Women's rebellion against the monolithic claims of conventional theorizing . . . does not represent the same sacrifice of privilege that it does for men. . . ." ("Refining Feminist Theory: Lessons from Aesthetics," in Hein and Korsmeyer, 5–6).

153. Mark Johnson's theory of the embodied nature of cognition is briefly described in chapter 6.

154. Beverly Diamond, "Strategies for Confronting Patriarchy in the Music School," in *Compendium of the International Conference on Music, Gender, and Pedagogics* (School of Music and Musicology at the University of Göteborg, Sweden: 1996), 26–36.

155. Eleanor Godway and Geraldine Finn, *Who Is this "We"? Absence of Community* (Montréal: Black Rose, 1994).

156. Roberta Lamb, "Tone Deaf," 132.

157. Jean-Francois Lyotard in Bernard Blistine, "A Conversation with Jean-Francois Lyotard," *Flash Art* 121 (March, 1985). Quoted in Neville Wakefield, *Postmodernism: The Twilight of the Real* (London: Pluto Press, 1990), 23.

158. Zygmunt Bauman, "The Fall of the Legislator," in *Postmodernism: A Reader*, ed. Thomas Docherty (New York: Columbia University Press, 1993), 129.

159. Ibid., 134.

160. Ibid.

161. Thomas Docherty, ed., *Postmodernism: A Reader* (New York: Columbia University Press, 1993), 36.

162. Ibid., 445.

163. Ibid., 135.

164. 'Ludic' and 'resistance' postmodernism are Teresa Ebert's terms: "Writing the Political: Resistance (Post)modernism," cited in Russell A. Potter's *Spectacular Vernaculars: Hip-Hop and the Politics of Postmodernism* (Albany: State University of New York Press, 1995), 2.

165. Lawrence Kramer, *Classical Music and Postmodern Knowledge* (Berkeley: University of California Press, 1995), 5.

166. Zygmunt Bauman, "The Fall of the Legislator," 139.

167. These are recurrent themes developed in Kramer, *Classical Music*.

168. Karlis Racevkis, *Postmodernism and the Search for Enlightenment* (University Press of Virginia, 1993), x.

169. Kramer, *Classical Music*, 34–35.

170. Donna Haraway cited in Kramer, *Classical Music*, 9.

171. David Elliott, *Music Matters* (New York: Oxford University Press, 1995), 210.

172. Ibid., 209.

173. Ibid., quoting Harold Osborne.

174. Ibid., 207.

175. It should be stressed that the claims outlined here are indeed speculative: offered with the intent of comparing or contrasting cultural pluralism and postmodernism's decidedly relativist bent.

176. Russell A. Potter, *Spectacular Vernaculars: Hip-Hop and the Politics of Postmodernism* (Albany: State University of New York Press, 1995), 20. Emphasis in the original.

177. Suzanne de Castell, "Textuality and the Designs of Theory," in *Critical Conversations in Philosophy of Education*, ed. Wendy Kohli (New York: Routledge, 1995), 242–43.

178. Potter, *Spectacular Vernaculars*. It is interesting to speculate about whether there can be a *post*-modern for people who never really subscribed to myths of modernity.

179. Ibid., 6.

180. Ibid., 8.

181. Ibid., 5.

182. Ibid., 108.

183. Andreas Huyssen, "Mapping the Postmodern," in *Feminism/Postmodernism*, ed. Linda J. Nicholson (New York: Routledge, 1990), 240–41.

184. Ibid., 248.

185. Kramer, *Classical Music*, 3–4.

186. Ibid., 5.

187. Ibid., 67. Kramer (ibid., 18) makes the same point another way: "The emergence of postmodernist musicologies will depend upon our willingness and ability to read as inscribed within the immediacy-effects of music itself the kind of mediating structures usually positioned outside music under the rubric of context. . . . [T]he differences between text and context, the aesthetic and the political or social, the 'inside' and the 'outside' of the musical moment . . . would be (re)constituted as provisional and permeable boundaries destined to disappear in and through the heteroglot weaving of musicological discourse.".

188. Ibid., 64.

189. Ibid.

190. Ibid., 49.

191. Ibid.

192. Ibid., 50. 'Observed or defied' because even a defied norm implicitly accepts the idea of normativity.

193. Ibid.

194. Ibid., 62.

195. Ibid., 235.

196. Ibid., 227.

197. Ibid., 230.

198. Note that feminism is in many respects an emphatically postmodern discourse—arguably the most audible, prominent, and influential. For that reason, my references to postmodernism in this closing section apply generally to feminism as well, even though I am fully aware of the wariness of many feminists feel toward postmodern sentiments because of its potential to undermine the idea of commonality even among women's experiences.

199. Charles Keil and Steven Feld, *Music Grooves* (Chicago: University of Chicago Press, 1994) 20.

Bibliography

Adorno, Theodor. *Aesthetic Theory*. Translated by C. Lenhardt. Edited by Gretel Adorno and Rolf Tiedemann. London: Routledge and Kegan Paul, 1984.

———. *Introduction to the Sociology of Music*. Translated by E. B. Ashton. New York: Continuum Publishing, 1989.

———. *Minima Moralia: Reflections from Damaged Life*. Translated by E. F. W. Jephcott. London: New Left Books, 1974.

———. "On the Fetish-Character in Music and the Regression of Listening." In *The Essential Frankfurt School Reader*. Edited by Andrew Arato and Eike Gebhart, 270–99. New York: Urizen Books, 1967.

———. "On the Social Situation of Music." *Telos* 35 (spring 1978): 128–64.

———. *Philosophy of Modern Music*. Translated by A. G. Mitchell and W. V. Blomster. New York: Seabury Press, 1973.

———. *Prisms: Cultural Criticism and Society*. Translated by Samuel and Shierry Weber. London: Neville Spearman, 1967.

Anderson, Warren D. *Ethos and Education in Greek Music: The Evidence of Poetry and Philosophy*. Cambridge, MA: Harvard University Press, 1966.

Arato, Andrew, and Eike Gebhart, editors. *The Essential Frankfurt School Reader*. New York: Urizen Books, 1967.

Aristotle. *DeCaelo*. Translated by J. L. Stocks. In *The Works of Aristotle*, vol. II, edited by W. D. Ross. Oxford: Clarendon Press, 1930.

———. *Meta physica*. Translated by W. D. Ross. In *The Works of Aristotle*, vol. VIII, edited by W. D. Ross. Oxford: Clarendon Press, 1928.

———. *Nicomachean Ethics*. Translated by W. D. Ross. In *The Works of Aristotle*, edited by W. D. Ross from *Great Books of the Western World*, vol. 2. Chicago: Encyclopaedia Britannica, 1952.

———. *On the Generation of Animals*. Translated by Arthur Platt. In *The Works of Aristotle*, vol. v, edited by J. A. Smith and W. D. Ross. Oxford: Clarendon Press, 1912.

———. *On Poetics*. Translated by Ingram Bywater. In *The Works of Aristotle*, edited by W. D. Ross, from *Great Books of the Western World*, vol. 2. Chicago: Encyclopaedia Britannica, 1952.

———. *Politics*. Translated by Benjamin Jowett. In *The Works of Aristotle*, edited by W. D. Ross, from *Great Books of the Western World*, vol. 2. Chicago: Encyclopaedia Britannica, 1952.

———. *Rhetoric*. Tranlated by W. Rhys Roberts. In *The Works of Aristotle*, edited by W. D. Ross, from *Great Books of the Western World*, vol. 2. Chicago: Encyclopaedia Britannica, 1952.

Aristoxenus. *Harmonics*. Edited and translated with an introduction by Henry S. Macran. Oxford: Clarendon Press, 1902.

Arnheim, Rudolf. *Entropy and Art: An Essay on Disorder and Order*. Berkeley: University of California Press, 1971.

Attali, Jacques. *Noise: The Political Economy of Music*. Translated by Brian Massumi. Minneapolis: University of Minnesota Press, 1985.

Augustine, *Confessions*. Translated by Edward Bouverie Pusey. In *Writings of St. Augustine*. New York: Fathers of the Church, 1947.

Augustine. *On Music*. Translated by Robert Catesby Taliaferro. In *Writings of Saint Augustine*, edited by Ludwig Schopp. NewYork: CIMA Publishing, 1947.

Bannerji, Himani, et al. *Unsettling Relations: The University as a Site of Feminist Struggles* (Toronto: Women's Press, 1991).

Barnes, Jonathan. *Aristotle*. Oxford: Oxford University Press, 1982.

Battersby, Christine. *Gender and Genius: Towards a Feminist Aesthetics*. London: The Women's Press, 1989.

Bauman, Zygmunt. "The Fall of the Legislator." In *Postmodernism: a Reader*, edited by Thomas Docherty, 128–40. New York: Columbia University Press, 1993.

Beardsley, Monroe C. "In Defense of Aesthetic Value." *Proceedings and Addresses of the American Philosophical Association* 52:6 (1979): 723–49.

——. "Semiotic Aesthetics and Aesthetic Education." *Journal of Aesthetic Education* 9 (1975): 5–26.

——. *Aesthetics: Problems in the Philosophy of Criticism*. Indianapolis, IN: Hackett Publishing, 1981.

——. *Aesthetics from Classical Greece to the Present: A Short History*. Tuscaloosa, AL: University of Alabama Press, 1966.

Berleant, Arnold. *Art and Engagement*. Philadelphia: Temple University Press, 1991.

——. "The Historicity of Aesthetics: Parts 1 and 2." *British Journal of Aesthetics* 26:2/3 (Spring 1986): 101–11, 195–203.

——. "Music as Sound and Idea." *Current Musicology* 6 (1968): 95–100.

Blocker, Harry. "Kant's Theory of the Relation of Imagination and Understanding in Aesthetic Judgements of Taste." *British Journal of Aesthetics* 5 (1965): 37–45.

Boethius. *Fundamentals of Music*. Translated by Calvin M. Bower. Edited by Claude V. Palisca. New Haven, CT: Yale University Press, 1989.

Bogden, Deanne. "Pythagoras' Rib or, What Does Music Education Want?" In *Philosophy of Music Education Review* 2:2 (Fall, 1994): 122–31.

Boretz, Benjamin. "Nelson Goodman's *Languages of Art* from a Musical Point of View." In *Perspectives on Contemporary Music Theory*, edited by Benjamin Boretz and Edward Cone. New York: W. W. Norton, 1972 (31–44).

Bovenschen, Silvia "Is There a Feminine Aesthetic?" Translated by Beth Weckmueller. In *Feminist Aesthetics*, edited by Gisella Ecker. London: Women's Press, 1985. 23–50.

Bowman, Wayne. "Justifying Music Education: Contingency and Solidarity." *Canadian Music Educator* 35:6 (Summer 1994) 27–32.

——. "Music Without Universals: Relativism Reconsidered." In *Critical Reflections on Music Education: Proceedings of the Second International Symposium on the Philosophy of Music Education*, edited by L. Bartel and D. Elliott. Toronto: Canadian Music Research Centre, 1996.

——. "Philosophy, Criticism, and Music Education: Some Tentative Steps Down a Less-Travelled Road." *Bulletin of the Council for Research in Music Education* 114 (Fall 1992): 1–19.

——. "A Plea for Pluralism:Variations on a Theme by George McKay." In *Basic Concepts in Music Education, II*, edited by Richard Colwell. Niwot, Colorado: University Press of Colorado, 1991 (94–110).

——. "The Problem of Aesthetics and Multiculturalism in Music Education." *Canadian Music Educator* 34:5 (May 1993): 23–31.

——. "Sound, Society, and Music 'Proper'." *Philosophy of Music Education Review* 2:1 (Spring 1994): 14–24.

——. "Sound, Sociality and Music." *The Quarterly Journal of Music Teaching and Learning* 5:3 (Fall 1994): 50–67.

——. "Tacit Knowing, Musical Experience, and Musical Instruction: The Significance of Michael Polonyi's Thought for Music Education." Ed.D. diss. University of Illinois, 1980.

——. "The Values of Musical Formalism." *Journal of Aesthetic Education* 25:3 (Fall 1991): 41–60.

——. "The Values of Musical Praxialism." Forthcoming in *Critical Matters in Music Education* (working title), edited by David Elliott.

Bredo, Eric. "Reality Construction and Aesthetics: Essay Review." *Journal of Aesthetic Education* 13 (1979): 109–19.

Buck-Morss, Susan. *The Origin of Negative Dialectics*. New York: Free Press, 1977.

Budd, Malcolm. "The Repudiation of Emotion: Hanslick on Music." *British Journal of Aesthetics* 20 (1980): 29–43.

——. *Music and the Emotions: The Philosophical Theories*. London: Routledge and Kegan Paul, 1985.

Butler, Judith. *Gender Trouble: Feminism and the Subversion of Identity*. New York: Routledge, 1990.

Burrows, David L. *Sound, Speech, and Music*. Amherst: University of Massachussetts Press, 1990.

Chadwick, Henry. *Boethius: The Consolations of Music, Logic, Theology, and Philosophy*. Oxford: Clarendon Press, 1981.

Chamberlain, David S. "Philosophy of Music in the Consolation of Boethius." *Speculum* 45:1 (1970): 80–97.

Citron, Marcia J. "Feminist Approaches to Musicology." In *Cecilia Reclaimed: Feminist Perspectives on Gender and Music*, edited by Susan C. Cook and Judy S. Tsou, 15–34. Urbana: University of Illinois Press, 1994.

Clifton, Thomas. *Music as Heard: A Study in Applied Phenomenology*. New Haven, CT: Yale University Press, 1983.

Coker, Wilson. *Music and Meaning: A Theoretical Introduction to Musical Aesthetics*. New York: Free Press, 1972.

Collingwood, R. G. *The Principles of Art*. Oxford: Clarendon Press, 1938.

Cook, Susan C., and Judy S. Tsou, eds. *Cecilia Reclaimed: Feminist Perspectives on Gender and Music*. Urbana: University of Illinois Press, 1994.

Cox, Renée. "Recovering *Jouissance*: An Introduction to Feminist Musical Aesthetics." In *Women and Music: A History*, edited by Karin Pendle, 331–40. Bloomington: Indiana University Press, 1991.

Crawford, Donald W. *Kant's Aesthetic Theory*. Madison: University of Wisconsin Press, 1974.

Cusick, Suzanne G. "Gender and the Cultural Work of a Classical Music Performance." *repercussions* 3:1 (Spring 1994): 77–110.

Dalhaus, Carl. *Esthetics of Music*. Translated by William W. Austin. Cambridge: Cambridge University Press, 1982.

De Castell, Suzanne. "Textuality and the Designs of Theory." In *Critical Conversations in Philosophy of Education*, edited by Wendy Kohli, 241–57. New York: Routledge, 1995.

Desmond, William. *Art and the Absolute: A Study of Hegel's Aesthetic*. Albany: State University of New York Press, 1986.

Dewey, John. *Art as Experience*. New York: Perigree, 1980.

———. *Democracy and Education: An Introduction to the Philosophy of Education*. New York: Macmillan, 1916.

Diamond, Beverly. "Strategies for Confronting Patriarchy in the Music School." In *Compendium of the International Conference on Music, Gender, and Pedagogics*, 26–36. School of Music and Musicology at the University of Göteborg, Sweden, 1996.

Dipert, Randall R. "Meyer's Emotion and Meaning in Music: A Sympathetic Critique of its Central Claims." *In Theory Only* 6:8 (1983): 3–17.

Docherty, Thomas, ed. *Postmodernism: A Reader*. New York: Columbia University Press, 1993.

Dufrenne, Mikel. *The Phenomenology of Aesthetic Experience*. Translated by Edward Casey et al. Evanston, IL: Northwestern University Press, 1973.

Ecker, Gisela, ed. *Feminist Aesthetics*. Translated by Harriet Anderson. London: Women's Press, 1985.

Eco, Umberto. *Interpretation and Overinterpretation*. Edited by Stefan Collini. Cambridge: Cambridge University Press, 1992.

Elias, Julias A. *Plato's Defence of Poetry*. Albany: State University of New York Press, 1984.

Eliot, T. S. *Four Quartets*. New York: Harcourt, Brace, Jovanovich, 1988.

———. *On Poetry and Poets*. Winchester, MA: Faber and Faber, 1957.

Elliott, David J. *Music Matters*. New York: Oxford University Press, 1995.

———. "Structure and Feeling in Jazz: Rethinking Philosophical Foundations." *Bulletin of the Council for Research in Music Education* 95 (1987): 13–38.

Epperson, Gordon. *The Musical Symbol: A Study of the Philosophic Theory of Music*. Ames: Iowa State University Press, 1967.

Ferrara, Lawrence. *Philosophy and the Analysis of Music: Bridges to Musical Sound, Form, and Reference*. New York: Greenwood Press, 1991.

Fraser, Nancy, and Linda J. Nicholson. "Social Criticism without Philosophy: An Encounter between Feminism and Postmodernism." In *Feminism/Postmodernism*, edited by Linda J. Nicholson, 19–38. New York: Routledge, 1990.

Friedrich, Carl J., ed. *The Philosophy of Kant: Immanuel Kant's Moral and Political Writings*. New York: Modern Library, 1949.

Frye, Northrop. *On Education*. Markham, Ontario: Fitzhenry and Whiteside, 1988.

Gay, Peter. *Freud, Jews, and Other Germans: Masters and Victims in Modernist Culture*. New York: Oxford University Press, 1978.

Godway, Eleanor M., and Geraldine Finn. *Who is this "We"? Absence of Community*. Montréal: Black Rose, 1994.

Goehr, Lydia. *The Imaginary Museum of Musical Works: An Essay in the Philosophy of Music*. New York: Oxford University Press, 1992.

———. "Political Music and the Politics of Music." *Journal of Aesthetics and Art Criticism* 52(1): 99–112 (1994).

Goodman, Nelson. *Languages of Art: An Approach to a Theory of Symbols*. Indianapolis, IN: Hackett Publishing, 1976.

———. *Ways of Worldmaking*. Hassocks, England: Harvester Press, 1978.

Gotshalk, D. W. "Form and Expression in Kant's Aesthetics." *British Journal of Aesthetics* 7 (1969) 250–60.

Göttner-Abendroth, Heide. "Nine Principles of a Matriarchal Aesthetic." Translated by Harriett Anderson. In *Feminist Aesthetics*, edited by Gisela Ecker, 81–94. London: Women's Press, 1985.

———. *The Dancing Goddess: Principles of a Matriarchal Aesthetic*. Translated by Maureen T. Krause (Boston: Beacon Press, 1991).

Gracyk, Theodore A. "Adorno, Jazz, and the Aesthetics of Popular Music." *Musical Quarterly* 76:4 (Winter 1992): 526–42.

Gurney, Edmund. *The Power of Sound*. New York: Basic Books, 1966.

Hall, Robert W. "On Hanslick's Supposed Formalism in Music." *Journal of Aesthetics and Art Criticism* 25:4 (Summer 1967): 433–36.

Hansen, Forest W. "Music, Feeling, and Meaning: A Study of Four Theories." Ph.D. diss., Johns Hopkins University, 1967.

———. "On Meyer's Theory of Musical Meaning." *British Journal of Aesthetics* 29:1 (Winter 1989): 10–20.

Hanslick, Eduard. *On the Musically Beautiful: A Contribution Towards the Revision of the Aesthetics of Music*. Translated and edited by Geoffrey Payzant. Indianapolis, IN: Hackett Publishing, 1986.

———. *The Beautiful in Music*. Translated by Gustav Cohen. Edited by Morris Weitz. New York: Liberal Arts Press, 1957.

Harding, Sandra G. "Is There a Feminist Method?" In *Feminism and Methodology: Social Science Issues*, edited by Sandra G. Harding. Bloomington: Indiana University Press, 1987.

Hare, R. M. *Plato*. New York: Oxford University Press, 1982.

Hassan, Ihab. "Toward a Concept of Postmodernism." In *Postmodernism: A Reader*, edited by Thomas Docherty. (New York: Columbia University Press, 1993) 146–56.

Hegel, G. W. F. *The Philosophy of Fine Art*. Translated by F. P. B. Osmaston. London: G. Bell and Sons, 1920.

———. *The Introduction to Hegel's Philosophy of Fine Art*. Translated by B. Bosanquet. London: Kegan Paul, Trench, and Co., 1886.

Heidegger, Martin. *Being and Time*. Translated by J. McQuarrie and E. Robinson. New York: Harper and Rowe, 1962.

Hein, Hilde, and Carolyn Korsmeyer, eds. *Aesthetics in Feminist Perspective*. Bloomington: Indiana University Press, 1993.

Hillman, James. *Emotion: A Comprehensive Phenomenology of Theories and their Meanings for Therapy*. London: Routledge, 1960.

Hospers, John. *Meaning and Truth in the Arts*. Hamden: Archon Books, 1964.

Howard, Vernon A. "Musical Meaning: A Logical Note." *Journal of Aesthetics and Art Criticism* 30 (1971): 215–19.

Huizinga, Johan. *Homo Ludens: A Study of the Play Element in Culture*. Boston: Beacon Press, 1950.

Husserl, Edmund. *Phenomenology and the Crisis of Philosophy*. Translated by Q. Lauer. New York: Harper and Rowe, 1955.

———. *Phenomenology of Internal Time-Consciousness*. Translated by James C. Churchill. Edited by Martin Heidegger. Bloomington: Indiana University Press, 1964.

Huyssen, Andreas. "Mapping the Postmodern." In *Feminism/Postmodernism*, edited by Linda J. Nicholson, 234–77. New York: Routledge, 1990.

Ihde, Don. *Listening and Voice: A Phenomenology of Sound*. Athens: Ohio University Press, 1976.

Innis, R. E. "Art, Symbol and Consciousness: A Polanyi Gloss on Susan Langer and Nelson Goodman." *International Philosophical Quarterly* 17 (1977): 455–76.

Irigaray, Luce. *This Sex Which Is Not One*. Translated by Catherine Porter. Ithaca, NY: Cornell University Press, 1985.

———. *Speculum of the Other Woman*. Translated by Gillian Gill. Ithaca, NY: Cornell University Press, 1985.

Izard, Carroll, ed. *Human Emotions*. New York: Plenum Press, 1977.

Jay, Martin. *Adorno*. Cambridge, MA: Harvard University Press, 1984.

Johnson, James R. "The Primacy of Form: A Study of the Philosophical Development of Suzanne K. Langer with Implications for Choral Music." Ph.D. diss., University of Illinois, 1988.

Johnson, Mark. *The Body in the Mind: The Bodily Basis of Meaning, Imagination, and Reason.* Chicago: University of Chicago Press, 1987.

Johnson, Pauline. *Marxist Aesthetics: The Foundation within Everyday Life for an Emancipated Consciousness.* London: Routledge and Kegan Paul, 1984.

Kaelin, Eugene. *An Existentialist Aesthetic: The Theories of Sartre and Merleau-Ponty.* Madison: University of Wisconsin Press, 1962.

Kaminsky, Jack. *Hegel on Art: An Interpretation of Hegel's Aesthetics.* Albany: State University of New York Press, 1962.

Kant, Immanuel. *The Critique of Judgement.* Translated by James Creed Meredith. Oxford: Clarendon Press, 1952.

———. *Observations on the Feeling of the Beautiful and Sublime.* Translated by John T. Goldthwait. Berkeley: University of California Press, 1960.

Keil, Charles M. "Motion and Feeling through Music." *Journal of Aesthetics and Art Criticism* 24 (1966): 337–49.

Keil, Charles, and Steven Feld. *Music Grooves.* Chicago: University of Chicago Press, 1994.

Kemal, Salim. "Systematic Ideas in Aesthetics (II): Expression and Idealism in Kant's Aesthetics." *British Journal of Aesthetics* 16:1 (Winter 1976): 68–79.

Kerman, Joseph. *Contemplating Music: Challenges to Musicology.* Cambridge: Harvard University Press, 1985.

Kivy, Peter. *The Corded Shell: Reflections on Musical Expression.* Princeton, NJ: Princeton University Press, 1980.

———. *Music Alone: Reflections on the Purely Musical Experience.* Ithaca, NY: Cornell University Press, 1990.

———. *Sound and Semblance: Reflections on Musical Representation.* Princeton, NJ: Princeton University Press, 1984.

Kneller, Jane. "Discipline and Silence: Women and Imagination in Kant's Theory of Taste." In *Aesthetics in Feminist Perspective*, edited by Hilde Hein and Carolyn Korsmeyer, 179–92. Bloomington: Indiana Unversity Press, 1993.

Knox, Israel. *The Aesthetic Theories of Kant, Hegel, and Schopenhauer.* New York: Humanities Press, 1958.

Kohli, Wendy, ed. *Critical Conversations in Philosophy of Education.* New York: Routledge, 1995.

Koskoff, Ellen, ed. *Women and Music in Cross-Cultural Perspective.* New York: Greenwood Press, 1987.

Kramer, Lawrence. *Classical Music and Postmodern Knowledge.* Berkeley: University of California Press, 1995.

Kristeva, Julia. *Desire in Language: A Semiotic Approach to Literature and Art.* Translated by Thomas Gora, Alice Jardine, and Leon Roudiez. Edited by Leon S. Roudiez. New York: Columbia University Press, 1980.

———. *Revolution in Poetic Language.* Translated by Margaret Waller. New York: Columbia University Press, 1984.

Kuhn, Thomas. *The Structure of Scientific Revolutions.* Chicago: University of Chicago Press, 1970.

Lamb, Roberta. "Aria Senza Accompagnamento: A Woman Behind the Theory." *The Quarterly Journal of Music Teaching and Learning* 4:4/5:1 (Winter 1993 and Spring 1994): 5–20.

———. "Discords: Feminist Pedagogy in Music Education." *Theory into Practice* 35:2 (Spring 1996): 124–131.

———. "Feminism as Critique in Philosophy of Music Education." *Philosophy of Music Education Review* 2:2 (Fall 1994): 59–74.

———. "Medusa's Aria: Feminist Theories and Music Education," In *Women and education*, edited by Jane Gaskell and Arlene McLaren, 299–319. Calgary: Detselig Enterprises, 1991.

———. "Music Trouble: Desire, Discourse, and the Pedagogy Project." Paper presented at Border Crossings: Future Directions in Music Studies, University of Ottawa, March 1995.

———. "Tone Deaf/Symphonies Singing: Sketches for a Musicale." In *Gender In/Forms Curriculum: From Enrichment to Transformation*, edited by Jane Gaskell and John Willinsky, 109–35. New York: Teachers College Press, 1995.

Langer, Susanne K. *Feeling and Form: A Theory of Art Developed from Philosophy in a New Key.* New York: Charles Scribner's Sons, 1953.

———. *Mind: An Essay on Human Feeling*, vols. 1–3. Baltimore: Johns Hopkins University Press, 1967, 1972, 1982.

———. *Philosophy in a New Key: A Study in the Symbolism of Reason, Rite, and Art.* Cambridge, MA: Harvard University Press, 1942.

——. *Problems of Art: Ten Philosophical Lectures*. New York: Charles Scribner's Sons, 1957.

Laszlo, Ervin. "Affect and Expression in Music." *Journal of Aesthetics and Art Criticism* 27:1 (1968): 131–34.

Lauter, Estella. "Re-Enfrachising Art: Feminist Interventions in the Theory of Art." In *Aesthetics in Feminist Perspective*, edited by Hilde Hein and Carolyn Korsmeyer, 21–34. Bloomington: Indiana Unversity Press, 1993.

Leibniz, G. W. "The Principles of Nature and Grace." 1714. In *The Philosophical Works of Leibnitz*, translated by G. M. Duncan, 209–17. New Haven, CT: Tuttle, Morehouse, and Taylor, 1890.

Leppert, Richard. "The Sonoric Body: Socio-Sexual Harmony—Acts of Violence." In *Compendium of the International Conference on Music, Gender, and Pedagogics*, 113–56. School of Music and Musicology at the University of Göteborg, Sweden, 1996.

Leppert, Richard and Susan McClary, eds. *Music and Society: The Politics of Composition, Performance, and Reception*. New York: Cambridge University Press, 1987.

Lippman, Edward A. *Musical Thought in Ancient Greece*. New York: Columbia University Press, 1964.

Lipsitz, George. *Dangerous Crossroads: Popular Music, Postmodernism and the Poetics of Place*. New York: Verso, 1994.

Lochhead, Judy. "Hearing New Music: Pedagagy from a Phenomenological Perspective." *Philosophy of Music Education Review* 3:1 (Spring 1995): 34–42.

Long. A. A. *Hellenistic Philosophy: Stoics, Epicureans, Sceptics*. New York: Charles Scribner's Sons, 1974.

Lorraine, Renée. "A Gynecentric Aesthetic." In *Aesthetics in Feminist Perspective*, edited by Hilde Hein and Carolyn Korsmeyer, 35–52. Bloomington: Indiana University Press, 1993.

Lukacs, Georgy. *History and Class Consciousness: Studies in Marxist Dialectics*. Translated by Rodney Livingstone. Cambridge, MA: MIT Press, 1971.

Lyotard, Jean-Francois. "Adorno as the Devil." *Telos* 19 (1974): 128–37.

Madison, Gary B. *The Phenomenology of Merleau-Ponty: A Search for the Limits of Consciousness*. Athens: Ohio University Press, 1981.

Magee, Bryan. *The Philosophy of Schopenhauer*. Oxford: Clarendon Press, 1983.

Mannheim, Karl. *Ideology and Utopia: An Introduction to the Sociology of Knowledge*. Translated by Louis Wirth and Edward Shils. New York: Harcourt Brace, 1985.

Margolis, Joseph. "On the Semiotics of Music." In *What is Music?* edited by Philip Alperson, 211–36. New York: Haven Press, 1987.

——, ed. *Philosophy Looks at the Arts: Contemporary Readings in Aesthetics*. Philadelphia: Temple University Press, 1987.

Martin, Biddy. "Feminism, Criticism, and Foucault." *New German Critique* 27 (fall 1982): 3–30.

McCarthy, Thomas. *The Critical Theory of Jurgen Habermas*. Cambridge, MA: MIT Press, 1978.

McClary, Susan. "Towards a Feminist Criticism of Music." *Canadian University Music Review* 10:2 (1990): 9–17.

——. *Feminine Endings: Music, Gender, and Sexuality*. Minneapolis: University of Minnesota Press, 1991.

McMahon, A. Philip. "Sextus Empiricus and the Arts." *Harvard Studies in Classical Philology* 42 (1931): 79–137.

Merleau-Ponty, Maurice. *Phenomenology of Perception*. Translated by Colin Smith. London: Routledge and Kegan Paul, 1962.

——. *Signs*. Translated by Richard McCleary. Evanston, IL: Northwestern University Press, 1964.

——. *The Primacy of Perception and Other Essays on Phenomenological Psychology, the Philosophy of Art, History, and Politics*. Edited by James M. Edie. Evanston, IL: Northwestern University Press, 1964.

——. *The Visible and the Invisible*. Translated by Alphonso Lingis. Edited by Claude Lefort. Evanston, IL: Northwestern University Press, 1968.

Meyer, Leonard B. "The Dilemma of Choosing: Speculations about Contemporary Culture." In *Value and Values in Evolution*, edited by E. A. Maziarz 117–141. New York: Gordon and Breach, 1979.

——. *Emotion and Meaning in Music*. Chicago: University of Chicago Press, 1956.

——. "Exploiting Limits: Creation, Archetypes, and Style Change." *Daedalus* 109:2 (1980): 177–205.

——. "Grammatical Simplicity and Relational Richness: The Trio of Mozart's g Minor Symphony." *Critical Inquiry* 2:2 (1976): 693–761.

——. "Innovation, Choice, and the History of Music." *Critical Inquiry* 9:3 (1983): 517–44.

———. "Process and Morphology in the Music of Mozart." *Journal of Musicology* 1:1 (1982): 67–94.

———. "Toward a Theory of Style." In *The Concept of Style*, edited by B. Lang, 21–71. Ithaca, NY: Cornell University Press, 1987.

———. *Explaining Music: Essays and Explorations*. Berkeley: University of California Press, 1973.

———. *Music, the Arts, and Ideas: Patterns and Predictions in Twentieth-Century Culture*. Chicago: University of Chicago Press, 1967.

Middleton, Richard. *Studying Popular Music*. Philadelphia: Open University Press, 1990.

Miller, R. D. *Schiller and the Ideal of Freedom: A Study of Schiller's Philosophical Works with Chapters on Kant*. Oxford: Clarendon Press, 1970.

Morton, Charlene A. "Feminist Theory and the Displaced Music Curriculum: Beyond the 'Add and Stir' Projects." *Philosophy of Music Education Review* 2:2 (Fall, 1994): 106–21.

———. "The Feminized Location of School Music and the Burden of Justification." Ed.D. diss., University of Toronto, 1996.

Murdoch, Iris. *The Fire and the Sun: Why Plato Banished the Artists*. Oxford: Oxford University Press, 1977.

Nagel, Ernest. Review of *Philosophy in a New Key*, by Susanne Langer. *Journal of Philosophy* 40 (1943): 323–29.

Nattiez, Jean-Jacques. *Music and Discourse: Toward a Semiology of Music*. Translated by Carolyn Abbate. Princeton, NJ: Princeton University Press, 1990.

Nauen, Franz Gabriel. *Revolution, Idealism and Human Freedom: Schelling, Hölderin, and Hegel, and the Crisis of Early German Idealism*. The Hague: Nijhoff, 1971.

Nicholson, Linda J., ed. *Feminism/Postmodernism*. New York: Routledge, 1990.

O'Connell, Robert J. *Art and the Christian Intelligence in St. Augustine*. Cambridge, MA: Harvard University Press, 1978.

Ortner, Sherry B. and Harriet Whitehead, eds. *Sexual Meanings: The Cultural Construction of Gender and Sexuality*. Cambridge: Cambridge University Press, 1981.

Paddison, Max. *Adorno, Modernism and Mass Culture: Essays on Critical Theory and Music*. London: Kahn and Averill, 1996.

———. *Adorno's Aesthetics of Music*. New York: Cambridge University Press, 1993.

Payzant, Geoffrey. "Hanslick, Sams, Gay, and *Tönend Bewegte Formen*." *Journal of Aesthetics and Art Criticism* 40 (1981): 41–48.

Pendle, Karin, ed. *Women and Music: A History*. Bloomington: Indiana University Press, 1991.

Plantinga, Leon. Review of *Music, the Arts, and Ideas*, by Leonard B. Meyer. *Journal of Music Theory* 13:1 (1969): 141–147.

Plato. *The Dialogues of Plato*. Translated by Benjamin Jowett. In *Great Books of the Western World*, vol. 1. Chicago: Encyclopaedia Britannica, 1952.

Plotinus. *The Six Enneads*. Translated by Stephen MacKenna and B. S. Page. Chicago: Encyclopaedia Britannica, 1952.

Polanyi, Michael. *Personal Knowledge: Towards a Post-Critical Philosophy*. Chicago: University of Chicago Press, 1958.

Portnoy, Julius. *The Philosopher and Music*. New York: Da Capo Press, 1980.

Post, Jennifer C. "Erasing the Boundaries Between Public and Private in Women's Performance Traditions." In *Cecilia Reclaimed: Feminist Perspectives on Gender und Music*, edited by Susan Cook and Judy Tsou, 34–51. Urbana: University of Illinois Press, 1994.

Potter, Russell A. *Spectacular Vernaculars: Hip-Hop and the Politics of Postmodernism*. Albany: State University of New York Press, 1995.

Pratt, Carroll C. "The Design of Music." *Journal of Aesthetics and Art Criticism* 12:3 (1954) 289–300.

Price, Kingsley, ed. *On Criticizing Music: Five Philosophical Perspectives*. Baltimore: Johns Hopkins, 1981.

Racevskis, Karlis. *Postmodernism and the Search for Enlightenment*. Charlottesville: University Press of Virginia, 1993.

Redfern, H. B. "Philosophical Aesthetics and the Education of Teachers." *Journal of Aesthetic Education* 22:2 (summer 1988): 35–46.

Regelski, Thomas A. "Prolegomenon to a Praxial Philosophy of Music and Music Education." *Finnish Journal of Music Education* 1:1 (1996) 23–39.

Reiss, Edmund. *Boethius*. Boston: Twayne, 1982.

Robinson, Jenefer, and Stephanie Ross. "Women, Morality, and Fiction." In *Aesthetics in Feminist Perspective*, edited by Hilde Hein and Carolyn Korsmeyer, 105–18. Bloomington: Indiana Unversity Press, 1993 (105–118).

Rorty, Richard. *Contingency, Irony, and Solidarity*. New York: Cambridge University Press, 1989.
———. *Essays on Heidegger and Others*. New York: Cambridge University Press, 1991
———. *Objectivity, Relativism, and Truth*. New York: Cambridge University Press, 1991.
Rosner, Burton S., and Leonard B. Meyer. "Melodic Processes and the Perception of Music." In *The Psychology of Music*, edited by Diana Deutsch 317–41. New York: Academic Press, 1982.
Rowell, Lewis. *Thinking about Music: An Introduction to the Philosophy of Music*. Amherst: University of Massachusetts Press, 1983.
Rudner, Richard. "On Semiotic Aesthetics." *Journal of Aesthetics and Art Criticism* (1951): 67–77.
Sallis, John. *Phenomenology and the Return to Beginnings*. Pittsburgh: Duquesne University Press, 1973.
Schafer, R. Murray. *The Tuning of the World*. Toronto: McClelland and Stewart, 1977.
Schantz, A. "A New Statement of Values for Music Education Based on the Writings of Dewey, Meyer, and Wolterstorff." Ph.D. diss., University of Colorado, 1983.
Schaper, Eva. "Friedrich Schiller: Adventures of a Kantian." *British Journal of Aesthetics* 4 (1964): 348–62.
Scheffler, Israel. *Inquiries: Philosophical Studies of Language, Science and Learning*. Indianapolis: Hackett Publishing, 1986.
Schiller, Friedrich. *On the Aesthetic Education of Man*. Edited and translated by Elizabeth M. Wilkinson and L. A. Willoughby. Oxford: Clarendon Press, 1982.
Schipper, Edith W. "*Mimesis* in the Arts in Plato's *Laws*." *Journal of Aesthetics and Art Criticism* 22 (1963): 199–202.
Schopenhauer, Arthur. *The World as Will and Representation*. 2 vols. Translated by E. F. J. Payne. Indian Hills, CO: Falcon's Wing Press, 1958.
Schor, Naomi. "This Essentialism Which is Not One: Coming to Grips with Irigaray." *differences* 1:2 (1989): 38–58.
Schrade, Leo. "Music in the Philosophy of Boethius." *Musical Quarterly* 33 (1947): 188–200.
Schueller, Herbert M. "Immanuel Kant and the Aesthetics of Music." *Journal of Aesthetics and Art Criticism* 14:2 (1955): 218–47.
Schueller, Herbert M. "Schelling's Theory of the Metaphysics of Music." *Journal of Aesthetics and Art Criticism* 15 (1957): 461–76.
Scruton, Roger. *The Aesthetic Understanding: Essays in the Philosophy of Art and Culture*. London: Methuen, 1983.
Sextus Empiricus. *Against the Musicians*. Translated by Denise D. Greaves. Lincoln: University of Nebraska Press, 1986.
Shapiro, H. Svi, and David Purpel, eds. *Critical Social Issues in American Education*. White Plains, NY: Longman Publishing, 1993.
Shaver, Phillip, J. Schwartz, D. Kirson, and C. O'Connor. "Emotion Knowledge: Further Exploration of a Prototype Approach." *Journal of Personality and Social Psychology*. 52:6 (1987): 1061–86.
Shepherd, John. "Music and the Last Intellectuals." *Journal of Aesthetic Education* 25 (1991): 112.
———. *Music as Social Text*. Cambridge: Polity Press, 1991.
———. *Whose Music: A Sociology of Musical Languages*. New Brunswick: Transaction Books, 1977.
Sherburne, Donald W. "Meaning and Music." *Journal of Aesthetics and Art Criticism* 24 (1966): 579–83.
Small, Christopher. *Music—Education—Society: An Examination of the Function of Music in Western, Eastern, and African Cultures with its Impact on Society and its Use in Education*. New York: Schirmer, 1977.
Smith, C. M. "Symbolic Systems, Cognitive Efficacy, and Aesthetic Education." *Journal of Aesthetic Education* 3 (1969): 123–36.
Smith, F. Joseph. *The Experiencing of Musical Sound: Prelude to a Phenomenology of Music* New York: Gordon and Breach, 1979.
Solie, Ruth A., ed. *Musicology and Difference: Gender and Sexuality in Music Scholarship*. Berkeley: University of California Press, 1993.
Sorbom, Goran. "Aristotle on Music as Representation." *Journal of Aesthetics and Art Criticism* 52:1 (Winter 1994): 37–46.
Sparshott, Francis E. "Aesthetics of Music: Limits and Grounds." In *What is music?* edited by Philip Alperson, 33–100. New York: Haven, 1987.
———. *The Theory of the Arts*. Princeton, NJ: Princeton University Press, 1982.

Speigelberg, Herbert. *The Phenomenological Movement*. The Hague: Nijhoff, 1965.

Spelman, Elizabeth. *Inessential Woman: Problems of Exclusion in Feminist Thought*. Boston: Beacon Press, 1988.

Stewart, David. *Exploring Phenomenology: A Guide to the Field and its Literature*. Athens: Ohio University Press, 1990.

Strauss, Erwin. *Phenomenology and Psychology*. New York: Basic Books, 1966.

Stravinsky, Igor. *An Autobiography*. New York: Simon and Schuster, 1936.

Stubley, Eleanor V. "Modulating Identities: The Play of Ensemble Performance (Being in the Body, Being in the Sound)." Paper presented to the Music Educators National Conference, Kansas City, MO, spring 1996.

Subotnik, Rose Rosengard. "The Challenge of Contemporary Music." In *What Is Music?* edited by Philip Alperson, 361–96. New York: Haven Press, 1987.

———. *Developing Variations: Style and Ideology in Western Music*. Minneapolis: University of Minnesota Press, 1991.

Tate, J. "Plato and 'Imitation'." *Classical Quarterly* 26:3 (1932): 161–69.

Titchener, John M., and M. E. Broyles. "Meyer, Meaning and Music." *Journal of Aesthetics and Art Criticism* 22:1 (1973): 17–25.

Van Peursen, Cornelis A. *Phenomenology and Analytical Philosophy*. Pittsburgh: Duquesne University Press, 1972.

Varela, Francisco J., Evan Thompson, and Eleanor Rocsch. *The Embodied Mind: Cognitive Science and Human Experience*. Cambridge: MIT Press, 1991.

Wakefield, Neville. *Postmodernism: The Twilight of the Real*. London: Pluto Press, 1990.

Walser, Robert. *Running with the Devil: Power, Gender, and Madness in Heavy Metal Music*. (Hanover, NH: Wesleyan University Press, 1993).

Walton, Kendall L. *Mimesis as Make Believe: On the Foundations of the Representational Arts*. Cambridge: Harvard University Press, 1990.

Weitz, Morris. "Symbolism and Art." *Review of Metaphysics* 7 (1954): 466–81.

Welsh, Paul. "Discursive and Presentational Symbols." *Mind* 64 (1955): 181–99.

West, M. L. *Ancient Greek Music*. New York: Oxford University Press, 1994.

Wilkinson, L. P. "Philodemus on *Ethos* in Music." *Classical Quarterly* 32 (1938): 174–81.

Winnington-Ingram, R. P. *Mode in Ancient Greek Music*. Chicago: Argonaut Publishing, 1968.

Wiseman, Mary Bittner. "Beautiful Exiles." In *Aesthetics in Feminist Perspective*, edited by Hilde Hein and Carolyn Korsmeyer, 169–78. Bloomington: Indiana Unversity Press, 1993.

Wittgenstein, Ludwig. *Philosophical Investigations*. Translated by G. E. M. Anscombe. New York: Macmillan, 1958.

Wolterstorff, Nicholas. *Works and Worlds of Art*. Oxford: Clarendon Press, 1980.

Zimmerman, Robert L. "Kant: The Aesthetic Judgment." *Journal of Aesthetics and Art Criticism* 21 (1963): 333–44.

Zuckerkandl, Victor. *Sound and Symbol: Music and the External World*. Translated by Willard R. Trask. New York: Pantheon Books, 1956.

Zuidervaart, Lambert. *Adorno's Aesthetic Theory: The Redemption of Illusion*. Cambridge, MA: MIT Press, 1991.

Subject Index

478

Name Index